T0350410

Machine Learning Techniques for Adaptive Multimedia Retrieval:

Technologies, Applications, and Perspectives

Chia-Hung Wei
Ching Yun University, Taiwan

Yue Li
Nankai University, China

INFORMATION SCIENCE REFERENCE

Hershey · New York

Director of Editorial Content:	Kristin Klinger
Director of Book Publications:	Julia Mosemann
Acquisitions Editor:	Lindsay Johnston
Development Editor:	Joel Gamon
Publishing Assistant:	Deanna Jo Zombro and Natalie Pronio
Typesetter:	Natalie Pronio and Casey Conapitski
Production Editor:	Jamie Snavely
Cover Design:	Lisa Tosheff

Published in the United States of America by
Information Science Reference (an imprint of IGI Global)
701 E. Chocolate Avenue
Hershey PA 17033
Tel: 717-533-8845
Fax: 717-533-8661
E-mail: cust@igi-global.com
Web site: http://www.igi-global.com

Library of Congress Cataloging-in-Publication Data

Machine learning techniques for adaptive multimedia retrieval : technologies,
applications, and perspectives / Chia-Hung Wei and Yue Li, editors.
      p. cm.
  Includes bibliographical references and index.
  Summary: "This book disseminates current information on multimedia
retrieval, advancing the field of multimedia databases, and educating the
multimedia database community on machine learning techniques for adaptive
multimedia retrieval research, design and applications"--Provided by
publisher.
  ISBN 978-1-61692-859-9 (hardcover) -- ISBN 978-1-61692-861-2 (ebook) 1.
Interactive multimedia--Databases. 2. Information retrieval. 3. Automatic
indexing. 4. Database management. 5. Machine learning. I. Wei, Chia-Hung,
1973- II. Li, Yue, 1980-
  QA76.9.D3M28424 2011
  006.3'1--dc22
                                        2010024361

British Cataloguing in Publication Data
A Cataloguing in Publication record for this book is available from the British Library.

All work contributed to this book is new, previously-unpublished material. The views expressed in this book are those of the authors, but not necessarily of the publisher.

Table of Contents

Section 1

Chapter 1
Chia-Hung Wei, Ching Yun University, Taiwan
Sherry Y. Chen, Brunel University, UK

Chapter 2
Dmitry Kinoshenko, Kharkiv National University of Radio Electronics, Ukraine
Vladimir Mashtalir, Kharkiv National University of Radio Electronics, Ukraine
Vladislav Shlyakhov, Kharkiv National University of Radio Electronics, Ukraine
Elena Yegorova, Kharkiv National University of Radio Electronics, Ukraine

Chapter 3
Jiaxiong Pi, University of Nebraska at Omaha, USA
Yong Shi, University of Nebraska at Omaha, USA
Zhengxin Chen, University of Nebraska at Omaha, USA

Chapter 4
Stefano Berretti, University of Firenze, Italy
Alberto Del Bimbo, University of Firenze, Italy
Pietro Pala, University of Firenze, Italy
Francisco Josè Silva Mata, Advanced Technologies Application Center, Cuba

Detailed Table of Contents

Section 1

As the size of multimedia database grows, it becomes impractical to manually annotate all contents and attributes of the media, and the difficulty in finding desired information increases. To copy with these challenges, content-based multimedia retrieval systems have been developed for various applications. The chapter not only provides a conceptual architecture for the design of content-based retrieval system, but also discusses essential components of retrieval system and their research issues, including feature extraction and representation, dimension reduction of feature vector, indexing, and query specifications. As content-based multimedia retrieval is a young research field and there exists many challenging research problems, this chapter also addresses several research issues for the future research.

Chapter 2

This chapter proposes a metric on partitions of arbitrary measurable sets and its special properties for metrical content-based image retrieval based on the 'spatial' semantic of images. The approach considers images represented in the form of nested partitions produced by any segmentations. Nested partitions representation expresses a degree of information refinement or roughening and so not only corresponds to rational content control but also ensures creation of specific search algorithms (e.g. invariant to image background) and synthesize hierarchical models of image search reducing the number of query and database elements match operations.

Jiaxiong Pi, University of Nebraska at Omaha, USA
Yong Shi, University of Nebraska at Omaha, USA
Zhengxin Chen, University of Nebraska at Omaha, USA

This chapter presents a study on using a useful spatial data structure, R*-tree, for similarity analysis and cluster analysis of image contents. This chapter not only describes an R*-tree based similarity analysis tool for similarity retrieval of images, but also discusses R*-tree based clustering methods for images. This has been a tricky issue: although objects stored in the same R* tree leaf node enjoys spatial proximity, it is well-known that R* trees cannot be used directly for cluster analysis. Nevertheless, R* tree's indexing feature can be used to assist existing cluster analysis methods, thus enhancing their performance of cluster quality. This chapter reports the progress of using R* trees to improve K-means and hierarchical clustering methods. Based on R*-Tree's feature of indexing Minimum Bounding Box (MBB) according to spatial proximity, this chapter extends R*-Tree's application to cluster analysis containing image data. Two improved algorithms, KMeans-R and Hierarchy-R, are proposed. Experiments have shown that KMeans-R and Hierarchy-R have achieved better clustering quality.

Stefano Berretti, University of Firenze, Italy
Alberto Del Bimbo, University of Firenze, Italy
Pietro Pala, University of Firenze, Italy
Francisco Josè Silva Mata, Advanced Technologies Application Center, Cuba

This chapter has a twofold objective. On the one hand, an original approach based on the computation of radial geodesic distances (RGD) is proposed to represent two-dimensional (2D) face images and three-dimensional (3D) face models for the purpose of face recognition. On the other hand, face representations based on RGDs are used for the purpose of face identification by using them in an operative framework that exploits state of the art techniques for manifold embedding and machine learning. This chapter also shows a general work flow that is not limited to face recognition applications, but can be used in many different contexts of recognition and retrieval. Experimental results are reported for 3D-3D and 2D-3D face recognition using the proposed approach.

Wing-Yin Chau, University of Warwick, UK
Chia-Hung Wei, Ching Yun University, Taiwan
Yue Li, Nankai University, China

With the rapid increase in the amount of registered trademarks around the world, trademark image retrieval has been developed to deal with a vast amount of trademark images in a trademark registration system. Many different approaches have been developed throughout these years in an attempt to develop an effective TIR system. Some conventional approaches used in content-based image retrieval, such as moment invariants, Zernike moments, Fourier descriptors and curvature scale space descriptors, have also been widely used in TIR. These approaches, however, contain some major deficiencies when addressing the TIR problem. Therefore, this chapter proposes a novel approach in order to overcome the major deficiencies of the conventional approaches. The proposed approach combines the Zernike moments descriptors with the centroid distance representation and the curvature representation. The experimental results show that the proposed approach outperforms the conventional approaches in several circumstances. Details regarding to the proposed approach as well as the conventional approaches are presented in this chapter.

Section 2

Chapter 6

Visual information has been immensely used in various domains such as web, education, health, and digital libraries, due to the advancements of computing technologies. Meanwhile, users realize that it has been more and more difficult to find desired visual content such as images. Though traditional content-based retrieval (CBR) systems allow users to access visual information through query-by-example with low level visual features (e.g. color, shape, and texture), the semantic gap is widely recognized as a hurdle for practical adoption of CBR systems. Wealthy visual information (e.g. user generated visual content) enables us to derive new knowledge at a large scale, which will significantly facilitate visual information management. Besides semantic concept detection, semantic relationship among concepts can also be explored in visual domain, other than traditional textual domain. Therefore, this chapter aims to provide an overview of the state-of-the-arts on discovering semantics in visual domain from two aspects, semantic concept detection and knowledge discovery from visual information at semantic level. For the first aspect, various aspects of visual information annotation are discussed, including content representation, machine learning based annotation methodologies, and widely used datasets. For the second aspect, a novel data driven based approach is introduced to discover semantic relevance among concepts in visual domain. Future research topics are also outlined.

Chapter 7

With nearly twenty years of intensive study on the content-based image retrieval and annotation, the topic still remains difficult. By and large, the essential challenge lies in the limitation of using low-level visual features to characterize the semantic information of images, commonly known as the semantic gap. To bridge this gap, various approaches have been proposed based on the incorporation of human knowledge and textual information as well as the learning techniques utilizing the information of different modalities. At the same time, contextual information which represents the relationship between different real world/conceptual entities has shown its significance with respect to recognition tasks not only through real life experience but also scientific studies. In this chapter, we first review the state of the art of the existing works on image annotation and retrieval. Moreover, a general Bayesian framework which integrates content and contextual information and its application to both image annotation and retrieval are elaborated. The contextual information is considered as the statistical relationship between different images and different semantic concepts for image retrieval and annotation, respectively. The framework has efficient learning and classification procedures and the effectiveness is evaluated based on experimental studies, which demonstrate its advantage over both content-based and context-based approaches.

This chapter presents a highly scalable and adaptable co-learning framework on multimodal data mining in a multimedia database. The framework enjoys a strong scalability in the sense that the query time complexity is a constant, independent of the database scale, and the mining effectiveness is also independent of the database scale, allowing facilitating a multimodal querying to a very large scale multimedia database. At the same time, this framework also enjoys a strong adaptability in the sense that it allows incrementally updating the database indexing with a constant operation when the database is dynamically updated with new information. Hence, this framework excels many of the existing multimodal data mining methods in the literature that are neither scalable nor adaptable at all. Theoretic analysis and empirical evaluations are provided to demonstrate the advantage of the strong scalability and adaptability. While this framework is general for multimodal data mining in any specific domains, to evaluate this framework, this study applies it to the Berkeley Drosophila ISH embryo image database for the evaluations of the mining performance. This study has compared the framework with a state-of-the-art multimodal data mining method to demonstrate the effectiveness and the promise of the framework.

Background knowledge has been actively investigated as a possible means to improve performance of machine learning algorithms. Research has shown that background knowledge plays an especially critical role in three atypical text categorization tasks: short-text classification, limited labeled data, and non-topical classification. This chapter explores the use of machine learning for non-hierarchical classification of search queries, and presents an approach to background knowledge discovery by using information retrieval techniques. Two different sets of background knowledge that were obtained from the World Wide Web, one in 2006 and one in 2009, are used with the proposed approach to classify a commercial corpus of web query data by the age of the user. In the process, various classification scenarios are generated and executed, providing insight into choice, significance and range of tuning parameters, and exploring impact of the dynamic web on classification results.

Section 3

The fast proliferation of video data archives has increased the need for automatic video content analysis and semantic video retrieval. Since temporal information is critical in conveying video content, in this chapter, an effective temporal-based event detection framework is proposed to support high-level video indexing and retrieval. The core is a temporal association mining process that systematically captures characteristic temporal patterns to help identify and define interesting events. This framework effectively tackles the challenges caused by loose video structure and class imbalance issues. One of the unique characteristics of this framework is that it offers strong generality and extensibility with the capability of exploring representative event patterns with little human interference. The temporal information and event detection results can then be input into the proposed distributed video retrieval system to support the high-level semantic querying, selective video browsing and event-based video retrieval.

This chapter tackles the analysis and characterization of the artistic animated movies in view of constituting an automatic content-based retrieval system. First, this study deals with temporal segmentation, and propose cut, fade and dissolve detection methods adapted to the constraints of this domain. Further, this chapter discusses a fuzzy linguistic approach for automatic symbolic/semantic content annotation in terms of color techniques and action content and this study tests its potential in automatic video classification. The browsing issue is dealt by providing methods for both, static and dynamic video abstraction. For a quick browse of the movie's visual content, this study creates a storyboard-like summary, while for a "sneak peak" of the movie's exciting action content proposed for a trailer-like video skim. Finally, this chapter discusses the architecture of a prototype client-server 3D virtual environment for interactive video retrieval. Several experimental results are presented.

Chapter 12

Hua-Tsung Chen, National Chiao-Tung University, Taiwan
Suh-Yin Lee, National Chiao-Tung University, Taiwan

The explosive proliferation of multimedia data necessitates the development of automatic systems and tools for content-based multimedia analysis. Recently, sports video analysis has been attracting more and more attention due to the potential commercial benefits, entertaining functionalities and mass audience requirements. Much research on shot classification, highlight extraction and event detection in sports video has been done to provide the general audience interactive video viewing systems for quick browsing, indexing and summarization. More keenly than ever, the audience desire professional insights into the games. The coach and the players demand automatic tactics analysis and performance evaluation with the aid of multimedia information retrieval technologies. It is also a growing trend to provide computer-assisted umpiring in sports games, such as the well-known Hawk eye system used in tennis. Therefore, sports video analysis is certainly a research issue worth investigation. This chapter proposes to review current research and give an insight into sports video analysis. The discussion on potential applications and encouraging future work is also presented.

Section 4

Chapter 13

Clement H.C. Leung, Hong Kong Baptist University, Hong Kong
Jiming Liu, Hong Kong Baptist University, Hong Kong
Alfredo Milani, University of Perugia, Italy & Hong Kong Baptist University, Hong Kong
Alice W.S. Chan, Hong Kong Baptist University, Hong Kong

With the rapid advancement of music compression and storage technologies, digital music can be easily created, shared and distributed, not only in computers, but also in numerous portable digital devices. Music often constitutes a key component in many multimedia databases, and as they grow in size and complexity, their meaningful search and retrieval become important and necessary. Music Information Retrieval (MIR) is a relatively young and challenging research area started since the late 1990s. Although some form of music retrieval is available on the Internet, these tend to be inflexible and have significant limitations. Currently, most of these music retrieval systems only rely on low-level music information contents (e.g., metadata, album title, lyrics, etc.), and in this chapter, this chapter presents an adaptive indexing approach to search and discover music information. Experimental results show that through such an indexing architecture, high-level music semantics may be incorporated into search strategies.

Nowadays MP3 music has become very popular with the availability of powerful computation and wide bandwidth connectivity. This chapter will be devoted to present techniques and algorithms, dealing with compressed audio, aimed at content analysis. Since content analysis in compressed domain is an innovative field of applications, the literature review will be extended to methods that extract music content from MP3, even if the algorithms are not focused on music information retrieval. This chapter focuses on a number of different algorithms dealing with common tasks of the MIR field such as tempo induction, tempo tracking, and automatic music synchronization. This chapter also presents an overview of the MusicXML, and IEEE1599 language to represent score and synchronization results and provides related applications, conclusions, and future works in the field of direct content analysis in compressed domain.

Most music is generally published in a cluster of songs, called an album. This study proposes to investigate whether or not there is a reason for assembling and enjoying full albums. Two different approaches are undertaken in order to investigate this, both based on audio features, calculated from the music, and related to the common music dimensions rhythm, timbre and chroma. In the first experiment, automatic segmentation is done on full music albums. If the segmentation is done on song boundaries, which is to be expected, as different fade-ins and –outs are employed, then songs are seen as the homogenous units, while if the boundaries are found within songs, then other homogenous units also exist. A second experiment on music sorting by similarity reveals findings on the sorting complexity of music albums. If the sorting complexity is high, then the albums are unordered; otherwise the album is ordered with regards to the features. A discussion of the results of the evaluation of the segment boundaries and sorting complexity reveals interesting findings.

Preface

Multimedia retrieval refers to a technology used to search for various types of digital multimedia information, such as texts, images, graphics, video, and audio, from multimedia databases. The technology makes the database users possible to locate desired multimedia information, analyze characteristics of multimedia sets, and discover knowledge hidden in vast amount of multimedia objects. As the size of multimedia databases grows, retrieval has been a key challenge in multimedia database management. The challenge in retrieving desired multimedia information comes from three aspects: The first aspect is the users' difficulty in specifying their information needs in the form of a predefined query. The second aspect is the problem of extracting semantics from the multimedia content. The third aspect is that user specific interests and the search context are usually neglected when objects are retrieved. To improve the performance of retrieval systems, it is necessary to apply machine learning methods to tune the mechanism of the retrieval system to the user's information needs in the search process. Machine learning is concerned with the design and development of algorithms and techniques that allow computers to learn like the human. Applying machine learning for multimedia retrieval makes retrieval systems more intelligent to sensibly tackle various problems and issues. Due to the importance of the field, a significant amount of research and efforts have been made around the world.

This book focuses on theories, methods, algorithms, and applications multimedia retrieval using machine learning techniques. The mission of this book is to disseminate state-of-the-art multimedia retrieval, advance the field of multimedia databases, and educate the multimedia database community. The individual chapters are contributed by different authors and present various solutions to the different kinds of problems concerning machine learning for multimedia retrieval. The prospective audience of the proposed book would be academics, scientists, practitioners and engineers who are engaged in efforts to understand the state of the art in multimedia retrieval research, design and applications. This book can also be used as a supplement in multimedia related courses for lecturers, upper-level undergraduates and graduate students. Moreover, fellow researchers and PhD students intending to broaden their scope or looking for a research topic in multimedia retrieval may find the book inspiring.

This book includes 15 chapters, which are organized into four sections. The first section provides fundamental techniques for multimedia and solutions to specific applications in image retrieval. In the second section, another four chapters discusses semantic analysis, annotation, and knowledge discovery. The third section introduces and presents approaches to video analysis, indexing, and retrieval. In the last section, three chapters are included to represent music information analysis and retrieval. The importance of each chapter is briefly described as follows:

As the size of multimedia database grows, it becomes impractical to manually annotate all contents and attributes of the media, and the difficulty in finding desired information increases. To copy with these challenges, content-based multimedia retrieval systems have been developed for various applications. In Chapter 1 of this book, Chia-Hung Wei and Sherry Y Chen provide a conceptual architecture for the design of content-based retrieval system, and discuss essential components of retrieval system and their research issues, including feature extraction and representation, dimension reduction of feature vector, indexing, and query specifications.

Dmitry Kinoshenko et al. proposes a metric on partitions of arbitrary measurable sets and its special properties for metrical content-based image retrieval based on the 'spatial' semantic of images. The approach considers images represented in the form of nested partitions produced by any segmentations. Nested partitions representation expresses a degree of information refinement or roughening and so not only corresponds to rational content control but also ensures creation of specific search algorithms and synthesize hierarchical models of image search reducing the number of query and database elements match operations.

The study of content-based information retrieval has been focused on such approaches as search-by-association, aimed search, and category search. In information and multimedia retrieval, any retrieval scheme is based on a query matching. R* trees can be utilized to find those similar data points. In Chapter 3, Jiaxiong Pi et al. not only utilize R* trees to improve K-means and hierarchical clustering methods, but also extend R*-Tree's application to cluster analysis for similarity retrieval of images.

In multimedia applications, 2D and 3D images can be used jointly to improve pattern recognition. In face recognition, Stefano Berretti et al. propose an original framework that performs recognition by using manifold embedding and machine learning techniques applied to the face representations extracted from 2D face images and from 3D face models. Objectives of Chapter 4 are twofold. On the one hand, an original approach based on the computation of radial geodesic distances (RGD) is proposed to represent two-dimensional (2D) face images and three-dimensional (3D) face models for the purpose of face recognition. On the other hand, face representations based on RGDs are used for the purpose of face identification by using them in an operative framework that exploits state-of-the-art techniques for manifold embedding and machine learning.

With the rapid increase in the amount of registered trademarks around the world, trademark image retrieval systems have been developed throughout these years. However, some conventional approaches to feature extraction, such as moment invariants, Zernike moments, Fourier descriptors and curvature scale space descriptors, contain some major deficiencies when addressing the trademark image retrieval problem. In Chapter 5, Wing-Yin Chau et al. propose a novel approach in order to overcome the major deficiencies of the conventional approaches. The proposed approach combines the Zernike moments descriptors with the centroid distance representation and the curvature representation. In Chapter 5, the experimental results show that the proposed approach outperforms the conventional approaches in several circumstances.

Visual information has been immensely used in various domains, such as education, health, and digital libraries, due to the advancements of computing technologies. Meanwhile, users realize that it has been more and more difficult to recognize visual content. Although traditional content-based retrieval systems allow users to access visual information through query-by-example with low level visual features (e.g. color, shape, and texture), the semantic gap is widely recognized as a hurdle for practical adoption of content-based retrieval systems. Rich visual information (e.g. user generated visual content) enables us to derive new knowledge at a large scale, which will significantly facilitate visual information management. Besides semantic concept detection, semantic relationship among concepts can also be explored in visual domain, other than traditional textual domain. In Chapter 6, Zhiyong Wang and Dagan Feng provide an overview of the state-of-the-arts on discovering semantics in visual domain from two aspects, semantic concept detection and knowledge discovery from visual information at semantic level. For the first aspect, various aspects of visual information annotation are discussed, including content representation, machine learning based annotation methodologies, and widely used datasets. For the second aspect, a novel data driven based approach is introduced to discover semantic relevance among concepts in visual domain. Future research topics are also outlined.

With nearly twenty years of intensive study on the content-based image retrieval and annotation, the related topics still remain difficult. The essential challenge lies in the limitation of using low-level visual features to characterize the semantic information of images, commonly known as the semantic gap. To bridge this gap, various approaches have been proposed based on the incorporation of human knowledge and textual information as well as the learning techniques utilizing the information of different modalities. In addition, contextual information which represents the relationship between different real world/conceptual entities has shown its significance with respect to recognition tasks through real life experience and scientific studies. In Chapter 7, Zhang and Guan firstly review the state of the art of the existing works on image annotation and retrieval. Moreover, they propose a general Bayesian framework which integrates content and contextual information and apply it for image annotation and retrieval. The contextual information is considered as the statistical relationship between different images and different semantic concepts for image retrieval and annotation, respectively. The framework has efficient learning and classification procedures and the effectiveness is evaluated based on experimental studies, which demonstrate its advantage over both content-based and context-based approaches.

In Chapter 8, Zhang et al. present a highly scalable and adaptable co-learning framework on multimodal data mining in a multimedia database. The framework demonstrates a strong scalability in the sense that the query time complexity is a constant, independent of the database scale. The mining effectiveness is also independent of the database scale, allowing facilitating a multimodal querying to a very large scale multimedia database. In addition, this framework also shows a strong adaptability in the sense that it allows incrementally updating the database indexing with a constant operation when the database is dynamically updated with new information. Hence, this framework excels many of the existing multimodal data mining methods in the literature that are neither scalable nor adaptable at all. Theoretic analysis and empirical evaluations are provided to demonstrate the advantage of the strong scalability and adaptability. While this framework is general for multimodal data mining in any specific domains, to evaluate this framework, this study applies it to the Berkeley Drosophila ISH embryo image database for the evaluations of the mining performance. This study has compared the framework with a state-of-the-art multimodal data mining method to demonstrate the effectiveness and the promise of the framework.

Background knowledge has been investigated as a potential means to improve performance of machine learning algorithms. In Chapter 9, Taksa and Zelikovitz explore the use of machine learning for non-hierarchical classification of queries, and present an approach to background knowledge discovery by using information retrieval techniques. Two different sets of background knowledge that were obtained from the World Wide Web, one in 2006 and one in 2009, are used with the proposed approach to classify a commercial corpus of Web query data by the age of the user. In the process, various classification scenarios are generated and executed, providing insight into choice, significance and range of tuning parameters, and exploring impact of the dynamic web on classification results.

The fast proliferation of video data archives has increased the need for automatic video content analysis and semantic video retrieval. In Chapter 10, Min Chen proposes an effective temporal-based event detection framework to support high-level video indexing and retrieval. The core of the framework is a temporal association mining process that systematically captures characteristic temporal patterns for identification of interesting events. This framework effectively tackles the challenges caused by loose video structure and class imbalance issues. Another characteristic of this framework is that it offers strong generality and extensibility with the capability of exploring representative event patterns with little human interference. The temporal information and event detection results can be input into the proposed distributed video retrieval system to support the high-level semantic querying, selective video browsing and event-based video retrieval.

In Chapter 11, Ionescu et al. present an automatic content-based retrieval system for tackling the analysis and characterization of the artistic animated movies in. They deal with temporal segmentation, and propose cut, fade and dissolve detection methods adapted to the constraints of this domain. Furthermore, this chapter discusses a fuzzy linguistic approach to automatic symbolic/semantic content annotation in terms of color techniques and action content. The browsing issue is dealt by providing methods for static and dynamic video abstraction. For a quick browse of the movie's visual content, Ionescu et al. create a storyboard-like summary, while for a "sneak peak" of the movie's exciting action content proposed for a trailer-like video skim.

Sports video analysis has been attracting more and more attention due to the potential commercial benefits, entertaining functionalities and mass audience requirements. Much research on shot classification, highlight extraction and event detection in sports video has been done to provide the general audience interactive video viewing systems for quick browsing, indexing and summarization. More keenly than ever, the audience desire professional insights into the games. The coach and the players demand automatic tactics analysis and performance evaluation with the aid of multimedia information retrieval technologies. It is also a growing trend to provide computer-assisted umpiring in sports games, such as the well-known Hawk eye system used in tennis. Therefore, sports video analysis is certainly a research issue worth investigation. In Chapter 12, Hua-Tsung Chen and Suh-Yin Lee review current research, give an insight into sports video analysis, and discuss potential applications and potential issues.

With the rapid advancement of music compression and storage technologies, digital music can be easily created, shared and distributed in computers and numerous portable digital devices. Music is often seen as a key component in many multimedia databases, and as they grow in size and complexity, their meaningful search and retrieval become important and necessary. Music information retrieval is a relatively young and challenging research area started since the late 1990s. Although some forms of music retrieval are available on the Internet, these tend to be inflexible and have significant limitations. In Chapter 13, Leung et al present an adaptive indexing approach to search and discover music information. High-level music semantics may be incorporated into search strategies through such an indexing architecture.

MP3 music has become very popular with the availability of powerful computation and wide bandwidth connectivity. Antonello D'Aguanno presents related techniques and algorithms to deal with compressed audio for content analysis. Chapter 14 focuses on a number of different algorithms dealing with common tasks of music information retrieval, such as tempo induction, tempo tracking, and automatic music synchronization. This chapter also presents an overview of the MusicXML, and IEEE1599 language to represent score and synchronization results and provides related applications, conclusions, and future works in the field of direct content analysis in compressed domain.

Most music is generally published in a cluster of songs, called an album, although many people enjoy individual songs, commonly called singles. In Chapter 15, Kristoffer Jensen investigates whether there is a reason for assembling full albums. Two different experiments are undertaken in order to investigate this issue. In the first experiment, automatic segmentation is done on full music albums. When the segmentation is done on song boundaries, different fade-ins and –outs are employed and songs are seen as the homogenous units. While the boundaries are found within songs, other homogenous units also exist. The second experiment on music sorting by similarity reveals the sorting complexity of music albums. If the sorting complexity is high, then the albums are unordered; otherwise the album is ordered with regards to the features.

Chia-Hung Wei
Ching Yun University, Taiwan

Yue Li
Nankai University, China

Acknowledgment

The editors would like to gratefully acknowledge all authors for their excellent contributions to this book. We would also like to appreciate the help of the advisory

We would also like to appreciate the help of the people involving in the collation and review process of the book. A further special note of appreciations goes to all the staff at IGI Global, whose contributions throughout the whole process from inception of the initial idea to publication are invaluable.

Chia-Hung Wei
Ching Yun University, Taiwan

Yue Li
Nankai University, China

Spring 2010

Section 1

Chapter 1
Techniques for Content–Based Multimedia Retrieval

Chia-Hung Wei
Ching Yun University, Taiwan

Sherry Y. Chen
Brunel University, UK

ABSTRACT

As the size of multimedia database grows, it becomes impractical to manually annotate all contents and attributes of the media, and the difficulty in finding desired information increases. To copy with these challenges, content-based multimedia retrieval systems have been developed for various applications. The chapter not only provides a conceptual architecture for the design of content-based retrieval system, but also discusses essential components of retrieval system and their research issues, including feature extraction and representation, dimension reduction of feature vector, indexing, and query specifications. As content-based multimedia retrieval is a young research field and there exists many challenging research problems, this chapter also addresses several research issues for the future research.

INTRODUCTION

In the past decade there has been rapid growth in the use of digital media, such as images, video, and audio. As the use of digital media increases, retrieval and management techniques become more important in order to facilitate the effective searching and browsing of large multimedia databases. Before the emergence of content-based retrieval, media was annotated with text, allowing the media to be accessed by text-based searching. Through textual description, media is managed and retrieved based on the classification of subject or semantics. This hierarchical structure, like yellow pages, allows users to easily navigate and browse, or search using standard Boolean queries. However, with the emergence of massive multimedia databases, the traditional text-based search suffers from the following limitations (Djeraba, 2003; Shah et al., 2004):

DOI: 10.4018/978-1-61692-859-9.ch001

- Manual annotations require too much time and are expensive to implement. As the number of media in a database grows, the difficulty in finding desired information increases. It becomes infeasible to manually annotate all attributes of the media content. Annotating a sixty-minute video, containing more than 100,000 images, consumes a vast amount of time and expense.
- Manual annotations fail to deal with the discrepancy of subjective perception. The phrase, "an image says more than a thousand words," implies that the textual description is sufficient for depicting subjective perception. To capture all concepts, thoughts, and feelings for the content of any media is almost impossible.
- Some media contents are difficult to concretely describe in words. For example, a piece of melody without lyric or irregular organic shape cannot easily be expressed in textual form, but people expect to search media with similar contents based on examples they provided.

In an attempt to address these limitations, content-based retrieval employs content information to automatically index data with minimal human intervention.

APPLICATIONS

Content-based retrieval has been proposed by different communities for various applications. These applications includes

- *Medical Diagnosis*: The medical community is currently developing picture archiving and communication systems (PACS), which integrate imaging modalities and interfaces with hospital and departmental information systems in order to manage the storage and distribution of images to radiologists, physicians, specialists, clinics, and imaging centers. A crucial requirement in PACS is to provide an efficient search function to access desired images. As images with the similar pathology-bearing regions can be found and interpreted, those images can be applied to aid diagnosis for image-based reasoning. For example, Wei & Li (2006) proposed a content-based retrieval system for locating mammograms with similar pathological characteristics.
- *Intellectual Property*: Trademark image registration has applied content-based retrieval techniques to compare a new candidate mark with existing marks to ensure that there is no repetition. Copyright protection can also benefit from content-based retrieval as copyright owners are able to search and identify unauthorized copies of images on the Internet. For example, Jiang et al. (2006) developed a content-based system using adaptive selection of visual features for trademark image retrieval.
- *Broadcasting Archives*: Every day broadcasting companies produce a lot of audio-visual data. To deal with these large archives, which can contain millions of hours of video and audio data, content-based retrieval techniques are used to annotate their contents and summarize the audio-visual data to drastically reduce the volume of raw footage. For example, Lopez & Chen (2006) developed a content-based video retrieval system to support news and sports retrieval.
- *Multimedia Searching on the Internet*: Although a large amount of multimedia has been made available on the Internet for retrieval, existing search engines mainly perform text-based retrieval. To access the various media on the Internet, content-based search engines can assist users in searching the media with the most similar contents based on queries. For example, Khan (2007)

designed a framework for image annotation and used ontology to enable content-based image retrieval on the Internet.

FRAMEWORK OF CONTENT-BASED RETRIEVAL SYSTEMS

The retrieval framework as shown in Figure 1 can be divided into off-line feature extraction and on-line retrieval. In the off-line feature extraction, the contents of the data in the database are pre-processed, extracted and described with a feature vector, also called a descriptor. A feature vector for each datum is stored alongside with its corresponding audio/video/image data in the database. In the on-line retrieval, the user can submit a query example to the retrieval system to search for desired data. The similarities between the feature vectors of the query example and those of the data in the database are computed and ranked. Retrieval is conducted by applying an indexing scheme to provide an efficient way of searching the database. Finally, the system ranks the similarity and returns the data that are most similar to the query example. If the user is not satisfied with the initial search results, human-centered computing is introduced into an interactive search process. The user can provide relevance information to the retrieval system in order to search further (following the arrows on the dashed lines in Figure 1). This interactive search process can be repeated until the user is satisfied with the search results or unwilling to offer any further feedback.

For the design of content-based retrieval system, a designer needs to consider four aspects: feature extraction and representation, dimension reduction of feature, indexing, and query specifications, which will be introduced in the following sections.

FEATURE EXTRACTION AND REPRESENTATION

Representation of media needs to consider which features are most useful and meaningful for representing the contents of media and which approaches can effectively code the attributes of the media. The features are typically extracted off-line so that efficient computation is not a significant issue, but large

Figure 1. A conceptual framework for content-based retrieval

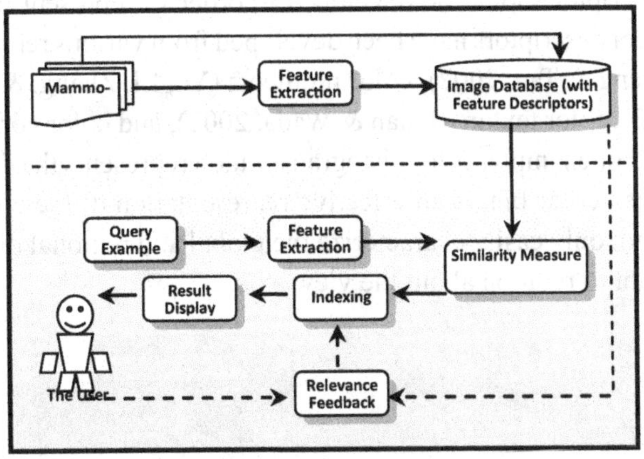

collections still need longer time to compute the features. Features of media content can be classified into low-level and high-level features.

Low-Level Features

Low-level features, such as color, shape, texture, object motion, loudness, power spectrum, bandwidth, and pitch, are extracted directly from media in the database (Liu et al., 2007). Features at this level are objectively derived from the media themselves, rather than referring to any external semantics. Features extracted at this level can answer queries such as "finding images with more than 20% distribution in blue and green color," which might retrieve several images with blue sky and green gras. Many effective approaches to low-level feature extraction have been developed for various purposes (Russ, 2006; Feng et al., 2003). In visual media, major low-level features are color, shape, and texture, which are described as follows.

Color

Color is a powerful descriptor that simplifies object identification (Gonzalez & Woods, 2002) and is one of the most frequently used visual features for content-based image retrieval. To extract the color features from the content of an image, a proper color space and an effective color descriptor have to be determined.

The purpose of a color space is to facilitate the specification of colors. Each color in the color space is a single point represented in a coordinate system. Several color spaces, such as RGB, HSV, CIE L*a*b, and CIE L*u*v, have been developed for different purposes. Although there is no agreement on which color space is the best for CBIR, an appropriate color system is required to ensure perceptual uniformity. Therefore, the RGB color space, a widely used system for representing color images, is not suitable for CBIR because it is a perceptually non-uniform and device-dependent system (Gevers, 2001). The most frequently used technique is to convert color representations from the RGB color space to the HSV, CIE L*u*v, or CIE L*a*b color spaces with perceptual uniformity (Li & Yuen, 2000). The HSV color space is an intuitive system, which describes a specific color by its hue, saturation and brightness value. This color system is very useful in interactive color selection and manipulation; The CIE L*u*v and CIE L*a*b color spaces are both perceptually uniform systems, which provide easy use of similar metrics for comparing color (Haeghen, Naeyaert, Lemahieu, & Philips, 2000).

An effective color descriptor should be developed in order to represent the color of the global or regional areas. Several color descriptors have been developed from various representation schemes, such as color histograms (Ouyang & Tan, 2002), color moments (Yu, Li, Zhang, & Feng, 2002), color edge (Gevers & Stokman, 2003), color texture (Guan & Wada, 2002), and color correlograms (Moghaddam, Khajoie, & Rouhi, 2003). For example, color histogram, which represents the distribution of the number of pixels for each quantized color bin, is an effective representation of the color content of an image. The color histogram can not only easily characterize the global and regional distribution of colors in an image, but also be invariant to rotation about the view axis.

Shape

Shape is one of the most important features in describing an image. People can easily identify different images and classify them into different categories solely from the outline of an object in a given image. As shape conveys some kind of semantic information which is meaningful to human recognition, it is used as a distinctive feature for the representation of an image object. In general, two large categories of shape descriptors can be identified: contour-based shape descriptors and region-based shape descriptors. Contour-based descriptors emphasize the closed curve that surrounds the boundary of an image object. The curve can be described by numerous models, including chain codes, polygons, circular arcs, and boundary Fourier descriptors. In addition, a boundary can be described by its features, for instance, inflection points. Region-based shape descriptors usually refer to the shape descriptions that are derived using all pixel information within the closed boundary of an image object. The region can be modeled in different ways, such as collections of primitives (rectangles, disks, etc.), and deformable templates.

Image retrieval based on shape similarity is still considered as one of the most difficult aspects of content-based image retrieval because the matching of geometric shapes is usually required to be invariant to scale, translation, and rotation. Since both contour-based descriptors and region-based descriptors reflect to perceptually meaningful representations, selecting a proper shape representation for particular images usually needs to consider either contour-based descriptors, region-based descriptors, or both, in the representation of shape.

Texture

Texture in image retrieval can be used for at least two purposes (Sebe & Lew, 2002). Firstly, an image can be considered as a jigsaw puzzle consisting of different texture regions. These regions can be used as examples to search for and retrieve images with similar areas. Secondly, text-based image retrieval requires effective image annotation methods to automatically describe image content in the form of captioning or keywords to a digital image. Texture can be employed for automatically annotating the content of an image. For example, the texture of a measles skin region can be used for annotating regions of interest with the same infection in medical image databases. Textural representation approaches can be classified into structural approaches and statistical approaches (Sebe & Lew, 2002). Structural approaches characterize texture by identifying a set of structural primitives and certain placement rules. Statistical approaches analyze textural characteristics according to the statistical distribution of image intensity. Approaches in this category include grey level co-occurrence matrix, fractal model, Tamura features, Wold decomposition, and so on (Feng, Siu, & Zhang, 2003). The following section will describe three of the most popular approaches to texture analysis, which are grey level co-occurrence matrix, grey level co-occurrence matrix, and Tamura features.

High-Level Features

High-level features, which are also called semantic features, such as timbre, rhythm, instruments, and events, involve different degrees of semantics contained in the media. High-level features are supposed to deal with the semantic queries, such as the query "finding a picture of water" or "searching for Mona Lisa Smile." The latter query contains higher-degree semantics than the former. As water in images displays the homogeneous texture represented in low-level features, such a query is easier to process. To retrieve the latter query, the retrieval system requires prior knowledge that identifies that Mona Lisa is a woman, who is a specific character rather than any other woman in a painting. The difficulty in processing high-level queries arises from external knowledge with the description of low-level features, known as the semantic gap. The retrieval process requires a translation mechanism that can convert the query of "Mona Lisa Smile" into low-level features. Two possible solutions have been proposed to minimize the semantic gap (Marques & Furht, 2002). The first is automatic metadata generation to the media. Automatic annotation still involves the semantic concept and requires different schemes for various media (Jeon et al., 2003). The second uses relevance feedback to allow the retrieval system to learn and understand the semantic context of a query operation. Feedback relevance is discussed in later this article.

DIMENSION REDUCTION OF FEATURE VECTOR

In an attempt to capture detailed information as much as possible, many multimedia databases contain large numbers of features. Such a feature-vector set is considered as high dimensionality. High dimensionality may cause the "curse of dimension" problem where the complexity and computational cost of the query increase exponentially with the number of dimensions (Bishop, 2006). Dimension reduction is a popular technique to overcome this problem and support efficient retrieval in large-scale databases. However, there is a trade-off between the efficiency obtained through dimension reduction and the completeness obtained through the information extracted. If each datum is represented by a smaller number of dimensions, the speed of retrieval is increased. However, some information may be lost. One of the most widely used techniques in multimedia retrieval is Principal Component Analysis (PCA). PCA is used to transform the original data of high dimensionality into a new coordinate system with low dimensionality, by finding the eigenvalues and eigenvectors of the source data. The eigenvalues represent the distribution of energy of the source data among each of the eigenvectors, which form a basis for the data. A subset of the eigenvectors are selected as basis vectors and projected onto the new basis. The new coordinate system removes the redundant data so the new set of data may better represent the essential information. Zuo et al. (2006) proposed a bidirectional PCA method to reduce the dimensionality in feature vectors.

INDEXING

The retrieval system typically contains two mechanisms: similarity measure and multi-dimensional indexing. Similarity measure is used to find the most similar objects. Multi-dimensional indexing is used to accelerate the retrieval performance in the search process.

Similarity Measure

Since each feature vector can be represented as a point in multi-dimensional space, the similarity measure for any two images is defined as the distance between their corresponding feature descriptors, normally represented by vectors. For any true distance metric, the distance from point I to point J, denoted by $D(I,J)$, possesses the following four key properties (Berry & Linoff, 2004):

- $D(I,J)=0$ if and only if $I=J$. The distance is 0 only if I and J are identical.
- $D(I,J)\geq 0$ for all I and all J. The distance between I and J can always be measured and greater than or equal to zero.
- $D(I,J)=D(J,I)$. The distance between I and J is equal to the distance between J and I. i.e., J and I possess commutativity when their distance is measured.
- $D(I,J)\leq D(I,K)+ D(K,J)\, D(I,J)$. Visiting an intermediate point K on the way from I to J never shortens the distance.

If points I and J are closer than another point K in distance, their corresponding images I and J are more similar than image K. This formal definition of distance is the basis for measuring similarity, but content-based image retrieval still works pretty well when some of these constraints are relaxed a bit. For example, the distance from an image I to another J is not always the same as the distance from J to I. However, the similarity measure is still useful for image retrieval purposes. It is should be noted the reverse meanings of distance and similarity, where distance is a measure of dissimilarity with the value of zero denoting exact an match and larger values indicating less similar images whereas similarity is usually defined in the range [0, 1] with 0 meaning no similarity and 1 perfect similarity.

The form of the extracted features determines the kind of measurement that will be used to compare their similarity (Smeulders, Worring, Santini, Gupta, & Jain, 2000). The commonly used similarity measures are introduced as follows. Let $D(I,J)$ represent the distance measure between the query example I and the image J in the database, and $f_i(I)$ denote as the i-th feature of I. If each dimension of image feature vector is of equal importance, the Minkowsky-form distance can be used for measuring the distance between two images. The Minkowsky-form distance metric is expressed as

$$D(I,J) = \left(\sum_i \left| f_i(I) - f_j(J) \right|^p \right)^{\frac{1}{p}} \tag{1}$$

where p is a positive integer. It is noted that when $p=2$, the distance is also called Euclidean distance. When the images, consisting of different features, are presented as multi-dimensional points, Euclidean distance is the most common metric used to measure the distance between two points in multi-dimensional space (Qian, Sural, Gu, & Pramanik, 2004). If each dimension of image feature vector is given different importance, the covariance matrix of the feature vectors should be taken into account. In that case, Mahalanobis distance is a proper metric, which is defined as

$$D(I,J) = \sqrt{\left(F_I - F_J \right)^T C^{-1} \left(F_I - F_J \right)} \tag{2}$$

where F is the feature vector and C is the covariance matrix of the feature vectors. For other forms of features, the aforementioned metrics may not be ideal similarity metrics or may not be compatible with human-perceived similarity. Appropriate metrics or schemes of similarity measure should be developed for specific applications. The study in Antani, Long, Thoma, & Lee (2003) used several approaches to encode the shape features for different classes of spine X rays. Each class used a specific similarity metric to compare the distance between two feature vectors.

Multidimensional Indexing

A retrieval query on a database of multimedia with multi-dimensional feature vectors usually requires fast execution of search operations. To support such search operations, an appropriate multi-dimensional access method has to be used for indexing the reduced but still high dimensional feature vectors. Popular multi-dimensional indexing methods include KD-tree (Friedman et al., 1977), R-tree (Guttman, 1984) and R*-tree (Beckmann et al., 1990). These multi-dimensional indexing methods perform well with a limit of up to 20 dimensions. Lo & Chen (2002) proposed an approach to transform music into numeric forms, and developed an index structure based on R-tree for effective retrieval.

RELEVANCE FEEDBACK

Relevance feedback was originally developed for improving the effectiveness of information retrieval systems. The main idea of relevance feedback is for the system to understand the user's information needs. For a given query, the retrieval system returns initial results based on predefined similarity metrics. Then, the user is required to identify the positive and/or negative search results that are relevant and/ or irrelevant to the query. The system subsequently analyzes the features of the user's feedback using a learning approach and then returns refined results. Two important issues to be addressed are how to obtain relevance feedback in an interactive search process and how to make use of relevance feedback to understand the user's information needs. The first issue regarding how to obtain relevance feedback in an interactive search process requires an interactive interface and interactive modes. A user-friendly interface is a prerequisite in an interactive search. This interface not only displays the search results, but also provides an interactive mechanism to communicate with the user and convey relevance feedback. The ways of obtaining relevance feedback usually fall into the following modes:

- **Binary choice:** The user can only select the most similar image as the positive example;
- **Positive examples:** This mode requires the user to select all relevant images as the positive examples at each round;
- **Both positive and negative examples:** In addition to selecting positive examples, the user can also label completely irrelevant images as negative examples in order to remove other irrelevant images in the next search round;
- **Degree of relevance for each retrieved image:** The degree of relevance for each retrieved image can be used to analyze the importance of image features, thereby inferring the search target.

The second issue concerns approaches to learning relevance feedback, i.e. when relevance feedback is submitted to the system, how the retrieval system can realize the user's information need by analyzing the relevance feedback and connect the user's information need with low-level features in order to improve the search results. Four relevance feedback approaches are query point movement, re-weighting, and classification, and probabilistic estimation approach.

Query Point Movement Approach

With this approach, it is assumed that there exists several images which completely convey the intentions of the user, and the high-level concept of those images has been modeled in a low-level feature space (Su, Zhang, Li, & Ma, 2003; Kushki, Androutsos, Plataniotis, & Venetsanopoulos, 2004). The query point movement approach is to move the point of the query toward the region of the feature space that contains the desired images. The development of the query point movement approach was based on the classic Rocchio algorithm, which was originally developed to improve the effectiveness of information retrieval systems Rocchio (1971). Suppose that the user provides a set of relevance feedback documents $D(=D^+ \cup D^-)$ to a given initial query q, where D^+ represents relevant documents and D^- represents irrelevant documents. The iterative estimation used for finding the ideal query point q' follows the equation,

$$q' = \alpha q + \beta \left(\frac{1}{N_{R'}} \sum_{i \in D'_R} D_i^+ \right) - \gamma \left(\frac{1}{N_{N'}} \sum_{i \in D'_N} D_i^- \right) \qquad (3)$$

where α, β, γ are weight parameters, ($\alpha+\beta+\gamma=1$), and N^+ and N^- are the numbers of the document set D^+ and D^-, respectively. The new query point q' is the point that is moved toward positive example points and away from negative example points.

Since α, β, γ control the importance of the previous query point, the average of document features at the set D^+, and the average of document features at the set D^-, respectively, the setting of the weight parameters implies different assumptions as follows:

- When $\alpha=0$, the initial query point q will be ignored. The new query point is obtained by using the currently available image set D. The original query often conveys information which should be retained. When α is greater, the position of the initial query point q in the feature space is more important for determination of the position of the new query point.
- When parameter $\beta=0$ indicates the relevant images D^+ will not be considered for refinement and the setting is unlikely to obtain effective retrieval refinement because the set of images does not reflect the common characteristics to interpret the user's information need. In addition to the requirement $\beta \neq 0$, the weight parameters should satisfy $\beta>\gamma$ in practical applications because information in D^+ is more valuable than that in D^-.
- When $\gamma=0$, the irrelevant images D^- will not be considered. When γ is greater, it means that the learning algorithm attempts to keep the centroid of the irrelevant images D^- as far as possible.

In addition to information retrieval systems, the query point movement approach has been applied in many CBIR systems, such as (Zhang & Zhang, 2006; Wang, Ding, Zhou, & Hu, 2006).

Re-Weighting Approach

The idea of the re-weighting approach is to adjust the weights assigned to each feature or modify the similarity measure (Rui, Huang, & Mehrotra, 1998), i.e. giving more important features larger weights, and less important features smaller weights. A direct way to implement this idea is to exploit statistical properties of the data distribution in the feature space or the user's relevance judgment for training examples.

When a given feature f_i is able to effectively represent a characteristic the relevant images have in common, the spread of the feature always concentrates on a specific area of the feature space. When this is not the case, i.e. when the feature has a widespread distribution, the feature is unlikely to be a discriminative descriptor for the set of relevant image set D^+. As a result, the inverse of the standard deviation for a given feature f_i can be used as the weight w_i to reflect the importance of the feature. In addition, the standard deviation σ_i can be replaced by variance to amplify the emphasis of the feature distribution. However, the way to compute the weights of the features does not take the different importance of individual feedback images into consideration. To alleviate this issue, another re-weighting technique is to assign the weight based on the user's relevance judgment (Rui & Huang, 1999). Let $\pi = [\pi_1, \pi_2, ..., \pi_n]$ represents the degree of relevance of each of n positive feedback images. An ideal query vector q_i for each feature i is described by the weighted sum of all positive feedback images as

$$q_i = \frac{\pi^T X_i}{\sum_{j=1}^{n} \pi_j} \qquad (4)$$

where X_i is the $n \times K_i$ (K_i is the length of feature i) training sample matrix for feature i obtained by stacking the n positive feedback training vectors into a matrix. The system uses q_i as the optimal query to evaluate the relevance of images in the database.

The first two approaches (query point movement approach and re-weighting approach) propose heuristic formulation with empirical parameter adjustment, mainly along the line of independent axis weighting in the feature space. The common characteristic of the two approaches is that parameter adjustment plays a vital role in the use of the two approaches because the parameters significantly affect the learning results. The two approaches can perform well only when appropriate parameters can be tuned for the particular application.

Classification Approach

The classification approach regards the image retrieval task as a classification problem, that is, one where the whole image set is classified into a positive set and a negative set. Those belonging to the positive class are considered as more similar images than those in the negative class. However, the actual goal of image retrieval is to measure the relevance degree of each image to a query example, rather than to classify images into different categories. A similarity measure needs to be included in order to rank the images in the search results.

As the image retrieval task is seen as a binary classification problem, there exists in an disadvantage—it is reasonable to assume positive examples to cluster in certain way, but negative examples usually do not cluster together since they can belong to any class (Zhou & Huang, 2003). The few negative examples are poor representations of the true distribution of all negative images. Assigning all negative examples into one class can mislead the algorithm and hurt the robustness in performance, especially when the number of relevance feedback provide is small. With the consideration, a two-class classifier is not directly suitable for relevance feedback. Due to the fact that positive examples are typically clustered in certain areas in the feature space and the negative examples are spread wide, Huang & Zhou (2001) defined learning from relevance feedback as a biased classification problem, where an uncertain number of classes are assumed but the user is only interested in one of them. To take into account how the bias is toward the positive examples, the ratio of positive scatter over negative scatter with respect to positive scatter is expected to be minimized, i.e., positive examples have minimal scatter while negative examples have maximal scatter with respect to positive ones. Huang & Zhou (2001) proposed biased discriminant analysis to find the optimal biased linear transformation, which allows the retrieval system to find the class where positive images are located. Then, the *k*-nearest neighbor algorithm can be performed to locate the nearest images that belong to the same class in the feature space.

When a classification approach is used for relevance feedback learning, the drawback is that a symmetrical training set of positive and negative examples are required to find the boundary of the training classes. Otherwise, the boundary of the training classes is likely to skew more toward the target class when the set of training data lacks symmetrical proportion.

Probabilistic Estimation Approach

This approach assumes that each candidate image in each search session is associated with the estimated probabilities $P(I \in D^+)$ and $P(I \in D^-)$. Images with the highest probabilities in the query example are deemed as the most relevant images to a given query. The Bayesian probabilistic approach has been applied in many studies for learning relevance feedback (Zhang, Qian, Li, & Zhang, 2003; de Ves, Domingo, Ayala, & Zuccarello, 2007). The image retrieval problem can also be formulated as a task of probability density estimation. Suppose a CBIR system collects a set of positive example images $D^+(n)$ and applies parametric density estimation, the task is to estimate the probability density of the relevant images, which is expressed as $p(x \mid D^+(n); \theta)$, where θ contains the parameters of the distribution. The Gaussian mixture model and the expectation-maximization algorithm have been proposed for solving the relevance feedback problem (Meilhac & Nastar, 1999). The major drawback of probability density estimation methods is in their lack of discriminative power to exclude negative examples with good generalization capabilities (Huang & Zhou, 2001).

QUERY SPECIFICATIONS

Queries in multimedia retrieval systems are traditionally performed by using an example or series of examples. The task of the system is to determine which candidates are the most similar to the given example. Based on the type of media, query examples in content-based retrieval systems can be images, videos, and songs, or generated from several different modes, such as sketch, painting, or singing. This design is generally termed as Query By Example (QBE) mode. The interaction starts with an initial selection of candidates. The initial selection can be randomly selected candidates or meaningful representatives selected according to specific rules. Subsequently, the user can select one of the candidates as an example and the system will return those results that are most similar to the example. However, the success of the query in this approach heavily depends upon the initial set of candidates. A problem exists in how to formulate the initial panel of candidates that contains at least one relevant candidate. This limitation has been defined as page zero problem (La Cascia et al., 1998). To overcome this problem, various solutions have been proposed for specific applications. For example, Sivic & Zisserman (2004) proposed a method that measures the re-occurrence of spatial configurations of view point invariant features to obtain the principal objects, characters and scenes, which can be used as entry points for visual search.

PERFORMANCE EVALUATION

In performance evaluation the four cases of relevant and irrelevant items that are retrieved and not retrieved are tabulated in Table 1. The most common evaluation measures used in CBIR are precision and recall, which often are presented as a precision versus recall graph. Precision P is the ratio of the number of relevant images retrieved to the total number images retrieved while recall R is the number of relevant images retrieved to the total number of relevant images stored in the database. Precision P and recall R are expressed using the following formulas:

$$P = \frac{A}{A + C} \tag{5}$$

$$R = \frac{A}{A + B} \tag{6}$$

In addition to precision and recall, a set of measures used in the TERC benchmark for evaluating effectiveness and efficiency (Muller, Muller, Squire, Marchand-Maillet, & Pun, 2001) are measured to compare systems based on the same image databases, and use the same queries and the same ground truth database.

r is the ratio of the total number of images in the database to the number of relevant images for each of the query tasks.

t is the time the system takes to perform a query.

$Rank_1$, $\overline{Rank}$: $Rank_1$ is the rank at which the first relevant image is retrieved, and $\overline{Rank}$ is the average rank.

$P(20)$, $P(50)$, and $P(n)$ are precision rates after 20, 50, and n images are retrieved, where n is the number of relevant images.

$P(R(0.5))$ and $R(100)$ are recalls at precision 0.5 and after 100 images are retrieved, respectively.

A CBIR system collects relevance feedback based on the users' relevant judgments on the initial search result. To show self-adaptability of the system to the user's query, the initial search result and the

Table 1. The four cases of relevant and irrelevant items retrieved and not retrieved

	Relevant	Irrelevant
Retrieved	A(true positive)	C(false positive)
Not-Retrieved	B(false negative)	D(true negative)

refined search results of the top *n* rounds at relevance feedback stage can be compared with the same measures aforementioned. The same measures can be used for comparing the performance among different CBIR systems. It is noted that, to make those measures comparable, it is presumed that the same image databases and the same queries are used.

FUTURE RESEARCH ISSUES AND TRENDS

Although remarkable progress has been made in content-based multimedia retrieval, there are still many challenging research problems. This section identifies and addresses some issues in the future research agenda.

Automatic Metadata Generation

Metadata (data about data) is the data associated with an information object for the purposes of description, administration, technical functionality and so on. Metadata standards have been proposed to support the annotation of multimedia content. Automatic generation of annotations for multimedia involves high-level semantic representation and machine learning to ensure accuracy of annotation. Content-based retrieval techniques can be employed to generate the metadata, which can be further used by the text-based retrieval.

Establishment of Standard Evaluation Paradigm and Test-Bed

The National Institute of Standards and Technology (NIST) has developed TREC (Text REtrieval Conference) as the standard test-bed and evaluation paradigm for the information retrieval community. In response to the research needs from the video retrieval community, the TREC released a video track in 2003, which became an independent evaluation (called TRECVID) (Smeaton et al., 2006). In music information retrieval, a formal resolution expressing a similar need was passed in 2001, requesting a TREC-like standard test-bed and evaluation paradigm (Pardo, 2006). The image retrieval community still awaits the construction and implementation of a scientifically valid evaluation framework and standard test bed.

Embedding Relevance Feedback

Multimedia contains large quantities of rich information and involves the subjectivity of human perception. The design of content-based retrieval systems has turned out to emphasize an interactive approach instead of a computer-centric approach. A user interaction approach requires human and computer to interact in refining the high-level queries. Relevance feedback is a powerful technique used for facilitating interaction between the user and the system. The research issue includes the design of the interface with regard to usability, and learning algorithms which can dynamically update the weights embedded in the query object to model the high level concepts and perceptual subjectivity.

Bridging the Semantic Gap

One of the main challenges in multimedia retrieval is bridging the gap between low-level representations and high-level semantics (Lew, Sebe, & Eakins, 2002). The semantic gap exists because low-level features are more easily computed in the system design process, but high-level queries are used at the starting point of the retrieval process. The semantic gap is not only the conversion between low-level features and high-level semantics, but also the understanding of contextual meaning of the query involving human knowledge and emotion. Current research intends to develop mechanisms or models that directly associate the high-level semantic objects and representation of low-level features.

CONCLUSION

The main contributions in this chapter were to provide a conceptual architecture for content-based multimedia retrieval, discuss the system design issues, and point out some potential problems in individual components. Some research issues and future trends were also identified and addressed. Although current content-based retrieval systems generally make use of low-level features, the ideal content-based retrieval system from a user's perspective involves the semantic level. Semantic metadata generation has been a challenging problem on content-based retrieval. Interactive design is a promising technique to bridge the semantic gap. Due to the efforts of the research community, a few systems have started to employ high-level features and are able to deal with some semantic queries. Therefore, more intelligent content-based retrieval systems can be expected in the near future.

REFERENCES

Beckmann, N., Kriegel, H.-P., Schneider, R., & Seeger, B. (1990). The R*-tree: An efficient and robust access method for points and rectangles. In *Proceedings of ACM SIGMOD International Conference on Management of Data* (pp. 322-331).

Berry, M. J. A., & Linoff, G. (2004). *Data Mining Techniques for Marketing, Sales, and Customer Relationship Management*. Indianapolis, USA: Wiley Publishing.

Bishop, C. M. (2006). *Pattern Recognition and Machine Learning*. New York: Springer.

de Ves, E., Domingo, J., Ayala, G., & Zuccarello, P. (2007). A novel Bayesian framework for relevance feedback in image content-based retrieval systems. *Pattern Recognition, 39*, 1622–1632. doi:10.1016/j.patcog.2006.01.006

Djeraba, C. (2002). Content-based multimedia indexing and retrieval. *IEEE MultiMedia, 9*(2), 18–22. doi:10.1109/MMUL.2002.998047

Feng, D., Siu, W. C., & Zhang, H. J. (2003). *Multimedia Information Retrieval and Management: Technological Fundamentals and Applications*. Berlin: Springer.

Feng, D., Siu, W. C., & Zhang, H. J. (Eds.). (2003). *Multimedia information retrieval and management: Technological fundamentals and applications*. Berlin: Springer.

Friedman, J. H., Bentley, J. L., & Finkel, R. A. (1977). An algorithm for finding best matches in logarithmic expected time. *ACM Transactions on Mathematical Software, 3*(3), 209–226. doi:10.1145/355744.355745

Gevers, T., & Stokman, H. (2003). Classifying color edges in video into shadow-geometry, highlight, or material transitions. *IEEE Transactions on Multimedia, 5*(2), 237–243. doi:10.1109/TMM.2003.811620

Gevers, T., & Stokman, H. (2003). Classifying color edges in video into shadow- geometry, highlight, or material transitions. *IEEE Transactions on Multimedia, 5*(2), 237–243. doi:10.1109/TMM.2003.811620

Gonzalez, R. C., & Woods, R. E. (2002). *Digital image processing.* Upper Saddle River, NJ: Prentice Hall.

Guan, H., & Wada, S. (2002). Flexible color texture retrieval method using multi- resolution mosaic for image classification. In *Proceedings of the 6th International Conference on Signal Processing: Vol. 1* (pp. 612-615).

Guttman, A. (1984). R-trees: A dynamic index structure for spatial searching. *Proceedings of ACM SIGMOD International Conference on Management of Data*, 47-54, Boston, MA, USA.

Haeghen, Y. V., Naeyaert, J. M. A. D., Lemahieu, I., & Philips, W. (2000). An imaging system with calibrated color image acquisition for use in dermatology. *IEEE Transactions on Medical Imaging, 19*(7), 722–730. doi:10.1109/42.875195

Huang, T. S., & Zhou, X. S. (2001). Image retrieval with relevance feedback: From heuristic weight adjustment to optimal learning methods. In *Proceedings of the IEEE International Conference on Image Processing* (pp. 2-5).

Jeon, J., Lavrenko, V., & Manmatha, R. (2003). Automatic image annotation and retrieval using cross-media relevance models. *Proceedings of the 26th Annual International ACM SIGIR Conference on Research and Development in Information Retrieval*, Toronto, Canada.

Jiang, H., Ngoa, C.-W., & Tana, H. K. (2006). Gestalt-based feature similarity measure in trademark database. *Pattern Recognition, 39*(5), 988–1001. doi:10.1016/j.patcog.2005.08.012

Khan, L. (2007). Standards for image annotation using semantic Web. *Computer Standards & Interfaces, 29*(2), 196–204. doi:10.1016/j.csi.2006.03.006

Kushki, A., Androutsos, P., Plataniotis, K. N., & Venetsanopoulos, A. N. (2004). Query feedback for interactive image retrieval. *IEEE Transactions on Circuits and Systems for Video Technology, 14*, 644–655. doi:10.1109/TCSVT.2004.826759

La Cascia, M., Sethi, S., & Sclaroff, S. (1998). Combining textural and visual cues for content- based image retrieval on the World Wide Web. In *Proceedings of the IEEE Workshop on Content-Based Access of Image and Video Libraries*, Santa BarBara, CA, USA.

Lew, M. S., Sebe, N., & Eakins, J. P. (2002). Challenges of image and video retrieval. *Proceedings of the International Conference on Image and Video Retrieval, Lecture Notes in Computer Science*, London, UK.

Li, C. H., & Yuen, P. C. (2000). Regularized color clustering in medical image database. *IEEE Transactions on Medical Imaging, 19*(11), 1150–1155. doi:10.1109/42.896791

Liu, Y., Zhang, D., Lu, G., & Ma, W.-Y. (2007). A survey of content-based image retrieval with high-level semantics. *Pattern Recognition, 40*(1), 262–282. doi:10.1016/j.patcog.2006.04.045

Lo, Y.-L., & Chen, S.-J. (2002). The numeric indexing for music data. *Proceedings of the 22nd International Conference on Distributed Computing Systems Workshops.* Vienna, Austria.

Lopez, C., & Chen, Y.-P. P. (2006). Using object and trajectory analysis to facilitate indexing and retrieval of video. *Knowledge-Based Systems, 19*(8), 639–646. doi:10.1016/j.knosys.2006.05.006

Marques, O., & Furht, B. (2002). *Content-based image and video retrieval.* London: Kluwer.

Meilhac, C., & Nastar, C. (1999). Relevance feedback and category search in image databases. *Proceedings of IEEE International Conference on Multimedia Computing and Systems,* 512-517.

Moghaddam, H. A., Khajoie, T. T., & Rouhi, A. H. (2003). A new algorithm for image indexing and retrieval using wavelet correlogram. In. *Proceedings of the International Conference on Image Processing, 3,* 497–500.

Muller, H., Muller, W., Squire, D. M., Marchand-Maillet, S., & Pun, T. (2001). Performance evaluation in content-based image retrieval: Overview and proposals. *Pattern Recognition Letters, 22,* 593–601. doi:10.1016/S0167-8655(00)00118-5

Ouyang, A., & Tan, Y. P. (2002). A novel multi-scale spatial-color descriptor for content-based image retrieval. In *Proceedings of the 7th International Conference on Control, Automation, Robotics and Vision: Vol.3* (pp. 1204-1209).

Pardo, B. (2006). Music information retrieval. *Communications of the ACM, 49*(8), 29–31.

Qian, G., Sural, S., Gu, Y., & Pramanik, S. (2004). Similarity between Euclidean and cosine angle distance for nearest neighbor queries. In *Proceedings of ACM Symposium on Applied Computing* (pp. 1232-1237).

Rocchio, J. J. (1971). Relevance feedback in information retrieval. In Salton, G. (Ed.), *The SMART Retrieval System-Experiments in Automatic Document Processing* (pp. 313–323). Englewood Cliffs, NJ: Prentice Hall.

Rui, Y., & Huang, T. (1999). *A novel relevance feedback technique in image retrieval* (pp. 67–70). New York: ACM Press.

Rui, Y., Huang, T. S., & Mehrotra, S. (1998). Human perception subjectivity and relevance feedback in multimedia information retrieval. In *Proceedings of IS&T / SPIE Storage and Retrieval of Image and Video Database* (pp. 25-36).

Russ, J. C. (2006). *The Image Processing Handbook.* New York: CRC Press. doi:10.1201/9780203881095

Sebe, N., & Lew, M. S. (2002). Texture features for content-based retrieval. In Lew, M. S. (Ed.), *Principles of Visual Information Retrieval* (pp. 51–85). London: Springer.

Shah, B., Raghavan, V., & Dhatric, P. (2004). Efficient and effective content-based image retrieval using space transformation. *Proceedings of the 10th International Multimedia Modelling Conference,* Brisbane, Australia.

Sivic, J., & Zisserman, A. (2004). Video data mining using configurations of viewpoint invariant regions. *Proceedings of the IEEE Conference on Computer Vision and Pattern Recognition,* Washington, DC, USA.

Smeaton, A. F., Over, P., & Kraaij, W. (2006). Evaluation campaigns and TRECVid. *Proceedings of the 8th ACM International Workshop on Multimedia Information Retrieval,* Santa Barbara, CA, USA.

Smeulders, A. W. M., Worring, M., Santini, S., Gupta, A., & Jain, R. (2000). Content-based image retrieval at the end of the early years. *IEEE Transactions on Pattern Analysis and Machine Intelligence, 22,* 1349–1380. doi:10.1109/34.895972

Su, Z., Zhang, H., Li, S., & Ma, S. (2003). Relevance feedback in content-based image retrieval: Bayesian framework, feature subspaces, and progressive learning. *IEEE Transactions on Image Processing, 12,* 924–937. doi:10.1109/TIP.2003.815254

Wang, Y., Ding, M., Zhou, C., & Hu, Y. (2006). Interactive relevance feedback mechanism for image retrieval using rough set. *Knowledge-Based Systems, 19,* 696–703. doi:10.1016/j.knosys.2006.05.005

Wei, C.-H., Li, C.-T., & Wilson, R. (2006). A content-based approach to medical image database retrieval. In Ma, Z. M. (Ed.), *Database Modeling for Industrial Data Management: Emerging Technologies and Applications* (pp. 258–291). Hershey, PA: Idea Group Publishing.

Yu, H., Li, M., Zhang, H.-J., & Feng, J. (2002). Color texture moments for content-based image retrieval. In *Proceedings of the International Conference on Image Processing 2002,* (Vol. 3, pp. 929-932).

Zhang, L., Qian, F., Li, M., & Zhang, H. (2003). An efficient memorization scheme for relevance feedback in image retrieval. In *Proceedings of the IEEE International Conference on Multimedia & Expo.*

Zhang, R., & Zhang, Z. (2006). BALAS: Empirical Bayesian learning in the relevance feedback for image retrieval. *Image and Vision Computing, 24,* 211–233. doi:10.1016/j.imavis.2005.11.004

Zhou, X. S., & Huang, T. S. (2003). Relevance feedback in image retrieval: A comprehensive review. *ACM Multimedia System Journal, 8,* 536–544. doi:10.1007/s00530-002-0070-3

Zuo, W., Zhang, D., & Wang, K. (2006). Bidirectional PCA with assembled matrix distance metric for image recognition. *IEEE Transactions on Systems, Man, and Cybernetics, 36,* 863–872. doi:10.1109/TSMCB.2006.872274

Chapter 2
Metrical Properties of Nested Partitions for Image Retrieval

Dmitry Kinoshenko
Kharkiv National University of Radio Electronics, Ukraine

Vladimir Mashtalir
Kharkiv National University of Radio Electronics, Ukraine

Vladislav Shlyakhov
Kharkiv National University of Radio Electronics, Ukraine

Elena Yegorova
Kharkiv National University of Radio Electronics, Ukraine

ABSTRACT

This chapter proposes a metric on partitions of arbitrary measurable sets and its special properties for metrical content-based image retrieval based on the 'spatial' semantic of images. The approach considers images represented in the form of nested partitions produced by any segmentations. Nested partitions representation expresses a degree of information refinement or roughening and so not only corresponds to rational content control but also ensures creation of specific search algorithms (e.g. invariant to image background) and synthesize hierarchical models of image search reducing the number of query and database elements match operations.

INTRODUCTION

As a promising and active research problem, the study of content-based information retrieval has been focused on such approaches as search by association, aimed search and category search. Somehow or other, any retrieval scheme is based on a query matching. There exist various querying modalities on qualitative level: given keywords, free-text (metadata) inducing by summarizing, datum exemplum, computer-generated or man made rough sketches, composite models. Different query forms require different processing methods but in any case measures of similarity (dissimilarity) are the kernel issues to assess on the base of data abstracted descriptions the certain semantic indistinguishability between a

DOI: 10.4018/978-1-61692-859-9.ch002

pair of media occurrences generally from large databases. It is clear that different distance measures have their own advantages and disadvantages but prospective key problem is to understand the semantics of a query, not simply the low-level underlying computational features. Synergy between machine learning and multimedia retrieval expresses in different ways. It should be emphasized automatic learning of a similarity metric or distance from ground-truth data, machine learning using both quantitative and qualitative responses for generation of relevance feedback-based search and learning algorithms ability to adapt and compensate for the noise and clutter in real contexts (Ma, 2009). Similarity measures have to be possessed of following main properties: agreement with semantics must be satisfactory for task-level system, robustness to noise and media transforms has to satisfy user requirements, computational complexity must provide approximate real time in large scale database, invariance to different backgrounds must allow to retrieve objects of interest. Further we shall focus an attention on content based image retrieval or more precisely on its core substantially defining effectiveness CBIR viz aspects of possible metrical interpretations of image content from segmentation point of view.

The elucidation of image content is complex and delicate even for human understanding (see e.g. Figure 1) so questions how to extract useful image features and how to use them for valid retrieval are of great importance. Thus, visual similarity may be problematic due to the semantic gap between low-level content and high-level concepts.

Comprehensive studies have been carried out with similarity between images given by image features such as color, texture, or shape and on the composition of these features. A number of region based retrieval systems are well investigated also (Lew at al 2006; Datta et al. 2008).

All similarity measures may be classified from the position of fulfillment axioms identity, symmetry and triangle inequality. If all axioms hold we have a metric, if an identity transforms to reflexivity, i.e. similarity equals to zero when comparing elements are the same, we get pseudometric. If symmetry is not valid we are dealing with a quasimetric. If triangle inequality does not hold we can operate a semimetric. If only reflexivity and triangle inequality are true we get a hemimetric. If triangle inequality is strengthened (instead of distances sum their maximum is used) we have an ultrametric. At last, if only reflexivity occurs we obtain a prametric. Certainly, all foregoing measures may be used in CBIR but we strongly need all axioms satisfying. Uppermost metric is most intuitive to compare arbitrary data comprehensively. Further, that is self-evident that to locate user-relevant information in large collections

Figure 1. Assessments of visual content: edge image (on the left), binary image (on the right)

of objects, fast algorithms of exact match or adequate proximity concepts can be grounded on a metric solely. A metric provides specialized search mechanisms which allow to eliminate iteratively inconsistent data subsets (Zezula et al. 2006). The obvious additional advantage of metric search is that the results can be ranked according to their estimated relevance.

We propose a next step with respect to low-level image features to define metrical image content (unfortunately, it is, as before, sufficiently far from human image understanding but it already reproduces a spatial sense of an image) in the form of nested partitions produced by segmentations. Such nested partitions carry some spatial content of scene with various levels of detailing, and take into consideration region relations in toto. It should be noted that there arise partitions in CBIR in a variety of ways. Under hierarchical clustering, for instance, nested partitions allow to construct images partitions into disjoint nested subsets so that firstly one can seek suitable class, then the most similar to the query subclass is chosen and so on. Consequently the exhaustive search is fulfilled only on the lower level of hierarchy (Kinoshenko et al., 2005). It is clear that nested partitions express in implicit form degree of information refinement or roughening. Therefore, metrical properties of nested partitions, which are investigated in the chapter, not only correspond to rational content control but provide creation of specific search algorithms e.g. invariant to image background.

The major points covered by this chapter may be summarized as follows. The next section presents previous works concerning metrics on partitions. Further, we have argued partitions set metric background. Sequent section is devoted to hierarchical set factorization then we discus geometrical properties of nested quotient sets and analyze metrical relations between nested partitions. Finally we provide experiments and future work discussion. Thus, chapter contribution consists in theoretical and ground and experimental exploration of metrical nested partitions properties providing the effective CBIR systems development.

STATE OF ART AND BACKGROUND

General 'ad exemplum' image retrieval methods require an index of proximity, or a likeness, or affinity, or association to be established between pairs of any images. Let $X = \{x_1, x_2, ..., x_n\}$ be a set of images in a database, and U is a problem oriented universum (a set of all possible images), $X \subseteq U$. Let also $y \in U$ be a query, which can be represented by an image or a sketch. Then retrieval process lies in finding k images closest to the query in the sense of a similarity function $\rho(\circ, \circ)$ with arguments symbolizing images in signal or feature space. They believe that a metric is the most sufficient form of such proximity function representation.

One of the most important characteristic of image retrieval efficiency is its reliability is sense of precise identification of the required images. So, denoting $\delta > 0$ as a threshold of retrieval similarity and $X^m = \left\{ x_{i_1}, x_{i_2}, ..., x_{i_m} \right\} \subseteq X$ as a set of retrieved images under (δ, k) search strategy where $(m \leq k)$, we can define image retrieval state of art as following

$$\forall x_{i_j} \in X^m, \ \forall x \in X \setminus X^m, \ \forall y \in U \quad \rho(y, x_{i_j}) \leq \delta, \ \delta \geq 0,$$

$$\rho(y, x_{i_j}) \leq \rho(y, x), \ \rho(y, x_{i_j}) \leq \rho(y, x_{i_{j+1}}), \ j = \overline{1, m-1}.$$

A step forward in the image retrieval field is ability to perform a content-based search not depending on physical features of the image but operating on a semantic level. Besides of the independence on the image preprocessing (segmentation) results it also requires operating on different levels of image detailing i.e. analyzing an image as a set of nesting partitions $x_1 \subset x_{1_1} \subset x_{1_2} \subset ... \subset x_{1_k}$.

The special properties of metric on partitions considered in this chapter ensure fulfillment of all the requirements stated above and allow to search for the content of images in whole and of separate objects they contain.

For image processing a large variety of metrics is used as a similarity measure. Along with traditional metrics, such as Minkovski metric and its special cases, many approaches were exploited for introducing some distances which would take into consideration specific character of visual information. Working with templates leads to development of new metrics in some manner satisfying image interpretation tasks.

Talking about most used techniques it is sufficient to mention the Minkovski-type dynamic partial function which can activate different features for different objects pairs (Li et al. 2003), content-based metric transforming local information into image structural similarities (Gao et al., 2005), distance function to consider histograms adjacent bins correlation (Triana et al., 2003), histogram distance (Zhong et. al. 2003), metric properties of Gaussian mixes (Sfikas et al., 2005), the Mahalanobis type metric used in the hierarchical classification (Partridge et al., 2002), the large deformation diffeomorphic mapping metric allowing to map a template segmentation to the target image space (Khan et al., 2005), Pixel Correspondence Metric for edge images taking into account edge strength as well as the displacement of edge pixel positions (Prieto et al., 2003), a metric considering similarity functions sets based on entropy properties and measure of frames changes (Cheng et al., 2005), fuzzy logic and pseudometrics used for neural semantic classification and retrieval (Wang et al., 2005; Li et al., 2000). Most of these are based on pixels groups analysis, some consider different regions features but all of them though can give some satisfactory results for some particular image sets and particular applications yet either depend on manually tuning parameters or within their limitations are not suitable to be used for complex objects. There arises a need for some alternative techniques which from one hand will not depend on the pixels characteristics and so will not be sensitive to varying environmental conditions, occlusions and colors, and from another hand will not be limited to pre-defined feature sets.

Among the most promising metrics which particularly have desirable properties one can name the Earth Mover's Distance (EMD) (Rubner, 2000), Region Matching Distance (RMD) (Hjaltason et al., 2003), variation of information (Meila, 2003), Van Dongen distance (Jiang et al., 2005), and partition metric introduced in (Mashtalir et al. 2006) and extended in (Kinoshenko et al., 2007).

The EMD is based on the idea of minimization of cost that must be paid to transform one distribution into the other combined with a representation scheme for distributions that is based on vector quantization. For that the total flow $F = [f_{ij}]$, with f_{ij} being the flow between clusters p_i and q_j, that minimizes the overall cost should be found as

$$WORK\left(P, Q, F\right) = \sum_{i=1}^{m} \sum_{j=1}^{n} d_{ij} f_{ij}$$

where $P = \{(p_1, w_{p1}), ..., (p_m, w_{pm})\}$ and $Q = \{(q_1, w_{q1}), ..., (q_n, w_{qn})\}$ are the signatures with m and n clusters respectively (here p_i, q_i are the clusters representatives and w_{pi}, w_i are the weights of the clusters), $d_{i,j} = d(p_i, q_j)$ is a base similarity measure of p_i and q_j clusters. 'Flow' here is a measure of how many parts of one region can be transformed into another region. The flow is subject to constraints of moving 'suppliers' order, amount of suppliers sent by clusters in P and received by clusters in Q according to their weights and constraint which forces to move the maximum amount of supplies possible. Then EMD is defined as the resulting work normalized by the total flow

$$EMD\left(P,Q\right) = \frac{\sum_{i=1}^{m}\sum_{j=1}^{n}d_{ij}f_{ij}}{\sum_{i=1}^{m}\sum_{j=1}^{n}f_{ij}},$$

where the normalization factor is the total weight of the smaller signature.

Being more robust than histograms matching this technique can be applied to variable-length representations of distribution, but its solution based on the transportation problem from linear optimization makes it rather slow to compute.

The RMD is used for approach which represents an image by a set of regions which practically shows better results than global approach. The region descriptors are made up of feature vectors representing color, texture, area and location of regions. The RMD similarity measure is based on the Earth Mover's Distance adopted for regions and is calculated as minimum value of function

$$RMD\left(P,Q,C\right) = \frac{\sum_{i\in\Phi}\sum_{j\in\Psi}c_{ij}d_{ij}}{\sum_{i\in\Phi}\sum_{j\in\Psi}c_{ij}}$$

where Φ,Ψ represent the sets of regions from two images P and Q, $c_{ij}\left(i\in\Phi, j\in\Psi\right)$ is the amount of 'flow' from region i in the first image to region j in the second image, C is the set of all permissible flow c_{ij}, and d_{ij} is the distance between regions i and j. The disadvantage which can be pointed out lies in still existing invariant features issue and inherited from EMD linear programming computational complexity.

Van Dongen distance is defined as

$$\rho_{VD} = 2N - \sum_{i=1}^{m}\max_{B_j\in\beta}card\left(A_i\bigcap B_j\right) - \sum_{j=1}^{n}\max_{B_i\in\beta}card\left(A_i\bigcap B_j\right)$$

And Meila metric can be presented as

$$\rho_{M} = \frac{1}{N}\Big(\sum_{i=1}^{m}card(A_i)\log\frac{card(A_i)}{N} + \sum_{j=1}^{n}card(B_j)\log\frac{card(B_j)}{N} -$$

$$-2\sum_{i=1}^{m}\sum_{j=1}^{n}card(A_i\bigcap B_j)\log\frac{N\,card(A_i\bigcap B_j)}{card(A_i)\,card(B_j)}\Big)$$

Another important requirement for the newly developed similarity measure is to be a metric. Due to existent and well-known 'curse of dimensionality' problem of high dimension feature vectors indexing (Rubner et al., 2000) more and more researchers in CBIR field use metric space approaches to speed up a search. There information about mutual distance between objects in the database is utilized and entire sets of images are discarded at the search stage by applying of triangular inequality (Chan et al., 2001; Weber et al., 1998; Liu et al., 2007).

In large databases the efficiency of image retrieval procedures with search 'ad exemplum' is determined by reliability (in terms of precise identification of the required images) and computational complexity (generally, in sense of matching operations amount) of algorithms used to pick up. To avoid the combinatorial explosion on retrieval search a large collection of preliminary processing algorithms is available to reduce the search. Often clustering-like algorithms are used for computing complexity depreciation. In other words, they propose hierarchical clustering methods which allow to convert images partitions into disjoint hierarchical subsets so that firstly one can seek suitable class, then the most similar to the query subclass is chosen and so on. The exhaustive search, if necessary, is fulfilled only on the lowest level of hierarchy. To select optimal clusters a metric on partitions is of great significance also.

Thus, there arise two open issues in the field of the image retrieval. First one is overcoming a semantic gap between low-level features extracted by computer and high-level concepts human operates. Second one is providing a high retrieval speed independent on the database volume. Promising approaches quite often are based on metrical properties that is why such similarity measures provide good enough solutions of problems above. A partition metric is evidently a candidate because it represents images as a finite subsets assemblage that takes into account mutual dependences of equivalence class corresponding to separate regions of interest and at the same time, it allows to compare image sets as clusters. Metrics on nested partitions take on special significance since they give possibilities to define and make use of hierarchical content descriptions.

METRIC ON PARTITION SETS

Let us consider some finite set Ω with measure $\mu(\Omega) < \infty$, i.e. for any $A \subset \Omega$ there exists a finite number $\mu(A)$ which is a measure (in finite case it can be length, area, volume, cardinality, etc.). And let $\mathfrak{F}_\Omega$ be a set of all finite subsets.

We shall introduce into consideration a set $\Pi_\Omega \subset \mathfrak{F}_\Omega$ of finite (as for the number of elements) partitions of set Ω such that $\beta \in \Pi_\Omega$, $\beta = \{B_j\}_{j=1}^m$, $B_j \in \mathfrak{F}_\Omega$ (Figure 2) and

$$\left. \begin{array}{r} \forall j, j' \in \{1,\ldots,m\} \;:\; j \neq j' \Rightarrow B_j \cap B_{j'} = \varnothing, \\ B_1 \cup \ldots \cup B_m = \Omega. \end{array} \right\} \tag{1}$$

On the Cartesian square $\Pi_\Omega \times \Pi_\Omega$ a functional

$$\rho(\alpha, \beta) = \sum_{i=1}^n \sum_{j=1}^m \mu(A_i \triangle B_j) \mu(A_i \cap B_j), \tag{2}$$

is a metric, where $\alpha, \beta \in \Pi_\Omega$, $\alpha = \{A_i\}_{i=1}^n$, $\beta = \{B_j\}_{j=1}^m$, and $A_i \triangle B_j = = (A_i \setminus B_j) \cup (B_j \setminus A_i)$ is a symmetrical difference. This result was primarily proved by induction for the finite sets, and then for

Figure 2. Example of set partition

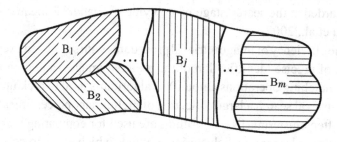

arbitrary measurable sets (Mashtalir et al., 2006). For functional (2) an equivalent representation was found:

$$\rho(\alpha, \beta) = \sum_{i=1}^{n} [\mu(A_i)]^2 + \sum_{j=1}^{m} [\mu(B_j)]^2 - 2\sum_{i=1}^{n}\sum_{j=1}^{m} [\mu(A_i \cap B_j)]^2 . \tag{3}$$

It should be emphasized that for clustering of images and their ensembles the main problems are connected with comparison of partitions with nesting structure. It is conditioned by need of searching of the segmentation results with proper level of detail, particularly while tending to the ground truth paradigm. Moreover, any scheme of regions splitting/merging under segmentation (especially when trying to interpret the synthesized quotient set in some object-oriented fields) requires criteria formalization. As the minimum task here is to define the breakpoint rules, one can take into consideration metric properties of nested partitions in the image or feature spaces (more often according to the shape descriptors). Also when having hierarchical indexing (for example hierarchical clustering of image families for search speed) we face up the task of strict quotient sets comparison (comparison of clusters on different strata). In other words, research of metrics specifics for nested quotient sets gives premises for generation of search algorithms that target on decrease of query and database elements matching operations number.

Let us first analyze the probability-based interpretation of the introduced metric. For any set $A \subset \Omega$ and arbitrary partition $\zeta = \{D_s\}_{s=1}^{p}$ on the finite subsets of set Ω, due to the measure's additivity property it fulfils

$$\mu(A) = \sum_{s=1}^{p} \mu(A \cap D_s) . \tag{4}$$

At that you can see that if we divide both parts of (4) on $\mu(\Omega)$, we shall get

$$\frac{\mu(A)}{\mu(\Omega)} = \sum_{s=1}^{p} \frac{\mu(A \cap D_s)}{\mu(\Omega)} = \sum_{s=1}^{p} \frac{\mu(A \cap D_s)}{\mu(D_s)} \frac{\mu(D_s)}{\mu(\Omega)} , \tag{5}$$

under condition that for every s it is true that $\mu(D_s) \neq 0$. Then it is easy to notice that we can refer to the theory probability terms and consider set $\{D_s\}_{s=1}^{p}$ as a set of hypotheses, then equality (5) represents a well known formula of total probability, i.e.

$$P(A) = \sum_{s=1}^{p} P(D_s)P(A/D_s), \tag{6}$$

where $P(A) = \dfrac{\mu(A)}{\mu(\Omega)}$, $P(D_s) = \dfrac{\mu(D_s)}{\mu(\Omega)}$ are probabilities of event A and hypotheses D_s, and

$$P(A/D_s) = \frac{\mu(A \cap D_s)}{\mu(\Omega)} \frac{\mu(\Omega)}{\mu(D_s)} = \frac{\dfrac{\mu(A \cap D_s)}{\mu(\Omega)}}{\dfrac{\mu(D_s)}{\mu(\Omega)}} = \frac{P(A \cap D_s)}{P(D_s)} \tag{7}$$

is a conditional probability of event A under fulfillment of hypothesis D_s.

One can see that if $\Omega \subset \mathbb{R}^n$ is some measurable set and there is a probability scheme corresponding to so-called geometrical probability, then probability of any event A is equal to

$$P(A) = \frac{\mu(A)}{\mu(\Omega)},$$

where μ is a measure corresponding to $\mathbb{R}^n$ ($n = 1$ is length, $n = 2$ is area, $n = 3$ is volume, etc.).

If we normalize $\rho(\alpha, \beta)$, namely divide it on $\mu^2(\Omega)$, we shall get

$$\rho*(\alpha, \beta) = \frac{\rho(\alpha, \beta)}{\mu^2(\Omega)} = \sum_{i=1}^{n}\sum_{j=1}^{m} \frac{\mu(A_i \Delta B_j)}{\mu(\Omega)} \frac{\mu(A_i \cap B_j)}{\mu(\Omega)} = \sum_{i=1}^{n}\sum_{j=1}^{m} P(A_i \Delta B_j)P(A_i \cap B_j), \tag{8}$$

where $P(A_i \Delta B_j)$ and $P(A_i \cap B_j)$ are probabilities of events $A_i \Delta B_j$ and $A_i \cap B_j$ correspondingly.

Using equality (3) we get the equivalent expression in form

$$\rho*(\alpha, \beta) = \sum_{i=1}^{n}[P(A_i)]^2 + \sum_{j=1}^{m}[P(B_j)]^2 - 2\sum_{i=1}^{n}\sum_{j=1}^{m}[P(A_i \cap B_j)]^2. \tag{9}$$

These results allow us to move to the nested partitions analysis. Generally speaking, the provided theory has quite wide range of application and, while practically applied in our work to finite-dimensional case of digital images, can be used in any problem-oriented field where there is a need to compare partitions of arbitrary measurable set. In particular, we apply approach of partitions comparison on image processing domain on "micro" level, when partition is a result of image segmentation (clustering), and on "macro" level, when subject of partition is a collection of images. We understood that our theoretical outcome could be effectively used in image retrieval field, applying mentioned above "micro" level to reduce of well-known semantic gap and "macro" level to create indexing structures for speed-up of querying. Next as for image retrieval, we saw possibility to use induced below integral inequality on partitions to search for regions of interest of query images by results of segmentation independently on the level of detail of compared images segmentations of query and those from database.

Figure 3. Example of nested partitions for the set of figure 1

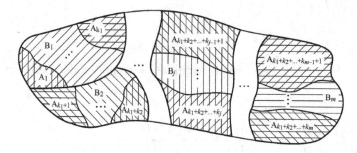

Talking mainly about segmentation and clustering notations and a means of definition of similarity between their outcomes, we carry out analysis of quotient sets from the probability interpretation and theoretical-set points of view. We do hope that a reader will have a chance to review our ideas from the different angle and as a result find out new applications of current fundamental theory of quotient sets matching.

HIERARCHICAL SET FACTORIZATION

Let us consider the situation when one partition is enclosed into another one, i.e. it practically 'details' some quotient set. We can formalize this as following.

Let two partitions $\alpha = \{A_i\}_{i=1}^n$ and $\beta = \{B_j\}_{j=1}^m$ of arbitrary set Ω be given. We shall talk about partially ordered sets regarding the nesting operation, i.e. quotient set hierarchy. For unambiguity we assume that $\alpha \subset \beta$.

From algebraic point of view it means that for any pair of elements $\omega_1, \omega_2 \in \Omega$ the following property takes place: from equality $E_\alpha(\omega_1, \omega_2) = 1$ we get equality $E_\beta(\omega_1, \omega_2) = 1$, where E_α, E_β is relation of equivalence on Cartesian square $\Omega \times \Omega$, induced by corresponding partitions.

In the set-theoretical sense $\alpha \subset \beta$ nesting means that for any $A_i \in \alpha$ can be found such $B_j \in \beta$, for which $A_i \subseteq B_j$. In general case α is a partition 'detailing' partition β, i.e. in any element of partition $B_j \in \beta$ there can be k_j elements of partition α, what is illustrated in Figure 3.

It is easy to see that partition β is decomposed on m subpartitions $\alpha_1, ..., \alpha_m$, i.e. $\alpha = \{\alpha_1, ..., \alpha_m\}$, where

$$
\begin{cases}
\alpha_1 = \{A_1, ..., A_{k_1}\}; \\
\alpha_2 = \{A_{k_1+1}, ..., A_{k_1+k_2}\}; \\
\cdots\cdots\cdots\cdots\cdots\cdots\cdots\cdots\cdots\cdots\cdots\cdots\cdots\cdots \\
\alpha_j = \{A_{k_1+k_2+...+k_{j-1}+1}, ..., A_{k_1+k_2+...+k_j}\}; \\
\cdots\cdots\cdots\cdots\cdots\cdots\cdots\cdots\cdots\cdots\cdots\cdots\cdots\cdots \\
\alpha_m = \{A_{k_1+k_2+...+k_{m-1}+1}, ..., A_{k_1+k_2+...+k_m}\};
\end{cases}
\tag{10}
$$

i.e. α_j ($j \in \overline{1,m}$) is a partition of set B_j and contains k_j elements of partition α with numbers from $k_1 + k_2 + \ldots + k_{j-1} + 1$ to $k_1 + k_2 + \ldots + k_j$.

Under that

$$B_j = \bigcup_{i=k_1+k_2+\ldots+k_{j-1}+1}^{k_1+k_2+\ldots+k_j} A_i \,,$$

where $k_1 + k_2 + \ldots + k_m = n$.

For any pair of A_i and B_j sets ($i \in \{1,\ldots,n\}$; $j \in \{1,\ldots,m\}$) three variants are possible:

a) $A_i \subset B_j$, when $k_j \neq 1$ and $A_i \in \alpha_j$;

b) $A_i = B_j$ when $k_j = 1$ and $\alpha_j = \{A_i\}$;

c) $A_i \cap B_j = 0$, when $A_i \notin \alpha_j$.

If a set of all pairs (i, j) is divided into three not intersecting subsets z_1, z_2, z_3, corresponding to mentioned relations, then functional $\rho(\alpha,\beta)$ takes form

$$\begin{aligned}
\rho(\alpha,\beta) = &\sum_{(i,j)\in z_1} \mu(A_i \triangle B_j)\mu(A_i \cap B_j) + \\
&+ \sum_{(i,j)\in z_2} \mu(A_i \triangle B_j)\mu(A_i \cap B_j) + \\
&+ \sum_{(i,j)\in z_3} \mu(A_i \triangle B_j)\mu(A_i \cap B_j).
\end{aligned} \qquad (11)$$

As in case b) we have $A_i \triangle B_j = \varnothing$, i.e. $\mu(A_i \triangle B_j) = 0$, and in case c) we obtain $A_i \cap B_j = \varnothing$, i.e. $\mu(A_i \cap B_j) = 0$, then in equality (11) two last summands will be equal to 0. In result we get

$$\rho(\alpha,\beta) = \sum_{(i,j)\in z_1} \mu(A_i \cap B_j)\mu(A_i \triangle B_j) \,. \qquad (12)$$

Taking into account that under $A_i \subset B_j$ $A_i \cap B_j = A_i$, $A_i \triangle B_j = B_j \setminus A_i$ are fulfilled, then from (12) it follows

$$\rho(\alpha,\beta) = \sum_{(i,j)\in z_1} \mu(A_i)\mu(B_j \setminus A_i) \,. \qquad (13)$$

Taking into consideration equalities (10), it is possible to make the following natural renumbering of the sets from partition α with the help of introducing double indexing

$$
\begin{cases}
\alpha_1 = \{A_{11},...,A_{1k_1}\}; \\
\alpha_2 = \{A_{21},...,A_{2k_2}\}; \\
\cdots\cdots\cdots\cdots\cdots\cdots\cdots \\
\alpha_j = \{A_{j1},...,A_{jk_j}\}; \\
\cdots\cdots\cdots\cdots\cdots\cdots\cdots \\
\alpha_m = \{A_{m1},...,A_{mk_m}\},
\end{cases}
$$

where $j = \overline{1,\, m}$, a $B_j = \bigcup_{i=1}^{k_j} A_{ji}$.

In this case

$$
B_j \setminus A_{ji} = \bigcup_{l=1\,(l \neq i)}^{k_j} A_{jl}, \tag{14}
$$

$j = \overline{1,\, m}$, $i = \overline{1,\, k_j}$. From (13) and (14) it follows

$$
\rho(\alpha,\,\beta) = \sum_{j=1}^{m}\sum_{i=1}^{k_j} \mu(A_{ji})[\sum_{i'=1\,(i' \neq i)}^{k_j} \mu(A_{ji'})], \tag{15}
$$

i.e. the distance between partitions α and β is determined by measures of elements of partition α. Partition β ("bigger" one) only determines in what "combination" values $\mu(A_{ji})$ take part in calculations.

Now we shall use relation (3). In the considered situation as for any A_i there is a single B_j for which A_i is a subset, then all these sums of type

$$
\sum_{j=1}^{m} [\mu(A_i \cap B_j)]^2
$$

transform into one summand, i.e.

$$
\sum_{j=1}^{m} [\mu(A_i \cap B_j)]^2 = [\mu(A_i \cap B_{j'})]^2 = [\mu(A_i)]^2.
$$

In this case for functional $\rho(\alpha,\beta)$ the following chain of equalities takes place

$$
\begin{aligned}
\rho(\alpha,\,\beta) &= \sum_{i=1}^{n} [\mu(A_i)]^2 + \sum_{j=1}^{m} [\mu(B_j)]^2 - 2\sum_{i=1}^{n}\sum_{j=1}^{m} [\mu(A_i \cap B_j)]^2 = \\
&= \sum_{i=1}^{n} [\mu(A_i)]^2 + \sum_{j=1}^{m} [\mu(B_j)]^2 - 2\sum_{i=1}^{n} [\mu(A_i)]^2 = \\
&= \sum_{j=1}^{m} [\mu(B_j)]^2 - \sum_{i=1}^{n} [\mu(A_i)]^2.
\end{aligned} \tag{16}
$$

Finally denoting $S(\alpha) = \sum_{i=1}^{n} [\mu(A_i)]^2$, we can formulate

Proposition 1. For any two finite partitions $\alpha, \beta \in \Pi_\Omega$ of arbitrary measurable set Ω, if $a \acute{I} b$, then

$$\rho(\alpha, \beta) = S_{(\beta)} - S_{(\alpha)}.$$

From the other hand any element of partition β, i.e. set B_j represents a union of non intersecting elements of partition α, viz

$$B_j = \bigcup_{i=1}^{k_j} A_{ji}, \; j = \overline{1, m},$$

then

$$\sum_{j=1}^{m} [\mu(B_j)]^2 = \sum_{j=1}^{m} (\sum_{i=1}^{k_j} \mu(A_{ji}))^2 = \sum_{j=1}^{m} \{\sum_{i=1}^{k_j} [\mu(A_{ji})]^2 + 2\sum_{i=1}^{k_j-1} \sum_{i'=i+1}^{k_j} \mu(A_{ji})\mu(A_{ji'})\}. \tag{17}$$

It is clear that

$$\sum_{j=1}^{m} \sum_{i=1}^{k_j} [\mu(A_{ji})]^2 = S(\alpha), \tag{18}$$

as in the left hand side of the equality all elements of α are summarized.

Then from (16) – (18) it follows

$$\rho(\alpha, \beta) = 2\sum_{j=1}^{m} \sum_{i=1}^{k_j-1} \sum_{i'=i+1}^{k_j} \mu(A_{ji})\mu(A_{ji'}). \tag{19}$$

Now we can formulate the second proposition.

Proposition 2. For any two finite partitions satisfying conditions of Proposition 1, functional of the distance between them can be expressed through the elements of nested (more detailed) partition in two ways: (15) and (19). At that for elements of partition α the natural equality is fulfilled

$$\sum_{j=1}^{m} \sum_{i=1}^{k_j} \{\mu(A_{ji})[\sum_{\substack{i'=1 \\ i' \neq i}}^{k_j} \mu(A_{ji'})]\} = 2\sum_{j=1}^{m} \sum_{i=1}^{k_j-1} \sum_{i'=i+1}^{k_j} \mu(A_{ji})\mu(A_{ji'}). \tag{20}$$

To give a point of how induced distances (15), (16), (19) can be used on practice, let us consider arbitrary scheme of regions splitting/merging under segmentation. For short let it be a stage of regions splitting, and $\mu(\alpha) = card(\alpha)$. For example, a region $B_j \subset \beta$, $card(B_j) = 6$ has to be split into

$k_j = 3$ subregions A_{j1}, A_{j2}, $A_{j3} \subset \alpha$, $card(A_{j1}) = 1$, $card(A_{j2}) = 2$, $card(A_{j3}) = 3$. The dissimilarity between partitions α and β, $\alpha \subset \beta$ is expressed by the distance between B_j and A_{j1}, A_{j2}, A_{j3}. The latest can be calculated as a difference between sum of measures of single region and its partitions by (15) or just using measures of detailing partitions. In this way, by (15) we get

$$\rho(\alpha,\beta) = 6^2 - (1^2 + 2^2 + 3^2) = 22,$$

by (16) $\rho(\alpha, \beta) = 1 \cdot (2 + 3) + 2 \cdot (1 + 3) + 3 \cdot (1 + 2) = 22$,

and by (19) $\rho(\alpha, \beta) = 2 \cdot (1 \cdot 2 + 1 \cdot 3 + 2 \cdot 3) = 22$.

We recommend to use (19) for calculation of the distance, as the amount of summation and multiplication operations here is $1 + k_j^2$, while for (15) it equals to $k_j (k_j - 1)$ and for (16) it equals to $\frac{k_j (k_j - 1)}{2} + 1$. Calculated distance $\rho(\alpha,\beta) = 22$ should be used by regions splitting/merging schema to make a decision if made splitting has to be applied and recursively processed or not.

A pair of finite partitions α, β, for which exists an enclosure $\alpha \subset \beta$, can be considered not as a pair of partitions but as consolidation of partition α. In this case we deal with the traditional procedure of agglomerative clustering, and elements of partition β can practically be considered as clusters. Now if we identify the hierarchical grouping procedure in form of $K(\alpha)$ as a functional map of partition α elements into partition β elements, i.e. we assume $\beta = K(\alpha)$, where $K(\alpha)$ is a set of arbitrary groups B_j, $j = 1,2,\ldots,m$ of partition α elements, then enclosure $\alpha \subset K(\alpha)$ will take place invariably.

Here we obtain a corollary from Proposition 1.

Corollary 1. For any finite partition of $\alpha \in \Pi_\Omega$ set Ω the following equality

$$\rho(\alpha, K(\alpha)) = S(K(\alpha)) - S(\alpha).$$

takes place. It can also be noted that for arbitrary partition $\alpha = \{A_1, A_2, \ldots, A_n\}$ of set B it takes place

$$\sum_{i=1}^{n} \mu(A_i)\mu(\overline{A}_i) = 2\sum_{i=1}^{n-1} \sum_{i'=i+1}^{n} \mu(A_i)\mu(A_{i'}), \tag{21}$$

where $\overline{A}_i = B \setminus A_i$, $i \in \{1, 2, \ldots, n\}$.

Indeed, when $i \neq i'$, summands on the left side of this equality represent different paired compositions $\mu(A_i)\mu(A_{i'})$. At that $\mu(A_i)\mu(A_{i'})$ are included into two summands for any pair of distinct numbers $i, i' \in \{1, 2, \ldots, n\}$, i.e.

$$\mu(A_i)\big[\mu(A_1) + \ldots + \mu(A_{i'-1}) + \mu(A_{i'+1}) + \ldots + \mu(A_n)\big],$$

$$\mu(A_{i'})\big[\mu(A_1) + \ldots + \mu(A_{i'-1}) + \mu(A_{i'+1}) + \ldots + \mu(A_n)\big].$$

In this way we get coefficient 2 and sum representing first part of equality (21). At that from equalities (20) and (21) we can formalize the next corollary.

Corollary 2. Equality (20) can be presented in a form

$$\sum_{i=1}^{k_j} \left\{ \mu(A_{ji}) \left[\sum_{\substack{i'=1 \\ i' \neq i}}^{k_j} \mu(A_{ji'}) \right] \right\} = 2 \sum_{i=1}^{k_j-1} \sum_{i'=i+1}^{k_j} \mu(A_{ji}) \mu(A_{ji'}).$$

It means that equality (20) practically takes place inside of each group (cluster) and does not in their summary form.

GEOMETRICAL PROPERTIES OF NESTED QUOTIENT SETS

Now let us consider the largest group (cluster) i.e. when partition β consists of one element viz set Ω itself. In this case we shall denote introduced map K(α) as O(α), i.e. O(α)={Ω} and introduce functional

$$\rho(\alpha, O) = G(\alpha). \tag{22}$$

There is a note to be made. If partition α is uniform, i.e.

$$\mu(A_i) = \frac{\mu(\Omega)}{n}, \tag{23}$$

where $i \in \{1, \ldots, n\}$, $\alpha = \{A_i\}_{i=1}^{n}$, then

$$G(\alpha) = S(\Omega) - S(\alpha). \tag{24}$$

Taking into consideration that functional S(α) is equal to

$$S(\alpha) = \sum_{i=1}^{n} [\mu(A_i)]^2, \tag{25}$$

and from (23) and (25) we get the chain of equalities

$$G(\alpha) = [\mu(\Omega)]^2 - \sum_{i=1}^{n} [\mu(A_i)]^2 = [\mu(\Omega)]^2 - n[\mu(A_i)]^2 = [\mu(\Omega)]^2 - \frac{[\mu(\Omega)]^2}{n} = \\ = [\mu(\Omega)]^2 (1 - 1/n). \tag{26}$$

So here we can finally formulate following.

Proposition 3. If α is an arbitrary set of initial measurable set Ω, satisfies the uniformity condition that is all partition elements have the same measure, then functional G(α) of distance from the largest partition of the initial set Ω in form of itself is equal to

$$G(\alpha) = [\mu(\Omega)]^2 - \frac{[\mu(\Omega)]^2}{n},$$ (27)

where n is number of elements of partition α.

It is evident that if number of arbitrary uniform partition elements tends to infinity then

$$\lim_{n \to \infty} G(\alpha) = [\mu(\Omega)]^2.$$

Practically the fact formalized in corollary means that, when decomposing initial set Ω on equally measured parts we shall move off the coarse partition in form of the set itself, but not further than on the distance $[\mu(\Omega)]^2$ no matter how small value $\varepsilon > 0$ we chose. Moreover starting from some $N(\varepsilon)$, under all $n \geq N$ all 'uniform' (equally measured) partitions lay in one-sided ε- neighborhood of $\mathfrak{D}$ 'circle' of radius $[\mu(\Omega)]^2$ with centre in 'point' O={Ω}. On Figure 4 conditionally shown the 'geometry' of this situation.

This way if ε is the accuracy for measuring distance between partitions then we can count that all uniform partitions α, which number of elements is

$$n > \frac{[\mu(\Omega)]^2}{\varepsilon},$$

lay inside the circle with centre in 'point' O of radius $[\mu(\Omega)]^2$.

The discussed 'geometry' has a number of specific properties, which we shall consider below.

We start with consideration of a circle with centre in 'point' O and with radius $[\mu(\Omega)]^2$. From (24) it follows that all partitions of initial set Ω lay inside the given circle including its bound (a single point), i.e. it is not possible that any partition moves off from O on the distance bigger than $[\mu(\Omega)]^2$. Then from the triangular inequality it follows that

$\rho(\alpha, \beta) \leq \rho(\alpha, O) + \rho(\beta, O),$

Figure 4. Geometrical interpretation of nested partitions

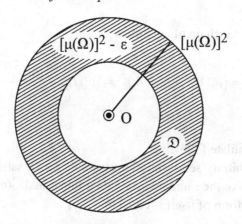

where α,β are arbitrary partitions of set Ω (Figure 5).

The above statements actually prove the forth proposition.

Proposition 4. Arbitrary partition α of measurable set Ω with finite number of elements regarding metric on quotient sets lies inside a 'circle' with centre in O = {Ω} and radius $[\mu(\Omega)]^2$, i.e. $\rho(\alpha,O) \leq [\mu(\Omega)]^2$, and for two arbitrary partitions α and *β* the following equation takes place

$$\rho(\alpha, \beta) \leq 2[\mu(\Omega)]^2.$$

Thus a set of partitions Π_Ω is limited.

Now if consider uniform partitions which elements are equally measured (we shall denote a set of such partitions as $\Re_\Omega$), we get the following proposition.

Proposition 5. For every sequence $\{\alpha_k\}_{k=1}^\infty \in \Re_\Omega$ for which $card\ \alpha_k \to \infty, \forall A_i \in \alpha_k\ \mu(A_i) \to 0$ takes place when *k* number is increasing, for any ε>0, starting with some $k \geq N(\varepsilon)$ we shall get

$$\rho(O,\alpha_k) \geq [\mu(\Omega)]^2 - \varepsilon,$$

what means that α_k and all next partitions are members of region $\mathfrak{D}$ (see Figure 4).

This fact follows directly from equation (26).

Now we shall consider two arbitrary partitions α,β $\in \Pi_\Omega$, where one is still enclosed into another one, i.e. $\alpha \subset \beta$ (or α 'details' *β*). Then from Proposition 1 we get

$$\rho(\alpha,\beta) = S(\beta) - S(\alpha). \tag{28}$$

From the other hand for any α,β $\in \Pi_\Omega$ enclosures $\alpha \subset O,\ \beta \subset O$, where O = {Ω} are fulfilled. Then from (28) it follows

$$\rho(\alpha,O) = S(O) - S(\alpha),$$

$$\rho(\beta,O) = S(O) - S(\beta).$$

Recalling definition of $G(\alpha)$ in equality (22) we get

Figure 5. Triangular inequality for nested partitions

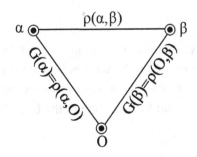

$$\begin{cases} G(\alpha) = S(O) - S(\alpha), \\ G(\beta) = S(O) - S(\beta). \end{cases} \tag{29}$$

In the set of equalities (29) we perform the subtraction of the second equality from the first one, and based on (28) we get

$$G(\alpha) - G(\beta) = S(\beta) - S(\alpha) = \rho(\alpha,\beta). \tag{30}$$

From Figure 5 and triangular inequality we get a set of equations

$$\begin{cases} G(\alpha) + G(\beta) \geq \rho(\alpha, \beta), \\ G(\alpha) + \rho(\alpha, \beta) \geq G(\beta), \\ G(\beta) + \rho(\alpha, \beta) \geq G(\alpha). \end{cases} \tag{31}$$

For any $\alpha,\beta \in \Pi_\Omega$ equations (31) are true as well as

$$\begin{cases} G(\alpha) - G(\beta) \leq \rho(\alpha, \beta), \\ G(\beta) - G(\alpha) \leq \rho(\alpha, \beta). \end{cases}$$

Given relations allow to formalize and prove the sixth proposition.

Proposition 6. On a set of partitions Π_Ω functionals $S(\alpha) = \sum_{i=1}^{n} [\mu(A_i)]^2$ and $G(\alpha) = \rho(\alpha, O)$, where $\alpha = \{A_i\}_{i=1}^{n} \in \Pi_\Omega$, $O = \{\Omega\} \in \Pi_\Omega$, have the next properties:

if $\alpha,\beta \in \Pi_\Omega$ and $\alpha \subset \beta$, then

$$\rho(\alpha,\beta) = S(\beta) - S(\alpha) = G(\alpha) - G(\beta); \tag{32}$$

regarding the nesting operation functional $S(\alpha)$ is decreasing and functional $G(\alpha)$ is increasing i.e. if $\alpha \subset \beta$, then

$G(\alpha) > G(\beta),$

$S(\alpha) < S(\beta);$

c)   all partitions which 'detail' given partition β, i.e. any $\alpha \subset \beta$ in the sense of metric $\rho(\alpha,\beta)$ lay on one 'line', passing through 'points' O and β what is illustrated on Figure 6, and along with the β 'detailing' process a 'point' α increase the number of its elements till the infinity and moves off the 'points' O and β along the initial line, tending to the bound point α_∞, i.e. to a partition with

Figure 6. Geometrical interpretation of nested partitions

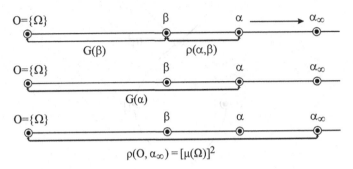

'infinite' elements number and with the measure values approaching 0, but situated on the finite distance from the point.

Proof. The first property followed from Proposition 2 and equality (30) proved above. The second one follows directly from the first one taking into consideration that $\rho(\alpha,\beta) \geq 0$ due to the metric property. Now we can finally move to the third property.

Indeed if $\alpha \subset \beta$, 'triangular' $O\alpha\beta$ (see Figure 4) 'shrinks' and transforms into a 'line", as from (32) it follows that $G(\alpha,\beta) + G(\beta) = G(\alpha)$, i.e. the third equation from set (31) transforms into equality. Thus, the 'point' α lies on a 'line', passing through 'points' O and β. At that it is 'moving off' from 'point' O, as $G(\alpha) > G(\beta)$. It is clear that during the 'detailing' the moving off process continues and α approaches the partition with infinite number of elements. But

$$\rho(\alpha,O) \rightarrow \rho(\alpha_\infty,O) = [\mu(\Omega)]^2$$

what follows from the limitation $\rho(\alpha,O) \leq [\mu(\Omega)]^2$ of Proposition 4. It completes the proof of the proposition.

Further we adduce some corollaries which follow from the facts we obtained.

Corollary 3. Any two 'lines' which pass through O and do not coincide, still intersect each other not just in 'point' O, but in infinite number of 'points'.

Proof. Let us consider two arbitrary partitions $\alpha,\beta \in \Pi_\Omega$ and partition $\alpha \cap \beta = \alpha\beta \in \Pi_\Omega$. It is obvious that $\alpha\beta \subset \alpha$ and $\alpha\beta \subset \beta$. Thus from the Proposition 6 it follows that 'line' which passes through 'points' O and α, and line which passes through 'points' O and β, generally do not match and intersect each other in 'point' $\gamma = \alpha\beta$. It is illustrated on Figure 7.

Obtained partition γ can be further comminuted what shall give us partitions $\alpha' \subset \gamma \subset \alpha$ and $\beta' \subset \gamma \subset \beta$. Continuing with this process, i.e. considering further detailing of partition $\gamma' = \alpha'\beta'$, we get $\gamma^{(\infty)}$ – a partition with infinite number of elements and primes. Thus the number of intersection 'points' is infinite, what grounds the given corollary (Figure 8).

Corollary 4. Π_Ω is a bundle of lines which start from the 'point' O (in terms of the introduced 'geometry').

It is really so as O contains (on enclosure) any partition of Π_Ω.

Drawing the conclusions we can formalize the main properties of nested quotient sets.

Property 1. Set of all partitions Π_Ω is limited and lies 'inside' of a circle with centre in O = $\{\Omega\}$ and radius equal to $[\mu(\Omega)]^2$.

Figure 7. Geometrical interpretation of nested partitions

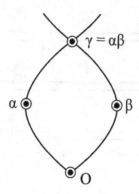

Figure 8. Intersection of clusters of 'lines' under partition detailing/splitting

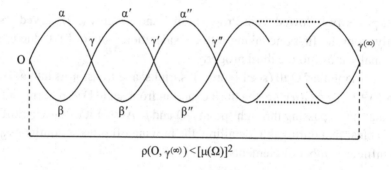

$$\rho(O, \gamma^{(\infty)}) < [\mu(\Omega)]^2$$

Property 2. A set Π_Ω is a bundle of 'lines' starting in point O.

Property 3. Any two elements of bundle of 'lines' Π_Ω intersect each other infinite number of times.

Property 4. A set of all points of intersection of any two lines in bundle Π_Ω while moving off O tends to one common conditional 'point' $\gamma^{(\infty)}$ – partition with infinite number of elements which measure value tends to 0.

Property 5. Boundary of set $\Re_\Omega$ consists of single 'point' α_∞.

Property 6. Diameter of 'circle' in which Π_Ω lies, does not exceed $2[\mu(\Omega)]^2$, i.e. $\max\limits_{\alpha,\, \beta \in \Pi_\Omega} \rho(\alpha, \beta) \leq 2[\mu(\Omega)]^2$.

The properties obtained above create premises for the detailed analysis of hierarchical representation of data of any nature. Further we shall analyze few particular aspects of metric probabilistic interpretations and relations which use some integrable functions, namely images, for the measure forming.

ANALYSIS OF METRICAL RELATIONS BETWEEN NESTED PARTITIONS

We shall consider probabilistic space $\langle \Omega, \mathcal{F}_\Omega, P \rangle$, where Ω is an arbitrary set in general case (set of elementary events), $\mathcal{F}_\Omega$ is an σ-algebra of its subsets including empty sets $\varnothing$ and Ω, closed regarding countable union operation, P is a probabilistic measure (probability), i.e. sigma-additive finite measure such that $P(\varnothing) = 0$, $P(\Omega) = 1$, $\forall A \in \mathcal{F}_\Omega$ $\exists P(A) : 0 \leq P(A) \leq 1$. Thus considering the results of nested quotient sets analysis can be interpreted as the hypotheses set.

Let a set of hypotheses $K_1 = \{H_1, H_2, \ldots, H_n\}$ is given, that defines the partition of elementary events set $\Omega = \{\omega_1, \omega_2, \ldots\}$, i.e. $H_i \in \mathcal{F}_\Omega$, $i = \overline{1, n}$; $\bigcup_{i=1}^n H_i = \Omega$; $H_i \cap H_j = \varnothing$ for any $i, j \in \{1, 2, n\}$ such that $i \neq j$. Let us assume that each of hypotheses is decomposed on subhypotheses i.e. $H_i = \{H_{i_1}, H_{i_2}, \ldots, H_{i_{l_i}}\}$ with the same properties.

Then cortege of elements $\mathcal{F}_\Omega$

$$K_2 = \{\{H_{11}, H_{12}, \ldots, H_{1l_1}\}, \{H_{21}, H_{22}, \ldots, H_{2l_2}\}, \ldots, \{H_{n1}, H_{n2}, \ldots, H_{nl_n}\}\}$$

represents the same probabilistic space hypotheses set enclosed into K_1, i.e. $K_2 \subset K_1$. This case completely fits the traditional urn scheme with intercepts in tasks of arbitrary elements choice. Thereby from (8) we get

$$\rho(K_1, K_2) = \sum_{i=1}^n \sum_{j=1}^{l_i} P(H_i \Delta H_{ij}) P(H_i \cap H_{ij}) \tag{33}$$

as for any H_i a non-empty intersection can be fulfilled only with its own sub-hypotheses (when intersecting with others it would not be a probable event, thus the corresponding summand is equal to zero).

In addition taking into account that $H_{ij} \subset H_i$, we find

$$H_i \Delta H_{ij} = H_i \setminus H_{ij}$$

or

$$H_i \setminus H_{ij} = \bigcup_{\substack{k=1 \\ k \neq j}}^{l_i} H_{ik}.$$

But then $P(H_i \Delta H_{ij}) = P(H_i) - P(H_{ij})$ or

$$P(H_i \setminus H_{ij}) = \sum_{\substack{k=1 \\ k \neq j}}^{l_i} P(H_{ik}).$$

Denoting $P(H_i) = P_i$ and $P(H_{ij}) = P_{ij}$, with consideration that $P(H_i \cap H_{ij}) = P_{ij}$ we finally find

$$\rho(K_1, K_2) = \sum_{i=1}^n \sum_{j=1}^{l_i} (P_i P_{ij} - P_{ij}^2), \tag{34}$$

$$\rho(K_1, K_2) = \sum_{i=1}^{n} \sum_{j=1}^{l_i} \sum_{\substack{k=1 \\ k \neq j}}^{l_i} P_{ij} P_{ik} \, . \tag{35}$$

We shall consider an example.

Let us have $K_1 = \{H_1, H_2, H_3\}$ and $K_2 = \{\{H_{11}, H_{12}\}, \{H_{21}, H_{22}\}, \{H_{31}, H_{32}, H_{32}\}\}$ (Figure 9). It is obvious that $K_2 \subset K_1$, and from (33) we get

$$
\begin{aligned}
\rho(K_1, K_2) &= P(H_1 \cap H_{11})P(H_1 \Delta H_{11}) + P(H_1 \cap H_{12})P(H_1 \Delta H_{12}) + \\
&\quad + P(H_2 \cap H_{21})P(H_2 \Delta H_{21}) + P(H_2 \cap H_{22})P(H_2 \Delta H_{22}) + \\
&\quad + P(H_3 \cap H_{31})P(H_3 \Delta H_{31}) + P(H_3 \cap H_{32})P(H_3 \Delta H_{32}) + P(H_3 \cap H_{33})P(H_3 \Delta H_{33}) = \\
&= P_{11}(P_1 - P_{11}) + P_{12}(P_1 - P_{12}) + P_{21}(P_2 - P_{21}) + P_{22}(P_2 - P_{22}) + P_{31}(P_3 - P_{31}) + \\
&\quad + P_{32}(P_3 - P_{32}) + P_{33}(P_3 - P_{33}).
\end{aligned}
$$

From the other hand taking into account (35) we get

$$
\begin{aligned}
\rho(K_1, K_2) &= P_{11}P_{12} + P_{12}P_{11} + P_{21}P_{22} + P_{22}P_{21} + P_{31}(P_{32} + P_{33}) \\
&\quad + P_{32}(P_{31} + P_{33}) + P_{33}(P_{31} + P_{32}) = \\
&= 2(P_{11}P_{12} + P_{21}P_{22} + P_{31}P_{32} + P_{31}P_{33} + P_{32}P_{33}).
\end{aligned}
$$

In the first case we have seven summands and in the second only five. In general case when we consider two partitions $\alpha = \{A_i\}_{i=1}^{n}$ and $\beta = \{B_j\}_{j=1}^{m}$ of arbitrary set Ω, we get n m summands, while under $\alpha \subset \beta$ a number of summands decrease. When using expression $\rho(\alpha, \beta) = S_{(\beta)} - S_{(\alpha)}$ from Proposition 1 we get n + m summands and when using (19), what is equivalent to (35), we get

$$\sum_{j=1}^{m} C^2_{card \, B_j} \, .$$

Figure 9. Example of hypotheses enclosing

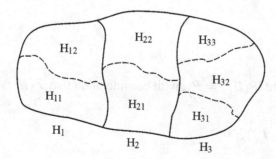

In the considered example $n + m = 7 + 3 = 10$, and

$$C^2_{card\ B_1} + C^2_{card\ B_2} + C^2_{card\ B_3} = C^2_2 + C^2_2 + C^2_3 = 5 \cdot$$

To draw the recommendations on counting the distances between nested quotient sets first we shall assume that all classes of equivalence are separated into the same number of elements

$$\begin{cases} B_1 = \{A_1, \dots, A_s\}; \\ B_2 = \{A_{s+1}, \dots, A_{2s}\}; \\ \dots\dots\dots\dots\dots\dots\dots\dots\dots\dots\dots \\ B_m = \{A_{(m-1)s+1}, \dots, A_{ms}\}. \end{cases}$$

We denote J' as the number of summands under finding functional $\rho(\alpha, \beta)$ in difference form and J'' according to formula (19). It is obvious that

$$J' = m + ms,$$

$$J'' = mC^2_s = \frac{ms(s-1)}{2}.$$

Consider the difference

$$J' - J'' = -m\frac{s^2 - 3s - 2}{2}.$$

As roots of the equation $s^2 - 3s - 2 = 0$ are equal to: $s_1 = -0,56$; $s_2 = 3,56$, and s is an integer, then

$$J' - J'' = \begin{cases} > 0, & s = 1, 2, 3; \\ < 0, & s = 4, 5, 6, \dots \end{cases} \tag{36}$$

Thus for two partitions $\alpha = \{A_i\}^n_{i=1}$ and $\beta = \{B_j\}^m_{j=1}$ such that $\alpha \subset \beta$, under condition that for every $B_j \in \beta$ not more than three elements $A_i \in \alpha$ can be found, expression (19) can be logically applied. In the other case it is preferable to use expression from Proposition 1. We shall note that these conclusions were made under assumption of quotient sets partition uniformity. Though decrease of separate equivalence classes number in the first case and its increase in another one only makes equations stronger (36).

Functional relations of quotient sets can be useful for image processing and most important for image context interpretation. In segmentation tasks the main information for data clustering is obtained from brightness distribution values. We shall assume that the measure is defined via positive integrated function on Ω, i.e. assuming that

$$\begin{cases} \alpha = \{[A_{11}, A_{12},..., A_{1r_1}],...,[A_{j1}, A_{j2},..., A_{jr_j}],...,[A_{j1}, A_{j2},..., A_{jr_m}]\}, \\ \beta = \{B_1, B_2,..., B_m\}, \end{cases}$$

where $B_j = \bigcup_{k=1}^{r_j} A_{jk}$, $A_{jk} \cap A_{jk'} = \varnothing$, $k \neq k' \in \{1, 2,..., r_j\}$, we shall count that

$$\mu(B_j) = \int_{B_j} f(x)dx,$$

$$\mu(A_{jk}) = \int_{A_{jk}} f(x)dx.$$

Then from relation $\rho(\alpha, \beta) = S_{(\beta)} - S_{(\alpha)}$ with consideration of metric non-negativity and expression (25) we get an integral inequality

$$\sum_{j=1}^{m}(\int_{B_j} f(x)dx)^2 \geq \sum_{j=1}^{m}\sum_{k=1}^{r_j}(\int_{A_{jk}} f(x)dx)^2 . \tag{37}$$

From (34) the next integral equation follows

$$\sum_{j=1}^{m}\sum_{k=1}^{r_j}(\int_{B_j} f(x)dx \int_{A_{jk}} f(x)dx - [\int_{A_{jk}} f(x)dx]^2) \geq 0 . \tag{38}$$

Equations (37) and (38) can serve as criteria (tending to equality is a necessary condition) for verifying of partitions nesting into a single equivalence class or cumulatively into quotient set what in common case corresponds to partial ordering relation.

Let us consider arbitrary partitions $\alpha, \beta \in \Pi_\Omega$. As all of them are enclosed into $O \in \Pi_\Omega$, we get the following triangular inequality

$$\rho(\alpha, \beta) \leq \rho(\alpha, O) + \rho(\beta, O).$$

Taking into account that

$$\rho(\alpha, \beta) = \sum_{i=1}^{n}\sum_{j=1}^{m} \int_{A_i \cap B_j} f(x)dx \int_{A_i \Delta B_j} f(x)dx,$$

$$\rho(\alpha, O) = (\int_{\Omega} f(x)dx)^2 - \sum_{i=1}^{n}(\int_{A_i} f(x)dx)^2,$$

we obtain

$$2(\int_{\Omega} f(x)dx)^2 \geq \sum_{i=1}^{n}(\int_{A_i} f(x)dx)^2 + \sum_{j=1}^{m}(\int_{B_j} f(x)dx)^2 + \sum_{i=1}^{n}\sum_{j=1}^{m} \int_{A_i \cap B_j} f(x)dx \int_{A_i \Delta B_j} f(x)dx. \tag{39}$$

Equation (38) allows to formulate a segmentation task (under a search of a level of detail of segmented image) as a task of mathematical programming under condition that template set is defined for example in a ground truth paradigm. In other words under $\alpha \subset \beta$ we have $\rho(\alpha, \beta) = \rho(\alpha, O) + \rho(\beta, O)$ and discrepancy in equation (39) allows to evaluate how partition $\alpha \in \Pi_\Omega$ tends to subpartition of partition $\beta \in \Pi_\Omega$.

If consider triangular inequality as the initial one

$$\rho(\beta, O) \le \rho(\alpha, \beta) + \rho(\alpha, O),$$

then corresponding integral equation takes form

$$\sum_{i=1}^{n} \left(\int_{A_i} f(x)dx \right)^2 - \sum_{j=1}^{m} \left(\int_{B_j} f(x)dx \right)^2 + \sum_{i=1}^{n} \sum_{j=1}^{m} \int_{A_i \cap B_j} f(x)dx \int_{A_i \Delta B_j} f(x)dx \ge 0. \tag{40}$$

This equation can also be used as quotient sets nesting criterion. Let us induce such nesting evaluation $\Theta_{\alpha_k}(\beta')$ for comparison of images segmentations, to be more precise, for search of region(s) of interest of query image in the collection (database) of images. Focusing on similarity of compared regions in terms of spatial features, we assume that

$$\mu(A) = \int_{A} f(x)dx = \sum_{(x,\,y) \in A} f(x, y) = card(A),$$

where $A \in \alpha$, $\forall (x,y) \in A$: $f(x,y) = 1$ (intensity function has constant value in every pixel). Then from triangular inequality $\rho(\alpha, O) \le \rho(\alpha, \beta) + \rho(\beta, O)$ follows expression (40) with exchanged first and second summands:

$$-\sum_{i=1}^{n} \left(\int_{A_i} f(x)dx \right)^2 + \sum_{j=1}^{m} \left(\int_{B_j} f(x)dx \right)^2 + \sum_{i=1}^{n} \sum_{j=1}^{m} \int_{A_i \cap B_j} f(x)dx \int_{A_i \Delta B_j} f(x)dx \ge 0. \tag{41}$$

Then in order to get more strict nesting evaluation value, we chose the minimal of left sides of (40) and (41). Thus, nesting evaluation $\Theta_{\alpha_k}(\beta')$ is expressed as follows:

$$\Theta_{\alpha_k}(\beta') = s_{\alpha_k,\beta'} + \sum_{i=1}^{n_k} \sum_{j=0}^{t} card(A_i \cap B_j) card(A_i \Delta B_j),$$

$$\rho(\alpha_k,\ O) = \sum_{i=1}^{n_k} card(A_i), \ \rho(\beta',\ O) = \sum_{i=0}^{t} card(B_i),$$

$$s_{\alpha_k,\beta'} = \min \left\{ [\rho(\alpha_k,\ O)]^2 - [\rho(\beta',\ O)]^2,\ [\rho(\beta',O)]^2 - [\rho(\alpha_k,\ O)]^2 \right\},$$

where $\alpha_k = \{A_i\}_{i=1}^{n_k}$ is partition of image with index k from database, B_0 and $B_1, B_2, ..., B_t$ – background region and regions of interest of query image correspondingly.

In the following section experimental results of usage induced nesting evaluation $\Theta_{\alpha_k}(\beta')$ in image retrieval task are shown.

EXPERIMENTS AND FUTURE WORK DISCUSSION

As various image processing applications practically require different levels of detailing, the problem of ability to operate the obtained image segmentation both on the level of partitions and coverings becomes a critical task for the image understanding. Efficient matching of image partitions collections stipulated by the properties of the metric on nested partitions does not only enables to evaluate the similarity of image segmentation, which allows image retrieval systems to cope with a wider variety of problems but also performing a measure for nested quotient sets it relieves the dependency on the segmentation results when obtaining partitions with low level and high level detailing (Figure 10).

Obtained nesting evaluations (37) and (38) and quotient sets similarities (39)-(40) created premises for solving region-based image retrieval.

To investigate the research results we chose 108 scene images in the following proportions: 72 images and their ground truth representation from the Berkley collection (Berkley segmentation dataset) and 36 images of a leaf with a different background from Caltech collection (Caltech archive) segmented with JSEG algorithm. We chose one image from the second group to be a query image and shall search for the region corresponding to the leaf object region (Figure 11).

Image similarity is defined via two partition matching methods: normalized metric on partitions and nesting evaluation.

Normalized metric on partitions is based on (2). We define measure μ(A) as area of region A and shall perform normalization within [0;1] as following

$$\rho^*(\alpha, \beta) = \frac{\sum_{i=1}^{n}\sum_{j=1}^{m} \mu(A_i \Delta B_j)\mu(A_i \cap B_j)}{(n \cdot m)^2}.$$

For each comparison variant we shall find 20 'closest' images.

Figure 12 illustrates values $\Theta_{\alpha_k}(\beta')$ of 108 database images partitions enclosing into the query goal partition. 20 images with minimal distance are marked with green circles, horizontal red line separates 20 chosen image and vertical line separates the Berkley collection images (left side) from the Caltech leaves images (right side).

Figure 10. Image and its partitions with different level of detail

Figure 11. Query image and partition for the search performance

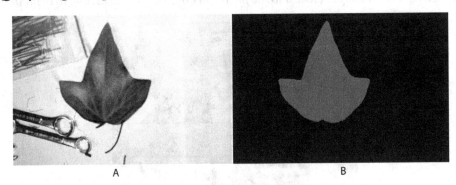

A   B

Figure 13 shows 20 most close images and their partitions representation in the distance ascending order.

It can be seen that first 8 closest images belong to the second image collection. In total the resulting group contains 14 images of the Caltech collection. At that the resulting partitions have high level of object (items 3, 17) and background (almost all 20 images) detailing. The closest result is the duplicate image with distance equal to 0.

Figure 14 shows 20 found images and coloring of their partitions used on the search stage. As in the previous case 8 closest images belong to the leaves images of Caltech. In total there were 13 such images found.

Figure 15 illustrates distances of 108 database images partitions and query goal partition according to the normalized partition metric.

Further experiments were carried out to see how partitions detailing level can influence the matching results. On the plots of distances (Figure 16) you can see that with increase of detailing the difference between quotient sets of images from Figure 9 decrease, what is proved by induced geometrical properties of partial ordered quotient sets.

Figure 12. Distance between query image and 108 database images based on enclosure evaluation $\Theta_{\alpha_k}(\beta')$

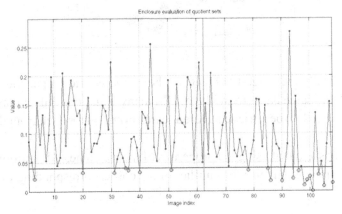

Figure 13. Search results 20 images closest to the partition on figure 10 according to evaluation $\Theta_{\alpha_k}(\beta')$

Figure 14. Search results 20 images closest to the partition on figure 10 according to normalized partition metric

As background is usually the biggest "object" in the image metric on partitions, we can perform a search for images with the same background layout. In many situations only a part of the image which corresponds to object(s) needs to be retrieved. Here a search criterion for background independent objects comes in handy.

It can be again emphasized that using the properties of metric on nested partitions 1) allows not only to search for the certain images but also for families of the cosets corresponding to the searched objects

Figure 15. Distance between query image partition and 108 database images partitions

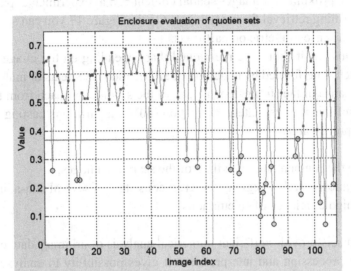

Figure 16. Distance between obtained partitions

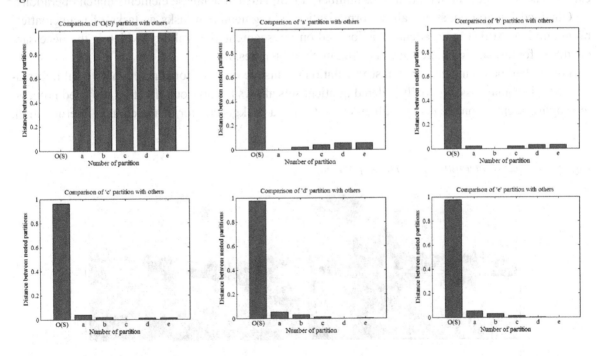

not depending on the background components, 2) makes the retrieval relatively independent from query or database images segmentation results.

From the image understanding point of view, the method allows to analyze objects represented at different levels of granularity and abstraction.

Still, the method has a disadvantage to mention. Metric is variant to geometrical transformations. Also it does not take into account similarity of images by visual features like color or texture. In current research we investigate proximity of images spatial content and at experimental part only this measure is utilized when performing retrieval from databases. On the Figure 17 you can see the example of images which are close in sense of metric on partitions.

Drawing the conclusions it should be mentioned that depending on the image retrieval functional requirements the search is performed by matching of all partitions elements or matching query with the region of interest. Because of the strong dependency of the second approach from the detailing of segmentation it is very sufficient to use integral equation (40) as a partitions nesting criterion. The basic advantages of this approach are:

- Low variance to the segmentation detailing of the searched images;
- Possibility to define a searched region of interest consistent of several non-adjacent raster regions;
- Simplicity and high efficiency of calculations.

Metric on quotient sets provides efficient numerical analysis of arbitrary data clusters. In the tasks of visual information processing and interpretation it gives possibility to analyze images ensembles grouped according to different criteria.

Providing hierarchical structures efficiency analysis the metric also allows to synthesize hierarchical models of image search reducing the number of template and database elements match operations.

Obtained integral equations allow formalization of segmentation tasks as tasks of mathematical programming. At that main attention is focused on the segmentation validity, which is the necessary condition for automatic image understanding methods synthesis.

For content based image retrieval segmentation results are used to store and extract visual information. Metrical analysis of partially ordered quotient sets allows to carry out effective stratified processing paying attention on the data detailing level. It gives a background for image context interpretation.

Figure 17. Spatial meaning of metric on partitions

Dependency of geometric transformations and utilization of spatial features only though can be mentioned as disadvantage and left for the future work consideration.

REFERENCES

Berkley Segmentation Dataset. (n.d.). Retrieved from http://www.eecs.berkeley.edu/Research/Projects/CS/vision/bsds

Caltech Archive. (n.d.). Retrieved from http://www.vision.caltech.edu/html-files/archive.html

Chan, K. L., Xiong, X., Liu, F., & Purnomo, R. (2001). Content-Based Image Retrieval Using Region Representation. In Klette, (Eds.), *Multi-Image Analysis, Lecture Notes in Computer Science* (*Vol. 2032*, pp. 238–250). Berlin: Springer-Verlag.

Chavez, E., Navarro, G., Baeza-Yates, R., & Marroquin, J. L. (2001). Searching in metric spaces. [CSUR]. *ACM Computing Surveys, 33*(3), 273–321. doi:10.1145/502807.502808

Cheng, W., Xu, D., Jiang, Y., & Lang, C. (2005). Information Theoretic Metrics in Shot Boundary Detection. In R. Khosla, et al. (eds.), *Knowledge-Based Intelligent Information and Engineering Systems,* (LNCS Vol. 3683, pp. 388-394). Berlin: Springer-Verlag.

Datta, R., Joshi, D., Li, J., & Wang, J. Z. (2008). Image retrieval: ideas, influences, and trands of the new age. *ACM Computing Surveys, 40*(2), 1–60. doi:10.1145/1348246.1348248

Gao, X., Wang, T., & Li, J. (2005). A Content-based Image Quality Metric. In D. Slezak et al. (eds.), *Rough Sets, Fuzzy Sets, Data Mining, and Granular Computing,* (LNCS Vol. 3642, pp. 231-240). Berlin: Springer-Verlag.

Hjaltason, G., & Samet, H. (2003). Index-driven similarity search in metric spaces. [TODS]. *ACM Transactions on Database Systems, 28*(4), 517–580. doi:10.1145/958942.958948

Jiang, X., Marti, C., Irniger, C., & Bunke, H. (2005). Image segmentation evaluation by techniques of comparing clusterings. In Fabio, R., & Sergio, V. (Eds.), *Image Analysis and Processing (ICIAP)* (*Vol. 3617*, pp. 344–351). LNCS. doi:10.1007/11553595_42

Khan, A., Aylward, E., Barta, P., Miller, M. I., & Beg, M. F. (2005). Semi-automated Basal Ganglia Segmentation Using Large Deformation Diffeomorphic Metric Mapping. In J.S. Duncan, G. Gerig (eds.), *Medical Image Computing and Computer-Assisted Intervention,* (LNCS Vol. 3749, pp. 238-245). Berlin: Springer-Verlag.

Kinoshenko, D., Mashtalir, V. & Shlyakhov, V. (2007). A partition metric for clustering features analysis. *International Journal 'Information theories and applications', 14*, 230-236.

Kinoshenko, D., Mashtalir, V., Vinarsky, V., & Yegorova, E. (2005). Hierarchical partitions for content image retrieval from Large-scale database. In *Machine Learning and Data Mining in Pattern Recognition,* (LNCS Vol. 3587, pp. 445-455). Berlin: Springer-Verlag.

Lew, M., Sebe, N., Djeraba, Ch., & Jain, R. (2006). Content-based multimedia information retrieval: state of art and challenges. *ACM Transactions of Multimedia Computing, Communications, and Applications, 2*(1), 1–19. doi:10.1145/1126004.1126005

Li, B., Chang, E., & Wu, Y. (2003). Discovery of a perceptual distance function for measuring image similarity. *Multimedia Systems, 8*(6), 512–522. doi:10.1007/s00530-002-0069-9

Li, J., Wang, J. Z., & Wiederhold, G. (2000). IRM integrated region matching for image retrieval. In *proc. ACM Multimedia'2000*, (pp. 147-156).

Liu, Y., Zhanga, D., Lua, G., & Ma, W.-Y. (2007). A survey of content-based image retrieval with high-level semantics. *Pattern Recognition, 40*(1), 262–282. doi:10.1016/j.patcog.2006.04.045

Ma, Z. (Ed.). (2009). *Artificial Intelligence for Maximizing Content-Based Image Retrieval*. Hershey, PA: Information Science Reference.

Mashtalir, V., Mikhnova, E., Shlyakhov, V., & Yegorova, E. (2006). A Novel Metric on Partitions for Image Segmentation. In *Proceedings of IEEE International Conference on Video and Signal Based Surveillance*, (pp. 18).

Meila, M. (2003). Comparing clustering by the Variation of Information. In B. Scheolkopf, M.K. Warmuth (eds.), *COLT/Kernel 2003*, (LNAI Vol. 2777, pp. 173–187). Berlin: Springer-Verlag.

Partridge, M., & Jabri, M. (2002). Hierarchical Feature Extraction for Image Recognition. *The Journal of VLSI Signal Processing, 32*(1-2), 157–167. doi:10.1023/A:1016379721504

Prieto, M. S., & Allen, A. R. (2003). A similarity metric for edge images. *IEEE Transactions on Pattern Analysis and Machine Intelligence, 25*(10), 1265–1277. doi:10.1109/TPAMI.2003.1233900

Rubner, Y., Tomasi, C., & Guibas, L. J. (2000). The Earth Mover's Distance as a Metric for Image Retrieval. *International Journal of Computer Vision, 40*(2), 99–121. doi:10.1023/A:1026543900054

Sfikas, G., Constantinopoulos, C., Likas, A., & Galatsanos, N. P. (2005). An Analytic Distance Metric for Gaussian Mixture Models with Application in Image Retrieval. In W. Duch, et al. (eds.), *Artificial Neural Networks: Formal Models and Their Applications*, (LNCS Vol. 3697, pp. 835-840). Berlin: Springer-Verlag.

Traina, A. J. M., Traina, C. Jr, Bueno, J. M., Chino, F. J. T., & Azevedo-Marques, P. (2003). Efficient Content-Based Image Retrieval through Metric Histograms. *World Wide Web (Bussum), 6*(2), 157–185. doi:10.1023/A:1023670521530

Wang, D., Ma, X., & Kim, Y. (2005). Learning Pseudo Metric for Intelligent Multimedia Data Classification and Retrieval. *Journal of Intelligent Manufacturing, 16*(6), 575–586. doi:10.1007/s10845-005-4363-1

Weber, R., Schek, H.-J., & Blott, S. (1998). A quantitative analysis and performance study for similarity-search methods in high-dimensional spaces. In *International Conference on Very Large Data Bases*, (pp. 194-205).

Zezula, P., Amato, G., Dohnal, V., & Batko, M. (2006). Similarity Search. In *The Metric Space Approach, Advances in Database Systems*, (220 p). New York: Springer Science+Business Media, Inc.

Zhong, D., & Defee, I. (2007). Perfomance of similarity measures based on histograms of local image feature vector. *Pattern Recognition Letters, 28*(15), 2003–2010. doi:10.1016/j.patrec.2007.05.019

Chapter 3
R*–Tree Based Similarity and Clustering Analysis for Images

Jiaxiong Pi
University of Nebraska at Omaha, USA

Yong Shi
University of Nebraska at Omaha, USA

Zhengxin Chen
University of Nebraska at Omaha, USA

ABSTRACT

Image content analysis plays an important role for adaptive multimedia retrieval. In this chapter, the authors present their work on using a useful spatial data structure, R*-tree, for similarity analysis and cluster analysis of image contents. First, they describe an R*-tree based similarity analysis tool for similarity retrieval of images. They then move on to discuss R*-tree based clustering methods for images, which has been a tricky issue: although objects stored in the same R* tree leaf node enjoys spatial proximity, it is well-known that R* trees cannot be used directly for cluster analysis. Nevertheless, R* tree's indexing feature can be used to assist existing cluster analysis methods, thus enhancing their performance of cluster quality. In this chapter, the authors report their progress of using R* trees to improve well-known K-means and hierarchical clustering methods. Based on R*-Tree's feature of indexing Minimum Bounding Box (MBB) according to spatial proximity, the authors extend R*-Tree's application to cluster analysis containing image data. Two improved algorithms, KMeans-R and Hierarchy-R, are proposed. Experiments have shown that KMeans-R and Hierarchy-R have achieved better clustering quality.

INTRODUCTION

Image content analysis has found many applications in various domains (such as in biomedical science) and plays an important role for adaptive multimedia retrieval. In order to effectively analyze the image contents, first we should be able to access and *manipulate* the images themselves (rather than staying with the metadata description of the images). Research effort has been made in this regard. For example,

DOI: 10.4018/978-1-61692-859-9.ch003

aimed at supporting a better coupling between enhanced image processing technique and an advanced image management for storage and retrieval, Li and Chen (2005) developed a system which supports the coupling of effective image management with enhanced image processing techniques, where image retrieval is conducted by using an image algebra. This approach is illustrated by a prototype medical image retrieval system on patient chromosome images, where similarity-based retrieval is conducted: when a query chromosome is provided, patient chromosomes in the database that are similar to the query chromosome are retrieved.

Upon manipulating images, the next important task for image content analysis is to effectively index the images. Various spatial data structures developed in the past can be useful for dealing with the spatial data store in images, including KD-trees (Bentley 1975), octrees (Aronov et al., 2003), TV-tree (Lin et al., 1994), X-tree (Berchtold et al. 1996), SR-tree (Katayama and Satoh, 1997), M-tree (Ciaccia et al. 1997), etc. In this chapter, we report our research of similarity search and clustering methods on images using on more traditional R*-tree data structure, because R*-tree (and its "relative" R-tree) is a popular and relative mature technique. This research is also a continuation of our own related research in the past (e.g., Schreck and Chen, 2000; Durby, Shi and Chen, 2004).

After a brief review on the basics of R*-trees, the presentation of our current work consists of two related topics: First, we describe an R*-tree based similarity analysis tool for similarity retrieval of images. We then move on to discuss R*-tree based clustering methods for images, presenting R*-tree based algorithms of KMean-R and Hiearchy-R. Experiments have shown that KMeans-R and Hierarchy-R have achieved better clustering quality. The contribution of R*-tree based clustering to image content analysis leads us to further consider ontology-related issues, as to be briefly addressed in a discussion section.

BASICS OF R* TREES

Just like a B-Tree, an R-Tree (Guttman 1984) relies on a balanced hierarchical structure, in which each tree node is mapped to a disk page. However, whereas B-Trees are built on single-value keys and rely on a total order on these keys, R-Trees organize rectangles according to a containment relationship. Each object to be indexed will be represented by Minimum Bounding Box (MBB) in the index structure except point for which an MBB simply degrades to a point. All indexed objects will eventually be put in leaf nodes. A leaf node contains an array of leaf entries. A leaf entry is a pair (*mbb*, *oid*), where *mbb* is the Minimum Bounding Box (MBB) and *oid* is the object ID. Each internal node is associated with a rectangle, referred to as the directory rectangle (*dr*), which is the minimal bounding box of the rectangle of its child nodes. The structure of R-Tree satisfies the following properties:

1 For all nodes in the tree (except for the root), the number of entries is between m and M, where $0 \leq m \leq M/2$.

2 For each entry (*dr*, *node-id*) in a non-leaf node N, *dr* is the directory rectangle of a child node of N, whose page address is *node-id*.

3 For each leaf entry (*mbb*, *oid*), *mbb* is the minimal bounding box of spatial component of the object stored at address oid.

4 The root has at least two entries (unless it is a leaf).

5 All leaves are at the same level.

R* tree is a variant of R tree for indexing spatial information. Minimization of both coverage and overlap is crucial to the performance of R-trees. The R*-tree attempts to reduce both, using a combination of a revised node split algorithm and the concept of forced reinsertion at node overflow. See references (Beckmann et al., 1990; Gaede & Günther, 1998) for more detail.

R*-TREE FOR SIMILARITY ANALYSIS

Since R*-Tree indexes spatial objects according to spatial proximity and close points tend to be put in the same leaf node, small amount leaf nodes will be traversed before similar points are found. As a result, fast similarity analysis can be achieved. However, due to the so-called "dimensionality curse," R*-Tree's performance degrades rapidly when dimension is larger than 10. Provided that some dataset/database is made up of time series with large length (>>10), and for R*-Tree to work efficiently, a dimensionality reduction technique is necessary. Over the years various dimensionality reduction techniques have been proposed; for example, Agrawal et al. (1993) adopted discrete Fourier transform (DFT) as a dimensionality reduction method., and Keogh et al. (2000) proposed a simple data transformation technique, Piecewise Aggregation Approximation (PAA). However, although principal component analysis (PCA) is a well-known method for dimensionality reduction, its application for time series analysis has not been reported.

We have explored using PCA for dimensionality reduction for time series data and developed a tool for similarity analysis using PCA and other methods. The following are general steps for performing PCA:

- Construct covariance matrix of column vectors;
- Calculate eigenvectors;
- Determine principle components and perform dimensionality reduction.

Compared with DFT and PAA, PCA has following virtues:

1   PCA is an orthogonal transformation and can guarantee distance conversation if all eigenvectors are used.
2   PCA operates on the whole dataset and can capture the primary features such as data distribution and variation of the dataset. After dimensionality reduction, those primary features can be maintained.

We have developed a similarity analysis tool which is made up of three modules, namely R*-Tree module, PCA module and B-Tree module. When this similarity analysis tool is used, given a spatial dataset and a given query, with similarity results will be returned through the phases as shown in Figure 1.

R*TREES FOR CLUSTER ANALYSIS

Similarity querying on R*-trees takes advantage of R*-tree's feature of grouping objects together based on spatial proximity. A natural extension of this study would be to push the task of retrieval a step further: to the task of clustering, where the entire dataset is clustered into groups based on similarity so that the commonality of the data in the same cluster can be revealed. However, using R*-tree for cluster

Figure 1. Data flow diagram in the similarity analysis tool when PCA module is used

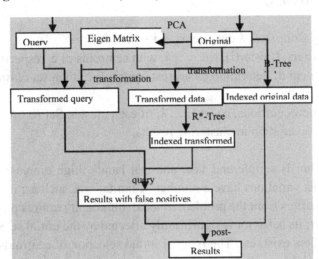

analysis should be done cautiously, as researchers already issued the following warning a decade ago (Ester et al., 1995):

1   IF R*-tree is used for clustering, then all clusters (i.e. the directory rectangles) have a rectangular shape and these rectangles have to be parallel to the axes of the coordinate system. This restriction does not comply with the objective of cluster analysis.

2   An R*-Tree is a balanced tree. For all nodes in the tree (except for the root), the number of entries is between m and M, where M is node capacity, m is set to a constant in [0, M/2]. Assuming that each node is a cluster, the number of members in every cluster is then between m and M. In reality, however, no bound is set for the number of cluster members.

3   The R*-Tree structure does not allow users to specify the number of clusters, it derives the number of cluster, k, indirectly from n and from the capacity of a page. This k may be inappropriate for a given application and may yield clusterings with a high total distance.

Although there is a mismatch of objectives and behavior between R*-tree structure and cluster analysis, the attractive indexing characteristics of R*-trees still lends itself for great potential of contribution to clustering tasks. Below we discuss issues related to this aspect by examining how to take advantage of R*-tree's indexing feature to get around of the problems mentioned above, and present two improved cluster analysis algorithms by incorporating R*-tree features.

From KMeans and KMeans-S to KMeans-R Algorithm

Among the partitioning algorithms, K-Means is a popular and widely studied clustering method for points in Euclidean space. For convenience of discussion, this algorithm is summarized below, where *IC* is the collection of initial centroids of *k* clusters. *S* is the collection of centroids of leaf nodes. KMeans(*IC*, *Data*, *k*) refers to the algorithm of clustering *Data* into *k* Clusters through KMeans with initial centroids of *IC*, and *k* clusters returned as the result.

Algorithm K-Means(IC, Data, k)

1. $IC= \Phi$
2. Pick randomly from *Data k* data items, c_i i=1, ..., k, $IC=IC \cup c_i$
3. Initialize *k* clusters, Cluster(i), i=1, ..., k, with centroids of c_i respectively.
4. For each data item d_i, determine its nearest centriods c_j, then set *cluster(j)=cluster(j)* $\cup c_j$
5. Set *IC= Φ*
6. Calculate the new centriods, n_{ci}, i=1,..., k, of each cluster. Set *IC=IC $\cup nc_i$*
7. Go to 4 until no variation in clustering results.

The K-Means algorithm is simple and fast, and can handle high-dimensionality relatively well. However, K-means and its variations have a number of limitations, such as: it has difficulty detecting the "natural" clusters; it suffers from the problem of local minima; it requires provision of total number of cluster, *k*, from the user; its behavior is significantly affected by the initial selection of centroids; and it has problem when outliers exist; etc. The issue of initial selection of centroids is partially addressed by a variant (referred to as KMeans-S here) where sampling techniques are used to determine optimized centroids in which sampled points are selected and clustered first to determine initial centroids for clustering the whole dataset.

Algorithm KMeans-S(Data, k)

1. Sample in *Data* and generate a subset of *Data, S*
2. $IC= \Phi$
3. Apply K-Means(*IC, S, k*) and obtain new *IC*
4. Apply K-Means(*IC, Data, k*)

Using R*-Trees cannot take care all of the shortcomings of KMeans or KMeans-S algorithms. However, it is reasonable to expect at least R* Trees can be used to assist better sampling. Note that when KMeans-S is used, the sampled points are not guaranteed to represent the whole dataset well. In our view, when data points are indexed through an R*-Tree, if we select one point from each leaf node, these selected data points collectively should represent the data in a way better than random sampling. As a result, the clustering result could be improved. Pushing this observation a step further, we take centroids of data in leaf nodes as a sample instead of using random points, one from each leaf node of the R*-tree. Those sampled centroids are then used as initial centroids for clustering. These points are better representatives of the dataset, because the collection of leaf nodes is a partition of a dataset and can reflect the distribution of the dataset. Since this approach incorporates R*-Tree into K-Means, it is referred to as KMeans-R, as shown below.

Algorithm KMeans-R(Data, k)

1. $IC=\Phi$, $S= \Phi$
2. Index *Data* by R*-Tree
3. For each leaf Ni of R*-Tree, obtain the centroid of its data elements, c_i, then set $S=S \cup c_i$
4. Apply K-Means(*IC,S,k*), obtain new centroids ICN of newly formed clusters, then set *IC=ICN*
5. Apply K-Means(*IC, Data, k*) return the clustering results.

We have the following observation involving these three clustering algorithms. KMeans-S uses the centroids of sampled dataset as initial centroids instead of randomly picked centroids as done in K-Means. Therefore in KMeans-S, centroids should better capture the spatial distribution of data. KMeans-R further improves initial centroids by using the centroids of leaf nodes. Since the quality of K-Means clustering can be affected by the selection of initial centroids, KMeans-R should perform better than KMeans-S and K-Means. Of course, this observation is only a heuristic; the algorithm developed based on this heuristic is to be confirmed through experimental studies (see a later section).

Hierarchical Clustering Extended with R*-Tree: The Hierarchy-R Algorithm

Unlike the K-Means method for which a user needs to specify the number of clusters beforehand, hierarchical clustering gives a series of clustering results at each level through merging process. Below we review the basics of this algorithm (Kaufmann & Rousseeuw, 1989), and then continue on to describe our extended version of the algorithm, Hierarchy-R.

In our implementation of hierarchical algorithms, *all paired distance* is used for the distance calculation between two clusters. For two sets of points $C_1(P_1, P_2, P_3, ...P_m)$ and $C_2(Q_1, Q_2, ..., Q_n)$, the all paired distance $d(C_1, C_2)$ between C_1 and C_2, can be formulated as,

$$d(C_1, C_2) = \frac{\left(\sum_{i=1}^{m} \sum_{j=1}^{n} d(P_i, Q_j) \right)}{mn}$$

where $d(P_i, Q_j)$ represents the distance between P_i in C_1 and Q_j in C_2.

For convenience of discussion, the basic algorithm of the hierarchical clustering is shown below, where *Data* is the input data with size of n. Note that *distMatrix* is a matrix of distance between any two clusters. In our implementation, it is initially set to an $m \times m$ lower triangle matrix with elements of 0s in main diagonals where *distMatrix*(i, j) is the element of ith row and j^{th} column of the matrix. We use *merge(Cluster*(i), *Cluster*(j)) as the method to merge two clusters. The nearest pair of clusters in a collection of clusters is the pair of clusters which have shortest all pair distance between. The pair can be easily identified as the two clusters corresponding to the row and the column of the minimum element blow the diagonal of *distMatrix*. Note that merging process stops when the desired number of clusters reaches by setting loop times. Clustering results are stored in remaining clusters.

Algorithm Hierarchy (Data)

1. Assign each points to a cluster, and generate n clusters, say, *Cluster*(1), *Cluster*(2), …, *Cluster*(n).
2. Start off the merging process as follows.
   2.1. Calculate and form initial an $n \times n$ all-pair distance matrix, *distMatrix*(n, n)
   2.2. Based on distance matrix, identify a pair of nearest clusters, say, *Cluster*(i) and *Cluster*(j), then merge them. Set *Cluster*(i) = *merge(Cluster*(i), *Cluster*(j)).
3. Recalculate distance matrix
   3.1. Assume *Cluster*(s) is the last one in the sequence of clusters, set *Cluster*(j) = *Cluster*(s) and then delete *Cluster*(s).

3.2. Recalculate the distance of *Cluster(i)* and *Cluster(j)* to other remaining clusters respectively

3.3. Based on above calculation, form an $(s-1) \times (s-1)$ distance matrix *distMatrix(s-1,s-1)*

4. Go to 2.2 until number of clusters is reduced to 1

If clustering starts off from individual points as done in original hierarchical clustering method, the number of start-up clusters will be large and thus clustering will be temporal and spatial expensive (O (m^2), where m is total number of objects). R*-trees can come for help. Although a leaf node in R* tree does not necessarily represent a cluster (as explained earlier), it is reasonable to hypothesize that when the node capacity is low for leaf nodes, the points in an R*-Tree's leaf node are likely belonging to same cluster. Therefore rather than start clustering process from individual points, we can first index those points and then cluster those minimal bounding boxes of leaf nodes. The corresponding algorithm is presented below. We would like to point out that the value of *m* cannot be big; otherwise the points in a leaf node could belong to two or more clusters. The value of *m* cannot be too small either, otherwise Hierarchy-R degrades to hierarchical clustering (*m*=1).

Algorithm Hierarchy-R(Data)

1. Index *Data* through R*-Tree and generate *m* leaf nodes.
2. Assign the points in each leaf node to a cluster, and generate *m* initial clusters, *Cluster*(1), *Cluster*(2), ..., *Cluster*(m).
3. Merge clusters as done in hierarchical clustering

CLUSTER EVALUATION

Evaluation Criteria

The "quality" of the clustering solutions obtained through each clustering method needs to be determined. In general, the evaluation measures which are applied to judge various aspects of cluster validity consists of three types: unsupervised (which measures the quality of a clustering structure using cluster cohesion and separation), supervised (which measures the extent to which the clustering structure discovered by a clustering algorithm matches some external structure) and relative (which compares different clusterings or clusters). Below we focus on a similarity-oriented, supervised measure of cluster validity for experiments on two datasets where prior knowledge about classes is available. Under such circumstance, Rand Index (RI), Adjusted Rand Index (ARI) and Information Gain (IG) can be used as criteria to evaluate clustering results. Essentially the evaluation problem is reduced to measuring the agreement of a clustering result against the given prior knowledge. Basics for the Randix Index (RI) can be found in Rand (1971) while the *Adjusted Rand Index (ARI)* was proposed by Hubert and Arabie (1985). As a widely used measure, Information Gain (IG) estimates the "amount of information" gained by clustering the dataset (Bradley and Fayyad, 1998). The weighted entropy of the entire clustering is given by:

$$\text{WeightedEntropy}(K) = \sum_{k=1}^{K} \left(\frac{CS_k}{M} \right) \text{ClusterEntropy}(k)$$

IG =Total Entropy – Weighted Entropy(K).

IG can be used as a criterion to evaluate the quality of a clustering method. The bigger IG is, the better the clustering method performs.

An Experiment of Cluster Analysis on Image Segmentation Dataset

We have conducted numerous experiments to compare the effectiveness of our proposed algorithms with existing methods. Below we report an application on the four clustering methods applied to an image segmentation dataset at UCI Website (Hettich & Bay, 1999). The dataset consists of data from seven images, where each image is made up of 300 instances. In our analysis, each image is regarded as a class. We rate the clustering quality first through studying the point redistribution in newly formed clusters. Table 1 shows the redistribution of points of original clusters in the newly formed clusters. For K-Means and KMeans-S, in the newly formed cluster V1, there are two main subgroups from U1 and U7, which means V1 is formed mainly through merging the most portions of U1 and U7. U3 in K-Means is split to V3 and V7 and U6 in KMeans-S is split to V6 and V7. In KMeans-R and Hierarchy-R, the dominance of numbers in diagonal indicates the newly formed clusters mainly from one class.

To compare the validity of each clustering method quantitatively, we used RI, ARI and IG for evaluation. Tables 2 and 3 show the greatest RI, ARI and IG have been achieved in KMeans-R, while the smallest happens in K-Means. The ratios of two ends are 1.05, 1.23 for RI and ARI, respectively. The IG increases from -0.736 in KMeans to -0.479 in KMeans-R. All three Indexes justify the superiority of KMeans-R in clustering although the difference is not significant as in yeast cell cycle dataset.

Table 1. Generated contingency table after cluster analysis for image segmentation dataset

	KMeans							KMeans-S						
	U1 U2 U3 U4 U5 U6 U7							U1 U2 U3 U4 U5 U6 U7						
V1	265	9	0	0	18	0	202	264	9	0	0	18	0	215
V2	0	183	0	1	49	82	12	0	136	0	0	49	7	9
V3	0	0	185	0	0	0	0	0	0	300	0	0	0	0
V4	0	0	0	297	0	0	0	0	0	0	297	0	0	0
V5	0	53	0	1	196	48	4	0	42	0	1	189	9	3
V6	35	55	0	1	37	170	66	36	53	0	0	30	169	72
V7	0	0	115	0	0	0	16	0	60	0	2	14	115	1
	KMeans-R							Hierarchy-R						
	U1 U2 U3 U4 U5 U6 U7							U1 U2 U3 U4 U5 U6 U7						
V1	247	2	0	0	12	0	61	236	9	0	0	13	0	80
V2	0	242	0	0	3	42	4	0	197	0	1	32	32	4
V3	0	0	300	0	0	0	0	0	0	300	0	0	0	0
V4	0	0	0	297	0	0	0	0	0	0	297	0	0	0
V5	0	3	0	2	241	11	40	0	31	0	1	215	21	40
V6	21	10	0	0	41	194	64	56	26	0	0	30	174	64
V7	32	43	0	1	3	53	131	8	37	0	1	10	73	112

Table 2. Calculated RI and ARI based on Table 1

	KMeans	KMeans-S	KMeans-R	Hierarchy-R
RI	0.864	0.884	0.909	0.889
ARI	0.553	0.616	0.680	0.610

Table 3. Calculated IG based on Table 1

	KMeans	KMeans-S	KMeans-R	Hierarchy-R
IG	-0.736	-0.615	-0.479	-0.674

Therefore, both RI and ARI have shown Hierarchy-R and KMeans-S achieve the same level of clustering quality, and IG values indicate KMeans-S slightly better. Overall, they are comparable.

TOWARD NEXT STEP: ONTOLOGY AND MULTIMEDIA INDEXING

Multimedia data storage (including images, videos, etc.) has experienced the path of using file systems only, to database storage of metadata (multimedia data is still stored outside the database), to authentic multimedia databases (where multimedia data is now stored in the databases). As such, they are now facing huge challenges. Among others, in order to *automatically* tune the mechanism of multimedia retrieval systems, as required by *adaptive* multimedia retrieval, demands at least two key aspects: the flexibility of accommodating new and evolving data, as well as the flexibility of dealing with diverse user information needs. Both of these tasks are related to multimedia indexing, and cannot be done without making use of ontologies. The importance of ontologies for image understanding has been long recognized (e.g., Petridis et al., 2005), and ontology derivation using clustering has also been addressed by researchers (e.g., Khan and Wang, 2002). Our work is related to this direction of research. In our view, clustering the contents of images naturally lends itself to achieve automatic semantic annotation, thus provides an effective mechanism for ontology construction and update. By ontology we mean the semantic organization of images (and other multimedia data) based on the contents of the stored data, including automatic generation, coding and transformation of metadata, content understanding, keyword/term extraction and content synthesis. Therefore, spatial indexing techniques such as R*-trees for image contents makes layered clustering for ontology construction possible, and has the potential of making contribution to adaptive multimedia retrieval at the level of multimedia indexing. This may also facilitate incorporation of additional knowledge into image content analysis, making a knowledge-driven multimedia retrieval possible.

CONCLUSION

As the 21st century enters its second decade, we are overwhelmed by the plethora of data. How to take advantage of this ocean of data is a big challenge. In this chapter, based on the fact that an R*-Tree indexes spatial objects according to spatial proximity, we have presented a similarity analysis tool and explored the possibility to extend the application scope of R*-Trees to cluster analysis. To take advantage of R*-Tree spatial properties and meanwhile confine its drawbacks, we proposed two clustering methods KMeans-R and Hierarchy-R as an improved version of K-Means and hierarchical clustering, respectively. Applied on a two-dimension synthetic dataset, both KMeans-R and Hierarchy-R have shown the capability to group those points in a natural cluster. We have also compared the clustering quality among KMeans-R, Hierarchy-R, K-Means and KMeans-S. Along with other experimental results not shown in this chapter, we have learned from our experimental results that

1   KMeans-R achieves superiority in clustering both datasets, and K-Means performs worst.
2   Hierarchy-R performs better than KMeans, and better than KMeans-S in one case and comparable in another case.

In addition, our proposed methods also have positive impact on time efficiency, because in both of them R* Trees have served as a preprocessor to feed in the algorithms the data with improved quality: for example, in case of Hierarchy-R, aggregation process starts with small sub-clusters (obtained from R* Tree leaves) rather than individual data objects. The time needed to form these sub-clusters from original data objects (as required in the plain hierarchical algorithm) can thus be saved.

There is still plenty of room for improvement of our research. In our study, we have mainly focused our study of KMeans-R and Hierarchy-R on clustering quality, A related issue deserves particular attention is scalability. Although improved efficiency of the proposed algorithms (as described above) should have positive impact on scalability (i.e., we will be able to process larger amount of data using our proposed algorithms than traditional algorithms), the issue of scalability should be addressed in a more direct fashion.

ACKNOWLEDGMENT

ZC's recent work is partly supported by a grant from National Natural Science Foundation of China (#70901011).

REFERENCES

Agrawal, R., Faloutsos, C., & Swami, A. (1993). Efficient similarity search in sequence databases. In *Proc. of the 4th Conference on Foundations of Data Organization and Algorithms*, (pp. 69-84).

Aronov, B., Bronnimann, H., Chang, A. Y., & Chiang, Y.-J. (2003). Cost-driven octree construction schemes: an experimental study. In *Proceedings of the nineteenth annual symposium on Computational geometry*, (pp. 227 – 236).

Beckmann, N., Kriegel, H. P., Schneider, R., & Seeger, B. (1990). The R*-Tree: An Efficient and Robust Access Method for Points and Rectangles. In *Proc. SIGMOD Conference,* (pp. 322-331).

Bentley, J. L. (1975). Multidimensional binary search trees used for associative searching. *Communications of the ACM, 18*(9), 509–517. doi:10.1145/361002.361007

Berchtold, S., Keim, D. A., & Kriegel, H.-P. (1996). The X-tree: An index structure for high-dimensional data. In *Proc. 22nd VLDM Conf.,* (pp. 28-39).

Bradley, P. S., & Fayyad, U. M. (1998). Refining initial points for K-Means clustering. In *Proceedings of the Fifteenth International Conference on Machine Learning*. San Francisco, CA: Morgan Kaufmann.

Ciaccia, P., Patella, M., & Zezula, P. (1997). M-tree: An Efficient Access Method for Similarity Search in Metric Spaces. *The VLDB Journal*, 426–435.

Dubey, P., Chen, Z., & Shi, Y. (2004) Using Branch-Grafted R-trees for Spatial Data Mining. In *Proc. ICCS 2004* (LNCS, pp. 657-660).

Ester, M., Kriegel, H. P., & Xu, X. (1995). Knowledge discovery in large spatial databases: Focusing techniques for efficient class identification. In *Proceedings of 4th International Symposium on Large Spatial Databases (SSD'95)*, Portland, ME, (LNCS, pp. 67-82). Berlin: Springer.

Frisch, A. M., & Allen, J. F. (1982). Knowledge retrieval as limited inference. In Loveland, D. (ed.), *Proceedings of the 6th Conference on Automated Deduction*, (pp. 274-291).

Gaede, V., & Günther, O. (1998). Multidimensional Access Methods. *ACM Computing Surveys, 30*(2), 170–231. doi:10.1145/280277.280279

Guttman, A. (1984). R-trees: A Dynamic Index Structure for Spatial Searching. In *Proc. ACM SIGMOD Int. Conf. on Management of Data*, (pp. 47-54).

Hettich, S., & Bay, S. D. (1999). *The UCI KDD Archive* [http://kdd.ics.uci.edu]. Irvine, CA: University of California, Department of Information and Computer Science.

Hubert, L. & Arabie, P. (1985). Comparing partitions. *Journal of Classification,* 193-218.

Katayama, N., & Satoh, S. (1997). The SR-tree: an index structure for high-dimensional nearest neighbor queries. In *Proc. 1997 ACM SIGMOD*, (pp. 369 – 380).

Kaufmann, L., & Rousseeuw, P. (1989). *Finding Groups in Data*. New York: John Wiley and Sons.

Keogh, E., Chakrabarti, K., Pazzani, M., & Mehrotra, S. (2000). Dimensionality reduction for fast similarity search in large time series databases. *Knowledge and Information Systems, 3*(3), 263–286. doi:10.1007/PL00011669

Khan, L. & Wang, L. (2002) Automatic Ontology Derivation Using Clustering for Image Classification. *Multimedia Information Systems*, (2002), 56-65.

Li, S., & Chen, Z. (2005) Enhanced Image Management Using an Image Algebra. In *Proc. ISIE 2005*.

Lin, K.-I., Jagadish, H. V., & Faloutsos, C. (1994). The TV-tree: An index structure for high-dimensional data. *The VLDB Journal, 3*(4), 517–542. doi:10.1007/BF01231606

Petridis, K., Precioso, F., Athanasiadis, T., Avrithis, Y., & Kompatsiaris, Y. (2005) Combined Domain Specific and Multimedia Ontologies for Image Understanding. In *Proc. 28th German Conference on Artificial Intelligence*, Koblenz, Germany.

Rand, W. M. (1971). Objective criteria for the evaluation of clustering methods. *Journal of the American Statistical Association, 66*, 846–850. doi:10.2307/2284239

Schreck, T., & Chen, Z. (2000). Branch grafting method for R-tree implementation. *Journal of Systems and Software, 53*(1), 83–93. doi:10.1016/S0164-1212(00)00057-1

Chapter 4

Face Recognition Based on Manifold Learning and SVM Classification of 2D and 3D Geodesic Curves

Stefano Berretti
University of Firenze, Italy

Alberto Del Bimbo
University of Firenze, Italy

Pietro Pala
University of Firenze, Italy

Francisco Josè Silva Mata
Advanced Technologies Application Center, Cuba

ABSTRACT

This chapter has a twofold objective. On the one hand, an original approach based on the computation of radial geodesic distances (RGD) is proposed to represent two-dimensional (2D) face images and three-dimensional (3D) face models for the purpose of face recognition. In 3D, the RGD of a generic point of a 3D face surface is computed as the length of the particular geodesic that connects the point with a reference point along a radial direction. In 2D, the RGD of a face image pixel with respect to a reference pixel accounts for the difference of gray level intensities of the two pixels and the Euclidean distance between them. The main contribution of this solution is to permit direct comparison between representations extracted from 2D and 3D facial data, thus opening the way to hybrid approaches for face recognition capable to combine and exploit advantages of different media so as to overcome limitations of traditional solutions based on 2D still images. On the other hand, face representations based on RGDs are used for the purpose of face identification by using them in an operative framework that exploits state of the art techniques for manifold embedding and machine learning. Due to the high dimensionality of face representations based on RGD, embedding into lower-dimensional spaces using

DOI: 10.4018/978-1-61692-859-9.ch004

manifold learning is applied before classification. Support Vector Machines (SVMs) are used to perform face recognition using 2D- and 3D-RGDs. This shows a general work flow that is not limited to face recognition applications, but can be used in many different contexts of recognition and retrieval. Experimental results are reported for 3D-3D and 2D-3D face recognition using the proposed approach.

INTRODUCTION

In recent years, a lot of research efforts have been devoted to define and develop methods capable to represent multimedia digital content with the aim to provide effective and efficient access to multimedia information. In doing so, various types of multimedia information have been considered, such as text, images, graphics, video and audio files, and 3D objects. In general, the set of technologies used to search for various types of digital multimedia are referred to as *multimedia information retrieval* (Lew et al., 2006; Datta et al., 2008).

Some issues have to be considered in multimedia information retrieval, independently from the particular searched media. In particular, there is the need for effective representations capable to capture relevant information in compact descriptors and to efficiently compare them so as to provide meaningful retrieval results in large databases. In so doing, one of the main challenge is extracting semantics from the multimedia content.

Among emerging media, 3D models of natural or artificial objects, or 3D scans of indoor or outdoor environments, have recently gained an increasing relevance as means to provide realistic representations of the reality. This is made possible mainly thanks to the availability of 3D scanning devices of increasing quality available at reasonable costs. As a consequence, large repositories of 3D objects are becoming common, and methods to effectively and efficiently access such archives are now required. 3D models are also largely used in recognition applications where they have shown the capability to improve recognition performance due to the use of three dimensional information. The main issues in recognition problems are very similar to those encountered in retrieval applications: definition of compact and effective descriptions of the objects; definition of measures of similarity between the descriptions capable to discriminate between different objects while capturing similarity between objects belonging to the same category; efficient computation of the similarity in large archives; semantic analysis of the objects so as to automatically classify 3D shapes.

In many applications, 2D and 3D informations are used jointly to improve recognition results. A particular applicative scenario is that of *face recognition* where the use of 3D face models has been experimented only recently. In the following, we focus on this particular problem and propose an original framework that performs recognition by using manifold embedding and machine learning techniques applied to the face representations extracted from 2D face images and from 3D face models. This aims to define innovative hybrid solutions to the recognition problem that exploit the complementary advantages carried out by different media to improve accuracy results.

The chapter is organized as follows. In the next section, we first define the face recognition problem and point out its main issues, and then summarize some of the previous works addressing hybrid face recognition techniques that use together 2D and 3D facial data. In section 3, 3D-RGDs are defined and used to capture geometric characteristics of a face. In this section, a 2D face representation based on the computation of 2D-RGDs in the intensity domain of an image is also presented, together with the issues related to the matching of 2D- and 3D-RGDs. In section 4, the face recognition process is encompassed into a framework which includes dimensionality reduction and SVMs classification of the difference between 2D- and 3D-RGDs. Based on this framework, in section 5 3D-3D face recognition results using 3D-RGDs are presented, and preliminary results for 2D-3D face recognition based on SVMs classification of RGDs are reported. Section 6 outlines future research directions and conclusions are drawn in the last section of the chapter.

BACKGROUND

Person identification based on facial data has been largely addressed in the last years mainly focusing on the detection and recognition of faces in 2D still images and videos (Zhao et al., 2003). However, in real application contexts the success of solutions based on 2D imaging is made difficult, in that invariance to pose and illumination conditions remains a largely unsolved problem. As a result, the accuracy of these 2D based solutions in many cases is not satisfactory to support automatic person recognition in real world application scenarios.

Recently, 3D facial data has been exploited as a means to improve the effectiveness of face recognition systems (Bowyer et al., 2006). Since 3D face models are less sensitive, if not invariant, to lighting conditions and pose variations, recognition based on 3D facial data entails the potential for better recognition accuracy and robustness to varying lighting and pose conditions.

However, a common drawback of solutions that perform recognition by matching 3D facial data is that, despite recent advances in 3D acquisition technologies and devices, acquisition of 3D facial data of a person can be accomplished only in controlled environments and requires a cooperative person to stay still in front of a 3D scanning device for a time that ranges from some seconds up to a few minutes. In addition, multiple scans from slightly different acquisition view-points are typically necessary in order to reconstruct parts of the face that can be self-occluded when acquired from a particular view. The 3D face model is then constructed from multiple scans by post-processing steps which include registration and merging of the scans, holes filling, smoothing, regularization, etc. Accordingly, the adoption of *pure* 3D face recognition solutions is cast to a set of very specific applications.

A viable solution that tries to combine together the advantages of 2D and 3D is to adopt hybrid 2D-3D matching schemes in which 3D facial data is compared against 2D face images. In this case, the operational cycle of the recognition system includes two distinct steps: *acquisition* and *recognition*. Acquisition and processing of 3D facial data of persons to be recognized is performed, off-line, only once. Instead, recognition takes place by comparing acquired 3D facial data to images or video frames taken on the fly as people transit through surveilled areas, monitored by video-camera systems.

Some of these 2D-3D matching solutions operate by transforming (projecting) the 3D geometry to 2D images so as to exploit well established representation techniques developed in 2D in order to perform recognition. As an example, in (Park et al., 2005), face recognition in videos is made invariant to pose and lighting by using 3D face models. 3D database models are used to capture a set of projection images taken from different points of view. Similarity between a target image and 3D models is computed by matching the query with the projection images of the models. In other solutions, 3D *morphable models* are mostly used to obtain 2D images representing particular views of the morphed model to be used in the 2D-2D match with face images (Blanz & Vetter, 2003).

Approaches based on *conformal transformations* exploit the property which allows any surface homeomorphic to a disc to be mapped to a 2D planar domain (Haker et al., 2000). The conformal mapping is one-to-one, onto, and angle preserving thus simplifying the 3D surface-matching to a 2D image-matching problem. In (Wang et al., 2005), this solution has been applied with an experimentation limited to a few face and brain models. In (Wang et al., 2006), least squares conformal geometric maps are applied to 3D faces, and results are provided for a relatively small database comprising 100 scans of 10 subjects.

Use of the eigenface approach based on Principal Component Analysis (PCA)—first introduced for 2D faces in (Turk & Pentland,1991)—has been reported in (Heseltine et al., 2004; Pan et al., 2005). In this latter approach, first a region of interest is defined as the intersection between a sphere centered on the nose tip with the face surface. Then, the region is parameterized into an isomorphic 2D planar circle trying to preserve the intrinsic geometric properties of the surface, and also mapping its relative depth values. *Eigenface* analysis is finally performed on the mapped relative depth image and used to compare faces.

Although these solutions show that 3D information can boost the recognition rates, none of them use the actual 3D geometry either as direct input or in the match. Rather, the 3D model is an intermediate source to render 2D views of a 3D model from different viewpoints and under different illumination conditions so as to best match 2D facial data represented in 2D images. In contrast, direct comparison of 2D facial data to 3D geometric information would enable more reliable matching as 3D geometric information is by its nature invariant to lighting and pose.

A possible way to extract 3D geometric information of a face model is to measure distances among 3D points of the model surface. The use of distances to capture 3D facial information is directly motivated by the relevance that face metrology has in studies conducted in medical disciplines. In particular, the form and values of these measurements are defined in *face anthropometry*, the biological science dedicated to the measurement of the human face. This field has been largely influenced by the seminal work of Farkas (Farkas,1994). In particular, Farkas proposed a total of 47 landmark points to describe the face, with a total of 132 measurements on the face and head. In these measurements, *geodesic, Euclidean*, and *angular* distances between facial landmarks are used. Until recently, the measurement process could only be carried out by experienced anthropometrists by hand, but recent works have investigated 3D scanners as an alternative to manual measurements. In particular, the possibility to effectively represent 3D facial information using geodesic distances with respect to reference points has been reported in some recent contributions on 3D face recognition (Bronstein et al., 2005; Samir et al., 2009; Ter Haar & Veltkamp, 2009).

In 2D, shading plays an important role in the human perception of surface shape. Artists have long used lighting and shading to convey vivid illusions of depth in paintings. Researchers in human vision have attempted to understand and simulate the mechanisms by which our eyes and brain actually use the shading information to recover the 3D shapes. In computer vision, the idea of using the gradual variation of shading in an image to recover 3D shape dates back to the first studies on shape-from-shading (Horn, 1977). A vast literature exists on this subject, and interesting results have been obtained (Zhang et al., 1999). However, in these solutions the final objective is the reconstruction of the 3D shape of the entire object. More related to our work are researches on computing geodesic distances in 2D images. For example, in (Ling & Jacobs, 2005) geodesic sampling is used treating a 2D image as a surface embedded in a 3D space. In this framework, image intensity is weighted relative to the distance in the x-y plane of the image. It is shown as this weight increases, geodesic distances on the embedded surface are less affected by image deformations so that, in the limit, distances are deformation invariant. Geodesic distance measures have also been used in object recognition. For example, in (Elad & Kimmel, 2003) they are used to build bending invariant signatures for real surfaces.

HYBRID FACE RECOGNITION USING 2D AND 3D FACIAL DATA

Grounding on previous considerations, in this work we propose an original framework to represent 2D and 3D facial data using *Radial Geodesic Distances* (RGDs) computed with respect to a reference point of the face (i.e., the tip of the nose). The objective is to define a face representation that can be extracted from 2D still face images as well as from 3D face models and used to directly compare them in order to perform recognition. In 3D, the RGD of a point of the 3D face surface is computed as the length of the particular geodesic that connects the point to the nose tip along a radial direction. In 2D, the RGD from a pixel to the fiducial point is computed based on the differences of the image gray level intensities along a radial path on the image. Matching between 2D- and 3D-RGDs result into feature vectors which are classified by a set of Support Vector Machines (SVMs). Since the feature vectors lay in a high-dimensional space, dimensionality reduction methods are applied before SVMs classification. Results on 3D-3D face recognition using 3D-RGDs, and preliminary results on 2D-3D face recognition, show the viability of the approach.

Radial Geodesics of 3D Face Models

The *Morse*'s theory (Milnor, 1963), first proposed the idea of defining smooth real valued function on the surface of a 3D model in order to capture its characteristics. In this theory, differential properties of the function are used to make explicit the topological properties of a surface, and different characteristics of the surface can be evidenced depending on the choice of the function. Possible choices include the simple elevation of surface points (particularly common for *terrain modeling*), the distance of surface points to some reference point of the model (e.g., the barycenter, curvature extrema or source points) (Hilaga et al., 2001), the average (either Euclidean or geodesic) distance of each surface point to all the other surface points (Berretti et al., 2009).

Use of a reference point to define values of the function is particularly critical to support analysis of generic models, in that models variability typically prevents the identification of a reference point that is guaranteed to be present, stable and reliably detectable in all models. However, if models are constrained to some specific class, and this is the case of facial models, some reference points can be detected reliably and computation of the function with respect to these points may boost the significance of function values. According to this, we use the *pronasale* (i.e., the most protruded point of the apex nasi) as the fiducial point of the 3D face. This point is known to be easily detectable and stable under different expressions (Chang et al., 2006; Farkas, 1994), and can be accurately determined using curvature information of the 3D model (Colombo et al., 2006; Mian et al., 2007). In the following, we will refer to this point as *nose tip*.

Following the *Morse*'s theory, in our case the function in a generic point of a 3D model surface is defined as the 3D *radial geodesic distance* (3D-RGD) between the point and the *nose tip*. By definition, a *geodesic* is the shortest path between two points on a curved space, and generalizes the concept of straight line to curved spaces. Instead, a *radial geodesic* is defined as the particular geodesic that connects one point of the face model surface to the nose tip along the radial direction connecting the

Figure 1. (a) The 2N*2N grid laying on the XY plane; (b) radial geodesics corresponding to the grid. Along each radial geodesic, the 3D-RGD is computed for the vertices of the model which are the nearest to the projections of the sampling points of the grid

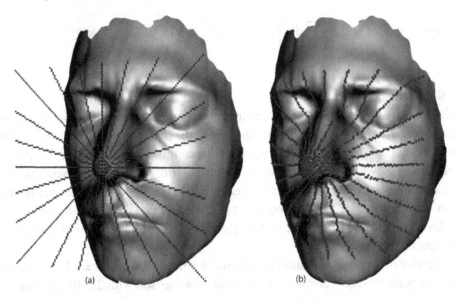

two surface points (radial geodesics separated by angles of 15° are reported on the face scans of figure 1(b)). According to this definition, the radial geodesic is a distance computed on the surface, but it is constrained to a predefined direction.

Based on this definition, a 3D face representation is constructed by considering K radial geodesics taken at fixed angular steps in the interval [0,360) degrees, with N sampling points per radial geodesic. In this way, a 3D face model is represented by a feature vector of size $K*N$, whose elements are the 3D-RGDs computed on the sampling points.

In order to make the 3D face representations extracted from the 3D scans of different subjects comparable among them, and with face representations extracted from 2D images, the sampling points along radial geodesics are selected based on a 2N*2N grid of points (see Figure 1(a)). By projecting points of the grid onto the 3D model surface a set of sampling points in 3D is identified. Values of the 3D-RGD are computed for each sampling point in 3D.

In practice, the surface S of a face model is approximated through a discrete mesh M with n vertices $v_1,...,v_n$, with the fiducial vertex v_f located at the nose tip. As a consequence, 3D-RGDs are computed for the vertices of the mesh that are the nearest to the projections of the grid points on the model. Before computation of geodesic distances, 3D face scans undergo to a mesh resampling that regularizes the size of the triangles of the mesh and make uniform the distribution of the vertices on the surface. Computation of the 3D-RGD for a sampled vertex v_i along a radial geodesic R^k is obtained as the length of the shortest piecewise linear path on mesh vertices connecting the vertex v_i with the nose tip vertex v_f along R^k: $\mu_{3D}^{k}(v_i,v_f) = L(P^k(v_i,v_f))$ (we will refer to this as $\mu_{3D}^{k}(i)$). In this expression, $P^k(v_i,v_f)$ is the sequence of vertices along R^k from v_i to v_f, defined as an ordered sequence of adjacent vertices, and $L(P^k(v_i,v_f))$ is the length of the path measured as the sum of the Euclidean distances between adjacent vertex pairs. Furthermore, all the vertices of the path are constrained by the additional condition: $P^k(v_i,v_f) = P^k(v_{i-1},v_f)$

U v_i for $i = 2,...,N$. This ensures that the set of vertices of a radial geodesic is repeatedly extended by adding the new vertex v_i to the current set:

$$\begin{cases} \mu_{3D}^k(i) = \mu_{3D}^k(i-1) + d(i, i-1) = \sum_{h=1}^{i} d(i, i-1) & i \geq 1 \\ \mu_{3D}^k(i) = 0 & i = 0 \end{cases} \quad (1)$$

being $d(i,i-1)$ the Euclidean distance between vertices v_i and v_{i-1} computed in 3D.

The 3D-RGDs values allow the differences occurring on the model for points along the radial geodesics to be captured. Figure 2(a), shows a 3D face model where the radial geodesic originated from the nose tip and oriented along the direction at 0 degrees is evidenced. In Figure 2(b), the 3D-RGD computed along this direction is shown for 60 sampling points of the grid. It can be observed that the 3D-RGD values capture information on the profile and the extent of the self-occlusion occurring at the base of the nose. It can be also observed a saturation effect of the RGD that occurs on the last three points of the radial geodesic. This is due to the fact that projections on the model of the last three points of the grid are coincident on the same vertex.

The final objective of this representation is to prove the 3D-RGDs capture salient face information, and can be used to perform face recognition through the comparison with 2D-RGDs computed for 2D images. As we will show in Section 5, the 3D face representation based on 3D-RGDs can be also used to directly perform 3D face recognition.

Radial Geodesics of 2D Face Images

2D face images capture intensity variations of the light reflected by the face surface. Therefore, pixel values are related to the reflectance properties and to the 3D geometry of the face. According to this, we

Figure 2. (a) A 3D face scan with the radial geodesic at 0 degrees; (b) Plot of the 3D-RGD (measured in mm) computed for the points of the radial geodesic shown in (a). Points on the horizontal axis are displaced each other by 1mm

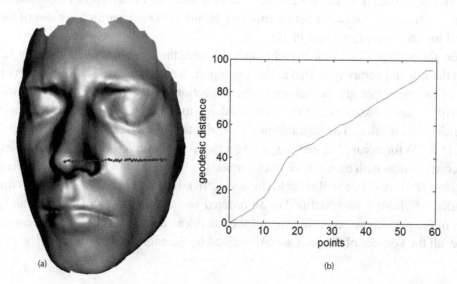

aim to define a 2D face representation based on the adjacency and intensity variations of image pixels that can be directly compared against the 3D face representation based on 3D-RGDs.

To this end, a face representation is constructed in 2D which has the same basic structure of the 3D representation. Similarly to 3D, the nose tip of the face image is used as fiducial point and radial geodesics on the image are considered. These originate from the nose tip and are extended along radial directions up to a fixed number of points in the image plane (see Figure 3). *2D radial geodesic distances* (2D-RGDs) are computed according to the intensity variations and proximity of image pixels. Considering a particular radial geodesic R^k, the following equation is used to compute the 2D-RGD:

$$\begin{cases} \mu_{2d}^k(i) = \sum_{h=1}^{i} \sqrt{(x_h - x_{h-1})^2 + (y_h - y_{h-1})^2 + f^k(\Delta I)} & i \geq 1 \\ \mu_{2d}^k(i) = 0 & i = 0 \end{cases} \tag{2}$$

where: i is the index of the pixel along the radial geodesic; x_h and y_h are the coordinates of the image pixels along the radial geodesic, and $\Delta I = |I(x_h, y_h) - I(x_{h-1}, y_{h-1})|$ is the absolute difference of intensity values between adjacent image pixels along the radial geodesic. The graph in the middle of Figure 3, provides a visual representation of Equation (2).

The function $f^k(\Delta I)$ in Equation (2) varies with the particular radial geodesic R^k and with the values of the intensity differences so as to establish the best correspondence between 2D and 3D geodesic measures. In particular, if the difference of intensity between two image pixels is zero (i.e., $\Delta I = 0$), $\mu_{2D}^k(i)$ is expected to reduce to the Euclidean distance between the pixels in the image plane.

Figure 3. The 2D-RGD computed according to the intensity values of the image. On the right, a particular radial path is shown, while the graphic on the left illustrates the meaning of the terms that appear in Equation (2)

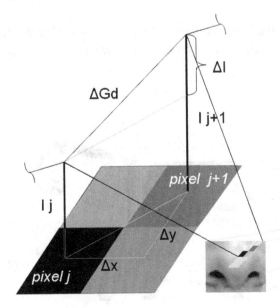
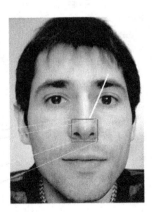

In order to determine the function $f^*(\Delta I)$ of Equation (2), which maps 2D- to 3D-RGDs for a 3D model, we rely on a reference image for each model. To this end, during the enrollment of a new subject into the gallery of 3D models, a frontal face image is also acquired and used as reference (3D scanners usually take this image separately from the depth information of the 3D scan).

The mapping determined for the reference image of an enrolled subject is then applied to generic images of any subject that must be compared with the 3D model. To this end, for any radial geodesic R^k, the function $f^*(\Delta I)$ is determined which best maps the N-dimensional vector $\mu_{2D}{}^k$ of the 2D-RGDs computed for the reference image, into the N-dimensional vector $\mu_{3D}{}^k$ of the 3D-RGDs. The function $f^*(\Delta I)$ to be estimated is found as solution of a *regression problem* of the form: $f\colon R \times R \times R \to R$, where the input domain is given by the coordinates of the set of image pixels along the radial path R^k, and by the values of image intensity of the same pixels. A supervised *feed-forward* neural network (Rojas, 1996) is used to this end.

We can observe that the 2D representation relies on the idea that 3D information of a face is captured by the intensity variations in 2D images. This is somewhat related to the studies on *Shape from Shading* (SfS). Researches in this area have shown that SfS works well for objects that are uniformly concave or convex, while if the object is more complex, having both concave and convex regions, then SfS can fail. In these situations, although the recovered surface normal direction is consistent with the measured image brightness, the recovered surface does not reflect the structure of the object (Castelan & Hancock, 2005). In particular, there may be inversions of the sign of the surface curvature with convex regions appearing concave and vice-versa. However, in the case of faces, the surface is largely convex, with the exception of the eye-sockets, the bridge of the nose and areas around the lips (Castelan & Hancock, 2005).

In our approach, the inversion of the sign or polarity of the surface curvature does not change the computation of the geodesic, because it only accounts for the absolute value of the trajectory length and the polarity does not change the values of the geodesic. Figure (4) shows the inversion problem. In particular, in the plot on the left, the intensity of pixels of the image in the middle of Figure (4) is used as third dimension (quote). In the image on the right of Figure (4), the plot is filled with the original gray level. For example, it can be noticed that in the eyes convex regions are converted into concave regions.

Figure 4. On the left, the intensity levels of the image in the middle are represented as third dimension of the image (quote). On the right, the image with intensity levels used as depth is filled with the original gray levels

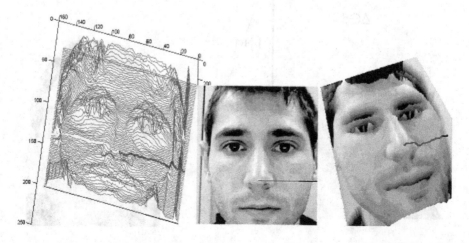

However, these regions do not affect the computation of geodesic distances in that only the length of the geodesic trajectories is relevant.

Face Image Normalization

In order to compare 2D- and 3D-RGDs, geometric normalization of 2D face images with respect to 3D face models is necessary. Normalization requires that at least one correspondence between a pair of image pixels and a pair of 3D points is identified, and that the distance computed between the pair of 3D points and the distance computed between the pair of 2D points are equal. If this is not the case, the image must be re-scaled accordingly. We used the Euclidean distance between the two *endocanthions* (i.e., the points at the inner commissure of the left and right eye fissure) computed in 3D to provide information of the real dimension of the face. These points have been verified to be easily detectable using curvature information, and stable with respect to face variations (Bronstein et al., 2006; Chang et al., 2006). We assumed this measure as an intrinsic characteristic of a 3D face model, and computed it during the enrollment of 3D face models into the *gallery* of known subjects. The algorithm in (Mian et al., 2007) has been used to detect endocanthions and the nose tip in 3D (these points are evidenced in Figure 5(a)). These points have been also used to align the models with respect to a global 3D reference system.

In 2D, image processing techniques have been used for the automatic detection of the face and for the identification of the two endocanthions and the nose tip. The face and eyes regions are first detected using a *Haar-cascade* detector (Viola & Jones, 2004) as shown in Figure 5(a). Some wrong detections can occur with this method (see for example the mouth region in Figure 5(a)), but these can be easily discarded with simple considerations about the position of the region with respect to the overall face region. Endocanthions are automatically identified by processing the eyes region of the face in order to extract corner points (a *Harris* corner detector has been used). Many corner points are usually identified on the border of the eyes, the irises and the pupils. The corners corresponding to the endocanthions are selected using heuristics on their reciprocal positions, and on their positions with respect to the eyes region (see Figure 5(c)). To validate the position of the two endocanthions, an iris detector based on the *Hough* transform is also used. This estimates the circles that best fit the irises and uses their positions

Figure 5. (a) The nose tip and the two endocanthions fiducial points evidenced on a 3D face scan. (b) Viola-Jones detection of the face and eyes regions. Figure (b) also shows a wrong detection (the mouth region is detected as another eyes region). The erroneuously detected region is then discarded using information on the position of the region with respect to the overall face region. (c) Detection of the two endocanthions in the image. (d) The three fiducial points are evidenced in the cropped face region of the image

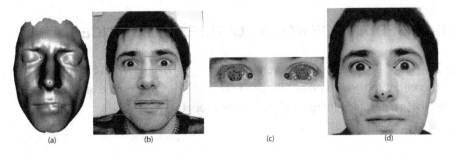

Figure 6. Detection of the fiducial points of 2D face images of three sample subjects: (a) eyes regions identified using a Haar cascade detector; (b) corners detected in the eyes region. The corners identified as the two endocanthions are highlighted in black; (c) normalized images with the nose tip and the two endocanthions highlighted in black

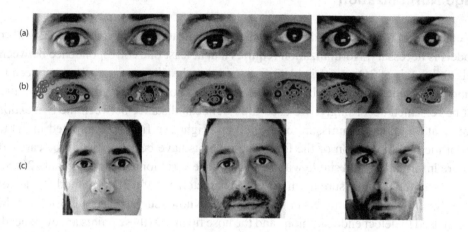

to validate the endocanthions extracted by the corner detector (detected fiducial points are reported in Figure 5(d) on the face region). As an example, Figure 6(a)-(b) show the eyes region, and the detected corners for the face images of three different subjects. The corners identified at the two endocanthions are highlighted in black in the figure.

When a face image must be compared against a 3D face model, the distance between the two endocanthions of the image is computed and the image is re-scaled according to the endocanthions distance associated to the model. This assumes that, given a 3D model, images of the same subject of the model are re-scaled accordingly and correspondence between 3D and 2D distances can be rightly established. In the same way, images of subjects different from the model are re-scaled with the endocanthions distance associated to the model, but this likely determines wrong correspondences between 3D and 2D measures.

Automatic detection of the nose tip in 2D is also necessary to extract the 2D-RGDs. Differently from the endocanthions, accurate detection of the nose tip is difficult to be performed in the image. We solved this problem by using information on the position of the nose tip in the 3D model. After normalization, the position of the nose tip in the image is estimated by using the Euclidean distances between the two endocanthions and the nose tip measured on the 3D model. As an example, Figure 6(c) shows the face regions of three persons with evidenced (in black) the nose tip and the two endocanthions that have been automatically detected.

MANIFOLD EMBEDDING OF RADIAL GEODESIC DISTANCES

In matching 2D- and 3D-RGDs the difference $e^k(i) = \mu^k_{2D}(i) - \mu^k_{3D}(i)$, is computed for every radial geodesic R^k. According to this, an *error vector* of size K*N is constructed and used to characterize the correspondence between a face image and a 3D face model.

In the experimented solution, K=72 radial geodesics at intervals of 5 degrees are used, each with 50 points, thus resulting in an error vector of size 3600. Since 2D-3D face recognition is based on SVMs classification of the error vectors, operating in this high dimensional space can be not effective due to the *curse of dimensionality*. To avoid this difficulty, error vectors undergo to a dimensionality reduction before to be used for face recognition.

The process of transforming data residing in a high dimensional space to a low dimensional subspace is based on the assumption that the data actually lies, at least approximately, on a *manifold* of smaller dimension than the data space. The goal is to find a representation of that manifold that allows the projection of the data vectors on it and obtains a low-dimensional, compact representation of the data. Ideally, the reduced representation should have a dimensionality that corresponds to the intrinsic dimensionality of the data. Based on the type of the transformation function that performs the mapping between the high and the low dimensional space, *linear* and *non-linear* techniques can be distinguished. Linear techniques assume that the data lies on or near a linear subspace of the high-dimensional space. Non-linear techniques do not rely on the linearity assumption as a result of which more complex embedding of the data in the high-dimensional space can be identified. Non linear techniques can be distinguished in *global* non-linear techniques, that attempt to preserve global properties of the data, and *local* non-linear techniques that solely preserve properties of small neighborhoods around the datapoints. Among linear techniques, we experimented the *Principal Component Analysis* (PCA), while we considered *Multidimensional Scaling* (MDS) and *Isomap* as global non-linear methods, and *Locally Linear Embedding* (LLE) and *Laplacian Eigenmaps* (LE) as local non-linear methods. More in detail, the used techniques can be shortly summarized as follows (Van der Maaten et al., 2007):

- *PCA* (Hotelling, 1933), constructs a low-dimensional representation of the data that describes as much of the variance in the data as possible. This is done by finding a linear basis of reduced dimensionality for the data, in which the amount of variance in the data is maximal;

- *MDS* (Cox & Cox, 1994), represents a collection of nonlinear techniques that map the high-dimensional data representation to a low-dimensional representation while retaining the pairwise distances between the datapoints as much as possible;

- *MDS* has proven to be successful in many applications, but it suffers from the fact that it is based on Euclidean distances, and does not take into account the distribution of the neighboring data-points. If the high-dimensional data lies on or near a curved manifold, MDS might consider two datapoints as near points, whereas their distance over the manifold is much larger than the typical interpoint distance. *Isomap* (Tenenbaum, 1998), resolves this problem by attempting to preserve pairwise geodesic (or curvilinear) distances between datapoints, that is the distance between two points measured over the manifold;

- *LLE* (Roweis & Saul, 2000), is similar to *Isomap* in that it constructs a neighborhood graph representation of the datapoints. In contrast to Isomap, it attempts to preserve solely local properties of the data, making *LLE* less sensitive to short-circuiting than Isomap. Furthermore, the preservation of local properties allows for successful embedding of nonconvex manifolds. In *LLE*, the local properties of the data manifold are constructed by writing the datapoints as a linear combination of their nearest neighbors. In the low-dimensional representation of the data, *LLE* attempts to retain the reconstruction weights in the linear combinations as well as possible;

- Similarly to *LLE*, LE find a low-dimensional data representation by preserving local properties of the manifold (Belkin & Niyogi, 2002). In *LE*, the local properties are based on the pairwise distances between near neighbors. *LE* compute a low-dimensional representation of the data in which the distances between a datapoint and its k nearest neighbors are minimized. This is done in a weighted manner, i.e., the distance in the low-dimensional data representation between a data-point and its first nearest neighbor contributes more to the cost function than the distance between the datapoint and its second nearest neighbor. Using spectral graph theory, the minimization of the cost function is defined as an eigenproblem.

SVMs Classification

Once face representations are embedded into a low-dimensional space, face recognition/authentication is managed as a classification problem using SVMs with a *radial basis function* kernel (Vapnik, 1998) (the *libsvm* package (Chang & Lin, 2001) through the *Weka* environment has been used: http://www. cs.waikato.ac.nz/~ml/weka/).

SVMs belongs to the class of maximum margin classifiers (Vapnik, 1998). In a *binary* classification problem, they find a decision surface that has maximum distance to the closest points in the training set (called *support vectors*). Given a set of points $x_i \in R^n$, $i = 1,...,l$, let us suppose each point x_i belongs to one of two classes identified by the label $y_i \in \{-1,1\}$. Assuming for simplicity that data is linearly separable, the goal of maximum margin classification is to separate the two classes by a hyperplane such that the distance to the support vectors is maximized. This *optimal separating hyperplane* has the form:

$$f(x) = \sum_{i=0}^{l} \alpha_i y_i x_i \cdot x + b \tag{3}$$

where α_i and b are the solutions of a quadratic programming problem. Classification of a new data point x is performed by computing the sign of the right side of Equation (3).

The construction can be extended to the case of nonlinear separating surfaces. Each point in the input space is mapped to a point $z = \Phi(x)$ of a higher dimensional space. In this *feature space*, the data is separated by a hyperplane. The main property of this construction is that the mapping $\Phi (.)$ is subject to the condition that the dot product of two points in the feature space $\Phi (x) * \Phi (y)$ can be rewritten as a *kernel function* $K(x,y)$. The decision surface has the equation:

$$f(x) = \sum_{i=0}^{l} \alpha_i y_i K(x,y) + b \tag{4}$$

where, similarly to Equation (3), α_i and b are the solutions of a quadratic programming problem. In both Equation (3) and Equation (4), it is relevant to note that f(x) does not depend on the dimensionality of the feature space.

Two main strategies can be used to solve *multi-class* problems with SVMs (Heisele et al., 2001) (in the following, q classes are considered, each corresponding to a 3D model in the gallery). In the *one-vs-all* approach, q SVMs are trained. Each SVM separates a single class from all the remaining classes. In the *pairwise* approach, $q(q-1)/2$ machines are trained, each separating a pair of classes. The pairwise classifiers are arranged in a tree, where each tree node represents a SVM. Regarding the training effort, the *one*-vs-*all* approach is preferable since only q SVMs have to be trained, compared to $q(q-1)/2$ SVMs in the pairwise approach. The run time complexity of the two strategies is similar. For recognition, the *one*-vs-*all* approach requires the evaluation of q SVMs, while the evaluation of $q-1$ SVMs is required for the pairwise approach.

RESULTS

In the following, we report on experiments of 3D-3D face recognition, and 2D-3D face authentication using the *Radial Geodesic Distance* (RGD) approach.

3D-3D Recognition Experiments

3D-3D face recognition shows the capability of 3D-RGDs to effectively discriminate between 3D face models and provides an indication of the significance of the representation. In this work, 3D-RGDs are not directly proposed as 3D face recognition approach. State of the art solutions for 3D face matching (Kakadiaris et al., 2007), (Mian et al., 2007), (Queirolo et al., 2010), (Berretti et al., 2010) can be addressed for this purpose. In these experiments, we directly used the 3D-RGDs in the space with K*N dimensions, without any dimensionality reduction. This is motivated by the objective to test the intrinsic information that is captured by the 3D-RGD representation.

According to this, to compare 3D-RGDs of two face models A and B, the *Euclidean* distance between 3D-RGDs in the space of size K*N has been evaluated:

$$D(\mu_{3D}(A), \mu_{3D}(B)) = \left[\sum_{j=1}^{K} \sum_{i=1}^{N} \left(\mu_{3D}^j(A, i) - \mu_{3D}^j(B, i) \right)^2 \right]^{1/2} \tag{5}$$

The *Gavab* face database (Moreno & Sànchez, 2004)has been used in these experiments (the databse is publicly available at: http://gavab.escet.urjc.es/). It includes 3D face models of 61 individuals (45 males and 16 females). The whole set of subjects are Caucasian and most of them are aged between 18 and 40. For each person, 7 different models are taken, differing in terms of acquisition pose or facial expression, resulting in 427 facial models. In particular, for each subject there are 2 neutral frontal and 2 neutral rotated models, and 3 frontal models in which the person laughs, smiles or exhibits a random expression. Models are coded in VRML with resolution of approximately 10000 vertices.

For each individual, one of the two scans with frontal view and neutral expression is used as reference model and included in the gallery. All the other scans of a subject are used as probes. According to this, we conducted a set of recognition experiments using 366 probes (with neutral and non-neutral facial expression) on a gallery of 61 models. Each probe is compared against all the gallery models producing a result list of gallery models ranked in increasing order of scored distance from the probe. The effectiveness of recognition has been measured according to the rank-k recognition rate, and presented with *Cumulative Matching Characteristics* (CMC) curves. In particular, a rank-k recognition experiment is successful if the gallery face representing the same individual of the current probe is ranked within the first k positions of the ranked list. CMC curves measure, for each k value, the corresponding percentage of successful rank-k experiments.

In order to tune the parameters of the 3D-RGD approach, the Gavab database has been first divided into a train set and a test set. In particular, we used the models of 11 subjects as train set (these subjects have been randomly selected in the database), while the models of the remaining 50 subjects have been used as test set. Then, operating on the test set, we performed a preliminary set of tests to investigate the importance of the number N of radial geodesics and of the number of points K along each radial geodesic.

Results of these tests are reported in Figure 7(a)-(b) for models with neutral expressions. In Figure 7(a) the CMC curves are reported for radial geodesics taken at intervals of 20 degrees in the range [0,360), with 10, 20, 30 and 40 points along the radial geodesics, respectively. These points were taken with uniform displacement between each other along the radial geodesics. In Figure 7(b), experiments have been performed using the same number of points, but with radial geodesics displaced by 10 degrees. In general, it can be observed that increasing the number of radial geodesics, the rank-*1* recognition rate improves independently from the number of points used along the radial geodesics (compare plots in Figure 7(a) against plot in Figure 7(b)). Similarly, it emerges that increasing the number of points along radial geodesics also improves the recognition rates (compare the plots for different number of points). However, though there is a remarkable increase of performances passing from 10 to 20 points, the relative increase from 20 to 30 points, and from 30 to 40 points are not so relevant. In particular, we can observe a sort of saturation that does not further improve the recognition rates. This suggests that a limited portion of the 3D face around the nose tip can provide significant structural information of the face.

Based on the results of the previous tests, matching of 3D-RGDs, has been performed using 72 radial geodesics displaced by 5 degrees, with 50 points each (3600 points total). Using this setting, *rank-1* recognition rates are reported in Table 1 for the 3D-RGD approach, and for the 3D face matching

Figure 7. CMC curves for 3D face recognition based on 3D-RGDs: (a) N = 18 radial geodesics displaced by 20 degrees; (b) N = 36 radial geodesics displaced by 10 degrees. In both the cases, curves for radial geodesics with different number of points are reported (from 10 to 40 points)

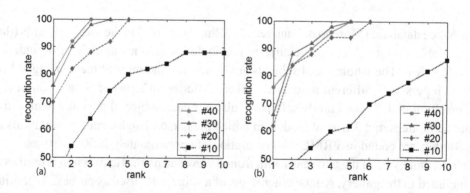

Table 1. Rank-1 recognition rates for probes with neutral and non-neutral facial expression

	rank-1 recognition rate	
	Neutral-frontal	**Non-neutral frontal**
3D-RGD	**86.9**	75.4
ICP	70.5	62.3

solution that uses the *Iterative Closest Point* (ICP) registration algorithm (Besl & Mc Kay, 1992). Results evidence that RGDs are able to improve results of the ICP, for 3D face models with both neutral and non-neutral facial expressions.

2D-3D Authentication Experiments

Preliminary authentication experiments have been performed to prove the viability of SVMs classification of the error vectors between 2D- and 3D-RGDs projected into an embedding subspace. Separate SVMs have been trained on five different projection subspaces, obtained using *PCA, MDS, Isomap, LLE* and *LE*, respectively (see the previous Section for a short summary of the five methods). Pairwise and *one*-vs-*all* classifiers have also been tested using different dimensions of the projection subspace. Percentage of correctly authenticated persons are reported in Table 2 for three experiments. Each experiment has been conducted using 10-fold cross validation of frontal face images acquired for each subject under controlled illumination conditions (10 images per subject).

In the first experiment (Exp.1), SVMs *binary* classifiers are trained in a three dimensional projection subspace, one classifier for each ordered pair of gallery models. According to this, person authentication is obtained by a cascade of binary classifiers that use the same dimensionality reduction approach.

In the second experiment (Exp.2), SVMs *one*-vs-*all* classifiers are trained in a three-dimensional projection subspace, one classifier for gallery model. In this case, person authentication is obtained as response of one classifier. Following the same approach, in the third experiment (Exp.3), a SVMs *one*-vs-*all* classifier is trained in a projection subspace with fifteen dimensions, one classifier for gallery model. Also in this case, person authentication is obtained by the response of one classifier. In general, it can be observed that the percentage of correctly classified persons is quite high. In particular, using *binary* classifiers (Exp.1), the dimensionality reduction methods have similar performance (maximum difference equal to 3.9%), with LLE scoring the best result (bold entries in the table evidence the approach that scores the highest percentage of correct classification in each experiment). Binary and *one*-vs-*all* classifiers have similar results (compare Exp.1 and Exp.2). The effect of increasing dimensionality of the embedding subspace does not emerge clearly from Exp.2 and Exp.3. In fact, the absolute maximum is obtained by the PCA approach in Exp.3, but ISOMAP and LE decrease their performance passing from Exp.2 to Exp.3. As final observation, though PCA performs reasonably well in the three experiments, non-linear methods like MDS and LLE seem able to provide better combination with the SVMs classification in several different conditions.

Table 2. For each experiment and projection method, the percentage of correctly classified persons using SVMs is reported

	PCA	MDS	Isomap	LLE	LE
Exp. 1	94.8	94.9	93.5	**97.4**	94.6
Exp. 2	91.9	96.2	95	95.6	**97.5**
Exp. 3	**99.4**	96.8	84.3	96.2	93.1

FUTURE RESEARCH DIRECTIONS

Future work will address different *feature selection* methods in order to identify the features with minimum redundancy to further improve dimensionality reduction for classification, and a larger experimentation for 2D-3D face authentication in a real application context. The 3D-3D face recognition approach will be also evaluated on larger benchmark data sets, like the Face Recognition Grand Challenge version 1.0 database (Phillips et al., 2005).

CONCLUSION

In this chapter, an original approach has been proposed for representing 2D face images and 3D face models, and to compare them for recognition and authentication purposes. 2D and 3D face representations are based on geodesic distances computed along radial directions originated from the nose tip. Manifold learning is then applied to the high dimensional error vectors originated by comparing 2D and 3D RGDs.

Experiments are reported for 3D-3D face recognition, together with preliminary experiments on 2D-3D face authentication using SVMs classification of the RGDs.

REFERENCES

Belkin, M., & Niyogi, P. (2002). Laplacian Eigenmaps and spectral techniques for embedding and clustering. *Advances in Neural Information Processing Systems, 14*, 585–591.

Berretti, S., Del Bimbo, A., & Pala, P. (2009). 3D Mesh Decomposition using Reeb Graphs. *Image and Vision Computing, 27*(10), 1540–1554. doi:10.1016/j.imavis.2009.02.004

Berretti, S., Del Bimbo, A., & Pala, P. (2010). 3D Face Recognition using Isogeodesic Stripes. *IEEE Transactions on Pattern Analysis and Machine Intelligence, 32*(12).

Besl, P., & Mc Kay, N. (1992). A method for registration of 3-d shapes. *IEEE Transactions on Pattern Analysis and Machine Intelligence, 14*(2), 239–256. doi:10.1109/34.121791

Blanz, V., & Vetter, T. (2003). Face recognition based on fitting a 3D morphable model. *IEEE Transactions on Pattern Analysis and Machine Intelligence, 25*(9), 1063–1074. doi:10.1109/TPAMI.2003.1227983

Bowyer, K., Chang, K., & Flynn, P. (2006). A survey of approaches and challenges in 3D and multi-modal 3D+2D face recognition. *Computer Vision and Image Understanding, 101*(1), 1–15. doi:10.1016/j.cviu.2005.05.005

Bronstein, A., Bronstein, M., & Kimmel, R. (2006). Robust expression-invariant face recognition from partially missing data. In *European Conference on Computer Vision,* (pp. 396–408), Gratz, Austria.

Bronstein, A. M., Bronstein, M. M., & Kimmel, R. (2005). Three dimensional face recognition. *International Journal of Computer Vision, 64*(1), 5–30. doi:10.1007/s11263-005-1085-y

Castelàn, M., & Hancock, E. R. (2005). Improved face shape recovery and re-illumination using convexity constraints. In *International Conference on Image Analysis and Processing* (pp. 487–494). Cagliari, Italy.

Chang, C.-C., & Lin, C.-J. (2001). *LIBSVM: a library for support vector machines*. Software available at: http://www.csie.ntu.edu.tw/~cjlin/libsvm.

Chang, K. I., Bowyer, K. W., & Flynn, P. J. (2006). Multiple nose region matching for 3D face recognition under varying facial expression. *IEEE Transactions on Pattern Analysis and Machine Intelligence*, *28*(6), 1695–1700. doi:10.1109/TPAMI.2006.210

Colombo, A., Cusano, C., & Schettini, R. (2006). 3d face detection using curvature analysis. *Pattern Recognition*, *39*(3), 444–455. doi:10.1016/j.patcog.2005.09.009

Cox, T., & Cox, M. (1994). *Multidimensional scaling*. London: Chapman & Hall.

Datta, R., Joshi, D., Li, J., & Wang, J. Z. (2008). Image Retrieval: Ideas, Influences, and Trends of the New Age. *ACM Computing Surveys*, *40*(2), 1–60. doi:10.1145/1348246.1348248

Elad, A., & Kimmel, R. (2003). On bending invariant signatures for surfaces. *IEEE Transactions on Pattern Analysis and Machine Intelligence*, *25*(10), 1285–1295. doi:10.1109/TPAMI.2003.1233902

Farkas, L. (1994). *Anthropometry of the Head and Face*. New York: Raven Press.

Haker, S., Angenent, S., Tannenbaum, A., Kikinis, R., Sapiro, G., & Halle, M. (2000). Conformal surface parameterization for texture mapping. *IEEE Transactions on Visualization and Computer Graphics*, *6*(2), 181–189. doi:10.1109/2945.856998

Heisele, B., Ho, P., & Poggio, T. (2001). Face recognition with support vector machines: Global versus component-based approach. In *International Conference on Computer Vision* (pp. 688–694), Vancouver, Canada.

Heseltine, T., Pears, N., & Austin, J. (2004). Three dimensional face recognition: an eigensurface approach. In *International Conference on Image Processing* (pp. 1421–1424), Singapore.

Hilaga, M., Shinagawa, Y., Kohmura, T., & Kunii, T. L. (2001). 3D Shapes. In *ACM SIGGRAPH* (pp. 203–212). Los Angeles, CA: Topology Matching for Fully Automatic Similarity Estimation of.

Horn, B. (1977). Understanding image intensities. *Artificial Intelligence*, *8*(2), 1250–1267. doi:10.1016/0004-3702(77)90020-0

Hotelling, H. (1933). Analysis of a complex of statistical variables into principal components. *Journal of Educational Psychology*, *24*, 417–441. doi:10.1037/h0071325

Kakadiaris, I. A., Passalis, G., Toderici, G., Murtuza, N., Lu, Y., Karampatziakis, N., & Theoharis, T. (2007). Three-dimensional face recognition in the presence of facial expressions: An annotated deformable approach. *IEEE Transactions on Pattern Analysis and Machine Intelligence*, *29*(4), 640–649. doi:10.1109/TPAMI.2007.1017

Lew, M. S., Sebe, N., Djeraba, C., & Jain, R. (2006). Content-based Multimedia Information Retrieval: State of the Art and Challenges. *ACM Transactions on Multimedia Computing, Communications, and Applications*, *2*(1), 1–19. doi:10.1145/1126004.1126005

Ling, H., & Jacobs, D. (2005). Deformation invariant image matching. In *International Conference on Computer Vision,* (pp. 1466–1473), Beijing, China.

Mian, A. S., Bennamoun, M., & Owens, R. (2007). An efficient multimodal 2D-3D hybrid approach to automatic face recognition. *IEEE Transactions on Pattern Analysis and Machine Intelligence, 29*(11), 1927–1943. doi:10.1109/TPAMI.2007.1105

Milnor, J. (1963). *Morse Theory*. Princeton, NJ: Princeton University Press.

Moreno, A. B., & Sànchez, A. (2004). GavabDB: A 3D Face Database. In *Workshop on Biometrics on the Internet,* (pp. 75-80), Vigo, Spain.

Pan, G., Han, S., Wu, Z., & Wang, Y. (2005). 3D face recognition using mapped depth images. In *Conference on Computer Vision and Pattern Recognition,* (pp. 175–181), San Diego, CA.

Park, U., Chen, H., & Jain, A. K. (2005). 3D model assisted face recognition in video. In *Canadian Conference on Computer and Robot Vision,* (pp. 322–329), Victoria, Canada.

Phillips, P. J., Flynn, P. J., Scruggs, T., Bowyer, K. W., Chang, J., Hoffman, K., et al. (2005). Overview of the Face Recognition Grand Challenge. In *IEEE Workshop on Face Recognition Grand Challenge Experiments,* (pp. 947-954), San Diego, CA.

Queirolo, C. C., Silva, L., Bellon, O. R. P., & Pamplona Segundo, M. (2010). 3D Face Recognition Using Simulated Annealing and the Surface Interpenetration Measure. *IEEE Transactions on Pattern Analysis and Machine Intelligence, 32*(2), 206–219. doi:10.1109/TPAMI.2009.14

Rojas, R. (1996). *Neural Networks - A Systematic Introduction*. Berlin: Springer-Verlag.

Roweis, S. T., & Saul, L. K. (2000). Nonlinear dimensionality reduction by Locally Linear Embedding. *Science, 290*(5500), 2323–2326. doi:10.1126/science.290.5500.2323

Samir, C., Srivastava, A., Daoudi, M., & Klassen, E. (2009). An Intrinsic Framework for Analysis of Facial Surfaces. *International Journal of Computer Vision, 82*(1), 80–95. doi:10.1007/s11263-008-0187-8

Tenenbaum, J. B. (1998). Mapping a manifold of perceptual observations. *Advances in Neural Information Processing Systems, 10*, 682–688.

Ter Haar, F. B., & Veltkamp, R. C. (2009). A 3D face matching framework for facial curves. *Graphical Models, 71*(2), 77–91. doi:10.1016/j.gmod.2008.12.003

Turk, M., & Pentland, A. (1991). Eigenfaces for recognition. *Journal of Cognitive Neuroscience, 3*(1), 71–86. doi:10.1162/jocn.1991.3.1.71

Van der Maaten, L., Postma, E., & Van Den Herik, H. (2007). *Dimensionality reduction: A comparative review*. Technical Report, Maastricht University.

Vapnik, V. (1998). *Statistical Learning Theory*. New York: John Wiley and Sons.

Viola, P., & Jones, M. J. (2004). Robust real-time face detection. *International Journal of Computer Vision, 57*(2), 137–154. doi:10.1023/B:VISI.0000013087.49260.fb

Wang, S., Wang, Y., Jin, M., Gu, X., & Samaras, D. (2006). 3D surface matching and recognition using conformal geometry. In *Conference on Computer Vision and Pattern Recognition* (pp. 2453–2460), New York.

Wang, Y., Chiang, M.-C., & Thompson, P. M. (2005). Mutual information-based 3D surface matching with applications to face recognition and brain mapping. In *International Conference on Computer Vision* (pp. 527–534), Beijing, China.

Zhang, R., Tsai, P.-S., Cryer, J., & Sham, M. (1999). Shape from shading: A survey. *IEEE Transactions on Pattern Analysis and Machine Intelligence, 21*(8), 690–706. doi:10.1109/34.784284

Zhao, W., Chellappa, R., Phillips, P. J., & Rosenfeld, A. (2003). Face recognition: A literature survey. *ACM Computing Surveys, 35*(4), 399–458. doi:10.1145/954339.954342

Chapter 5
Trademark Image Retrieval

Wing-Yin Chau
University of Warwick, UK

Chia-Hung Wei
Ching Yun University, Taiwan

Yue Li
Nankai University, China

ABSTRACT

With the rapid increase in the amount of registered trademarks around the world, trademark image retrieval has been developed to deal with a vast amount of trademark images in a trademark registration system. Many different approaches have been developed throughout these years in an attempt to develop an effective TIR system. Some conventional approaches used in content-based image retrieval, such as moment invariants, Zernike moments, Fourier descriptors and curvature scale space descriptors, have also been widely used in TIR. These approaches, however, contain some major deficiencies when addressing the TIR problem. Therefore, this chapter proposes a novel approach in order to overcome the major deficiencies of the conventional approaches. The proposed approach combines the Zernike moments descriptors with the centroid distance representation and the curvature representation. The experimental results show that the proposed approach outperforms the conventional approaches in several circumstances. Details regarding to the proposed approach as well as the conventional approaches are presented in this chapter.

1. INTRODUCTION

With the invention of the digital cameras, personal computers and the Internet, people are now allowed to create, share and distribute multimedia content effortlessly. As a consequence, the amount of digital data has been increased tremendously in past decades. Automatic searching for the multimedia content becomes prominent at reducing search efforts. As a result, content-based image retrieval (CBIR) and multimedia content description interface (MPEG-7) has been emerged to cope with this problem.

DOI: 10.4018/978-1-61692-859-9.ch005

1.1 Background and Motivation

Prior to the existence of CBIR and MPEG-7, the traditional approach to retrieving digital data requires a lot of manual processes. Digital data are first categorised according to their manners and are annotated manually afterwards by assigning keywords or names with respect to their content. This approach, however, is not efficacious enough. Faults or slips may appear because of different perception of the digital data throughout the annotation process. This leads to the development of CBIR and MPEG-7. The purposes of CBIR and MPEG-7 are both designed to bridge the semantic gap between human percept images and machine percept images. CBIR is relatively pragmatic by comparing to MPEG-7. Instead of producing a collection of standardised descriptions of the digital asset to increase interoperability, CBIR concerns more on pictorial data management in an individual system.

Although CBIR does not allow any search across different repositories, it can be widely applied in different areas. For instance, in the medical field, CBIR can be used to deal with different types of radiographs such as mammograms and brain tomograms; in the law enforcement field, CBIR can be used to cope with the criminal database and last but not least, CBIR can also be applied for the trademark registration in the management of intellectual property.

As CBIR covers many different aspects, this chapter was only focused on trademark image retrieval (TIR). According to Alwis and Austin (1998), a trademark is a distinctive sign which can be uniquely identified for products and services in the commercial environment. With the use of trademark, a company can differentiate its own product from other companies' products. By concerning the rapid increase in the amount of registered trademarks around the world, TIR has been developed to deal with a vast amount of trademark images in a trademark registration system. Concerning Eakins, Graham, and Boardman (1997), the traditional classification of registered trademark images is based on their shape features and types of objects depicted by employing manually-assigned codes. Currently, the traditional classification has been proven to be infeasible in dealing with a gigantic amount of trademark images that contain little or no representational meanings (Alwis and Austin, 1998).

As mentioned previously, the techniques used in the CBIR system for a trademark image database are mainly focused on shape extraction. Therefore it is sensible to utilise different shape descriptors to characterise the trademark images in a TIR system. The intention of ensuring the existing trademarks is sufficiently distinctive from new candidate trademark images, TIR techniques are incorporated into the existing trademark registration system to surmount the traditional classification and augment the competence in retrieving perceptually and conceptually relevant trademark design in an enormous trademark image database.

1.2 Challenges

Although it is easy to spot a trademark in our daily lives, it is difficult to classify and search for the similar trademarks when there are an enormous amount of trademark images present. The process of classifying and retrieving trademark images is indeed very challenging. Since trademark images can have a significant amount of variations from one another, this complicates the comparison between different trademark images.

Trademarks can be categorised into few different natures. A trademark can either be identified as a word-only mark, a device-only mark or a device-and-word mark (see Figure 1). For a word-only mark, the design of the trademark consists purely of text words or phrases. For a device-only mark, the

Figure 1. Examples of different kinds of trademark: **(a)** *a word only mark,* **(b)** *a device only mark,* **(c)** *a device-and-word mark*

trademark only contains symbols, icons or images. If a trademark comprises both words and any iconic symbols or images, it can be regarded as a device-and-word mark (Eakins, 2001). Since different algorithms have to be used in describing different kinds of trademark images, a TIR system can only design to accommodate either device-only mark, word-only mark or device-and-word mark. Although several TIR systems have designed to handle all kinds of trademark images, the performance of these systems is rather unfavorable when comparing to those systems which are specifically designed to handle only one kind of trademark. Another challenge in TIR is difficult to model human similarity perception into the system. As human perception of an image involves collaboration between different sensoriums, it is difficult to integrate and model a human perception mechanism into a TIR system. In this chapter, only machine percept image mechanism is implemented. Within the implementation, device-marks and device-and-word marks have been considered. Further details of the used approaches will be discussed fully later in this chapter.

1.3 Assumptions

Since TIR requires profound techniques, many groups of researchers have been investigated in this area over the past ten years in an attempt to build an effective TIR system. According to Eakins (2001), some studies proposed or exploited techniques derived from mainstream image processing, typically involving extraction and matching of features. Some studies proposed very specific techniques to solve one aspect of the problem instead of attempting to build and test a completed system. The major interests in this chapter were set in two parts: (1) to investigate different feature representation techniques; (2) to build a simple TIR system with a proposed feature representation algorithm.

1.4 Objectives

The major objective of this chapter is to present a comprehensive feature representation algorithm for a TIR system. In order to accomplish this objective, the chapter has been divided into four different stages together with some achievable goals. The four stages are as follows: Stage 1: To investigate different shape feature representation algorithms. This includes both regional-based and contour-based shape descriptors; Stage 2: To implement different shape feature representation algorithms that are investigated in stage 1; Stage 3: Design the complete TIR system, including local feature representation for the trademark images, global feature representation for the trademark images, and combine both local and global feature representation techniques; Stage 4: Conduct performance evaluation.

2. LITERATURE REVIEW

2.1 Existing Trademark Image Retrieval Systems

Several remarkable TIR systems have been developed previously. TRADEMARK, STAR and ARTISAN are certainly the three most prominent TIR systems. According to Alwis and Austin (1998), different methodologies have been employed in these trademark systems. The TRADEMARK system implemented using the graphical features' vectors (GF-vector), while the STAR system adopted the mainstream CBIR techniques. The techniques adopted in this system include the Fourier descriptors, grey level projection and moment invariants. The ARTISAN system, however, introduced an innovative approach that incorporates with principles derived from Gestalt psychology.

2.1.1 TRADEMARK

TRADEMARK is the first literally addressed TIR system. It is also the first system that has been developed based on the visual interaction with the user. The system interprets the image content automatically and calculates the similarity based on human perception (Alwis, & Austin, 1998). Basically, TRADEMARK uses GF-vector as the principal feature of a trademark image. The trademark images were first normalised to an 8×8 pixel grid. Then, the GF-vector of an image was calculated from various pixel distributions. During the query stage, users can choose to submit either hand-drawn sketches or example images. Afterwards, distances between the GF-vector of a query image and the stored images were computed using the city-block algorithm (Kato, 1992).

2.1.2 STAR

STAR is hitherto one of the most sophisticated and comprehensive TIR systems. It has been designed to deal with word-only marks, device-only marks and device-and-word marks. The STAR system works by considering both shape components and the spatial layout of an image (Wu, Lam, Mehtre, Gao, & Narasimhalu, 1996), however, recognition of some perceptually significant components has been considered to be too difficult to be done by some automated process (Alwis, & Austin, 1998), and therefore, in certain extent, manual operation is needed for the segmentation of some abstract trademark images.

Shape, structure and semantics have been used in STAR for similarity matching. For the shape and structure components description, Fourier descriptors, moment invariants and grey level projections have been used. For the semantics, keywords and Vienna Classification codes have been used to represent the semantic components of each image in STAR (Alwis, & Austin, 1998).

2.1.3 ARTISAN

ARTISAN was developed in collaboration with the UK Patent Office to overcome the problem of classifying the trademarks in the Trade Marks Registry (Eakins et al., 1997). It has been designed to cope

Figure 2. Examples of typical abstract trademark images

with device-only trademarks which consist of some abstract geometric designs (see Figure 2). Since the aim of ARTISAN is to reproduce the judgment of an experienced trademark examiner, unlike STAR and TRADEMARK, it employs principles derived from Gestalt psychology to segment trademark images into different components before the shape representation stage. With the use of Gestalt psychology, ARTISAN can ensure the judgments are closed to the judgments that made by human trademark examiners, and therefore, grouping can be easily made by a number of trademark examiners later such that each image component can be grouped into perceptually significant regions or classes.

2.2 Shape Representation

Most of the image processing techniques adopted by the researchers in addressing the problem of TIR are from the MPEG-7 standard. MPEG-7 standard consists of several different components. According to Manjunath and Sikora (2002), by separating the MPEG-7 into several different parts, this allows various clusters of technology to be used standalone with regards to the MPEG's toolbox principles. Although there are many different descriptors and description schemes presented in MPEG-7 that are useful in tackling the problem of TIR, only a few MPEG-7 shape descriptors and system performance evaluation techniques have been researched. For the MPEG-7 shape descriptors, the algorithms have been researched include Zernike moments and curvature scale space descriptor (CSSD). Other conventional algorithms such as moment invariants and Fourier descriptors have also been investigated in this study.

Shape is one of the most important features in describing an image. Human can easily identify different images and classify them into different categories solely from the outline of an object in a given image. As shape often carries some kind of semantic information, which is meaningful to human recognition, it is used as a distinctive feature for classification of an image object.

In general, there are two types of shape descriptors have been described in literature. They are the region-based shape descriptors and contour-based shape descriptors according to Zhang and Lu (2003). Region-based shape descriptors usually refer to the shape descriptions that have been derived using all pixel information within a shape region of an image object. On the contrary, contour-based descriptors only exploit the shape boundary of an image object. There are several kinds of shape descriptors presented in these two types (see Figure 3). In the following sections, different kinds of shape description techniques are presented. These include moment invariants and Zernike moments that are under the region-based descriptors section; chain codes, Fourier descriptors and curvature scale space descriptor (CSSD) that are under contour-based descriptors section.

Figure 3. Classification of shape description techniques

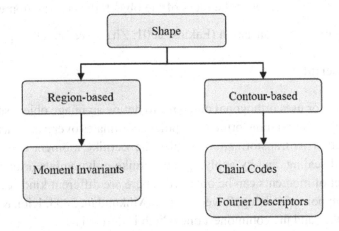

2.2.1 Region-Based Descriptors

As mentioned earlier, region-based shape descriptors describe a shape based on both boundary and interior pixel information. With this property, it can be used to depict some complex objects as well as some simple objects that with or without holes (see Figure 4) (Bober, Preteux, & Kim, 2002). Generally, the implementations for most of the region-based descriptors are based on the calculation of an object moments, and the major advantage for this is that, they work well in describing non-connected and disjoint image objects (Zhang, & Lu, 2003), however, since the contour features of an image object are not emphasised in any region-based descriptors, and therefore, it is not applicable to use region-based descriptors to depict image objects without interior pixel information.

Moment Invariants Descriptor

Moment invariants, also called geometric moments, are derived from a set of central moments of different image objects. The central moments of order $p+q$ of 2D objects can be represented by function $f(x, y)$ and defined as:

$$\mu_{pq} = \sum_{x}\sum_{y}(x - \bar{x})^{p}(y - \bar{y})^{q}f(x,y)\, p,q=0,1,2,... \tag{1}$$

Figure 4 Examples of shapes which are applicable and inapplicable to region-based descriptors: (a) shapes that are applicable to region-based descriptors, (b) shapes that are inapplicable to region-based descriptors

with $\bar{x} = \dfrac{\mu_{10}}{m}$ and $\bar{y} = \dfrac{\mu_{01}}{m}$, where m is the mass of the object, the central moments (μ_{pq}) is therefore invariant to scaling, rotation and translation (Eakins, 2001; Zhang, & Lu, 2003).

Zernike Moments Descriptor

Zernike moments descriptor uses orthogonal moments to define an image object shape (Teague, 1980). Generally, the image object is first transformed into polar coordinates over a unit circle, and then Zernike polynomials are applied. This transformation enables the Zernike moment descriptor is invariant to translation, rotation and scaling, and by applying the Zernike polynomials orthogonally over the unit circle, an orthogonal set of moments can be obtained. There are different kinds of expression used for defining the Zernike polynomial (Chong, Raveendran, & Mukundan, 2003; Kim, & Kim, 2000; Teague, 1980; Zhang, & Lu, 2003) and the commonest one which is defined as

$$V_{pq}(x,y) = V_{pq}(\rho,\theta) = R_{pq}(\rho)\exp(jq\theta) \tag{2}$$

where

$$R_{pq}(\rho) = \sum_{s=0}^{(p-|q|)/2} \frac{(-1)^s \left[(p-s)!\right]\rho^{p-2s}}{s!\left(\dfrac{p+|q|}{2}-s\right)!\left(\dfrac{p-|q|}{2}-s\right)!} \tag{3}$$

with p is a non-negative integer, and q is a non-zero integer which subjects to the constraints $n-|m|$ is even and $|m| \leq n$; (ρ,θ) is the polar coordinates of the transformed image object. A set of Zernike moments can then be obtained through the equation with $V_{pq}(x,y)$. Zernike polynomials can calculate up to 15th order, the higher the order, the more details of an image can be described. Furthermore, different names are given to different orders. The name for each order usually conveys their corresponding nature (see Figure 5, Table 1).

2.2.2 Contour-Based Descriptors

While region-based descriptors capture both interior contents and the boundary information of an image object, contour-based descriptors, however, only interested in exploiting the boundary information of an image object. There are generally two different approaches for contour-based representation, and they are the conventional and structural shape representations. The major difference between the conventional and structural shape representations is that, the structural approach breaks down the shape of an image object into different boundary segments called primitives, while the conventional approach retains the overall shape of an image object during calculation. There are several contour-based descriptors presented in this section, and they are chain codes, Fourier descriptors and CSSD accordingly. For the classification of these descriptors, only chain codes are classified under the structural shape representation, while the others are classified as conventional shape representation (Zhang, & Lu, 2003).

Figure 5 Zernike polynomials up to 4th order

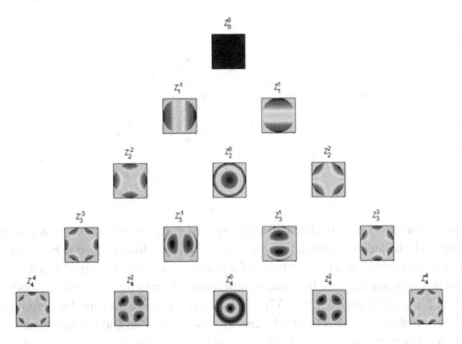

Chain Codes

Chain codes have been commonly used in image representations. Generally, it is used to represent the boundary points of an image object by a sequence of connected straight line segments with specified length and direction. There are 4 or 8 connectivity of the segments that chain codes can be chosen from (see Figure 6) (Gonzalez, & Woods, 2002). Although chain codes are invariant to rotation, translation and scaling, however, they cannot be used alone in any TIR systems. This is because they are not applicable in describing any disjoint or non-connected image objects, and therefore, they are usually being used with other techniques in TIR.

Fourier Descriptors

There are altogether four different approaches can be used to express the Fourier descriptors. They are complex coordinates, centroid distance, curvature function and cumulative angles respectively. In gen-

Table 1. Common name of Zernike polynomials up to 4th order

Radial order (p)	Azimuthal frequency (q)	Common name
0	0	Piston
1	-1, 1	Tilt
2	-2, 2	Astigmatism
2	0	Defocus
3	-1, 1	Coma
3	-3, 3	Trefoil
4	0	Spherical Aberration

Figure 6. Examples of chain codes: (a) 4-directional chain code, (b) 8-directional chain code

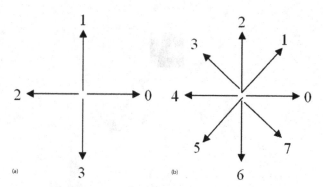

eral, the Fourier descriptors are calculated by applying the Fourier transform on the boundary points of an image object. The boundary points of an image object are, therefore, needed to be obtained by chain codes before the transformation has been done. Afterwards, the results are normalised according to different approaches such that they are invariant to translation and rotation (Gonzalez, Woods, & Eddins, 2004; Zhang, & Lu, 2002; Zhang, & Lu, 2003). Since chain codes have been used in deriving the Fourier descriptors, they are therefore, sensitive to the change of starting point and rotation of an image object. Additionally, the lower frequency descriptors capture the gross essence of a shape while the higher frequency descriptors give detail descriptions of a shape (Kauppinen, Seppänen, & Pietikäinen, 1995).

Curvature Scale Space Descriptor (CSSD)

CSSD is one of the contour-based shape descriptors in the MPEG-7 standard. Basically, it uses the curvature information of a contour to describe an image object. Concerning Bober et al. (2002), the extraction of CSS representation begins with applying Gaussian smoothing progressively on the boundary of an image object. In other words, the contour of an image object is convoluted by Gaussian smoothing. Then, the inflection points are obtained by finding the zero-crossings of the curvature function. With different amount of convolutions on the contour, different number of the inflection points can be obtained and thus, a 2-D graph can be plotted against the amount of Gaussian smoothing regarding to the inflection points (Bober et al., 2002; Mokhtarian, & Mackworth, 1986; Zhang, & Lu, 2003). CSSD has some useful properties. These properties are invariant to rotation, translation and scaling. Some researchers have also shown that CSSD has been tolerant on other deformations in the object, such as skewing and elongation. In addition, CSSD is also robust to some regional changes on a shape as it retains the local information of an image object. CSSD also outperforms region-based descriptors in tackling some deformation images. However, by comparing to the region-based descriptors, CSSD is incapable to cope with some simple shapes such as circle, triangle and polygons (Bober et al., 2002).

3. SYSTEM DESIGN AND ARCHITECTURE

After some in depth investigations on different aspects in TIR in the previous chapter, it is time to discuss about the system design and the architecture during the implementation stage. General design guidelines have been created before the implementation stage. Most of them came from the research conducted in the early stages. A series of algorithms and ideas which were included in the general guidelines have been researched and implemented using MATLAB. Various options for implementing a good TIR system have been explored before reaching the final design decision. This chapter presents a review of the design phase and the architecture of the system which can help in explaining the operation of the system and the ideas behind working algorithms.

3.2 Architecture of Traditional Content-Based Image Retrieval

The architecture of the TIR system developed in this study was based on a traditional CBIR system framework. In a traditional CBIR system, there are two critical processes, namely, the feature extraction and the image retrieval phase. The feature extraction phase is considered as an offline process while the image retrieval phase is considered as an online process. During the offline process, there is no interaction between the user and the system. Some tasks such as image feature extraction and database construction are done in this phase. Throughout the image feature extraction in the offline process, feature descriptors are used to represent a given image, and then they are stored in the database together with the images for later use.

Online process is commenced after the offline process has been finished. User interaction is involved in this process. Initially, the user inputs a query image, and then the system starts with extracting the features from the query image. Afterwards, the system performs similarity measure between the query image and the images stored in database. In the similarity measure, the feature descriptors located in the database are being compared with the feature descriptors of the query image.

There are several methods can be used to perform the comparison. The most commonly used method is the Euclidean distance. Alternative methods such as Manhattan distance (also known as city-block distance), quadratic form distance and Mahalanobis distance can also be used as the similarity measurement (Feng, Long, & Zhang, 2002; Furht, & Marques, 2002).

After the similarities have been obtained, the system ranks the results by allocating different indices to the images. Then, the system rearranges the indices and displays the K-most similar images to the user where K is a number that specified by the user (see Figure 7).

3.3 Creation of Trademark Image Database

One of the significant issues concerns with the CBIR problem is the sample used for system performance evaluation. Since there is no pre-existing trademark image database, a database with 1003 trademark images has been created in this study. During the creation of the trademark image database, several rules have to follow: (1) all the trademark images should be in the size of 200×200; (2) all the trademark images should be belonged to the same format; (3) all the trademark images should be classified into different classes regarding to their visual properties; (4) all the trademark images should be black and white images; (5) each class should has at least 20 trademark images. Otherwise, we assign the images into a miscellaneous class. The database contains 14 different classes and the classification is shown in Figure 8.

Figure 7. A traditional CBIR system with application of TIR

Input Query
Feature
The User
Display
Indexing
Similarity
Image Retrieval
Feature Extraction
Trademark
Feature
Image Database with

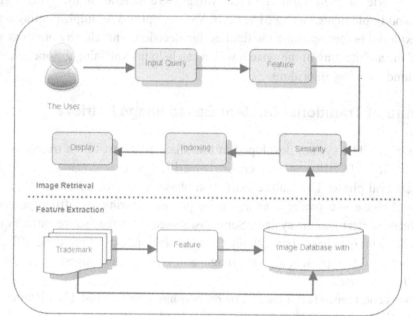

Figure 8. Classification of the trademark images

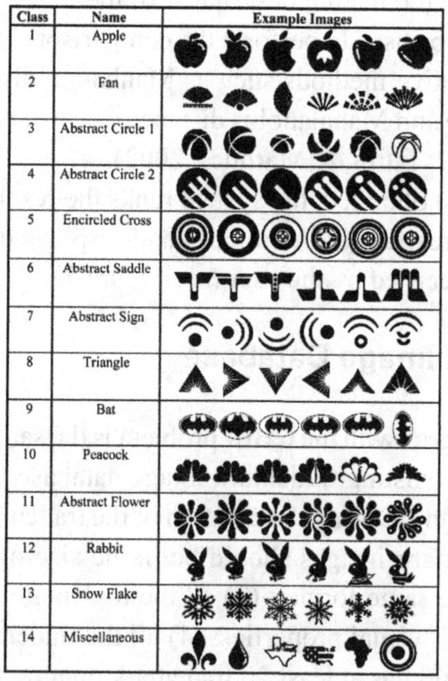

Class
Name
Example Images
1
Apple
2
Fan
3
Abstract Circle 1
4
Abstract Circle 2
5
Encircled Cross
6
Abstract Saddle
7
Abstract Sign
8
Triangle
9
Bat
10
Peacock
11
Abstract Flower
12
Rabbit
13
Snow Flake
14
Miscellaneous

3.4 Choice of Algorithms

Several existing algorithms have been commonly used in TIR. For instance, moment invariants, Zernike moments, Fourier descriptors and curvature scale space are the four most renowned algorithms that have been investigated in this study. By detailed inspections on these algorithms, Zernike moments demonstrate the best performance on the designated database while comparing with other algorithms and yet, some deficiencies have still been discovered when implementing the Zernike moments. Further researches were carried out in an attempt to improve the searching ability of the system. After all these investigations, a new fast and robust algorithm has been proposed at the end of the study.

The aim of this section is to present a summarisation of the conventional algorithms after some detailed inspections on their adequacies and deficiencies over the designated database.

3.4.1 Moment Invariants Descriptor

Moment invariants is said to be invariant to scaling, translation and rotation (Feng et al., 2002; Eakins, 2001; Fisher, 2004; Gonzalez, & Woods, 2002; Zhang, & Lu, 2003), and hence, some experiments were carried out over the designated database on these properties. The seven moment invariants in Figure 9 were computed according to the equations described in Gonzalez and Woods (2002). The results for image 2 and 3 are in reasonable agreement with the rotation invariants computed for image 1, but, the results for image 5 and 6 show inconformity with image 4 (also shown in Figure 10, *Apple 1, 2 and 3*). These demonstrate that the seven moment invariants computed for a scaled and translated image may vary from the values obtained from the original image. The major cause of this can be attributed to the amount of noises introduced during the translation and scaling of the original image. Apart from the variability on translation and scaling, another deficiency of moment invariants is its susceptibility to any regional changes. Small changes to the original image may produce discordant results of the seven moment invariants. In addition, moment invariants are inaccurate in describing similar size images, and this can be shown in Figure 10 with the seven moment invariants of the *Abstract Shape* are close to the vicinity of the seven moment invariants of the *Apple 3*.

Upon applying the moment invariants over the entire designated database, further results were obtained. Figure 11 was obtained by averaging the moment invariants derived from different images within a significant class and Figure 12 was obtained by averaging the moment invariants and the standard deviation among the seven moments. Figure 11 gives further prove that moment invariants is also incapable in describing general shapes while Figure 12 shows the inadequacy of employing moment

Figure 9. The seven moment invariants for different images

Image		1st	2nd	3rd	4th	5th	6th	**7th**
1		1.021	10.945	11.737	8.515	19.315	14.581	19.184
2		1.016	11.580	11.597	11.633	24.445	24.445	23.532
3		1.028	9.959	12.768	7.686	18.964	13.105	17.978
4		0.811	8.371	11.191	6.027	15.521	10.756	14.831
5		1.526	15.951	18.230	12.171	27.481	22.408	28.183
6		1.596	8.407	10.343	8.923	18.825	13.498	20.876

Figure 10. A graph of the seven moment invariants of four different images which demonstrates the weaknesses of moment invariants

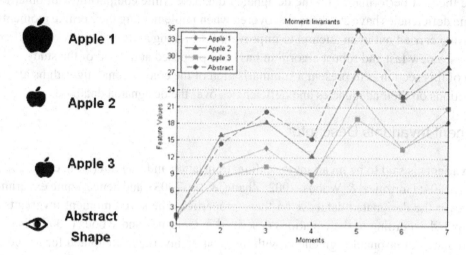

Figure 11. A graph of average moment invariants over five different classes

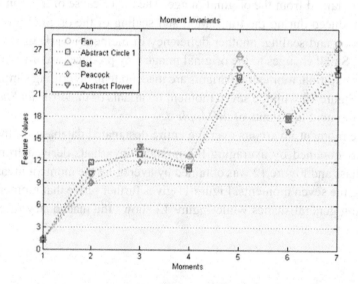

invariants over the designated database, since most of the moment invariants from different classes are overlapped.

3.4.2 Zernike Moments Descriptor

Experiments that were used in testing the moment invariants have also been used to examine the Zernike moments descriptor. In general, reasonable agreements can be found with the rotation, translation and scaling invariants computed for a set of images. Having accomplished some simple tests on the properties of the Zernike moments descriptor, it was then tested on its distinctiveness over the designated database. The average values and the standard deviations of each Zernike moment in each class were

Figure 12. A graph of average moment invariants and its range in all fourteen classes

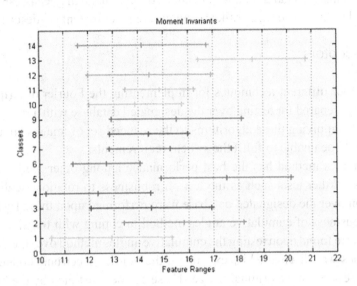

Figure 13. A graph of mean values for the zero order of Zernike moments and its range in all fourteen classes

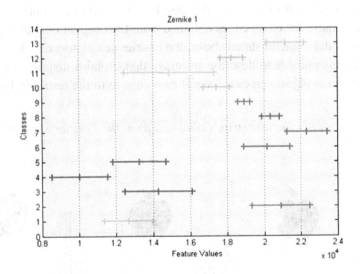

computed in order to examine their uniqueness. By detail inspection on these values, the zero order moment is appeared to be the most distinctive moment by comparing to the other moments. A graph has also been created in order to check the range covered by the zero order moment in each of the fourteen classes (see Figure 13).

As readily seen from the graphs and the values obtained, Zernike moments appear to be capable to cope with the designated database, but still, there are also some minor problems were discovered during the experiments, such as Zernike moments are unable to give agreeable results when dealing with some skewed and stretched images; small amount of changes on the image may cause significant changes to certain moments and last but not least, Zernike moments are incompetent for describing hollow images.

3.4.3 Fourier Descriptors

Given that there are four different techniques for implementing the Fourier descriptors, four different implementations were prepared for testing over the designated database with a reduced set of images. If the results produced by applying these algorithms to the reduced set of images are unsatisfactory, then those algorithms should be unable to fulfil the system requirements.

The cumulative angles method has the best performance among other methods over the reduced database. Afterwards, further tests such as the test on robustness to rotation, scaling, translation and non-rigid deformation over the designated database were performed upon these findings.

In spite of the robustness of cumulative angles method in coping with translated images, there are several deficiencies were found upon testing the cumulative angles method over the designated database. One of the deficiencies was discovered by examining the Fourier spectrums created after performing several rotations and resizes on the original image. These can be illustrated by the histograms obtained from the Fourier spectrums. Certain disagreements between the histograms present in Figure 14 on *Apple 3* and *4* and also *Circle 1* and *2* can be found. These disparities can be attributed to the use of chain codes in extracting the boundary points from the image object. Since chain codes are direction dependent, therefore, the starting point of the rotated image is different from the one in the original image. As a result, this differentiates the chain codes obtained from the original image and its rotated version.

Apart from the major deficiencies stated above, the Fourier descriptors developed from the cumulative angles method are also unable to describe an image that contains disjoint shapes. Furthermore, a little alteration in the image object can cause significant change to the resulting Fourier spectrum and

Figure 14. A graph that shows the histograms obtained from the Fourier spectrums produced by different images

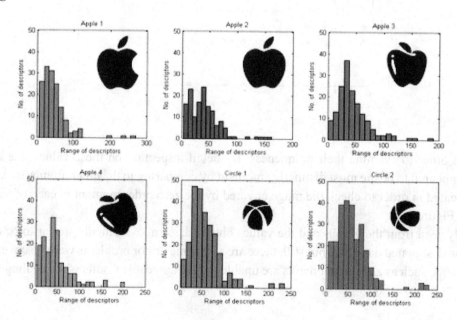

this explains the reason why the Fourier descriptors are sensitive to noise. Indeed, all of these problems can be attributed to the use of chain codes during the boundary extraction. Although there are so many problems have been identified on using the Fourier descriptions, some of these problems can be solved when it is used with any regional-based shape descriptors. In fact, there are several researches have been suggested that using a combination of region-based and contour-based shape descriptors can actually improve the searching ability of a TIR system (Alwis, & Austin, 1998; Eakins, 2001; Wu et al., 1996).

3.4.4 Curvature Scale Space Descriptor

CSSD is considered to be robust to rotation, scaling, translation, skewing and elongation (Bober et al., 2002). Several tests were performed based on these properties over the designated database to find out the adequacy of employing this algorithm into the TIR system.

After testing on several sets of images, CSSD can obtain the same number of zero-crossings curvature within a set of rotated (see Figure 15), translated, skewed and elongated images, however, different numbers of zero-crossings curvature were recorded within a set of scaled image. The major cause of this can be attributed to the aliasing on the image during the reduction and enlargement processes.

In spite of the variability on scaling, CSSD is well performed on describing hollow shape images. As CSSD is only interested in the contour of an image object rather than its interior content, image objects with the same shape can yield the same number of zero-crossings curvature. Thus it allows hollow images to be compared with filled images.

Further investigations were performed on CSSD over the designated database. The results obtained, however, were not desirable. Figure 16 shows some of the experimental results after applying CSSD on different types of trademark image. Even though, image 3 and 4 in Figure 16 are in entirely different shapes, but same number of zero-crossings curvature has been obtained. This demonstrates that CSSD is difficult to be applied on general cases.

The experimental results also show that CSSD is sensitive to regional changes. This can be demonstrated by image 4 and 5 in Figure 16. Small changes on the image objects can result in a great difference on the contour. As a result, the numbers of corner points obtained after the convolution can be different. This example also reveals that CSSD is defective in describing an image composed of complex shapes.

Another defect of CSSD is its incapability of coping with encircled image objects. The major cause of this can be attributed to the nature of a circle. Since a circle has the same non-zero curvature ubiq-

Figure 15. A set of rotated images with 19 zero-crossings curvature: **(a)** *original image;* **(b)** *after a rotation of 90°;* **(c)** *after a rotation of 180°;* **(d)** *after a rotation of 270°*

Figure 16. The number of zero-crossings curvature obtained according to different types of image

	Image	No. of corner points
1		9
2		9
3		19
4		19
5		33
6		34

uitously, therefore, the number of corners acquired is independent to the number of circles exist in an image (see Figure 17).

3.5 Discussions

Investigations were made upon four different shape representation techniques, including two region-based and two contour-based shape representations. Different tests were performed regarding to their given properties. Large amount of information was collected during the tests. Critical analyses were carried out to find the best approach among the four algorithms in tackling the TIR problem. In the previous section, adequacies and deficiencies of each approach over the designated database have been presented. Based on these findings, choice can be made between the four approaches.

Throughout numerous inspections, some common deficiencies can be found from the results. These, however, can be helped in developing guidelines for further improvements. For instance, the four approaches are all susceptible to any local changes on a given image. Three of the four approaches, excepting the CSSD are unable to handle skewed and stretched images. The results also show that the contour-based shape representations are typically difficult to apply on general cases and are insufficient for describing any disjoint or non-connected shapes. In contrast, region-based shape descriptors are well in defining images with non-connected components and disjoint objects.

In general, Zernike moments descriptor outperforms other shape descriptors especially in the robustness to translation, rotation and scaling. The experiments show that it can capture the gross essence of the trademark images in the designated database, and in the meanwhile maintaining certain details of the images, therefore, it was chosen to be the basis algorithm for the problem. Even though Zernike moments have a good performance over the designated database, there are still some deficiencies on the algorithm have to be solved. As a result, further research has been performed to explore the techniques that can be used to describe the local features of an image in order to tackle the problems.

Figure 17. An example of encircled image objects and their zero-crossings curvature

4. SYSTEM IMPLEMENTATION

The intention of building up a TIR system is to provide automatic search on the trademark images in an extensive trademark image database. A number of techniques have been researched based on the TIR, but still, none of the approaches are shown to be exhaustive. In fact, some deficiencies can be found from different approaches. As a result, a novel approach is proposed for constructing a fast and robust TIR system.

There are two major elements in the image feature extraction and retrieval stage for the development of a fast and robust TIR system. They are the image feature representation and the feature matching respectively. The image feature representation is laid within the feature extraction stage while the feature matching is placed inside the image retrieval stage. Since an appropriate choice of feature matching techniques can enhance the system performance, while an inappropriate choice may lead to obtaining unfavorable results from the system, even though a correct approach has been employed in the feature representation. Nonetheless, any efficient feature matching techniques are indeed relied on the approaches employed in representing the images in the database, and therefore, the two major elements are interdependent. The feature extraction stage in the proposed algorithm involves two important sections; which are the image preprocessing and the features representation. In the features representation section, it can be subdivided into two main areas. Correspondingly, the local features representation and the global features representation.

As for the image retrieval stage in the proposed algorithm, the most important section is the feature matching. Within the feature matching, a multi-level matching strategy is employed. Since it involves both the local features and the global features comparisons, the use of it can further enhance the system performance. This chapter, therefore, is mainly aimed at presenting detail specification for the proposed algorithm. Detail descriptions regarding to the feature extraction stage and the image retrieval stage are presented successively in the following sections.

4.1 Feature Extraction

The system architecture for the proposed algorithm in the feature extraction stage is subdivided into two major areas. They are the image preprocessing and the feature representation. Within the feature representation, two methods have been used for describing the local features of the images in the local features extraction stage, whereas the global features extraction stage only relies on the use of Zernike moments to extract the global features of the images (see Figure 18).

Within the image preprocessing, the system commences with the extraction of the edge from an inputted image by using the canny edge detector. Then, the system put the edge obtained into a unit circle and transforms its coordinates from Cartesian into polar coordinates. These steps ensure the invariability of the algorithm to rotation, scaling and translation.

After the image has been preprocessed, the system proceeds to the features representation. The major purpose of feature representation is to describe the preprocessed image by different types of feature vector. There are two different types of feature can be obtained. Specifically, they are the local feature and the global feature vectors. The local feature vectors capture the interior details of the shapes from the preprocessed image while the global feature vectors capture the gross essence of the shapes.

The local feature descriptors are obtained by calculating the curvature and the centroid distance of each boundary point in the preprocessed image. The curvature is computed upon the Cartesian coordinate system, whereas the centroid distance is computed upon the polar coordinate system.

The curvature of each boundary point in the preprocessed image is calculated by the reciprocal of the radius of an osculating circle on the Cartesian plane. For instance, when the magnitude of the curvature is approaching zero, a straighter line can be identified. According to the illustration and formula in Figure 19, a straight line can be identified when all the points on the curve have zero curvature, while on the contrary, a circle can also be identified when all the points on the curve have 1/r curvature. Given a plane curve $y=f(x)$, the curvature k can be expressed as (Müller, & Rigoll, 1999)

Figure 18. The feature extraction stage in the proposed algorithm

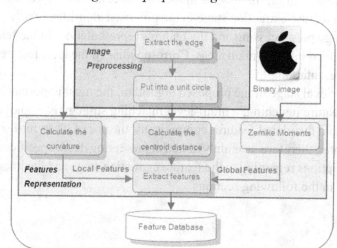

Figure 19. The curvature at point P

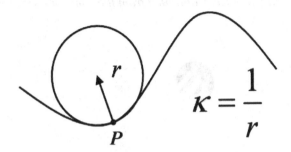

$$\kappa = \frac{y''}{[1+(y')^2]^{3/2}} \tag{4}$$

where y', y'' are the 1st and 2nd order derivatives with respect to x. After obtaining all the curvature values of each boundary point of the image, the curvature feature is expressed as $\sigma(k_1, k_2.., k_n)$, where σ stands for standard deviation. The curvature feature not only captures interior minutiae, but also overcomes a problem caused by anisotropic stretch.

As for the distance to centroid features, the edge map projected at the polar coordinates will be employed to express the interior structure of the corresponding trademark image. The features are obtained by calculating the distance from the centroid(x_0, y_0) to each boundary point (see Figure 20). As the edge maps are projected in a fixed unit circle, a histogram of all the distance to centroid s can be generated (see Figure 21).

Given an image space containing n distance bins in a fixed unit circle, the distance histogram of the edge map of image I is represented as $H(I)=[h_1,...,h_n]$, where h_i is the total number of boundary points in the ith distance bin. The total distance can be expressed as

Figure 20. The centroid distances from the centre of mass to the boundary points of the image

Figure 21. Histograms of centroid distances from different trademark images: (a) encircled cross; (b) abstract circle 2; (c) apple; (d) histograms obtained from the same class; (e) histograms obtained from different classes

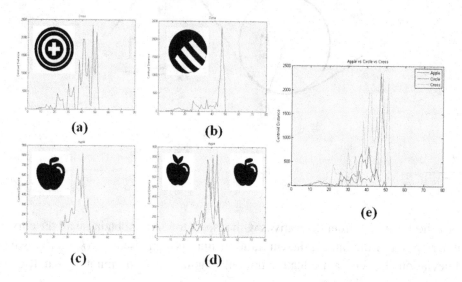

$$D = \sum_{i=1}^{n} h_i d_i \qquad (5)$$

where d_i is the average of the values in the ith distance bin. As a result, we can obtain the two features μ_D and σ_D, which present the mean and standard deviation of the distance from the boundary points to the centroid, respectively.

In addition, this representation enables the proposed algorithm to be invariant to rotation (see Figure 22), translation and scaling. Within the global feature representation, the system follows the steps described previously when deriving the Zernike moments descriptors. The Zernike moments descriptors obtained are then stored into the feature database with the local feature descriptors. As a result, there are eighteen feature vectors altogether for describing an image.

4.2 Image Retrieval

The most important part within the image retrieval stage is the feature matching. In the proposed algorithm, multi-level matching strategy was used for enhancing the accuracy of the search. As mentioned in the previous section, there are altogether eighteen features for each image stored in the database. In order to improve the system performance, the features are compared separately in different level.

The proposed algorithm utilises two levels of feature matching. In the first level of the feature matching, centroid distance features have been utilised. Meanwhile, the curvature feature and the Zernike moments descriptors have been applied to the second level of the feature matching. By utilising the Euclidean distance to compute the similarity between the query image features and the features stored in the database in each level, the relevance values between two images can then be obtained. In order to discriminate the relevant images from the irrelevant images through the relevance values, a threshold

Figure 22. An example that illustrates the centroid distance features are invariant to rotation

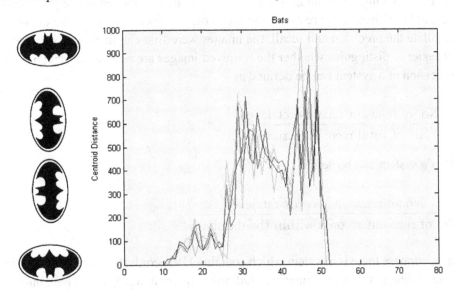

of 0.3 has been set up for both levels. In other words, if the relevance value obtained for a candidate image is greater than 0.3 in either one of the levels, a value 10 will be added to its current relevance value, whereas a value 20 will be added to its current relevance value if the values obtained are greater than 0.3 in both levels. Afterwards, the final value obtained for each image can then be used to rank the images in ascending order. The candidate images with a smaller relevant value are placed on the top while the candidate images with a larger relevant value are placed at the bottom.

5. PERFORMANCE EVALUATION

In this section, the results obtained from the proposed system under various conditions are presented. Precisions and recalls were computed for the proposed system. In order to compare the performance of the proposed system, four test systems have been set up. Basically, the structure of the test system is the same as the proposed system. Conventional algorithms such as the moment invariants, Zernike moments, Fourier descriptors and CSSD were implemented in each test system to replace the proposed algorithm. In addition, multi-level matching strategy has been removed from the test system. The analysis of the proposed algorithm and the conventional algorithms was examined based upon the graphs generated from the average precisions and recalls. According to the precision and recall graphs produced, the proposed algorithm outperforms the conventional algorithms over the designated database.

5.1 System Performance Evaluation Scheme

The system performance evaluation scheme used in this study is the precision and recall. In accordance with Müller et al. (Müller, Müller, Squire, Marchand-Millet, & Pun, 2001), precision and recall can give a good indication of the system performance, especially when they are both taken into consideration. Either one of them alone is not enough for evaluating a system thoroughly. Since precision can be maintained in a high level by retrieving fewer images while recall can be maintained in a high level by reducing the size of the database, therefore, precision and recall often works together in the evaluation process. In order to calculate the precision and recall, the images were first classified into different classes. By doing so, it is easier to distinguish whether the retrieved images are relevant or irrelevant to the query image. The precision of a system can be defined as

$$\text{Precision} = \frac{\text{No. of relevant records retrieved}}{\text{No. of total records retrieved}} \tag{6}$$

and the recall of a system can be defined as

$$\text{Recall} = \frac{\text{No. of relevant records retrieved}}{\text{No. of relevant records within the database}} \tag{7}$$

For example, suppose there is a system which contains 119 records that have been considered as relevant images according to the query image (excluding the query image itself). Then, during the search, 45 records were retrieved in total, in which only 32 relevant records were returned. The precision of the system is then equal to 32/45 (i.e. 0.71). In the meantime, the recall of the system is equal to 32/119 (i.e. 0.27). Therefore, the precision and the recall rate of the system for the given query image is 0.71 and 0.27 respectively.

Upon computing the precision and recall for each inputted query image, average precision and recall can be obtained. Normally, the precision and recall graphs are produced by 10 or more iterations, so a set with 10 or more precisions and recalls data are required. In order to obtain the precision and recall data set, the test sets used must contain more than 100 images. This ensures the results for the evaluation are representative of the system. In this study, 10 iterations were used to plot the precision and recall graphs. The values for the number of total records retrieved were varied from 9 to 99 where each of the iteration was 9 apart.

5.2 Presentation of Results

The results regarding to both conventional and the proposed algorithms are presented in this section. The evaluation techniques used in obtaining the precision and recall graphs have already been discussed in the previous section. Apart from traversing the entire database to obtain the average precision and recall rates with a given set of query images, the average precision and recall rates for different classes were also computed. For instance, the algorithms were evaluated according to five different classes in order to examine their limitations relatively. The classes that were used in the evaluation process included class 1 (*Apple*), class 3 (*Abstract circle 1*), class 9 (*Bat*), class 10 (*Peacock*) and class 12 (*Rabbit*). In total, 20 images in each class were selected as the query images throughout the whole evaluation process.

5.2.1 Research Results

The evaluation for each of the conventional algorithms was based on the five different classes. According to the graphs obtained for each algorithm (see Figure 23-Figure 26), Zernike moments outperform other algorithms in four out of five classes. However, in class 10, moment invariants give a better performance than Zernike moments. This can be attributed to the fact that Zernike moments tend to capture the gross essence of the shapes.

It can also be seen that class 2 and class 8 both contain images, which have similar outline as class 10, so during the search, Zernike moments tend to retrieve the images which belong to class 2, 8 and 10. As a consequence, a comparatively low precision and recall rates were obtained (see Figure 27).

By inspecting the graphs, Fourier descriptors, CSSD and moment invariants have similar performance in class 1 (see Figure 23, Figure 25-Figure 26). This is because the images in class 1 are some simple shape objects which contain fewer disjoint or non-connected components. Apart from the complexity of the images, the size of the image objects can also affect the performance obtained from those algorithms. Therefore, by unifying the size of the images, a better performance can be obtained from the system.

Figure 23. Precision and recall graph for moment invariants over the five classes

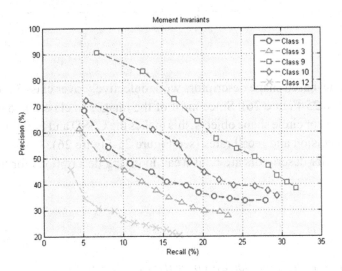

Figure 24. Precision and recall graph for Zernike moments over the five classes

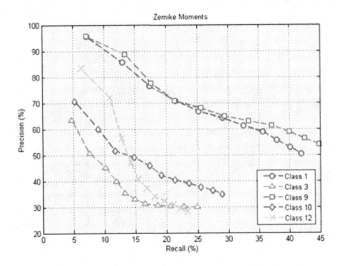

Figure 25. Precision and recall graph for Fourier descriptor (cumulative angle) over the five classes

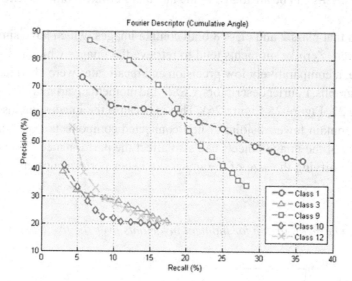

Generally, the contour-based shape descriptors work defectively over class 3 and class 10 according to the graphs (see Figure 25-Figure 26). Since most of the images in class 3 and class 10 are made up of disjoint, non-connected or circle shape objects, this makes the CSSD and Fourier descriptors produced a comparatively low precision and recall rates (see Figure 25-Figure 26). This can be attributed to the fact that CSSD and Fourier descriptors are both weak in giving descriptions for the images with these kinds of attribute.

Figure 26. Precision and recall graph for CSS over the five classes

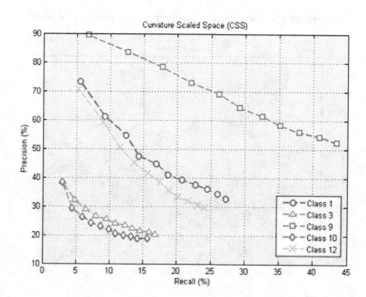

Figure 27. Some retrieval results for Zernike moments

Query Image	Rank 1	Rank 2	Rank 3	Rank 4	Rank 5	Rank 6

5.2.2 Proposed Algorithm Results

The evaluation scheme for the proposed algorithm was similar to the one for the conventional algorithms. The only different is that the proposed system was tested after the implementation of each feature representations. In other words, the system was tested after the implementation of centroid distance, curvature function and Zernike moments respectively. The precision and recall graphs for the proposed algorithm show that the local feature descriptors are not distinctive enough for retrieving the relevant images from class 3, class 10 and class 12 when the Zernike moments was excluded (see Figure 28-Figure 29). But, after Zernike moments have been added into the second level of the feature matching, the precision and recall rates show a huge increment. This is because Zernike moments tend to capture the overall shape instead of some internal details of the shape. While the local features tend to describe a shape with internal details, therefore, the values of the features vary a lot even though only small changes have been made upon the images. Furthermore, a rapid drop on the result is recorded on the graph for class 12 in Figure 30. This can be attributed to the variety of the images within class 12 (see Figure 31). Last but

Figure 28. Precision and recall graph for proposed algorithm (only centroid distance features) over the five classes

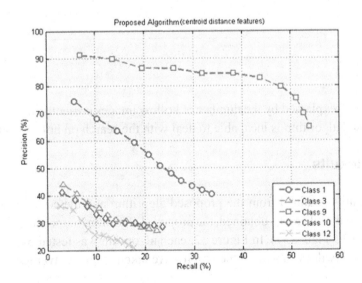

Figure 29. Precision and recall graph for proposed algorithm (centroid distance and curvature features) over the five classes

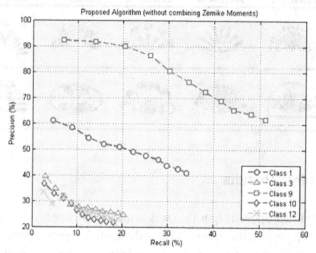

Figure 30. Precision and recall graph for proposed algorithm over the five classes

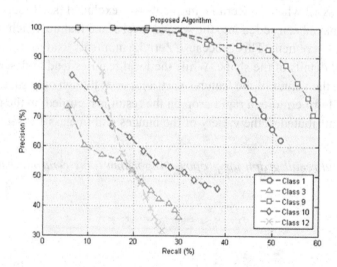

not least, this can also be explained by the number of hollow images present in class 12, and hence, this shows that the proposed algorithm is incapable to deal with the search on hollow shape images.

5.3 Analysis of Results

In this section, the results obtained from the proposed algorithm and the conventional algorithms are compared. According to the all graphs obtained, the proposed algorithm outperforms all the conventional algorithms (see Figure 32-Figure 37). In Figure 32, each algorithm was tested over the entire database to obtain the results. The values shown on the graph were taken from the average of all the precisions

Figure 31. Variety of images within class 12

Figure 32. Precision and recall graph for all the algorithms over the entire database

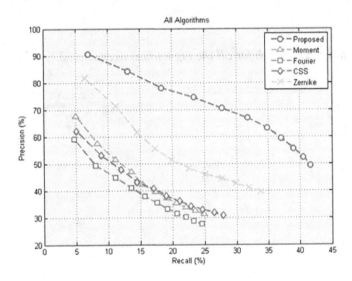

and recalls obtained in each iteration. Apart from the proposed algorithm, the Zernike moments also outperform other algorithms over the designated database. This further proves that the decision was made correctly in choosing Zernike moments as the basis algorithm.

In Figure 33, the graph shows that the proposed algorithm has an excellent performance upon retrieving the class 1 images. However, the moment invariants gave the poorest result among all the algorithms. In fact, this class was designed to test the invariability to rotation, scaling, translation and non-rigid deformation of each algorithm. This graph also demonstrates that the moment invariants are too sensitive to the change of size of the images.

In Figure 34, the graph shows that the contour-based shape representation had a poor performance in retrieving relevant images from this class. There are several reasons can be used to explain this problem. As mentioned above, Fourier descriptors are poor in describing disjoint or non-connected image object, however, most of the images within class 3 are either a disjoint or non-connected, and therefore, this greatly reduces the precision and recall rates for the Fourier descriptors. Besides, this graph also

Figure 33. Precision and recall graph for all the algorithms over class 1

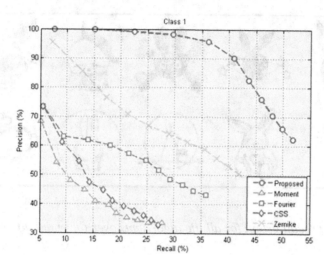

Figure 34. Precision and recall graph for all the algorithms over class 3

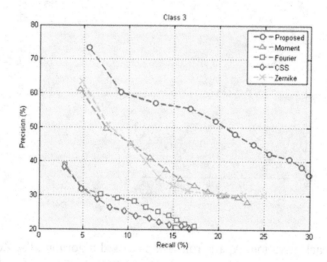

shows that CSSD is incapable to cope with circle objects. Since most of the images within this class are circle images, therefore, a low precision and recall rates were attained for CSSD.

In Figure 35, it shows that the proposed algorithm is well performed when describing any encircled image objects. This can be attributed to the use of centroid distance features. Since the centroid distance features tend to produce more distinctive results for encircled image objects, therefore after the first level of feature matching, the images from class 9 which are relevant to the query image tend to have a relevance value closed to zero but the irrelevant images tend to have a larger relevance value. These values separate the relevant and irrelevant images apart. As a result, the precision and recall rate for this class has been increased.

In Figure 36, it shows that the contour-based shape representations have a poor performance when retrieving the relevant images in this class. This can be attributed to the properties of contour-based

Figure 35. Precision and recall graph for all the algorithms over class 9

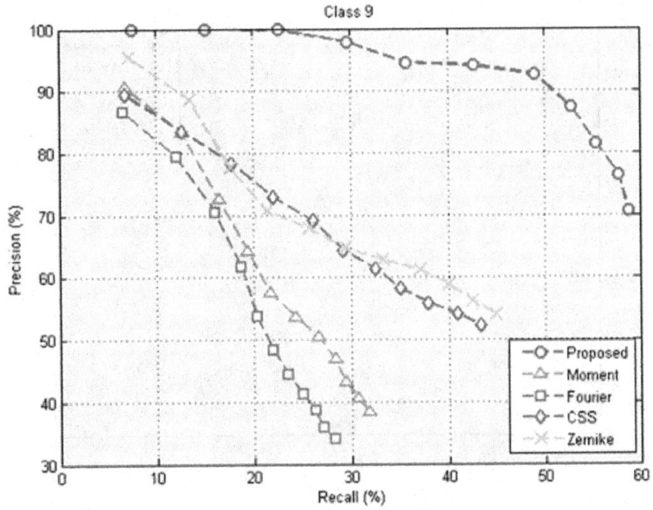

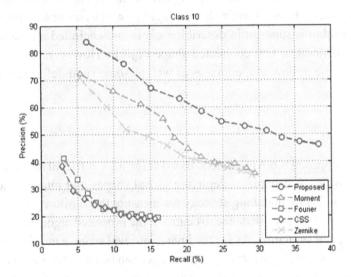

Figure 36. Precision and recall graph for all the algorithms over class 10

shape representations. Since the contour-based shape representations interested in the contour of the image objects, and therefore they are unable to distinguish the images which composed with similar shapes, even though their natures are different.

In Figure 37, it shows a sharp fall on the result curve obtained from the proposed algorithm after it reaches 13% of the recall rate. This can be explained by the number of disturbances present within class *12*. The disturbances include some hollow shape images as well as some rigid deformed images. Half of the classes are made up with these images, therefore, this shows that the proposed algorithm is incapable for describing hollow shape images and also some rigid deformed images.

Figure 37. Precision and recall graph for all the algorithms over class 12

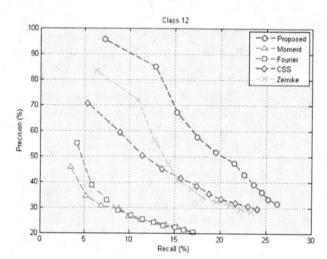

In conclusion, the proposed algorithm is well performed overall. It outperforms the conventional algorithms that have been introduced in this report. The results obtained also show that the proposed algorithm can be used to describe any simple shape images as well as some sophisticated images. Moreover, the proposed algorithm is superior in describing circle and encircled image objects. It is also capable of handling any disjoint or non-connected shape objects. However, the proposed algorithm is incapable to deal with some hollow shape images as well as some rigid deformed images.

6. CONCLUSION

In this work, we have proposed a novel content-based trademark retrieval system, with a feasible set of feature descriptors, which is capable of depicting global shapes and interior / local features of the trademarks, and effective feature matching strategy for measure the similarity between feature sets. By utilising the curvature feature and the distance to centroid, the proposed algorithm is robust against rotation, translation, scaling and stretching. As for the image retrieval stage, a multi-level matching strategy was used in feature matching. With this strategy, the images can be compared with the query image both locally and globally, and therefore enabling the system to be insensitive to noise or small regional changes.

The performance of the proposed algorithm was evaluated in terms of the precision and recall rate. The graphs show that the proposed algorithm outperforms other conventional algorithms including moment invariants, Fourier descriptors, Zernike moments and CSSD. Nevertheless, the proposed scheme is unable to relate the trademarks with similar semantic meanings but is better with different low level features. We are currently investigating ways of incorporating relevance feedback into the proposed system in order to tackle this challenge.

In summary, the proposed algorithm outperforms those conventional algorithms that have been introduced in this work. The results obtained also show that the proposed algorithm can be used to describe any simple shape images as well as some sophisticated images. Moreover, the proposed algorithm is superior in describing circular and encircled image objects. It is also capable of handling any disjoint or non-connected shape objects. However, the proposed algorithm is incapable to dealing with some hollow shape images as well as some rigid deformed images.

REFERENCES

Alwis, S., & Austin, J. (1998). A novel architecture for trademark image retrieval systems. In *Challenge of Image Retrieval*. Retrieved from http://citeseerx.ist.psu.edu/viewdoc/download?doi=10.1.1.100.1494&rep=rep1&type=pdf doi: 10.1.1.100.1494

Bober, M., Preteux, F., & Kim, W.-Y. Y. (2002). Shape descriptors. In B. S. Manjunath, P. Salembier & T. Sikora (Ed.), *Introduction to MPEG-7,* (pp. 231-260). Chichester, UK: Wiley.

Chong, C.-W., Raveendran, P., & Mukundan, R. (2003). Translation invariants of Zernike moments. *Pattern Recognition, 36*(8), 1765–1773. doi:10.1016/S0031-3203(02)00353-9

Curvature. (n.d.). In *Wikipedia.* Retrieved April 13, 2007, from http://en.wikipedia.org/wiki/Curvature

Eakins, J. P. (2001). Trademark image retrieval. In Lew, M. S. (Ed.), *Principles of visual information retrieval* (pp. 319–354). Berlin: Springer-Verlag.

Eakins, J. P., Graham, M. E., & Boardman, J. M. (1997). Evaluation of a trademark image retrieval system. In *Proceedings of the information retrieval research, the 19th annual BCS-IRSG colloquium on IR research,* Aberdeen, UK: BCS Information Retrieval Specialist Group.

Feng, D., Long, F., & Zhang, H. (2002). Fundamentals of content-based image retrieval. In Feng, D., Siu, W. C., & Zhang, H. (Eds.), *Multimedia information retrieval and management: Technological fundamentals and applications* (pp. 7–13). Berlin: Springer-Verlag.

Fisher, R. B. (2004, January 16). *Moment invariants.* Retrieved from http://homepages.inf.ed.ac.uk/rbf/CVonline/LOCAL_COPIES/FISHER/mominv.htm

Furht, B., & Marques, O. (2002). *Content-based image and video retrieval.* New York: Kluwer Academic.

Gonzalez, R. C., & Woods, R. E. (2002). *Digital image processing.* Upper Saddle River, NJ: Prentice Hall.

Gonzalez, R. C., Woods, R. E., & Eddins, S. L. (2004). *Digital image processing using MATLAB.* Upper Saddle River, NJ: Prentice Hall.

Kato, T. (1992). Database architecture for content-based image retrieval. In Jamberdino, A. A., & Niblack, W. (Eds.), *Image storage and retrieval systems* (pp. 112–113). Berlin: Springer-Verlag.

Kauppinen, H., Seppänen, T., & Pietikäinen, M. (1995). An experimental comparison of autoregressive and Fourier-based descriptors. *IEEE Transactions on Pattern Analysis and Machine Intelligence, 17*(2), 201–207. doi:10.1109/34.368168

Kim, W.-Y., & Kim, Y.-S. (2000). A region-based shape descriptor using Zernike moments. *Signal Processing Image Communication, 16*(1-2), 95–102. doi:10.1016/S0923-5965(00)00019-9

Manjunath, B. S., & Sikora, T. (2002). Overview of visual descriptors. In Manjunath, B. S., Salembier, P., & Sikora, T. (Eds.), *Introduction to MPEG-7* (pp. 180–185). Chichester, UK: Wiley.

Mokhtarian, F., & Mackworth, A. (1986). Scale-based description and recognition of planar curves and two-dimensional shapes. *IEEE Transactions on Pattern Analysis and Machine Intelligence, 8*(1), 34–43. doi:10.1109/TPAMI.1986.4767750

Müller, H., Müller, W., Squire, D. McG., Marchand-Millet, S., & Pun, T. (2001). Performance evaluation in content-based image retrieval: Overview and proposals. *Pattern Recognition Letters, 22*(5), 593–601. doi:10.1016/S0167-8655(00)00118-5

Müller, S., & Rigoll, G. (1999). Improved stochastic modelling of shapes for content-based image retrieval. *IEEE Workshop on Content-based Access of Image and Video Libraries, CBAIVL'99*, (pp. 23-27).

Teague, M. R. (1980). Image analysis via the general theory of moments. *Journal of the Optical Society of America, 70*(8), 920–930. doi:10.1364/JOSA.70.000920

Wu, J. K., Lam, C. P., Mehtre, B. M., Gao, Y. J., & Narasimhalu, A. D. (1996). Content-based retrieval for trademark registration. *Multimedia Tools and Applications, 3*(3), 245–267. doi:10.1007/BF00393940

Zhang, D., & Lu, G. (2002). A comparative study on shape retrieval using Fourier descriptors with different shape signatures. *Signal Processing Image Communication, 17*(10), 825–848. doi:10.1016/S0923-5965(02)00084-X

Zhang, D., & Lu, G. (2003). A comparative study of curvature scale space and Fourier descriptors for shape-based image retrieval. *Journal of Visual Communication and Image Representation, 14*(1), 41–60. doi:10.1016/S1047-3203(03)00003-8

Zhang, D., & Lu, G. (2003). Evaluation of MPEG-7 shape descriptors against other shape descriptors. *Multimedia Systems, 9*(1), 15–30. doi:10.1007/s00530-002-0075-y

Section 2

Chapter 6
Discovering Semantics from Visual Information

Zhiyong Wang
University of Sydney, Australia

Dagan Feng
University of Sydney, Australia & Hong Kong Polytechnic University, China

ABSTRACT

Visual information has been immensely used in various domains such as web, education, health, and digital libraries, due to the advancements of computing technologies. Meanwhile, users realize that it has been more and more difficult to find desired visual content such as images. Though traditional content-based retrieval (CBR) systems allow users to access visual information through query-by-example with low level visual features (e.g. color, shape, and texture), the semantic gap is widely recognized as a hurdle for practical adoption of CBR systems. Wealthy visual information (e.g. user generated visual content) enables us to derive new knowledge at a large scale, which will significantly facilitate visual information management. Besides semantic concept detection, semantic relationship among concepts can also be explored in visual domain, other than traditional textual domain. Therefore, this chapter aims to provide an overview of the state-of-the-arts on discovering semantics in visual domain from two aspects, semantic concept detection and knowledge discovery from visual information at semantic level. For the first aspect, various aspects of visual information annotation are discussed, including content representation, machine learning based annotation methodologies, and widely used datasets. For the second aspect, a novel data driven based approach is introduced to discover semantic relevance among concepts in visual domain. Future research topics are also outlined.

DOI: 10.4018/978-1-61692-859-9.ch006

1. INTRODUCTION

In the last decades we have witnessed tremendous growth in visual information such as images and videos, due to the advancements of computing technologies. It has never been easier than today to take images through digital cameras or video shots through camcorders, ranging from personal collections to professional archives such as news. And the rapid development of the Web has further accelerated this process by allowing any users to publish or share their visual contents conveniently. There are about 3 billion images are hosted by Flickr[1] and about 12.7 billion videos were watched in a month by America Internet users only[2]. And millions of images are uploaded every day to popular photo sharing web sites like Flickr. Therefore, efficient access to such enormous amount of visual information has emerged as a challenging issue.

Since 1980s, visual information retrieval has been a very active research topic with the endeavor from two communities, database management and computer vision (Tamura & Yokoya, 1984) (Chang, Shi, & Yan, 1987) (Chang, Yan, Dimitroff, & Arndt, 1988). These two communities study image retrieval from different aspects, one being text or alphanumeric based and the other visual based, respectively. Unlike textual information which can be characterized in terms of its semantic primitives (i.e. terms), visual information lacks such primitives even with the state-of-the-art techniques in computer vision. Therefore, in order to leverage the success of relational database, visual information in general is manually annotated with textual descriptions for retrieval purpose. However, manual annotation suffers from the follow issues:

- Manual annotation is very time consuming and labor intensive, which is not scalable to the dramatically growing visual information.
- Manual annotation is subjectively dependent on annotators and not general for all the possible front-end users, especially for the users using different languages.
- It is very difficult and challenging to describe image content with only several keywords. As said a picture is worth a thousand words. Sometimes some aspects of image content such as texture are even beyond words.

In order to overcome these problems, it would be more ideal to characterize visual content with perceptual attributes (i.e. visual features) such as color, shape, texture, and motion. In the early 1990s, content based image retrieval (CBIR) was proposed to allow users to search for target visual information in terms of its true content represented with visual features by making use of techniques from image processing and computer vision domains. CBIR has been an interesting and promising research area for decades and many query strategies have been proposed, such as query by example (QBE) and query by sketch (Veltkamp & Tanase, 2000). As reviewed in (Gupta & Jain, 1997) (Idris & Panchanathan, 1997) (Loncaric, 1998) (Brunelli, Mich, & Modena, 1999) (Y. Rui, Huang, & Chang, 1999) (Smeulders, Worring, Santini, Gupta, & Jain, 2000) (Antani, Kasturi, & Jain, 2002) (D. Feng, Siu, & Zhang, 2003) (C. G. M. Snoek & Worring, 2005) (Datta, Li, & Wang, 2005) (Lew, Sebe, Djeraba, & Jain, 2006) (Y. Liu, Zhang, Lu, & Ma, 2007) (Datta, Joshi, Li, James, & Wang, 2008) (Ren, S. Singh, M. Singh, & Y. S. Zhu, 2009), most of works have focused on the following issues, feature extraction to characterize visual content, feature transformation including dimension reduction and feature selection to achieve compact and optimal representation, similarity measurement for efficient matching (Santini & Jain, 1999), high dimensional indexing for efficient search (Valle, Cord, & Philipp-Foliguet, 2008), and relevance feedback for interactive and personalized user experiences (X. S. Zhou & Huang, 2003).

In spite of the significant progress of content based retrieval (CBR) in many domains ranging from general images to medical images (Muller, Michoux, Bandon, & Geissbuhler, 2004), the semantic gap, which describes the discrepancy between the similarity measured in terms of semantic meaning of visual information and the similarity measured in terms of low level visual features, is widely recognized as a hurdle for practical adoption of CBR systems (Hauptmann, 2005) (Lew et al., 2006) (Datta et al., 2008). For example, given a query with a red *apple* image, a CBIR system may return many images which have nothing to do with *apple*. Related studies (Markkula & Sormunen, 2000) (Rodden, Basalaj, Sinclair, & Wood, 2001) have also confirmed this issue in visual information access with such low-level features and most of users still prefer to express their information needs in keywords. Similarly, Hughes et al. (Hughes, Wilkens, Wildemuth, & Marchionini, 2003) revealed that users preferred textual information to visual information when validating their search results in video retrieval. The semantic gap also results in the difficulty for users in interpreting the retrieval results and in making informed decision to refine their query. In addition, dealing with visual information by using low level features prevents the exploration of visual knowledge, since knowledge inference generally happens at the semantic level. As shown in Figure 1, visual information should be transformed from data to content, to semantics, and ultimately to knowledge. Scientific research has also concluded that 80% of human cognition is obtained from visual information (Bertoline, 1998). Hence, it has been desirable that visual information can be automatically labeled with a set of linguistic terms so that both computers and human beings can be brought to the same ground of visual perception and the semantic gap can be reduced, or eventually eliminated. In order to address the issue of the semantic gap, automatic annotation of visual information at the semantic level has emerged as an active research topic for the communities of multimedia computing, information retrieval, and machine learning.

Due to the nature of automatic image and video annotation, machine learning based classification approaches have been widely employed for such a task. Although images or videos can be assigned with

Figure 1. Data flow of discovering visual semantics. Note that the relationship among concepts is for illustration purpose only

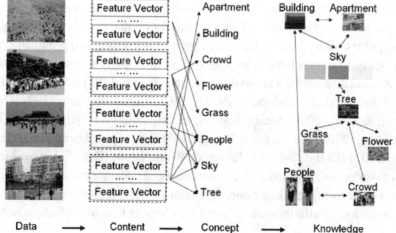

semantic labels by treating each concept (e.g. image category or object category) as a class or label and training a number of classifiers (Winn, Criminisi, & Minka, 2005) for the concepts, automatic annotation also leads to unique new challenges:

- Traditional classification approaches assume that one input will be exclusively assigned to one of the predefined classes. For example, in image classification domain, images will be classified into either *Indoor* or *Outdoor* (Payne & Singh, 2005), which is named multi-class classification. However, annotation allows one image or video to be associated with several related labels. For example, an image of *Opera House* could be labeled with *Outdoor*, *Opera House*, *Sydney*, *Scenery*, *Sightseeing*, and more. The correlation among the labels will definitely increase the learning difficulty of the classifiers, which imposes more challenges on machine learning methods.
- For some training samples, no correspondence between the concept and the specific image regions or objects is available. For example, when an image is labeled with *sky* in a training set, no information on which part is *sky* is provided.
- Annotation is supposed to be a task of a larger scale (e.g. much more labels or classes) and sufficient training samples should be available for learning purpose.

Great opportunities have also emerged while we are facing technical challenges imposed by the rapidly increased proliferation of visual information for efficient information access:

- It has been much more convenient to obtain a large number of training samples so as to achieve broad coverage. For example, some commercial search engines provide APIs (Application Programming Interface) for public users so that a large image repository with thousands of images can be systematically established. It is also possible to combine the results from several search engines or even write your own application to download images from the Web so that a much larger image repository can be created.
- An enormous amount of visual information is now accompanied with textual information (e.g. news photos with captions), which provides us valuable resources to solve the problem and even enables further discovery of visual knowledge. For example, in the Web, a given image can generally be interpreted with its surrounding text, on which most commercial search engines accomplish their search tasks for images, so that we can achieve the transformation from semantic concept to visual knowledge.

Due to the promising potential in discovering semantics in visual information, many researchers from various disciplines such as machine learning, multimedia data processing, information retrieval and knowledge engineering have collaboratively contributed to this area and significant progresses have been achieved in many domains ranging from consumer domains such as personal photos (Schreiber, Dubbeldam, Wielemaker, & Wielinga, 2001) to professional domains such as medical images (Luo, Fan, Gao, & Xu, 2004)(J. Yao, Antani, Long, Thoma, & Zhang, 2006)(Deselaers & Deserno, 2008).

In this chapter, we present an overview of the state of the art in discovering semantics from visual information by following the data flow of information transformation from data to knowledge as shown in Figure 1. In Visual Information Representation, we mainly explain visual information representation on two aspects, content descriptor and content representation. In Annotation Methodologies, we review the existing methods on automatic image and video annotation in four major categories. In Section 4, we report the recent development on deriving visual knowledge from annotated visual information. And in the last section, we conclude our observations on this topic and discuss its future trends.

VISUAL INFORMATION REPRESENTATION

Content Descriptor

Unlike textual information which can be characterized in terms of its semantic primitives (i.e. terms), visual information itself generally has to be characterized through visual features such as color, shape (e.g. object contour), texture (e.g. stripe pattern of a zebra), and motion, which are distinguishing primitive attributes of visual content. With rapid development and progress in content based retrieval and computer vision, a large number of visual descriptors have been proposed to efficiently characterize visual contents in the literature. And in general practice, multiple visual descriptors are combined to achieve better characterization by taking different aspects of a given visual content into account. However, utilizing which visual descriptors is dependent on specific applications (Lecce & Guerriero, 1999) and how to achieve optimal combination is also an open issue. Therefore, in this section, we only review several popular visual descriptors. Readers can refer to other surveys in the literature for more comprehensive details on visual descriptors (Idris & Panchanathan, 1997) (Loncaric, 1998) (Brunelli et al., 1999) (Y. Rui et al., 1999) (Smeulders et al., 2000) (Antani et al., 2002) (D. Feng et al., 2003) (C. G. M. Snoek & Worring, 2005) (Datta et al., 2005) (Lew et al., 2006) (Y. Liu et al., 2007) (Datta et al., 2008) (Ren et al., 2009). In order to have a standard and systematic solution for exchange various multimedia features, the Motion Picture Experts Group (MPEG) initiated MPEG-7 in 1996. MPEG-7, namely Multimedia Content Description Interface, is geared towards enhancing the data that describes the contexts and contents of multimedia information, the so-called meta-data. Many AudioVisual descriptors, such as Color Layout Descriptor and Edge Histogram Descriptor, have also been specified in MPEG-7(B. Manjunath, Salembier, & Sikora, 2002).

Color provides a strong cue in human perception and has been the most widely used visual feature in representing visual content. In general, they are two issues in dealing with color, color space and color descriptor. Color space defines a coordinate system to describe each color. The most popular color space is RGB. However, RGB color space is not perceptual uniform, which leads to the fact that the similarity between two colors in color space does not comply with the distance perceived by human beings. Therefore, many other color spaces and variant tri-tuple representations have been proposed such as HSV. However, choosing which color space is still application dependent. The most popular color descriptor is color histogram proposed by Swain and Ballard (Swain & Ballard, 1991). Basically, color histogram characterizes the distribution (i.e. percentage) of each color in a given image and results in a N-dimension feature vector $[f_1, f_2, ..., f_N]$, where N is the number of colors. In general practice, N is set to a value ranging from tens (e.g. 64) to hundreds (e.g. 512) through a proper quantization method, since higher dimension (i.e. more colors) does not always guarantee more effective characterization though leading to increased computational complexity. However, since color histogram does not include spatial information, an image with red balloon and an image with many small red dots may have the same color histogram. Many other color descriptors were developed, such as color coherence vector (CCV) (Pass & Zabih, 1999), color correlogram (Huang, Kumar, Mitra, Zhu, & Zabih, 1999), and color anglogram

(Tao & Grosky, 2001). Color constancy is also addressed in order to eliminate the effects of illumination change on color values (Finlayson, Funt, & Barnard, 1995).

Shape features are generally used to describe objects and have a long history in computer vision and pattern recognition due to tremendous efforts on many object recognition applications. In 1970s, Dudani et al.(Dudani, Breeding, & McGhee, 1977) proposed to identify aircraft with moment invariants (Hu, 1962). Existing shape features can be categorized into either boundary based (e.g. Fourier Descriptor (Persoon & Fu, 1997)) or region-based methods (e.g. moments invariants (Hu, 1962) and its many variants). Since most of shape descriptors are only applicable to well segmented objects by representing object contours or regions, some approaches were proposed to transform original images and to perform feature extraction on the transformed data so as to avoid erroneous object segmentation. Recently, Oliva and Torralba (Oliva & Torralba, 2001) proposed to model the shape of the scene with the spatial envelope to avoid segmentation and defined a very low dimensional representation of the scene in terms of perceptual attributes including naturalness, openness, roughness, expansion, and ruggedness, which was successfully utilized to identify some semantic categories such as streets, highways, and coasts. A good review on shape content analysis can be found in (Loncaric, 1998).

Texture is used to describe a visual pattern defined through visual primitive and structure among primitives, though there is no commonly agreed definition on what texture is. And various texture descriptors have been investigated through exploring either structural properties or statistical properties of visual patterns. Using gray level co-occurrence matrices (GLCM) as texture features was first proposed by Haralick et al (Haralick, Shanmugam, & Dinstein, 1973) and has become one of the most well known and widely used. And many texture descriptors can be derived through GLCM, such as energy, entropy, contrast, homogeneity, and correlation. Based on psychological studies on human perception on texture, Tamura (Tamura, Mori, & Yamawaki, 1978) designed a set of descriptors including coarseness, contrast, directionality, linelikeness, regularity, and roughness. Gabor feature (B. S. Manjunath & Ma, 1996) obtained through Gabor filters for texture has demonstrated very good performance in content based image retrieval. LBP (Local Binary Pattern) (Ojala, Pietikinen, & Harwood, 1996) (Ojala, Pietikainen, & Maenpaa, 2002) is also a very effective texture descriptor exploring texture spectrum formed by local 3x3 neighborhood patterns.

The recently emerged SIFT (Scale Invariant Feature Transform) descriptor (Lowe, 2004) in computer vision domain has attracted a lot of attentions in both object recognition and image annotation, since it is robust to scale, translation, and orientation. Firstly, key points as shown in Figure 2 will be identified in an image through Harris affine detector (Mikolajczyk & Schmid, 2002). Then a histogram of gradient locations and orientations is built for each key point. Therefore, SIFT descriptor, a 128-dimensional vector of an affine invariant region identified by each key points, has been widely used in object recognition and categorization due to its superior performance to others in related literature (Mikolajczyk & Schmid, 2003). Very often an image can have thousands of key points, which is problematic in computational complexity. Therefore, some approaches were proposed to optimize SIFT descriptors. For example, PCA-SIFT was proposed to create a compact SIFT descriptor (i.e. lower dimension) (Ke & Sukthankar, 2004) and Pavel et al. proposed a matching tree based method to eliminate noisy key points in object recognition(Pavel, Wang, & Feng, 2009) as shown in Figure 2(b).

A video is a sequence of frames and can be characterized with the above visual features by treating each frame as an image. Due to the redundancy between frames, videos are often firstly partitioned into shots (i.e. a sequence of frames recorded continuously and representing a continuous action in time or space) and a number of key frames (i.e. representative frames) are chosen for each shot to reduce com-

Figure 2. Illustration of SIFT descriptor. (a) unfiltered key points; (b) filtered key points

putational complexity. Meanwhile, temporal attributes such as motion are unique for videos. In (Ngo, Zhang, Chin, & Pong, 2000), Ngo et al. proposed a temporal slice based descriptor to characterize various types of motion pattern (e.g. panning and tilting). As reviewed in (Brunelli et al., 1999) (C. G. M. Snoek & Worring, 2005) (Ren et al., 2009), many spatial-temporal features (e.g. motion trajectory) have been proposed to characterize such an aspect of videos. In (Basharat, Zhai, & Shah, 2008), spatial-temporal volumes were proposed to characterize video contents. In order to achieve computational efficiency, some features were even obtained from compressed domain (Yeo, Ahammad, Ramchandran, & Sastry, 2008). Acoustic features from audio modality are also very useful in characterizing video contents such as highlights in sports videos. Therefore, various multi-modal features and fusion schemes have been developed(C. G. M. Snoek & Worring, 2005). And recently, PicSOM, a self-organizing map (SOM) based content based information retrieval framework was employed to infer semantics by associating visual aural descriptors with textual features(Sjoberg, Laaksonen, Honkela, & Polla, 2008).

Content Representation

The abovementioned visual descriptors can be directly applied to the whole piece of visual information and serve as a global descriptor. On the other hand, a descriptor characterizes visual information partially in terms of space or time is named a local descriptor. The diversity of information needs from different users demands finer granularity (e.g. objects and regions) of content representation. Existing content representation approaches can be grouped into two categories, flat vector based and structure based. Besides the global descriptor based representation, approaches of the former category generally partition an image or keyframe into regions (shown in Figure 3) and extract visual descriptors for each region so that an image or video is represented with a collection of feature vectors. Most of existing approaches simply concatenate those feature vectors into a super feature vector and the bag of visual words model has recently attracted a lot of attention in visual information annotation. Therefore, only bag of visual words based approaches are introduced for the flat vector based category.

Figure 3. Illustration of region based and block based partitions. (a) segmentation based partition; (b) fixed size block based partition

Bag of Visual Words Based Representation

The Bag of words model is a classical representation for textual documents by assuming that positions of words in a document is not important for document content. With such a model, great success has been achieved in many natural language processing applications such as document classification and information retrieval (Manning, Raghavan, & Schtze, 2008), though the assumption is not true at all. Denote a collection of documents $D = \{d_i | i = 1, 2, ..., m\}$ and a vocabulary $V = \{w_i | i = 1, 2, ..., n\}$. Using the bag of words model, document d_i will be represented with a vector $F_i = [f_{i,j} | j = 1; 2; ..., n]$, where $f_{i,j}$ is the statistics of word w_j in the document d_i. In general, $f_{i,j}$ will be calculated with the popular TF-IDF equation such as one implementation shown in Equation 1, where TF (Term Frequency) stands for how frequently a term appears in a document and IDF (Inverse Document Frequency) stands for how popular the term is in the given collection of documents:

$$f_{i,j} = tf_{i,j} * idf_j = tf_{i,j} * \log \frac{m}{df_j}$$

(1)

where df_j denotes the number of documents including keyword w_j.

Csurak et al. firstly introduced this idea into object recognition by constructing a visual codebook from SIFT descriptors and represent an image with those visual keywords (Csurka, Dance, Fan, Willamowski, & Bray, 2004), which is dubbed as Bag of Visual Words model. And many variants were also proposed lately (Sivic, Russell, Efros, Zisserman, & Freeman, 2005) (Fei-Fei & Perona, 2005). In order to adopt such a model, two issues should be resolved, selecting suitable representation primitives and clustering those primitives. Most of the existing annotation approaches obtain a visual vocabulary through traditional clustering such as *k*-means and SOM.

Besides the SIFT descriptors, it would be more desirable to treat objects in an image as primitives. However, due to the limits of the state-of-the-art in computer vision, image segmentation at object level in a general context is still an open issue. Region level representation is an alternative, though it is still very challenging to achieve a reasonable segmentation (as show in Figure 3(a) which is obtained through method proposed in (Ma & Manjunath, 2000)). In addition, it was demonstrated that region based segmentation cannot always achieve better performance than fixed partition (e.g. 5x5 partition shown in Figure 3(b) (Barnard, Duygulu, Guru, Gabbur, & Forsyth, 2003) (Z. Wang, Feng, & Chi, 2004). Therefore, most of the recent research works resort to fixed partition rather than regions obtained through error-prone segmentation, particularly in video annotation. However, it is still problematic in selecting an optimal partition resolution (i.e. how many partitions). In order to solve this issue, Wu et al. proposed to conduct a multilayer partition (Wu, Hu, Li, Yu, & Hua, 2009).

As mentioned at the beginning of this section, the Bag of Words model ignores the position information of words appearing in a document. Similarly, the bag of visual words model ignores spatial information in the feature vector of a given image. Therefore, some researchers have worked on this issue recently. In (Savarese, Winn, & Criminisi, 2006), Savarese et al. proposed to use correlograms to capture spatial information. And a constellation of bags of words through a hierarchical model was proposed for human action recognition (Niebles & Fei-Fei, 2007). In (Lazebnik, Schmid, & Ponce, 2006), Lazebnik et al. proposed a spatial pyramid partition to balance the partition granularity and the number of partitions.

Structural Representation

Besides the flat vector based representation, structural representation provides more flexibility in characterizing visual content. In (Salembier & Garrido, 2000), a binary tree was proposed for image segmentation and retrieval. Wang et al. proposed to represent image content in tree structures and discover semantic classes of images by using Structured Self-Organizing Map (SD-SOM) (Z. Wang, Hargenbuchner, Tsoi, Cho, & Chi, 2002). Various tree representation schemes such as the binary tree shown in Figure 4 were evaluated in (Z. Wang et al., 2004), which also demonstrated that region based tree structure could also increase the learning difficulty due to the variant structures. Similarly, a tree structure based shape representation shown in Figure 5 was proposed in (Zhiyong Wang & Feng, 2002) for object classification.

Since videos have underlying editing and logical structure which is analogous to textual documents, it is straightforward to adopt some structural representation such as key frame level, shot level, object level, and scene level. In (Xie, Chang, Divakaran, & Sun, 2003), Xie et al. proposed a hierarchical structure to represent videos. However, most of the existing annotation approaches still focus on key frame level based representation.

Note that it is very challenging to process structured based representation, although structural representation is very flexible and several neural network models (such as Backpropagation through Structure (Frasconi, Gori, & Sperduti, 1998) and SD-SOM (Hagenbuchner, Sperduti, & Tsoi, 2003)) were proposed for such data structures.

Figure 4. Illustration of structural representation for an image

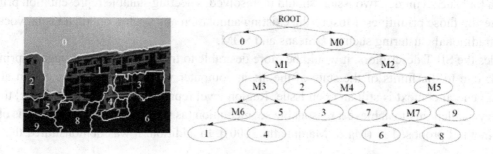

Figure 5. Illustration of structural representation for a shape. (a) original shape; (b)-(d) smoothed shape with different δ values, 10, 15, and 20, respectively; (e) constructed tree representation corresponding to the importance of each segment during the smoothing evolution

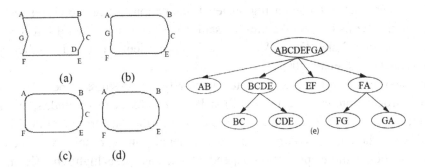

ANNOTATION METHODOLOGIES

A significant number of methods have been proposed for automatic image annotation, which can be generally classified into four categories, namely multi-class classification based, multi-label classification based, dual-modality modeling based, and knowledge based. The multi-class classification based methods assume that each semantic concept corresponds to a class of a pattern recognition problem and independent to each other. Hence, a corresponding classifier will be trained through training datasets for each class. Different with the methods of the first category where each training sample is exclusively associated with one class during the training process, the multi-label classification based methods learn the association between training samples and multiple concepts (i.e. class labels). By treating visual and semantic aspects as two aspects of one piece of information, the methods of the third category are proposed to model such a dual-modal attribute. And knowledge based methods aim to integrate external knowledge into annotation process, since interpreting visual information heavily relies on knowledge accumulated by individual users.

Multi-Class Classification Based Methods

Due to the nature of image annotation, many traditional pattern classification techniques have been widely employed for such a task. For example, Campbell et al. proposed to label image regions with semantic terms (e.g sky, vegetation, and road) by using a three-layer neural network (Campbell, Mackeown, Thomas, & Troscianko, 1997). Vailaya et al. proposed to classify vacation images hierarchically (e.g. City vs. Landscape, and Mountain vs. Coast) with a Bayesian approach (Vailaya, Figueiredo, Jain, & Zhang, 2001). Li and Wang proposed to model the semantic concepts of images with 2D Multi-resolution Hidden Markov Models (MHMMs) and semantic terms were selected from each image category to annotate images (J. Li & Wang, 2003). Support Vector Machine has also been widely used in concept detection due to its superior classification performance (Goh, Li, & Chang, 2005) (Gao, Fan, Xue, & Jain, 2006) (Yang & Dong, 2006). In order to mimic the success of language model in textual information retrieval and classification, various visual language models were also proposed by treating an image as a set of ordered visual words to capture the co-occurrence of visual words. In (Wu, Li, Li, Ma, & Yu, 2007), depending on how the spatial proximity of local visual words is considered, three types of language models were utilized, including unigram, bigram and trigram. In (Tirilly, Claveau, & Gros, 2008), an image is described as visual sentences consisting of visual words and geometric properties of keypoints and the Probabilistic Latent Semantic Analysis (PLSA) were adopted to eliminate useless visual words. Meanwhile, many approaches focus on region level annotation. Since the correspondence between regions and annotation terms lacks in the training samples, this issue is generally solved through either multiple instance learning (Yang, Dong, & Fotouhi, 2005) or identifying region saliency (Tang, Hare, & Lewis, 2006) (Fu, Chi, & Feng, 2009).

Classifying videos in terms of semantic content generally includes three types of applications, genre classification, event detection, and object recognition. Popular video genres include sports, news, cartoon, commercials, music, etc. The first attempt to genre classification was presented in (Fischer, Lienhart, & Effelsberg, 1995), where news, commercial, cartoon, tennis, and car racing were considered. Event and object classification is more application dependent, such as sports highlights (Xiong, Radhakrish-nan, Divakaran, & Huang, 2005), hunts in wildlife videos (Haering, Qian, & Sezan, 2000), activities in movies (Ke, Sukthankar, & Hebert, 2007) (Laptev, Marszalek, Schmid, & Rozenfeld, 2008). Due to the temporal properties, video classification adopts many learning algorithms from speech processing domain. For example, in (Huang, Liu, Wang, Chen, & Wong, 1999) Hidden Markov Model (HMM) was utilized for video classification and in (Xiong et al., 2005) Coupled Hidden Markov Model was adopted to fuse audio and visual features for sports highlight detection.

However, most of these multi-class approaches adopt a single label paradigm where an image or video is exclusively labeled with one class according to the output of the classifier. Therefore, in the regime of image and video annotation, these approaches suffer from the following issues:

- selecting a large set of suitable labels. For example, selecting *Indoor*, *Outdoor*, and *Scenery* as labels will impose difficulties to classifiers, since most *Scenery* images are definitely of *Outdoor* category. Therefore, the classes to be investigated have to be selected either empirically or based on specific application domains. In (Vailaya et al., 2001), a hierarchy of a small number of labels (e.g. *City* vs. *Landscape*) was established to organize vacation images. However, how to construct a hierarchy of a large number of labels is another open issue, though ontology can aid this process in some applications (Naphade et al., 2006);
- obtaining training data in a large quantity. Since images are of rich contents and belong to multiple classes, it is challenging to manually label images with only one label;
- capturing correlation among labels, since one label could provide useful hints about the others.

In order to solve the insufficiency of the training data, semi-supervised learning algorithms were applied to leverage a large amount of unlabeled data to boost classification accuracy (Zhu, 2008). In (M. Wang et al., 2006) (M. Wang, Hua, Mei, et al., 2009), a non-parametric based semi-supervised learning algorithm was proposed for video annotation, which is based on kernel density estimation approach.

3.2. Multi-Label Classification Based Methods

Due to the above mentioned issues of multi-class classification based methods, multi-label classification methods have been investigated for image annotation so that a training instance can be associated with multiple labels. Multi-label classification based methods have been demanded by many modern applications such as document classification (Ghamrawi & McCallum, 2005) (Ueda & Saito, 2003).

Tsoumakas et al. categorized the approaches of multi-label classification into two categories, problem transformation methods and algorithm adaptation methods (Tsoumakas & Katakis, 2007). The former extend traditional classification approaches by transforming multi-label classification problems either into one or more single-label classification or regression problems (Boutell, Luo, Shen, & Brown, 2004) (J. Li &Wang, 2006). For example, Boutell et al. investigated multi-label scene classification by incorporating multi-label information for cross-training using Support Vector Machines (SVM) (Boutell et al., 2004). And Carneiro et al. proposed to model each concept with hierarchical GMM clustering (Carneiro, Chan, Moreno, & Vasconcelos, 2007). However, these methods did not take the mixture characteristics into account explicitly. The latter extend specific learning algorithms to handle multi-labeled data directly (Ueda & Saito, 2003) (Ghamrawi & McCallum, 2005) (Qi et al., 2007) (M. Wang, Zhou, & Chua, 2008) (M.-L. Zhang & Zhou, 2007) by exploiting the co-occurrence of labels, which assumes that training dataset provides sufficient coverage on the co-occurrence of labels. These methods share the same motivation with Coherent Language Model (R. Jin, Chai, & Si, 2004) and correlated Label Propagation (Kang, Jin, & Sukthankar, 2006) which explores the concept correlation (X. Zhou, Wang, Zhang, Zhang, & Shi, 2007).

Dual-Modality Modeling Based Methods

Rather than be annotated with predefined semantic classes, more and more images are accompanied with abundant textual information which can be utilized to represent semantic content of images. For example, image archives in museums have been well annotated, and images in web pages are explained by their surrounding text on which most commercial search engines currently rely. In addition, joint visual-text modeling is helpful for automatic retrieval of multimedia documents (Iyengar et al., 2005). Therefore, many approaches also consider image annotation as a problem of associating a bag of words with images by exploiting the co-occurrence of two modalities, visual attributes and textual attributes, of images. The challenge lies in how to model the association between these two modalities.

The co-occurrence of such two modalities was first investigated by Mori et al. (Mori, Takahashi, & Oka, 1999). The method looked at the co-occurrence of annotation words and image features, so that when an unseen image is presented, annotation can be automatically generated based on visual features and co-occurrence knowledge. In (Pan, Yang, Duygulu, & Faloutsost, 2004), four types of correlation schemes were employed to discover correlations between image features and keywords. LSA (latent semantic analysis) and PLSA (probabilistic LSA) were also proposed for image annotation by following similar motivations (Monay & Gatica-Perez, 2003) (Monay & Gatica-Perez, 2004). In (Barnard, Duygulu, Freitas, et al., 2003), a translation model was proposed to translate a vocabulary of image blobs to a vocabulary of linguistic terms based on the joint probability of image blobs and terms. Based on cross-lingual information retrieval, a cross-media relevance model (CMRM) was proposed to allow for both image annotation and retrieval (Jeon, Lavrenko, & Manmatha, 2003). In (Lavrenko, Manmatha, & Jeon, 2003), a continuous relevance model (CRM), a continuous version of CMRM, was proposed to handle continuous visual features, which avoided the quantization step adopted in other relevance models. In (Blei & Jordan, 2003), a correspondence LDA (Latent Dirichlet Allocation) model was proposed to extend the generative nature of LDA and apply correspondence constraints to image annotation. Based on these works, some variant approaches have also been proposed for image annotation and retrieval. Feng et al. (S. L. Feng, Manmatha, & Lavrenko, 2004) utilized Bernoulli relevance model. Zhang et al. proposed a probabilistic semantic model in which the visual features are associated with semantic terms through a hidden layer (R. Zhang, Zhang, Li, Ma, & Zhang, 2005). In (J. Liu et al., 2007), a dual cross-media relevance model was proposed for image annotation by exchanging the role of word and images. In summary, these approaches attempted to estimate the joint probability of $P(W, I)$ from different perspectives, where W denotes the annotation terms, and I denotes the representation of visual information.

Recently, graph-based approaches have been widely utilized to efficiently solve various machine learning problems and can be also applied to image and video annotation. By viewing individual images/videos and words as vertices and relationship among them as edges, annotation tasks can be tackled with many graph based schemes. In (Pan, Yang, Faloutsos, & Duygulu, 2004), GCap (Graph-based Captioning) approach was proposed to annotate images, where images, annotations, and regions were represented as three types of vertices, and linked together according to their known association into one graph. However, how to optimally weight these vertices from different modalities in one graph is challenging. In addition, the relationship among annotated keywords was not taken into account. In (Bailloeul, Zhu, & Xu, 2008), an enhanced GCap (EGCap) was proposed by taking the advantage of the canonical correlation analysis technique to shorten the semantic gap in the image space and define a new metric in the text space to correlate annotations. In (J. Liu, Li, Ma, Liu, & Lu, 2006), a similarity graph was constructed so that manifold learning was adopted to propagate the labels of labeled data into unlabeled data through the similarity graph. Instead of using a single graph, Optimized Multi-Graph-based Semi-supervised Learning (OMG-SSL) was proposed to simultaneously tackle insufficiency of training data and the curse of high dimensionality (M. Wang, Hua, Yuan, & Rong Dai, 2007) (M. Wang, Hua, Hong, et al., 2009). OMG-SSL integrates multiple graphs into a regularization and optimization framework to sufficiently explore their complementary nature.

In order to fully utilize the textual information accompanying visual information, some researchers from other domains such as Data Mining, Web Search and Natural Language Processing also work on this topic. In (Moxley, Mei, Hua, Ma, & Manjunath, 2008), Moxley et al. proposed to mine annotation terms from the speech transcripts of videos with similar visual contents. Similarly, Velivelli and Huang proposed to obtain semantic terms from speech transcripts for a video by using Maximum Entropy approach (Velivelli & Huang, 2006). In (Cai, He, Wen, & Ma, 2004) Cai et al. tried to achieve meaningful segmentation of web pages by utilizing their visual presentation so that more accurate surrounding text can be obtained for web images. And some researchers proposed to utilize the search results and accompanying textual information for web image annotation (X. Rui, Yu, Wang, & Li, 2007) (X.-J. Wang, Zhang, Li, & Ma, 2008). And in (Deschacht & Moens, 2007), Deschacht and Moens tried to identify salient terms for a given image by parsing captions syntactically. In (Ah-Pine et al., 2009), trans-media similarity is defined by integrating the similarities of mono-modality so that image annotation problem can be solved by evaluating the similarity between texts and images, which makes the proposed method extensible to any information modality.

Knowledge Based Methods

Ontology, as a representation of knowledge, has been widely used to facilitate many classification problems such as image classification (Benitez & Chang, 2003) (Fu, Chi, Feng, & Song, 2004). In general, an ontology defines a specification of a conceptualization (Antoniou & Harmelen, 2008) and contains concepts and their relationships and rules. Inspired by the methods exploring the semantic relationship among concepts, some researchers resorted to utilizing existing ontologies to derive semantic correlation among concepts, rather than explore a relatively small dataset. One of the first attempts for image annotation was made for describing photographs of apes by Schreiber et al. in 2001 (Schreiber et al., 2001). In 2002, Hyvonen et al. developed an ontology for describing graduation photographs at the University of Helsinki. In (Hollink, Little, & Hunter, 2005), Hollink et al. reported MPEG-7 based semantic inference to annotate medical images. Hoogs et al. (Hoogs, Rittscher, Stein, & Schmiederer, 2003) also proposed to perform video annotation by enriching WordNet with visual attributes. And in (Bertini, Bimbo, & Torniai, 2006), MPEG-7 descriptors were also adapted to a multimedia ontology for video annotation. General ontology WordNet (Fellbaum, 1998) is the most popular one to derive correlation among concepts for broad domains (Y. Jin, Khan, Wang, & Awad, 2005) (Shi, Chua, Lee, & Gao, 2006) (C. G. M. Snoek et al., 2007) (Fan, Luo, Gao, & Jain, 2007). Recently, in order to facilitate the research progress on multimedia annotation, a multimedia ontology, LSCOM (Large-Scale Concept Ontology for Multimedia) (Naphade et al., 2006), has been recently manually defined to annotate multimedia content (Zha, Mei, Wang, & Hua, 2007) (C. G. M. Snoek et al., 2007).

DATASETS FOR ANNOTATION

Datasets with ground truth information provide inputs for learning. In addition, in order to benchmark the progress in automatic annotation on visual content, it is essential to have standards datasets. There are four types of datasets, datasets from computer vision domain, datasets from image retrieval domain, datasets from various evaluation forums, and datasets collected from the Web.

As mentioned in Section 1, automatic annotation has a close tie with image/scene classification, object recognition, and content based retrieval, some standards datasets in these areas have been used for annotation. Oliva and Torralba utilized a dataset of 2688 images from 8 categories (e.g. coasts, forest, mountain, open country, highway, inside of cities, tall buildings, and streets) for scene classification (Oliva & Torralba, 2001). The dataset used for scene retrieval (Vogel & Schiele, 2004) consists of 702 natural scenes from 6 categories. Microsoft Research Cambridge dataset consists of 35 categories (Winn et al., 2005) and the dataset from the University of Washington contains 21 categories of images[3]. However, these datasets are generally of a small number of categories.

Corel dataset contains images of which each is associated with several linguistic terms and has been widely used for both content based image retrieval and image classification (J. Li & Wang, 2003). In (Duygulu, Barnard, Freitas, & Forsyth, 2002) (Barnard, Duygulu, Freitas, et al., 2003), 5000 Corel images with 374 distinct keywords were used for image annotation, among which 4500 images were used for training and 500 images for testing. Some datasets provide ground truth information on image region level. Carbonetto et al. (Carbonetto, Freitas, & Barnard, 2004) created a dataset with 55 keywords corresponding to image regions by using part of Corel dataset. Barnard et al. (Barnard et al., 2008) created a dataset by manually labeling 1014 segmented images with 1297 keywords including two special keywords unknown and background. However, it is argued in (Muller, Marchand-Maillet, & Pun, 2002) that Corel dataset may not be suitable for studying image annotation and retrieval. LotusHill dataset (B. Yao, Yang, & Zhu, 2007) provides 50000 labeled and segmented images.

Therefore, many forums have been set up to create standardized datasets. TRECVID[4] is such a major forum. In 2001, the National Institute of Standards and Technology (NIST) started the TREC Video Track (i.e. TRECVID) to progress in content based video retrieval through an open evaluation. For example, TRECVID 2005 dataset contains keyframes over 60000 shots from about 85 hours international broadcast news videos and LSCOM (Naphade et al., 2006) has been developed as a vocabulary of more than

1000 concepts for broadcast videos. MediaMill challenge concept data (C. G. Snoek, Worring, Gemert, Geusebroek, & Smeulders, 2006) also defined an annotation corpus for the TRECVID 2005 video collection. There are also some similar forums such as ImageCLEF[5] and PASCAL[6].

In order to create a large scale ground truth datasets for annotation, some research groups obtain ground truth data in a collaborative way. Russell et al. at MIT developed an on-line annotation application LabelMe aimed to collecting keywords describing image regions for research on object recognition (Russell, Torralba, Murphy, & Freeman, 2008). Users are allowed to specify the region areas by clicking through a number of polygons and to enter keywords in an uncontrolled manner. A verification step by the database administrator will be carried out to improve the quality of data collected. And Google Image Labeler utilizes ESP (Extra Sensory Perception) games developed by von Ahn and Dabbish (Ahn & Dabbish, 2004)(Ahn, Liu, & Blum, 2006), though only a small portion of the dataset (i.e. 30000 images (B. Yao et al., 2007)) is available for public access. Meanwhile, these commercial search engines provide APIs for public users to access a small number of images (e.g. 1000) for each query, so that various datasets can be created conveniently, though there is a concern on the data quality returned by those search engines. Fei-Fei et al. created Caltech101 dataset of 101 categories by using Google Image Search engine (Fei-Fei, Fergus, & Perona, 2004). In order to increase the diversity of the dataset, a new dataset Caltech256 has also been available (Griffin, Holub, & Perona, 2007). And Torralba et al. performed object and scene recognition by using 80 million tiny images obtained from the Web (Torralba, Fergus, & Freeman, 2008). The more recent efforts on images are MSRA-MM from Microsoft Research Asia (M.Wang, Yang, & Hua, 2009) and ImageNet from the Vision Lab of Princeton University (Deng et al., 2009). MSRA-MM is the dataset created by Microsoft Research Asia, which contains 65443 images and 10277 videos collected from Microsoft Live Search. ImageNet is a large scale database established by collecting web images for synsets obtained from WordNet. Currently, it is the largest dataset for object recognition with 3.2 million clean images (i.e. irrelevant images removed manually) for 5247 synsets.

Cambridge-driving Labeled Video Database (CamVid) (Brostow, Fauqueura, & Cipolla, 2009) is the first collection of videos with object class semantic labels. Such dataset provides ground truth labels that associate each pixel with one of 32 semantic classes.

SEMANTIC RELEVANCE AMONG CONCEPTS IN VISUAL DOMAIN

Exploring semantic relevance between concepts has been indispensable in the natural language processing domain (Bollegala, Matsuo, & Ishizuka, 2007) and played an important role in many applications such as language modeling and information retrieval (Y. Li, Bandar, & McLean, 2003). For example, concept relevance has been utilized to improve the relevance of the search in information retrieval through query expansion (Mitra, Singhal, & Buckley, 1998). Therefore, it is expected that many tasks such as visual information annotation and visual information retrieval can be better conducted, if such relevance information can be effectively utilized. It is also worthwhile to explore visual semantic relevance automatically since semantic relevance between concepts evolves over time and across domains (Bollegala et al., 2007), although semantic relevance information can be directly borrowed from that of the natural language processing domain and LSCOM (Large Scale Concept Ontology for Multimedia) (Naphade et al., 2006) has been manually created. In addition, three of the most critical sources of knowledge are visual, audio and textual information. Scientific research has got the conclusion that 80% of human cognition is obtained from visual information (Bertoline, 1998). As a result, learning from visual data would be a helpful step to achieve artificial intelligence. Intuitively, visual similarity could imply semantic relevance to some degree. As a result, measuring high-level concept relevance in visual domain is gaining more and more focus recently, which could be further applied to natural language processing (Inkpen & Desilets, 2005) and information retrieval (Leslie, Chua, & Ramesh, 2007) (Varelas, Voutsakis, Raftopoulou, Petrakis, & Milios, 2005).

Benitez and Chang proposed to extract semantic knowledge from annotated images by clustering images with visual features (Benitez & Chang, 2002a) (Benitez & Chang, 2002b). Taking both visual attributes and existing knowledge base WordNet into account, Hoogs et al. (Hoogs et al., 2003) established an enhanced knowledge base for video annotation, since concepts included in WordNet are not always visually meaningful. In (Hollink & Worring, 2005) Hollink and Morring further extended this idea by combining two existing knowledge corpora, WordNet and MPEG-7 to build a visual ontology. Koskela et al. (Koskela, Smeaton, & Laaksonen, 2007) proposed a clustering-based framework to analyze concept similarity by modeling semantic concepts with cluster histograms. They also investigated various methods for assessing concept similarity by accounting for different information sources such as semantic network WordNet. Their experiments were conducted with TRECVID 2005 data set and the concepts defined in LSCOM. However, there is information loss while visual feature vectors were quantized to build a discrete codebook of clusters by through clustering (e.g. k-means and Self-Organizing Map (SOM)). In addition, clustering was conducted on the images of all the concepts, which makes their method not scalable to a large number of concepts.

In order to harvest the abundant visual information in the Web, it has been emerging to investigate this issue in a much broader domain, rather than small and domain specific datasets. Wu et al. (Wu, Hua, Yu, Ma, & Li, 2008) proposed to measure concept similarity by utilizing a visual language model (VLM) to represent visual characteristics of a concept. Since images used for experiments were collected from the photo sharing website Flickr, the proposed similarity method was coined as Flickr Distance. Wang et al. (Z. Wang, Guan, Wang, & Feng, 2008) proposed to represent each concept through a Gaussian Mixture Model (GMM) on a continuous visual feature space so as to avoid information loss in clustering. As shown in Figure 6, sample images of each concept will be clustered with a GMM model and the relevance between each concept pair will be measured in terms of the distance between two GMMs. It has been demonstrated that the concept relationship discovered through the GMM framework complies well with human cognition. It is also observed that removing noisy samples can benefit concept modeling (Guan, Wang, Tian, & Feng, 2009). As shown in Figure 7, a concept hierarchical tree (right tree)

Figure 6. Diagram of the GMM based concept relevance discovery

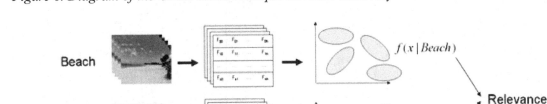

constructed from noise pruned dataset complies better with human cognition than from original noisy dataset. For example, *Sky*, *Weather*, and *Airplane* which closely related in the right figure are dispersed in the left figure.

SUMMARY

In this chapter, we discuss the necessity, challenges, and potentials of discovering semantics from visual content by reviewing the evolution of visual information retrieval from traditional relational database supported systems, to content based systems, and to automatic annotation based systems. Based on such an account, the key aspects of automatic annotation for semantics discovery are reviewed, including content representation, annotation methodologies, and annotation datasets. We also introduce techniques exploring visual knowledge from large scale visual content repositories, which is one step further than semantic annotation.

Empowered with wealthy visual resources and advanced machine learning techniques, we believe that research on discovering semantics from visual information is promising; particularly, the following three aspects will play an essential role in the future research of this topic. Firstly, appropriate content representation for annotation is still highly demanded, though much success has been achieved. In particular, most of the current approaches simplified video annotation with key frame annotation and temporal attributes were not well exploited, which constrains the exploration of video content at a higher

Figure 7. Concept trees obtained on 38 LSCOM concepts without (left tree) and with (right tree) dataset pruning, respectively

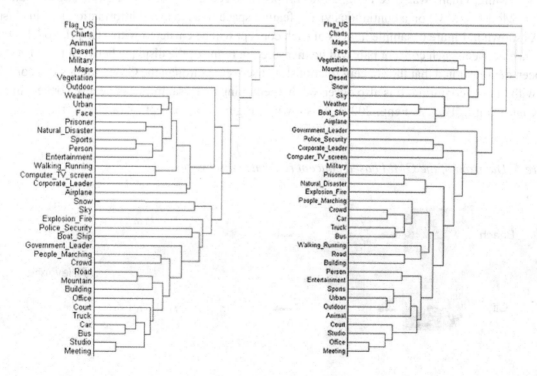

semantic level. It is anticipated that structural information derived from temporal domain is very useful for such a purpose. In addition, how to fuse different descriptors adaptively also remains challenging.

Secondly, the increasing proliferation of visual content available in the Web provides a great opportunity to perform semantic discovery in an ever larger scale. Therefore, it is essential to focus on scalable approaches and how to efficiently utilize such contents which are very noisy, compared with relatively small and closed datasets. In (Nister & Stewenius, 2006), a scalable vocabulary tree was constructed for efficient access of millions of images represented with bag of visual words. And Wang et al. proposed a scalable Markov model-based method for image annotation (C. Wang, Zhang, & Zhang, 2008). Noise pruning was also recently addressed in measuring the semantic relatedness from web images (Guan et al., 2009).

Lastly, the discovery process could be more user-centric, since users are the front end consumers of visual information. As a result, semantics information related to user experiences is also important, such as affective aspects (Hanjalic & Xu, 2005) and aesthetics (Dorai & Venkatesh, 2001). And how to identify a reasonable number of truly related concepts for users and to meet the dynamic preferences of users will become critical, when more and more concepts can be easily tagged to visual content. Otherwise, users will be flooded with information.

ACKNOWLEDGMENT

The work presented in this chapter is partially supported by the grants from ARC and Hong Kong Polytechnic University.

REFERENCES

Ah-Pine, J., Bressan, M., Clinchant, S., Csurka, G., Hoppenot, Y., & Renders, J.-M. (2009). Crossing textual and visual content in different application scenarios. *Multimedia Tools and Applications, 42,* 31–56. doi:10.1007/s11042-008-0246-8

Antani, S., Kasturi, R., & Jain, R. (2002). A survey on the use of pattern recognition methods for abstraction, indexing and retrieval of images and video. *Pattern Recognition, 35,* 945–965. doi:10.1016/S0031-3203(01)00086-3

Antoniou, G., & van Harmelen, F. (2008). *A semantic web primer* (2nd ed.). Cambridge, MA: MIT Press.

Bailloeul, T., Zhu, C., & Xu, Y. (2008, October). Automatic image tagging as a random walk with priors on the canonical correlation subspace. In *ACM International Conference on Multimedia Information Retrieval* (p. 75-82), Vancouver, British Columbia, Canada.

Barnard, K., Duygulu, P., de Freitas, N., Forsyth, D., Blei, D., & Jordan, M. (2003, March). Matching words and pictures. *Journal of Machine Learning Research, 3,* 1107–1135. doi:10.1162/153244303322533214

Barnard, K., Duygulu, P., Guru, R., Gabbur, P., & Forsyth, D. (2003, June). The effects of segmentation and feature choice in a translation model of object recognition. In *The IEEE International Conference on Computer Vision and Pattern Recognition,* (Vol. 2, p. 675-682).

Barnard, K., Fan, Q., Swaminathan, R., Hoogs, A., Collins, R., & Rondot, P. (2008, May). Evaluation of localized semantics: Data, methodology, and experiments. *International Journal of Computer Vision*, *77*(1-3), 199–217. doi:10.1007/s11263-007-0068-6

Basharat, A., Zhai, Y., & Shah, M. (2008, June). Content based video matching using spatiotemporal volumes. *Computer Vision and Image Understanding*, *110*(3), 360–377. doi:10.1016/j.cviu.2007.09.016

Benitez, A. B., & Chang, S.-F. (2002a, August). Perceptual knowledge construction from annotated image collections. In *IEEE International Conference on Multimedia & Expo (ICME)*. Lausanne, Switzerland.

Benitez, A. B., & Chang, S.-F. (2002b, August). Semantic knowledge construction from annotated image collections. In *IEEE International Conference on Multimedia & Expo (ICME)*. Lausanne, Switzerland.

Benitez, A. B., & Chang, S.-F. (2003, September). Image classification using multimedia knowledge networks. In *IEEE International Conference on Image Processing (ICIP)*. Barcelona, Spain.

Bertini, M., Bimbo, A. D., & Torniai, C. (2006). Automatic annotation and semantic retrieval of video sequences using multimedia ontologies. In *ACM International Conference on Multimedia* (p. 679-682), Santa Barbara, CA.

Bertoline, G. (1998). Visual science: An emerging discipline. *Journal for Geometry and Graphics*, *2*(2), 181–187.

Blei, D. M., & Jordan, M. I. (2003, August). Modeling annotated data. In *The 26th annual International ACM SIGIR Conference*.

Bollegala, D., Matsuo, Y., & Ishizuka, M. (2007). Measuring semantic similarity between words using web search engines. In *International Conference on World Wide Web (WWW)*.

Boutell, M. R., Luo, J., Shen, X., & Brown, C. M. (2004). Learning multi-label scene classification. *Pattern Recognition*, *37*, 1757–1771. doi:10.1016/j.patcog.2004.03.009

Brostow, G. J., Fauqueura, J., & Cipolla, R. (2009, January). Semantic object classes in video: A high definition ground truth database. *Pattern Recognition Letters*, *30*(2), 88–97. doi:10.1016/j.patrec.2008.04.005

Brunelli, R., Mich, O., & Modena, C. M. (1999). A survey on the automatic indexing of video data. *Journal of Visual Communication and Image Representation*, *10*, 78–112. doi:10.1006/jvci.1997.0404

Cai, D., He, X., Wen, J.-R., & Ma, W.-Y. (2004). Block-level link analysis. In *the 27th annual International ACM SIGIR Conference on Research and Development in Information Retrieval (SIGIR'04)*, (pp. 440–447).

Campbell, N. W., Mackeown, W. P. J., Thomas, B. T., & Troscianko, T. (1997). Interpreting image databases by region classification. *Pattern Recognition*, *30*(4), 555–563. doi:10.1016/S0031-3203(96)00112-4

Carbonetto, P., de Freitas, N., & Barnard, K. (2004, May). A statistical models for general contextual object recognition. In *The Eighth European Conference on Computer Vision (ECCV2004)*.

Carneiro, G., Chan, A. B., Moreno, P. J., & Vasconcelos, N. (2007, March). Supervised learning of semantic classes for image annotation and retrieval. *IEEE Transactions on Pattern Analysis and Machine Intelligence*, *29*(3), 394–410. doi:10.1109/TPAMI.2007.61

Chang, S. K., Shi, Q. Y., & Yan, C. W. (1987, May). Iconic indexing by 2-d strings. *IEEE Transactions on Pattern Analysis and Machine Intelligence, 9*(3), 413–428. doi:10.1109/TPAMI.1987.4767923

Chang, S. K., Yan, C. W., Dimitroff, D. C., & Arndt, T. (1988, May). An intelligent image database system. *IEEE Transactions on Software Engineering, 14*(5), 681–688. doi:10.1109/32.6147

Csurka, G., Dance, C. R., Fan, L., Willamowski, J., & Bray, C. (2004). Visual categorization with bags of keypoints. In *International Workshop on Statistical Learning in Computer Vision,* (p. 1-22).

Datta, R., Joshi, D., Li, J., James, & Wang, Z. (2008). Image retrieval: Ideas, influences, and trends of the new age. *ACM Computing Surveys, 40*(2), 5:1-5:49.

Datta, R., Li, J., & Wang, J. Z. (2005, November). Content-based image retrieval - approaches and trends of the new age. In *ACM SIGMM International Workshop on Multimedia Information Retrieval,* (pp. 253-262).

Deng, J., Dong, W., Socher, R., Li, L.-J., Li, K., & Fei-Fei, L. (2009, June). Imagenet: A large-scale hierarchical image database. In *IEEE International Conference on Computer Vision and Pattern Recognition (CVPR)*, Miami Beach, FL, USA.

Deschacht, K., & Moens, M.-F. (2007, June). Text analysis for automatic image annotation. In *the 45th annual meeting of the Association of Computational Linguistics,* (pp. 1000-1007), Prague, Czech Republic.

Deselaers, T., & Deserno, T. M. (2008). Medical image annotation in imageclef 2008. In *CLEF Workshop 2008.*

Dorai, C., & Venkatesh, S. (2001, October - December). Computational media aesthetics: Finding meaning beautiful. *IEEE MultiMedia, 8*(4), 10–12. doi:10.1109/93.959093

Dudani, S. A., Breeding, K. J., & McGhee, R. B. (1977, January). Aircraft identification by moment invariants. *IEEE Transactions on Computers, 26*(1), 39–45. doi:10.1109/TC.1977.5009272

Duygulu, P., Barnard, K., de Freitas, N., & Forsyth, D. (2002). Object recognition as machine translation: learning a lexicon for a fixed image vocabulary. In *The seventh European Conference on Computer Vision,* (pp. 97112).

Fan, J., Luo, H., Gao, Y., & Jain, R. (2007, August). Incorporating concept ontology for hierarchical video classification, annotation, and visualization. *IEEE Transactions on Multimedia, 9*(5), 939–957. doi:10.1109/TMM.2007.900143

Fei-Fei, L., Fergus, R., & Perona, P. (2004). Learning generative visual models from few training examples: An incremental bayesian approach tested on 101 object categories. In *International Workshop on Generative Model based Vision.*

Fei-Fei, L., & Perona, P. (2005). A bayesian hierarchical model for learning natural scene categories. In *IEEE International Conference on Computer Vision and Pattern Recognition (CVPR)* (p. 524-531). Washington, DC: IEEE.

Fellbaum, C. (Ed.). (1998). *WordNet: an electronic lexical database.* Cambridge, MA: MIT Press.

Feng, D., Siu, W. C., & Zhang, H. J. (Eds.). (2003). *Multimedia information retrieval and management - technological fundamentals and applications*. Berlin: Springer.

Feng, S. L., Manmatha, R., & Lavrenko, V. (2004). Multiple Bernoulli relevance models for image and video annotation. In *IEEE International Conference on Computer Vision and Pattern Recognition (CVPR)* (Vol. 2).

Finlayson, G. D., Funt, B. V., & Barnard, K. (1995, June). Color constancy under varying illumination. In *IEEE International Conference on Computer Vision (ICCV)* (pp. 720-725). Cambridge, MA, USA.

Fischer, S., Lienhart, R., & Effelsberg, W. (1995). Automatic recognition of film genres. In *ACM International Conference on Multimedia* (pp. 295-304).

Frasconi, P., Gori, M., & Sperduti, A. (1998). A general framework for adaptive processing of data structures. *IEEE Transactions on Neural Networks, 9*, 768–785. doi:10.1109/72.712151

Fu, H., Chi, Z., & Feng, D. (2009, January). An efficient algorithm for attention-driven image interpretation from segments. *Pattern Recognition, 42*(1), 126–140. doi:10.1016/j.patcog.2008.06.021

Fu, H., Chi, Z., Feng, D., & Song, J. (2004, December). Machine learning techniques for ontology-based leaf classification. In *International Conference on Control, Automation, Robotics and Vision* (p. 681-686), Kunming, China.

Gao, Y., Fan, J., Xue, X., & Jain, R. (2006). Automatic image annotation by incorporating feature hierarchy and boosting to scale up svm classifiers. In *ACM International Conference on Multimedia* (p. 901-910).

Ghamrawi, N., & McCallum, A. (2005). Collective multi-label classification. In *ACM International Conference on Information and Knowledge Management* (p. 195-200). New York: ACM.

Goh, K.-S., Li, B., & Chang, E. Y. (2005, October). Using one-class and two-class svms for multi-class image annotation. *IEEE Transactions on Knowledge and Data Engineering, 17*(10), 1333–1346. doi:10.1109/TKDE.2005.170

Griffin, G., Holub, A., & Perona, P. (2007). *Caltech-256 object category dataset.* Technical Report No. 7694, California Institute of Technology.

Guan, G., Wang, Z., Tian, Q., & Feng, D. (2009, October). Improved concept similarity measuring in visual domain. In *IEEE International Workshop on Multimedia Signal Processing*. Rio de Janeiro, Brazil.

Gupta, A., & Jain, R. (1997, May). Visual information retrieval. *Communications of the ACM, 40*(5), 70–79. doi:10.1145/253769.253798

Haering, N., Qian, R., & Sezan, M. (2000, September). A semantic event-detection approach and its application todetecting hunts in wildlife video. *IEEE Transactions on Circuits and Systems for Video Technology, 10*(6), 857–868. doi:10.1109/76.867923

Hagenbuchner, M., Sperduti, A., & Tsoi, A. C. (2003, May). A self-organizing map for adaptive processing of structured data. *IEEE Transactions on Neural Networks, 14*(3), 491505. doi:10.1109/TNN.2003.810735

Hanjalic, A., & Xu, L. Q. (2005). Affective video content representation and modeling. *IEEE Transactions on Multimedia, 7*, 143–154. doi:10.1109/TMM.2004.840618

Haralick, R. M., Shanmugam, K., & Dinstein, I. (1973). Textural features for image classification. *IEEE Transactions on Systems, Man, and Cybernetics, SMC-3*(6), 610–621. doi:10.1109/TSMC.1973.4309314

Hauptmann, A. G. (2005, July). Lessons for the future from a decade of informedia video analysis research. In *ACM International Conference on Image and Video Retrieval* (p. 1-10). Singapore.

Hollink, L., Little, S., & Hunter, J. (2005, October). Evaluating the application of semantic inferencing rules to image annotation. In *International Conference on Knowledge Capture*, Banff, Alberta, Canada.

Hollink, L., & Worring, M. (2005). Building a visual ontology for video retrieval. In *ACM International Conference on Multimedia* (pp. 479 - 482), Hilton, Singapore.

Hoogs, A., Rittscher, J., Stein, G., & Schmiederer, J. (2003, June). Video content annotation using visual analysis and a large semantic knowledgebase. In *IEEE International Conference on Computer Vision and Pattern Recognition (CVPR)* (pp. 327-334).

Hu, M. K. (1962). Visual pattern recognition by moment invariants. *I.R.E. Transactions on Information Theory, 8*(2), 179–187. doi:10.1109/TIT.1962.1057692

Huang, J., Kumar, S. R., Mitra, M., Zhu, W.-J., & Zabih, R. (1999, December). Spatial color indexing and applications. *International Journal of Computer Vision, 35*(3), 245–268. doi:10.1023/A:1008108327226

Huang, J., Liu, Z., Wang, Y., Chen, Y., & Wong, E. K. (1999). Integration of multimodal features for video classification based on hmm. In *IEEE International Workshop on Multimedia Signal Processing* (pp. 53-58), Copenhagen, Denmark.

Hughes, A., Wilkens, T., Wildemuth, B. M., & Marchionini, G. (2003). Text or pictures? an eyetracking study of how people view digital video surrogates. In *ACM International Conference on Image and Video Retrieval*.

Idris, F., & Panchanathan, S. (1997, June). Review of image and video indexing techniques. *Journal of Visual Communication and Image Representation, 8*(2), 146–166. doi:10.1006/jvci.1997.0355

Inkpen, D., & Desilets, A. (2005). Semantic similarity for detecting recognition errors in automatic speech transcripts. In *International Conference on Human Language Technology and Empirical Methods in Natural Language Processing* (pp. 4956), Morristown, NJ.

Iyengar, G., Duygulu, P., Feng, S., Ircing, P., Khudanpur, S. P., Klakow, D., et al. (2005, November). Joint visual-text modeling for automatic retrieval of multimedia documents. In *ACM International Conference on Multimedia,* (pp. 21-30), Singapore.

Jeon, J., Lavrenko, V., & Manmatha, R. (2003). Automatic image annotation and retrieval using cross-media relevance models. In *The ACM SIGIR Conference on Research and Development in Information Retrieval*.

Jin, R., Chai, J. Y., & Si, L. (2004). Effective automatic image annotation via a coherent language model and active learning. In *ACM International Conference on Multimedia*.

Jin, Y., Khan, L., Wang, L., & Awad, M. (2005). Image annotations by combining multiple evidence & wordnet. In *ACM International Conference on Multimedia*.

Kang, F., Jin, R., & Sukthankar, R. (2006). Correlated label propagation with application to multi-label learning. In *IEEE International Conference on Computer Vision and Pattern Recognition,* (pp. 1719 - 1726).

Ke, Y., & Sukthankar, R. (2004, June). PCA-SIFT: A more distinctive representation for local image descriptors. In *IEEE International Conference on Computer Vision and Pattern Recognition.* Washington, DC: IEEE.

Ke, Y., Sukthankar, R., & Hebert, M. (2007, October). Event detection in crowded videos. In *IEEE International Conference on Computer Vision* (p. 1-8), Rio de Janeiro, Brazil.

Koskela, M., Smeaton, A. F., & Laaksonen, J. (2007, August). Measuring concept similarities in multimedia ontologies: Analysis and evaluations. *IEEE Transactions on Multimedia, 9*(5), 912–922. doi:10.1109/TMM.2007.900137

Laptev, I., Marszalek, M., Schmid, C., & Rozenfeld, B. (2008, June). Learning realistic human actions from movies. In *IEEE International Conference on Computer Vision and Pattern Recognition* (p. 1-8), Anchorage, AK.

Lavrenko, V., Manmatha, R., & Jeon, J. (2003). A model for learning the semantics of pictures. In *The 16th annual Conference on Neural Information Processing Systems.*

Lazebnik, S., Schmid, C., & Ponce, J. (2006). Beyond bags of features: Spatial pyramid matching for recognizing natural scene categories. In *IEEE International Conference on Computer Vision and Pattern Recognition.*

Lecce, V. D., & Guerriero, A. (1999, December). An evaluation of the effectiveness of image features for image retrieval. *Journal of Visual Communication and Image Representation, 10*(4), 351–362. doi:10.1006/jvci.1999.0423

Leslie, L., Chua, T.-S., & Ramesh, J. (2007). Annotation of paintings with high-level semantic concepts using transductive inference and ontology based concept disambiguation. In *ACM International Conference on Multimedia,* (pp. 443-452). New York: ACM.

Lew, M. S., Sebe, N., Djeraba, C., & Jain, R. (2006). Content-based multimedia information retrieval: State of the art and challenges. *ACM Transactions on Multimedia Computing, Communications, and Applications, 2*(1), 1–19. doi:10.1145/1126004.1126005

Li, J., & Wang, J. Z. (2003). Automatic linguistic indexing of pictures by a statistical modeling approach. *IEEE Transactions on Pattern Analysis and Machine Intelligence, 25*(9), 1075–1088. doi:10.1109/TPAMI.2003.1227984

Li, J., & Wang, J. Z. (2006). Real-time computerized annotation of pictures. In *the ACM International Conference on Multimedia.*

Li, Y., Bandar, Z. A., & McLean, D. (2003, August). An approach for measuring semantic similarity between words using multiple information sources. *IEEE Transactions on Knowledge and Data Engineering, 15*(4), 871882.

Liu, J., Li, M., Ma, W.-Y., Liu, Q., & Lu, H. (2006, October). An adaptive graph model for automatic image annotation. In *ACM International Workshop on Multimedia Information Retrieval* (pp. 61-70), Santa Barbara, CA.

Liu, J., Wang, B., Li, M., Li, Z., Ma, W., Lu, H., et al. (2007, September). Dual cross-media relevance model for image annotation. In *the ACM International Conference on Multimedia* (pp. 605 - 614), Augsburg, Germany.

Liu, Y., Zhang, D., Lu, G., & Ma, W.-Y. (2007). A survey of content-based image retrieval with high-level semantics. *Pattern Recognition, 40*, 262–282. doi:10.1016/j.patcog.2006.04.045

Loncaric, S. (1998). A survey of shape analysis techniques. *Pattern Recognition, 31*(8), 983–1001. doi:10.1016/S0031-2023(97)00122-2

Lowe, D. G. (2004). Distinctive image features from scale-invariant keypoints. *International Journal of Computer Vision, 60*(2), 91–110. doi:10.1023/B:VISI.0000029664.99615.94

Luo, H., Fan, J., Gao, Y., & Xu, G. (2004). Multimodal salient objects: General building blocks of semantic video concepts. In *ACM International Conference on Image and Video Retrieval,* (pp. 374-383).

Ma, W.-Y., & Manjunath, B. S. (2000). EdgeFlow: a technique for boundary detection and image segmentation. *IEEE Transactions on Image Processing, 9*(8), 1375–1388. doi:10.1109/83.855433

Manjunath, B., Salembier, P., & Sikora, T. (Eds.). (2002). *Introduction to MPEG-7: multimedia content description interface.* Chichester, UK: Wiley.

Manjunath, B. S., & Ma, W. Y. (1996). Texture features for browsing and retrieval of image data. *IEEE Transactions on Pattern Analysis and Machine Intelligence, 18*(8), 837–842. doi:10.1109/34.531803

Manning, C. D., Raghavan, P., & Schtze, H. (2008). *Introduction to information retrieval.* Cambridge, UK: Cambridge University Press.

Markkula, M., & Sormunen, E. (2000, January). End-user searching challenges indexing practices in the digital newspaper photo archive. *Information Retrieval, 1*(4), 259–295. doi:10.1023/A:1009995816485

Mikolajczyk, K., & Schmid, C. (2002). An afine invariant interest point detector. In *European Conference on Computer Vision* (pp. 128-142), Copenhagen, Denmark.

Mikolajczyk, K., & Schmid, C. (2003). A performance evaluation of local descriptors. In *IEEE International Conference on Computer Vision and Pattern Recognition.*

Mitra, M., Singhal, A., & Buckley, C. (1998). Improving automatic query expansion. In *International ACM SIGIR Conference on Research and Development in Information Retrieval.*

Monay, F., & Gatica-Perez, D. (2003, November). On image auto-annotation with latent space models. In *ACM International Conference on Multimedia,* (pp. 275-278), Berkeley, CA.

Monay, F., & Gatica-Perez, D. (2004, November). PLSA-based image auto-annotation: constraining the latent space. In *ACM International Conference on Multimedia,* (pp. 348-351). New York: ACM.

Mori, Y., Takahashi, H., & Oka, R. (1999). Image-to-word transformation based on dividing and vector quantizing images with words. In *The first International Workshop on Multimedia Intelligent Storage and Retrieval Management (MISRM99)*.

Moxley, E., Mei, T., Hua, X.-S., Ma, W.-Y., & Manjunath, B. S. (2008, June). Automatic video annotation through search and mining. In *IEEE International Conference on Multimedia and Expo,* (pp. 685-688), Hannover, Germany.

Muller, H., Marchand-Maillet, S., & Pun, T. (2002). The truth about corel-evaluation in image retrieval. In *ACM International Conference on Image and Video Retrieval,* (pp. 38-49).

Muller, H., Michoux, N., Bandon, D., & Geissbuhler, A. (2004). A review of content-based image retrieval systems in medical applications-clinical benefits and future directions. *International Journal of Medical Informatics, 73*(1), 1–23. doi:10.1016/j.ijmedinf.2003.11.024

Naphade, M., Smith, J. R., Tesic, J., Chang, S.-F., Hsu, W., & Kennedy, L. (2006, July-September). Large-scale concept ontology for multimedia. *IEEE MultiMedia, 13*(3), 86–91. doi:10.1109/MMUL.2006.63

Ngo, C., Zhang, H., Chin, R. T., & Pong, T. (2000, June). Motion characterization by temporal slice analysis. In *IEEE International Conference on Computer Vision and Pattern Recognition* (pp. 768-773), Hilton Head Island, SC.

Niebles, J. C., & Fei-Fei, L. (2007). A hierarchical model of shape and appearance for human action classification. In *IEEE International Conference on Computer Vision and Pattern Recognition*.

Nister, D., & Stewenius, H. (2006). Scalable recognition with a vocabulary tree. In *IEEE International Conference on Computer Vision and Pattern Recognition*.

Ojala, T., Pietikainen, M., & Maenpaa, T. (2002, July). Multiresolution gray-scale and rotation invariant texture classification with local binary patterns. *IEEE Transactions on Pattern Analysis and Machine Intelligence, 24*(7), 971–987. doi:10.1109/TPAMI.2002.1017623

Ojala, T., Pietikinen, M., & Harwood, D. (1996). A comparative study of texture measures with classification based on featured distribution. *Pattern Recognition, 29*(1), 51–59. doi:10.1016/0031-3203(95)00067-4

Oliva, A., & Torralba, A. (2001). Modeling the shape of the scene: a holistic representation of the spatial envelope. *International Journal of Computer Vision, 42*, 145–175. doi:10.1023/A:1011139631724

Pan, J.-Y., Yang, H.-J., Duygulu, P., & Faloutsost, C. (2004, June). Automatic image captioning. In *IEEE International Conference on Multimedia and Expo (ICME)* (Vol. 3, pp. 1987-1990). Taipei, Taiwan.

Pan, J.-Y., Yang, H.-J., Faloutsos, C., & Duygulu, P. (2004, July). Gcap: Graph-based automatic image captioning. In *International Workshop on Multimedia Data and Document Engineering*, Washington, DC.

Pass, G., & Zabih, R. (1999). Comparing images using joint histograms. *Multimedia Systems, 7*(3), 234–240. doi:10.1007/s005300050125

Pavel, F. A., Wang, Z., & Feng, D. D. (2009, October). Reliable object recognition using sift features. In *IEEE International Workshop on Multimedia Signal Processing*. Rio de Janeiro, Brazil.

Payne, A., & Singh, S. (2005, October). Indoor vs. outdoor scene classification in digital photographs. *Pattern Recognition, 38*(10), 1533–1545. doi:10.1016/j.patcog.2004.12.014

Persoon, E., & Fu, K. sun. (1997). Shape discrimination using fourier descriptors. *IEEE Transactions on Systems, Man, and Cybernetics, SMC-7*(3), 170–179.

Qi, G.-J., Hua, X.-S., Rui, Y., Tang, J., Mei, T., & Zhang, H.-J. (2007, September). Correlative multi-label video annotation. In *The ACM International Conference on Multimedia*, Augsburg, Germany.

Ren, W., Singh, S., Singh, M., & Zhu, Y. S. (2009). State-of-the-art on spatio-temporal information based video retrieval. *Pattern Recognition, 42*, 267–282. doi:10.1016/j.patcog.2008.08.033

Rodden, K., Basalaj, W., Sinclair, D., & Wood, K. (2001, March). Does organisation by similarity assist image browsing? In *ACM SIGCHI Conference on Human Factors in Computing Systems*, (pp. 190-197), Seattle, WA.

Rui, X., Yu, N., Wang, T., & Li, M. (2007). A search-based web image annotation method. In *IEEE International Conference on Multimedia and Expo*, Beijing, China.

Rui, Y., Huang, T. S., & Chang, S.-F. (1999, March). Image retrieval: Current techniques, promising directions, and open issues. *Journal of Visual Communication and Image Representation, 10*(1), 39–62. doi:10.1006/jvci.1999.0413

Russell, B., Torralba, A., Murphy, K., & Freeman, W. T. (2008, May). Labelme: a database and web-based tool for image annotation. *International Journal of Computer Vision, 77*(1-3), 151–173. doi:10.1007/s11263-007-0090-8

Salembier, P., & Garrido, L. (2000, April). Binar partition tree as an efficient representation for image processing, segmentation, and information retrieval. *IEEE Transactions on Image Processing, 9*, 561–576. doi:10.1109/83.841934

Santini, S., & Jain, R. (1999). Similarity measures. *IEEE Transactions on Pattern Analysis and Machine Intelligence, 21*(9), 871–883. doi:10.1109/34.790428

Savarese, S., Winn, J., & Criminisi, A. (2006). Discriminative object class models of appearance and shape by correlations. In *IEEE Conference on Computer Vision and Pattern Recognition*.

Schreiber, A. T., Dubbeldam, B., Wielemaker, J., & Wielinga, B. (2001, May-June). Ontology-based photo annotation. *IEEE Intelligent Systems, 16*(3), 66–74. doi:10.1109/5254.940028

Shi, R., Chua, T.-S., Lee, C.-H., & Gao, S. (2006). Bayesian learning of hierarchical multinomial mixture models of concepts for automatic image annotation. In *ACM International Conference on Image and Video Retrieval*.

Sivic, J., Russell, B. C., Efros, A. A., Zisserman, A., & Freeman, W. T. (2005). Discovering object categories in image collections. In *IEEE International Conference on Computer Vision*. Washington, DC: IEEE.

Sjoberg, M., Laaksonen, J., Honkela, T., & Polla, M. (2008, August). Inferring semantics from textual information in multimedia retrieval. *Neurocomputing, 71*(13-15), 2576–2586. doi:10.1016/j.neucom.2008.01.029

Smeulders, A. W. M., Worring, M., Santini, S., Gupta, A., & Jain, R. (2000). Content-based image retrieval at the end of the early years. *IEEE Transactions on Pattern Analysis and Machine Intelligence, 22*(12), 1349–1380. doi:10.1109/34.895972

Snoek, C. G., Worring, M., van Gemert, J. C., Geusebroek, J.-M., & Smeulders, A. W. M. (2006, October). The challenge problem for automated detection of 101 semantic concepts in multimedia. In *ACM International Conference on Multimedia,* (pp. 421 - 430), Santa Barbara, CA.

Snoek, C. G. M., Huurnink, B., Hollink, L., de Rijke, M., & Schreiber, G. (2007, August). Adding semantics to detectors for video retrieval. *IEEE Transactions on Multimedia, 9*(5), 975–986. doi:10.1109/TMM.2007.900156

Snoek, C. G. M., & Worring, M. (2005). Multimodal video indexing: A review of the state-of-the-art. *Multimedia Tools and Applications, 25*, 5–35. doi:10.1023/B:MTAP.0000046380.27575.a5

Swain, M. J., & Ballard, D. H. (1991, November). Color indexing. *International Journal of Computer Vision, 7*(1), 11–32. doi:10.1007/BF00130487

Tamura, H., Mori, S., & Yamawaki, T. (1978). Textural features corresponding to visual perception. *IEEE Transactions on Systems, Man, and Cybernetics, SMC-8*(6), 460–473. doi:10.1109/TSMC.1978.4309999

Tamura, H., & Yokoya, N. (1984). Image database systems: A survey. *Pattern Recognition, 17*(1), 29–43. doi:10.1016/0031-3203(84)90033-5

Tang, J., Hare, J., & Lewis, P. (2006). Image auto-annotation using a statistical model with salient regions. In *IEEE International Conference on Multimedia and Expo,* (pp. 525-528).

Tao, Y., & Grosky, W. I. (2001, December). Spatial color indexing using rotation, translation, and scale invariant angle. *Multimedia Tools and Applications, 15*(3), 247–268. doi:10.1023/A:1012486900033

Tirilly, P., Claveau, V., & Gros, P. (2008). Language modeling for bag-of-visual words image categorization. In *ACM International Conference on Image and Video Retrieval.*

Torralba, A., Fergus, R., & Freeman, W. T. (2008, November). 80 million tiny images: A large data set for nonparametric object and scene recognition. *IEEE Transactions on Pattern Analysis and Machine Intelligence, 30*(11), 1958–1970. doi:10.1109/TPAMI.2008.128

Tsoumakas, G., & Katakis, I. (2007). Multi-label classification: An overview. *International Journal of Data Warehousing and Mining, 3*(3), 1–13.

Ueda, N., & Saito, K. (2003). Parametric mixture models for multi-labeled text . In *Advances in neural information processing systems* (p. 15). Cambridge, MA: MIT Press.

Vailaya, A., Figueiredo, M. A. T., Jain, A. K., & Zhang, H. J. (2001). Image classification for contentbased indexing. *IEEE Transactions on Image Processing, 10*(1), 117–130. doi:10.1109/83.892448

Valle, E., Cord, M., & Philipp-Foliguet, S. (2008). High-dimensional descriptor indexing for large multimedia databases. In *ACM Conference on Information and Knowledge Management* (pp. 739-748), Napa Valley, California, USA.

Varelas, G., Voutsakis, E., Raftopoulou, P., Petrakis, E. G., & Milios, E. E. (2005). Semantic similarity methods in wordnet and their application to information retrieval on the web. In *ACM International Workshop on Web Information and Data Management* (pp. 10-16). New York: ACM.

Velivelli, A., & Huang, T. S. (2006, June). Automatic video annotation by mining speech transcripts. In *IEEE International Conference on Computer Vision and Pattern Recognition Workshop* (pp. 115-122), New York.

Veltkamp, R. C., & Tanase, M. (2000). *Content-based image retrieval systems: A survey* (Technical Report UU-CS-2000-34), Department of Information and Computing Sciences, Universiteit Utrecht.

Vogel, J., & Schiele, B. (2004). Natural scene retrieval based on a semantic modeling step. In *ACM International Conference on Image and Video Retrieval*, Dublin, Ireland.

von Ahn, L., & Dabbish, L. (2004, April). Labeling images with a computer game. In *ACM SIGCHI Conference on Human Factors in Computing Systems* (p. 319 - 326). Vienna, Austria.

von Ahn, L., Liu, R., & Blum, M. (2006, April). Peekaboom: A game for locating objects in images. In *ACM SIGCHI Conference on Human Factors in Computing Systems* (p. 55 - 64). Montreal, Quebec, Canada.

Wang, C., Zhang, L., & Zhang, H.-J. (2008). Scalable markov model-based image annotation. In *ACM International Conference on Content-based Image and Video Retrieval,* (pp. 113-118), Niagara Falls, Canada.

Wang, M., Hua, X.-S., Hong, R., Tang, J., Qi, G.-J., & Song, Y. (2009, May). Unified video annotation via multigraph learning. *IEEE Trans. on Circuits and Systems for Video Technology, 19*(5), 733–746. doi:10.1109/TCSVT.2009.2017400

Wang, M., Hua, X.-S., Mei, T., Hong, R., Qi, G., & Song, Y. (2009, March). Semi-supervised kernel density estimation for video annotation. *Computer Vision and Image Understanding, 113*(3), 384–396. doi:10.1016/j.cviu.2008.08.003

Wang, M., Hua, X.-S., Song, Y., Yuan, X., Li, S., & Zhang, H.-J. (2006, October). Automatic video annotation by semi-supervised learning with kernel density estimation. In *ACM International Conference on Multimedia* (pp. 967-976), Santa Barbara, CA.

Wang, M., Hua, X.-S., Yuan, X., & Rong Dai, Y. S. andLi. (2007, September). Optimizing multi-graph learning: Towards a unified video annotation scheme. In *ACM International Conference on Multimedia,* (pp. 862-871), Ausburg, Bavaria, Germany.

Wang, M., Yang, L., & Hua, X.-S. (2009). *MSRA-MM: Bridging research and industrial societies for multimedia information retrieval,* (Technical Report MSR-TR-2009-30). Microsoft Research Asia.

Wang, M., Zhou, X., & Chua, T.-S. (2008, July). Automatic image annotation via local multi-label classification. In *ACM International Conference on Image and Video Retrieval* (pp. 17-26). Niagara Falls, Ontario, Canada.

Wang, X.-J., Zhang, L., Li, X., & Ma, W.-Y. (2008, November). Annotating images by mining image search results. *IEEE Transactions on Pattern Analysis and Machine Intelligence, 30*(11), 1919–1932. doi:10.1109/TPAMI.2008.127

Wang, Z., Chi, Z., & Feng, D. (2002, November). Structural representation and bpts learning for shape classification. In *International Conference on Neural Information Processing,* (pp. 134-138).

Wang, Z., Feng, D., & Chi, Z. (2004). Comparison of image partition methods for adaptive image categorization based on structural image representation. In *The 8th International Conference on Control, Automation, Robotics, and Vision (ICARCV04)* (pp. 676-680).

Wang, Z., Guan, G., Wang, J., & Feng, D. (2008, October). Measuring semantic similarity between concepts in visual domain. In *IEEE International Workshop on Multimedia Signal Processing,* (pp. 628-633), Carins, Australia.

Wang, Z., Hargenbuchner, M., Tsoi, A. C., Cho, S. Y., & Chi, Z. (2002). Image classification with structured self-organizing map. In *IEEE International Joint Conference on Neural Networks (IJCNN2002)*.

Winn, J., Criminisi, A., & Minka, T. (2005, October). Object categorization by learned universal visual dictionary. In *The IEEE International Conference on Computer Vision* (p. 1800-1807).

Wu, L., Hu, Y., Li, M., Yu, N., & Hua, X.-S. (2009). Febuary). Scale-invariant visual language modeling for object categorization. *IEEE Transactions on Multimedia, 11*(2), 286–294. doi:10.1109/TMM.2008.2009692

Wu, L., Hua, X.-S., Yu, N., Ma, W.-Y., & Li, S. (2008, October). Flickr distance. In *ACM International Conference on Multimedia* (pp. 31 40). New York: ACM.

Wu, L., Li, M., Li, Z., Ma, W.-Y., & Yu, N. (2007, September). Visual language modeling for image classification. In *ACM International Workshop on Multimedia Information Retrieval*, Augsburg, Bavaria, Germany.

Xie, L., Chang, S.-F., Divakaran, A., & Sun, H. (2003, July). Unsupervised discovery of multilevel statistical video structures using hierarchical hidden markov models. In *IEEE International Conference on Multimedia and Expo (ICME)*, Baltimore, MD.

Xiong, Z., Radhakrishnan, R., Divakaran, A., & Huang, T. S. (2005, September). Audiovisual sports highlights extraction using Coupled Hidden Markov Models. *Pattern Analysis & Applications, 8*(1-2), 62–71. doi:10.1007/s10044-005-0244-7

Yang, C., & Dong, M. (2006). Region based image annotation using asymmetrical support vector machine based multiple-instance learning. In *IEEE International Conference on Computer Vision and Pattern Recognition,* (pp. 2057-2063).

Yang, C., Dong, M., & Fotouhi, F. (2005, November). Region based image annotation through multipleinstance learning. In *The ACM International Conference on Multimedia,* (pp. 435438).

Yao, B., Yang, X., & Zhu, S.-C. (2007, August). Introduction to a large scale general purpose ground truth dataset: methodology, annotation tool, and benchmarks. In *IEEE International Conference on Computer Vision and Pattern Recognition,* (pp. 169-183), Ezhou, China.

Yao, J., Antani, S., Long, R., Thoma, G., & Zhang, Z. (2006). Automatic medical image annotation and retrieval using secc. In *IEEE Symposium on Computer-based Medical Systems*.

Yeo, C., Ahammad, P., Ramchandran, K., & Sastry, S. S. (2008, August). High-speed action recognition and localization in compressed domain videos. *IEEE Transactions on Circuits and Systems for Video Technology, 18*(8), 1006–1015. doi:10.1109/TCSVT.2008.927112

Zha, Z.-J., Mei, T., Wang, Z., & Hua, X.-S. (2007). Building a comprehensive ontology to refine video concept detection. In *International Workshop on Multimedia Information Retrieval* (pp. 227- 236), Augsburg, Bavaria, Germany.

Zhang, M.-L., & Zhou, Z.-H. (2007, July). ML-KNN: A lazy learning approach to multi-label learning. *Pattern Recognition, 40*(7), 2038–2048. doi:10.1016/j.patcog.2006.12.019

Zhang, R., Zhang, Z., Li, M., Ma, W.-Y., & Zhang, H.-J. (2005, October). A probabilistic semantic model for image annotation and multi-modal image retrieval. In *The IEEE International Conference on Computer Vision,* (pp. 846-851).

Zhou, X., Wang, M., Zhang, Q., Zhang, J., & Shi, B. (2007). Automatic image annotation by an iterative approach: incorporating keyword correlations and region matching. In *ACM International Conference on Image and Video Retrieval,* (pp. 25-32), Amsterdam, The Netherlands.

Zhou, X. S., & Huang, T. S. (2003, April). Relevance feedback in image retrieval: A comprehensive review. *Multimedia Systems, 8*(6), 536–544. doi:10.1007/s00530-002-0070-3

Zhu, X. (2008, July). *Semi-supervised learning literature survey.* Technical Report TR-1530, University of Wisconsin Madison, Madison, WI.

ENDNOTES

[1]   Flickr, http://www.flickr.com.

[2]   Internet 2008 in Numbers, http://royal.pingdom.com/2009/01/22/internet-2008-in-numbers/.

[3]   University of Washington Dataset, http://www.cs.washington.edu/research/imagedatabase/groundtruth/.

[4]   TRECVID, http://www-nlpir.nist.gov/projects/trecvid/.

[5]   ImageCLEF, http://imageclef.org/.

[6]   The PASCAL Visual Object Classes, http://pascallin.ecs.soton.ac.uk/challenges/VOC/.

Chapter 7
Collaborative Bayesian Image Annotation and Retrieval

Rui Zhang
Ryerson University, Canada

Ling Guan
Ryerson University, Canada

ABSTRACT

With nearly twenty years of intensive study on the content-based image retrieval and annotation, the topic still remains difficult. By and large, the essential challenge lies in the limitation of using low-level visual features to characterize the semantic information of images, commonly known as the semantic gap. To bridge this gap, various approaches have been proposed based on the incorporation of human knowledge and textual information as well as the learning techniques utilizing the information of different modalities. At the same time, contextual information which represents the relationship between different real world/conceptual entities has shown its significance with respect to recognition tasks not only through real life experience but also scientific studies. In this chapter, the authors first review the state of the art of the existing works on image annotation and retrieval. Moreover, a general Bayesian framework which integrates content and contextual information and its application to both image annotation and retrieval are elaborated. The contextual information is considered as the statistical relationship between different images and different semantic concepts for image retrieval and annotation, respectively. The framework has efficient learning and classification procedures and the effectiveness is evaluated based on experimental studies, which demonstrate its advantage over both content-based and context-based approaches.

INTRODUCTION

Ever-lasting growth of multimedia information has been witnessed and experienced by human beings since the beginning of the information era. An immediate challenge resulting from the information explosion

DOI: 10.4018/978-1-61692-859-9.ch007

is how to intelligently manage and enjoy the multimedia databases. In the course of the technological development of multimedia information retrieval, various approaches have been proposed with the ultimate goal of enabling semantic-based search and browsing. Among those intensively explored topics, content-based image retrieval (CBIR), born at the crossroad of computer vision, machine learning and database technologies, has been studied for more than a decade, yet still remaining difficult (Smeulders, Worring, Santini, Gupta, Jain, 2001), (Datta, Joshi, Li, Wang, 2008). In a nutshell, the content-based approaches to image retrieval primarily rely on the pictorial information, a.k.a. low level visual features such as color, texture, shape and layout, which can be automatically extracted from images for similarity measure. The essential challenge is that the low level visual features accurately characterizing the semantic meaning of images are difficult to discover. Therefore, semantically relevant images may be located far away from each other in the space of the pictorial information. To reduce the gap between the high level semantics and low level features, human knowledge was expected to help refine the representation of the semantic meaning in a user's query. To this end, the relevance feedback (RF), a technique originally proposed for traditional document retrieval, was adapted to solve the problem of image retrieval (Crucianu, Ferecatu, Boujemaa, 2004), (Zhou, Huang, 2003). To enable more efficient search within a large scale database, content-based image classification has been proposed for structured indexing. Existing along with the advantages of content-based approaches is the inherent difficulty in terms of the query formulation based on representation completely different from the human language. To human beings, identifying discriminative visual features for expressing high level semantic meaning, such as someone's first day at a university or the most exciting scene in a movie, is a fairly difficult task. Therefore, automatic image annotation aiming at constructing the correspondence between visual features and textual words has also been intensively studied. After so many years of research on the above-mentioned topics, it can be identified that none of the individual modalities, e.g. visual content, text, and metadata[1] such as time, location, etc, is sufficient for effectively accomplishing the goal. Therefore, it has become a leading trend (Guan, Muneesawang, Wang, Zhang, Tie, Bulzacki, & Ibrahim, 2009) within the research community to collect and integrate the sources of information with respect to the modalities that are distinct from and complementary to each other, which is known as the information fusion. In fact, as long as we believe that human beings are incomparable in terms of recognizing high level semantics, information fusion is indeed a promising direction not only for the topics covered herein but also for the general domain of pattern classification, as human beings are the most proficient user of the synergy across distinct modalities.

While research on image annotation and retrieval involves the effort from many different aspects, such as computer vision, machine learning, and even psychology, each of which has its own active research frontier, we intend to devote this chapter to a review of the representative works on image annotation and retrieval as well as the elaboration of our recent trend-aligned endeavor regarding this topic. The goal is to provide a general picture on the state of the art in order to draw the attention from the prospective readers and motivate more interesting ideas and development in the research community. The rest of this chapter is organized as follows. In section II, landmark achievements after the year of 2000 in the related research fields are reviewed. For those developed in 1990s, readers are referred to the literature mentioned in the section of introduction. In section III, we focus on a general Bayesian framework and its application to both image annotation and retrieval. Following the elaboration of the Bayesian framework, we continue with further discussion on the experimental results. Finally, the chapter is concluded with a summary including some future research directions.

RELATED WORKS

Image Retrieval

Conventional CBIR systems exploiting low-level visual features, e.g. QBIC (Flickner, Sawhney, Niblack, Ashley, Huang, Dom, Gorkani, Hafner, Lee, Petkovic, Steele, & Yanker, 1995) and VisualSEEk (Smith, Chang, 1996), have proven effective to the extent of pre-attentive similarity due to the semantic gap. To incorporate human knowledge into the retrieval process, an SVM-based active learning framework (Tong, Chang, 2001) was proposed, in which users are asked to classify the most ambiguous images into either the relevant or the irrelevant category. In addition, an interactive neural network-based learning framework (Muneesawang, Guan, 2004) was developed, in which the most informative images are used to refine the query model. To enable multiple levels of the degree of relevance, a soft RF (Yap, Wu, 2005) scheme was proposed. We refer to the above RF techniques based on each individual user's feedback as short term relevance feedback (STRF) as the learning only continues until the end of a single search request. Approaches in this category alleviate the semantic gap by incorporating human users' knowledge into the process of labeling training samples yet still suffering from the problem of sample sparseness, as average users are normally willing to select only a few relevant and irrelevant images. In addition, as irrelevant images may be distinct from the relevant ones in many different ways, training samples of the two categories in the context of RF are very likely imbalanced. Along with the demand for the real-time performance of a practical search engine, the above-mentioned problems can be considered as the major factors leading to the performance bottleneck. Having recognized that learning the semantics of images is a very long task, long term relevance feedback (LTRF) based on users' feedback across multiple queries has been proposed. Based on single value decomposition, the concept of semantic space (He, King, Ma, Li, & Zhang, 2003) was introduced, which captures the high level similarity between images. Content-free image retrieval (CFIR) (Uchihashi, Kanade, 2005) directly exploiting statistical dependence across the images in a database was proposed, where semantically similar images identified by human users in the past retrieval sessions are connected to one another using a maximum entropy model. An inherent limitation of CFIR is the cold start problem, resulting from deficient or even unavailable training data.

Recently, we have attempted to tackle the problem of semantic gap by integrating low-level visual properties of images and high-level human knowledge (Zhang, Guan, 2009). The work is motivated by noticing that the two kind of knowledge can be complementary to each other and the necessity of a mathematically justifiable framework to join them together. To this end, we proposed a general framework based on the Bayes' theorem, in which the low level content and high level knowledge associated with images are utilized to calculate the likelihood and the *a priori* probability, respectively. In particular, we consider the statistical relation across images as the high level knowledge, which is referred to as context. While either content or context component can help refine the similarity measured based on the other component, the framework can incrementally update the context component (Zhang, Guan, 2008) with continuously accumulated high level knowledge. The approach is named collaborative Bayesian image retrieval (CLBIR) because it uses a collaborative filtering approach for extracting contextual information from past retrieval results, which is similar to that of CFIR.

Image Annotation

As mentioned earlier, query formulation based on the low level visual content may be burdensome for human beings, especially when images related high level semantics are expected in a search result. Unlike low-level visual features, human language was created to record human knowledge and to express ourselves. Hence, textual information expressed using natural language lends itself to characterizing the semantics in images. Feng (Jing, Li, Zhang, & Zhang, 2005) proposed a multi-modal image retrieval, which enables both query-by-keyword and query-by-example with the measured similarity linearly combined at a subsequent step. Nonetheless, existing behind the performance improvement of the multi-modal retrieval is the lack of textual annotation with sufficient semantic richness. Considering the unreliability of the text surrounding the images on the Internet and the infeasibility of manually annotating large scale image databases, automatic image annotation intended to facilitate semantic-based search and browsing has been studied over the years (Hanbury, 2008). Early works (Szummer, Picard, 1998), (Vailaya, Figueiredo, Jain, & Zhang, 2001) are based on image classification using global features and hence only prove effective with respect to general semantic categories, such as indoor versus outdoor and city view versus natural scene. Essentially, most of the existing approaches to automatic image annotation solve the problem based on $P(\omega|x)$, where ω denotes a concept, not as restricted to a single word as it is for object recognition, and x denotes the visual feature, or visual word if quantized, of an image or a region of it. They fall into two categories according to the way $P(\omega|x)$ is obtained, i.e. either directly estimated or through $P(\omega|x)/P(x)$. Mori and et. al. (1999) considered the $P(\omega|x)$ as the histogram of the words associated with all the training image regions in the same cluster to which x belongs. For an entire image, the $P(\omega|x_1,x_2,...,x_N)$ is a mixture of the histograms of the individual regions belonging to the image, where $x_1,x_2,...,x_N$ denotes the N visual words of the image. In addition, the image annotation has also been considered as machine translation from textual word to visual word (Duygulu, Barnard, Freitas, & Forsyth, 2002), assuming $P(\omega|x)$ as a mixture of $P(\omega|x_i)$ where x_i is a visual word of a given image. A cross-media relevance model (CMRM) was proposed (Jeon, Lavrenko, 2003), where $P(\omega|x_1,x_2,...,x_N)$ is estimated through $P(\omega|x_1,x_2,...,x_N)/ P(x_1,x_2,...,x_N)$, both of which are further decomposed into probabilities conditional on training images. As opposed to the decomposition of the distribution of either textual or visual words into the distribution conditional on training images, the probabilistic latent semantic analysis (pLSA) (Hofmann, 1999) was employed to learn a hierarchical semantic structure of a set of images and their associated text (Barnard, Forsyth, 2001), where the textual and visual words are modeled as a mixture of distributions conditional on latent variables, which either represents a concept class or its level of generality. Carneiro and et. al. developed a supervised learning-based approach (Carneiro, Chan, Moreno, & Vasconcelos, 2007), by which each training image is modeled using a mixture distribution and the mixtures of the training images belonging to the same semantic class are used as samples to learn a class-specific semantic model. Although the above methods estimate the $P(\omega|x)$ through different ways, a common aspect shared by them is that, the visual words, resulting from the quantization of the visual features, are unified with the textual words into the bag-of-words (BOW) representation, but taking values from a separate discrete alphabet. As an example of the models not based on the BOW representation, an approach based on 2-dimensional hidden Markov models (2D-HMMs) in the visual feature space for representing semantics (Li, Wang, 2003) was proposed and the concepts are ranked based on the likelihood $P(x|\omega)$. In addition, Blei and et. al. employed the latent dirichlet allocation (LDA) (Blei, Ng, & Jordan, 2003) to jointly model the data of different nature (Blei, Jordan, 2003). Their correspondence LDA makes a trade-off between the flexibility of LDA and the correspondence of the multinomial Gaussian mixture. The approaches studied in (Barnard, Forsyth, 2001), (Barnard, Duygulu, Forsyth, Freitas, Blei, & Jordan, 2003) and (Blei, Jordan, 2003) are commonly referred to as topic modeling techniques as hidden variables are introduced to capture the similarity of a certain group of data in a single or across multiple domains. The distributions of data with respect to different topics can be viewed as the basis vectors spanning a topic space and each image can be represented using a convex combination of the topics. According to the study in the field of cognitive psychology (Biederman, Mezzanotte, & Rabinowitz, 1982), probabilistic relation across different objects serves as an important contributing factor in scene perception, which is commonly referred to as the contextual information in the research area of pattern recognition. Distinguished from the above-mentioned approaches, contextual object recognition based on Markov random field was proposed (Carbonetto, Freitas, & Barnard, 2004). The statistical relation among the semantic concepts is modeled through a hidden layer of nodes with a pre-defined neighborhood system. The expressiveness of the model, however, is enhanced at the cost of intractable computation. Accordingly, the training is based on the maximization of pseudo-likelihood, which usually ends up locally optimal. In fact, the correspondence LDA (Blei, Jordan, 2003) also takes a certain form of contextual information into consideration in that each of the visual features is assumed to be generated by some value of the hidden variable generating a textual word. Rabinovich and et. al. (2007) proposed a method based on the conditional random field (CRF), where the content and context components are learned separately. It still assumes the conditional independence between visual observations given words, a problem of generative models which is supposed to be resolved by discriminative models. Mei and et. al. (2008) considered the prior annotation of a training image as a nonseparable entity, which is propagated to new images as a whole such that the relation across the words is considered.

To combine and utilize the content and contextual information in an efficient way for image annotation, we proposed to integrate the two modalities using a Bayesian framework (Zhang, Wu, Yap, Guan, 2008), which is named collaborative Bayesian image annotation (CBIA). First, in terms of the types of information involved in the annotation process, our framework is distinct from most of the existing works without considering context. Second, pertaining to the way of information integration, our framework employs the Bayes' theorem, where the content and context are exploited to evaluate the likelihood of a feature vector and *a priori* probability of each individual class. It can be distinguished from the other existing approaches. As opposed to the linear information fusion methods, there is no need to heuristically or empirically adjust the system parameters. Third, compared with the existing works taking into account the contextual information, the advantage of our framework lies in its relatively low complexity with respect to the modeling of the context. By separately modeling the content and context, we avoid the adaptation of the partition function in an undirected graphical model.

THE GENERAL BAYESIAN FRAMEWORK

The Integration of Content and Context

In general, the content and contextual information are integrated through a Bayesian classification framework. To be specific, the content and context refer to the visual properties and the statistical relation across different images or semantic concepts, respectively, depending on the targeted application. Considering the context as the knowledge characterizing the high-level semantic information, the underlying rationale of the integration is that the online observation of visual content refines the *a priori* information encoded in the context model, especially when there is not sufficient high-level knowledge, and the contextual information extracted from past user history can be used to bridge, to some extent, the semantic gap associated with the low-level visual features.

In term of the notation in the general framework, an observation is denoted as x, a vector in a d-dimensional feature space, i.e. $x \in R^d$. The class label of an observation is denoted as ω, where $\omega \in W$, $W = \{1, 2, \ldots, W\}$ and W is the number of classes. Based on the maximum *a posteriori* probability (MAP) criterion which minimizes the classification error, the true class label is estimated with:

$$\hat{\omega} = \arg \max_{\omega \in W} P\left(\omega | x, I\right) \tag{1}$$

where $\hat{\omega}$ is an estimate of ω. In the literature, I is sometimes referred to as background information, which exists with a well-formulated problem. Generally speaking, it represents a set of indexes in the current framework. The specific meaning and the availability of this term in our work will be explained later during the discussion on the retrieval and annotation systems. Using the Bayes' theorem, the *a posteriori* probability can be written as:

$$P(\omega | x, I) \propto P(x | \omega, I) P(\omega | I) \tag{2}$$

with the equality replaced by the proportionality due to the unimportance of the probability density function (PDF) of an observation when the theorem is employed to solve a classification problem. Based on the meaning of the background information I, we can assume the conditional independence between the observation x and I given the true class label of the observation, i.e. $x \perp I | \omega$. Therefore, the *a posteriori* probability can be calculated through:

$$P(\omega | x, I) \propto P(x | \omega) P(\omega | I) \tag{3}$$

The first term on the right-hand side of (3) is the PDF of the feature vector of a certain class, which is referred to as the content model characterizing the visual properties. The second term is essentially a conditional distribution of the class label of one observation given that of another, which is regarded as the contextual information in that it characterizes the statistical relation between two different classes. According to (3), the content and contextual information are integrated through the decision-level fusion by multiplying the output of the two models. Before proceeding to the discussion on the retrieval and annotation frameworks, we briefly talk about the learning of the Bayesian framework.

Learning of the Content Model

The visual content models for different semantic classes are learned through a supervised fashion. Since the visual content model plays the role of evaluating the likelihood of a visual feature with respect to a class, any parametric or non-parametric model which can produce a quantitative metric characterizing the consistency of the visual feature with the model is applicable. In our study, we employ the support vector machine (SVM) for visual content modeling. Moreover, a theoretical requirement is that the output of the visual content model must comply with the definition of a PDF. To this end, we employ the exponential function, i.e. $h(s)=e^s$, $s \in R$, to convert the discriminant function of an SVM into a PDF. The selection of the above exponential function is based on the following consideration. First, it is monotonically increasing, resulting in the preservation of the physical interpretation of the algebraic distance between a sample and the decision boundary. Second, it is positive. Since the total integral of a function to be equal to unity, appropriate normalization is necessary. Finally, denoting the discriminant function of the SVM corresponding to the ω-th class as $f_\omega(x)$ and substituting it for the variable s in the exponential function followed by normalization, we obtain:

$$p\left(x|\omega\right) = \frac{1}{A}e^{f_\omega(x)}$$

(4)

where $A = \int e^{f_\omega(x)}dx$.

Learning of the Context Model

Our objective is to calculate $P(\omega|I)$ in (3) which is the *a priori* probability of a class indexed by ω given I. Without knowing I, the probability mass of ω is uniformly distributed over the class ensemble W. Due to the statistical dependence across the classes, however, the distribution will be updated once I is available. As a result, the classes that are more strongly correlated with I will have higher probabilities than others. Since the random variables are discrete in nature, the problem is essentially the estimation of a conditional probability mass function (PMF). A typical train of thought leads to the conventional approach to calculating the conditional probability; i.e., $P(\omega|I)=P(\omega,I)/P(I)$, for which we need a set of training samples belonging to $W \times W_1 \times W_2 \times ... \times W_{|I|}$, where W_i is the same as W and $i \in I=\{I_i|i=1,2,...,|I|\}$. However, in the case of neither retrieval nor annotation is such kind of training data easy to acquire because the data are in the form of past retrieval results for the former and the co-occurrence of semantic concepts for the latter. As a result of the above analysis, we propose the following way of modeling the contextual information. We represent a training sample as a random vector, denoted as $Y=[Y_1,Y_2,...,Y_W]$, where Y_ω is a binary random variable defined as:

$$Y_\omega = \begin{cases} 1, & \text{if concept } \omega \text{ exists in a scene or if image } \omega \text{ is relevant to a query} \\ 0, & \text{otherwise} \end{cases}$$

(5)

Given a set of T training samples represented as $\{Y_1,Y_2,...,Y_T\}$, we can estimate the $P(Y)$ and then calculate the conditional probability $P\left(Y_\omega \mid Y_{I_1},Y_{I_2},...Y_{I_{|I|}}\right)$, which is simply represented as $P(Y_\omega|YI)$ in what follows. To approximate the *a priori* probability in (3), we use:

$$P\left(\omega|I\right) = \frac{P\left(Y_\omega|Y_I\right)}{\sum_{\nu=1}^{W}P\left(Y_\nu|Y_I\right)}.$$

(6)

As the size of the concept ensemble grows, the computational intensity of the calculation of $P(Y_\omega | YI)$ based on $P(Y)$ increases exponentially. Therefore, it would be more efficient if we can directly estimate $P(Y_\omega | Y_I)$ based on a set of training samples. To this end, we employ a general approach for estimating the conditional probability, which is known as the maximum entropy (MaxEnt) approach based on Renyi's entropy (Zitnick, 2003). Essentially, the problem is solved by finding the conditional distribution $P(Y_\omega | Y_I)$ with the maximum entropy, among the distributions which are consistent with a set of statistics extracted from the training samples. Therefore, it can be considered as constrained optimization, which is formulated as:

$$\max_{P(Y_\omega | Y_I) \in [0,1]} - \sum_{y_\omega, y_I} \hat{P}\left(Y_I = y_I\right) P\left(Y_\omega = y_\omega | Y_I = y_I\right)^2,$$

subject to

$$\frac{\sum_{y_I} \hat{P}\left(Y_I = y_I\right) P\left(Y_\omega = y_\omega | Y_I = y_I\right) f_k}{\hat{P}(f_k)} = \hat{P}\left(f_\omega | f_k\right), k \in \{0\} \bigcup I, \tag{7}$$

where $\omega \in W$ and $\omega \notin I$ because $P(Y_\omega = 1 | YI\_1) \equiv 1$ for $\omega \in I$. In addition, $\hat{P}(\bullet)$ represents the empirical probabilities directly estimated from the training samples, $f\omega\_ Y\omega$ and $f_k = Y_k$ when $k \neq 0$ and $f_k = 1$ otherwise. Using a matrix-based representation, solving the above optimization leads to the result that:

P=M×N-¹×f (8)

where,

$$\boldsymbol{P} = \left(P\left(Y_{a_1} | Y_I\right), P\left(Y_{a_2} | Y_I\right), \ldots, P\left(Y_{a_{|W \setminus I|}} | Y_I\right) \right)^T \tag{9}$$

$$\boldsymbol{M} = \begin{pmatrix} \hat{P}\left(f_{a_1} | f_0\right) & \hat{P}\left(f_{a_1} | f_{I_1}\right) & \cdots & \hat{P}\left(f_{a_1} | f_{I_{|I|}}\right) \\ \hat{P}\left(f_{a_2} | f_0\right) & \hat{P}\left(f_{a_2} | f_{I_1}\right) & \cdots & \hat{P}\left(f_{a_2} | f_{I_{|I|}}\right) \\ \vdots & \vdots & \ddots & \vdots \\ \hat{P}\left(f_{a_{|W \setminus I|}} | f_0\right) & \hat{P}\left(f_{a_{|W \setminus I|}} | f_1\right) & \cdots & \hat{P}\left(f_{a_{|W \setminus I|}} | f_{I_{|I|}}\right) \end{pmatrix} \tag{10}$$

$$\boldsymbol{N} = \begin{pmatrix} 1 & 1 & \cdots & 1 \\ \hat{P}\left(f_{I_1} | f_0\right) & 1 & \cdots & \hat{P}\left(f_{I_1} | f_{I_{|I|}}\right) \\ \vdots & \vdots & \ddots & \vdots \\ \hat{P}\left(f_{I_{|I|}} | f_0\right) & \hat{P}\left(f_{I_{|I|}} | f_{I_1}\right) & \cdots & 1 \end{pmatrix} \tag{11}$$

and

$$f = \left(f_0, f_{I_1}, \ldots, f_{I_{|I|}} \right)^T \tag{12}$$

where $W \backslash I = \{a_1, a_2, \ldots, a_{|W \backslash I|}\}$.

A BAYESIAN IMAGE ANNOTATION FRAMEWORK

In the CBIA framework, a concept corresponds to a semantic class and is represented using ω. As illustrated in Figure 1, the framework is composed of a set of modules with different functionalities, which are enabled to run under two different states, i.e. on-line and off-line modes. The off-line phase is principally composed of the operations for the purpose of system training. First, a set of training images are processed using a two-stage image segmentation (Zhang, Wu, Yap, Guan, 2008). The objective of using this segmentation is to classify each segment into a foreground or a background class. In this way, the decision rule in (3) can be re-written as:

$$\hat{\omega} = \begin{cases} \max_{\omega \in W_F} P(\omega | x, I), & \text{if } x \text{ is extracted from a foreground segment} \\ \max_{\omega \in W_B} P(\omega | x, I), & \text{if } x \text{ is extracted from a background segment} \end{cases} \tag{13}$$

Simply put, the benefit of the two-stage image segmentation lies in the reduction of the number of semantic classes, leading to the alleviation of the semantic gap to some extent. Second, the resulting

Figure 1. The block diagram of the collaborative Bayesian image annotation framework

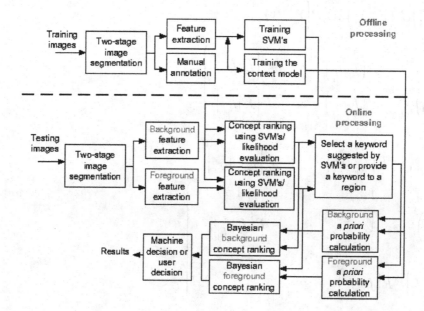

image regions are manually annotated based on their semantics. Third, to encode the content information, a set of low-level features are extracted from the image regions, based on which a set of SVMs, corresponding to the concepts in our pre-defined vocabulary, are obtained via supervised learning. Meanwhile, the keywords associated with the annotated images are used to build a statistical model, characterizing the contextual information. In the on-line mode, an image undergoes the same procedure of content analysis as those training images at first. Afterwards, the concepts are ranked for each of the image regions using the trained SVMs. To enable the integration of content and context, a user is asked to select a region with the correct concept appearing in the list suggested by the SVMs, or provide the concept of a region if none of the regions has a correctly suggested one. It is this input from the user that is considered as the background information I in the formulation of the Bayesian framework. The user's feedback will serve as the input of the context model, which generates the possibility of the appearance of other concepts given the one provided by the user. With the modification of the content model and the context model elaborated previously, the two types of information are integrated through the Bayesian framework.

A BAYESIAN IMAGE RETRIEVAL FRAMEWORK

Shown in Figure 2 is the system block diagram of the CLBIR framework. Upon the arrival of a search request, the system will calculate the *a posteriori* probability of each database image given the query images according to (3), which is used to generate a ranked list of the database images. In terms of retrieval, I and ω in (3) denote the indexes of query images and a database image, and x represents the center of the feature vectors of the query indexed by I. The likelihood can be evaluated based on a content-based method with proper modification and the *a priori* probability can be estimated from the past retrieval results. The underlying rationale of applying the Bayesian framework to image retrieval can be illustrated using Figure 3. The links between relevant images in Figure 3(b) are estimated by utilizing the co-occurrence of relevant images in the past retrieval results, which was originally proposed by Zitnick (2003) and adapted by Zhang and et. al. (2009) to make it applicable to a CLBIR framework, as discussed in the elaboration of the general framework. As mentioned earlier, the two types of similarity measure are complementary to each other. Specifically, the content-based component suffers from the semantic gap which can be alleviated using the contextual information. If there is no available contextual information, the system can still work using the content-based component and incrementally accumulate the retrieval results. When the context model is obtained with an incremental learning algorithm (Zhang, Guan, 2008), the system can integrate the two types of information. In our experiments, we employ both nearest neighbor CBIR (NN-CBIR) and SVM active learning CBIR (SVMAL-CBIR) as the content-based component. In fact, potential candidate for the content model is not confined to the above-mentioned two approaches, as explained during the formulation of the general Bayesian framework. Meanwhile, STRF, such as query movement or active learning, is also enabled to refine the result within each single query session. One of the advantages of the system is that various content-based methods can be plugged in to handle the content information so that we can make the best of many advanced CBIR systems. From the practical point of view, the system is assumed to start from a state with no available retrieval history, i.e. a state with no contextual information. In this case, the context model of the framework makes no contribution and hence the retrieval is conducted simply based on the content-based component and the incremental learning of the context model plays the role of LTRF.

Figure 2. The block diagram of the collaborative Bayesian image retrieval framework

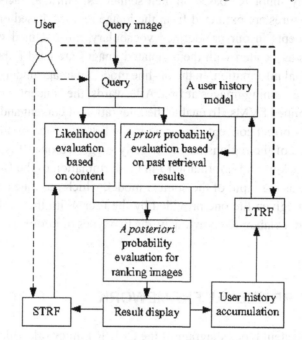

EXPERIMENTS

Experiments for Image Annotation

Database and Concept Vocabulary

To evaluate the performance of the proposed framework and compare it with several other alternative approaches, we used an image database consisting of 5000 images featuring 50 different categories of animals, which were collected from Flickr™ and Google™. In each category, there are 100 images. It covers a wide variety of species of animals, with some examples shown in Figure 4. Based on the scope of the semantic content of the database, we defined a concept vocabulary including 65 keywords, each of which uniquely represents a type of object possibly appearing in the images of the database, and therefore, $W=65$. The specific keywords can be found in Table 1. In addition to the concept corresponding to the 50 kinds of animals, there are 15 concepts representing the real-world objects that possibly appear in the living environment of the animals.

Training and Testing Sets

After the preprocessing, each region of an image is manually assigned a keyword, selected from the concept vocabulary. With no special consideration, we selected 750 images, with 15 from each of the 50 animal categories, to train a set of SVMs for the pre-defined concepts. For each semantic category, the training set is composed of the visual features of the image segments containing the objects of the semantic category. For feature selection, we employ color moments and wavelet moments, resulting in

Figure 3. The similarity measure in the content and context domains. (a) Semantic gap exists in the content domain. (b) There might not be sufficient data to extract accurate contextual information

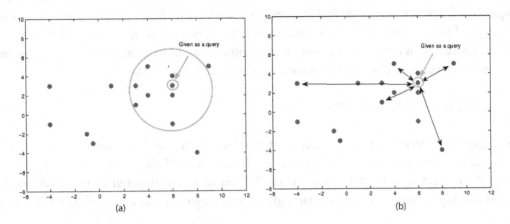

(a) (b)

a 26-dimensional feature vector for each segment of the images. Since the essential notion of context in the presented work is the possibility of the co-occurrence of the objects of different semantic categories, to model the contextual information and test the annotation framework, only images containing more than one semantic concept can be used. According to this requirement, only 534 of the 750 images used to train the SVMs are useful for training the context model. In addition, other than the images for training the SVMs and the context model, there are 2855 images available for performance evaluation and comparison in the database. The above usage of the images for training and testing purposes is summarized in Table 2. Since the annotation is considered as a pattern classification problem in which each sample, for either training or testing, is the feature vector of an image segment, it is more informative to look into the sizes of training and testing sets in terms of the number of image segments. To this end,

Table 1. The foreground and background concepts included in the concept vocabulary

Foreground concepts					
1. bear	2. black panther	3. camel	4. cat	5. chimpanzee	6. cow
7. crocodile	8. deer	9. dog	10. dolphin	11. duck	12. eagle
13. elephant	14. fish	15. flamingo	16. fox	17. frog	18. giraffe
19. goat	20. gorilla	21. guinea pig	22. hippo	23. horse	24. hyena
25. iguana	26. kangaroo	27. koala bear	28. leopard	29. lion	30. mongoose
31. monkey	32. orangutan	33. ostrich	34. owl	35. panda	36. parrot
37. peacock	38. pelican	39. penguin	40. polar bear	41. porcupine	42. puma
43. rabbit	44. rhinoceros	45. seal	46. snake	47. squirrel	48. tiger
49. tortoise	50. zebra				
Background concepts					
51. branch	52. cage	53. dry grass	54. fabric	55. flower	56. grass
57. ground	58. plant	59. sand	60. sky	61. snow	62. stone
63. tree	64. underwater	65. water			

the number of image segments belonging to each semantic category is shown in Figure 5. In addition, it has been calculated that there are in total 7927 segments used as testing samples with 2.78 segments per image on average. It is due to the fact that images containing different kinds of animals may include the same type of background objects that there are significantly more segments of background concepts than those of foreground concepts. It should also be noted that, unlike the SVM training, for learning the contextual information, concept-to-segment alignment is not needed.

Performance Evaluation Criteria

First, as a general criterion for all statistical pattern classification systems, the average classification accuracy can be employed to measure the overall performance of the annotation framework. In the context of the presented work, the average classification accuracy, denoted as P_{avg}, is defined as the average probability of assigning a keyword to a given image segment which is consistent with the ground

Figure 4. The sample images in the database employed for performance evaluation

Table 2. The information on the training and testing sets in terms of the number of images

Dataset	Number of images
Training set for the content model	750
Training set for the context model	534
Testing set	2855

truth. To approximate P_{avg}, the ratio of N_{CS}, the number of correctly classified segments, to N_{TS}, the total number of testing segments, is evaluated; i.e., where $N_{TS}=7927$. The above measure is also extended in the following way. When there is a large concept vocabulary, if a machine can suggest a relatively small set of relevant keywords containing the correct one and leave the final decision to human users, it is still helpful in terms of annotation efficiency. To study the performance under such a circumstance, we employ $P_{avg}(k) \approx N_{CS}(k)/N_{TS}$, where $N_{CS}(k)$ is the total number of correctly classified segments by examining the top k concepts on the ranked lists of all annotation tasks. It can be seen that, when $k=1$, it is just the performance of the machine-based decision. Second, considering that the goal of developing annotation techniques is to enable semantic-based retrieval and browsing, it is worthwhile to study to what extent the annotation framework affects retrieval and how effective it is compared with retrieving the images annotated using other methods. For this evaluation, we study the performance with respect to those foreground concepts because it reflects the ability of the framework to provide users with images relevant to some type of animal. For category ω, the precision and recall, defined as $PR_{\omega}=N_{C,\omega}/N_{R,\omega}$ and $RC_{\omega}=N_{C,\omega}/N_{G,\omega}$, are employed to evaluate the performance, where $N_{C,\omega}$ denotes the numbers of images correctly annotated by the system and thus relevant to the query ω, $N_{G,\omega}$ is the number of images belonging to the class ω according to the ground truth, and $N_{R,\omega}$ is the number of images annotated by the system with the concept ω, regardless of being correct or wrong. Finally, the average precision and recall, defined as $PR_{avg} = \frac{1}{W}\sum_{\omega=1}^{W} PR_{\omega}$ and $RC_{avg} = \frac{1}{W}\sum_{\omega=1}^{W} RC_{\omega}$, are compared among all approaches considered in our experiments.

Numerical Results

To demonstrate the advantage of the Bayesian framework over others, we compare in total three cases, including content-based annotation using SVMs (SVMA), context-based annotation (CTXA), and the CBIA. Since the two-stage image segmentation brings about the availability of the information showing whether a segment contains a foreground or background concept, we consider two types of classification/annotation for each of the above three approaches to justify the improvement resulting from the two-stage image segmentation. The first type does not utilize the information obtained via the two-stage

Figure 5. The information on the training and testing sets in terms of the number of image segments. (a) The number of training and testing samples for the SVMs in each semantic class. (b) The co-occurrence information in the training samples for the concept network

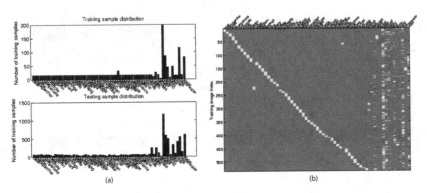

image segmentation and hence the class label of a to-be-classified sample may be any of the concepts in the vocabulary shown in Table 1. This is referred to as all classification and ALL for short. On the other hand, the second type takes advantage of the information so that only foreground/background concepts are considered when annotating a foreground/background segment. We referred to this as separate classification and SEP for short. In summary, six approaches are compared with each other in our study, i.e. SVMA ALL, SVMA SEP, CTXA ALL, CTXA SEP, CBIA ALL, CBIA SEP. In terms of the Pavg(k, we also take CMRM into account in the comparative study.

Prior to the discussion on the numerical results in terms of the annotation performance evaluated using the afore-mentioned criteria, Figure 6 and Figure 7 are used to illustrate the underlying rationale of the CBIA framework. For both examples, the results are obtained using the CBIA SEP because this is the most comprehensive approach one among all of the six considered in the experiments. The first example indicates a situation in which the contextual information corrects the content information, using the example of annotating an image containing a lion. Shown in Figure 6(a) is the segmentation result. The a priori probabilities P(ω|I) of the foreground and background concepts calculated based on the context model are separately shown in Figure 6(b). The likelihood P(x|ω) of the foreground segment with respect to each foreground class ω and the a posteriori probability P(ω|x,I) of each of them are displayed in Figure 6(c).

Figure 6. Illustration of the rationale of the CBIA framework, in which the contextual information helps correct the content information. (a) The segmentation and ground truth. (b) The a priori probabilities of the image segments. (c) The likelihood and the a posteriori probabilities of the image segments

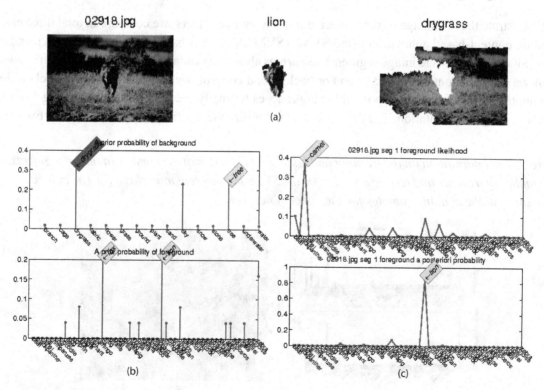

It can be observed based on the curve of likelihood that the camel is recognized as the concept assigned to the foreground segment using SVM. With the information captured by the context model, however, this value is down-weighted, while the value corresponding to lion is raised. Therefore, the Bayesian framework selects the lion as the concept for the foreground segment because it's a posteriori probability is the highest. In contrast to the first example, the second one illustrates a case in which the content information corrects the contextual information using the annotation of an image containing a bear. Given water as the background concept, a priori information naturally results in higher probabilities of the aquatic animals or amphibians listed in Table 1, such as dolphin and seal, which leads to a wrong decision in this example. However, the observation on the visual property of the segment refines the a priori knowledge in the way such that the a posteriori probability of bear becomes the highest.

Shown in Figure 8(a) is the comparison among the six approaches in terms of $P_{avg}(k)$. Based on the observation that the sizes of training and testing sets for foreground and background are considerably different, as shown in Figure 5(a), and the intended usage of the image database, not only do we evaluate the overall performance, we also study the performance of annotating foreground and background individually. It can be observed that, as the most comprehensive framework in question, the CBIA SEP outperforms all others regardless of how many concepts on the ranked list are examined by users, which includes the case of machine-based decision making, i.e. $k=1$. The overall performance comparison also shows that, when $k \geq 5$, SVMA SEP exhibits better performance than CBIA ALL. With respect to this observation, the separate evaluations on the foreground and background shown in Figure 8(b) and Figure 8(c) reveal more information. It can be seen that the background annotation performance of

Figure 7. Illustration of the rationale of the CBIA framework, in which the content information helps correct the contextual information. (a) The segmentation and ground truth. (b) The a priori probabilities of the image segments. (c) The likelihood and the a posteriori probabilities of the image segments

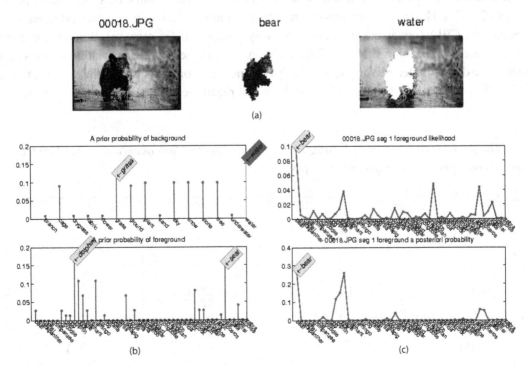

SVMA SEP increases much faster than CBIA ALL as the examined portion of the ranked list of concepts becomes larger. It can be explained as follows. Based on the SEP type classification, the information of being a background segment obtained using the two-stage image segmentation reduces the size of the set of semantic labels from 65 to 15, which almost accounts for 77% of the concept vocabulary. On the other hand, if a segment contains a foreground object, the semantic label set only shrinks by 23%. Among the 50 foreground concepts, semantic gap is still very severe, whereas the gap within the 15 background concept is not. However, the above explanation only makes sense when the final decision is left to users. As long as machine-based decision is employed, the proposed CBIA framework has best performance, for both ALL and SEP type classification. In general, the comparison indicates that the CBIA framework resolves the drawbacks of both content-based and context-based methods, especially when the two-stage image segmentation is employed to enable SEP type classification. Moreover, the performance of annotation using CMRM is also considered in the comparison, which also indicates better performance of the CBIA framework.

The comparison in terms of precision and recall is shown in Figure 9. For all compared approaches, the actual number of images in each semantic category is the same and therefore the difference in terms of the recall values stems from the distinct abilities of various approaches to successfully annotate the foreground segments of the images. At the first glance, it seems that the performance of SVMA SEP is better than that of CBIA ALL, which is inconsistent with the analysis based on the $P_{avg}(k)$, where $k=1$. In fact, although each image has one and only one foreground segment resulting in the fact that the number of foreground segments is the same as the number of images, the above conclusion is not true, which can be explained as follows. The average recall RC_{avg} is defined as the arithmetic average of the class-specific recall $RC_{avg,\omega}$, whereas the average classification accuracy Pa_{vg} is defined as the expectation of the class-specific accuracy. In other words, the evaluation of the average recall does not involve any information on the sample distribution over the semantic classes, which, if considered, will give rise to another conclusion that the average accuracy values of the SVMA SEP and CBIA ALL are respectively 21.37% and 22.17%. However, the comparison shown in Figure 9 still demonstrates effectiveness and advantage of the CBIA framework in terms of the way it improves the retrieval. When it comes to the comparison based on precision shown in Figure 9(a), retrieval based on the annotation using ALL type classification exhibits better performance, which is somewhat contradictory to the way it affects the annotation. Since both of the class-specific precision and recall are defined based on $N_{C,\omega}$, if the Pav_{gr} e-

Figure 8. The performance evaluated using the average classification accuracy. (a) All concepts. (b) Foreground concepts. (c) Background concepts

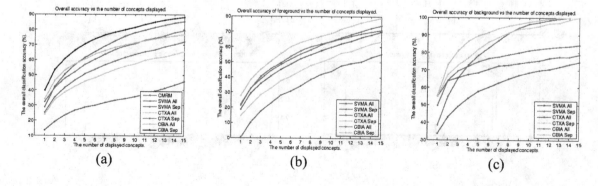

lated to ALL classification is higher than that related to SEP classification and the relation in terms of $RCav_{g_i}$s reversed, then it is very likely that $N_{R'_\omega}$ related to ALL classification is lower than that related to SEP classification. Therefore, for both SVMA and CBIA, we evaluate the ratio of $N_{R'_\omega}$ using ALL classification to $N_{R'_\omega}$ using SEP classification and the result shown in Figure 10 verifies our analysis. Considering the observation one step further, we find that it can be explained as follows. When ALL classification is employed, there are in total 65 semantic categories into which the 2855 images/foreground segments are classified. However, there are only 50 classes if SEP classification is used but the total number of images is unchanged. Therefore, on average, the number of images classified into each class using ALL classification tends to be lower than that of SEP classification. In other words, in the case of ALL classification, there are many foreground segments that are classified into the semantic classes corresponding to background concepts. Nonetheless, it is worth noting that the comparison based on precision and recall justifies the advantage of the CBIA framework over the content- and context-based approaches, especially when the most comprehensive framework CBIA SEP is considered.

Experiments for Image Retrieval

Experimental Setup

To guarantee the diversified image content, which is a typical situation of image retrieval in a large general domain, we randomly selected 200 classes from the COREL image collection, with 50 images in each class. The resultant 10000 images and the vendor-defined categories were used as the database and the ground truth for evaluating the performance. From the database, 10 queries were selected from each of the 200 classes, resulting in 2000 queries, each of which is composed of two different images. Under the query-by-example retrieval paradigm, the average of the features of the two images was used as the feature of each query. The queries were further divided into three mutually exclusive subsets, denoted by T_A, $T_{B,1}$, and $T_{B,2}$, where $T_A = 1000$, $T_{B,1} = 400$, and $T_{B,2} = 600$ are the respective sizes of the subsets.

Figure 9. The performance evaluated using precision and recall. It is the performance of a simple retrieval approach based on keyword matching. Also note that the recall of CTXA ALL is not zero but a very small value; otherwise, the precision would be zero as well. (a) Average precision. (b) Average recall

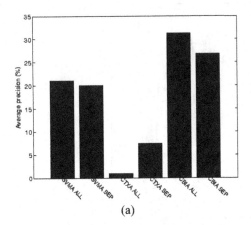

(a)

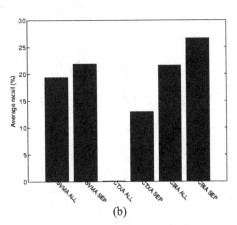

(b)

We employed global color histogram in Hue-Saturation-Value (HSV) space, color layout in YCbCr space and Gabor wavelet as low-level features. The experimental procedure is summarized as follows.

1. T_A was used when the user history model was not available, i.e. before initial LTRF was conducted. In such a case, only STRF is involved, and the NN-CLBIR and the SVMAL-CLBIR are essentially the same as the NN-CBIR and SVMAL-CBIR because the *a priori* distribution of the candidate images is uniform. The retrieval results corresponding to T_A were used to perform the initial LTRF.
2. After the initial LTRF, the CLBIR systems are expected to present better performance thanks to the accumulated high-level knowledge characterized by the user history model, while the STRF still improves the results with respect to each specific query. $T_{B,1}$ was used to demonstrate the performance improvement.
3. During the operation of the CLBIR systems, the new retrieval results after a certain LTRF are gradually accumulated until the next LTRF is carried out. In our experiments, the retrieval results corresponding to $T_{B,1}$ were used to perform the second LTRF, i.e. an incremental update of the system. To show the effectiveness of the incremental update, the performance was evaluated using $T_{B,2}$. Since the query subsets are mutually exclusive, we guaranteed that the trained system using LTRF were tested based on previously unseen samples.

Numerical Results

Shown in Figure 11(b) is the comparison between NN-CBIR and NN-CLBIR in terms of the average precision as a function of the number of retrieval iterations, which is defined as:

$$PR_{avg}(n) = \frac{1}{K}\sum_{k=1}^{K}PR(k,n)$$

and $PR(k,n)=N_C(k,n)/N_R(k,n)$, where k and n are the index of a query and the number of retrieval iterations, and $N_C(k,n)$ and $N_R(k,n)$ are the numbers of relevant images and retrieved images for the k-th

Figure 10. The ratio of $N_{R,\omega}$ using ALL classification to $N_{R,\omega}$ using SEP classification

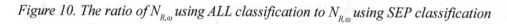
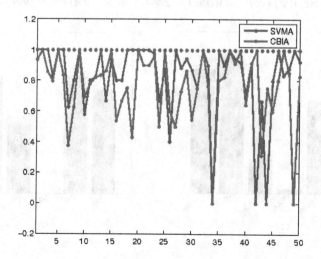

query after n iterations. We adopted N_R=48 in this case. First, using query set TB,1, the improvement due to the initial LTRF, which was based on the retrieval results corresponding to TA, can be observed, indicating the ability of the CLBIR systems to utilize the past retrieval results. Meanwhile, the improvement resulting from STRF can also be observed, which is shared by both CBIR and CLBIR systems. Second, after the second LTRF, the performance of NN-CLBIR using query set TB,2 is further enhanced resulting from more accumulated knowledge through LTRF. Based on the same query set, the performance of NN-CBIR remains similar. To test the performance in terms of ranking ability, we employed the precision-versus-recall curve (PRC), where the recall is defined as $RC(k,n)=N_C(k,n)/N_G(k,n)$, where $N_G(k)$ is the number of images in the semantic class of query k. The precision is averaged over all queries at each different recall value for a certain number of retrieval iteration n. The PRC after the initial retrieval was shown in Figure 11(a). Higher precision value at a certain recall indicates more relevant images being ranked ahead of irrelevant ones. Based on this fact, the advantage of the integration of user history as high-level knowledge with the content analysis can be demonstrated based on the comparison in Figure 11(a). The comparison shown in Figure 11(c) and Figure 11(d) is for the same purpose of performance evaluation as that described above, whereas the difference lies in the approach to the content analysis for the likelihood computation, which is based on the output of the SVM employed for active learning-based STRF. In this case, we adopted N_R=20 for the evaluation of $PR_{avg}(n)$. Since the initial retrieval is just random ranking, the precision was evaluated starting from the first STRF iteration. Again, we can observe the improvement resulting from the information integration through the Bayesian framework.

Figure 11. Objective evaluation on the performance improvement resulting from the Bayesian integration of content and context. a) and c) Comparison in terms of the PRC after the first retrieval iteration. b) and d) Comparison in terms of the precision as a function of the number of RF iterations

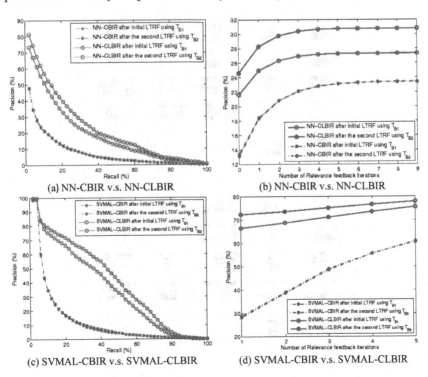

Subjective Evaluation

In addition to the objective evaluation, an interface for the framework has been implemented to facilitate subjective evaluation of the effectiveness of the proposed framework. Illustrated in Figure 12(a) are the top 20 retrieved images using NN-CBIR. Shown in Figure 12(b) and Figure 12(c) are the results using NN-CLBIR with the context model trained using 1000 and 1400 past retrieval results. It is not difficult to observe the improvement resulting from integrating the content and context using the Bayesian framework by comparing Figure 12(a) and Figure 12(b). Furthermore, the improvement obtained by incrementally update the context model can also be verified based on the comparison between Figure 12(b) and Figure 12(c).

Figure 12. Subjective performance evaluation. (a) A retrieval result of NN-CBIR. (b) A retrieval result of NN-CLBIR based on the user history model trained using 1000 past retrieval results. (c) A retrieval result of NN-CLBIR based on the user history model trained using 1400 past retrieval results

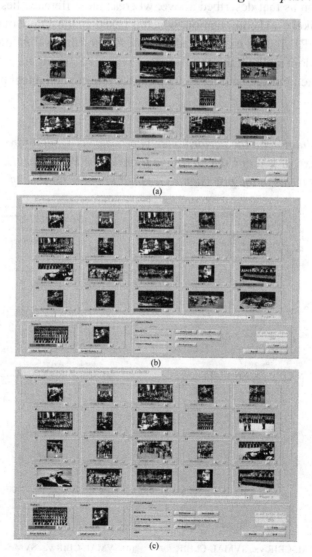

(a)

(b)

(c)

CONCLUSION

In this chapter, the current leading trend within the research area of image annotation and retrieval is discussed with a detailed review on the representative works. Recognizing the critical role of integrating information of multiple modalities, we focus on the integration of content and context and present an in-depth discussion on our recent work, in which a Bayesian framework is proposed for the tackling the problem of semantic gap. In addition, the Bayesian framework is compared with a few others either based on experimental results or the underlying principle. The advantages of the Bayesian framework are demonstrated by the numerical results of the experiments of various tasks, such as annotation and retrieval. As for future work, there are many interesting open problems which are worth investigating. In terms of the CBIA framework, it still relies some input from the user to effectively incorporate the contextual information. In terms of the CLBIR framework, when the size of a database grows, which is a very practical issue for retrieval, being able to update the context model efficiently is very necessary. Building context model over a pre-clustered database is a potential solution. In general, establishing context model effectively and efficiently for a large collection of entities and its integration with a large database of multimedia data is valuable. In addition, the potential contribution of the integration of content and context to multimedia data mining, such as learning a hierarchical semantic structure of image collection should also be considered.

REFERENCES

Barnard, K., Duygulu, P., Forsyth, D., Freitas, N., Blei, D. M., & Jordan, M. I. (2003). Matching words and pictures. *Journal of Machine Learning Research, 3,* 1107–1135. doi:10.1162/153244303322533214

Barnard, K., & Forsyth, D. (2001). Learning the semantics of words and pictures. In *Proceedings from ECCV '01: The International Conference on Computer Vision,* (vol. 2, pp. 408–415).

Biederman, I., Mezzanotte, R. J., & Rabinowitz, J. C. (1982). Scene perception: detecting and judging objects undergoing relational violations. *Cognitive Psychology, 14*(2), 143–177. doi:10.1016/0010-0285(82)90007-X

Blei, D. M., & Jordan, M. I. (2003). Modeling annotated data. In *Proceedings from ACM SIGIR '03: The International ACM SIGIR Conference on Research and Development in Informaion Retrieval,* (pp. 127–134). New York: ACM.

Blei, D. M., Ng, A. Y., & Jordan, M. I. (2003). Latent dirichlet allocation. *Journal of Machine Learning Research, 3,* 993–1022. doi:10.1162/jmlr.2003.3.4-5.993

Carbonetto, P., Freitas, N., & Barnard, K. (2004). A statistical model for general contextual object recognition. In *Proceedings from ECCV '04: The European Conference on Computer Vision,* (pp. 350–362).

Carneiro, G., Chan, A. B., Moreno, P. J., & Vasconcelos, N. (2007). Supervised learning of semantic classes for image annotation and retrieval. *IEEE Transactions on Pattern Analysis and Machine Intelligence, 29,* 394–410. doi:10.1109/TPAMI.2007.61

Crucianu, M., Ferecatu, M., & Boujemaa, N. (2004). Relevance feedback for image retrieval: a short survey. *Report of the DELOS2 EuropeanNetwork of Excellence.*

Datta, R., Joshi, D., Li, J., & Wang, J. Z. (2008). Image retrieval: Ideas, influences, and trends of the new age. *ACM Computing Surveys, 40*(2), 5:1 – 5:60.

Duygulu, P., Barnard, K., Freitas, N., & Forsyth, D. A. (2002). Object recognition as machine translation: Learning a lexicon for a fixed image vocabulary. In *Proceedings from ECCV '02: The European Conference on Computer Vision,* (pp. 97–112).

Flickner, M., Sawhney, H., Niblack, W., Ashley, J., Huang, Q., & Dom, B. (1995). Query by Image and Video Content: The QBIC System. *Computer, 28*(9), 23–32. doi:10.1109/2.410146

Guan, L., Muneesawang, P., Wang, Y., Zhang, R., Tie, Y., Bulzacki, A., & Ibrahim, M. T. (2009). Multimedia multimodal methodologies. In *Proceedings from ICME '09: The International Conference on Multimedia and Expo.*

Hanbury, A. (2008). A survey of methods for image annotation. *Journal of Visual Languages and Computing, 19*(5), 617–627. doi:10.1016/j.jvlc.2008.01.002

He, X., King, O., Ma, W.-Y., Li, M., & Zhang, H.-J. (2003). Learning a semantic space from user's relevance feedback for image retrieval. *IEEE Transactions on Circuits and Systems for Video Technology, 13*(1), 39–48. doi:10.1109/TCSVT.2002.808087

Hofmann, T. (1999). Probabilistic latent semantic analysis. In *Proceedings of UAI '99: The Conference on Uncertainty in Artificial Intelligence.*

Jeon, R. M. J., & Lavrenko, V. (2003). Automatic image annotation and retrieval using cross-media relevance models. In *Proceedings from ACM SIGIR '03: The 26th Annual International ACM SIGIR Conference on Research and Development in Informaion Retrieval,* (pp. 119 – 126).

Jing, F., Li, M., Zhang, H.-J., & Zhang, B. (2005). A unified framework for image retrieval using keyword and visual features. *IEEE Transactions on Image Processing, 14,* 979–989. doi:10.1109/TIP.2005.847289

Li, J., & Wang, J. Z. (2003). Automatic linguistic indexing of pictures by a statistical modeling approach. *IEEE Transactions on Pattern Analysis and Machine Intelligence, 25*(9), 1075–1088. doi:10.1109/TPAMI.2003.1227984

Mei, T., Wang, Y., Hua, X.-S., Gong, S., & Li, S. (2008). Coherent image annotation by learning semantic distance. In *Proceedings of CVPR '08: The IEEE Conference on Computer Vision and Pattern Recognition,* Anchorage, AK.

Mori, Y., Takahashi, H., & Oka, R. (1999). Image-to-word transformation based on dividing and vector quantizing images with words. In *Proceedings of International Workshop on Multimedia Intelligent Storage and Retrieval Management.*

Muneesawang, P., & Guan, L. (2004). An interactive approach for CBIR using a network of radial basis functions. *IEEE Transactions on Multimedia, 6*(5), 703–716. doi:10.1109/TMM.2004.834866

Rabinovich, A., Vedaldi, A., Galleguillos, C., Wiewiora, E., & Belongie, S. (2007). Objects in context. In *Proceedings from ICCV '07: The International Conference on Computer Vision.*

Smeulders, A. W. M., Worring, M., Santini, S., Gupta, A., & Jain, R. (2001). Content-based image retrieval at the end of the early years. *IEEE Transactions on Pattern Analysis and Machine Intelligence, 22*(12), 1349–1380. doi:10.1109/34.895972

Smith, J. R., & Chang, S.-F. (1996). *Visualseek: A fully automated content-based image query system* (pp. 87–98). ACM Multimedia.

Szummer, M., & Picard, R. W. (1998). Indoor-outdoor image classification. In *Proceedings of IEEE International Workshop on Content-Based Access of Image and Video Database*, (pp. 42–51.)

Tong, S., & Chang, E. (2001). Support vector machine active learning for image retrieval. In *Proceedings of ACM MM '01: The Ninth ACM International Conference on Multimedia*, (pp. 107–118).

Uchihashi, S., & Kanade, T. (2005). Content-free image retrieval based on relations exploited from user feedbacks. In *Proceedings of ICME: The International Conference on Multimedia and Expo*, (pp. 1358 – 1361).

Vailaya, A., Figueiredo, M. A. T., Jain, A. K., & Zhang, H.-J. (2001). Image classification for content-based indexing. *IEEE Transactions on Image Processing, 10*(1), 117–130. doi:10.1109/83.892448

Yap, K. H., & Wu, K. (2005). A soft relevance framework in content-based image retrieval systems. *IEEE Transactions on Circuits and Systems for Video Technology, 15*(12), 1557–1568. doi:10.1109/TCSVT.2005.856912

Zhang, R., & Guan, L. (2008). A new relevance feedback framework for content-free image retrieval. In *Proceedings from MMSP '08: The IEEE international workshop on Multimedia Signal Processing.*

Zhang, R., & Guan, L. (2009). A collaborative Bayesian image retrieval framework. In *Proceedings from ICASSP '09: The International Conference on Acoustic, Speech, and Signal Processing.*

Zhang, R., Wu, K., Yap, K. H., & Guan, L. (2008). A collaborative bayesian image annotation framework. In *Proceedings of PCM '08: The IEEE Pacific-Rim Conference on Multimedia*, (pp. 348–357).

Zhou, X. S., & Huang, T. (2003). Relevance feedback in image retrieval: A comprehensive review. *Multimedia Systems, 8*, 536–544. doi:10.1007/s00530-002-0070-3

Zitnick, C. (2003). *Computing conditional probabilities in large domains by maximizing Rényi's quadratic entropy*. Doctoral dissertation, Robotics Institute, Carnegie Mellon University, Pittsburgh, PA.

ENDNOTE

[1] Strictly speaking, metadata is defined as data for explaining data and therefore may include both visual content and text. We separate them from the others in that they have been and still are considered as the main stream modalities for tackling image retrieval and annotation.

Chapter 8

A Highly Scalable and Adaptable Co–Learning Framework on Multimodal Data Mining in a Multimedia Database

Zhongfei (Mark) Zhang
SUNY Binghamton, USA

Zhen Guo
SUNY Binghamton, USA

Christos Faloutsos
Carnegie Mellon University, USA

Jia-Yu (Tim) Pan
Google Inc., USA

ABSTRACT

This chapter presents a highly scalable and adaptable co-learning framework on multimodal data mining in a multimedia database. The co-learning framework is based on the multiple instance learning theory. The framework enjoys a strong scalability in the sense that the query time complexity is a constant, independent of the database scale, and the mining effectiveness is also independent of the database scale, allowing facilitating a multimodal querying to a very large scale multimedia database. At the same time, this framework also enjoys a strong adaptability in the sense that it allows incrementally updating the database indexing with a constant operation when the database is dynamically updated with new information. Hence, this framework excels many of the existing multimodal data mining methods in the literature that are neither scalable nor adaptable at all. Theoretic analysis and empirical evaluations are provided to demonstrate the advantage of the strong scalability and adaptability. While this framework is general for multimodal data mining in any specific domains, to evaluate this framework, the authors apply it to the Berkeley Drosophila ISH embryo image database for the evaluations of the mining performance. They have compared the framework with a state-of-the-art multimodal data mining method to demonstrate the effectiveness and the promise of the framework.

DOI: 10.4018/978-1-61692-859-9.ch008

INTRODUCTION

Multimodal data mining in a multimedia database is a challenging topic in data mining research (Zhang et al, 2006). In this context, a multimedia database refers to a data collection in which there are multiple modalities of unstructured data such as text and imagery. By multimodal data mining in a multimedia database it is meant that the knowledge discovery to the multimedia database is initiated by a query that may consist of multiple modalities of unstructured data such as text and imagery. In this chapter, we focus on a multimedia database as an image database in which each image has a few textual words given as annotation. We then address the problem of multimodal data mining in such an image database as the problem of retrieving similar data and/or inferencing new patterns to a multimodal query from the database.

Specifically, in the context of this chapter, multimodal data mining refers to two aspects of activities. The first is the multimodal retrieval. This is the scenario where a multimodal query consisting of either textual words alone, or imagery alone, or in any combination is entered and an expected retrieval data modality is specified that can also be text alone, or imagery alone, or in any combination; the retrieved data based on a pre-defined similarity criterion are returned back to the user. The second is the multimodal inferencing. While the retrieval based multimodal data mining has its standard definition in terms of the semantic similarity between the query and the retrieved data from the database, the inferencing based mining depends on the specific applications. In this chapter, we focus on the application of the fruit-fly image database mining. Consequently, the inferencing based multimodal data mining may include many different scenarios. A typical scenario is the across-stage multimodal inferencing. There are many interesting questions a biologist may want to ask in the fruit fly research given such a multimodal mining capability. For example, given an embryo image in stage 5, what is the corresponding image in stage 7 for an image-to-image three-stage inferencing? What is the corresponding annotation for this image in stage 7 for an image-to-word three-stage inferencing? The multimodal mining technique we have developed in this chapter also addresses this type of across-stage inferencing capability, in addition to the multimodal retrieval capability.

Based on the motivation to develop such a technique for the multimodal data mining in a multimedia database, we propose a co-learning framework. This co-learning framework is based on the Multiple Instance Learning (MIL) theory (Dietterich et al, 1997; Maron & Lozano-Perez, 1998; Auer, 1997). While this co-learning framework is general for any specific domains, to demonstrate the effectiveness of this framework, we apply this framework to the Berkeley Drosophila (fruit-fly) ISH embryo image database[1]. In addition, we have also compared this co-learning framework on this database with a state-of-the-art multimodal data mining method to demonstrate the effectiveness and the promise of the framework.

This chapter is organized as follows. This Introduction section is followed by a brief literature review for the most related work. Then the co-learning framework based on the MIL theory is presented. A theoretic analysis on the scalability of the framework when the database is updated is reported. Finally, the extensive evaluations on the retrieval and across-stage inferencing based on the Berkeley Drosophila ISH data are documented in comparison with a state-of-the-art multimodal retrieval method. We also report the empirical evaluations using the same data set to demonstrate the scalability advantage of the framework. The chapter is concluded at the end.

RELATED WORK

In the machine learning community, MIL has become a focused topic in recent years and has received extensive attention in the literature ever since the classic work of (Dietterich et al, 1997; Auer, 1997; and Maron and Lozano-Perez, 1998). Recent developments on MIL include (Andrews et al, 2003; Andrews and Hofmann; 2004; and Rahmani and Goldman, 2006). (Yang and Lozano-Perez, 2000) and (Zhang et al, 2002) were among the first to apply MIL to image retrieval, which led to more subsequent work on this topic (Zhang et al, 2006; Zhu et al, 2006).

(Chen et al, 2006) recently added the embeded instance selection principle into the classic MIL algorithm resulting in a better learning performance, and also applied this method to image retrieval.

On the other hand, image data mining, and in particular image retrieval, has been studied for over a decade. One of the notorious bottleneck of image retrieval is the semantic gap (Smeulders et al, 2000). Recently, it is reported that this bottleneck may be effectively reduced using multimodal approaches (Barnard et al, 2003; Duygulu et al, 2002; Feng et al, 2004; Zhang et al, 2005) by taking the advantage that in many applications imagery data do not exist in isolation but typically co-exist with other modalities of information such as text. It is demonstrated in the literature (Jeon and Manmatha, 2004; Feng et al, 2004; Zhang et al, 2005) that given such a presence of the multimodal data, there are effective methods to reduce the semantic gap by exploiting the synergy among the different modalities of the data.

Following this line of reasoning, multimodal data mining, and in particular, multimodal data retrieval, has recently received substantial attention since Barnard and Duygulu et al. started their pioneering work on image annotation (Barnard et al, 2003, Duygulu et al, 2002). Recent work includes (Jeon et al, 2003; Jeon and Manmatha, 2004; Chang et al, 2003; Wang et al, 2004; Pan et al, 2004; Monay and Gatica-Perez, 2004; Zhang et al, 2005; Liu and Tang, 2005; Wu et al, 2005; Li et al, 2006; Li and Wang, 2006; Datta et al, 2006; Wang et al, 2006).

(Fergus et al, 2005) trained the PLSA based image annotation method for the Google image search data for further enhancing the image search performance.

Yang et al (Yang et al, 2005; Yang et al, 2006) proposed similar frameworks to our work in the sense that MIL theory was used for image retrieval where text annotation was available in the training data. However, in comparison, they focused on decomposing an image into regions, and more importantly, they failed to address the scalability and adaptability issues at all.

HIGHLIGHTS OF THIS WORK

The main contribution of this work is that this proposed co-learning framework is not just yet another multimodal data mining technique; more importantly, this framework is highly scalable in the sense that the query time complexity is a constant, independent of the database scale, and the mining effectiveness is also independent of the database scale, allowing facilitating a multimodal querying to a very large scale of a multimedia database. At the same time, this framework is also highly adaptable in the sense that it allows incrementally updating the database indexing with a constant operation when the database is dynamically updated with new information. Hence, this framework excels many of the existing multimodal data mining methods in the literature that are neither scalable nor adaptable at all. Theoretic analysis and empirical evaluations are provided to demonstrate the advantage of the strong scalability and adaptability.

CO-LEARNING FRAMEWORK

We first consider the scenario that the whole database is initially used as the training set to develop the database indexing before the database is allowed to evolve under the assumption that the word vocabulary stays the same. We will relax this assumption in the adaptability analysis in Section Adapbility Analysis.

In the rest of the chapter, we use calligraphic letters to denote the set variables or functions, and to use regular letters to denote regular variables or functions. A database $\mathbf{D} = \{\mathbf{I}, \mathbf{W}\}$ consists of two parts, an image collection $\mathbf{I}$ and a vocabulary collection $\mathbf{W}$. A collection of images $\mathbf{I} = \{I_i, i = 1, ..., N\}$ is the whole database image set used as the training set; $N = |\mathbf{I}|$; for each image I_i, there are a set of words annotating this image $W_i = \{w_{ij}, j = 1, ..., N_i\}$; the whole vocabulary set of the database is $\mathbf{W}$, $M = |\mathbf{W}| = |\bigcap_{i=1}^{N} W_i|$. We define a block as a subimage of an image such that the image is partitioned into a set of blocks and all the blocks of this image share the same resolution.

We define a VRep (visual representative) as a representative of a set of all the blocks for all the images in the database that appear visually similar to each other. A visual similarity is typically defined in a low-level image feature space. Depending on specific application domains and the specific implementation, this visual similarity may vary. We intentionally leave the specific definition of the visual similarity to the specific application and implementation to make the proposed framework a general one capable of being applied to any such domains. Given a specific definition of the visual similarity in a specific feature space, a VRep of an image may be represented as a feature vector in the feature space.

Before we present the framework, we first make a few assumptions.

- A semantic concept corresponds to one or multiple words, and a word corresponds to one semantic concept for each image. Consequently, semantic concepts may be represented in words.
- A semantic concept corresponds to one or multiple VReps, and a VRep corresponds to one or multiple semantic concepts.
- A word corresponds to one or multiple VReps, and a VRep corresponds to one or multiple words.
- An image may have one or more words for annotation.

Based on these assumptions, we first describe how to obtain the VReps. Then we introduce the framework based on the MIL theory for establishing the direct mapping between the VRep space and the word space for the database indexing.

Obtain VReps for Each Image

For each image I_i, we partition it into a set of exclusive blocks B_{ij}, i.e.,

$$I_i = \bigcup_{j=1}^{n_i} B_{ij} \tag{1}$$

where n_i is a function of the resolution of I_i such that the resolution of B_{ij} is no less than a threshold. If all the images in the database are in the same resolution, all the n_i's are the same as a constant. Since all the blocks are exclusive and each block may be represented as a feature vector in a feature space, for all the blocks of all the images in the database, a nearest neighbor clustering in the feature space leads to a partition of the whole block feature vectors in the feature space into a finite number of clusters such that each cluster is represented by its centroid; let L be the number of such clusters. This centroid is a VRep corresponding to this cluster for all the images in the database. Consequently, the whole VRep set in the database is

$$V=\{v_i|i=1,...,L\} \tag{2}$$

Thus, each image I_i may be represented by a subset of V. Each VRep is represented as a feature vector in the feature space and corresponds to a subset of all the images in the database such that this VRep appears in those images in the subset, i.e., for each VRep v_i, there is a subset I_{v_i} of the images in the database such that

$$I_{v_i} = \{I_h \mid h = 1,...,n_{v_i}\} \tag{3}$$

where $n_{v_i} = |I_{v_i}|$. This is similar to building a visual codebook described in (Jurie and Triggs, 2005; Pan et al, 2006; Zhang & Zhang, 2007).

Establish the Direct Mapping between the Word Space and the VRep Space

Once we have obtained all the VReps for the images in the database, we sort all the textual vocabulary words in **W** (say alphabetically), and for each word w_k, there is a corresponding set of images, S_k, such that this word wk appears in the annotation of each of the images in the set. Since each image is represented as a set of decomposed blocks, S_k may be represented as

$$S_k = \{I_{k_i} \mid I_{k_i} = \bigcup_{j=1}^{n_{k_i}} B_{kij} \tag{4}$$

where $B_{k_{ij}}$ is the jth block in image I_{k_i}. For each block $B_{k_{ij}}$ in image I_{k_i}, a feature vector $f_{k_{ij}}$ in the feature space is used to represent the block. Consequently, we have the relationship between the word space and the VRep space through the connection of the image space as illustrated in Figure 1.

In order to further establish the direct relationship between the word space and the VRep space, we map the problem to an MIL problem \cite{b:dietterich97}. A classic MIL problem is to learn a function $y=F(x)$, where we are given by multiple samples of x represented as bags, and each bag has ambiguities represented by the multiple instances of x. Here the problem is that each bag is an image, and that all the instances of this bag are the blocks represented by the corresponding feature vectors; the y here is a word vector instead of a value in the range of [0, 1] in the classic version of MIL, consisting of all the words given in the training set that correspond to a specific VRep; the function to be learned each time is the function of a VRep mapping to the words.

Specifically, for each word $w_k \in$ **W**, we use MIL to apply to the whole image database to obtain the optimal block feature vector t_k, as depicted in Figure 2. Given the distribution of all the $f_{k_{ij}}$ corresponding to the image set S_k in the feature space, using the Diverse Density algorithm of MIL (Maron & Lozano-Perez, 1998), we immediately obtain the optimal block feature vector as the t_k

Figure 1. The relationship between the word space and the VRep space through the connection of the image space

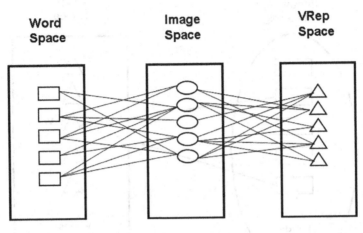

$$t_{k} = \arg \max_{t} \prod_{t} P(t \in I \mid I \in S_{k}) \prod_{t} P(t \in I \mid I \notin S_{k}) \qquad (5)$$

where $P(.\mid.)$ is a posterior probability that can be easily obtained from the occurrence frequency counts in the database. Now we have established the one-to-one mapping between the word w_{k} and the block feature vector t_{k}. Then we use the nearest neighbor clustering to identify all the closest VReps $v_{k_{l}}$ such that

$$\mid t_{k} - v_{k_{l}} \mid < T_{k} \qquad (6)$$

where T_{k} is a threshold. Denote the ranked list of those VReps that satisfy this constraint and are ranked w.r.t. the distances to t_{k} as V_{k},

$$w_{k} \leftrightarrow V_{k} = \{v_{k_{l}} \mid l = 1, ..., n_{w_{k}}\} \qquad (7)$$

where $n_{w_{k}}$ is the number of such VReps satisfying this constraint.

Further, we may obtain the corresponding ranked list of images for each word w_{k}. Given w_{k}, there is a corresponding set of VReps V_{k} that are close to t_{k} subject to the threshold T_{k}. In addition, according to Equaiton 3, each such VRep $v_{k_{l}}$ has an associated image set $I_{k_{l}}$ such that all the images in the set have this VRep. For each such image $I_{k_{li}} \in I_{k_{l}}$, using the mixture of Gaussian model (Dillon & Goldstein, 1984), we compute the posterior probability $P(I_{k_{li}} \mid w_{k})$. Then, we rank all the images in the set $I_{k_{l}}$ by the posterior probability $P(I_{k_{li}} \mid w_{k})$. We denote such a ranked list of images in the database as L_{k}. Hence, for each word w_{k}, there is a corresponding ranked list of images in the database

Figure 2. The direct mapping from a word to a set of ranked VRep

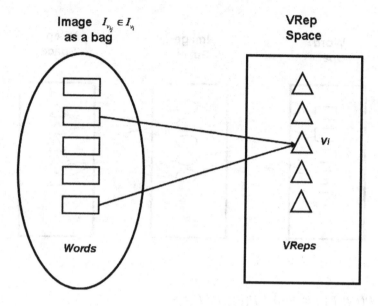

$$L_k = \{I_{k_h} \mid h = 1,...,\mid L_k\mid\}\tag{8}$$

i.e.

$$w_k \leftrightarrow L_k\tag{9}$$

Similarly, we use MIL to learn the function $y=F'(x)$ where x's are the ambiguous instances of the annotation words for an image and y is the set of the corresponding VReps to a word; here again the bag is an image. Specifically, for each VRep v_i, according to Equation 3, there is a corresponding image set I_{v_i}; and for each image $I_{v_{ij}} \in I_{v_i}$, there is a corresponding annotation word set $W_{v_{ij}}$

$$W_{v_{ij}} = \{w_{v_{ij}}^h \mid h = 1,...,\mid W_{v_{ij}}\mid\}\tag{10}$$

as depicted in Figure 3. Thus, using the Diverse Density algorithm of MIL (Maron & Lozano-Perez, 1998) again, we obtain the optimal annotation word w_k corresponding to the image set I_{v_i}

$$w_k = \arg\max_w \prod_w P(w \in W_{v_{ij}} \mid I \in I_{v_i}) \times \prod_w P(w \in W_{v_{ij}} \mid I \in I_{v_i})\tag{11}$$

Similarly, we may use the same algorithm to compute the ith best annotation word corresponding to VRep v_i. Consequently, for every VRep v_i, there is a corresponding ranked list of annotation words L_{v_i}, i.e.,

$$v_i \leftrightarrow L_{v_i}\tag{12}$$

Figure 3. The direct mapping from a VRep to a set of ranked words

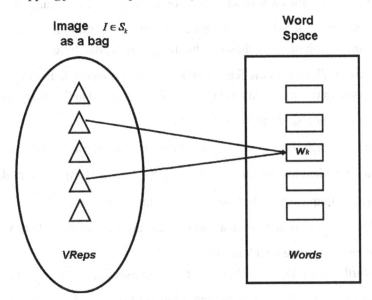

Finally, for every VRep $v_i \in V$, we compute the prior probability $P(v_i)$ by determining the relative occurrence frequency of v_i in the whole image database. Similarly, for every word $w_k \in \mathbf{W}$, we compute the prior probability $P\{w_k\}$ by determining the relative occurrence frequency of w_k for all the images in the database.

Given this learned direct correspondence relationship between the word space and the VRep space, we have completed indexing the database as part of the framework. Now we are ready for multimodal data mining.

Word to Image Retrieval

If a query is given by several words for retrieving images from the database, we assume that the query consists of words w_{q_k}, $k = 1, ..., p$. We also assume that all the query words are within the textual vocabulary of the training data. Since each w_{q_k} has a corresponding ranked list of images L_k, we just need to merge these p ranked lists L_k, $k=1, ..., p$ by $P\{I_{k_i} \mid w_{q_k}\}$ for all the different images I_{k_i}. Since the bottleneck of the computation is on merging the p ranked lists, the total computation is in $O(p|L_k)$, which is independent of the database scale $O(M, N)$. Hence, this retrieval is $O(1)$.

Image to Image Retrieval

If a query is given by several images for retrieving images from the database, we assume that the query consists of images I_{q_k}, $k = 1, ..., p$. These images may or may not be necessarily from the database; however, we assume that these images follow the same feature distributions of those in the database. For each query image I_{q_k}, we partition it into p_k blocks following the definition in Equation 1, and extract the feature vector $f_{q_{kl}}$ for each block $B_{q_{kl}}$. For each $f_{q_{kl}}$, we compute the distances to all the VReps v_i in the feature space. Based on the distances and the assumption that the features in the query images follow the same distributions of those of the images in the database, each $B_{q_{kl}}$ is replaced with the corresponding closest VRep v_i in the feature space. From Equation 3, each v_i has a corresponding image set I_{v_i}; we assume that there are in total r_k such VReps v_i found in the query image I_{q_k} and $r_k \leq p_k$. Let S_{q_k} be the largest common set of the r_k image sets I_{v_i}.

On the other hand, for each VRep v_i of I_{q_k}, we immediately have a ranked word list U_{v_i} based on $P(w_k|v_i)$. We merge the r_k ranked lists based on $P(w_k \mid v_i)P(v_i \mid I_{q_k})$ to form a new ranked list U_{q_k}, where $P(v_i|q_k)$ is the occurrence frequency of the VRep v_i appearing in the image I_{q_k}. For all the words in the list U_{q_k} (in the implementation we may truncate to the top few words for the list), we use the word-to-image retrieval scheme to generate a ranked image list.

L_{q_k}. L_{q_k} is then further trimmed such that only those images that are in S_{q_k} survive with the same relative ranked order in L_{q_k}. Finally, we merge the p ranked lists L_{q_k}, $k=1,...,p$. Given an appropriate hashing function for all the images in the database, this retrieval may be done in $O(p \mid U_{q_k})$, which again is independent of the database scale $O(M, N)$. Hence, this retrieval is $O(1)$.

Image to Word Retrieval

If the query is given by several images for word retrieval, i.e., for automatic annotation, we assume that the query consists of p images, I_{q_k}, $k=1,...,p$. Similar to the image-to-image retrieval, each query image I_{q_k} is decomposed into several VReps, and assume that the p query images have in total s_k VReps $v_i=1,...,s_k$. Let $P(v_i|I_q)$ be the relative frequency of the VRep v_i in all the query images I_{q_k}, $k=1,...,p$. Since each VRep v_i has a corresponding ranked list of words U_{v_i} based on $P(w_k|v_i)$, the final retrieval is the merged ranked list of words based on $P(w_k|v_i)P(v_i|I_q)$ from the s_k ranked lists U_{v_i}. Similarly, this retrieval is done in $O(s_k|U_{v_i}|)$, which is again independent of the database scale $O(M, N)$. Hence, this retrieval is $O(1)$.

Multimodal Querying for Image Retrieval

If the query is given by a combination of a series of words and a series of images, without loss of generality, we perform the image retrieval as follows. W use the word-to-image retrieval and he image-to-image retrieval, respectively, and finally merge the retrievals together based on their corresponding posterior probabilities. Clearly, this retrieval is in $O(\max\{p \mid L_k \mid, p \mid U_{q_k} \mid, s_k \mid U_{v_i} \mid\}) = O(1)$ independent of the database scale $O(M, N)$.

Figure 4. An example of an across 3 stages' image-to-image inferencing

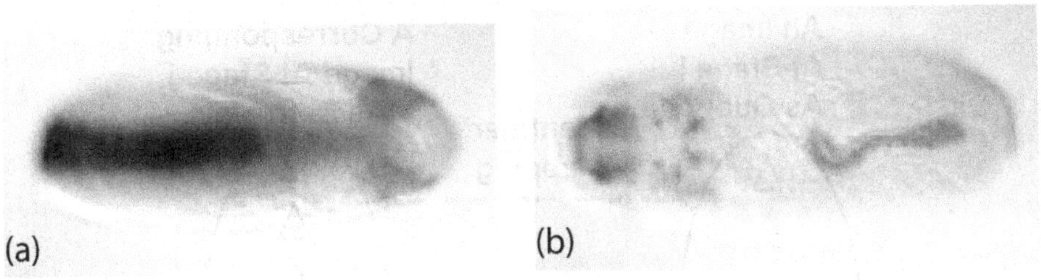

(a)　　　　　　　　　　　　　　(b)

Across-Stage Inferencing

For a fruit-fly embryo image database such as the Berkeley Drosophila ISH embryo image database, we have embryo images classified in advance into different stages of the embryo development with separate sets of textual words as annotation to those images in each of these stages. In general, images in different stages may or may not have the direct semantic correspondence (e.g., they all correspond to the same gene), not even speaking that images in different stages may necessarily exhibit any visual similarity. Figure 4 shows an example of a pair of identified embryo images at stages 9-10 (Figure 4(a)) and stages 13-16 (Figure 4(b)), respectively, that they both correspond to the same gene as a result of the image-to-image inferencing between the two stages[2]. However, it is clear that they exhibit a very large visual dissimilarity.

Consequently, it is not appropriate to use any pure visual feature based similarity retrieval method to identify such image-to-image correspondence across stages.

Furthermore, we also expect to have the word-to-image and image-to-word inferencing capabilities across different stages, in addition to the image-to-image inferencing.

Given this consideration, this is exactly where the proposed co-learning framework for multimodal data mining can be applied to complement the existing pure retrieval based methods to identify such correspondence. Typically in such a fruit-fly embryo image database, there are textual words for annotation to the images in each stage. These annotation words in one stage may or may not have the direct semantic correspondence to images in another stage. However, since the data in all the stages are from the same fruit-fly embryo image database, the textual annotation words between two different stages share a semantic relationship, which can be obtained by a domain ontology.

In order to apply the co-learning framework to this across-stage inferencing problem, we treat each stage as a separate multimedia database, and map the across-stage inferencing problem to a retrieval based multimodal data mining problem by applying the co-learning framework to the two stages such that we take the multimodal query as the data from one stage and pose the query to the data in the other stage for the retrieval based multimodal data mining. Figure 5 illustrates the application of the co-learning framework to the two stages' (stage i and stage j where $i \neq j$) image-to-image inferencing. Through the repetitive two-stage inferencings, any number of stages' inferencing may be made.

Clearly, in comparison with the retrieval based co-learning multimodal data mining framework analyzed in the previous sections, the only additional complexity here in the across-stage inferencing is the inferencing part using the domain ontology in the word space. Typically this ontology is small in scale. In fact, in our evaluations for the Berkeley Drosophila ISH embryo image database, this ontology is handcrafted and is implemented as a look-up table for word matching through an efficient hashing func-

Figure 5. An illustrative diagram for image-to-image across two stages' inferencing

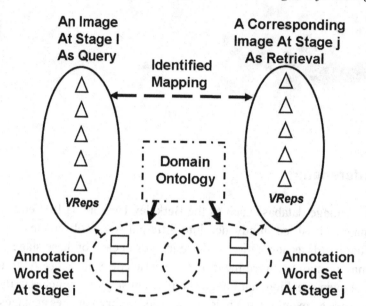

tion. Thus, this part of the computation may be ignored. Consequently, the complexity of the across-stage inferencing based multimodal data mining using this co-learning framework is the same as that of the retrieval based multimodal data mining, which is independent of the database scale.

Scalability Analysis

As is given in the analysis presented in the previous sections, the co-learning framework for multimodal data mining in a multimedia database enjoys a constant complexity, independent of the database scale. Similarly, the mining effectiveness is also independent of the database scale. This advantage is supported and verified in the empirical evaluations (see Section Experimental Evaluations). Note that many existing multimodal data mining methods for multimedia databases in the literature have a complexity dependent upon the databases' scales, typically linear, and their mining effectiveness degrades substantially when the databases scale up. With this advantage, the co-learning framework substantially advances the literature and excels these existing methods in the sense that it pushes to a new horizon a major step forward towards a real world application with a very large scale database.

ADAPTABILITY ANALYSIS

In this section, we show through the complexity analysis that the framework is adaptable very well when the database undergoes dynamic changes. This analysis is also consistent with the empirical evaluations we report in Section Experimental Evaluations. Specifically, we show that the database indexing updating only takes $O(1)$ computation for the following three exhaustive cases. The first two cases consider the scenario when images are added into or deleted from the database while the accompanying annotation words stay with the same vocabulary of the database; the last case considers the scenario when the vocabulary also changes. For all the cases, we assume that any newly added images follow the same feature distributions as those already in the database.

Case 1: When a New Image is Added into the Database

Let I^{new} be the new image. We first consider the new image added with no annotation. We show that the following steps complete updating the indexing of the database and that in each of the steps only a local change is necessary, i.e., the updating complexity is a constant w.r.t. the database size *(N, M)*.

- **Step 1: Determining VReps:** Following the definition in Equation 1, we partition the image into blocks; based on the assumption that any newly added images follow the same distributions in the feature space as those of the images in the database, from the VRep definitions in the feature space of the images in the database in Equation 2, each block of I^{new} is replaced with the nearest VRep in the feature space. This step takes $O(L)$ time. Since $L<<M,N$, this step is $O(1)$.

- **Step 2: Updating VRep-to-image mapping:** For each VRep v_i of I^{new}, we revise the corresponding image set I_{v_i} in Equation 3 by adding I^{new} into the set I_{v_i} to become $I_{v_i}^{new}$ and thus revise the occurrence frequency as the prior probability $P(v_i)$ (through both incrementing the numerator and the denominator of the previous prior probability). We assume that the list I_{v_i} is indexed by an array, such that the insertion of a new image takes a constant time. Thus, this step is $O(1)$.

- **Step 3: Determining annotation words:** In order to determine the annotation words for I^{new}, i.e., to determine the image-to-word mapping for I^{new}, since each VRep in I^{new} has a corresponding ranked list of words in the original database indexing already, the annotation words for I^{new} is the merged ranked list of all the ranked lists of words corresponding to the VReps in I^{new} based on $P(w_k|v_i)P(v_i|I^{new})$ where $P(v_i|I^{new})$ is the relative occurrence frequency of VRep v_i in I^{new}. Let $A_{I^{new}}$ be this merged ranked list for I^{new}. In practice, this list may be truncated to a top few words as the appropriate annotation words for I^{new} based on the ranking weight $P(w_k|v_i)P(v_i|I^{new})$. The total time is $O(L)$. Since $L<<M,N$, this step is $O(1)$.

- **Step 4: Updating word-to-VRep mapping:** For updating the word-to-VRep mapping in the database indexing, in order to avoid redoing the indexing from the scratch, we approximate the original mapping in the database indexing from a word to a set of VReps in Equation 7 using the weighted VReps instead of the actual block feature vectors of all the images in the feature space in the original database. Thus, we just need to revise the weights (i.e., the occurrence frequencies) of those VReps that appear in I^{new}. From Equation 12, each VRep *vi* appearing in I^{new} has a corresponding ranked list of annotation words L_{v_i}. Given all the VReps appearing in I^{new}, we immediately have a merged ranked list of annotation words from all the ranked lists L_{v_i}. Since in practice we truncate each ranked word list L_{v_i} to the top few words, these truncated ranked lists are merged together. Let C^t be such a merged list. Consequently, we only need to update the word-to-VRep mapping for those words in C^t. Specifically, for each $w_k \in C^t$, we check the corresponding VRep set V_k in Equation 7 and increment the frequency counts by one for those VReps in V_k that appear in I^{new}; we then update the optimal centroid t_k^{new} based on the updated VRep frequencies in V_k in the feature space. Finally, we use the same threshold T_k to update the new nearest neighborhood V_k^{new} of t_k^{new} based on Equation 6. Thus, the complexity of this step is $O(|C'|L)$. Since $|C'| << M,N$, and $L << M,N$, this step is $O(1)$.

- **Step 5: Updating word-to-image mapping:** In order to update the word-to-image mapping list in Equation 8 and the prior probability $P(w_k)$, we only need to focus on those words $w_k \in A_{I^{new}}$ obtained in Step 3. For each word $w_k \in A_{I^{new}}$, we have the updated corresponding VRep set V_k^{new} obtained in Step 4. We only need to check those VReps $v_i \in V_k^{new}$ that were updated for the corresponding image set $I_{v_i}^{new}$ in Step 2. Let L^u be the number of such VReps in V_k^{new}. Thus, the posterior probability $P(I^{new}|w_k)$ is approximated as

$$P(I^{new} \mid w_k) = \frac{L^u}{L} \tag{13}$$

and the prior probability $P(wk)$ is approximated as

$$P(w_k) = \frac{L^u}{N} \tag{14}$$

Finally, the word-to-image mapping ranked list L_k in Equation 8 is updated by inserting I^{new} based on the weight $P(I^{new}|w_k)$ determined in Equation 13. Clearly, this step takes $O(L)$ which is $O(1)$ due to $L << M,N$.

When the new image is added with annotation words, $A_{I^{new}}$ in Step 3 is given and thus Step 3 is skipped; Step 4 now may be only focused on determining the word-to-VRep mapping for those annotation words given in the new image, which can be similarly shown to be done in $O(1)$ time; the rest of the procedure is exactly the same. Consequently, the constant updating conclusion still holds true.

Case 2: When an Existing Image Is Deleted from the Database

Let I^{del} be the image in the original database that needs to be deleted. Let $v_i, i=1,...,r_d$ be the VReps of I^{del}. Let $w_k, k=1,...,s_d$ be the annotation words accompanying I^{del}. We show that the following steps complete the indexing updating with a constant time.

- **Step 1: Updating VRep-to-image mapping:** For each $v_i, i=1,...,r_d$, we remove I^{del} in the corresponding image list I_{v_i} in Equation 3. We then update the prior probability $P(v_i)$ by decrementing the numerator (the occurrence frequency of images with v_i) and the denominator (i.e., N). We assume that the list I_{v_i} is indexed by an array, such that deleting an image from the list takes a constant time. Thus, this step is $O(1)$.
- **Step 2: Updating word-to-VRep mapping**: Similar to Step 4 in Case 1, we update the word-to-VRep mapping. Here instead of incrementing the occurrence frequencies of those v_i in the feature space, we decrement the occurrence frequencies of the v_i. In practice, it is sufficient to focus on

updating the mapping for w_k, $k=1,...,s_d$. Since $s_d<<M$, as is the complexity of Step 4 in Case 1, this step is $O(1)$.

- **Step 3: Updating word-to-image mapping:** To update the word-to-image mapping, according to Equation 8, we just need to remove I^{del} from the ranked list L_k for each word w_k. The prior probability $P(w_k)$ can also be updated immediately by decrementing the occurrence frequency of w_k. Assuming that the ranked list L_k is indexed in an array, the removal of an image from this list is a constant operation. Thus, this step is $O(1)$.

Case 3: When the Database Vocabulary Changes

Since we only consider the scenario in which text vocabulary in a database is the accompanying information for the annotation of the images in the database, there are only two subcases for the dynamic change of the text vocabulary in the database: (1) when a new image is added into the database with textual annotations using new text vocabulary; and (2) when an existing text word is deleted from the text vocabulary in the database at the time when its accompanying image is deleted from the database. Clearly, Subcase 2 is a special case of Case 2 discussed above. Thus, we only need to discuss Subcase 1 here.

Let I^{new} be the new image to be added into the database. Let w_l, $l=1, ..., r_l$ be the annotation words of I^{new} that are from the existing vocabulary in the database, and let w_k, $k=1, ..., r_k$ be the annotation words new to the database text vocabulary. We show that following a procedure similar to that discussed in Case 1 above, the database indexing may be updated with a constant time. Specifically, Steps 1, 2, and 5 are exactly the same to the corresponding steps in Case 1, and Step 3 is skipped as the annotation words for I^{new} are given. Thus, we just need to show the remaining Step 4.

- **Step 4: Updating word-to-VRep mapping:** For each w_l, the updating is exactly the same as that in Step 4 of Case 1. For each w_k, since all the VReps corresponding to w_k in the feature space are those appearing in I^{new}, following the same procedure the co-learning framework to establish the direct mapping between the word space and the VRep space with the same constraint in Equation 6 and the threshold T_k, we obtain the optimal VRep feature vector t_k as well as its neighborhood, from which we immediately obtain a list of the VReps corresponding to wk defined similarly to V_k in Equation 7. Let V_k be such a VRep list corresponding to w_k, $k=1, ..., r_k$. Since the number of the VReps appearing in w_k, $k=1, ..., r_k$ is finite, and since $r_k<<M$, the complexity of this step is $O(1)$.

In summary, we have shown that regardless of how the database changes, the updating of the indexing may be done incrementally with a constant time without needing to redo the indexing from the scratch. This allows that the database indexing can always be updated in a timely manner with an incremental change of the database content. This adaptability advantage of the framework enables it to excel many of the peer methods in the literature that do not adapt at all, i.e., the database must be reindexed (or retrained) from the scratch even if the database is only incrementally updated.

EXPERIMENTAL EVALUATIONS

While this co-learning framework is general for any specific domains, in order to demonstrate and evaluate its mining effectiveness, we use the Berkeley Drosophila ISH embryo image database as the testbed for the evaluations of the mining performance of the framework.

We evaluate this framework's performance using this database for both the retrieval based and the across-stage inferencing based multimodal data mining. To demonstrate the effectiveness and the promise of the framework for multimodal data mining, we compare this framework with a state-of-the-art multimodal data mining method MBRM (Feng et al, 2004).

In the testbed, there are in total 16 stages of the embryo images archived in six different folders with each folder containing two to four stages of the images; there are in total 36,628 images and 227 words in all the six folders; not all the images have annotation words. For the retrieval based multimodal data mining evaluations, we use folder 5884 as the multimedia database, which corresponds to stages 11 and 12. There are about 5,500 images that have annotation words and there are 64 annotation words in this folder. We split the whole folder's images into two parts (one third and two thirds), with the two thirds used in the training to establish the indexing and the one third used as the evaluation testing. For the across-stage inferencing based multimodal data mining evaluations, we use folders 5884 and 5885 for the two stages' inferencing evaluations, and use folders 5883, 5884, and 5885 for the three stages' inferencing evaluations. Consequently, each folder here is considered as a "stage" in the across-stage based multimodal data mining evaluations. In each of the inferencing scenarios, we use the same split as we do in the retrieval based multimodal data mining evaluations for each folder for training and testing.

In order to facilitate the across-stage inferencing capabilities, we handcraft the ontology of the words involved in the evaluations. This is simply implemented as a simple look-up table indexed by an efficient hashing function. For example, *cardiac mesoderm primordium* in folder 5884 is considered as the same as *circulatory system* in folder 5885. With this simple ontology and word matching, the co-learning framework may be well applied to this across-stage inferencing problem for the multimodal data mining.

Figures 6 and 7 report the precisions and recalls averaged over 63 queries, respectively, for both the retrieval based and the two-stage inferencing based multimodal data mining using the co-learning framework in comparison with MBRM for the word to image mining scenario.

Similarly, Figures 8 and 9 report the precisions and recalls averaged over 1648 queries, respectively, for both the retrieval based and the two-stage inferencing based multimodal data mining using the co-learning framework in comparison with MBRM for the image to word mining scenario. Clearly, for the word-to-image mining scenario, our framework outperforms MBRM substantially in the retrieval based mining performance, and performs slightly better than

MBRM in most cases for the two-stage inferencing mining performance; for the image-to-word mining scenario, our framework has almost the same performance as that of MBRM in the retrieval based mining performance, but MBRM performs slightly better than the framework in the two-stage inferencing based mining performance.

Since MBRM does not have the capability for image-to-image retrieval, we adapt it to the across-stage image-to-image inferencing using the same ontology we have manually handcrafted to ensure a fair comparison. Figure 10 and Figure 11, respectively, document the averaged (over 1648 queries) performance comparison between the co-learning framework and MBRM for the three-stage image to image inferencing, where we see that both methods have a comparable performance overall. Figure 4 showcases such an inferencing example across the three stages using the co-learning framework. Figure

Figure 6. Precisions of the word to image retrieval and 2-stage inferencing between the co-learning framework and MBRM

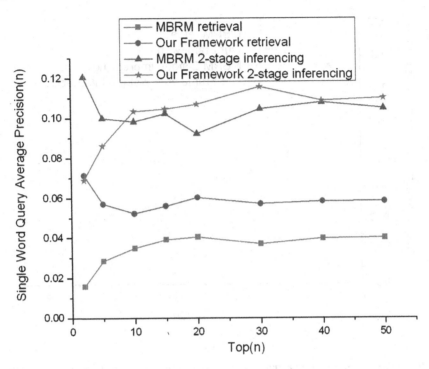

Figure 7. Recalls of the word to image retrieval and 2-stage inferencing between the co-learning framework and MBRM

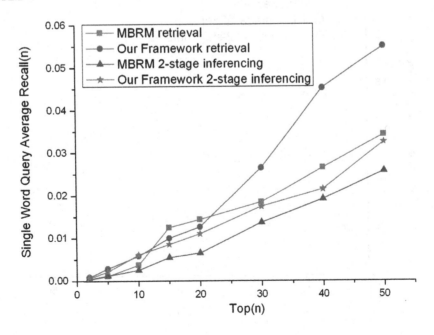

Figure 8. Precisions of the image to word retrieval and 2-stage inferencing between the co-learning framework and MBRM

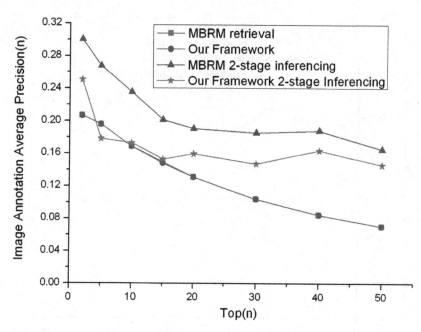

Figure 9. Recalls of the image to word retrieval and 2-stage inferencing between the co-learning framework and MBRM

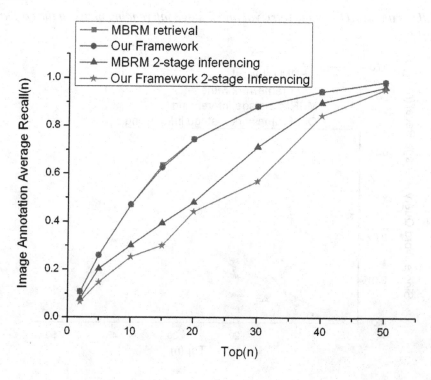

4(a) is an embryo image in folder 5883 (stages 9 to 10) and Figure 4(b) is the corresponding embryo image identified by the framework in folder 5885 (stages 13 to 16). Note the substantial visual difference between the two images which would fail any purely visual feature based similarity retrieval method for this type of inferencing.

To demonstrate the scalability advantage, Figure 12 and Figure 13 report the precision and recall averaged over 1648 queries, respectively, for image-to-word retrieval based multimodal data mining performance of the co-learning framework for folder 5885 where the database scales up from the 30% of the original data to the 100% of all the data in the folder.

Figure 14 and Figure 15 report the similar averaged (over 63 queries) performance evaluations for the word-to-image retrieval based multimodal data mining scenario. Since MBRM does not allow incrementally updating the indexing, it completely fails and thus its performance is not reported in the figures. On the other hand, the co-learning framework shows a strong scalability for the mining effectiveness with almost about the same performance when the database scales up from 30% to 100%. These empirical evaluations are consistent with the scalability analysis. In order to verify the strong scalability for the time complexity, we report that the average image-to-word query response times over 1648 queries for the three different scales of the database respectively are all the same as 0.0051 second, and the average word-to-image query response times over 63 queries for the three different scales respectively are all the same as 0.026 second, under a Linux environment with 2.2 GHz CPU and 1 GB memory. In comparison, since MBRM is not adaptable, we retrained the indexing for three different "static" databases corresponding to the 30%, 70%, and 100% of the data, and ran MBRM for the same 1648 image-to-word queries and for the same 63 word-to-image queries to measure the averaged response

Figure 10. Precisions of the image to image, 3-stage inferencing between the co-learning framework and MBRM

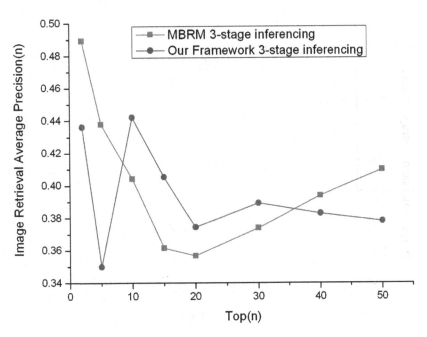

times for the three different databases, respectively, under the same Linux environment to ensure a fair comparison.

Figure 11. Recalls of the image to image, 3-stage inferencing between the co-learning framework and MBRM

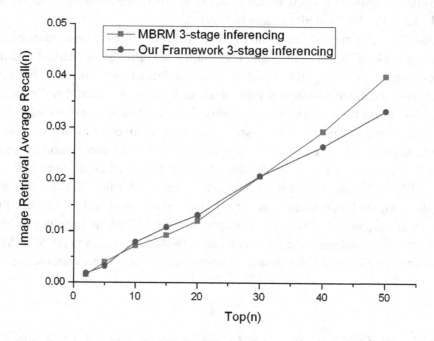

Figure 12. Precisions of the image to word retrieval of the co-learning framework for three scales

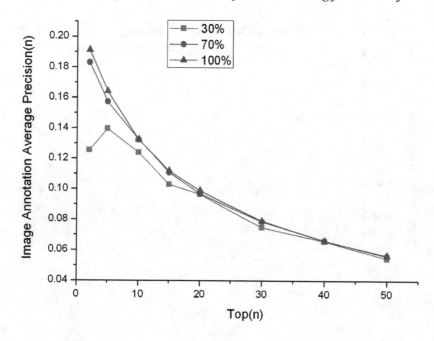

Figure 13. Recalls of the image to word retrieval of the co-learning framework for three scales

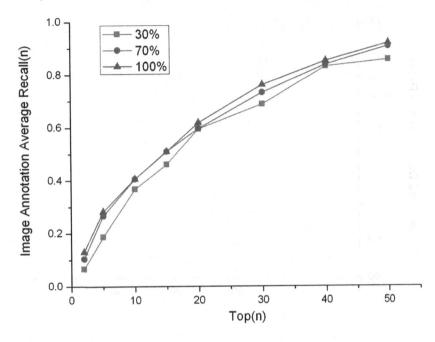

Figure 14. Precisions of the word to image retrieval of the co-learning framework for three scales

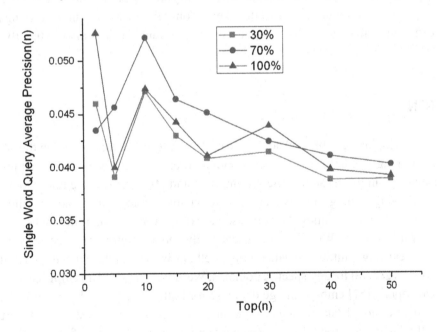

For image-to-word, the average MBRM response times are 0.013, 0.018, and 0.021 seconds, respectively, and for word-to-image, the average MBRM response times are 0.41, 0.53, and 0.60 seconds, respectively. This clearly shows that the co-learning framework is highly independent of the database scale while MBRM is not. We note that when we scaled up the database from the 30% data to the whole

Figure 15. Recalls of the word to image retrieval of the co-learning framework for three scales

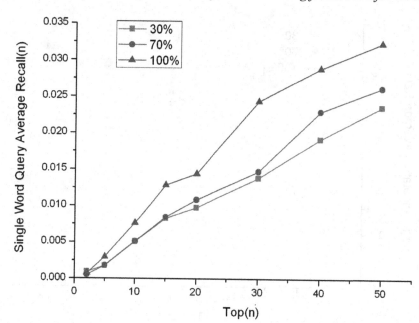

100% data, we followed the steps outlined in the adaptability analysis to incrementally update the indexing. Given the fact shown in Figures 12 to 15 that there is only little variation in the mining performance for the three different scales, the strong adaptability of the framework is also indirectly verified and supported.

CONCLUSION

We have presented a highly scalable and adaptable co-learning framework based on the MIL theory for multimodal data mining. We have demonstrated both theoretically and empirically that this framework has a strong scalability in the sense that the mining time and effectiveness are both independent of the database scale, allowing mining in a very large scale database, and a strong adaptability in the sense that it allows an incremental updating the database indexing with a constant time when the database is updated with new information. With the strong scalability and adaptability this co-learning framework excels many of the existing multimodal data mining methods in the literature that do not scale or adapt at all. The framework is general for any specific domains. We have conducted an empirical validation using the Berkeley Drosophila ISH embryo image database for both the retrieval based and the across-stage inferencing based multimodal data mining evaluations, in comparison with a state-of-the-art multimodal data mining method to demonstrate the effectiveness and the promise of this framework.

ACKNOWLEDGMENT

This work is supported in part by NSF (IIS-0535162, IIS-0812114, CCF-1017828, DBI-0640543), AFRL Information Institute (FA8750-05-2-0284), and AFOSR (FA9550-06-1-0327).

REFERENCES

Andrews, S., & Hofmann, T. (2004). *Multiple-instance learning via disjunctive programming boosting.* NIPS.

Andrews, S., Tsochantaridis, I., & Hofmann, T. (2003). *Support vector machines for multiple-instance learning.* NIPS.

Auer, P. (1997). On learning from multi-instance examples: empirical evaluation of a theoretical approach. In *Proc. ICML.*

Barnard, K., Duygulu, P., Freitas, N. D., Blei, D., & Jordan, M. I. (2003). Matching words and pictures. *Journal of Machine Learning Research*, 3, 1107–1135. doi:10.1162/153244303322533214

Chang, E., Goh, K., Sychay, G., & Wu, G. (2003). Cbsa: Content-based soft annotation for multimodal image retrieval using bayes point machines. *IEEE Trans. On Circuits and Systems for Video Technology, 13*(1).

Chen, Y., Bi, J., & Wang, J. (2006). MILES: multiple-instance learning via embedded instance selection. *IEEE Trans. PAMI, 28*(12).

Datta, R., Ge, W., Li, J., & Wang, J. (2006). Toward bridging the annotation-retrieval gap in image search by a generative modeling approach. *Proc. ACM Multimedia.*

Dietterich, T., Lathrop, R., & Lozano-Perez, T. (1997). Solving the multiple instance problem with axis-parallel rectangles. *Artificial Intelligence, 89*, 3171. doi:10.1016/S0004-3702(96)00034-3

Dillon, W. R., & Goldstein, M. (1984). *Multivariate Analysis, Methods and Applications.* New York: John Wiley and Sons.

Duygulu, P., Barnard, K., Freitas, J. F. G. D., & Forsyth, D. A. (2002). Object recognition as machine translation: Learning a lexicon for a fixed image vocabulary. In *Proc. The 7th European Conference on Computer Vision*, (Vol. IV, pp. 97–112), Copenhagen, Denmark.

Feng, S. L., Manmatha, R., & Lavrenko, V. (2004). Multiple Bernoulli relevance models for image and video annotation. In *Proc. The International Conference on Computer Vision and Pattern Recognition*, Washington, DC.

Fergus, R. Li, F.-F., Perona, P., & Zisserman, A. (2005). Learning object categories from Google's image search. In *Proc. ICCV.*

Jeon, J., Lavrenko, V., & Manmatha, R. (2003). Automatic image annotation and retrieval using cross-media relevance models. In *Proc. ACM SIGIR.*

Jeon, J., & Manmatha, R. (2004). Using maximum entropy for automatic image annotation. In *Proc. International Conf. Image and Video Retrieval*.

Jurie, F., & Triggs, B. (2005). Creating efficient codebooks for visual recognition. In *Proc. ICCV*.

Li, J., & Wang, J. (2006). Real-time computerized annotation of pictures. In *Proc. ACM Multimedia*.

Li, X., Chen, L., Zhang, L., Lin, F., & Ma, W.-Y. (2006). Image annotation by large-scale content based image retrieval. In *Proc. ACM Multimedia*.

Liu, W., & Tang, X. (2005). Learning an image-word embedding for image auto-annotation on the nonlinear latent space. In *Proc. ACM Multimedia*.

Maron, O., & Lozano-Perez, T. (1998). *A framework for multiple instance learning*. NIPS.

Monay, F., & Gatica-Perez, D. (2004). PLSA-based image auto-annotation: constraining the latent space. In *Proc. ACM Multimedia*.

Pan, J.-Y., Balan, Y., Xing, E., Traina, A., & Faloutsos, C. (2006). Automatic mining of fruit fly embryo images, *Proc. ACM KDD*.

Pan, J.-Y., Yang, H.-J., Faloutsos, C., & Duygulu, P. (2004). Automatic multimedia cross-modal correlation discovery. In *Proc. ACM KDD*.

Rahmani, R., & Goldman, S. (2006). MISSL: multiple-instance semi-supervised learning. In *Proc. ICML*.

Smeulders, A. W. M., Worring, M., Santini, S., Gupta, A., & Jain, R. (2000). Content-based image retrieval at the end of the early years. *IEEE Transactions on Pattern Analysis and Machine Intelligence, 22*, 1349–1380. doi:10.1109/34.895972

Wang, X.-J., Ma, W.-Y., Xue, G.-R., & Li, X. (2004). Multi-model similarity propagation and its application for web image retrieval. In *Proc. the 12th annual ACM international conference on Multimedia*, (pp. 944–951), New York City.

Wang, X.-J., Zhang, L., Jing, F., & Ma, W.-Y. (2006). AnnoSearch: Image auto-annotation by search. In *Proc. CVPR*.

Wu, Y., Chang, E., & Tseng, B. (2005). Multimodal metadata fusion using casual strength. In *Proc. ACM Multimedia*.

Yang, C., Dong, M., & Fotouhi, F. (2005). Region based image annotation through multiple instance learning. In *Proc. ACM Multimedia*.

Yang, C., Dong, M., & Hua, J. (2006). Region-based image annotation using asymmetrical support vector machine-based multiple instance learning. In *Proc. CVPR*.

Yang, C., & Lozano-Perez, T. (2000). Image database retrieval with multiple-instance learning techniques. In *Proc. ICDE*.

Zhang, H., Rahmani, R., Cholleti, S., & Goldman, S. (2006). Local image representations using pruned salient points with applications to CBIR. In *Proc. ACM Multimedia*.

Zhang, Q., Goldman, S., Yu, W., & Fritts, J. (2002). Content-based image retrieval using multiple instance learning. In *Proc. ICML*.

Zhang, R., & Zhang, Z. (2007). Effective image retrieval based on hidden concept discovery in image database. *IEEE Transactions on Image Processing, 16*(2). doi:10.1109/TIP.2006.888350

Zhang, R., Zhang, Z., Li, M., Ma, W.-Y., & Zhang, H.-J. (2005). A probabilistic semantic model for image annotation and multi-modal image retrieval. In *Proc. ICCV*.

Zhang, Z., Masseglia, F., Jain, R., & Del Bimbo, A. (2006). KDD/MDM 2006: The 7th KDD multimedia data mining workshop report. *ACM KDD Explorations, 8*(2), 92–95. doi:10.1145/1233321.1233336

Zhu, Q., Yeh, M.-C., & Cheng, K.-T. (2006). Multimodal fusion using learned text concepts for image categorization. In *Proc. ACM Multimedia*.

ENDNOTES

[1] http://www.fruitfly.org/cgi-bin/ex/bquery.pl?qpage=entryqtype=summary.

[2] The Berkeley Drosophila ISH embryo image database is given in such a way that images from several real stages are mixed together to be considered as all from one "stage". Thus, stages 9-10 are considered as one stage, and so are stages 13-16.

Chapter 9
Non–Topical Classification of Query Logs Using Background Knowledge

Isak Taksa
Baruch College, City University of New York, USA

Sarah Zelikovitz
The College of Staten Island, City University of New York, USA

Amanda Spink
Queensland University of Technology, Australia

ABSTRACT

Background knowledge has been actively investigated as a possible means to improve performance of machine learning algorithms. Research has shown that background knowledge plays an especially critical role in three atypical text categorization tasks: short-text classification, limited labeled data, and non-topical classification. This chapter explores the use of machine learning for non-hierarchical classification of search queries, and presents an approach to background knowledge discovery by using information retrieval techniques. Two different sets of background knowledge that were obtained from the World Wide Web, one in 2006 and one in 2009, are used with the proposed approach to classify a commercial corpus of web query data by the age of the user. In the process, various classification scenarios are generated and executed, providing insight into choice, significance and range of tuning parameters, and exploring impact of the dynamic web on classification results.

INTRODUCTION

Text classification in the framework of machine learning is an active area of research, encompassing a variety of learning algorithms (Ensuli et al., 2008), classification systems (Banerjee, 2008) and data representations (Wu et al., 2008). Three non-standard issues in machine learning are the focus of the research in this chapter: short text classification problems, limited labeled data, and non-topical classification.

DOI: 10.4018/978-1-61692-859-9.ch009

Figure 1. Steps in a classification process

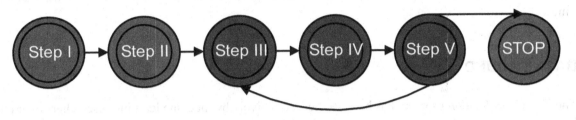

This chapter studies the classification of search queries, which is one example of text classification that is particularly complex and challenging. Typically, search queries are short, reveal very few features per single query and are therefore a weak source for traditional machine learning (Gabrilovich at el., 2009).

We examine the issues of non-hierarchical (Cesa-Bianchi et al., 2006) classification and investigate a method that combines limited manual labeling, computational linguistics and information retrieval to classify a large collection of search queries. We discuss classification proficiency of the proposed method on a large search engine query log, and the implication of this approach on the advancement of short-text classification. We also compare results of two classification tasks executed in 2006 and 2009 to examine the impact of the growing internet collection on consistency of classification results.

We start with a search engine query log which is viewed as a set of textual data on which we perform classification (Jansen et al., 2009; Zimmer and Spink, 2008). Observed in this way, each query in a log can be seen as a document that is to be classified according to some pre-defined set of labels, or *classes*. Viewing the initial log with the search queries as a document corpus $D = \{d_1, d_2...d_p...d_n\}$, we create a set of classes that indicate a personal demographic characteristic of the searcher, $C = \{c_1, c_2...c_p...c_m\}$. Using Web searches, our approach retrieves a set of background knowledge to learn additional features that are indicative of the classes, C. This allows for the categorization of the queries. This approach consists of the following five steps:

1. Select (from the print and the online media) a short set of manually chosen terms $T_{init} = \{t_1, t_2,..., t_j...,t_m\}$ consisting of terms t_j that are known a priori to be descriptive of a particular class c_j;
2. Use this initial set T to classify a small subset of (search queries) set D thereby creating an initial set of classified queries $Q_{init} = \{q_1, q_2...q_j...q_i\}$;
3. Submit these queries q_j to a commercial search engine and use the returned search results to build a temporary corpus of background knowledge $B_{temp} = \{b_1, b_2...b_j...b_{i*10}\}$;
4. Use an algorithm to select from B more class related terms T;
5. Use this newly created set T to classify more documents (search queries) in corpus D thereby adding more classified queries to set Q.

While steps I and II are executed only once, steps III through V are repeated continuously until the classification process is terminated (Figure 1).

We focus on validating our approach to the classification of a set of short documents, namely search queries. This approach uses a combination of techniques: we first look at developing a method to obtain relevant background knowledge for a set of web queries; then we build the background knowledge to acquire ranked terms for improved information retrieval; we then investigate the impact of the new terms' selection algorithms on the effectiveness of the classification process. Finally, we examine the influence of various sets of background knowledge acquired from the Web at different classification times.

BACKGROUND

The *Text Classification* problem has been studied extensively by machine learning researchers over the last decade. We can define the categorization as follows: Given a set of documents *D* and a set of *m* classes (or labels) *C*, define a function *F* that will assign a value from the set of *C* to each document in *D*. For example, *D* might consist of the set of all *Classified Advertisements*, and *C* could be the set of types of classified advertisements (automobile, home furnishing, help wanted, etc.) Although the text classification problem can be defined so easily, in practice there is often not enough information to find the function *F*.

A text document can be expressed as a feature-value vector, where the features correspond to particular words (or phrases), and the value corresponds to the presence/absence of the word (or some weight that corresponds to the word). When documents are expressed in this fashion, the machine learning community can apply well-known algorithms to this problem (Sebastiani 2002). The straightforward approach deals with text classification problems as *supervised* learning problems. In this case the human expert simply has to label a set of examples with appropriate classes. This set of labeled examples is called the *training set*, which we will refer to as the set *T*. Once a training corpus of correctly labeled documents is available, there are a variety of techniques that can be used to create a set of rules or a model of the data that will allow future documents to be classified correctly. The techniques can be optimized and studied independently of the domains and specific problems that they will be used to address. A plethora of different learning algorithms including Bayesian classifiers (Genkin et al, 2007), nearest neighbor (Han et al, 2001), and support vector machines (Joachims, 2002), have been applied to many different representations of textual documents, successfully allowing for the classification of documents in varied domains.

Topical text categorization problems, such as the example given above, that have a sufficient number of training examples, are now well-understood by machine learning researchers. However, non-standard problems have been the focus of more recent research. A common problem when using machine learning for text classification is dealing with an insufficient number of training examples to correctly classify instances with unknown classes. If there are too few examples, machine learning algorithms often cannot represent the classes properly, and therefore have a high error rate when attempting to classify new examples. In essence, few examples do not allow for the creation of a model of the data that generalizes well for new examples in the domain. There are a number of approaches that may be taken to aid in the creation of more accurate classifiers. Researchers have noted that although it is often the case that there are very few labeled examples, there are often many unlabeled examples readily available (Nigam et al., 2006; Joachims, 2002). An approach that has been taken by a number of researchers has been to choose, in some way, a *small* number of additional training examples that should be hand-labeled in order to add particular examples to the *labeled* training set that will improve learning. Uncertainty sampling has been used in this way (Lewis and Catlett, 1994) where specific examples are chosen out of a large pool of unlabeled examples to be given to humans to be classified. These hand labeled examples then become part of the training corpus. In this way fewer examples must be given to an expert to be labeled than if the examples were simply randomly sampled.

The *semi-supervised* learning paradigm is used when there are unlabeled examples that are too expensive or inconvenient to label. In text classification research semi-supervised learning has been used in various ways and in conjunction with a variety of classifiers (Zhu, 2007) to improve classification. Work using naïve Bayes text classifiers use the labeled training examples to assign probabilistic classes to many unlabeled examples. These newly classified examples are then used in the classifier creation process (Nigam et al., 2006; Schneider, 2005). Unlabeled examples have also been used to create new features for the set of labeled examples. In this, the set of labeled examples is enhanced by the information provided in the set of unlabeled examples (Szummer and Jaakkola, 2000).

Semi-supervised Support Vector Machines (SVMs) have been studied extensively as well. (Sindhwani and Keerthi, 2006; Liu et al., 2004). Feature creation can be a helpful way of harnessing external knowledge (Gabrilovich and Markovitch, 2007).

Other non-standard qualities of a set of data can cause many machine learning algorithms to be useless. Specifically, for short-text classification problems, labeled and unlabeled examples may be too short to learn new features, and too short to obtain proper word statistics. Machine learning algorithms depend on the co-occurrences of terms to provide understanding as to the probability of which terms fall into which classes. Text classification problems with short text entries in the training set do not allow for these types of generalizations. Furthermore, unlabeled examples or new examples to be classified might not share any terms with the training set.

Other approaches have been taken in these hard-to-classify domains. There have been studies of the incorporation of domain knowledge by the selection and creation (Li and Liu 2003), cross-referencing query and domain documents (Wen et al., 2002), or reweighing of features using related information such as ontologies (Gabrilovich and Markovich, 2005) or user feedback (Raghavan et al., 2006). Domain knowledge has also been incorporated into text classifiers by modification of the classifiers to include prior results (Dayanik et al., 2006; Schapire et al., 2002). There has also been work done using query-expansion type techniques to incorporate additional knowledge into text classifiers (Sahami and Heilman, 2006) and query formulation techniques using terms found in previously retrieved documents (Zhu et al., 2003).

Often, with short text classification problems, there are related textual documents that are not examples that can be classified. We term this set of related documents research *background knowledge* and use it to aid a short-text classifier. Background knowledge has been previously used (Chan et al, 2008; Zelikovitz et al., 2007) to improve classification of unknown instances. These sets of background text are not of the same length and form as the training and unlabeled examples, but can be used to find common co-occurrences of terms, as well as terms that are indicative of specific classes.

Short text classification is a challenging type of classification because very little information (i.e. words) is known for each example that is to be classified. Researchers have recognized that since short text examples tend to share few terms, it is particularly difficult to classify new instances and common comparisons between texts often yield no useful results. Simply comparing a training set to unknown examples using traditional methods such as cosine similarities can therefore be useless. An example of short text classification that is receiving interest lately is the query classification (Beitzel et al 2008; Sahami and Heilman, 2006). Different approaches have been taken in these short text classification tasks to provide longer related knowledge to each one, by using web searches, synonyms, and statistical methods (Sarawagi, 2005) or unsupervised learning methods (Gliozzo, 2009). Other researchers (Bobicev and Sokolova, 2008) use language modeling methods to obtain more information from the short text.

Non-topical text classification is a non-standard type of text classification that is harder to approach than the classification of documents into unambiguous topics. An example of non-topical text classification is classification of documents by sentiment. In this type of problem the set of classes, C, is not the set of distinct topics, but instead is the set of possible attitudes (positive, negative) that the document conveys. Classification of movie review articles for recommendation systems is a practical example of this type of categorization. Work has been done in this area to adapt algorithms that are used for topical classification to deal with the particular issues that are specific to this type of classification (Tan et al, 2009). In addition, there has been work that has been done on representation of text that is not the simple word and value pairs to fit this type of problem (Lippincott and Passanneau, 2009, Choi et al, 2009). Another example of a non-topical classification is classification of documents by some attribute of the writer or user (Ozmutu et al. 2008) or personality trait (Kaban 2008). Although in particular cases statistical machine learning methods work well (Kaban 2008), often with these types of classification problems a training set is not enough to correctly classify unknown instances. Adjustment of algorithms (Tan et al., 2009) to incorporate domain knowledge is helpful in many of these tasks.

METHODOLOGY

Our approach in this chapter is different from the traditional machine learning approaches described above. Instead of actually incorporating the background knowledge set into the learning algorithm, we use background knowledge for the purpose of finding previously unknown class related terms. As described earlier, we begin with only a small set of manually selected class related terms (or phrases). These terms are used to label a small set of documents – search queries extracted from a large Excite query log collected in the morning and afternoon hours of December 20, 1999 and contains close to 2.5 million queries (Excite, 1999). This small set of labeled documents is then used as search queries to retrieve a much larger set of longer, related documents. We analyze the larger set of related documents to learn additional class related terms for the classification task. The task was performed twice, in December 2006 and November 2009. In our discussion we will refer to these two tasks as Task-6 and Task-9.

Bootstrapping From Known Class-Related Terms

To create the set of classes we used Levinson's *Life Structure Theory*. After studying a group of men and women Levinson introduced his theory (Levinson, 1986) as consisting of equilibrium/disequilibrium periods during which a man builds/questions his life structure. At the center of his theory is the *life structure*, the underlying pattern of an individual's life at any particular time. For our classes we use Levinson's seasonal cycles as shown in Table 1.

Using the abbreviations we get a set of classes as follows: $C = \{EA, AW, SD, MA, CL, LA\}$. We aquired terms that are indicative of each of these classes. In particular, we obtained the terms (words or phrases) from well-known printed publications (Seventeen, Parenting, Family Circle, American Association of Retired Persons Magazine, etc.) and popular blogs (MySpace, The Chronicle, BloggingMommies, etc.). For each of the classes in set C, we manually selected a list of 10 words and phrases that are indicative of each of these classes. A partial example of these terms can be seen in Table 2. To preserve the evenness we used the same initial set of age indicative terms for both tasks.

Table 1. Age categories

Levinson's Life Structure Theory		
AGE	*STAGE*	*SEASONAL CYCLE*
17-22	Early adult transition	Early adulthood (EA)
22-28	Enter adult world	Adult world (AW)
28-33	Age 30 transition	
33-40	Settle down	Settle down (SD)
40-45	Midlife transition	
45-50	Enter middle adulthood	Middle adulthood (MA)
50-55	Age 50 transition	
55-60	Culmination of middle adulthood	Culmination (CL)
60-65	Late adult transition	
65+	Late adulthood	Late adulthood (LA)

Table 2. Age indicative query terms

CLASS	AGE INDICATIVE TERMS/PHRASES
EA (17-22)	Cliff notes, Prom, College admission, Spring break, Internship, Summer job
AW (22-33)	Job, Wedding, Pregnancy, Child care, Housing, Mortgage, Graduate school
SD (33-45)	Investments, Family vacation, Summer home, 401(K), Prep schools, Schools
MA (45-55)	Retirement, Travel, Personal health, Elder care, Cosmetic surgery, Politics
CL (55-65)	Inheritance tax, Estate planning, Wills, Grand parenting, Cruises, Heart attack
LA (65+)	Philosophy, Persistent pain, Hip replacement, Medicare, Leisure

Using the list of terms for each class, we culled a set of queries from the Excite log that contained these age-indicative terms. We began with a very small set of returned labeled queries; 60 in all, 10 per

Table 3. Excite log queries

CLASS	QUERY
EA (17-22)	cliff notes Wuthering heights
AW (22-33)	Hotel catered wedding
SD (33-45)	Investment policy statement
MA (45-55)	retirement community Florida
CL (55-65)	IRS inheritance tax
LA (65+)	Arthritis pain

Table 4. Top search result for query "Cliff Notes Wuthering Heights" in Task-6 and Task-9

Task-6	Task-9
Call it a Cliff Note, Cliffs Note, or CliffsNotes, if you're looking for the original literature study guide series then you've come to the right place. Use the links below to find free summaries, character analyses, essay suggestions, important quotes, and more to help you get the very most from your study time.	**Wuthering Heights Emily Brontë** In Emily Brontë's Wuthering Heights, realism and gothic symbolism combine to form a romance novel that's full of social relevance. Follow the self-destructive journey of Heathcliff as he seeks revenge for losing his soul mate, Catherine, to Edgar. Themes — such as good versus evil, chaos and order, selfishness, betrayal, and obsession — intertwine as the story unfolds. Emily Brontë's Wuthering Heights is a symbolic and psychological study of the nature of love.

each of the six classes. This set of queries is our set of classified training documents that we use to start the classification of many other queries that do not contain the original list of class related terms. An example of a query selected from the log for each of the classes in the set C is shown in Table 3.

Automatic Retrieval of Background Sets

We submitted the classified queries to the Google search engine to automatically create a background set of knowledge. For each of the classified queries we created a pool of documents, each of which was the text of a search result obtained by submitting the classified query to Google. We restricted search results to documents written in the English language. Google returned the top results of the search on the classified query that were downloaded and stored. We saved the textual sections of the pages that were downloaded, and each one became a document, classified according to the class of the query that generated it. We limited our search results to the top 10 results returned for each query since the users are generally satisfied if the desired page is found within the top 10 results (Metaxas et al., 2009; Taksa, 2005). After downloading search results we had a set of ten text documents for each one of our queries. These were then used as a corpus for analysis. This method allows for the retrieval of documents that are class related, but are much longer than the original queries. The queries from the search log are an average length of ~3 words, whereas the new documents that were downloaded had an average length of several thousand words, and hence more could be learned from them. It is important to note that with widespread portalization (Cormode and Krishnamurthy, 2008; Dix, 2007) and commercialization (Hernandes et al., 2009; Krafft, 2009), website designers allocate more space to products on sale, at the expense of actual information. For example, an actual query *Cliff Notes Wuthering Heights* classified as an EA *(17-22)* and submitted to Google as part of Task-6 and Task-9, returned two very distinct top results (Table 4). While Task-6 offered other terms that high school students might use to search for more relevant results, namely *essay*, or *study guide*, or even alternate spellings of *Cliff Notes*, Task-9, besides displaying ads for PizzaHut and Cablevision, jumped directly into discussing the literary text, offering relatively unrelated terms – such as *love* and *romance*, which could be relevant to many other classes.

Finding New Class Related Terms

Each page that was returned by Google was labeled with the class category of the query that produced it. This set of pages can be looked at as a new and different document *training* corpus with known labels. The training set T consists of the returned search pages, and the classes C are the classes that were used to label the original small set of hand-labeled queries. However, the properties of this training corpus are markedly different than the original query training set. Essentially, this newly created training corpus does not consist of short-text examples. As opposed to our original data set, where examples were queries only a few words long, this larger returned corpus contains entries that are web-page length. Hence there is much more generalization that we can do from the words in this larger returned document corpus.

What is especially interesting is the new, larger, document corpus vocabulary. A serious disadvantage of short-text corpora is that they do not contain a rich enough vocabulary to facilitate learning, however, with a longer document corpus we can learn much about the domain from the set of words that are in it. In essence, our method of page retrieval allows us to swap a short-text corpus for one with longer entries from which we can learn.

Our approach studies the set of terms that composes the returned document corpus to find those particular terms that are related to our classification problem. We began by using the information gain (IG) criterion to rank *all* terms in the corpus; no stemming was used to facilitate query creation later. For a supervised text classification task, each term that is present in the training corpus can be seen as a feature that can be used individually for classification. For example, suppose that the term *investment* occurs in the training corpus. We can partition the training corpus into two disjoint subsets, one of which contains the word *investment*, and one of which does not. Given the training set of classified examples, T, we can partition it by the presence or absence of each term, t that exists in these examples. We can then determine how closely related this term is to the classification task.

To do this, we borrow a concept from Information Theory, called *information gain*, which has been used by machine learning researchers for the purposes of classification (Quinlan, 1986). Given a probability distribution $P=(p_1,p_2,...,p_n)$ then the information conveyed by this distribution, also called the *entropy* of P, is:

$Entropy(P)= -(p_1 \times \log(p_1) + p_2 \times \log(p_2) + ...p_n \times \log(p_n))$

Essentially, this measure is a measure of the randomness of the distribution. High entropy signifies that the distribution is random, whereas low entropy signifies that there is some pattern in the data. In the field of information theory, the entropy is a measure of how many bits it takes to transmit a message with the probability distribution P. If we wish to discover the entropy of a training set T, then the probability distribution P is simply the set of probabilities that a training example fits into any of the classes of set C. From these training set probabilities we can compute *entropy (T)*.

Each term t gives a partition of the training set T, $\{T_0,T_1\}$, where T_0 consists of those training examples that contain the term t, and T_1 consists of those training examples that do not contain the term t. For each of these subsets, we can compute individual entropies, and the summation of those entropies, weighted by the probability distribution gives us the information needed to identify the class of a training example after the partition is done.

The information gain (*IG*) for a term t tells us how much information is gained by partitioning the training set T on the term t. It is defined as the subtraction:

$$IG(t) = entropy(T) - (entropy(T_0) \times \frac{|T_0|}{|T|} + entropy(T_1) \times \frac{|T_1|}{|T|})$$

Terms with high information gain create partitions of the original training set that overall have lower entropy, and therefore are reflective of the particular classification scheme.

Table 5. Terms with highest IG for class AW (22-33)

SEQ#	Task-6		Task-9	
	TERM	*IG*	*TERM*	*IG*
1	Bride	0.61277	Gown	0.51355
2	Planner	0.55563	Dinner	0.50064
3	Menu	0.55034	Babysitter	0.46023

The computation of the *IG* value for each of these terms allows us to learn important features in this background corpus. However, our challenge was to determine which of these features best reflected each class. To discover which terms give us information about particular classes, we sorted all terms in the corpus in descending order based upon the *IG* value. We labeled each of the terms with the class whose training examples most reflected this term, i.e. whose training examples actually most often contained that term. See Table 5 for a partial list of the terms with the highest information gain (IG) for the class *AW (22-33)*. It is interesting to note that there were only 27 common terms between the two lists.

We then chose the top terms for each of the classes. At this point we selected a list of fifty terms (per class) to classify queries that were not classified before. An example of some of the derived terms for all of the classes can be seen in Table 6.

It is important to note that some of the text documents did not contain the terms that were associated with their class. We are not concerned with this fact, however, because we are simply looking for good indicative terms that are related to particular classes.

DISCUSSION

To assess the effectiveness of the proposed approach we designed and implemented several evaluation scenarios (Table 6). By successively modifying parameters (one at a time) that describe each scenario, we identified parameters that affect classification process.

Table 6. Derived classification terms

CLASS	Task-6	Task-9
	NEW TERMS/PHRASES	*NEW TERMS/PHRASES*
EW (17-22)	Essay, guide, college, character	Financial aid, application, dorm, phone, tuition
AW (22-33)	Bride, planner, menu, romantic, flowers	Gown, dinner, babysitter, honeymoon, elections
SD (33-45)	Dividends, long term, interest, monthly	Credit, custody, dating, unemployment
MA (45-55)	Golf, builder, luxury, villa, condominium	House, health, vacation, exercise
CL (55-65)	Bequest, valuation, income, gift, publication	IRA, employment, eyeglasses, interest
LA (65+)	Chronic pain, joints, painkillers,	Nursing, pain, food, insurance, Prices

Table 7. Classification scenarios

TYPE	SCENARIO	Number of queries to retrieve background knowledge	Query selection process	Number of top classification terms	Terms selection process
		I	II	III	IV
Base	**Scenario-A**	10	Random	50	Top
	Scenario-B	20	Random	50	Top
Group α	**Scenario-C**	10	"Longer"	50	Top
	Scenario-D	10	"Lighter"	50	Top
Group β	**Scenario-E**	10	Random	30	Top
	Scenario-F	10	Random	100	Top
Group γ	**Scenario-G**	10	Random	50	"Lightest" of the top 100
	Scenario-H	10	Random	50	"Heaviest" of the top 100

Creating Evaluation Scenarios

Five parameters describe every scenario. The first parameter, not shown in the table and constant for all scenarios, is the number of manually selected class terms used to bootstrap the process. As specified above, the number is 10. Other parameters are modifiable, and their values are listed in Table 7. We started with Scenario-A (base scenario) and modified only one of the parameters at a time to generate three groups of additional scenarios. The first, ***Group α,*** varies the quantity of queries (*Column I*) and query selection process (*Column II*). The second, ***Group β***, uses two contrasting numbers (*Column III*) of newly acquired terms for the classification process. The third, ***Group γ***, modifies the order (*Column IV*) of top 100 classifications terms used for the classification process.

The first parameter *Number of queries to retrieve background knowledge* (column I) represents the number of queries that are selected from the queries classified in the prior iteration of our algorithm. These queries are submitted to Google to retrieve "background knowledge". In all the scenarios this number is 10 except for Scenario-B where the number is 20. We want to examine whether increasing the size of the retrieved background knowledge would generate better quality classification terms.

The next parameter *Query selection process* (column II) specifies the process of selecting new search queries from amongst the newly classified queries. In most scenarios the process is random, which

Table 8. Sample queries

QUERY #1	Catered hotel wedding
QUERY #2	Wedding reception menu ideas
QUERY #3	Wedding planner in dallas
QUERY #4	Party planner in dallas

Table 9. Determining query's size and weight

QUERY#1		QUERY#2		QUERY#3		QUERY#4	
TERM	**FREQ.***	**TERM**	**FREQ.***	**TERM**	**FREQ.***	**TERM**	**FREQ.***
catered	8.2/5.8	reception	101/86	planner	59/54	planner	59/54
wedding	176/213	wedding	176/213	Dallas	117/132	dallas	117/132
hotel	453/591	ideas	344/384	wedding	176/213	party	553/703
		menu	664/736				

*frequency in millions (Task-6/Task-9)

means that from a pool of queries classified we select (via a random number generator) a small set of queries to add to our labeled training set. The process is changed for Scenario-C. The majority of the queries in the log are 2 to 3 words long. We sort the queries that match our list of class-related terms in descending order of their length (number of terms in the query, excluding stop words). We use the top 10 longest queries for the retrieval of the background knowledge. For example, in Table 8, we list four sample queries that have terms related to wedding planning. Query #2 is the longest query – it has four meaningful terms.

On the other hand, for Scenario-D we are looking for "lighter" queries. We take the four queries in Table 7 and submit each term to Google to find document frequency for every term. See results in Table 9. We use this frequency as the query weight. For example, the "lightest" query in this table is Query#1 (its "lightest" term has the smallest frequency). The heaviest is Query#2 (same reasoning). To break the tie between Query#3 and Query#4 we have to go down to the third term.

The next parameter *Number of top classification terms* (column III) represents the number of new terms that will be used in the next classification iteration. After calculating the Information Gain (IG) for every term in background knowledge, we sort the list in descending order of IG. The list is long and we use the top 50 terms only. For Scenario-E we use only the top 30 terms and for Scenario-F we use the top 100 terms.

The final parameter *Terms selection process* (column IV) specifies the selection of new classification terms from the sorted list produced by IG calculations. For all scenarios we use Top-50, but for the last two scenarios we take the Top-100 and go to Google to find their frequencies. For Scenario-G we sort the Top-100 list in ascending order of the frequencies and pick the 50 "lightest" queries and for Scenario-H the other half of the list or the 50 "heaviest" queries.

Appraising Classification Results

To start (bootstrap) Scenario-A (and all other scenarios), we used a manually selected set consisting of 60 terms (10 per each class). Even though this set is negligible in size, it allowed for classification of over 8% of the query log. The number of queries that can be classified for the bootstrap step and subsequent six unsupervised iterations are shown in Table 10.

The second row of numbers in all cells shows the number of classified queries (per iteration) as a percent of the class total after all classification iterations. These numbers indicate: a) highly fluctuating individual class/iteration classification results and b) steady decline of iteration classification results for all classes combined.

Table 10. Scenario A: Classification results

CLASS	Bootstrap Step	NUMBER OF CLASSIFIED QUERIES						
		Unsupervised Iterations						
		1	2	3	4	5	6 29,374 11,472 9,656	Class Total
EA (17-22)	84,541 (32%)	52,540 (20%)	22,427 (8%)	38,464 (15%)	26,275 (10%)	15,264 (6%)	23,374 (9%)	262,885 (100%)
AW (22-33)	37,344 (25%)	23,421 (16%)	14,438 (10%)	21,783 (15%)	13,642 (9%)	21,643 (15%)	14,472 (10%)	146,743 (100%)
SD (33-45)	49,473 (31%)	34,212 (21%)	22,427 (14%)	18,953 (12%)	11,378 (7%)	14,562 (9%)	9,656 (6%)	160,661 (100%)
MA (45-55)	28,136 (17%)	32,652 (20%)	26,538 (16%)	21,642 (13%)	22,455 (13%)	18,713 (11%)	17,210 (10%)	167,346 (100%)
CL (55-65)	11,350 (27%)	6,427 (15%)	8,259 (19%)	6,230 (15%)	3,174 (8%)	4,215 (10%)	2,721 (6%)	42,376 (100%)
LA (65+)	6,713 (33%)	3,247 (16%)	1,521 (8%)	2,874 (14%)	3,943 (19%)	1,379 (7%)	562 (3%)	20,239 (100%)
Iteration Total	217,557 (27%)	152,499 (19%)	95,610 (12%)	109,946 (14%)	80,867 (10%)	75,776 (9%)	67,995 (9%)	800,250 (100%)
% of all log's queries	*8.70*	*6.09*	*3.82*	*4.40*	*3.23*	*3.03*	*2.72*	*32.01*

Table 11 exhibits classification results of all eight scenarios. Overall, only one scenario demonstrated slightly better results than the base Scenario-A. All other scenarios, while demonstrating measurable improvements for individual classes, failed to produce any improvement for the complete scenario.

In the first of three groups, *Group a*, we tried two different approaches: the increased number of newly classified queries used to retrieve the background knowledge (Scenario-B) and different methodologies of selecting these queries (Scenario-C and Scenario-D). Scenario-B showed a slight overall improvement over the base Scenario-A (1%), while demonstrating an individual improvement in two out of the six classification classes. On the other hand, Scenario-C (longer queries) showed improvement in only one class and Scenario-D ("lighter" queries) showed no improvements in individual classes. Both scenarios fell by 7% and 6% respectively in overall performance vs. the base Scenario-A. There are several interesting observations that came from these experiments. The largest class *EA (17-22)* was the biggest beneficiary of either Scenario-B (more queries) or Scenario-C (longer queries) used to generate background knowledge. While these approaches were beneficial for one class, they produced inferior results for others. Similarly, looking for less frequent queries (Scenario-D), either produced negative improvement or no improvement at all. This is intuitively the case because many of the less frequent queries are variations of more common popular queries, and our background sets were unable to produce new, previously unknown terms, with high information gain. For example, no matter what literary work follows the term *Cliff Notes*, the "Top 10" results are either identical or very similar. Although a query containing *Cliff Notes* and some obscure work might be uncommon in the query log, the set of 10 background texts that it returned are not new.

Table 11. Comparison of all Task-6 classification results (class/scenario) *

CLASS	SCENARIO							
	A	B	C	D	E	F	G	H
EA (17-22)	262,885	**291,575**	**270,536**	254,210	255,471	**274,213**	259,574	247,533
AW (22-33)	146,743	129,073	133,278	139,541	129,843	126,913	144,526	137,728
SD (33-45)	160,661	**165,240**	153,544	159,257	158,474	157,618	146,711	156,390
MA (45-55)	167,346	162,548	132,549	148,232	143,269	161,431	129,550	152,479
CL (55-65)	42,376	45,216	37,050	38,672	25,846	35,341	29,535	39,542
LA (65+)	20,239	14,753	16,492	13,561	15,847	19,540	15,236	17,220
CLASS TOTAL	*800,250*	*808,405*	*743,449*	*753,473*	*728,750*	*775,056*	*725,132*	*750,892*
% CHANGE	0%	1%	-7%	-6%	-9%	-3%	-9%	-6%

* Items in bold font show increase vs. the base Scenario-A.

In the second group, **Group β**, we examined the influence, or actually lack of any, by varying the number of new classification terms produced by the retrieved background knowledge. Instead of the usual 50 terms, used throughout all other scenarios, we first reduced this number to 30 (Scenario-E) and overall scenario results dropped by 9% vs. the base scenario. And after increasing this number to 100 (Scenario-F), the drop in performance was only 3%. While the overall scenario's performance went down, only one class showed improved performance when this number was increased to a 100.

In the third group, **Group γ**, we used two distinct ordering schemas of the terms produced by the retrieved background knowledge. As usual, we selected the 100 terms with the highest information gain (IG). But instead of using the top 50 (as we did in other scenarios) we reordered the top 100 terms according to the document frequencies returned by Google for each term. We used the frequency as the "weight" of the term and sorted the top 100 list in ascending order of the term's "weight" for Scenario-G and descending order for Scenario-H. In both scenarios we used the top 50 terms. Again, both scenarios produced results inferior to the base Scenario-A. While investigating the effectiveness of these two scenarios, we observed that the most common terms in our Excite corpus are often scattered throughout the *IG* sorted list of words. Many of the most common terms in the Excite corpus do not have high information gain in any iteration. This is intuitive, because many common search terms are generic in the sense that queries of all classes of *C* may contain them. These terms are not really useful when classifying documents and our *IG* method that ranks terms will discover that these terms are not class related.

Furthermore, as we reflect on the nature of the data that we are using for our approach, there are several objective factors that make this classification task and our approach to it, a difficult one. First, according to a topical study of the same log, a large number of queries are intra-class in nature (e.g. 20.3% People and places, 7.5% Sex and pornography, 6.8% Non-English or unknown) (Spink et al., 2004), and therefore are not easily classifiable according to our original set of classes, *C*. In particular, many of the queries in the Excite log may contain no terms that can be deemed class related, or may

Table 12. Comparison of Task-6 and Task-9 classification results (Scenario A only)

| | Task-6 | Task-9 | | |
| | | | a | b | c |
Class	Scenario-A	Scenario-A	Found in same class in Task-6	Found in other classes in Task-6	Newly classified queries
EA (17-22)	262,885	267,678	208,631	26,089	32,958
AW (22-33)	146,743	159,544	113,467	29,731	16,346
SD (33-45)	160,661	161,318	132,136	22,953	6,229
MA (45-55)	167,346	126,563	116,837	3,915	5,811
CL (55-65)	42,376	46,103	34,631	3,453	8,019
LA (65+)	20,239	24,172	16,953	6,034	1,185
CLASS TOTAL	**800,250**	**785,378**	**622,655**	**92,175**	**70,548**

contain terms that fit two or more classes. It would be impossible to classify these types of queries. The other important factor that affects the match of queries in the log and terms in the background set, is the fact that we are using today's Web collection and search engine to produce the background set, but the query log was collected in 1999. The Web collection grew tenfold in the last seven years; search engines are fine-tuned to return results that reflect contemporary culture and language (Spink et al., 2004). This conjecture is partially supported by comparing results of the two tasks executed three years apart. While the numbers of queries classified via Scenario-A in both tasks are almost identical, there is a disparity in the classification results: a) only 79% of Task-9 results are identically classified (found in same class in Task-6), b) 12% of Task-9 results are cross-classified (found in different classes in Task-6), and c) 9% of Task-9 results came from previously unclassified queries.

Finally it is essential to keep in mind the season (Chaw at al., 2005). Five days before Christmas the users are searching for very specific things, such as *candles* for a party, *recipes* for holiday meals, tree *decorations and ornaments* or holiday *gifts* or *presents* for friends.

CONCLUSION AND FUTURE RESEARCH

Starting with a small, manually selected set of terms, we develop and present an approach that classifies a set of web queries. This text classification task is difficult for three reasons: the dataset does not contain many labeled examples, the text examples are extremely short, and classification is non-topical, by characteristics of the users. By iteratively applying our approach and improving performance of the ranking algorithm we are able to classify many queries in a large query log. However, analysis of several distinct background discovery scenarios did not produce a clear winner.

We also conduct two separate classification tasks (three years apart) that demonstrate temporal inconsistency of information retrieval as a source for background knowledge. On the plus side, the discovery of this inconsistency is an excellent source for a new research direction: use of different search engines (at different times) to identify new classification terms.

An important and necessary area of further research is how to evaluate the quality of the classification results. There are several ways to explore this. We can use a limited number of the classified queries to retrieve web sites and manually compare these sites to well known age-related sites. Alternatively, we can use a large number of the classified queries to retrieve web sites and algorithmically compare these sites to a set of age-related web sites to check for cross-classification of results.

REFERENCES

Banerjee, S. (2008). Improving text classification accuracy using topic modeling over an additional corpus. *Proceedings of the 31st International ACM SIGIR conference on research and development in information retrieval*, 867-868.

Beitzel, S., Jensen, E., Chowdhury, A., & Frieder, O. (2008). Analysis of varying approaches to topical web query classification. *Proceedings of the 3rd international Conference on Scalable information Systems*, 1-5.

Bobicev, V., & Sokolova, M. (2008). An effective and Robust Method for Short Text Classification. *Proceedings of the 21st Conference of the Association of the Advancement of Artificial Intelligence*, 1444-1445.

Cesa-Bianchi, N., Gentile, C., & Zaniboni, L. (2006). Hierarchical Classification: Combining Bayes with SVM. *Proceedings of the 23rd International Conference on Machine Learning*, 177–184, Pittsburgh, PA.

Chan, J., Koprinska, I., & Poon, J. (2008). Semi-Supervised Classification using Bridging. *International Journal of Artificial Intelligence Tools*, *17*(3), 415–431. doi:10.1142/S0218213008003972

Chau, M., Fang, X., & Sheng, O. R. L. (2005). Analysis of the Query Logs of a Web Site Search Engine. *Journal of the American Society for Information Science and Technology*, *56*(13), 1363–1376. doi:10.1002/asi.20210

Choi, Y., Kim, Y., & Myaeng, S. (2009). Domain-specific sentiment analysis using contextual feature generation. *Proceeding of the 1st international CIKM Workshop on Topic-Sentiment Analysis for Mass Opinion*, 37-44.

Cormode, G., & Krishnamurthy, B. (2008). Key differences between Web1.0 and Web2.0. *First Monday*, *13*(6).

Dayanik, A., Lewis, D. D., Madigan, D., Menkov, V., & Genkin, A. (2006). Constructing informative prior distributions from domain knowledge in text classification. *Proceedings of the 29th Annual international ACM SIGIR Conference on Research and Development in Information Retrieval*, 493–500. New York: ACM Press.

Dix, A. (2007). Designing for appropriation. *BCS-HCI '07: Proceedings of the 21st British HCI Group Annual Conference on HCI*, 27-30.

Esuli, A., Fagni, T., & Sebastiani, F. (2008). Boosting multi-label hierarchical text categorization. *Information Retrieval*, *11*, 287–313. doi:10.1007/s10791-008-9047-y

Excite. (1999). Excite and other more recent data sets can be downloaded from http://ist.psu.edu/faculty_pages/jjansen/academic/transaction_logs.html

Gabrilovich, E., Broder, A., Fontoura, M., Joshi, A., Josifovski, V., Riedel, L., & Zhang, T. (2009). Classifying search queries using the Web as a source of knowledge. *ACM Transactions on the Web*, *3*(2), 1–28. doi:10.1145/1513876.1513877

Gabrilovich, E., & Markovitch, S. (2005). Feature generation for text categorization using world knowledge. *Proceedings of the Nineteenth International Joint Conference of Artificial Intelligence*, 1048–1053.

Gabrilovich, E., & Markovitch, S. (2007). Harnessing the Expertise of 70,000 Human Editors: Knowledge-Based Feature Generation for Text Categorization. *The Journal of Machine Learning Research*, *8*, 2297 – 2345.

Genkin, A., Lewis, D., & Madigan, D. (2007). Large Scale Bayesian Logistic Regression for Text Categorization. *Technometrics*, *49*(3), 291–304. doi:10.1198/004017007000000245

Ghani, R. (2002). Combining Labeled and Unlabeled Data for MultiClass Text Categorization. *Proceedings of the Nineteenth International Conference on Machine Learning*, 187–194. San Francisco: Morgan Kaufmann.

Gliozzo, A., Strapparava, C., & Dagan, I. (2009). Improving Text Categorization Bootstrapping via Unsupervised Learning. [TSLP]. *ACM Transactions on Speech and Language Processing*, *6*(1), 1–24. doi:10.1145/1596515.1596516

Goldman, S., & Zhou, Y. (2000). Enhancing Supervised Learning with Unlabeled Data. *Proceedings of the Seventeenth International Conference on Machine Learning*, (pp. 327–334). San Francisco: Morgan Kaufmann.

Han, E. H., Karypis, G., & Kumar, V. (2001). Text categorization using weight-adjusted k-nearest neighbor classification. In D. Cheung, Q. Li and G. Williams (eds.), *Proceedings PAKDD-01, 5th Pacific–Asia Conference on Knowledge Discovery and Data Mining*, (LNCS 2035, 53–65. Berlin: Springer.

Hernandez, B., Jiménez, J., & Martín, M. J. (2009). Key website factors in e-business strategy. *International Journal of Information Management*, *29*(5), 362–371. doi:10.1016/j.ijinfomgt.2008.12.006

Jansen, B. J., Zhang, M., Booth, B., Park, D., Zhang, Y., Kathuria, A., & Bonner, P. (2009). To What Degree Can Log Data Profile a Web Searcher? *Proceedings of the American Society for Information Science and Technology*, Vancouver, British Columbia.

Joachims, T. (2002). The Maximum-Margin Approach to Learning Text Classifiers, *Ausgezeichnete Informatikdissertationen*. In Wagner, D. (Eds.), *GI-Edition - Lecture Notes in Informatics (LNI)*. Bonn, Germany: Köllen Verlag.

Kaban, A. (2008). A Probabilistic Neighborhood Translation Approach for Non-standard Text Classification. In *Proceedings Discovery Science (DS08)*, (LNAI 5255, 332-343).

Krafft, J. (2009). Profiting in the info-coms industry in the age of broadband: Lessons and new considerations. *Technological Forecasting and Social Change*, 77(2), 265–278. doi:10.1016/j.techfore.2009.07.002

Levinson, D. J. (1986). *The Seasons of a Man's Life*. New York: Ballantine Books.

Lewis, D. D., & Catlett, J. (1994). Heterogeneous Uncertainty Sampling for Supervised Learning. *Proceedings of the Eleventh International Conference on Machine Learning*, 148–156. San Francisco: Morgan Kaufmann.

Li, X., & Liu, B. (2003). Learning to Classify Text Using Positive and Unlabeled Data. *Proceedings of the Eighteenth International Joint Conference on Artificial Intelligence*, 587–594. San Francisco: Morgan Kaufmann.

Lippincott, T., & Passonneau, R. (2009). Semantic Clustering for a Functional Text Classification Task. In *Proceedings of the 10th international Conference on Computational Linguistics and Intelligent Text Processing*, (LNCS 5449, 509-522.

Liu, X., Croft, W. B., Oh, P., & Hart, D. (2004). Automatic recognition of reading levels from user queries. *Proceedings of the 27th ACM International Conference on Research and Development in Information Retrieval*, 548–549, Sheffield, UK.

McCallum, A., & Nigam, K. (1998). A comparison of event models for naïve Bayes text classification. In *AAAI-98 Workshop on Learning for Text Categorization*.

Metaxas, P., Ivanova, L., & Mustafaraj, E. (2009). New Quality Metrics for Web Search Results. *Web Information Systems and Technologies LNBIP*, 18(3), 278–292. doi:10.1007/978-3-642-01344-7_21

Nigam, K., McCallum, A., & Mitchell, T. (2006) Semi-Supervised Text Classification Using EM. In O. Chapelle, B. Sch¨olkopf, & A. Zien (Eds.), *Semi-Supervised Learning*, 31-51. Cambridge, MA: MIT Press.

Ozmutlu, S., Ozmutlu, H. C., & Spink, A. (2008). Analytical approaches for topic analysis and identification of Web search engine transaction logs. In Jansen, B. J., Spink, A., & Taksa, I. (Eds.), *Handbook of Web Log Analysis*. Hershey, PA: Idea Group Publishing.

Quinlan, J. R. (1986). Induction of Decision Trees. *Machine Learning*, 1, 81–106. doi:10.1007/BF00116251

Raghavan, H., Madani, O., & Jones, R. (2006). Active Learning with Feedback on Both Features and Instances. *Journal of Machine Learning Research*, 7, 1655–1686.

Sahami, M., & Heilman, T. D. (2006). A Web-based Kernel Function for Measuring the Similarity of Short-text Snippets. *Proceedings of the Fifteenth International World Wide Web Conference*, 377–386. New York: ACM.

Sarawagi, S. (Ed.). (2005). *SIGKDD Explorations, Newsletter of the ACM Special Interest Group on Knowledge Discovery and Data Mining*. Reading, MA: AddisonWelsley.

Schapire, R. E., Rochery, M., Rahim, M., & Gupta, N. (2002) Incorporating Prior Knowledge into Boosting. *Proceedings of the International Conference on Machine Learning*, 538–545. San Francisco: Morgan Kaufmann.

Schneider, K.-M. (2005). Techniques for Improving the Performance of Naïve Bayes for Text Classification. In *Sixth International Conference on Intelligent Text Processing and Computational Linguistics*, (LNCS 3406, 682–693).

Sebastiani, F. (2002). Machine learning in automated text categorization. *ACM Computing Surveys*, *34*(1), 1–47. doi:10.1145/505282.505283

Sindhwani, S., & Keerthi, S. (2006) Large scale semi-supervised linear SVMs. *Proceedings of the 29th annual international ACM SIGIR conference on Research and Development in Information Retrieval*, 477–484. New York: ACM Press.

Spink, A., & Jansen, B. J. (2004). *Web search, public searching of the web*. New York: Kluwer.

Spink, A., Jansen, B. J., Wolfram, D., & Saracevic, T. (2002). From E-Sex to E-Commerce: Web Search Changes. *IEEE Computer*, *35*(3), 107–109.

Szummer, M., & Jaakkola, T. (2000). Kernel expansions With Unlabeled Examples. [Cambridge, MA: MIT Press.]. *Advances in Neural Information Processing Systems*, *13*, 626–632.

Taksa, I. (2005). Predicting the Cumulative Effect of Multiple Query Formulations. *Proceedings of the IEEE International Conference on Information Technology: Coding and Computing*, (Volume II, April 2005, 491–496.

Tan, S., Cheng, X., Wang, Y., & Xu, H. (2009). Adapting Naïve Bayes to Domain Adaptation for Sentiment Analysis. *Proceedings of the European Conference on Information Retrieval*, (LNCS 5478, 337-349.

Wen, J.-R., Nie, J.-Y., & Zhang, H.-J. (2002). Query clustering using user logs. *ACM Transactions on Information Systems*, *20*(1), 59–81. doi:10.1145/503104.503108

Wu, X., Kumar, V., Ross Quinlan, J., Ghosh, J., Yang, Q., & Motoda, H. (2008). Top 10 algorithms in data mining. *Knowledge and Information Systems*, *14*(1), 1–37. doi:10.1007/s10115-007-0114-2

Zelikovitz, S., Cohen, W. W., & Hirsh, H. (2007). Extending WHIRL with Background Knowledge for Improved Text Classification. *Information Retrieval*, *10*(1), 35–67. doi:10.1007/s10791-006-9004-6

Zhu, T., Greiner, R., & Haeubl, G. (2003). Learning a model of a web user's interests. *Proceedings of the 9th International Conference on User Modeling*, (LNCS 2702, 65–75. Berlin: Springer.

Zhu, X. (2007). *Semi-Supervied Learning Literature Survey*. Madison, WI: Computer Sciences Technical Report, University of Wisconsin-Madison.

Zimmer, M., & Spink, A. (2008). *Web Searching: Interdisciplinary Perspectives*. Dordrecht, The Netherlands: Springer.

KEY TERMS AND DEFINITIONS

Background Knowledge: Body of text, images, databases, or other data that is related to a particular machine learning classification task. The background knowledge may contain information about the classes; it may contain further examples; it may contain data about both examples and classes.

Entropy: Measurement that can be used in machine learning on a set of data that is to be classified. In this setting it can be defined as the amount of uncertainty or randomness (or noise) in the data. If all data is classified with the same class, the entropy of that set would be 0. The entropy of a set T that has a probability distribution of classes $\{p_1, p_2, \ldots p_n\}$ can be defined as $-(p_1 \times \log(p_1) + p_2 \times \log(p_2) + \ldots p_n \times \log(p_n))$.

Information Gain: The amount of information in a given set of data can be defined as $(1 - entropy)$. If any observation about the given data is made, new information can then be recomputed. The difference between the two information values is the "information gain". In other words, the change of entropy is the information that is gained by the observation. If we partition a set T into T_1 and T_0, based upon some characteristic of the data then the information gain of that partition can be defined as

$$IG(t) = entropy\,(T) - (entropy\,(T_0) \times \frac{|T_0|}{|T|} + entropy\,(T_1) \times \frac{|T_1|}{|T|}).$$

Labeled Set: Set of item-label pairs. The item consists of an actual example that can be classified, and the label is the classification. In a supervised learning paradigm this set is sometimes referred to as the "training set".

Machine Learning: The area of artificial intelligence that studies the algorithms and processes that allow machines to learn. These algorithms use a combination of techniques to learn from examples, from prior knowledge, or from experience.

Text Classification: Process of assigning classes (or labels) to textual data. Textual data can range from short phrases to much longer documents. Sometimes referred to as "text categorization", a text classification task can be defined as follows: Given a set of documents $D = \{d_1, d_2 \ldots, d_n\}$ and a set of classes $C = \{c_1, c_2, \ldots, c_m\}$ assign a label from the set C to each element of set D.

Unlabeled Set: Set of examples whose labels or classes are unknown. If the class of an unlabeled example is learned, it can then be added to a "labeled set".

Section 3

Chapter 10
Temporal–Based Video Event Detection and Retrieval

Min Chen
University of Montana, USA

ABSTRACT

The fast proliferation of video data archives has increased the need for automatic video content analysis and semantic video retrieval. Since temporal information is critical in conveying video content, in this chapter, an effective temporal-based event detection framework is proposed to support high-level video indexing and retrieval. The core is a temporal association mining process that systematically captures characteristic temporal patterns to help identify and define interesting events. This framework effectively tackles the challenges caused by loose video structure and class imbalance issues. One of the unique characteristics of this framework is that it offers strong generality and extensibility with the capability of exploring representative event patterns with little human interference. The temporal information and event detection results can then be input into our proposed distributed video retrieval system to support the high-level semantic querying, selective video browsing and event-based video retrieval.

INTRODUCTION

With the proliferation of multimedia data and ever-growing requests for multimedia applications, new challenges emerge for efficient and effective managing and accessing large audio-visual collections. Discovering events from video streams improves the access and reuse of large video collections. Events are real-world occurrences that unfold over space and time, and play important roles in classic areas of multimedia and new experiential applications such as eChronicles, life logs, and event-centric media managers (Westermann & Jain, 2007). However, with current technologies, there is little or no metadata

DOI: 10.4018/978-1-61692-859-9.ch010

associated with events captured in videos, making it very difficult to search through a large collection to find instances of a particular pattern or event (Xie, Sundaram, & Campbell, 2008).

To address this need, semantic event classification, which is the process of mapping video streams to pre-defined semantic event categories, has been an active area of research with notable recent progress. (Westermann & Jain, 2007) (Xie et al., 2008) provide some extensive surveys. In essence, most existing event detection frameworks involve two main steps (Leonardi, Migliorati, & Prandini, 2004): video content processing (or called video syntactic analysis) and decision-making process. During the first step, the video clip is segmented into certain analysis units (mostly in shots which refer to unbroken sequences of frames taken by a single camera) and their representative features ranging from low-level, mid-level, and feature aggregations (Xie et al., 2008) are extracted. While good features are deemed important, coming up with the "optimal features" remains an open problem and some prefer a featureless approach that leaves the task of determining the relative importance of input dimensions to the learner. The second step then extracts the semantic index from the feature descriptors. In the literature, several generative models such as hidden Markov model (HMM), dynamic Bayesian network (DBN), linear dynamic systems are commonly used for capturing events that unfold in time. Generally speaking, the events detected by the abovementioned methods are semantically meaningful and usually significant to the users. The major disadvantage, however, is that many rely on specific artifacts (so-called domain knowledge or a priori information) (Chen, Chen, Shyu, & Wickramaratna, 2006) and hinder the generalization and extensibility of the framework. In addition, current techniques on video semantic analysis and representation are mostly shot-based (Chen, & Zhang, 2007). However, events are inherently related to the concept of time (Westermann & Jain, 2007) and therefore normally a single analysis unit separately from its *context* has less capability of conveying semantics (Zhu, Wu, Elmagarmid, Feng, & Wu, 2005).

In this chapter, we propose an automatic process in developing an extensible framework, in terms of event pattern discovery, representation, and usage. It fully utilizes contextual correlation and temporal dependencies to improve event detection and retrieval accuracy. The main contributions of this framework are summarized as follows:

- A temporal association mining approach is proposed to properly locate and model important *context* to help identify and define events. This is a challenging task especially when dealing with videos with loose content structure (e.g., sports videos) where such *context* might appear randomly (to some degree) with regard to the targeted events. For example, as we look at the two soccer video sequences shown in Figure 1 where x_t represents the shot with goal event, the shot before it (i.e., x_{t-1}) can contain a close-up view (in sequence 1) or global view (in sequence 2). Similarly, x_{t-2} shots in these two sequences are also quite different from each other.

- Many types of events appear rarely in video sequences (e.g., accidents in traffic videos, distress events in surveillance videos, and goal events in soccer videos). Such class-imbalance problem causes some potential difficulties for many traditional classification techniques, that is few training examples from the targeted event class and non-event class constitutes the majority to dominate the learning process. Our framework tackles this issue effectively and outperforms many well-known classification approaches as demonstrated by the comparative experiments.

- One purpose of event detection is to support semantic video retrieval and navigation. Currently, many multimedia systems support shot level video retrieval and temporal neighbor browsing (Mu, 2006). That is to retrieve interested shots based on certain query criteria and allow users to navigate around these select shots. However, in many cases, an event is a better semantic unit as compared to a shot. Therefore, in our framework, event-based retrieval is realized using the event detection results and an enhanced temporal query model that allow users to view an event including its associated event causes and effects.

BACKGROUND AND RELATED WORK

Essentially, a video clip can be viewed as a time series $X = \{x_t, t = 1,..., N\}$, where t is the time index and N is the total number of observations. If we let $x_i \in X$ be an interesting event, the problem of event detection in our framework is decomposed into three subtasks. First, an event x_i should possess its own characteristics or feature set that needs to be extracted. Second, from the temporal evolution point of view, usually an event x_i is the result of past activities and might cause effects in the future as well. Therefore, an effective approach is required to explore the time-ordered structures (or temporal patterns) in the time series that are significant for characterizing the events of interests. Finally, a decision making process is carried out to fuse the information obtained in the previous two subtasks and automatically detect the interesting events.

Intuitively, the problem of finding temporal patterns can be converted as to find adjacent attributes (i.e., X) which have strong associations with (and thus characterize) the target event (i.e., Y). We can thus see a mapping between the temporal pattern discovery and the association rule mining (ARM). As we know, Association rules are an important type of knowledge representation revealing implicit relationships among the items present in a large number of transactions. Given $I = \{i_1, i_2, ..., i_n\}$ as the item space, a transaction is a set of items which is a subset of I. An association rule is an implication of the form [$X \rightarrow Y$, *support, confidence*], where X and Y are sets of items (or itemsets) called antecedent and consequence of the rule with $X \subset I$, $Y \subset I$, and $X \cap Y = \emptyset$. The *support* of the rule is defined as the percentage of transactions that contain both X and Y among all transactions in the input data set; whereas the *confidence* shows the percentage of transactions that contain Y among transactions that contain X. The intended meaning of this rule is that the presence of X in a transaction implies the presence of Y in the same transaction with a certain probability. Therefore, traditional ARM aims to find frequent and strong association rules whose support and confidence values exceed the user-specified minimum *support* and minimum *confidence* thresholds.

However, the problem of temporal pattern discovery for video event detection also has its own unique characteristics that differ greatly from the traditional ARM.

- **Problem 1.** An itemset in traditional ARM contains only distinct items without considering the quantity of each item in the itemset. However, an event is normally characterized by not only the associated attribute types but also their occurrence frequency. For example, in a traffic video, a police car passing through an intersection is considered normal whereas ten police cars going toward the same direction within a short temporal window may signal an abnormal event nearby.
- **Problem 2.** In traditional ARM, the order of the items appeared in a transaction (enclosed by a pair of braces {}) is considered as irrelevant. Therefore, a transaction $\{a, b\}$ is treated the same as $\{b, a\}$. In fact, this is a helpful feature to deal with the issue of loose video structure as discussed in the previous section. For example, as can be seen from Figure 1, the x_{t-1} and x_{t-2} shots in sequence 1 contain a global view followed by a close-up view (denoted as {global view, close-up view}) whereas in sequence 2 are {close-up view, global view}. Therefore, if the order of the

items is considered irrelevant, we might identify a common pattern between sequences 1 and 2. Of course this is just a simplified case. The complete algorithm is detailed in next section. However, for an event E (e.g., x_t shot in Figure 1), if we name its cause Ec (e.g., $\{x_{t-1}, x_{t-2}\}$) and effect Ee (e.g., $\{x_{t+1}, x_{t+2}\}$) and we have a rule of $<Ec, Ee>\rightarrow E$, the order between Ec and Ee is obviously important (enclosed by a pair of angle brackets $< >$) in characterizing E since the cause should always occur ahead of the effect.

To our best knowledge, such issues have not been addressed in other existing video event detection approaches. A slightly similar work is presented in (Zhu et al., 2005), where ARM is applied to the temporal domain to facilitate event detection. However, it uses the traditional itemset idea. In addition, it searches the whole video to identify the frequent itemsets. Under the situation of rare event detection, useful patterns are most likely overshadowed by the irrelevant itemsets. In our earlier work (Chen, Chen, & Shyu, 2007), a hierarchical temporal association mining approach was proposed to tackle these issues by checking the associations in multiple levels. The framework can achieve promising results in event detection. However, its complexity also leads to a higher computational cost and certain inflexibility, especially when integrating with video retrieval systems.

PROPOSED FRAMEWORK

The ultimate goal of our research is to develop a general framework which can automatically analyze videos, detect events, and finally offer an efficient and user-friendly system for video retrieval and distribution. As illustrated in Figure 2, the proposed system essentially consists of two modules – event detection module and event retrieval module.

The former can be divided into three major components based on their functionalities, namely *syntactic analysis*, *temporal pattern discovery*, and *data mining*, which match with the three subtasks discussed in the previous section. In the *syntactic analysis* component, an unsupervised video shot boundary detection approach (Chen, Shyu, & Zhang, 2005) is used to temporally segment the raw soccer video sequences into a set of consecutive video shots. The detected shot boundaries are thus passed for feature extraction, where the shot-level multimodal features (visual and audio features) are extracted. Here, visual features are captured with the assistance of color analysis and object segmentation techniques, whereas audio features are exploited in both time-domain and frequency-domain. A complete

Figure 1. Two sample video sequences where each shot is represented by its key frame

list of multimodal features and their detailed feature descriptions can be found in (Chen, Shyu, Zhang, & Chen, 2006). In the *temporal pattern discovery* component, an extended ARM algorithm (E-ARM) is proposed to explore the temporal patterns significant for characterizing the events and results in a set of temporal rules, which are effectively employed to capture the candidate video events and to alleviate the class-imbalance issue. Then the events of interests are detected automatically in the *multimodal data mining* component, where C4.5 decision tree based multimodal data mining process is performed. We chose C4.5 not only because it is one of the most commonly used algorithms in the machine learning and data mining communities but also because it has become a de facto standard against which every new algorithm is judged (Chen et al., 2007). Finally the development of the second module, i.e., the event retrieval module, mainly involves the development of an advanced temporal query paradigm which can model a large variety of temporal queries of video events. To achieve this goal, the raw video, video shots, their associated temporal information and multimodal features are formally modeled and stored in an object-relational database efficiently so that basic queries can be easily supported. In addition, a temporal query language is used to specify the relative queries between sets of events.

In essence, the components *syntactic analysis* and *data mining* are similar to the general two-step procedure discussed in the Introduction Section. The focus of this chapter is therefore on the exploration and representation of the temporal patterns, that is the extended ARM (E-ARM) and the video retrieval system.

Extended Arm (E-ARM)

In this study, E-ARM is proposed to explore the most significant temporal patterns and the following important concepts are addressed.

- *Concept 1*. How are the items and transaction defined for E-ARM?
- *Concept 2*. How can E-ARM deal with the unique problem of temporal pattern discovery?
- *Concept 3*. Can the *support* and *confident* criteria be defined automatically instead of manually set as in the traditional ARM?

Figure 2. The proposed integrated video analysis and retrieval system

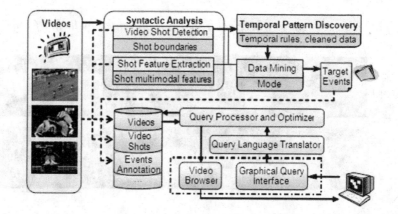

Concept 1: Items and Transaction

Many of the existing temporal analysis approaches (Feng, & Huang, 2005) (Povinelli & Feng, 2003) focused on finding the significant pattern to *predict* the events. For example, as discussed in (Povinelli & Feng, 2003), given a training time series $X = \{x_t, t = 1,..., N\}$, the task of defining a temporal pattern p is to identify $X_t = \{x_{t-(Q-1)\tau},..., x_{t-\tau}, x_t\}$ from X, where x_t represents the present observation and $x_{t-(Q-1)\tau},..., x_{t-\tau}$ are the past activities. Their goal is to capture the temporal patterns that occur in the past and are completed in the present, with the capability of *forecasting* some event occurring in the future. However, as far as video event detection is concerned, we intend to identify the temporal patterns that *characterize* the events. We consider not only the causes (Ec) that lead to the event (E), but also the effects (Ee) which the event might have. Therefore, the problem can be formalized as to identify the temporal rule $<Ec, Ee> \rightarrow E$ where $Ec \subseteq \{x_{t-i\tau}, i=1, ..., a\}$ and $Ee \subseteq \{x_{t+j\tau}, j=1, ..., b\}$. Here τ called *granularity indicator*, represents the granularity level (i.e., shot-level, frame-level or clip-level in video analysis) at which the observations are measured, x_t represents the unit which contains the targeted event, and the parameters a and b define the starting and ending positions of the temporal observations (or called the size of cause window Wc and effect window We), respectively. Intuitively, as compared to the original market basket scenario where the items of a transaction represent a set of things purchased by a user during one shopping process, the items and transaction in event detection can be defined as the set of units occurring within a temporal window of the targeted event. Theoretically, event detection can be performed at various granularities such as frame level, shot level, or clip level. However, since a shot is normally regarded as a self-contained unit, in this study, we define the item at the shot level and therefore a transaction contains $(a+b+1)$ shots (including the event shot). Now the question is how to determine the value of a and b, that is the size of the temporal window. In our earlier work (Shyu, Xie, Chen, & Chen, 2008), an advanced approach was proposed to identify the significant temporal window with regard to the target event, which can be incorporated into this framework to define the window size. Alternatively, they can be set to any reasonably small values such as 3 or 4 since generally only the temporally adjacent shots have strong association with the target event.

Concept 2: E-ARM for Temporal Pattern Discovery

Mathematically, let $D = \{X_i\}$ ($i = 1, ..., N$) be the video database that contains N video clips for training. From each video clip X_i, a common set of feature descriptors F are extracted using the *syntactic analysis* component. We then have the following definitions.

Definition 1. A video X_i is an ordered collection of units $<X_{ij}, j = 1, ..., n_i>$, where n_i is the number of units in X_i and each unit X_{ij} is a 2-tuple (F_{ij}, C_{ij}). Here F_{ij} indicates the unit attributes and $C_{ij} = \{yes, no\}$ is the class label indicating the eventness of X_{ij}.

As mentioned in *Concept 1*, the unit is defined at the shot level where the unit attributes can be features at low-level, middle-level or high-level. Note that if the feature values are continuous, certain discretization process should be conducted to create a set of discrete values to be used by E-ARM. As usual, the task is to find all frequent and strong patterns from the transactions given the target event E. Different from traditional ARM, in order to address Problems 1 and 2 mentioned in the previous section, we propose to use the *bag* concept which is mathematically defined as a variation of a set that can contain the same item more than once. In addition, instead of finding association rule in the form of [$X \rightarrow Y$, *support*, *confidence*] in traditional ARM, E-ARM aims to discover temporal rules of $<Ec, Ee> \rightarrow E$.

Consequently, the antecedent X in traditional ARM is treated as a single unit whereas the counterpart in E-ARM consists of two related yet separate parts Ec and Ee. The E-ARM algorithm therefore differs largely from the traditional ARM and involves three major steps.

- Search for frequent temporal patterns

We proceed by first finding all frequent cause and effect patterns Pc and Pe. Different from traditional ARM, to alleviate the problem of class imbalance problem, the frequent patterns are searched for the minority class (i.e., event class) only. In other words, we fetch $\{X_{i(j-k)}, k = 1, ..., a\}$ and $\{X_{i(j+m)}, m = 1, ..., b\}$ (denoted as Pc_{ij} and Pe_{ij}, respectively) only when $C_{ij} = $ 'yes.' For example, assuming in Figure 1 the size of cause window Wc and effect window We is a and b where $a=b=2$ and x_t shot in sequence 1 is an event but is not in sequence 2, we will then not include sequence 2 in this step. The discrimination power of the patterns is validated against the nonevent class only when we get to step 2. Following the bag concept, we define *itembag* (the counterpart of *itemset* in the traditional ARM) as follows:

Definition 2. An *itembag* B is a combination of unit attributes. B matches the characterization of an event in window Wc or We if B is the subset of Pc_{ij} or Pe_{ij} where $C_{ij} = $ 'yes.'

For example, if a Wc for an event E contains attributes $\{G, C, C\}$, then we call $B = \{C, C\}$ a match of the characterization of event E, whereas $B = \{G, G\}$ is not. Consequently, we revise the traditional *support* definition as follows.

Definition 3. An *itembag* B has *support* s in D if $s\%$ of all $Pc_E = \{Pc_{ij}\}$ (or $Pe_E = \{Pe_{ij}\}$) for target event E are matched by B. B is frequent if s exceeds the predefined *min_sup*.

Mathematically, *support* is defined as

$$Support = Count(B, Pc_E)/|Pc_E| \text{ or } Support = Count(B, Pe_E)/|Pe_E| \tag{1}$$

From Equation (1), we can see that our definition of support is not simply an extension of the one used in traditional ARM. It is restricted to $Pc_E = \{Pc_{ij}\}$ or $Pe_E = \{Pe_{ij}\}$ which are associated with the target events (i.e., $C_{ij} = $ 'yes'). An *itembag* appearing in D periodically might not be considered as frequent if it is not covered by Pc_E or Pe_E. The pseudo code for finding frequent *itembag* is listed in Table 1. The general idea is to maintain in memory, for each target event E at X_{ij}, all the units within its associated Pc_{ij} and Pe_{ij}, which are then stored in B_c and B_e (steps 1 to 19), and Extended *Apriori* algorithm (will be presented in Table 2) is applied to find the frequent cause and effect patterns Pc and Pe from B_c and B_e (steps 20 to 21). Then the final step (step 22) is used to generate the complete temporal pattern where the ordering between cause and effect patterns needs to be observed. In addition, the *Apriori* like principle can be applied which states that for a particular pattern to be frequent, its element(s) must be frequent as well. Therefore we have $P = <Pc, Pe>$, i.e., only frequent cause pattern Pc and effect pattern Pe are considered in producing the frequent temporal pattern P.

In terms of the extended *apriori* algorithm (see Table 2), for the construction of 1-*itembags*, the traditional *Apriori* algorithm works (step 1) because a *bag* functions just like a *set* when it contains only 1 item. To construct *itembags* with more than 1 item, we need to consider each unit attribute as a distinct element even though some attributes might have the same values. For example, $\{G, C, C\}$ is treated as containing 3 distinct elements since in the transactions and *itembags* we allow the existence of duplicated elements. Because we consider the ordering of the units and the inter-arrival times between the units and target events within each time window to be irrelevant in finding the frequent cause and effect

Table 1. Logic to find all frequent patterns

Input: training video database D, cause window size a, effect window size b, minimum support min_sup, target-event type E
Output: frequent cause patterns Pc, effect patterns Pe and temporal patterns P
FrequentPatterns(D, a, b, min_sup, E)
1) $Bc = \varnothing; B = \varnothing; Be = \varnothing$
2) for each video sequence $X_i \in D$
3) for each unit $X_{ij} = (F_{ij}, C_{ij}) \in X_i$
4) for each unit $X_{ik} = (F_{ik}, C_{ik}) \in B$
5) if $(j - k) > a$
6) Remove X_{ik} from B
7) endif
8) endfor
9) if X_{ij} is a target event // i.e., C_{ij} = 'yes'
10) $Bc = Bc \cup \{F_{ik} \mid (F_{ik}, \cdot) \in B\}$
11) $PS = j+1$
12) while $(PS - j) < b$
13) $Be = Be \cup \{F_{ik} \mid k = PS\}$
14) PS is set to its next shot until it is the end of X_i
15) Endwhile
16) endif
17) $B = B \cup X_{ij}$
18) Endfor
19) endfor
20) Use extended *Apriori* over Bc to find Pc with min_sup
21) Use extended *Apriori* over Be to find Pe with min_sup
22) $P = <Pc, Pe>$

patterns, for the sake of simplicity, all the units inside the *itembags* are sorted in the algorithm (step 2.1) then merged (steps 2.2 and 2.3). Note that the computational cost for such procedures is minimal because the transactions are constructed only for minority class and the number of elements in such transactions is small (without loss of generality, the window size is reasonably small as we discussed in *concept* 1).

- Identify strong temporal patterns

To validate that the temporal patterns obtained from Step 1 effectively characterize the event of interests, a restrict solution is to adopt the traditional association measure called *confidence*, where a similar idea presented in (Vilalta & Ma, 2002) can be adopted. The general idea is to count the number of times each of the patterns occurs outside the windows of the target events.

Definition 4. A temporal pattern P has *confident c* in D if c% of all transactions matched are associated with the target event E. P is strong if c exceeds min_conf.

Table 2. The procedure of extended apriori algorithm

1) Construct 1-*itembags*. Count their *supports* and obtain the set of all frequent 1-*itembags* as in traditional *Apriori* algorithm
2) A pair of frequent k-*itembags* are merged to produce a candidate $(k+1)$-*itembags*. The merges are conducted in three steps:
2.1) Sort all the frequent k-itembags
2.2) A pair of frequent k-*itembags* are merged if their first $(k-1)$ items are identical, and
2.3) A frequent k-*itembag* can be merged with itself only if all its elements are the same.
3) The *supports* are counted and the frequent *itembags* are obtained as the traditional *Apriori* algorithm. Go to step 2.
4) The algorithm terminates when no further merge can be conducted.

Intuitively, we take inputs of a set of transactions, which correspond to all $Pc_{\_N} = \{Pc_{ij}\}$ and $Pe_{\_N} = \{Pe_{ij}\}$ with $C_{ij} = $ '*no.*' In fact, such lists can be obtained using the algorithm presented in Table 1 when we scan through the unit sequence and store them in $Bc_{\_N}$ and $Be_{\_N}$, respectively. Let x_1 and x_2 be the number of times the pattern P is matched in $<Bc, Be>$ and $<Bc_{\_N}, Be_{\_N}>$, respectively. We have *confidence* of P defined as

$$confidence(P) = x_1/(x_1+x_2) \qquad (2)$$

This metric is thus applied to compare with *min_conf* and to validate whether the temporal patterns are strong.

- Build temporal rules

Once we obtain the frequent and strong temporal patterns, we will build temporal rules to facilitate the event detection. The principle is defined as follows.

Definition 5. Given two patterns, P_i and P_j, $P_i \succ P_j$ (also called P_i has a higher rank than P_j) if

1. The *confidence* of P_i is greater than that of P_j, or
2. Their *confidences* are the same, but the *support* of P_i is greater than that of P_j, or
3. Both the *confidences* and *supports* of P_i and P_j are the same, but P_i is more specific than P_j (i.e., $P_j \subset P_i$).

The rules are in the form of $P_i \rightarrow E$ (targeted event). Let R be the set of generated rules, the basic idea is to choose a set of high ranked rules in R to cover all the target events in D. When given unseen videos for event detection, such temporal rules are applied to clear data and generate a candidate event set to feed into the data classification stage.

Concept 3: Define Support and Confident Criteria

The richness of the generated patterns is partially dependent on *min_sup*, which in most existing works is defined manually based on domain knowledge. However, given a training database, it is infeasible to expect users to possess the knowledge of the complete characteristics of the training set. Therefore, the proposed approach addresses this issue by refining the *support* threshold $Tsup_{k+1}$ iteratively based on the statistical analysis of the frequent patterns obtained using threshold $Tsup_k$.

Given k^{th} threshold $Tsup_k$, let R_k be the number of members in the largest frequent *itembags*, we have $sup_{kr} = \{supports$ of all r-*itembags*$\}$, where $r=1, \ldots, R_k$. The steps to calculate *min_sup* are shown in Table 3.

The idea is that the learned frequent patterns in the previous round can help reveal certain knowledge regarding the training data set and thus help refine the *support* threshold intelligently. Specifically, we study the biggest fluctuation between the *supports* of two adjacent *itembags*. Since $(r+1)$-*itembags* are rooted from r-*itembags*, if the difference is greater than $R_k/2$, the support threshold is adjusted to avoid the possible over-fitting issue and improve framework efficiency. Note that the initial support threshold $Tsup_0$ can be set to a reasonably small value.

For the confidence threshold, a similar criterion is adopted to examine the biggest difference between two adjacent sequential patterns with the condition that the generated rules in R should be able to cover

Table 3. The procedure of calculating min_sup

$diff(r) = \text{mean}(sup_{k_r}) - \text{mean}(sup_{k_{r+1}}), r=1,\ldots,R_k-1$

$r_k = \arg\max_r \left(diff(r) \right)$ If $diff(r_k) > R_k/2$

$Tsup_{k+1} = (\text{mean}(sup_{k_r}) + (\text{mean}(sup_{k_{r+1}}))/2$
else $min\_sup = SupTH_k$

all target events in D. In other words, if the newly defined confidence threshold $Tcon_{k+1}$ causes the missing of target events in D, $Tcon_k$ is then used as *min_conf*.

Distributed Video Retrieval System

In our earlier work (Chen, Shyu, & Zhao, 2005), a distributed video retrieval system was developed with the application on soccer videos, therefore called *SoccerQ* system. *SoccerQ* adopts multi-threaded client/server architecture so multiple requests from diverse users can be handled simultaneously. The client side application integrates both soccer event query and video browsing panels. When issuing a query, the request and the related parameters are transmitted to the server side. According to the request, the server side database engine performs the computation intensive functionalities including graphical query translation, query optimization, query processing, video supply, etc. The huge amount of multimedia data is efficiently organized by adopting the PostgreSQL DBMS. *SoccerQ* also features a set of useful tools for multimedia data processing and distribution. For example, it provides an automatic video shot segmentation tool. In addition, the retrieved video or video shots can be downloaded to the client side and displayed as a media object in a multimedia presentation.

The design in SoccerQ supports temporal queries which can be categorized into five models, such as the temporal relationship between event E and video V, relationship between event E_1 and event E_2, etc. Correspondingly, the visual query language was designed such that the users can easily specify the relative temporal queries. However, the event is purely shot-based in the system without its associated cause and effect information.

In this work, we propose to add another level of retrieval, i.e., event-based retrieval based on the temporal association information discovered in the event detection module. A sample query supported through this distributed system is illustrated below.

Query 1: *"Find all the corner kick shots from all the women's soccer videos where the corner kick is the cause of a goal event."*

As shown in Figure 3, the query criteria are specified in the graphical query panel in the upper-right corner. Essentially, the problem of checking whether a "corner kick" shot is the cause of a "goal" event can be converted into applying the temporal rule <{"corner kick", ·}{·}> →"goal" over the video database. The key frames of four result shots are displayed in the video browsing panel. An option is provided for the user to view the video segment containing event cause/effect by double clicking the corresponding frame (e.g., the frame marked by the red box).

Figure 3. Soccer retrieval interface with example temporal query and results

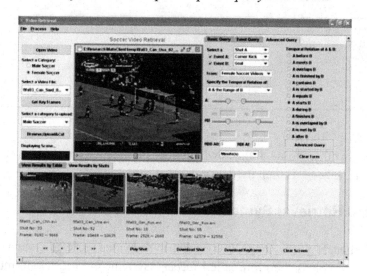

EXPERIMENTS

The proposed framework was tested upon 27 soccer videos with a total duration of more than 9 hours. These videos were obtained from a variety of sources with various production styles. Soccer videos are one of the most widely adopted testbeds for event detection due to their popularity and loose structures. As shown in Table 4, in the experiment we target to detect goal and corner events from the soccer videos, where they account for only 41 and 95 shots, respectively, out of 4,885 shots. As discussed earlier, it is quite challenging to detect such rare concepts.

In order to better evaluate our proposed framework, the random subsampling (or repeat hold-out) scheme (Perlich, Provost, & Simonoff, 2003) is used. That is, the entire video data set is randomly partitioned into two disjoint sets, called the training and the test data sets, respectively. A classification model is then induced from the training data set and its performance is evaluated on the test data set. The proportion of data reserved for training and testing is two-thirds and one-third of the entire data, respectively. This process is repeated five times. Accordingly, for each empirical study, totally five decision models are constructed and tested with the corresponding testing data sets.

Table 4. Performance Comparison between SCM and Other Well-known Classification Algorithms

Concept	Measure	Temporal-based (%)	SVM (%)	NN (%)	KNN (%)
goal	R	**85.1**	61.6	62.2	54.1
	P	69.0	21.2	**71.9**	74.1
	F	**76.2**	31.5	66.7	62.5
corner	R	**63.5**	43.6	52.1	27.4
	P	39.6	11.3	26.3	**55.3**
	F	**48.8**	17.9	35.0	36.6

In feature extraction process, 15 low-level features including 5 visual features (pixel-change, histo-change, grass_ratio, background_mean, background_var) and 10 audio features (1 volume feature, 5 energy features and 4 spectrum flux features) are extracted at the shot-level. In addition, two middle-level features (camera view and excitement label) are derived from low-level features and used to derive the temporal rules. This data pruning process filters out many inconsistent and irrelevant shots and produces a candidate event set where the goal shots and corner shots accounted for about 6% and 11% of the remaining data set.

The resulting candidate pool was then passed to the C4.5 decision tree based multimodal data mining process for further classification. The average performance across five models is calculated and is then compared with a set of well-known classification methods, such as SVM, Neural Network (NN), K-nearest Neighbor (KNN), which are enclosed in the WEKA package (WEKA). Three evaluation metrics, recall (R), precision (P), and F1 measure (F), are adopted. In the literature, the pair of recall and precision is generally used. However, as it is always possible to sacrifice one metric value in order to boost the other, the F1 measure, which is a combination of recall and precision and is defined as 2RP/(R+P), is deemed as a better performance metrics.

For the methods implemented in WEKA, minimal parameter tuning was required or allowed as their default values are mostly appropriately configured for optimal performance. However, we tried different parameter combinations and conducted several rounds of testing so that the best performance is reported. The parameter setups are as follows. For SVM, John Platt's sequential minimal optimization algorithm (Platt, 1998) was used for training a support vector classifier. The value of the complexity parameter C was set to 1, a quadratic polynomial kernel was employed, the filterType option was set to perform data set standardization, and the lowerOrderTerms option was set so that lower order polynomials were also included. For Neural Network (NN), a normalized Gaussian radial basis function network was picked, which used the K-means clustering algorithm to provide the basis functions and learned a linear regression on top of that. The random seed to pass on to K-means was set to 1 and the minimum standard deviation for the clusters was set to 0.1. IBk, Weka's implementation of both NN and KNN classifiers, was configured to perform data set normalization and to ignore distance weighting options.

The best performance (P, R, and F) for each event across all the classification methods are shown in bold fonts in Table 4. From this table, we have the following observations. First, our proposed temporal-based event detection framework always achieves the best recall values in both test cases. In event detection, the recall metric is normally considered as more important than the precision metric. In other word, we would like to be able to classify as many data instances to the correct events as possible even at the cost of including a small number of false positives. Second, though some other classification approaches can yield better precision than the proposed work, our F1 measure is always the best in all the cases, which captures the system overall performance in a more complete manner. In summary, the proposed framework is very promising in the sense that it works automatically for event detection with limited dependency on domain knowledge.

CONCLUSION

In this chapter, we introduce an integrated temporal-based event detection and video retrieval system. The event detection module integrates the strength of feature extraction, temporal analysis, and multimodal data mining. Especially, the E-ARM algorithm offers a robust solution to explore and employ the characteristic temporal patterns with respect to the events of interests. This approach effectively addresses the issues of loose video structure and skewed data distribution. It also largely relaxes the dependency on domain knowledge and contributes to the ultimate goal of automatic content analysis. In addition, a distributed video retrieval system called *SoccerQ* is presented, which is built on top of the event detection module and supports a large variety of video temporal queries, including the proposed event-based retrieval, and semantic video browsing via a visual query interface and an enhanced temporal query model. The proposed framework has many implications in video indexing and summarization, video database retrieval, and semantic video browsing, etc.

REFERENCES

Chen, M., Chen, S.-C., & Shyu, M.-L. (2007) Hierarchical temporal association mining for video event detection in video databases. In *Proceedings of the Second IEEE International Workshop on Multimedia Databases and Data Management, in conjunction with IEEE International Conference on Data Engineering,* (pp. 137-145).

Chen, M., Chen, S.-C., Shyu, M.-L., & Wickramaratna, K. (2006). Semantic event detection via temporal analysis and multimodal data mining. *IEEE Signal Processing Magazine. Special Issue on Semantic Retrieval of Multimedia, 23*(2), 38–46.

Chen, S.-C., Shyu, M.-L., & Zhang, C. (2005). Innovative shot boundary detection for video indexing. In Deb, S. (Ed.), *Video data management and information retrieval* (pp. 217–236). Hershey, PA: Idea Group Publishing.

Chen, S.-C., Shyu, M.-L., Zhang, C., & Chen, M. (2006). A multimodal data mining framework for soccer goal detection based on decision tree logic. *International Journal of Computer Applications in Technology, 27*(4), 312–323. doi:10.1504/IJCAT.2006.012001

Chen, S.-C., Shyu, M.-L., & Zhao, N. (2005) An enhanced query model for soccer video retrieval using temporal relationships. In *Proceedings of the 21st International Conference on Data Engineering (ICDE 2005),* (pp. 1133-1134).

Chen, X., & Zhang, C. (2007) Interactive mining and semantic retrieval of videos. In *Proceedings of the 2007 International Workshop on Multimedia Data Mining, in conjunction with the ACM SIGKDD International Conference on Knowledge Discovery & Data Mining.*

Feng, X., & Huang, H. (2005). A fuzzy-set-based reconstructed phase space method for identification of temporal patterns in complex time series. *IEEE Transactions on Knowledge and Data Engineering, 17*(5), 601–613. doi:10.1109/TKDE.2005.68

Leonardi, R., Migliorati, P., & Prandini, M. (2004). Semantic indexing of soccer audio-visual sequences: a multimodal approach based on controlled Markov chains. *IEEE Transactions on Circuits and Systems for Video Technology, 14*(5), 634–643. doi:10.1109/TCSVT.2004.826751

Mu, X. (2006) Supporting semantic visual feature browsing in content-based video retrieval. In *Proceedings of the 29th International ACM SIGIR Conference on Research and Development in Information Retrieval,* (pp. 734-734).

Perlich, C., Provost, F., & Simonoff, J. S. (2003). Tree induction vs. logistic regression: a learning-curve analysis. *Journal of Machine Learning Research, 4*, 211–255. doi:10.1162/153244304322972694

Platt, J. (1998). Fast training of support vector machines using sequential minimal optimization. In Schoelkopf, B., Burges, C., & Smola, A. (Eds.), *Advances in kernel methods - support vector learning* (pp. 185–208). Cambridge, MA: MIT Press.

Povinelli, R. J., & Feng, X. (2003). A new temporal pattern identification method for characterization and prediction of complex time series events. *IEEE Transactions on Knowledge and Data Engineering, 15*(2), 339–352. doi:10.1109/TKDE.2003.1185838

Shyu, M.-L., Xie, Z., Chen, M., & Chen, S.-C. (2008). Video semantic event/concept detection using a subspace-based multimedia data mining framework. *IEEE Transactions on Multimedia. Special Issue on Multimedia Data Mining, 10*(2), 252–259.

Vilalta, R., & Ma, S. (2002) Predicting rare events in temporal domains. In *Proceedings of IEEE International Conference on Data Mining,* (pp. 474-481).

WEKA. (Version 3.6) [Software], (n.d.). Available from http://www.cs.waikato.ac.nz/ml/weka/

Westermann, U., & Jain, R. (2007). Toward a common event model for multimedia applications. *IEEE MultiMedia Magazine, 14*(1), 19–29. doi:10.1109/MMUL.2007.23

Xie, L., Sundaram, H., & Campbell, M. (2008). Event mining in multimedia streams. *Proceedings of the IEEE, 96*(4), 623–647. doi:10.1109/JPROC.2008.916362

Zhu, X., Wu, X., Elmagarmid, A. K., Feng, Z., & Wu, L. (2005). Video data mining: semantic indexing and event detection from the association perspective. *IEEE Transactions on Knowledge and Data Engineering, 17*(5), 665–677. doi:10.1109/TKDE.2005.83

Chapter 11
Analyzing Animated Movie Contents for Automatic Video Indexing

Bogdan Ionescu
University Politehnica of Bucharest, Romania

Patrick Lambert
University of Savoie, France

Didier Coquin
University of Savoie, France

Alexandru Marin
University Politehnica of Bucharest, Romania

Constantin Vertan
University Politehnica of Bucharest, Romania

ABSTRACT

In this chapter the authors tackle the analysis and characterization of the artistic animated movies in view of constituting an automatic content-based retrieval system. First, they deal with temporal segmentation, and propose cut, fade and dissolve detection methods adapted to the constraints of this domain. Further, they discuss a fuzzy linguistic approach for automatic symbolic/semantic content annotation in terms of color techniques and action content and we test its potential in automatic video classification. The browsing issue is dealt by providing methods for both, static and dynamic video abstraction. For a quick browse of the movie's visual content the authors create a storyboard-like summary, while for a "sneak peak" of the movie's exciting action content they propose a trailer-like video skim. Finally, the authors discuss the architecture of a prototype client-server 3D virtual environment for interactive video retrieval. Several experimental results are presented.

DOI: 10.4018/978-1-61692-859-9.ch011

INTRODUCTION

Recent advances in multimedia technology, especially in high-speed networking, storage devices and portable devices, have determined an exponential increase in popularity of digital video libraries. Accessing the relevant information proves to be a difficult and time consuming task, considering that usually video databases may contain as many as thousands and thousands of videos. To cope with this issue, content-based video indexing systems are specially designed to provide efficient content-based retrieval facilities, ideally in a manner close to human perception.

Video indexing primarily involves *content annotation*, which basically means adding some extra content-related information to the actual data (i.e. indexes/attributes). This information provides key-cues about the data content, allowing thus the automatic cataloging. Content annotation is mandatory, as non-indexed data is practically inexistent for the system (and eventually for the user) since there is no trace of it. Besides the content annotation, a video indexing system provides also *searching capabilities*, i.e. retrieving data according to the user specifications, which is done by comparing data indexes from the database against the ones extracted from the user's query; and *browsing capabilities*, i.e. providing a visual interface for accessing and visualizing data contents, which is usually performed with the help of automatic content abstraction techniques. Most of the research in the field addresses mainly the data annotation task, which is also the most difficult to perform (Naphade, Huang, 2002; Snoek, Worring, 2005). The challenge is to find methods to extract meaningful attributes, which tend to maximize the relevance and the information coverage, while minimizing the amount of data to deal with, and thus the dimensionality of the data feature space. Nevertheless, in order to be useful and efficient, the annotation *must be performed automatically*, without the human intervention.

Unfortunately, due to the diversity of the existing video materials, which involves a large variety of specific processing constraints, the issue of automatic understanding of video contents is still an open issue. Despite some few attempts (Qian, Haering, Sezan, 1999; Chan, Qing, Yi, Yueting, 2001; Kim, Frigui, Fadeev, 2008), there is still no generic solution available for indexing all kind of video materials. The chosen compromise consists in reducing the high complexity of this task by adopting some simplifying assumptions, e.g. particular setups, "a priori" information, hypothesis, etc., which are facilitated by the specificity of each application domain. This makes the existing systems highly application dependent. Many domains have been addressed, while new ones are still emerging, e.g. basketball sequences (Saur, Tan, Kulkarni, Ramadge, 1997), soccer sequences (Leonardi, Migliorati, Prandini, 2004), medical sequences (Fan, Luo, Elmagarmid, 2004), news footage (Lu, King, Lyu, 2003), TV programs (Kawai, Sumiyoshi, Yagi, 2007), animal hunt in wildlife documentaries (Haering, Qian, Sezan, 2000), etc.

In this chapter we address the indexing issue for a new application domain, which becomes more and more popular: the animated movie entertainment industry. While the very few existing approaches are limited to dealing either with the analysis of classic cartoons or with cartoon genre detection (Roach, Mason, Pawlewski, 2001; Snoek, Worring, 2005; Ianeva, Vries, Rohrig, 2003; Geetha, Palanivel, 2007), our approach is different, as it addresses the artistic animated movies. One reference in the field is IAFF - The International Animated Film Festival (CITIA, 2009), which stood as validation platform for our approaches. CITIA, the company managing the festival, has composed one of the world's first digital animated movie libraries. Today, this library accounts for more than 31.000 movie titles, 22.924 companies and 60.879 professionals, which are to be available online for a general and professional use. Managing thousands of videos is a tedious task; therefore an automatic content-based retrieval system is required. For the moment, the existing indexing capabilities for animated movies (the CITIA

Animaquid Indexing System) are limited to use only textual information (e.g. synopsis, descriptions, etc.), provided mainly by movie authors, which in many cases do not totally apply to the rich artistic content of the animated movies.

Animated movies are different from conventional movies and from cartoons in many respects which should be particularly addressed, (Ionescu, Coquin, Lambert, Buzuloiu, 2008, see Figures 2, 8 and 9):

- we mainly deal with fiction or abstract movies and therefore, there usually are no physical rules;
- characters, if any, can take any shape or color;
- depending on the animation technique, the motion could be discontinuous;
- a large variety of animation techniques are employed;
- usually, there are a lot of color effects (Ionescu, Buzuloiu, Lambert, Coquin, 2006);
- the movies are artistic creations, therefore artistic concepts are used, e.g. painting concepts, theatrical concepts, etc.;
- colors are selected and mixed by the artists to express particular feelings or to produce particular sensations (Ionescu, Lambert, Coquin, Buzuloiu, 2006);
- the content is very varied: some animation experts say that more than 30% of the animated movies from IAFF cannot be summarized because their content is singular.

Therefore, deriving high level information from the color concepts, from the visual sensations induced by the movie or from the action content should be an ideal way of accessing its content in a video database. However, the developed methods have to cope with the peculiarity of this domain.

BACKGROUND

Video indexing primarily means *content annotation*. Content annotation is the process which allows the system to automatically understand video contents by marking its relevant features. These features, i.e. numeric attributes, parameters, textual data, known as indexes, usually describe the physical properties of the scene at pixel, image, or group of images levels, and are then used by the system to retrieve the useful information. Due to the fact that video sequences are the temporal extension of static images, the existing video annotation techniques are first of all inspired from static image indexing techniques, i.e. using *color, texture and shape* information. Besides the extension of these features to the temporal dimension, video annotation involves in particular the analysis of the *temporal structure, motion information* and *sound*.

Color is one fundamental feature to describe the image's local or global content (color histograms, Calic, Izquierdo, 2002; color ratio models, Adjeroh, Lee, 2001). However, very few approaches address color information at temporal level. *Texture* information is used to describe the physical properties of the materials from the scene at image level, while some approaches try to extend the notion of texture to the temporal level (Rahman, Murshed, 2008). In the case of video sequences, due to the movement of objects (i.e. non rigid objects), *shape* information must provide some invariance to progressive geometrical transformations, (Lee, 2005; Yilmaz, Javed, Shah, 2006). The *temporal structure* is specific to video sequences and it is related to the way the sequence was conceived. The way the video transitions are inserted - in terms of frequency, class of the transition (sharp, gradual), distribution - is specific to each type of video and provides meaningful information about its content (Xie, Chang, Divakaran, Sun,

2003; Petra, Jenny, Jean-Philippe, 2006). *Motion information* is the fundamental information of a video sequence and methods are to be standardized thanks to the MPEG-7 standard ("Multimedia Content Description Interface", Jeannin, Divakaran, 2001). The motion annotation is performed either locally, i.e. the spatio-temporal annotation: motion segmentation, objects tracking and motion characterization, or globally: camera motion analysis, motion activity (Smith, Drummond, Cipolla, 2004; Lee, Yang, Lee, 2001). *Sound information* is also specific to video data. The existing approaches are performing both in the temporal and frequency domains, and audio content is in general described in terms of volume, zero crossings, tonality, spectral parameters, etc. Higher-level applications include automatic classification of sounds into predefined categories, e.g. voice, music, violence, etc. (Wang, Liu, Huang, 2000). *Other common sources of information* are the detection and analysis of human presence in the scene (Burak Ozer, Wolf, 2002), as well as the detection and translation of the inline text (Kim, Jung, Park, Kim, 2000).

Due to the nature of video sequences, the natural trend of the existing video annotation systems is towards multi-modal approaches, which do not use only one source of information, but combine several modalities in order to provide the closest description of the real scenes. Also, while the previous generation of annotation systems provided low-level content descriptions (in general meaningless numeric data), the actual systems are focusing on semantic content-descriptions, and thus approaching the human perception (Naphade, Huang, 2002; Snoek, Worring, 2005; Yong, Bhandarkar, Kang Li, 2007).

This is precisely the target of the content-based retrieval system discussed with this chapter, which addresses the particular domain of animated movies. The remainder of the chapter is organized as follows: first, we deal with temporal segmentation, and propose cut, fade and dissolve detection methods, which were specifically tuned to the animation domain. Further, we discuss a fuzzy linguistic approach for automatic symbolic/semantic content annotation in terms of color techniques and action content. The browsing issue is dealt by providing methods for both static, storyboard-like and dynamic, trailer-like video abstraction. Finally, we present the prototype of a 3D virtual environment for interactive video indexing.

TEMPORAL SEGMENTATION

The temporal segmentation of the movie is a fundamental processing step, required by most of the existing video analysis techniques, as it provides the movie basic temporal unit structure, or shot structure. Roughly speaking, the temporal segmentation means detecting the video transitions which make the connection between different shots (continuous sequences of images). The most frequent transitions are the sharp transitions, or cuts (e.g. 30 minutes of video accounts in general for up to 300 cuts), and represent the direct concatenation of two different shots. On the other hand, the gradual transitions - fades, dissolves, mattes, wipes, etc. (Han, Gao, Ji, 2005) - are short visual effects, with an occurrence frequency at least one order measure less than the cuts.

For our application, we first jointly detect cuts and an animated movie specific color effect, denoted SCC ("short-in-time dramatic color change"). From the existing gradual transitions, we detect only the most representative ones for the animated movies: fades and dissolves.

Cut Detection

Due to their high occurrence frequency in a movie, cuts have been the most extensively studied video transitions. The present methods easily achieve detection ratios close to 94% (TRECVID, 2009). They exploit the sharp visual discontinuity produced by a cut, which can be measured using the different modalities of a sequence:

- *contour/edge information* (Huan, Xiuhuan, Lilei, 2008): object contours in the image before a cut transition are very different from the ones in the image after the cut. These methods, which in general use as visual discontinuity function, some edge/contour changing ratios (e.g. ECR - Edge Change Ratio, EMR - Edge Matching Rate, etc.), come with high complexity and are very sensitive to motion. On the other hand, their main advantage is their usability for the detection of some gradual transitions;
- *motion information* (Lupatini, Saraceno, Leonardi, 1998, Porter, Mirmehdi, Thomas, 2000): the global/local movement of the scene is interrupted during a cut transition. The existing methods are relying on the results of the motion estimation, which, in the case of a cut, should be discontinuous. These methods come also with high computational complexity and are interesting in the case of the movies with predominant motion content;
- *compressed domain* (Jiang, Li, Xiao, Chen, 2007): cut patterns are also visible in the compressed domain. These methods, measure the discontinuity produced by a cut using the information extracted directly from the compressed domain, e.g. thresholding some DCT coefficients or the number of MPEG macro-blocks, etc. They have the main advantage of performing in real time, as data decompression is no longer needed;
- *pixel intensity information* (Santos, Borges, Gomes, 2008): a cut produces an important visual discontinuity in the image flow. In this case, it is measured using the visual features of the image, and thus the pixel intensity information. The basic detection principle is to threshold the image changes, which are quantified by computing some distance measures between consecutive frames. These methods prove to be the most reliable ones, due to their reduced computational complexity, invariance to motion (e.g. frames are divided into blocks and the distance is computed between each corresponding block in order to reduce the changes caused by movement), intensity fluctuations (frame difference is computed in some particular color spaces which provide a separation between intensity information and chrominance, e.g. YCbCr), geometrical transformations (frame distance is computed between color histograms to take advantage of their invariance properties) etc.

Almost every animation movie has its own particular color palette, being the artist's signature. The proposed cut detection approach exploits this feature and measures the visual discontinuity produced by cuts using Euclidean distances between color histograms (Ionescu, Buzuloiu, Lambert, Coquin, 2006). Besides the color information, we adopt several other improvements.

One important issue, when dealing with animated movies, is the movement of objects in the scene, which tends to be the predominant movement. Large-sized moving objects (e.g. characters) may produce noticeable differences in the histograms of successive frames, and therefore frames are first divided into quadrants (thorough tests have shown that only the objects of the size of an image quadrant or higher will significantly change the global color histogram). Further, for each quadrant we compute a color histogram.

To reduce the false positives, we perform the spatial localization of the color changes by computing for each retained frame (frames are temporally sub-sampled), 4 Euclidean distances (between the 4 quadrant histograms and the corresponding ones from the next retained neighbor frame). Moreover, to simplify the cut/non-cut decision, the 4 values are transformed into one by taking the mean value, denoted $D_{mean}()$.

Another problem, also present in natural movies, is the continuous camera/objects motion which is a source of false positives, as it introduces significant and repetitive visual changes in the visual flow. A cut is represented in the dissimilarity function, $D_{mean}()$, with a "Low-High-Low" (L-H-L) values pattern (see Figure 1), therefore we employ second order derivatives to reduce the continuous changes, while preserving the isolated peaks, thus: $\ddot{D}_{mean}(k+1) = D_{mean}(k+1) - 2 \cdot D_{mean}(k) + D_{mean}(k-1)$, where k is the time index.

For the final frame classification, $\ddot{D}_{mean}()$ values are compared to a certain threshold, $\tau_{cut.}$. The threshold value should be adapted to the color characteristics of each movie, as each animated movie has a particular color signature; therefore, we propose an adaptive threshold which is computed as the average value of all the significant $\ddot{D}_{mean}()$ values, where a significant value is a value which is a local maxima greater than the temporal average. This strategy assures that τ_{cut} is high enough to avoid most of the fluctuations generated by visual changes other than cuts (Ionescu, Buzuloiu, Lambert, Coquin, 2006).

Finally, because animation movies contain a lot of special visual effects, the occurrence of false cuts is very likely. To cope with this issue, every detected cut is additionally checked in view of detecting a color effect specific to animation movies, called "short color change" or SCC (e.g. thunders, explosions, lightening). This effect is the equivalent of camera flash-lights from the natural movies, and has a simple pattern, thus: it starts with an important change in color (an important histogram distance, i.e. greater than $\tau_{cut)}$ and ends with almost the same frame as the starting one (histogram distance close to zero, see Figure 2). Several experimental results are presented at the end of the chapter.

Fade Detection

A fade is a short optical effect (typically less than 2 seconds) which consists on the gradual emerging of an image, from a constant image, typically black, what we call a fade-in sequence, or the inverse process, the progressive dissolution of an image into a constant background, called a fade-out (Lienhart, 2001), see Figure 3. Compared to cut detection, fade detection approaches are less numerous and less

Figure 1. Cut emphasizing using second order derivative: left image describes the principle (negative values are set to 0 and marked with X), right image presents an example for an animated movie (Adaptation from Academy Publisher Journal of Multimedia, 2(4), 2007)

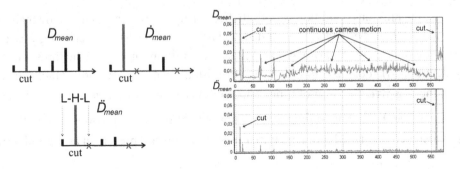

Figure 2. Short color changes detection:D()is the Euclidean distance between frame histograms, I(k) is the frame at time index k, (l<10, max size of a SCC). Several SCC examples are presented at the right (each SCC is depicted with the middle image, images from (CITIA, 2009), Adaptation from Academy Publisher Journal of Multimedia, 2(4), 2007)

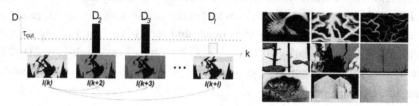

reliable, average detection ratios being situated around 75% (TRECVID, 2009). That is mainly due to the complexity of this effect, which significantly augments when perturbations occur, e.g. motion, intensity fluctuations, etc. The existing fade detection methods vary from *pixel-based techniques* (also the most reliable), which use the hypothesis that during a fade transition the pixel intensity has a linear increase/decrease (Truong, Dorai, 2000), *techniques using edge/contour information* which use statistics on the amount of entering/existing contour pixels (Lupatini, Saraceno, Leonardi, 1998) to *mixed approaches* which exploit other sources of information such as the visual rhythm by histogram (Guimaraes, Couprie, Araujo, Leite, 2003) or use the compressed domain (Li, Qu, Zhang, 2008).

The proposed fade detection method is a pixel intensity-based approach, inspired by the method proposed in (Fernando, Canagarajah, Bull, 1999). The advantage of our approach mainly consists of the way we jointly use the luminance and chrominance information in the YCbCr color space in order to improve the invariance of the detection to image noise and global intensity fluctuations. This method was not particularly tuned for the animated movies, but performed very well when tested in our system.

For each frame k, we compute three parameters: $\bar{Y}_k$ (average intensity), $\sigma^2(I_k)$ (variance of Y) and $\left|\bar{Cb}_k - \bar{Cr}_k\right|$ (the absolute difference between the mean values of the two chromatic components).

After smoothing the obtained values (e.g. using median filtering), the fade-in detection starts with the localization of fade start images, thus having the following properties: the image is uniform ($\sigma^2(I_k)$ close to 0), the next neighbor image at time index $k+1$ is not uniform (this positions the start image right before the gradual transition begins) and $D(k+2,k+1)>0.2\cdot D(k+1,k)$, where $D(k+2,k+1) = \bar{Y}_{k+2} - \bar{Y}_{k+1}$ (which avoids the confusion with cuts).

The next step consists on the validation of the transition. Starting from the next neighbor image (at $k+1$), for each image at the moment $k+i$, with $i>1$, we check that $\bar{Y}_{k+i}$ and $\left|\bar{Cb}_{k+i} - \bar{Cr}_{k+i}\right|$ have a gradual augmentation, that is: $\bar{Y}_{k+i} > 0.98 \cdot \bar{Y}_{k+i-1}$ or $\left|\bar{Cb}_{k+i} - \bar{Cr}_{k+i}\right| > 0.98 \cdot \left|\bar{Cb}_{k+i-1} - \bar{Cr}_{k+i-1}\right|$. If for the image at $k+i$, the previous condition is not satisfied, or if i is greater than the fade maximum length (around 30 frames), then the detection is ended. A last check consists of verifying that the detected transition has more than 3 images, which represents a fade minimum length (the threshold values were empirically determined). For detecting fade-out transitions, we use the same algorithm but applied backwards, in the negative direction of time. Thorough tests show that $\left|\bar{Cb}_k - \bar{Cr}_k\right|$ is less sensitive to motion than $\bar{Y}_k$, while $\bar{Y}_k$ is more efficient in the absence of movement, and therefore the two parameters are used disjunctively (see Figure 3). Experimental results are presented at the end of the chapter.

Figure 3. Temporal evolution of: $\sigma^2(I_k)$ (blue line), $\bar{Y}_k$ (red line) and $\left|\bar{Cb}_k - \bar{Cr}_k\right|$ (green line). A fade-in and fade-out example is depicted at the right, movie "Coeur de Secours" (CITIA, 2009)

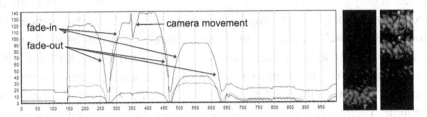

Dissolve Detection

The most common gradual transitions and also one of the most difficult to detect are the dissolves. A dissolve represents the gradual transition at the pixel-intensity level of a certain image into another (see Figure 4). Compared to fades, dissolves are much more complex transitions which support many variations. The most common are the cross-dissolves, which are basically the superposition of a fade-out and a fade-in transition, and additive-dissolves, which are the addition of a fade-out and a fade-in (Lienhart, 2001). Similar to the detection of fades, the existing dissolve detection techniques are using either *pixel-based techniques* (also the most reliable ones), e.g. the mathematical model of a dissolve which states that the temporal evolution of the variance of the pixel intensities should have a parabolic shape (Truong, Dorai, Venkatesh, 2000; Su, Tyan, Mark Liao, Chen, 2005); *contour/edge-based techniques* which use the hypothesis that the edges of the start image are fading-out, while the edges of the end image are fading-in (Lienhart, 1999), to approaches which perform directly in *the compressed domain*, e.g. measuring the temporal evolution of the distance between DCT coefficients and of the dispersion of the motion vectors (Boccignone, De Santo, Percannella, 2000). The main difficulty when dealing with dissolve detection is the presence of motion.

The animated movies are often created image by image, thus the visual flow is not continuous as in natural movies. This renders useless the general assumptions on the gradual or parabolic evolution of some intensity parameters. Therefore, the proposed method exploits the pixel intensity in terms of the amount of fading-out and fading-in pixels, which during a dissolve transition is relatively high (Su, Tyan, Mark Liao, Chen, 2005). The novelty of our method mainly consists of using the shape analysis of the discontinuity function for the localization of the dissolves, instead of just thresholding, as most of the

Figure 4. Temporal evolution of FP_k (blue line). The middle frames of the detected dissolves are marked with the red line. Dissolve examples are depicted at the right, movie "Le Moine et le Poisson" (CITIA, 2009)

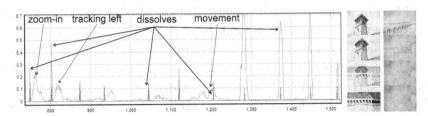

existing approaches. This way we reduce the false detections caused by steep fluctuations, due to noise or motion. Also, due to the restraint visual continuity of animated movies, fading-out and fading-in pixels are searched in only a reduced time window, of only several frames (empirically determined).

For the detection we use only the intensity information provided by the luminance component, Y, of the YCbCr color space. For each analyzed frame at time index k, I_k, we determine the number of fading-out pixels (i.e. Y_k decreases) and fading-in pixels (i.e. Y_k increases) during the next 3 frames (empirically determined), denoted FOP_k and respectively FIP_k. Further, a normalized discontinuity function is determined by taking the mean of the two ratios, thus: $FP_k = (FOP_k + FIP_k)/H \cdot W$, where $H \cdot W$ is the image size. For determining whether the FP_k amplitude is high enough for a dissolve transition we use twin thresholding, thus: if FP_k for the frame I_k is greater than a first threshold $\tau_{CT=}0.4$ (Certain Threshold), and if this value is a local maxima, then a dissolve is declared in the time interval [k-30/2;k+30/2] (Ik is the middle frame of the dissolve, we consider a maximum dissolve size of 30 images). On the other hand, if FPk is greater than a second threshold $\tau_{TT-0}.1$ (Tolerant Threshold), but still beneath τ_{CT}, then the image Ik i_s only a potential dissolve image and the validation consists on shape analysis of FPk i_n the neighborhood of this image.

The values of FPk $_s$hould decrease both on the positive and negative time axis. Therefore, we seek for the time moments Tle$_{ft<k}$ and Tri$_{ght>k}$, when FPk $_s$tarts to increase, thus: $FP_{T_{left}} < FP_{T_{left}-1}$ and $FP_{T_{right}} < FP_{T_{right}+1}$. To quantify the relevance of FP_k with the respect to neighbor values, we compute:

$$D_{left} = \left| FP_k - FP_{T_{left}} \right|, D_{right} = \left| FP_k - FP_{T_{right}} \right|$$

A dissolve occurs in the time interval [k-30/2;k+30/2] if the distance values are greater than a fraction of FP_k, that is: $D_{left} > 0.5 \cdot FP_k$ and $D_{right} > 0.5 \cdot FP_k$. This last condition assures that FP_k is a local maximum, significant enough compared to neighbor values (it has an increase of at least 50% compared to local neighbor maxima). The proposed method involves the choice of several threshold values, which have been experimentally determined after the analysis of several representative dissolve examples from various animated movies. Experimental results are presented at the end of the chapter.

COLOR AND ACTION DESCRIPTORS

In this section we address the content description of the animated movies in terms of color techniques and action content. The goal is to provide a content annotation system able to understand the message transmitted by these artistic creations. Besides the interest in automatic indexing, these descriptions are useful for analysis purposes, e.g. providing animation experts with detailed information about the used techniques.

Very little research has been done in this field, especially in the animated movie domain (Snoek, Worring, 2005). Many of the existing color characterization methods have focused naturally on the static image indexation task as they describe local image properties. Most of them describe the image color content with low-level parameters (Smeulders, Worring, Santini, Gupta, Jain, 2000). However, few methods try to tackle the "semantic gap" issue and thus to capture the semantic meaning of the color content. For example, in (Lay, Guan, 2004) the color artistry concepts are extracted for the indexing task of artwork static images. The relationships between colors are analyzed in a perceptual color space, namely LCH (luminosity, chroma, and hue), and several color techniques are used: contrasting color schemes, Itten's seven color contrasts, and color harmony schemes. A similar approach is the query by image content (QBIC) system proposed in (IBM QBIC, 2006). It supports two types of syntactic color search: the dominant color search and the color layout search where the user specifies an arrangement of a color structure. However, these approaches are applied to static images. The understanding of the color content of a movie requires a temporal color analysis. In the video indexing field, color content analysis, together with other low-level features, such as texture, shape, and motion, has extensively been used for the low-level characterization of the image local properties. Few approaches tackle the description of the color perception of video material by adding a temporal dimension to the local image based analysis. Such a system which takes the temporal color information into account is proposed in (Colombo, Del Bimbo, Pala, 1999). The art images and commercials are analyzed at emotional and expressional levels. Various features are used, not only the color information but also motion, video transition distribution, and so on, all in order to identify a set of primary induced emotions, namely, action, relaxation, joy, and uneasiness. The colors are analyzed at a region-based level by taking the spatial relationships of the object in the image into account. The proposed system is adapted to the semantic analysis of commercials. Another connected approach is the one proposed in (Detyniecki, Marsala, 2003), where fuzzy decision trees are used for data mining of news video footage. In this case, color histograms are used to successfully retrieve two types of semantic information: the textual annotations and the presence of the journalist.

Our approach is different. We are addressing here the problem of delivering a global color and action content characterization of the animated movies. To do so, we use high-level descriptions (textual) obtained through a fuzzy representation mechanism using the expertise of the animation domain. The proposed approach is carried out in two steps, namely a low-level description and a high-level description, which are described with the following.

Low-Level Descriptions

The first step is the description of the movie's content with several low-level statistical parameters, which capture the physical properties of the movie at *visual level* (Ionescu, Coquin, Lambert, Buzuloiu, 2008), as well as at *structural level* (Ionescu, Coquin, Lambert, Buzuloiu, 2007).

Color Description

To capture the color content, we use the *global weighted color histogram* proposed in (Ionescu, Lambert, Coquin, Dârlea, 2005), defined thus:

$$h_{GW}(c) = \sum_{i=0}^{M} \left[\frac{1}{N_i} \sum_{j=0}^{N_i} h_{shot_i}^j(c) \right] \cdot w_i \qquad (1)$$

where c is the color index (colors are first reduced using an error diffusion approach on the Webmaster non-dithering 216 color palette, which has the advantage of providing an efficient color naming system), M is the number of shots, N_i is the number of the retained frames for shot i (representing $p\%$ of its frames, usually $p\%[15\%,25\%]$), $h_{shot_i}^j$ () is the color histogram of the frame j from the shot i, and w_i is the weight of the shot i, thus N_{shot_i} / N_{total} (the total number of frames of shot i divided by the total number of frames of all the movie shots).

The next parameter captures the movie *global elementary color distribution*, by projecting each color on to its elementary hue, thus:

$$h_E(c_e) = \sum_{c=0}^{215} h_{GW}(c)\Big|_{Name(c_e)\subset Name(c)} \qquad (2)$$

where c_e is an elementary color index from the elementary colors set of the Webmaster palette, i.e. {"orange", "red", "pink", "magenta", "violet", "blue", "azure", "cyan", "teal", "green", "spring", "yellow", "gray", "white", "black"}, *Name*() is the operator which returns a color name from the palette color dictionary. Using the two histograms, h_{GW}() and h_E(), and the color naming system, we determine further several color parameters: *the color variation*, P_{div} (the amount of significant colors used), *color diversity*, P_{div} (the amount of significant elementary colors used), *the light color ratio*, P_{light} (the amount of bright colors):

$$P_{light} = \sum_{c=0}^{215} h_{GW}(c)\Big|_{W_{light}\subset Name(c)} \qquad (3)$$

where c is a color index with the property that its name, returned by *Name*(), contains one of the words denoting bright colors, i.e. W_{light}={"light","pale","white"}. Using the same reasoning as for the computation of P_{light}, we define: *the dark color ratio* P_{dark}, *the hard color ratio* P_{hard} (amount of saturated colors), *the weak color ratio* P_{weak}, *the warm color ratio* P_{warm} and *the cold color ratio* P_{cold}. The last parameters are two color relationship ratios, thus *adjacent color ratio*, P_{adj} and *complementary color ratio*, P_{compl} which are defined using the analogy of the Webmaster palette with Itten's color wheel (Itten, 1961).

Action Description

To *describe the movie contents at structural level*, we use several parameters computed on the movie video shot distribution. The first parameter, denoted *the movie global rhythm*, $\bar{v}_T$ is defined as the average number of shot changes over all the movie time windows of size T seconds (a common values is T=5s). Defined in this way, $\bar{v}_T$ is a measure of the movie global tempo, which in animated movies reflects the type of action of the movie, e.g. static, dynamic, slow, etc. The next parameter is *the action ratio*, which is defined thus $A_{movie}=T_{action}/T_{movie}$, where T_{action} is the total length of the movie's action segments (defined below, see Equation 5) and T_{move} is the movie length. This measure defines the character of the movie, e.g. high action content, no action, etc.

Action segments are determined using the four step algorithm proposed in (Ionescu, Coquin, Lambert, Buzuloiu, 2007), which uses the hypothesis that action is related to a high frequency of shot changes:

- step a - *thresholding*: we defined a binary action signal, thus:

$$action(i) = \begin{cases} 1 & \xi_T(i) > \overline{v}_T \ (\text{action}) \\ 0 & otherwise \ (\text{no action}) \end{cases} \tag{4}$$

where, i is the frame index, $\xi_T(i)$ represents the number of shot changes which occur in the time window T starting with frame i,

- step b - *merging*: SCCs color effects are marked as action segments (i.e. *action(i)=1*) and neighbor action clips, at a time distance below T seconds are merged together (reduce the over-segmentation).
- step c - *clearing*: the small action clips, with a length below T, are being removed (remove unnoticeable and irrelevant action segments),
- step d - *removing*: action segments containing less than 4 video shots, are being removed (very likely to be the result of false detections). An example is depicted in Figure 5.

The gradual transitions, besides their importance to temporal segmentation, also have a semantic meaning in the animated movies. For instance, a dissolve is usually used to change the time of the action; similarly, a fade is used to change the action or, used in a fade group introduces a pause before changing the action place. In animated movies, high amounts of such transitions are related somehow to the movie mystery (Ionescu, Coquin, Lambert, Buzuloiu, 2007), therefore, we compute a *gradual transitions ratio*, R_{trans}. Also, movies using high amounts of SCC effects are in general uncommon (see Figure 2), therefore we compute the *SCC color ratio* parameter, R_{SCC}. The two parameters are defined as follows:

$$R_{trans} = (T_{fades} + T_{disolve})/T_{movie}, \ R_{SCC} = T_{SCC}/T_{movie} \tag{5}$$

where T_{fades}, $T_{disovles}$ and T_{SCC} represent the total length of fades, dissolves and SCC transitions.

High-Level Descriptions

To determine higher-level descriptions of the movie content we use a linguistic representation of data using fuzzy sets (Ionescu, Coquin, Lambert, Buzuloiu, 2007; Ionescu, Coquin, Lambert, Buzuloiu, 2008).

Figure 5. Action highlighting: the oX axis is the time axis, a-d denote the processing steps, the red line is a temporal annotation graph (vertical lines correspond to video transitions) and the green line represents the action() binary signal (movie "François le Vaillant" (CITIA, 2009), Adaptation from Springer LNCS, 4398)

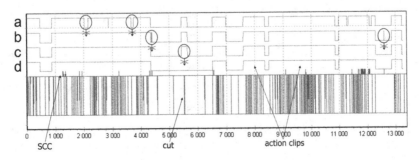

Fuzzy sets, compared to crisp sets, provide many advantages for our application: e.g. are similar to the way the human brain is functioning, they allow to represent numeric low-level information with textual data, while normalization is provided by the degree of truth.

First, we provide a symbolic level of description by associating a textual concept to each of the previously determined numeric parameters. Each concept is described with several fuzzy symbols while the fuzzy meaning is given by membership functions. For instance, the *"light color content"* concept is associated to P_{light} (see equation 3) and it is described with three symbols: "low", "mean" and "high". Membership functions are piecewise linear functions defined using 4 thresholds, {t1=33, t2=50, t3=60, t4=66} (e.g. P_{light}>66% means a high amount of light colors, etc., see Figure 6); the *"movie rhythm"* concept is associated to $\bar{v}_T$ parameter (see the previous section) and it is described with three symbols: "slow", "average" and "fast". In this case, membership functions are defined using the thresholds {t1=0.5, t2=0.7, t3=1, t4=1.2} (see Figure 6, e.g. a reduced rhythm is represented with movies like "A Crushed World" ($\bar{v}_T = 0.46$), "Amerlock" ($\bar{v}_T = 0.04$) while a high movie tempo with movies like "Ferrailles" ($\bar{v}_T = 1.92$) or "Le Moine et le Poisson" ($\bar{v}_T = 2.37$), etc.).

A semantic level of description is attended for the color content using fuzzy rule bases. New concepts are emerging through a uniform mechanism according to the combination/projection principle using conjunction operators for the generalized modus ponens. The proposed semantic descriptions concern mainly some of the Itten's color contrasts (Itten, 1961) and color harmony schemes (Birren, 1969), which are to be found in the animated movies. An example is presented in Figure 6. For instance, the "light-dark contrast" concept is defined by the following rule: IF ("light color content" is "mean") AND ("dark color content" is "mean") THEN "there is a light-dark contrast". The new membership function of the new semantic concept is given thus:

$$\mu_{contL-D}(P_{light}, P_{dark}) = \min\{\mu_{LCmean}(P_{light}), \mu_{DCmean}(P_{dark})\} \tag{6}$$

where μ_{LCmean} and μ_{DCmean} are the membership functions of the symbols "mean" light color content and "mean" dark color content.

Figure 6. Fuzzy representation of data: (left) examples of membership functions, (right) example of a fuzzy rule base (NDA-no description available, Adaptation from Eurasip JIVP-CIVP, 1)

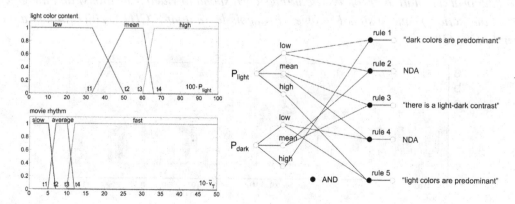

VIDEO ABSTRACTION

Browsing a database in the search for a specific movie can be inefficient and time consuming, as it requires visualizing movie contents. For addressing this issue, movie abstracts are one efficient solution, as they propose compact representations of the original video, significantly shorter, which preserve at least some of the essential parts of the original video.

There are two fundamentally different kinds of video abstracts. The *still-image abstracts*, known as video summaries, are a small collection of salient images (i.e. key frames) that best represent all the underlying content or only certain scenes of interest. Basically, the existing methods differ in the way the key frames are extracted (Truong, Venkatesh, 2007; Money, Agius, 2008). For instance, in (Doulamis, Doulamis, Kollias, 2000) key frames are extracted using derivatives on a curve of characteristic frame vectors, in (Ronh, Jin, Wu, 2004) where the key frame extraction process is compared to TF-IDF (Term-Frequency Inverse Document Frequency) text searching mechanism, and key frames are selected at shot level as frames having a reduced frame coverage of the rest of the movie, while (Li, Schuster, Katsaggelos, Gandhi, 2004) uses the Sequence Reconstruction Error (SRE) which measures the capacity of the summary of reconstructing the original movie contents.

On the other hand, the *moving-image abstracts*, or video skims, consist on a collection of image sequences. Therefore, a video skim is, itself, a video sequence. One simple and straightforward method to create a movie skim is to include some of the neighborhood frames (i.e. a frame interval) of the key frames extracted using a video summary technique. However, the complexity of a video skim yields some more developed approaches. The existing video skimming techniques are addressing two different approaches, thus: summary sequences, which are classic abstracts covering the entire movie contents, and movie highlights, which only summarize some of the most interesting parts of the movie. Video highlighting techniques are related to the characteristics of the events, which are to be considered as representatives for the underlying movie content (Truong, Venkatesh, 2007). Therefore, the existing approaches are application dependent. Several approaches have been tackled, for instance (Xiong, Radhakrishnan, Divakaran, 2003) addresses the skimming of sport videos and the video highlight extraction is performed on the events which trigger particular reactions from the public, e.g. applause or cheering or (Coldefy, Bouthemy, 2004) which considers only the movie segments which produce certain reactions from the narrator/commentator, e.g. exciting.

Due to their major differences in terms of the information they provide in the context of indexing, e.g. video summaries provide essential visual cues and are easy to compute and visualize, while video skims are much complex but more exciting as they provide dynamic contents, both types of abstracts are as much necessary, being used extensively with content-based video indexing systems to reduce the browsing time, to improve the quality of the search as well as to reduce the computational complexity by replacing the original movie in the processing steps (Zhu, Mei, Hua, 2005).

In this section we tackle the issue of generating automatic action-based movie trailers, which are a particular case of video highlights: a short promotional film composed of clips showing highlights of a movie due for release in the near future (Smeaton, Lehane, O'Connor, Brady, Craig, 2006; Kawai, Sumiyoshi, Yagi, 2007), and storyboard-like summaries for the animated movies. Having for each movie a brief description of the action content or a collection of key frames which follow the movie event evolution should be an ideal way of accessing its content in an indexing system, like Animaquid (CITIA, 2009).

Currently, the manual production of this type of video abstract is quite a costly creative process, in terms of human resources and also, as it is time consuming. For instance, to produce a trailer for a short animated movie (less than 10 minutes), an expert may need as long as up to 5-6 hours (CITIA, 2009). Therefore, automatic approaches are more than welcome. Unfortunately, building automatic movie trailers, similar to the ones a human may generate, is still an open issue. This requires the full understanding of the movie grammar, which is limited with today's scientific progress (Smeaton, Lehane, O'Connor, Brady, Craig, 2006). However, to cope with this issue, the few existing approaches are either developed in restraint conditions, e.g. they are application dependent and use "a priori" data or the expertise of the domain (close captions, electronic guides, etc.), or aim to only assist the manual movie trailer production.

Little work has been reported to date on automatically generating movie trailers (Chen, Kuo, Chu, Wu, 2004; Smeaton, Lehane, O'Connor, Brady, Craig, 2006; Kawai, Sumiyoshi, Yagi, 2007). The approach proposed in (Chen, Kuo, Chu, Wu, 2004) is based on sets of rules or grammars which encapsulate the theory of the film composition. They analyze action movies in terms of shot change detection, the MPEG-7 measurement of motion activity and a set of audio features based on the energy of the audio signal, which combined, form a feature, referred to as movie tempo. The movie trailer is composed of those video shots which have a tempo value greater than a certain threshold. A similar approach is proposed in (Smeaton, Lehane, O'Connor, Brady, Craig, 2006) in which shots are selected from the movie to assist in the creation of video trailers. A set of audiovisual features are extracted from the movie temporal structure (video transitions), audio track (type) and motion information (motion intensity, camera movement), to model the characteristics of typical trailer shots. The relevant shots are then obtained through a Support Vector Machine classification process. One particularity of this approach consists in its validation, which is performed by comparing the proposed trailers against genuine commercial trailers. Another example is the method proposed in (Kawai, Sumiyoshi, Yagi, 2007), which tackles the production of TV program trailers (short video clips to advertise the program) using descriptions from electronic program guides. Two methods are discussed. The first one, is based on the sentence similarity between the close captions and the introductory text of the target program. The similarity is evaluated with Bayesian belief networks. The second method extracts several sentences which have the same textual features as those of a general introductory text, and determines the corresponding video sections.

Our movie trailer approach is based on highlighting the movie action segments by analyzing the movie, both at inter-shot level (a high frequency of video transitions) and inter-frame level (visual activity) (Ionescu, Lambert, Coquin, Ott, Buzuloiu, 2006). Globally, this is not a particularly new idea (e.g. Smeaton, Lehane, O'Connor, Brady, Craig, 2006), however, the novelty of this work is rather in the efficiency of this relatively standard approach, when transposed and adapted to the specificity of the animation domain (e.g. short animated movies, movies without dialog or commentary, etc.). To solve the problem of producing trailers for movies with a predominant static content, for which the notion of trailer is rather ambiguous, we adapt the action detection to movie contents, as we cannot speak of action segments or exciting scenes.

For the proposed video summary, the key frames are extracted according to the visual activity of each scene, in a storyboard manner, which is captured with histograms of cumulative inter-frame distances (Ott, Lambert, Ionescu, Coquin, 2007). The performance of our approaches has been confirmed through several user studies, directly by the "consumers of the product", i.e. the end-users.

Action and Shot Visual Activity

The first analysis is an inter-shot analysis. *Action segments* are highlighted using the method proposed in (Ionescu, Coquin, Lambert, Buzuloiu, 2007), which was previously used for the characterization of the action content (see Equation 4 and Figure 5). This provides a rough localization within the movie of almost all the representative/action parts.

The next analysis is the inter-frame analysis. This aims at providing more details on the *visual activity* at shot level. For each retained frame i of the shot k (frames are temporarily and spatially subsampled and color reduced), we compute its color histogram, denoted $H^i_{shot_k}$. To evaluate the visual distance between frames, we use a normalized version of the classical Manhattan, thus:

$$d_M(H^i_{shot_k}, H^j_{shot_k}) = \frac{1}{2 \cdot N_p} \sum_c \left| H^i_{shot_k}(c) - H^j_{shot_k}(c) \right| \qquad (7)$$

where N_p represents the number of pixels and i and j are two frame indexes. Further, we compute a normalized inter-frame distance for the current frame i of the shot k as:

$$D_{shot_k}(i) = \frac{1}{Card(S) - 1} \sum_{j \in S, i \neq j} d_M(H^i_{shot_k}, H^j_{shot_k}) \qquad (8)$$

in which S is the set of the retained frames for shot k and $Card()$ returns the size of a set. This measure gives us information on the correlation between the frame i and the other frames.

To capture the visual activity of the shot, we compute what we call a histogram of cumulative inter-frame distances, thus:

$$\aleph^D_{shot_k}(d_q) = \sum_{i \in S} \delta(D^q_{shot_k}(i) - d_q) \qquad (9)$$

in which S is the frame set for the shot k, d_q is a quantified value of the normalized cumulative inter-frame distance, denoted $D^q_{shot_k}$ (we use N_b=100 bins), q represents the bin index and $\delta(x)$=1 if x=0and 0 otherwise.

After observing and analyzing several examples of $\aleph^D_{shot_k}$ histograms, we conclude that, despite the diversity of histograms, they can be projected basically into only a limited number of patterns which are related to the type of shot content (see also Figure 10):

- *pattern 1* - histograms with small distance: all the values of the cumulative distance are small and therefore there is a reduced variability of the visual content (shot content is almost constant);
- *pattern 2* - histograms with both small and high distances: most of the cumulative distances are small, but there are a few frames which are very different from the others (the visual content is mainly constant, but with some important visual changes, e.g. a scene with a moving object/character);
- *pattern 3* - multi-modal histograms: the shot contains different groups of similar frames (in general several static scenes connected by camera movement);
- *pattern 4* - single-mode histograms: the histogram has only one mode, but the cumulative distances are high (a constantly changing content, e.g. continuous motion, color effects).

Histogram pattern is determined using signal shape analysis techniques (Cheng, Sun, 2000).

Trailer-Like and Storyboard-Like Abstracts

Once we have determined the action and the visual activity at shot level, the *trailer-like video abstract* is computed as follows:

$$trailer = \bigcup_{m=1}^{M} \bigcup_{n=1}^{N_m} seq_{p\%}^{n} \tag{10}$$

in which M is the number of action clips, N_m represents the number of video shots within the action clip m, $seq_{p\%}^{n}$ is an image sequence which contains $p\%$ of the shot n frames. As the action takes place most likely in the middle of a shot, the sequence is shot centered. The choice of parameter p is related to histogram $\aleph_{shot_k}^{D}$. We adapt the amount of the retained shot information to its visual activity, thus: for histograms of pattern 1 or 2 (similar color content) we use p, around 15%, while for histograms of patterns 3 or 4 (high visual activity), we use $p=35\%$ (values empirically determined having as constraint the visual continuity of the trailer, and to preserve an optimal trailer length). Defined in this way, the proposed trailer captures the movie's most "uncommon" parts, even for movies with a predominant static content, for which the notion of trailer is rather ambiguous (action detection is adapted to movie contents).

The *proposed video summary*, aims at presenting one image for each individual movie scene, in the storyboard manner. The number of key frames is adapted to the variability of the shot visual content, i.e. extracting one key frame for each group of similar content images. This is done by taking into account the shape of the histogram $\aleph_{shot_k}^{D}$. For shots with histogram of pattern 1, we extract only one key frame k (the median one), thus:

$$k = \arg\min_{i \in S}\{D_{shot}(i)\} \tag{11}$$

where S is the frame set and $D_{shot}()$ is given by Equation 8. For shots of pattern 2 we extract two key frames: the first will capture the content with a reduced visual variability (according to equation 11), while the second image, l, aims at representing the changing content, thus:

$$l = \arg\max_{i \in S}\{D_{shot}(i)\} \tag{12}$$

being the most different one. For shots with histograms of pattern 3, i.e. multi-modal, we select one key frame for each histogram peak, as being the median image given by equation 11 when applied only to the frames which contributed to the peak value of the histogram. Finally, single-mode histograms (pattern 4) are the most difficult to deal with due to the high variability. Normally this requires a high number of images. However, we use a compromise and we retain the most common image and the most different one (Equations 12 and 13). Several experimental results are presented and discussed with the following section.

A 3D NAVIGATION SYSTEM ARCHITECTURE

All the proposed content analysis and characterization techniques have been integrated with a 3D client-server software prototype called VideoVerse. The proposed 3D content-retrieval application is a complex environment which manages the graphical content browsing capabilities, the video database, content description algorithms, video abstraction and sequence classification techniques. Its software architecture is depicted in Figure 7.

The client is written in Java, and therefore can run either standalone or within a browser, thus greatly widening its portability and availability. Its main component is the application core (see Figure 7.a), which controls all the other functions: Graphical User Interface (GUI), user interaction, communication with the server and image caching. We have adapted the underlying data model to the content of the presented media. The main component of the GUI is a 3D world created using the Java3D technology, which provides Application Programmer Interface (API), both for display and user interaction, and achieves good performance due to hardware support.

Movies are presented in a 3D universe as small icons mapped to a multilayered invisible globe. Its architecture is presented in Figure 7.c, while a screenshot is depicted in Figure 7.d. In this environment, mouse zoom, drag and rotate inputs provide an interaction system similar to the well-known Google Earth interface. Lighting and fog effects along with a natural background were also added to increase the experience of this environment. This basically provides a 3D polar coordinate system, very useful for the indexing task, as movies can be represented according to some clustering techniques (e.g. as in Figure 9). A simple mouse click on a desired movie will bring insight a 2D interface which presents detail information about the movie contents. The 2D Movie Panel is based on the SwingX framework and contains controls both for viewing the metadata associated with a sequence, e.g. textual synopsis, temporal structure, color and action content, trailer and storyboard like abstracts, and also for inspecting

Figure 7. VideoVerse application architecture: (a) Client architecture, (b) Server architecture, (c) 3D world graph (TG-Transform Group, LOD-Level Of Detail), (d) 3D interface screenshot. Movies from (CITIA, 2009)

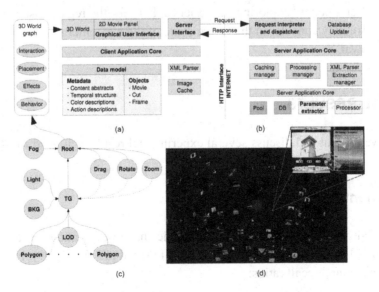

the sequence at will. In order to address low bandwidth situations, an open-source streaming framework called MediaFrame was used. Also, since the number of available video sequences might be very large, special techniques were implemented for reducing the application load: image and metadata caching, Level Of Detail (LOD) rendering etc.

The server is also a Java application, and is built using Java Enterprise Edition (JEE) solutions. It runs on top of an application server (e.g. Tomcat), and can serve a virtually unlimited number of clients simultaneously. A layered architectural approach has been implemented, as one can see in Figure 7.b. The application core controls and manages all the other components. The database updater is responsible for properly importing into the system any new video sequences from the video pool. This procedure implies several steps:

- running offline the parameter extraction algorithms on the new sequence, i.e. performing the content annotation and abstraction,
- adding the sequence to the database and thus updating the database entries,
- processing the sequence according to the output of the parameter extractor.

A caching manager has also been devised for handling the situations of repeated client demands for the same resource. The processing manager and extraction manager are responsible for operating the corresponding external components. The parameter extractor, which consists on the previously mentioned annotation techniques, is implemented in fast C++ code, while the processing module is also available in fast native code based on the *ffmpeg* framework.

It should also be mentioned that the application has been designed having in mind the possibility of further development into a large-scale system. All the metadata exchange in the system (both internally and over Internet) is done through XML objects which provide robustness and scalability, the client application has a thorough Model Controller View (MVC) design, and many functional and graphical extension points are available.

After several experimental tests conducted on various movie databases, we may notice that for some particular setups, e.g. very large amounts of videos, memory constraints, limited computational power, etc., Java3D tends to fail, introducing, sometimes, unpleasant delays in the response of the GUI to user actions. To offer a better "exploring" experience, both for the regular usage and for illustration of scientific results, we may consider in the future some of the new emerging technologies, such Flash with 3D support or JavaFX.

EXPERIMENTAL RESULTS

With this section we present and discuss several experimental results achieved for the previously presented techniques.

Temporal Segmentation

The proposed cut, fade and dissolve detection approaches have been validated on an animated movie database from IAFF - The International Animated Film Festival (CITIA, 2009). For the evaluation we use the classic precision and recall ratios:

$$precision = \frac{GD}{GD + FD}, \quad recall = \frac{GD}{N_{total}} \tag{13}$$

where GD represents the number of good detections, FD the number of false detections and N_{total} the total number of the real transitions. To constitute the detection ground truth, all the transitions have been manually labeled using a specially–developed software.

The proposed cut detection method has been tested on more than 158 minutes of video containing up to 3166 cuts (Ionescu, Lambert, Coquin, Buzuloiu, 2007). Our method was compared with two other approaches: a classical histogram-based method, which uses directly the frames color histograms in order to detect the cuts, and a motion-based method, which uses the discontinuity of the motion vectors obtained with a block-based estimation method. *Using the proposed method we have obtained both high precision and recall ratios, above 92%* (see Table 1). The recall obtained with the classic histogram method was improved of 4% (+125 cuts), while the precision of the motion-based method was improved of 5.5% (+178 cuts). Moreover, using the proposed cut detection in conjunction with the SCC detection procedure, the precision was up to 96% and thus improved with 1% (see Table 1). The obtained false detections are mostly owing to the very fast camera motions, while the misdetections are due to color similarity between the cut frames and to the occurrence of the gradual transitions (i.e. fades, dissolves).

Fade detection was tested on 102 minutes of video containing a total number of 37 fade-ins and 56 fade-outs. The results are presented in Table 2 (movies: 1-"A Crushed World", 2-"A Viagem", 3-"François le Vaillant", 4-"Paradise", 5-"Gazoon", 6-"The Buddy System", 7-"Le Moine et le Poisson", 8-"Casa", 9-"Circuit Marine", 10-"Ferrailles", 11-"The Hill Farm", 12-"L'Egoiste", 13-"Le Chat d'Appartement", 14-"Le Château des Autres"). Globally, we have achieved good detection ratios, both, *recall and precision ratios, above 90%*: fade-in precision 81.9% and recall 97.2%, fade-out precision 91.4% and recall 94.6%. The false detections were mainly due to objects entering the scene, which caused an intensity variation similar with the one generate by a real fade, or due to the sharp transitions followed by global motion. On the other hand, the misdetections are occurring mainly for very short fades, which have an augmentation of the luminance up to 90% in only one or two frames.

Dissolve detection was tested on 61 minutes of video containing 452 dissolves. The results are synthesized with Table 3. Overall, the proposed dissolve detection algorithm *achieved 360 good detections and only 23 false detections, that is a recall of 79.6% and a precision of 94%*. The achieved results are very good considering the difficulty of the test sequences which are rich in global visual effects and object motion (e.g. movies "Coeur de Secours", "Paradise", "M. Pascal"), most of the dissolves having atypical patterns. Due to shape analysis of the discontinuity function, most of the peaks corresponding

Table 1. Comparison between the proposed method and two other methods (GD-good detections, FD-false detections, SCC-short color change detection)

Method	Count	GD	FD	Precision %	Recall %
conventional histogram-based	3166	2806	199	93.37	88.63
motion discontinuity-based	3166	2993	355	89.39	94.53
proposed	3166	2931	157	94.92	92.6
proposed + SCC detection	3166	2931	127	95.97	92.6

to other visual changes were disregarded and the proposed method was able to retrieve many of the dissolves superposed with visual effects or motion (see Figure 4). However, the non-detections were due to very complex scene changes, while the false detection to visual effects having an intensity signature similar to the dissolves.

In order to determine the shot segmentation, video transitions are synchronized with the respect to the movie time axis and video shots are then determined as being the video segments which lie between two successive video transitions. For our application, several additional rules were adopted, e.g. cuts detected during gradual transitions are removed (a source of cut false detections), shots containing only black frames are removed (e.g. black frames between a fade-out - fade-in sequence), gradual transition frames are removed (irrelevant for the shots), SCC color effects do not determine a shot change.

Color and Action Descriptions

The proposed content description approach has been tested on 52 animated movies from (CITIA, 2009). The evaluation was confronted with the problem of the high subjectivity of such a type of content descriptions. However, to cope with this issue, we have substituted the absence of a real ground truth with the manual analysis of the results using all the content-related available information as reference (e.g. synopsis, content descriptions, etc.). Several examples are presented in Figure 8, while the obtained textual descriptions are detailed with Table 4.

Table 2. Fade detection results (GD-good detections, FD-false detections). Total number of fade-in 37 and fade-out 56, movies (CITIA, 2009)

Movie	1	2	3	4	5	6	7	8	9	10	11	12	13	14
fade-in, overall precision 81.9%, recall 97.2%														
count	7	4	2	7	0	1	5	1	0	0	5	0	3	2
GD	7	4	2	7	0	1	5	0	0	0	5	0	3	2
FD	0	1	1	1	0	0	0	1	0	1	3	0	0	0
fade-out, overall precision 91.4%, recall 94.6%														
count	6	4	4	7	0	1	5	3	0	7	6	5	5	3
GD	6	4	4	7	0	0	5	3	0	6	6	5	5	2
FD	1	1	0	0	0	0	0	0	0	0	3	0	0	0

Table 3. Dissolve detection results (GD-good detections, FD-false detections). Total number of dissolves 452, overall precision 94% and recall 79.6%, movies (CITIA, 2009)

Movie	Ex-Enfant	Le Moine et le Poisson	M. Pascal	Une Bonne Journée	Paradise	Coeur de Secours	The Sand Castle
Count	75	61	98	19	60	67	72
GD	65	47	76	19	44	47	62
FD	8	2	2	0	7	2	2
Precision %	89.04	95.91	97.44	100	86.27	95.92	96.88
Recall %	86.66	77.05	77.55	100	73.33	70.15	86.11

Table 4. Color and action content descriptions (the number in the brackets represents the fuzzy degree of truth, NDA-no description available, movies from CITIA, 2009)

Descriptions	"Le Moine et le Poisson"	"Amerlock"	"Och, och"	"François le Vaillant"
movie rhythm	fast (1)	slow (1)	mean (0.82)	fast (1)
action content	high (1)	low (1)	high (0.71)	high (1)
movie mystery	high (1)	low (1)	mean (1)	low (0.53)
color variability	average (1)	low (0.98)	mean (0.79)	high (1)
dark colors are predominant	(0)	(0)	(1)	(1)
light colors are predominant	(0)	(0.95)	(0)	(0)
there is a light-dark contrast	(0.93)	(0)	(0)	(0)
warm colors are predominant	(1)	NDA	NDA	(0)
cold colors are predominant	(0)	NDA	NDA	(0.97)
there is a warm-cold contrast	(0)	NDA	NDA	(0)
adjacent colors are predominant	(0.7)	(0.51)	(0.27)	(0)
complementary colors are predominant	(0)	(0.02)	(0)	(0)
there is a adj.-compl. scheme	(0.3)	(0.02)	(0.73)	(1)

For instance, the movie "Le Moine et le Poisson" is described as having a fast rhythm and a high action content, which is also visible from the movie synopsis "a monk chases repetitively a fish" while the mystery is high, as the chase becomes more and more symbolical. In terms of colors, the predominant colors are the "Yellow", contrasted by "Black", therefore the colors are mainly warm, both light and dark and the color variability is average (see Figure 8).

On the other hand, the movie "Amerlock" uses as animation technique the plasticine modeling. It has only one setup where a piece of plasticine takes progressively different shapes, therefore the action content is low, while the movie tempo is reduced. The use of this particular technique, limits the color palette to only a few colors and the color variability is low. The predominant colors are "Blue"

Figure 8. Color and action characterization examples. For each movie we present several representative images, the global weighted histogram and the action content annotation (green line, see also Figure 5). Movies from (CITIA, 2009)

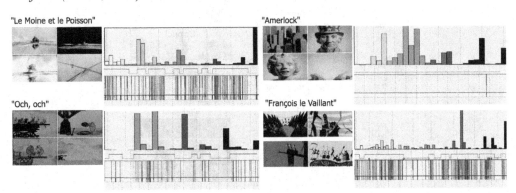

(background), "Azure", "Gray" and "Red" and most of the colors are bright, while only an insignificant amount of colors are cold and warm (see Figure 8).

The proposed content descriptions have been used in an attempt to classify animated movies from (CITIA, 2009) in terms of color artistry content and action content. The objective is to test the discriminating power of our attributes for a prospective use as indexes in our content-based retrieval system. The classification was tackled using k-means unsupervised clustering, while the input data consisted on the fuzzy degree of the linguistic descriptions.

The first classification consisted of using both action and color information. The low homogeneity of the obtained clusters proves that in general color is not related to the action content. A second attempt uses only the action information. This allows us to retrieve two particular movie types, thus movies with slow rhythm (e.g. "Amerlock", "Sculptures", "The Wall") and movies with high action content (e.g. "Circuit Marine", "François le Vaillant"). The final classification was performed using only color information. Several results are synthesized in Figure 9 (the number of clusters varies from 2 to 4 and for each relevant cluster we present several movies for visualization purpose). One important result is the separation of the dark cold color movies (that could be referred to as sad movies, cluster 4 in Figure 9) and colorful movies (or joyful movies, cluster 2 in Figure 9), from the other movies.

The results of the last two classification tests show that, although, addressed jointly (e.g. classification using the action parameters of the movies from the dark cold color movie cluster 4) may lead to the retrieval of a particular animation technique, i.e. sand and plasticine modeling, which is characterized with a very reduced color palette, dark cold colors and a reduced rhythm. More details are provided in (Ionescu, Coquin, Lambert, Buzuloiu, 2007; Ionescu, Coquin, Lambert, Buzuloiu, 2008). Whether these first attempts proved the real potential of the linguistic content descriptions, more elaborated methods should be addressed in order to attend human perception.

Figure 9. Color-based classification of 52 animated movies, the cluster repartition is plotted using only the first three principal components (movies from (CITIA, 2009); Adaptation from Eurasip JIVP-CIVP, 1)

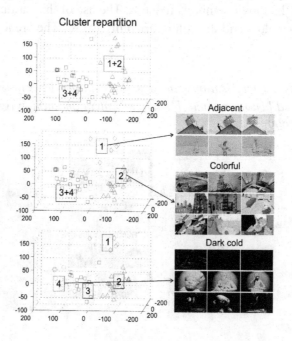

Video Abstraction

The evaluation of video abstraction techniques is in general a subjective task, as it mainly relies on human perception. A consistent evaluation framework is actually missing. However, among the existing approaches i.e. the description of the results, the use of objective metrics and user studies (Truong, Venkatesh, 2007), the user studies is probably the most useful and realistic form of evaluation, as it involves directly the "consumer of the product" in the evaluation process: the end-users.

An evaluation campaign has been conducted on 10 animated movies, involving 27 people (students, didactic personnel and several animation experts, ages from 21 to 49). The test protocol consists in showing the participants, first, the entire movie and then, the proposed movie trailer and video summary, and asking to answer several questions concerning the quality of the content representation and the length of the proposed abstracts.

The proposed movie trailer was perceived as providing *almost all* of the movie's important parts, with a global average score over all the sequences, of 7.7 (scale from 1=*not at all*, to 10=*all of them*) and a standard deviation of 1.3. This corresponds to our goal, as video trailers do not aim at providing all the action contents or exciting parts. The trailer length was considered *appropriate* with a global average score of 2.6 (scale from 0=*very short*, to 4=*very long*) and a standard deviation of 0.6.

In Table 5 we compare the length of the proposed trailer against the original movie. One may notice that the trailer provides a good reduction of the original movie contents with an average compression around 9:1 (max value up to 21:1). The only cases when the trailer tends to be less efficient are for the movies with a predominant action content (i.e. action ratio >85%).

In what concerns *the proposed video summary*, in Figure 10 we have presented several examples of shot summarization. Multi-modal histograms conclude with one key frame for each individual group of

Figure 10. Shot summarization using histograms of cumulative inter-frame distances (for each shot we present several representative images for visualization purpose). Selected key frames are marked with red rectangles. Movies from (CITIA, 2009)

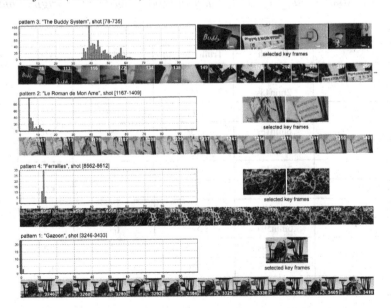

similar pictures, e.g. the shot [78:735] (movie "The Buddy System"), which contains a 3D continuous camera motion with several focuses on some interesting points of the scene, is summarized with one representative frame for each focus point. Shots containing only one group of similar frames and several visual changes, are summarized with one common image and one image which captures the variability of the content, see shot [1167:1409] (movie "Le Roman de Mon Ame").

Due to histogram invariance, constant shots are summarized with only one image, despite any object motion of other small movements (see shot [3246:3433], movie "Gazoon"). The evaluation campaign revealed that the proposed video summary was perceived as preserving *almost entirely* the movie contents (average score 6.9, scale 1=*not at all* to 10=*entirely*, and standard deviation 1.7), while preserving in general an appropriate length (average score 6.1, scale 1=*too short*, 10=*very long*, and standard deviation 1.5). However, the summary was less efficient for movies with a very complex content, when the number of "don't know" answers was important, or the dispersion of the answers was high.

FUTURE RESEARCH DIRECTIONS

Future research consists, first, in enhancing the proposed content annotation system. At low-level, we should consider other sources of information than color and temporal structure, like the motion information. However, methods will have to cope with some specific constrains, e.g. the native discontinuity of motion of some animation techniques or the abundance of color effects. At semantic level, we seek out to increase the discriminating power of the proposed content-based descriptions, and thus, the indexing capabilities of the content-based retrieval system. We are currently studying the automatic detection of the movie's genre and of the animation technique, information highly demanded by users when searching for a specific animated movie. A possible solution may be provided by machine learning techniques, e.g. Support Vector Machines. However, content descriptions have to be properly selected (i.e. maximizing the information coverage while minimizing the feature space), as well as the distance measures. While

Table 5. A comparative study of the proposed trailer approach against the original movie (movies from CITIA, 2009)

Movie	Length	Trailer length	# shots	A_{movie}	Compression ratio
"Francois le Vaillant"	8min56s	1min25	164	70%	6:1
"La Bouche Cousue"	2min48s	16s	39	52.2%	10:1
"Ferrailles"	6min15s	1min31s	138	98%	4:1
"Casa"	6min15s	42s	49	87%	9:1
"Circuit Marine"	5min35s	55s	125	87%	6:1
"Gazoon"	2min47s	35s	31	89%	4:1
"La Cancion du Microsillon"	8min56s	52s	97	55%	10:1
"Le Moine et le Poisson"	6min	55s	99	74%	7:1
"Paroles en l'Air"	6min50s	57s	63	77%	7:1
"The Buddy System"	6min19s	1min	77	77%	6:1
"David"	8min12s	23s	27	40%	21:1
"Greek Tragedy"	6min32s	24s	29	48%	16:1

for numeric data the existing literature proposes many solutions, quantifying the distance between two movies is still an open issue.

CONCLUSION

In this chapter we tackle the analysis and characterization of the animated movies in view of constituting an automatic indexing system. With the proposed system, movies are to be retrieved in a human-like manner, i.e. using linguistic semantic concepts, through a 3D interactive environment, we call VideoVerse.

First, we address the temporal segmentation issue, by proposing cut, fade and dissolve detection algorithms. Several solutions have been adopted, in order to overcome some of the difficulties of the animated movies, e.g. reducing the influence of movements, of intensity fluctuations, of some color effects, etc. Cut detection achieved average detection ratios above 94%, while gradual transitions around 90%. The proposed methods tend to fail only due to some very complex scenes or due to the superposition of motion and visual effects.

Next, we discuss the content description of the animated movies in terms of color techniques (color contrasts, color harmony schemes) and action content (rhythm, action, mystery). The aim is to automatically understand the artistic content of these movies. To do so, we use high-level descriptions (textual) obtained through a fuzzy representation mechanism using the expertise of the animation domain. Through tests proved that the proposed descriptions are mostly coherent with the real movie contents (validation performed manually). Some interesting results have been obtained in an attempt to automatically classify the animated movies using the proposed content descriptions with a k-means unsupervised clustering, e.g. retrieval of the dark cold color movies (referred as sad) or the prospective detection of some animation techniques (e.g. plasticine modeling). Nevertheless, whether these first results prove the potential of the linguistic descriptions to video retrieval, additional analysis and more elaborated machine learning techniques should addressed to widen the retrieval capabilities.

Browsing a database requires visualizing movie contents. One efficient solution is provided by automatic video abstraction. We propose two kinds of abstract, which were specifically tuned to the animation domain. The first one is a trailer-like dynamic abstract, which summarize only the movie's most exciting parts, while the second one, is a static video summary, in which, key frames are selected in a storyboard manner (one image for each different scene). To overcome the general subjectivity of the video abstraction evaluation process, we have conducted a user campaign. The results show that the proposed trailer provides almost all the movie's important parts (which also corresponds to our goal), while the video summary preserves almost entirely the movie content, being close to a storyboard. However, the only drawback of our approach was sometimes the length of the abstracts, which for some particular movies tends to be long.

Finally, we discuss the architecture of a 3D interactive environment for video retrieval. With the proposed system, movies are presented in a 3D universe as small icons mapped to a multilayered invisible globe and user interaction is provided similar to the well-known Google Earth interface. Besides the graphical experience proposed with this system (the user surfs in an universe of movies), this is a fully operational and modular client-server architecture, which can run, either standalone or within a browser, and which manages graphical content browsing capabilities, the video database, content description algorithms, video abstraction and sequence classification techniques.

ACKNOWLEDGMENT

The work has been co-funded by the Sectoral Operational Programme Human Resources Development 2007-2013 of the Romanian Ministry of Labour, Family and Social Protection through the Financial Agreement POSDRU/89/1.5/S/62557 and under Rhône-Alpes region Research Cluster 2, LIMA - Loisirs IMAges project. The authors would like to thank CITIA - The City of Moving Images and Folimage Animation Company for providing them access to their animated movie database and for the technical support.

REFERENCES

Adjeroh, D. A., & Lee, M. C. (2001). On ratio-based color indexing. *IEEE Transactions on Image Processing, 10*(1), 36–48. doi:10.1109/83.892441

Birren, F. (1969). *Principles of color - a review of past traditions and modern theories of color harmony.* New York: Reinhold.

Boccignone, G., De Santo, M., & Percannella, G. (2000). Automated threshold selection for the detection of dissolves in MPEG video. *IEEE International Conference on Multimedia and Expo, 3,* 1535–1538.

Burak Ozer, I., & Wolf, W. H. (2002). A hierarchical human detection system in uncompressed domains. *IEEE Transactions on Multimedia, 4*(2), 283–300. doi:10.1109/TMM.2002.1017740

Calic, J., & Izquierdo, E. (2002). A multiresolution technique for video indexing and retrieval. *IEEE International Conference on Image Processing, 1,* 952–955.

Chan, S. S. M., Qing, L., Yi, W., & Yueting, Z. (2001). A hybrid approach to video retrieval in a generic video management and application processing framework. *IEEE International Conference on Multimedia and Expo,* (pp. 389 - 392).

Chen, H. W., Kuo, J.-H., Chu, W.-T., & Wu, J.-L. (2004). Action movies segmentation and summarization based on tempo analysis. *ACM International Workshop on Multimedia Information Retrieval,* (pp. 251-258). New York: ACM.

Cheng, H., & Sun, Y. (2000). A hierarchical approach to color image segmentation using homogeneity. *IEEE Transactions on Image Processing, 9*(12), 2071–2082. doi:10.1109/83.887975

CITIA. (2009). *City of Moving Images - The International Animated Film Festival,* http://www.citia. info/, & *Animaquid Indexing System,* http://www/toondra.com/, Annecy-France.

Coldefy, F., & Bouthemy, P. (2004). Unsupervised soccer video abstraction based on pitch, dominant color and camera motion analysis . In *ACM Multimedia* (pp. 268–271). New York: ACM.

Colombo, C., Del Bimbo, A., & Pala, P. (1999). Semantics in visual information retrieval. *IEEE MultiMedia, 6*(3), 38–53. doi:10.1109/93.790610

Detyniecki, M., & Marsala, C. (2003). Discovering knowledge for better video indexing based on colors. *IEEE International Conference on Fuzzy Systems,* (Vol. 2, pp. 1177–1181), St. Louis, USA.

Doulamis, A. D., Doulamis, N., & Kollias, S. (2000). Non-sequential video content representation using temporal variation of feature vectors. *IEEE Transactions on Consumer Electronics, 46*(3). doi:10.1109/30.883444

Fan, J., Luo, H., & Elmagarmid, A. K. (2004). Concept-oriented indexing of video databases: toward semantic sensitive retrieval and browsing. *IEEE Transactions on Image Processing, 13*(7), 974–991. doi:10.1109/TIP.2004.827232

Fernando, W. A. C., Canagarajah, C. N., & Bull, D. R. (1999). Fade and dissolve detection in uncompressed and compressed video sequence. *IEEE International Conference on Image Processing,* (pp. 299-303), Kobe, Japan.

Geetha, M. K., & Palanivel, S. (2007). HMM based automatic video classification using static and dynamic features. *International Conference on Computational Intelligence and Multimedia Applications,* (Vol. 3, pp. 277 – 281).

Guimaraes, S. J. F., Couprie, M., Araujo, A. A., & Leite, N. J. (2003). Video segmentation based on 2D image analysis. *Pattern Recognition Letters, 24,* 947–957. doi:10.1016/S0167-8655(02)00218-0

Haering, N., Qian, R., & Sezan, I. (2000). A semantic event-detection approach and its application to detecting hunts in wildlife video. *IEEE Transactions on Circuits and Systems for Video Technology, 10*(6), 857–868. doi:10.1109/76.867923

Han, B., Gao, X., & Ji, H. (2005). A unified framework for shot boundary detection. In *Pattern Recognition,* (LNCS 3801, pp. 997-1002). Berlin: Springer.

Huan, Z., Xiuhuan, L., & Lilei, Y. (2008). Shot boundary detection based on mutual information and canny edge detector. *IEEE International Conference on Computer Science and Software Engineering,* (pp. 1124-1128).

Ianeva, T. I., Vries, A. P., & Rohrig, H. (2003). Detecting cartoons: a case study in automatic video-genre classification. *IEEE International Conference on Multimedia and Expo, 1,* 449-452.

IBM QBIC. (2006). *Hermitage Museum.* Retrieved from http://www.hermitagemuseum.org.

Ionescu, B., Buzuloiu, V., Lambert, P., & Coquin, D. (2006). Improved cut detection for the segmentation of animation movies. *IEEE International Conference on Acoustic, Speech and Signal Processing,* (Vol. 2, pp. 14-19), Toulouse, France.

Ionescu, B., Coquin, D., Lambert, P., & Buzuloiu, V. (2007). Fuzzy semantic action and color characterization of animation movies in the video indexing task context . In Marchand-Maillet, S. (Eds.), *LNCS 4398* (pp. 119–135). Berlin: Springer.

Ionescu, B., Coquin, D., Lambert, P., & Buzuloiu, V. (2008). A fuzzy color-based approach for understanding animated movies content in the indexing task. *Eurasip Journal on Image and Video Processing, special issue on Color in Image and Video Processing, 1,* 20-36.

Ionescu, B., Lambert, P., Coquin, D., & Buzuloiu, V. (2006). Fuzzy color-based semantic characterization of animation movies. In *IS&T CGIV - 3th European Conference on Colour in Graphics, Imaging, and Vision,* University of Leeds, United Kingdom.

Ionescu, B., Lambert, P., Coquin, D., & Buzuloiu, V. (2007). The cut detection issue in the animation movie domain. *Academy Publisher Journal of Multimedia, 2*(4), 10–19.

Ionescu, B., Lambert, P., Coquin, D., & Dârlea, L. (2005). Color-based semantic characterization of cartoons. *IEEE ISSCS - International Symposium on Signals, Circuits and Systems, 1*, (pp. 223-226), Iaşi, Romania.

Ionescu, B., Lambert, P., Coquin, D., Ott, L., & Buzuloiu, V. (2006). Animation movies trailer computation . In *ACM Multimedia*. Santa Barbara.

Itten, J. (1961). *The art of color: The subjective experience and objective rational of color*. New York: Reinhold.

Jeannin, S., & Divakaran, A. (2001). MPEG-7 visual motion descriptors. *IEEE Transactions on Circuits and Systems for Video Technology, 11*(6), 720–724. doi:10.1109/76.927428

Jiang, J., Li, Z., Xiao, G., & Chen, J. (2007). Real-time shot-cut detection in a compressed domain. *SPIE Journal of Electronic Imagining, 16*(4).

Kawai, Y., Sumiyoshi, H., & Yagi, N. (2007). Automated production of TV program trailer using electronic program guide. *ACM International Conference on Image and Video Retrieval*, (pp. 49-56), Amsterdam.

Kim, D.-J., Frigui, H., & Fadeev, A. (2008). A generic approach to semantic video indexing using adaptive fusion of multimodal classifiers. *International Journal of Imaging Systems and Technology, 18*(2-3), 124–136. doi:10.1002/ima.20147

Kim, K. I., Jung, K., Park, S. H., & Kim, H. J. (2000). Support vector machine-based text detection in digital video. *Pattern Recognition, 34*(2), 527–529. doi:10.1016/S0031-3203(00)00095-9

Lay, J. A., & Guan, L. (2004). Retrieval for color artistry concepts. *IEEE Transactions on Image Processing, 13*(3), 125–129. doi:10.1109/TIP.2003.822971

Lee, K. (2005). *Semantic feature extraction based on video abstraction and temporal modeling. Pattern Recognition and Image Analysis* (Vol. 3522, pp. 392–400). Berlin: Springer.

Lee, M.-S., Yang, Y.-M., & Lee, S.-W. (2001). Automatic video parsing using shot boundary detection and camera operation analysis. *Pattern Recognition, 34*, 711–719. doi:10.1016/S0031-3203(00)00007-8

Leonardi, R., Migliorati, P., & Prandini, M. (2004). Semantic indexing of soccer audio-visual sequences: a multimodal approach based on controlled Markov chains. *IEEE Transactions on Circuits and Systems for Video Technology, 14*(5), 634–643. doi:10.1109/TCSVT.2004.826751

Li, Z., Qu, H., & Zhang, J. (2008). Real-time fade detection in compressed domain. *IEEE International Conference on Image and Signal Processing, 2*(2), 535-539.

Li, Z., Schuster, G., Katsaggelos, A. K., & Gandhi, B. (2004). Optimal video summarization with a bit budget constraint. *IEEE International Conference on Image Processing*, (Vol. 1, pp. 617-620), Singapore.

Lienhart, R. (1999). Comparison of automatic shot boundary detection algorithms. *SPIE Storage and Retrieval for Still Image and Video Databases VII, 3656*, 290–301.

Lienhart, R. (2001). Reliable transition detection in videos: A survey and practitioner's guide. *International Journal of Image and Graphics*, *1*(3), 469–486. doi:10.1142/S021946780100027X

Lu, S., King, I., & Lyu, M. (2003). Video summarization using greedy method in a constraint satisfaction framework. In *International Conference on Distributed Multimedia Systems*, (pp. 456–461), Miami, Florida, USA.

Lupatini, G., Saraceno, C., & Leonardi, R. (1998). Scene break detection: A comparison. In *Research Issues in Data Engineering, Workshop on Continuous Media Databases and Applications*, (pp. 34–41), Orlando, FL, USA.

Money, A. G., & Agius, H. (2008). Video summarization: A conceptual framework and survey of the state of the art. *International Journal of Visual Communication and Image Representation*, *19*, 121–143. doi:10.1016/j.jvcir.2007.04.002

Naphade, M. R., & Huang, T. S. (2002). Extracting semantics from audiovisual content: The final frontier in multimedia retrieval. *IEEE Transactions on Neural Networks*, *13*(2), 793–810. doi:10.1109/TNN.2002.1021881

Ott, L., Lambert, P., Ionescu, B., & Coquin, D. (2007). Animation movie abstraction: Key frame adaptative selection based on color histogram filtering. In *Computational Color Imaging Workshop at the International Conference on Image Analysis and Processing*, Modena.

Petra, K., Jenny, B.-P., & Jean-Philippe, D. (2006). Scene similarity measure for video content segmentation in the framework of a rough indexing paradigm. *International Journal of Intelligent Systems*, *21*(7), 765–783. doi:10.1002/int.20159

Porter, S. V., Mirmehdi, M., & Thomas, B. T. (2000). Video cut detection using frequency domain correlation. *International Conference on Pattern Recognition*, (pp. 413–416), Barcelona, Spain.

Rahman, A., & Murshed, M. (2008). Temporal texture characterization: A review. *Studies in Computational Intelligence*, *96*, 291–316. doi:10.1007/978-3-540-76827-2_12

Roach, M., Mason, J. S., & Pawlewski, M. (2001). Motion-based classification of cartoons. *International Symposium on Intelligent Multimedia, Video and Speech Processing*, (pp. 146-149), Hong-Kong, China.

Ronh, J., Jin, W., & Wu, L. (2004). Key frame extraction using inter-shot information. *IEEE International Conference on Multimedia and Expo, 1*, Taiwan. Qian, R., Haering, N., & Sezan, I. (1999). A computational approach to semantic event detection. *Computer Vision and Pattern Recognition, 1*, 206.

Santos, S. M., Borges, D. L., & Gomes, H. M. (2008). An evaluation of video cut detection techniques. In *Progress in Pattern Recognition, Image Analysis and Applications*, (LNCS 4756, pp. 311-320). Berlin: Springer.

Saur, D. D., Tan, Y. P., Kulkarni, S. R., & Ramadge, P. J. (1997). Automated analysis and annotation of basketball video. In *SPIE Symposium on Storage and Retrieval for Image and Video Databases V*, (Vol. 3022, pp. 176–187).

Smeaton, A. F., Lehane, B., O'Connor, N. E., Brady, C., & Craig, G. (2006). Automatically selecting shots for action movie trailers. In *ACM International Workshop on Multimedia Information Retrieval*, (pp. 231-238), Santa Barbara.

Smeulders, A. W. M., Worring, M., Santini, S., Gupta, A., & Jain, R. (2000). Content-based image retrieval at the end of the early years. *IEEE Transactions on Pattern Analysis and Machine Intelligence*, *22*(12), 1349–1380. doi:10.1109/34.895972

Smith, P., Drummond, T., & Cipolla, R. (2004). Layered motion segmentation and depth ordering by tracking edges. *IEEE Transactions on Pattern Analysis and Machine Intelligence*, *26*(4), 479–492. doi:10.1109/TPAMI.2004.1265863

Snoek, C. G. M., & Worring, M. (2005). Multimodal video indexing: A review of the state-of-the-art. *Multimedia Tools and Applications*, *25*(1), 5–35. doi:10.1023/B:MTAP.0000046380.27575.a5

Su, C. W., Liao, H.-Y. M., Tyan, H. R., Fan, K. C., & Chen, L. H. (2005). A motion-tolerant dissolve detection algorithm. *IEEE Transactions on Multimedia*, *7*(6), 1106–1113. doi:10.1109/TMM.2005.858394

TRECVID. (2009). *Video retrieval evaluation campaing*. Retrieved from http://www-nlpir.nist.gov/projects/trecvid/

Truong, B. T., & Dorai, C. (2000). Automatic genre identification for content-based video categorization. *IEEE International Conference on Pattern Recognition*, *4*, 230–233, Barcelona, Spain.

Truong, B. T., Dorai, C., & Venkatesh, S. (2000). New enhancements to cut, fade, and dissolve detection processes in video segmentation. In *ACM Multimedia*, (pp. 219–227).

Truong, B. T., & Venkatesh, S. (2007). Video abstraction: A systematic review and classification. *ACM Transactions on Multimedia Computing Communications and Applications*, *3*(1), 3. doi:10.1145/1198302.1198305

Wang, Y., Liu, Z., & Huang, J.-C. (2000). Multimedia content analysis using both audio and visual clues. *IEEE Signal Processing Magazine*, *17*(6), 12–36. doi:10.1109/79.888862

Xie, L., Chang, S.-F., Divakaran, A., & Sun, H. (2003). Unsupervised mining of statistical temporal structures in video . In *Video Mining*. Amsterdam: Kluwer Academic Publishers.

Xiong, Z., Radhakrishnan, R., & Divakaran, A. (2003). Generation of sports highlights using motion activity in combination with a common audio feature extraction framework. *IEEE International Conference on Image Processing*, *1*, 5-8, Barcelona, Spain.

Yilmaz, A., Javed, O., & Shah, M. (2006). Object tracking: A survey. *ACM Computing Surveys*, *38*(4). doi:10.1145/1177352.1177355

Yong, W., & Bhandarkar, S. M. Kang Li, (2007). Semantics-based video indexing using a stochastic modeling approach. *IEEE International Conference on Image Processing*, *4*, 313-316.

Zhu, C.-Z., Mei, T., & Hua, X.-S. (2005). Video booklet - natural video browsing. In *ACM Multimedia*, (pp. 265-266), Singapore.

ADDITIONAL READING

Agoston, G. A. (1987). *Color theory and its application in art and design. Optical Sciences*. Springer-Verlag.

ARGOS. (2006). Evaluation campaign for surveillance tools of video content. http://www.irit.fr/argos.

Beaver, F. E. (2007). *Dictionary of film terms: The aesthetic companion to film art* (4th ed.). Paperback.

CSAIL. (2006). Color name dictionaries. http://swiss.csail.mit.edu/~jaffer/Color/Dictionaries.html.

Del Bimbo, A. (1999). *Visual information retrieval*. San Francisco, California: Morgan Kaufmann Publishers, Inc.

FFMpeg. (2009). Cross-platform solution to record, convert and stream audio and video. http://www.ffmpeg.org/.

Furht, B., Smoliar, S. W., & Zhang, H. (1995). *Video and image processing in multimedia systems. Norwell*. Kluwer.

Hanjalic, A. (2002). Shot-boundary detection: unraveled and resolved? *IEEE Transactions on Circuits and Systems for Video Technology, 12*(2), 90–105. doi:10.1109/76.988656

Ionescu, B. (2009). *Content-based semantic retrieval of video documents, application to navigation, research and automatic content abstraction. LAPI - Image Processing and Analysis Laboratory*, CNCSIS Project RP-2, http://alpha.imag.pub.ro/VideoIndexingRP2/.

IRISA. (2005). Motion2D. http://www.irisa.fr/vista/Motion2D/, Rennes, France.

Jain, A. K., Murty, M. N., & Flynn, P. J. (1999). Data clustering: A review. *ACM Computing Surveys, 31*(3), 264–323. doi:10.1145/331499.331504

Java3D (2009). http://download.java.net/media/java3d/javadoc/1.5.2/index.html.

Kay, P. & Regier, T. (2003). Resolving the question of color naming universals. *National Academy of Sciences*, 100(15), 9085-9089.

Klir, G. J., & Yuan, B. (1995). *Fuzzy sets and fuzzy logic: Theory and applications*. New Jersey: Prentice Hall.

Papoulis, A. (1991). *Probability, random variables, and stochastic processes* (3rd ed.). Mc Graw Hill, Inc., New-York.

Paragios, N., Chen, Y., & Faugeras, O. (2006). *Handbook of mathematical models in computer vision*. New York, USA: Springer Science. doi:10.1007/0-387-28831-7

Witten, I. H., & Frank, E. (2005). *Data minning - Practical machine learning tools and techniques* (2nd ed.). Elsevier, Morgan Kaufman Publishers.

KEY TERMS AND DEFINITIONS

Animated Movies: Are fiction cartoon movies with artistic connotations. Compared to classic cartoons, they involve a great deal of animation techniques, e.g. 3D synthesis, color salts, glass painting, object animation, paper drawing, plasticine modeling, etc. Besides entertainment, they aim at transmitting the author's particular feelings or concepts.

Temporal: Segmentation: Is a fundamental processing step which aims at parsing the video into its fundamental temporal units, i.e. video shots. A video shot is defined as time-continuous sequences of images, which is typically recorded between a camera turn-on and turn-off.

Fuzzy Sets: Are sets whose elements have degrees of membership. In this case, the belonging of a data to a certain class is no longer a problem of affirmation/negation (e.g. crisp sets), but a problem of degree of truth.

Video Abstraction: Is the process of generating compact representations of the original video, significantly shorter, which preserve at least some of its essential parts. Video abstraction techniques are addressing video summaries, i.e. still-image abstracts and video skims, i.e. moving-image abstracts.

Video Browsing: Is the process of accessing movie contents in a large collection of video materials. This task is usually tackled by the navigation system, which provides the user with visual browsing and searching capabilities, ideally, addressed in a human-like manner, and thus accessible to everyone.

Video Indexing: Means automatic annotation of large collections of video footage and consists on generating additional content-related information. These features, e.g. numeric attributes, parameters, textual data, known as indexes, describe usually the physical properties of the underlying video content and are used by the system to automatically cataloguing the data.

Video Trailer: Is a particular case of video highlights (a video skim which summarize only some featured movie parts), being formally defined as a short promotional film, composed of clips showing highlights of a movie due for release in the near future. In general, a video trailer presents some of the most exciting action parts of a movie, in a dynamic way, in order to catch the viewer's attention.

Video Transitions: Are visual effects which make the transition between consecutive shots. Globally, video transitions are divided into sharp transitions, i.e. cuts (direct concatenation of two shots), and gradual transitions (e.g. fades, dissolves, wipes, mattes, etc.).

Chapter 12
Sports Video Analysis

Hua-Tsung Chen
National Chiao-Tung University, Taiwan

Suh-Yin Lee
National Chiao-Tung University, Taiwan

ABSTRACT

The explosive proliferation of multimedia data necessitates the development of automatic systems and tools for content-based multimedia analysis. Recently, sports video analysis has been attracting more and more attention due to the potential commercial benefits, entertaining functionalities and mass audience requirements. Much research on shot classification, highlight extraction and event detection in sports video has been done to provide the general audience interactive video viewing systems for quick browsing, indexing and summarization. More keenly than ever, the audience desire professional insights into the games. The coach and the players demand automatic tactics analysis and performance evaluation with the aid of multimedia information retrieval technologies. It is also a growing trend to provide computer-assisted umpiring in sports games, such as the well-known Hawk eye system used in tennis. Therefore, sports video analysis is certainly a research issue worth investigation. In this chapter, the authors propose to review current research and give an insight into sports video analysis. The discussion on potential applications and encouraging future work is also presented.

1. INTRODUCTION

The advances in video production technology and the consumer demand have led to the ever-increasing volume of multimedia information. The rapid evolution of digital equipments allows the general users to archive multimedia data much easier. The urgent requirements for multimedia applications therefore motivate the researches in various aspects of video analysis for content-based multimedia information retrieval.

DOI: 10.4018/978-1-61692-859-9.ch012

Recently, sports video is attracting considerable attention due to potential commercial benefits and entertaining functionalities. There has been lots of research directed toward automatic indexing and summarization of broadcast sports video. As the pace of life in the information society accelerates, most viewers desire to retrieve the significant events or designated scenes and players, rather than watch a whole game in a sequential way. Various algorithms of shot classification and highlight extraction in sports video have been developed based on the combination of low-level visual/auditory features and game-specific rules. Some research efforts focus on ball/player tracking for event detection, since semantic events are mainly caused by ball-player and player-player interactions.

Most existing works in sports video analysis are audience-oriented. However, more keenly than ever, the audience desire professional insights into the games. The coach and the players demand automatic tactics analysis and performance evaluation with the aid of multimedia information retrieval technologies. Traditional interactive video viewing systems which provide quick browsing, indexing and summarization of sports video no longer fulfill their requirements. The professionals prefer better understanding of the tactic patterns and statistical data so that they are able to improve performance and better adapt the operational policy during the game. To achieve this purpose, the current trend is to employ some personnel for game annotation, match recording, tactics analysis and statistics collection. However, it is obviously time-consuming and labor-intensive. Hence, automatic tactics analysis and statistics collection in sports games via video analysis technology are undoubtedly compelling.

In this chapter, we propose to review current research and take baseball for example to give an insight into sports video analysis. The rest of this chapter is organized as follows. Section 2 reviews the related work on sports video analysis. Section 3 elaborates the baseball video analysis work with applications (Chen et al. 2006b; Chen et al. 2007a). Section 4 gives the further research directions and finally, section 5 concludes this chapter.

2. RELATED WORK ON SPORT VIDEO ANALYSIS

The contents of sports video are well-structured since the broadcasters present the game process in similar ways due to the game rules. Therefore, many domain-specific features and knowledge can be employed and incorporated into sports video analysis. The possible applications have been found in many kinds of sports, e.g., baseball, soccer, tennis, volleyball, etc. The major research issues are described as follows.

Shot Classification

In a sports game, the positions of cameras are fixed around the field and each camera has a specific assignment for broadcasting the game. The rules of presenting the game progress are similar in different channels. The broadcasting technique that a few dominant shots constitute most parts of a sports game leads to the requirement of *shot classification*. Duan et al. (2003 & 2005) employ a supervised learning scheme to perform a top-down shot classification based on mid-level representations, including motion vector field model, color tracking model and shot pace model. Hua et al. (2002) integrate color distribution, edge distribution, camera motion, sound effects and closed captions with maximum entropy scheme to classify baseball scenes. Kumano et al. (2005) divide a frame into blocks and analyze the mean, variance and log variance of the luminosity within each block for pitch scene discrimination. Lu and Tan (2003) propose a recursive peer-group filtering scheme to identify prototypical shots for each dominant scene, and examine time coverage of these prototypical shots to decide the number of dominant scenes for each sports video. Mochizuki et al. (2005) provide a baseball indexing method based on patternizing baseball scenes using a set of rectangles with some image features and a motion vector.

Highlight Extraction

To provide the audience a quick browse of the game, *highlight extraction* attempts to abstract a long game into a compact summary. Assfalg et al. (2003) present a system for automatic annotation of highlights in soccer video. Domain knowledge is encoded into a set of finite state machines, each of which models a specific highlight. The visual cues used for highlight detection are ball motion, playfield zone, players' position and colors of players' uniforms. Xie et al. (2004) utilize dominant color ratio and motion intensity to model the structure of soccer video based on the special syntax and content characteristics of soccer video. Ekin et al. (2003) integrate low-level algorithms, such as dominant color region detection, shot boundary detection and shot classification, with higher-level algorithms for goal detection, referee detection and penalty-box detection. Summaries (highlights) are generated using cinematic features and object-based features. Zhu et al. (2007a) present a multimodal approach to organize the highlights extracted from racket sports video based on human behavior analysis using a nonlinear affective ranking model.

Many research efforts of highlight extraction work on the baseball domain. Rui et al. (2000) propose an approach utilizing audio features, including energy, Mel-frequency cepstral coefficients, entropy and pitch, to accomplish human speech endpoint detection, ball hit detection and excited human speech modeling in baseball video. Cheng and Hsu (2006) fuse visual motion information with audio features, including zero crossing rate, pitch period and Mel-frequency cepstral coefficients, to extract baseball highlight based on hidden Markov model. Han et al. (2003) and Gong et al. (2004) classify baseball highlights by integrating image, audio and speech cues using a framework based on maximum entropy model (MEM). Chang et al. (2002) utilize the transition of image features in each frame for automatic video indexing with hidden Markov model (HMM).

Chen et al. (2007c) present a novel method to reduce a baseball video sequence from one batter to the next batter into a compact *pitch-by-pitch* highlight clip. The concept of pitch-by-pitch extraction is shown in Figure 1. First, batter change events are detected via superimposed caption recognition for producing batter-to-batter clips. Then, ball trajectories are extracted based on the spatial-temporal relationship of the ball candidates detected over frames. Finally, trajectory information is used to approximate the pitcher's motion degree to select the frames for pitch-by-pitch highlight generation.

Trajectory-Based Analysis

Object tracking is widespread used in sports analysis. Since significant events are mainly caused by ball-player and player-player interactions, balls and players are tracked most frequently. Yu et al. (2003 & 2006) present a trajectory-based algorithm for ball detection and tracking in soccer video. The ball size is first estimated from feature objects (the goalmouth and ellipse) to detect ball candidates. Potential trajectories are generated from ball candidates by a Kalman filter based verification procedure. The true ball trajectories are finally selected from the potential trajectories according to a confidence index, which indicates the likelihood that a potential trajectory is a ball trajectory. With the extracted ball trajectory, the actions of ball touching and passing are detected and the team ball possession is analyzed. Zhu et al. (2007b) analyze the temporal-spatial interaction among the ball and players to construct a tactic rep-

Figure 1. Concept of pitch-by-pitch extraction

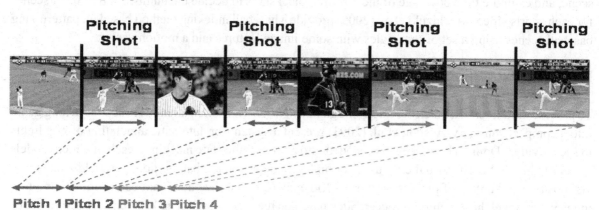

resentation called *aggregate trajectory* based on multiple trajectories. The interactive relationship with play region information and hypothesis testing for trajectory temporal-spatial distribution are exploited to analyze the tactic patterns. Wang et al. (2005) use the ball trajectory and landing position as features to classify tennis games into 58 winning patterns. Shum and Komura (2004) track the baseball using dynamic programming and estimate the 3D ball trajectory from single view video sequences based on the physical characteristics of the ball motion.

Despite a lot of research efforts in sports video processing, little work was done in volleyball video analysis due to the high density of players on the court and the complicated overlapping of player-player or ball-player, which lead to great complexity of object tracking for advanced analysis. For ball detection and trajectory extraction in volleyball video, Chen et al. (2007b) present a physics-based scheme which utilizes the motion characteristics to extract ball trajectory from lots of moving objects. The block diagram of the volleyball tracking work with applications to set type recognition and action detection is illustrated in Figure 2. The volleyball tracking work detects the court lines, performs camera calibration and then proportionally estimates the ball size from the distance of the court line intersections. Many false ball candidates can be discarded by the ball size constraint. The distribution of the remaining ball candidates over frames is analyzed to identify the true ball trajectory. Finally, set type recognition and

Figure 2. Block diagram of the volleyball tracking work with set type recognition and action detection

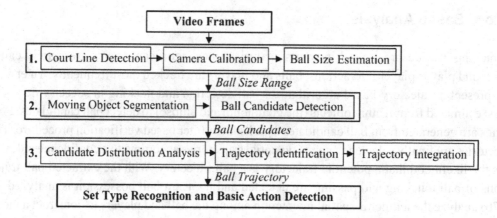

Figure 3. Illustration of set type diagram

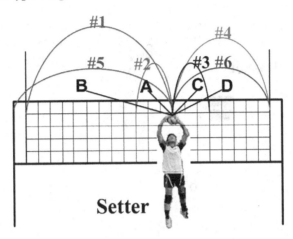

basic action detection can be done based on the obtained trajectory. In volleyball games, *attack* is the most effective way to gain points and the *set type* dominates the attack. Therefore, set type recognition is crucial for tactics analysis. Figure 3 illustrates of ten common set types and Figure 4 demonstrates ball tracking, action detection and set type classification in volleyball video.

In basketball, shooting is one of the important scoring events. Chen et al. (2009a) and Tien et al. (2007) confront the challenge of ball tracking and 3D trajectory reconstruction in broadcast basketball video in order to automatically gather the game statistics of *shooting locations*. Shooting location, the location where a player shoots the ball, is one of the important game statistics providing abundant information about the shooting tendency of a basketball team. An example of statistical graph for shooting locations is given in Figure 5, where each shooting location is marked as an **O** (score) or **X** (miss). The statistical graph for shooting locations not only provides the audience rich information about the game but also assists the coach in guiding the defense strategy. With the statistical graph for shooting locations, the coach is able to view the distribution of shooting locations at a glance and to quickly comprehend where the players have higher possibility of scoring by shooting. Thus, the coach can enhance the defense

Figure 4. Demonstration of ball tracking, action detection and set type classification in volleyball video. (a) Serve. (b) Reception. (c) Set. (d) Attack

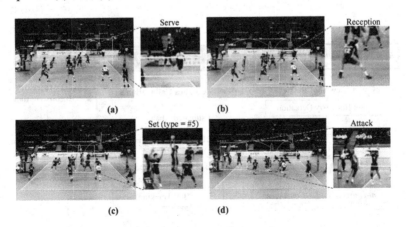

Figure 5. Statistical graph of shooting locations

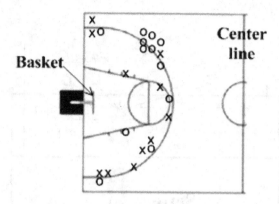

strategy of the team by preventing the opponents from shooting at the locations they stand a good chance of scoring. Increasing basketball websites, such as NBA official website, provide text- and image-based web-casting, including game log, match report, shooting location and other game statistics. However, these tasks are achieved by manual efforts. It is time-consuming and inefficient to watch a whole long video, take records and gather statistics. Hence, Chen et al. propose a physics-based ball tracking system for 3D trajectory reconstruction so that automatic shooting location estimation and statistics gathering can be achieved. Whether the shooting action gains points or not can be derived from the change of the scoreboard by close caption detection technique (Chen et al., 2006a). Thus, the statistical graph of shooting locations, as Figure 5, can be generated automatically.

Figure 6 shows the flowchart of the system for ball tracking and 3D trajectory reconstruction in basketball video. Basketball video contains several prototypical shots: close-up view, medium view, court view and out-of-court view. The system starts with *court shot retrieval*, because court shots can present complete shooting trajectories. Then, *2D ball trajectory extraction* is performed on the retrieved court shots based on visual features and the velocity constraint. To reconstruct 3D trajectories from 2D ones, the motion equations are set up with the parameters: velocities and initial positions, to define the 3D trajectories based on physical characteristics. The 3D ball positions over frames can be represented

Figure. 6. Flowchart of the proposed system for ball tracking and 3D trajectory reconstruction in basketball video

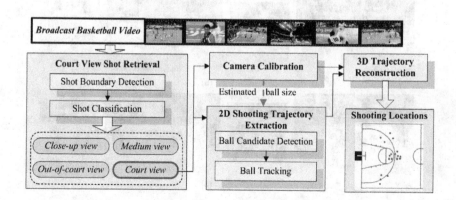

by equations. *Camera Calibration*, which provides the geometric transformation from 3D to 2D, is used to map the equation-represented 3D ball positions to 2D ball coordinates in frames. With the 2D ball coordinates over frames being known, the parameters of the 3D motion equations can be approximated. Finally, the 3D positions and velocities of the ball can be derived. Having the reconstructed 3D information, the shooting locations can be estimated more accurately from 3D trajectories than from 2D trajectories, which lack the z-coordinate (height) of ball.

The major contribution of this work is that 3D information is constructed from single view 2D video sequences based on the integration of multimedia features, basketball domain knowledge and the physical characteristics of ball motion. Besides, trajectory-based high-level basketball video analysis is also provided. The 3D ball trajectories facilitate the automatic collection of game statistics about shooting locations in basketball, which greatly help the coaches and professionals to infer the *shooting tendency* of a team.

Computed-Assisted Umpiring Based on Multiple Cameras

The players and professional personnel desire assistance for umpiring with high technology. *Computer-assisted umpiring* not only improves the fairness of the games but also promotes the level of the sports, which would attract more audience and bring in more commercial benefits. Hence, researchers invest considerable efforts in this area.

Having been used in Wimbledon 2003, Hawk-Eye system (Owens et al., 2004) produces computer-generated replays viewed through 360 degrees to illustrate the game by taking into account the trajectory, skid and compression of the ball. 2D tracking is first performed on each of the specifically-located cameras. These 2D tracks are then sent to a 3D reconstitution module to construct the 3D tracks, and impact points between separate tracks (might occur at a bounce or a strike) are determined. Finally, the complete track is visualized for display and analysis.

ESPN K-Zone system (Gueziec, 2002) extracts the trajectory for each pitch and uses computer-generated graphics to create a shaded, translucent box which outlines the strike zone boundaries for viewers. Two cameras linked to two PCs are used to observe the ball and each PC extracts a 2-D trajectory using Kalman filtering. Communicating over a local Ethernet connection, the two pitch-tracking computers combine two 2-D positions which correspond to the same time code into a 3-D position. Then, the successive 3-D positions are fed into another Kalman filter to determine the final trajectory. An operator uses a third camera and PC to locate the strike zone's top and bottom boundaries for each batter. Finally, the system reports the baseball trajectory's point of impact with the plane of strike zone and draws the intersection on the TV screen.

QuesTec (2007) provides UIS (Umpire Information System) to support the previously announced strike zone initiatives of MLB (Major League Baseball). Two remote-controlled cameras are mounted in the stands off the first- and third-base lines to track each pitch. The entire process includes detection of the start of the pitch, tracking of the ball, location computations, and identification of non-baseball objects moving through the field of view. The ball's movement inside a 3-D space in front of the pitcher is tracked. The speed, placement and curvature of the pitch along its path are also measured. Two other cameras are placed low and close to the field for measuring the batter's strike zone. Thus, whether a pitch is in or out of the strike zone can be judged. Moreover, a 3-D view of the ball from the pitcher's release until it crosses the homeplate is created for the viewers.

Other Semantic Sports Video Analysis

Luo et al. (2003) interpret and analyze human motion in sports video using video object extraction, semantic event modeling and the Dynamic Bayesian Network (DBN) for characterizing the spatial-temporal nature of the semantic objects. Zhu et al. (2007a & 2007c) recognize the player actions by considering the movement of body parts for semantic and tactic analysis in tennis video. The *affective* features which simulate a user's emotion are extracted from player actions and trajectories for highlight ranking. Xu et al. (2008) incorporate web-casting text into sports video analysis for semantic annotation and personalized retrieval. Personalized summary from general or specific viewpoints related to a particular game, event, player or team is created according to user's preference. Bertini et al. (2006) perform automatic annotation of soccer video based on camera motion, playfield zone and players' positions. Different coding strategies are applied to different video parts according to the relative importance for content-based compression.

Despite a lot of research efforts in baseball video processing, little work has been done in analyzing the detailed process and ball movement of the batting content. Chen et al. (2008) propose a novel system to automatically summarize the progress of each batting in baseball video. The flowchart of the proposed baseball exploration system is shown in Figure 7. For a given baseball video sequence, the *field shots*, in which the camera follows the batted ball in the field, are first segmented. Then, the visual features in a field shot are extracted via analyzing the distribution of dominant colors and white pixels. As depicted in Figure 8, the baseball field is characterized by a well-defined layout of specific colors. Utilizing the baseball domain knowledge, the field lines and field objects are detected: *left line (LL)*, *right line (RL), pitcher's mound (PM), home base (HB), first base(1B), second base (2B), third base (3B)* and *auditorium (AT)*, as shown in Figure 9.

In order to comprehend the detailed content of ball movement and region transition, the *play region*, the currently focused region in the baseball field, is recognized via classifying each field frame into one of the twelve typical play region categories: IL (infield left), IC (infield center), IR (infield right), B1 (first base), B2 (second base), B3 (third base), OL (outfield left), OC (outfield center), OR (outfield

Figure 7. Framework of the proposed baseball exploration system

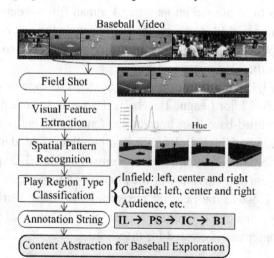

Figure 8. Prototypical baseball field: (a) Full view of a real baseball field (b) Illustration of field objects and lines

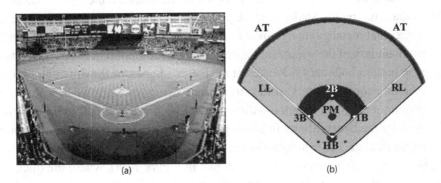

right), PS (player in soil), PG (player in grass) and AD (audience), as shown in Figure 10. Finally, an annotation string which describes the transition of play regions is generated from each field shot to abstract the content of the batting.

Figure 9. Detection of field lines and field objects

Figure 10. Twelve play region categories

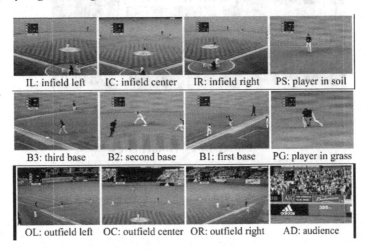

On the other hand, Chen et al. (2009b & 2009 c) also present a contour-based approach for strike zone shaping and visualization in broadcast baseball video. In baseball, the pitch content usually dominates the game situation, and the *strike zone* plays a crucial role in each pitch. In baseball rules, the strike zone is a conceptual rectangular area over the *home plate* through which a pitch passing is judged as a *strike*. The top boundary of the strike zone is defined as the midpoint between the batter's shoulders and the belt, and the bottom boundary is located at the batter's knees, as illustrated in Figure 11. To gain strikes, pitchers should acquire mastery of the strike zone. Moreover, the strike zone also provides the reference for positioning the pitch location—the relative location of the ball in/around the strike zone when the ball passes by the batter. Sports fans and professionals have a fervent interest in the statistical information about the pitches. For example, the sequence of pitches which a pitcher uses to face a batter can be summarized as a *pitch location image*, as shown in Figure 12(a), where the thick rectangle represents the strike zone, the circles mark the pitch locations and the numbers indicate the order of the pitches. After accumulating a mass of pitches, the statistics of the pitch locations can be compiled and visualized as Figure 12(b), where the number in each region is the count of pitches thrown in the region.

Figure 13 illustrates the proposed strike zone shaping work. The home plate is first detected, which determines the vertical boundaries of the strike zone, in the pitch scene. With the specifications of the baseball field, the *batter boxes* can be proportionally estimated from the home plate width. Then, the batter is contoured in the *batter region* (BR), which is outlined above the batter box, and locate the feature points (shoulders, hip and knees) on the batter's contour to set the top and bottom boundaries of the strike zone. The hip is located instead of the belt, because the belt is not obvious and the top of the hip has about the same y-coordinate as the belt. Since the algorithms are contour-based, the strike zone can be shaped adaptively to the batter's stance no matter what color of the uniform the batter is dressed in. Finally, strike zone shaping and visualization enrich the viewing experience of baseball games.

Manifold interesting sports video analyses have been proposed in various sports domains. In the following section, we take baseball for example to give a further insight into sports video analysis.

Figure 11. Illustration of strike zone definition and batter regions

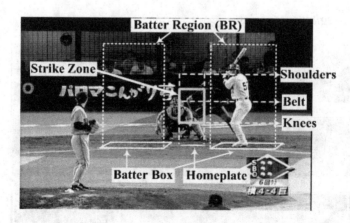

Figure 12. Visualization of statistical data about the pitches

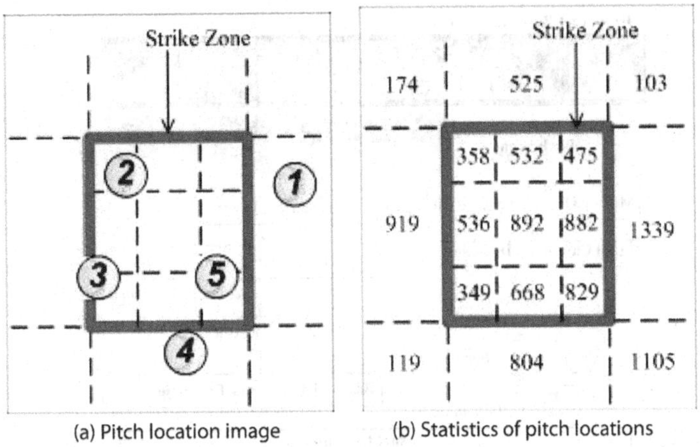

(a) Pitch location image

(b) Statistics of pitch locations

3. TRAJECTORY-BASED BALL TRACKING WITH VISUAL ENRICHMENT IN BROADCAST BASEBALL VIDEO

In baseball games, pitching contents play the key role in the resultant victory or defeat. In this section, we propose to elaborate the work (Chen et al. 2006b; Chen et al. 2007a): trajectory-based ball tracking and pitching evaluation in broadcast baseball video.

Overview of the Trajectory-Based Ball Tracking Method

Based on the game-specific properties and visual features, a trajectory-based ball tracking method in broadcast baseball video is proposed, as depicted in Figure 14. First, moving objects in each frame are segmented. Each frame then generates *ball candidates* including the ball and some ball-like objects which

Figure 13. Block diagram of the proposed strike zone shaping

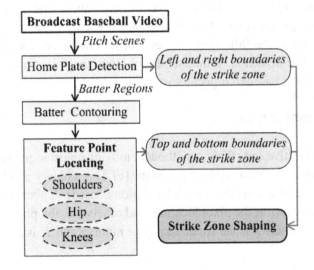

Figure 14. Block diagram of the ball tracking method with visual enrichment

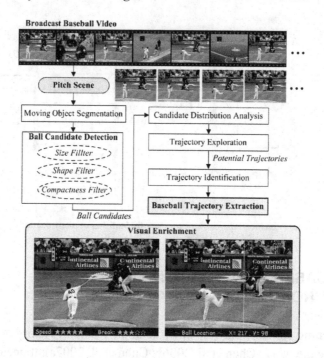

satisfy the constraints of size, shape and compactness. Identifying whether a single object is a ball within a single frame is difficult due to the ball deformation or noises. Therefore, the physical characteristic of ball motion that the ball moves parabolically helps to identify whether a *potential trajectory* is the true ball trajectory. The X- and Y-distributions of ball candidates in a sequence of frames are analyzed to explore the trajectory which fulfills the physical characteristic. Finally, the baseball trajectory is extracted and the ball position in each frame can be located. In addition, visual enrichment and pitching evaluation can be presented based on the extracted ball trajectory.

There are two key contributions in this work. The first is a trajectory-based ball tracking scheme which allows the ball trajectory to be extracted reliably by utilizing the physical characteristics of ball motion, even though there are many ball-like objects in each frame. The second is a trajectory-based pitching evaluation which provides speed estimation and breaking measurement to the audience for enriched visual presentation. In the following, we describe in turn the processing stages: moving object segmentation, ball candidate detection, candidate distribution analysis, trajectory exploration, trajectory identification and finally, baseball trajectory extraction.

Moving Object Segmentation

Frame differencing is an effective and efficient method for moving object segmentation since there is little camera motion in pitch shots. A *Frame Difference Image* (FDI) is a binary image formed by comparing every two successive frames (here the intensity information is used). A pixel value of FDI is set to 255 if a significant difference occurs at the pixel location, and otherwise, the pixel value of FDI is set to 0, as defined in Equation (1), where n is the frame sequence number and T_d is a threshold.

$$FDI_n(x,y) = \begin{cases} 255, & \text{if } \left|Intensity_n(x,y) - Intensity_{n-1}(x.y)\right| > T_d \\ 0 & \text{otherwise} \end{cases} \tag{1}$$

An example of moving object segmentation is shown in Figure 15. Figure 15(a) is the original frame and Figure 15(b) shows the FDI. Because FDI takes the absolute value of intensity difference between frames, the ball is included in a white region larger than the original ball size. The baseball is white and bright, so the intensity of the ball in a video frame should be higher. That is, the baseball is included in the positive regions of intensity difference between frames. Hence, the *Positive Frame Difference Image* (PFDI), defined as Equation (2), is used to effectively segment positive regions of intensity difference which contains the ball, as shown in Figure 15(c). Morphological operations are then performed to remove noises and make the regions filled, as shown in Figure 15(d). Regions formed by region growing and ball candidate will be detected among these regions in the following processing stage.

$$PFDI_n(x,y) = \begin{cases} 255, & \text{if } \left|Intensity_n(x,y) - Intensity_{n-1}(x.y)\right| > T_d \\ 0 & \text{otherwise} \end{cases} \tag{2}$$

Ball Candidate Detection

The ball in the frames might show in a shape different from a circle due to deformation. On the other hand, many non-ball objects might look like a ball. Hence, to recognize which is the true one is a difficult task. The following filters based on visual features are designed to sieve out the ball candidates from the moving objects. After sieving, the remaining objects which satisfy the constraints are considered as the *ball candidates*.

Figure 15. Illustration of segmenting the moving objects where the ball is included

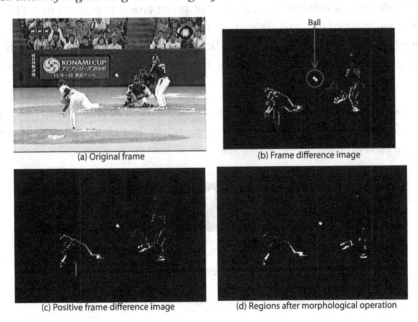

(a) Original frame

(b) Frame difference image

(c) Positive frame difference image

(d) Regions after morphological operation

Size Filter: Even though the ball size would vary due to the capturing conditions of cameras and the ball deformation, it should fall within a specific range. The size filter discards the moving objects whose sizes are out of a pre-defined range.

Shape Filter: The ball might have a shape different from a circle in a frame, but the deformation is not so dramatic. Therefore, the shape filter discards the objects with aspect ratios out of a pre-defined range.

Compactness Filter: An object in a different shape (star-shaped, cross-shaped, triangular, etc.) may pass through the size filter and shape filter because of its acceptable size and proper aspect ratio. For this reason, the compactness filter is built to further remove those objects with the degree of compactness D_c less than a threshold T_c (D_c less than half cannot be claimed to be "compact", so T_c is set to 50%). The degree of compactness D_c is defined in Equation (3). Objects with low D_c would be filtered out while objects with high D_c would be retained, as shown in Figure 16.

$$D_c = \text{object size} / \text{bounding box area} \qquad (3)$$

Thus, the ball candidates (the remaining objects sifted through the filters) are obtained. During a pitch, the ball is at a distance away from other moving objects in most frames, so the candidates close to other moving objects might be over-segmented regions of the pitcher or the batter. To improve the accuracy of ball tracking, the ball candidates are classified into *isolated* and *contacted* candidates according to their nearest objects in the frame. A ball candidate is classified as *isolated* if there exists no neighboring object within a distance shorter than the average ball size and it is classified as *contacted*, otherwise.

Candidate Distribution Analysis

The distributions of ball candidates in both Y- and X- directions are analyzed to explore the trajectory more reliably. Figure 17(a) presents the 2D distribution of ball candidates. The *y-t* distribution, YTD, plots the y-coordinate of each ball candidate over time (indexed by the frame serial number *n*). For each isolated (or contacted) candidate, a black dot (or green cross) is marked in YTD at point (n, y_c), where y_c is the y-coordinate of the candidate in the frame. The left-bottom corner of the frame is taken as the origin for presentation clarity of the parabolic curves. Similarly, the *x-t* distribution, XTD, plots the x-coordinate of each ball candidate over time. For each isolated (or contacted) candidate, a black

Figure 16. Illustration of the compactness filter: (a) Compactness degree D_c is defined as the ratio of the object size to the area of the bounding box. (b) Objects with low D_c would be removed while objects with high D_c would be retained

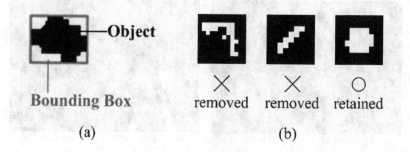

(a)   (b)

dot (or green cross) is marked in XTD at point (n, x_c), where x_c is the x-coordinate of the candidate in the frame. The motion characteristics of ball candidates in both vertical and horizontal directions can be clearly perceived in YTD and XTD.

Trajectory Exploration

In fact, the ball trajectory may not be a perfect parabolic curve. However, the effectiveness and efficiency of ball tracking can be improved by utilizing the motion characteristics. A *potential trajectory* is explored via finding a sequence of ball candidates which form a near parabolic curve in YTD and a near straight line in XTD concurrently. The prediction functions for YTD and XTD are modeled as Equation (4) and Equation (5).

$$y = a \bullet n^2 + b \bullet n + c, a < 0 \tag{4}$$

$$x = d \bullet n + e \tag{5}$$

Figure 17. Illustration of the y-t and x-t distributions for different process stages. In the figure, n is the frame serial number, y_c in YTD and x_c in XTD are the y- and x-coordinates of each candidate in the original frame, respectively

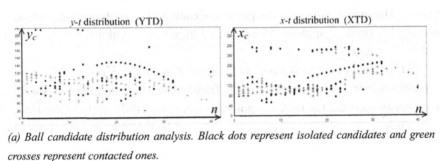

(a) Ball candidate distribution analysis. Black dots represent isolated candidates and green crosses represent contacted ones.

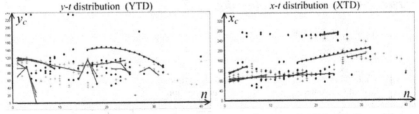

(b) Trajectory exploration. Potential trajectories are shown as the linked ball candidates.

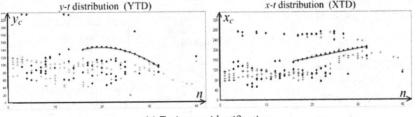

(c) Trajectory identification.

The procedure of trajectory exploration is summarized in Figure 18. All ball candidates are first linked to the nearest neighbor in the next frame. The ball position in the next frame can be predicted by the prediction functions. The prediction is considered *matched* if a ball candidate close to the predicted position is found. The trajectory then grows by adding the candidate found and the prediction functions are updated by re-computing the optimal approximate function for the coordinates of the candidates detected so far. If there exists no candidate close to the predicted position, the frame is regarded as a *missing frame* and the predicted position is taken as the ball position. Trajectory growing terminates when the number of consecutive missing frames reaches a predefined limit. The potential trajectories produced from this procedure are shown as the linking of ball candidates in YTD and XTD, as depicted in Figure 17(b).

Trajectory Identification

Given the set of potential trajectories, the next step is to identify the true ball trajectory. Most of the false trajectories can be removed by the following properties: *trajectory length, estimation error* and the *ratio of isolated candidates over all candidates on the trajectory.*

Trajectory length: The distance between the pitcher and the catcher in the baseball field is strictly defined in the rule (about 18.39 meters). It takes about 367.8 ms for a ball to fly from the pitcher to the catcher at the speed of 180 km/h. That is, a ball trajectory would last for at least 11 frames. To the best of our knowledge, the highest ball speed in baseball games is no more than 170 km/h. Hence, the potential trajectories shorter than 11 frames can be discarded.

Prediction error: The average distance (in pixels) of each ball candidate position from the predicted position is considered as *prediction error*. The potential trajectories with prediction error greater than a threshold would be eliminated.

Ratio of isolated candidates over all candidates on the trajectory: Since the pitched ball is at a distance away from other moving objects in most of the frames, the true ball trajectory should contain more isolated candidates than contacted ones. On a potential trajectory, if the ratio of the isolated candidates over all candidates is less than 50%, the trajectory could not be the true one and should be discarded.

Figure 18. Procedure of ball trajectory exploration

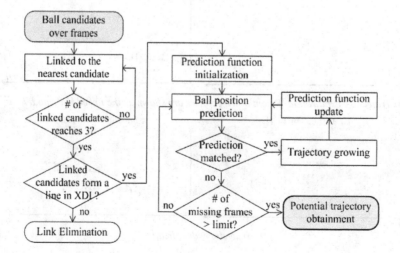

After the elimination process, much fewer potential trajectories remain. Among the remaining potential trajectories, the trajectory with the longest *length of consecutive isolated candidates* is identified as the ball trajectory. Figure 17(c) shows the final ball trajectory after trajectory identification.

Baseball Trajectory Extraction

The scheme of baseball trajectory extraction is summarized in Figure 19. First, the moving objects with high intensity are segmented out. Utilizing the constraints of size, shape and compactness, ball candidates are detected from the segmented moving objects. The distributions of ball candidates in both Y- and X-directions are analyzed. Then, the ball trajectory is identified from the potential trajectories based on the properties of trajectory length, prediction error, the ratio of isolated candidates over all candidates on the trajectory and the length of consecutive isolated candidates. Finally, the ball position in each frame is computed and the extracted trajectory can be superimposed on the frame for enriched visual presentation.

Trajectory-Based Pitching Evaluation and Visual Enrichment

The audience desires to perceive comprehensive information about games. With the baseball trajectory extracted, pitch evaluation, such as *speed estimation* and *breaking measurement*, can be achieved.

Speed Estimation: The distance from the pitcher's mound to the home plate is strictly defined in the game rules. Hence, as defined in Equation (6), the ball speed (*Ball_Speed* in km/h) can be computed via dividing the distance from the pitcher's mound to the home plate (18.39 m = 0.01839 km) by the

Figure 19. Summarization of baseball trajectory extraction

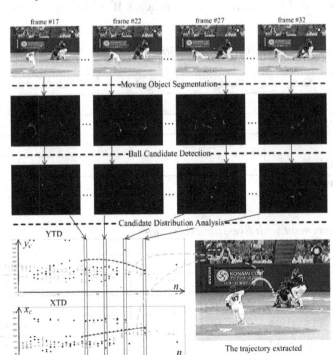

time interval of the ball trajectory (*frame#* in frame). The ball speed estimation and the five-star evaluation are given in Table 1, which lists the time interval of the trajectory, the estimated ball speed and the respective evaluation.

$$Ball\_Speed~(km~/~h) = \frac{0.01839~(km)}{(frame\#~/~30~/~3600)~(h)} \tag{6}$$

Breaking Measurement: A *breaking ball* is a pitch which does not travel straight like a *fastball*, and it would have a sudden drop when approaching the batter. The more the drop height is, the harder the batter can hit the ball. Hence, the drop height is measured by utilizing the curvature of the parabolic curve, the coefficient *a* in Equation (4), in YTD. The breaking measurement and the five-star evaluation are given in Table 2, where the larger the curvature of the trajectory | *a* | is, the higher the evaluation is.

The pitching evaluation in this work aims at providing visual enrichment for entertainment effects based on the ball trajectory. In fact, there are no regulations about how fast a pitched ball can be considered as five-star or what the curvature of a five-star breaking ball is in baseball rules. Thus, the parameter settings, supported by experienced experts in baseball games, in Table 1 and Table 2 for speed estimation and breaking measurement are comparative values, not absolute values.

Two examples of the trajectory-based pitching evaluation and visual enrichment are demonstrated in Figure 20. Figure 20(a) is a MLB (Major League Baseball) pitch shot with a right-handed pitcher and a right-handed batter, who swings at the ball. Figure 20(b) is a MLB pitch shot with a left-handed pitcher and a left-handed batter, who does not swing. In the left figure of each example, the enriched frame shows the sight when the pitcher is about to throw the ball. The superimposed trajectory clearly presents the ball motion of the pitch. In addition, the pitching evaluation displayed at the bottom of the frame provides more details about the pitch. In the right figure of each example, the final ball location of the trajectory is spotlighted with a crosshair (or reticle). If the batter swings at the pitched ball, the

Table 1. Ball speed estimation with five-star evaluation

Frame#	Ball_Speed (km/h)	Evaluation	Frame#	Ball_Speed (km/h)	Evaluation
12	164	★★★★★	17	116	★★☆☆☆
13	151	★★★★☆	18	109	★★☆☆☆
14	141	★★★☆☆	19	104	★☆☆☆☆
15	131	★★★☆☆	20	98	★☆☆☆☆
16	123	★★☆☆☆	21	94	★☆☆☆☆

Table 2. Breaking measurement with five-star evaluation

Curvature: |a|	Evaluation
|a| > 0.5	★★★★★
0.4 < |a| ≤ 0.5	★★★★☆
0.3 < |a| ≤ 0.4	★★★☆☆
0.2 < |a| ≤ 0.3	★★☆☆☆
|a| ≤ 0.2	★☆☆☆☆

Figure 20. Demonstration of trajectory-based pitching evaluation and visual enrichment. Left: the super-imposed ball trajectory and pitching evaluation. Right: the final ball location spotlighted with a crosshair

(a) MLB (Major League Baseball) pitch shot with a right-handed pitcher
and a right-handed batter who swings at the ball

(b) MLB pitch shot with a left-handed pitcher and
a left-handed batter who does not swing

enriched frame catches up and reflects the situation how the ball is hit or missed, as demonstrated in the right of Figure 20(a). On the other hand, in baseball rules the *strike zone* is defined as that area over the homeplate the upper limit of which is a horizontal line at the midpoint between the shoulders and the belt, and the lower limit is a line at the knees. Hence, if the batter does not swing, the crosshair can provide a reference for the strike/ball judgment, as shown in the right of Figure 20(b). Moreover, the ball trajectory and the final ball location can also provide assistant information for the professional personnel to infer the tactics which each pitcher usually adopts in specific situations, such as "the pitcher prefers throwing a breaking ball to the inside corner of the strike zone when there are runner(s) on the base(s) and a fast ball to the outside corner when there is no runner."

Experimental Results

The ball tracking work has been tested on broadcast baseball videos (352 x 240, MPEG-1) of MLB, JPB and CPBL captured from different sports channels, as listed in Table 3. Note that only pitch shots are processed. The ball position in each video frame is manually recognized as *ground truth*. A ground truth ball is called "detected" if it matches a ball candidate. A ground truth ball falling on the obtained trajectory is called "tracked", since the ball position can be predicted on the trajectory by the motion

Table 3. Testing video used in the experiments

Baseball video	Source channel
MLB (Major League Baseball)	PTS channel of Taiwan
JPB (Japan Professional Baseball)	NHK channel of Japan
CPBL (Chinese Professional Baseball League)	VL sports channel of Taiwan

Figure 21. Illustration of ball detection and ball tracking

(a) Ball detection. Ball is missed in two frames when passing over the white uniform

(b) Ball tracking. Missed ball positions can be recovered by applying the predicted positions of the obtained trajectory

characteristics even though it does not match a ball candidate. The experimental results of ball detection and tracking are reported in Table 4, where "video" represents the video sources, "pitch shot" shows the number of pitch shots, "total frames" represents the number of total frames in all pitch shots and "ball frame" represents the number of the frames containing the ball. The row "ball detected (%)" gives the number (percentage) of balls detected, "false alarm" gives the number of false-detected ball positions, and "ball tracked (%)" gives the number (percentage) of balls tracked.

Some misses occur because the ball might not be detected when it passes over a left-handed batter in a white uniform. Fortunately, the missed ball position can be recovered via position prediction of the trajectory. An example of ball detection is shown in Figure 21(a). In the example, the ball is missed in two frames when passing over the white uniform. Figure 21(b) presents the ball tracking result. The missed ball position can be recovered via ball position prediction of the obtained trajectory. Although there are some tracking errors, the proposed scheme promotes the accuracy of ball tracking up to 96%, overall. Some examples of ball tracking with visual enrichment are demonstrated in Figure 22. The ball tracking work performs well in baseball video from different channels, no matter whether the pitcher/batter is left- or right- handed.

Table 4. Performance of ball detection and tracking

Video	MLB	JPB	CPBL	Overall
Pitch shot	30	32	24	86
Total frame	1380	2089	942	4411
Ball frame	424	466	352	1242
Ball detected (%)	387 (91.27%)	435 (93.35%)	326 (92.61%)	1148(92.43%)
False alarm	11	12	7	30
Ball tracked (%)	409 (96.46%)	453 (97.21%)	338 (96.02%)	1200(96.62%)

Figure 22. Demonstration of ball tracking and visual enrichment in various baseball videos

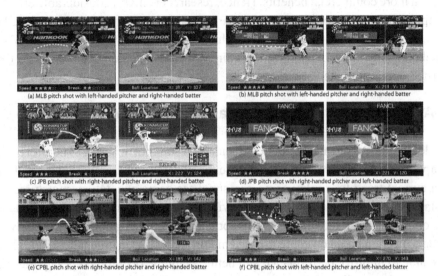

(a) MLB pitch shot with left-handed pitcher and right-handed batter

(b) MLB pitch shot with left-handed pitcher and right-handed batter

(c) JPB pitch shot with right-handed pitcher and right-handed batter

(d) JPB pitch shot with right-handed pitcher and left-handed batter

(e) CPBL pitch shot with right-handed pitcher and right-handed batter

(f) CPBL pitch shot with left-handed pitcher and left-handed batter

Summarization of the Trajectory-Based Ball Tracking Work

Since pitching contents are the crucial factors of the resultant victory or defeat in a baseball game, the professional personnel and the audience urgently require advanced information about the pitches. Ball tracking in baseball videos is a challenging task due to the small size and high speed of the ball. In this work, ball tracking is achieved by applying the physical characteristic of ball motion. Trajectory-based pitching evaluation and visual enrichment can be provided in near real-time before the next pitch coming up.

The methods described can be further adapted to other kinds of sports. For example, the ball detection algorithm can be adapted for detecting the ball in basketball, volleyball or other sports videos via adjusting the ball size filter. Moreover, the trajectory exploration method can be adapted for object tracking in other kinds of videos via modeling different motion characteristics with appropriate prediction functions. That is, the proposed methods not only perform well for ball tracking in different kinds of sports videos but also can be well adapted for object tracking in other kinds of videos. Overall, the described methods have good adaptability.

FUTURE RESEARCH DIRECTIONS

The future research directions of sports video analysis are manifold. By content-based media analysis, we refer to research in the following areas.

Computer-Assisted Umpiring

Umpiring with the assistance of computer technology is a growing trend. Computer-assisted umpiring not only improves the fairness of the games but also promotes the sports level, which attracts more audience and brings in more commercial benefits. Hence, researchers invest considerable efforts in this area. Currently, computer-assisted umpiring systems have been developed and have worked well in tennis and baseball games. However, different kinds of sports have their respective domain knowledge. Except for tennis and baseball, many kinds of sports still require researchers to delve into this area for developing computer-assisted umpiring systems.

Computer-Aided Game Strategy Study and Competitive Intelligence Collection

The more you know the opponents, the better chance you stand of winning. Therefore, game strategy study and competitive intelligence collection before the play is of vital importance for the coaches and players. It is a current trend to employ some personnel for game annotation, match recording, tactics analysis and statistics collection. However, it is obviously time-consuming and labor-intensive. Hence, developing automatic or semi-automatic systems for computer-aided game strategy study and competitive intelligence collection based on content-based media analysis is in urgent demand. The coaches and players will be able to improve performance and better adapt the operational policy during the game.

On the other hand, not all of the sports games are broadcasted on TV. As the rapid evolution of digital equipments, general users are allowed to capture the video more easily. It is common nowadays for sports professionals to set up a camera to capture the games they are interested in for game strategy study. Hence, besides broadcast sports video, analyzing the user-captured sports video is another practical research direction.

Integrated Sports Game Analysis System

The majority of existing sports video analysis focuses on single task, such as shot classification, event detection and object tracking. It is one future research direction to design an integrated sports game analysis system. Take baseball for example, we can combine the ball tracking work (Chen et al. 2006b; Chen et al. 2007a) with strike zone shaping (Chen et al. 2009b; Chen et al. 2009c). In this way, the pitch locations can be automatically indicated and logged. Moreover, we can involve the baseball exploration system (Chen et al., 2008) for batting content understanding. Then, we are able to further deduce the relationship between a sequence of pitch locations and the resultant batting content. An integrated sports game analysis system will be certainly appreciated by the sports professionals and the audience.

CONCLUSION

Sports content is expected to be a key driver for compelling new infotainment applications and services due to the mass requirements and specific needs. The inherent structures of sports video which are amenable for automatic processing inspire much research. In this chapter, we review the development of sports video analysis and describe several research issues, including: shot classification, highlight extraction, trajectory-based analysis, computer-assisted umpiring based on multiple cameras and other semantic sports video analysis. We also give an insight into the trajectory-based baseball tracking work. The techniques developed have many applications in video archive and retrieval, broadcasting, training, grading and entertainment. Hence, sports video analysis is a quite interesting and practical research area, worth investigation and delving into.

REFERENCES

Assfalg, J., Bertini, M., Colombo, C., Bimbo, A. D., & Nunziati, W. (2003). Semantic annotation of soccer videos: automatic highlights identification. *Computer Vision and Image Understanding*, *92*(2-3), 285–305. doi:10.1016/j.cviu.2003.06.004

Bertini, M., Cucchiara, R., Bimbo, A., & Prati, A. (2006). Semantic adaptation of sport videos with user-centred performance analysis. *IEEE Transactions on Multimedia*, *8*(3), 433–443. doi:10.1109/TMM.2006.870762

Chang, P., Han, M., & Gong, Y. (2002). Extract highlights from baseball game video with hidden Markov models. In. *Proceedings of IEEE International Conference on Image Processing*, *1*, 609–612. doi:10.1109/ICIP.2002.1038097

Chen, D. Y., Hsiao, M. H., & Lee, S. Y. (2006a). Automatic closed caption detection and filtering in MPEG videos for video structuring. *Journal of Information Science and Engineering*, *22*(5), 1145–1162.

Chen, H. S., Chen, H. T., Tsai, W. J., Lee, S. Y., & Yu, J. Y. (2007c). Pitch-By-Pitch Extraction from Single View Baseball Video Sequences. In *Proceeding of IEEE International Conference on Multimedia and Expo*, (pp. 1423-1426).

Chen, H. T., Chen, H. S., Hsiao, M. H., Chen, Y. W., & Lee, S. Y. (2006b). A trajectory-based ball tracking framework with enrichment for broadcast baseball videos. In. *Proceedings of the International Computer Symposium*, *2006*, 1145–1150.

Chen, H. T., Chen, H. S., Hsiao, M. H., Tsai, W. J., & Lee, S. Y. (2007a). A trajectory-based ball tracking framework with visual enrichment for broadcast baseball videos. *Journal of Information Science and Engineering*, *24*(1), 143–157.

Chen, H. T., Chen, H. S., & Lee, S. Y. (2007b). Physics-based ball tracking in volleyball videos with its applications to set type recognition and action detection. In *Proceedings of IEEE Int. Conference on Acoustic Speech Signal Processing*, (Vol. 1, pp. 1097-1100).

Chen, H. T., Hsiao, M. H., Chen, H. S., Tsai, W. J., & Lee, S. Y. (2008). A baseball exploration system using spatial pattern recognition. In *Proceedings of IEEE International Symposium on Circuits and Systems*, (pp. 3522-3525).

Chen, H. T., Tien, M. C., Chen, Y. W., Tsai, W. J., & Lee, S. Y. (2009a). Physics-based ball tracking and 3D trajectory reconstruction with applications to shooting location Estimation in Basketball Video. *Journal of Visual Communication and Image Representation*, *20*(3), 204–216. doi:10.1016/j.jvcir.2008.11.008

Chen, H. T., Tsai, W. J., & Lee, S. Y. (2009b). Stance-based strike zone shaping and visualization in broadcast baseball video: providing reference for pitch location positioning. In *Proceedings of International Conference on Multimedia and Expo*, (pp. 302-305).

Chen, H. T., Tsai, W. J., & Lee, S. Y. (2009c). Contour-based strike zone shaping and visualization in broadcast baseball video: providing reference for pitch location positioning and strike/ball judgment. *Multimedia Tools and Applications*, *47*(2), 239–255. doi:10.1007/s11042-009-0321-9

Cheng, C. C., & Hsu, C. T. (2006). Fusion of audio and motion information on HMM-based highlight extraction for baseball games. *IEEE Transactions on Multimedia, 8*(3), 585–599. doi:10.1109/TMM.2006.870726

Duan, L. Y., Xu, M., Chua, T. S., Tian, Q., & Xu, C.-S. (2003). A mid-level representation framework for semantic sports video analysis. In *Proceedings of 11th ACM International Conference on Multimedia,* (pp. 33- 44).

Duan, L. Y., Xu, M., & Tian, Q. (2005). A unified framework for semantic shot classification in sports video. *IEEE Transactions on Multimedia, 7*(6), 1066–1083. doi:10.1109/TMM.2005.858395

Ekin, A., Tekalp, A. M., & Mehrotra, R. (2003). Automatic soccer video analysis and summarization. *IEEE Transactions on Image Processing, 12,* 796–807. doi:10.1109/TIP.2003.812758

Gong, Y., Han, M., Hua, W., & Xu, W. (2004). Maximum entropy model-based baseball highlight detection and classification. *Computer Vision and Image Understanding, 96*(2), 181–199. doi:10.1016/j.cviu.2004.02.002

Gueziec, A. (2002). Tracking pitches for broadcast television. *Computer, 35,* 38–43. doi:10.1109/2.989928

Han, M., Hua, W., Xu, W., & Gong, Y. (2003). An integrated baseball digest system using maximum entropy method. In *Proceedings of 10th International Conference on Multimedia,* (pp. 347-350).

Hua, W., Han, M., & Gong, Y. (2002). Baseball scene classification using multimedia features. In *Proceeding of IEEE International Conference on Multimedia and Expo,* (Vol. 1, pp. 821-824).

Kumano, M., Ariki, Y., Tsukada, K., Hamaguchi, S., & Kiyose, H. (2005). Automatic extraction of PC scenes based on feature mining for a real time delivery system of baseball highlight scenes. In *Proceeding of IEEE International Conference on Multimedia and Expo,* (Vol. 1, pp. 277-280).

Lu, H., & Tan, Y. P. (2003). Unsupervised clustering of dominant scenes in sports video. *Pattern Recognition Letters, 24*(15), 2651–2662. doi:10.1016/S0167-8655(03)00108-9

Luo, Y., Wu, T. D., & Hwang, J. N. (2003). Object-based analysis and interpretation of human motion in sports video sequences by dynamic Bayesian networks. *Computer Vision and Image Understanding, 92*(2-3), 196–216. doi:10.1016/j.cviu.2003.08.001

Mochizuki, T., Tadenuma, M., & Yagi, N. (2005). Baseball video indexing using patternization of scenes and hidden Markov model. In. *Proceedings of IEEE International Conference on Image Processing, 3,* 12–15.

Owens, N., Harris, C., & Stennett, C. (2004). Hawk-eye tennis system. *International Conference on Visual Information Engineering,* (pp. 182- 185).

QuesTec. (2007). *Umpire Information System.* Retrieved from http://www.questec.com/q2001/prod_uis.htm

Rui, Y., Gupta, A., & Acero, A. (2000). Automatically extracting highlights for TV baseball programs. In *Proceedings of the 8th ACM international conference on Multimedia,* (pp. 105-115).

Shum, H., & Komura, T. (2004). A spatiotemporal approach to extract the 3D trajectory of the baseball from a single view video sequence. In. *Proceedings of IEEE International Conference on Multimedia and Expo, 3,* 1583–1586.

Tien, M. C., Chen, H. T., Chen, Y. W., Hsiao, M. H., & Lee, S. Y. (2007). Shot classification of basketball videos and its applications in shooting position extraction. In. *Proceedings of IEEE International Conference on Acoustics, Speech, and Signal Processing, 1,* 1085–1088.

Wang, J. R., & Parameswaran, N. (2005). Analyzing tennis tactics from broadcasting tennis video clips. In *Proceedings of 11th IEEE International Multimedia Modelling Conference,* (pp. 102-106).

Xie, L., Xu, P., Chang, S. F., Divakaran, A., & Sun, H. (2004). Structure analysis of soccer video with domain knowledge and hidden Markov models. *Pattern Recognition Letters, 25*(7), 767–775. doi:10.1016/j.patrec.2004.01.005

Xu, C., Wang, J., Lu, H., & Zhang, Y. (2008). A novel framework for semantic annotation and personalized retrieval of sports video. *IEEE Transactions on Multimedia, 10*(3), 421–436. doi:10.1109/TMM.2008.917346

Yu, X., Leong, H. W., Xu, C., & Tian, Q. (2006). Trajectory-based ball detection and tracking in broadcast soccer video. *IEEE Transactions on Multimedia, 8*(6), 1164–1178. doi:10.1109/TMM.2006.884621

Yu, X., Xu, C., Leong, H. W., Tian, Q., Tang, Q., & Wan, K. W. (2003). Trajectory-based ball detection and tracking with applications to semantic analysis of broadcast soccer video. In *Proceedings of 11th ACM International Conference on Multimedia,* (pp. 11-20).

Zhu, G., Huang, Q., Xu, C., Rui, Y., Jiang, S., Gao, W., & Yao, H. (2007b). Trajectory based event tactics analysis in broadcast sports video. In *Proceedings of 15th ACM International Conference on Multimedia,* (pp. 58-67).

Zhu, G., Huang, Q., Xu, C., Xing, L., Gao, W., & Yao, H. (2007a). Human behavior analysis for highlight ranking in broadcast racket sports video. *IEEE Transactions on Multimedia, 9*(6), 1167–1182. doi:10.1109/TMM.2007.902847

Zhu, G., Xu, C., Huang, Q., Gao, W., & Xing, L. (2007c). Player action recognition in broadcast tennis video with application to semantic analysis of sports game. In *Proceedings of 14th ACM International Conference on Multimedia,* (pp. 431- 440).

Section 4

Chapter 13
Adaptive Indexing for Semantic Music Information Retrieval

Clement H.C. Leung
Hong Kong Baptist University, Hong Kong

Jiming Liu
Hong Kong Baptist University, Hong Kong

Alfredo Milani
University of Perugia, Italy & Hong Kong Baptist University, Hong Kong

Alice W.S. Chan
Hong Kong Baptist University, Hong Kong

ABSTRACT

With the rapid advancement of music compression and storage technologies, digital music can be easily created, shared and distributed, not only in computers, but also in numerous portable digital devices. Music often constitutes a key component in many multimedia databases, and as they grow in size and complexity, their meaningful search and retrieval become important and necessary. Music Information Retrieval (MIR) is a relatively young and challenging research area started since the late 1990s. Although some form of music retrieval is available on the Internet, these tend to be inflexible and have significant limitations. Currently, most of these music retrieval systems only rely on low-level music information contents (e.g., metadata, album title, lyrics, etc.), and in this chapter, the authors present an adaptive indexing approach to search and discover music information. Experimental results show that through such an indexing architecture, high-level music semantics may be incorporated into search strategies.

INTRODUCTION

Multimedia is any combination of text, art, sound, animation, and video delivered by computer or other electronic or digitally manipulated means (Vaughan, 2006). Through the rapid growth of multimedia technology, multimedia content can be created, shared and distributed easily. The amount of available digital music is continuously increasing, promoted by a growing interest of users and by the development

DOI: 10.4018/978-1-61692-859-9.ch013

of new technology for the ubiquitous enjoyment of music (Orio, 2006). According to Vaughan (2006), "Sound is perhaps the most sensuous element of multimedia". While music is an art form of sound organized in time, Orio (2006) also points out that the pervasiveness of music information is due to the fact that the enjoyment of music does not require the need for translation. Thus, unlike text-oriented web documents, it crosses the barriers of national languages and cultural backgrounds. Therefore, meaningful music retrieval is important and necessary.

Currently, searching information from multimedia content is still very challenging. According to Goth (2004), "Most of the multimedia content out there right now is not really very searchable", and this situation has not improved significantly since. Since multimedia content can be represented in various forms in numerous formats and in different dimensions, compared with text-based information retrieval (IR), multimedia retrieval is far more difficult since its content cannot be extracted automatically due to current technology limitations (Leung & Liu, 2007). Also, Sebe & Tian (2007) state that we need robust techniques to index/retrieve multimedia information in accessing huge multimedia databases, as well as semantic visual interfaces integrating the above components into unified multimedia browsing and retrieval systems.

BACKGROUND

Music information retrieval (MIR) is a relatively young research area, emerged in the late 1990s (Crawford, 2005; Downie, 2003; Fingerhut, 2004), devoted to fulfill users' music information needs (Orio, 2006). The ultimate task of a MIRS is the accurate transfer of musical information from a database to a user (Lesaffre, 2006). Since music can have different characteristics and its content can be represented in various ways and formats, it is not easy to deal with the retrieval problem in a large music database. In an effective "concept-based" multimedia retrieval system, efficient and meaningful indexing is necessary (Go'mez & Vicedo, 2007; Goth, 2004). Due to current technological limitations, it is impossible to extract the semantic content of music data objects automatically (Snoek et. al., 2006; Yang & Hurson, 2005). Meanwhile, the discovery and insertion of new indexing terms are always costly and time-consuming. Therefore, novel indexing mechanisms are required to support flexible music search and retrieval. Here, we present an innovative method which enables the retrieval of music information by a novel indexing approach.

CURRENT MIR APPROACHES

Music Information Representations

In the digital world, music information can be represented in various forms and different formats. Different formats can only capture limited information in different dimension about the music (Futrelle & Downie, 2002). Typically, the most common music information representation approaches consist of symbolic, audio, visual, and metadata.

Symbolic music representation describes musical notation information by musical symbols. Audio music representation records raw audio data by sampling music which can be uncompressed, losslessly compressed, or lossy compressed. Visual music representation presents music information in visual im-

Table 1. Examples of music representation approaches

Representation	Examples
Symbolic	Musical notation in scores, MIDIs, Parsons code, etc.
Audio	Music recordings, audio streaming, etc.
Visual	Color Music
Metadata	Album information, MusicXML, etc.

agery, such as videos or using computer graphics. Metadata music representation describes the structure or schema of the music information. Table 1 shows some of the examples of these music representation approaches. In addition, some snapshots for each of the representation approaches are shown in Figure 1. Since the information recorded by different representation approaches are limited and varied, it is not easy to have a unified music representation method.

Limitations

Currently, the most common music information retrieval (MIR) approaches mainly focus on music content (e.g., melody, rhythm), and its metadata (e.g., file format, album type). For example, melody search from users entering via a piano keyboard interface (e.g., Musipedia), query by humming QBH (Dannenberg et. al, 2007), contour-based parsons code search (Musipedia), rhythm-based tapping search (Musicpedia), collaborative social tagging (Bischoff et. al., 2008), etc. However, all these approaches only support limited music information formats in the search domain and do not provide high-level semantic concept search (e.g. human perceptions of the music, music style) on the music. Knees et al. (2007) propose a

Figure 1. Snapshots of music representation approaches

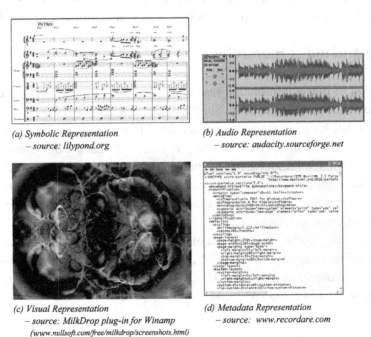

(a) Symbolic Representation
  – source: lilypond.org

(b) Audio Representation
  – source: audacity.sourceforge.net

(c) Visual Representation
  – source: MilkDrop plug-in for Winamp
  (www.nullsoft.com/free/milkdrop/screenshots.html)

(d) Metadata Representation
  – source: www.recordare.com

music search engine based on the automatic derive descriptions by making use of methods from Web Retrieval and Music Information Retrieval (MIR). Their method makes use of the information found in the ID3 tags, such as the values of the fields "artist", "album" and "title", of the music files. However, this approach only focuses on the metadata (e.g., title, album, track number, etc.) of the music files while these kinds of information is easily extracted compared with the semantic information (e.g., music style, musical arrangements, chord progressions, etc.) relating to the music files. Yang et al. (2009) suggest a creative MIR approach based on personal emotion. This idea is a little closer to our proposed method. However, our proposed method is not just exclusively concerned with the human personal subjective perception, but also with the general human perception of the community since we collect their perceptions through analyzing their search history and behviour. Here, we base our innovative concept-based approach on music search by adaptive collaborative indexing.

ADAPTIVE INDEXING APPROACH

In this section, we shall introduce our adaptive indexing approach for concept-based music information retrieval. Our approach concerns music discovery by collaborative semantic indexing and user relevance feedback. It enables the semantic search of music information resources by the collective discovery and meaningful indexing of their semantic concepts. Therefore, we focus on high-level human perception incorporating subtle emotional impression on the music (e.g., music styles, music characteristics, mood etc.) rather than its metadata which can be extracted easily. Through the successive use of our model, semantic properties can be discovered and incorporated by user relevance feedback and users' search behaviour. Eventually, through the growth and evolution of our index hierarchy, the semantic index can be dynamically constructed, validated, built-up, and converge towards communities' expectations. In the course of building up the indexes, the relationships among keywords (e.g., synonym) may be taken into consideration. The distance between indexes can be easily calculated, for example, by the Wiki Distance. Once we determine the distance between indexes, we can simply obtain similar music information. This book chapter is mainly focused on the adaptive indexing approach for the semantic MIR.

Index Structure and Index Hierarchy

Assuming a collection of music information resources $\{M_j\}$ where their semantic contents and characteristics cannot be extracted automatically. Such music resources may be wave files, mp3 files, midi files, music scores, MusicXML, or other resources related to music. Each M_j has a set of index set I_j, which consists of a number of index elements $\{e_{j.1}, e_{j.2}, ..., e_{j.x}\}$. Each index element is composed of three items: a music information resource M_i, an index term T_j, and the index score $S_{i,j}$ for T_j in M_i. This index score implies the significance of an index term T_j to the music resource M_i; the higher the index score, the more important is the index term to the music resource. Figure 2 shows the index structure. In this figure, the music information resource M_1, an index term T_1, and the index score $S_{1.1}$ form an index element $e_{1.1}$. Then, M_1 would form a set of index elements $\{e_j\}$ with a set of index terms $T=\{T_1, T_2, ..., T_n\}$, and the corresponding scores $S_1 = \{S_{1.1}, S_{1.2} ..., S_{1.n}\}$, while each set of index elements would form an index set I_x. Thus, the family of index sets $I = \{I_1, I_2, ..., I_x\}$ would be formed for the collection of music information resources $M = \{M_1, M_2,.., M_x\}$.

Figure 2. Index structure: Music information, index & index element

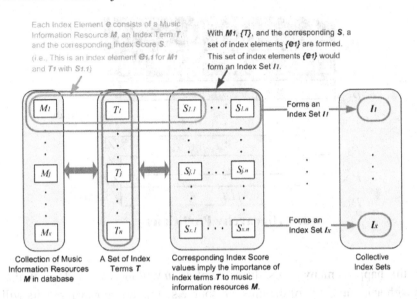

An index hierarchy refers to the collective index sets I of all M stored in the database. This collection of index sets can be partitioned into N levels based on the index scores S of the index elements. The N levels $L_1, L_2, ..., L_N$ of the index hierarchy are determined by the index score values and a set of partitioning parameters $P_1, P_2, ..., P_N$. For a given index element E which consists of an index term T_x for a music information resource M_y with index score value X, the index level of this index element can be determined by the following algorithm:

If $P_i \leq X < P_{i+1}$, where $i = 1, 2, ..., N$-1.
Then, E would be placed in level Li of the index hierarchy.
Otherwise, E would be placed in level N if $P_N \leq X$.

Figure 3 shows the structure of the index hierarchy. In this index hierarchy, the higher the level, the more significant are the associated index terms.

Index Growth through Inclusion of Existing Index Terms

Consider a particular music resource m, which is minimally indexed with term $t = w$ (i.e. t consists of the single word w, e.g. "jazz"). Suppose a user enters a query using $Q = w \cup u$, which signifies a situation where $w \cup u$ forms a single meaningful compound index term (e.g. "Latin jazz"). In general, u may be added before or after w and serves to further qualify w (hence narrowing down the search possibilities). From this query, all music resources with w in its index will be returned – there may be some music resources with $w \cup u$ or $w \cup u'$ (e.g. Latin jazz or soul jazz). After some browsing through these returned music resources, the user finally selects a particular music resource. As a result of this selection, it is inferred that the selected music resource will have the property represented by the more complete index term $w \cup u$ (i.e. Latin jazz). Thus the term $w \cup u$ will be added to the index hierarchy of this music

Figure 3. Index hierarchy structure

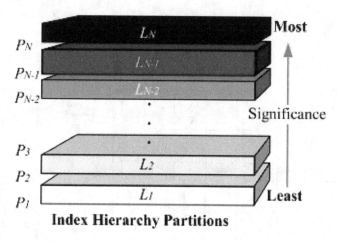

Index Hierarchy Partitions

resource, and if this happens many times, the score of $w \cup u$ will increase and this will cause $w \cup u$ to be installed along with w in the index of the music resource so that the retrieval results will be much more accurate. The original index term w will remain in the index hierarchy, and may be retained or gradually dropped in accordance with the score updating algorithm. In general, a music resource which is minimally indexed with term $T = w$ may be successfully augmented to $w \cup u_1 \cup ... \cup u_k$ through this mechanism.

Index Growth through Addition of New Index Terms

Consider a particular music resource m, which is indexed with term t, where t may be simple (i.e., single word) or compound (i.e., multiple words). When a query is entered using the term t, many music resources of different types will be returned, all of which will have the term t in their index. Among the results set is the required music resource m, and this is the only relevant music resource for the user. Other music resources that have been returned are not relevant for this user query. Due to the volume of music resources returned, it will take considerable time and effort for the user to navigate through them to get to the target music resource m, which is inefficient.

Next, suppose the same music resource m can have another index term t' which is not yet included in the current index but represents an additional property of m. Occasionally, users would include both terms t and t' in a query with a view of increasing the precision of the search. Since t' is not indexed, the initial search results will still be the same as before. As the user is interested in m and not other music resources, he will eventually select m from among the resources returned. This suggests that t' may be a potential index term and will enter the index hierarchy at the lowest level with a score of P_1. Once it has been installed in the index hierarchy, repeated search using it and subsequent selection will serve to raise its score and may eventually elevate it to the main index. In so doing, a music resource which is indexed with a single term may subsequently have a number of index terms associated with it. In general, a music resource having an initial set of index terms $t_1, t_2, ..., t_n$, may have new index terms t_1' $t_2', ..., t_m'$ added to it through repeated usage.

Relevance Feedback and Index Score Update

Relevance feedback (RF) is a classical information retrieval (IR) technique where users relay their agreement with the system's evaluation of document relevance back to the system, which then uses this information to provide a revised list of search results (Vinay, 2005). It allows user to mark either relevant (positive feedback) or irrelevant (negative feedback) to the resource(s) of the result list by their relevance judgments. The user relevance feedback collected would be useful for refining the index scores, such that it helps tuning the index hierarchy to fit user preferences. Our model collects both explicit and implicit relevance feedback from the user community. The explicit feedback relates to relevance, indicating the relevance of the resource retrieved for a query, and is collected directly from user judgements.

Based on our index growth example mentioned in the previous section, a diagram illustrating our index evolution workflow affected by user relevance feedback (votes and selections) is shown in Figure 4. Our index evolution workflow can be viewed from different perspectives; index view and model view. These two views share the same timeline which indicates the sequential order of the index growth against time. Initially (at time = T_0), we assume that our target music information resource m is only indexed with an index term "jazz". When a user submits a query Q_0: "Latin" and "jazz", all the music resources that are indexed with the term "jazz" (including m) would be returned in the result R_0. When the user is interested in m in R_0 and selects it since the user judges that resource would be relevant to Q_0, then, the new term "Latin" would be added to m in the lower level in the index hierarchy after user selection feedback. After that, users would submit queries which consist of "Latin" and "jazz". Through successive usage, these user selections would promote the new index term "Latin" of m to the upper level in the index hierarchy. Thus, the index term "Latin" would become properly indexed. Therefore, users can retrieve m by the query which has only the term "Latin".

Tables 2 and 3 describes a situation of index score update (increase) after receiving a user selection (positive) feedback. Here, the music objects O_1 and O_2 are both indexed with the index term t_1 and with index score S_0 initially (in Table 2). The score increment parameter after receiving a positive user selection feedback is defined as Δ_+, where the increment parameter should be a positive real number. When a user submits a query $Q(t_1)$, the music objects which related to t_1 would be returned in the query result (i.e., O_1, O_2, etc.). When a user selects O_2 eventually on the query result list, the index score of O_2 of t_1 would be increased by Δ_+ (Table 3).

Explicit User Feedback: User Vote

Our model enables users to indicate relevance explicitly using a binary vote relevance system. The binary vote relevance feedback indicates that a music information resource is either relevant or irrel-

Table 2. Initial index values

Music Object	Index Term	Index Score
O_1	t_1	S_0
O_2	t_1	S_0
. . .	. . .	. . .

Figure 4. Explanation of index evolution workflow modulated by user relevance

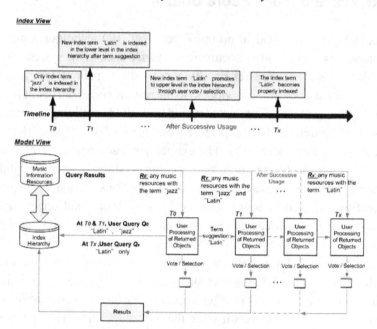

evant for a specific query. Once a user submits a query, our system will return a list of query results to the user. In the spirit of Web 2.0 (Boll (2007), Giannakidou et. al. (2008), and Yesilada et. al. (2008)) with collaborative user involvements, our system allows users to provide their relevance feedback for the music information resources of the query results. Their feedback can be either *positive* or *negative*. When positive relevance feedback is received, the related index scores would increase. Similarly, the related index scores would decrease when negative relevance feedback is received.

Implicit User Feedback: User Selection

Although the idea of exploiting user's feedback to rate relevance seems promising, it is not easy to convince a community of users to spend their time to explicitly rate resources. Therefore, our model also collects implicit relevance feedback from them. The implicit feedback is inferred from user behaviour and their history, such as noting which resource(s) that users do and do not select for viewing, and the duration of time spent in viewing a resource. All such information can be collected automatically and would reflect user satisfaction and expectation of the query result. When users click on a resource in

Table 3. Index values after receiving a user selection (positive) feedback

Music Object	Index Term	Index Score
O_1	t_1	S_0
O_2	t_1	$S_0 + \Delta_+$
.	.	.
.	.	.
.	.	.

the answer vector, we can infer that the selected resource may be relevant to the user query. Our system will treat it as a kind of *positive feedback* from the user implicitly. On the contrary, when users do not select any resource in the answer vector, we can infer that they may think that the resources in the answer vector are irrelevant to their input query or they are not interested in those resources. Our system will treat it as a kind of *negative feedback* from the user implicitly. The index score update approach is similar to the explicit user feedback; the related index score would increase when receiving a positive user feedback, and the related index score would decrease when receiving a negative user feedback.

EXPERIMENTS ON INDEX CONVERGENCE

In order to evaluate the effectiveness of our large scale indexing approach, we adopt a simulation approach based on the target score values S_T. The goal of the series of experiments is to investigate the relationship between the initial S_T and the convergence of the index.

In the scoring system, 0 denotes the minimum score and 1 denotes the maximum score. Initially, each index term of a resource is associated with a static target score value S_T where $0 < S_T < 1$. The simulation model simulates the following processes: user queries submission, answer vector computation and user relevance feedback simulation on the basis of S_T. In the following series of tests, we make use 2,000 resources in 5,000 queries, answer vector size 10 with different initial random S_T values. For the measurement of the evaluation, we introduce relative answer relevance R to measure the single query optimality. R is the ratio between the total target score of a query answer and the best possible answer of length k; the aim of this measure is to express how optimal is the current query answer with respect to the resources currently in the database.

Experimental Results & Discussions

In the experiments, we assign initial S_T with random values x which follow uniform distributions in different ranges:

1. $U(0, 0.5)$
2. $U(0, 1)$
3. $U(0.3, 0.8)$
4. $U(0.5, 1)$

Where U signifies the uniform distribution with:

$$U(a,b) = \begin{cases} \dfrac{1}{b-a} & \text{for } a \leq x \leq b, \\ 0 & \text{for } x < a \text{ or } x > b, \end{cases}$$

Its mean and variance are respectively $\dfrac{a+b}{2}$, $\dfrac{(b-a)^2}{12}$.

Figures 5, 6, 7, and 8 show the average R values for the preceding 100 queries. Here, we sum the R-values obtained for the 901-th to the 1000-th query and then divide the sum by 100. From these run

Figure 5. Test with initial S_t following the uniform distribution $U(0,0.5)$

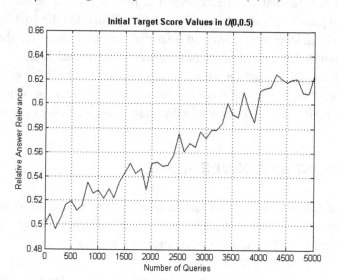

results, the values of **R** of these runs are increasing. In other words, all of the runs are convergent disregarding their initial S_T. In addition, the convergence behaviour of run with $0 < x < 0.5$ is similar to the one of run with $0 < x < 1$. However, the convergence rate of the run with $0 < S_T < 1$ is the fastest since its curve gives the greatest slope.

By comparing all of the runs, with different distributional characteristics of the initial S_T, we can conclude the following. All of the runs would be convergent irrespective of the initial value of S_T. When the S_T value of the run starts with a lower mean value, it attains a faster converging rate since more room is provided for the index to become convergent. In addition, some experimental evaluation has been carried out to determine the evolution time and feasibility of such indexing, and the following cases are considered.

Figure 6. Test with initial S_t following the uniform distribution $U(0,1)$

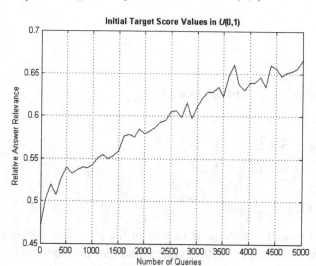

Figure 7. Test with initial S_t following the uniform distribution U(0.3,0.8)

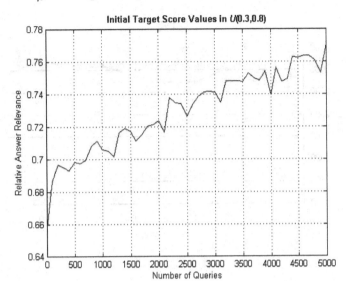

Case 1

Initial number of index terms per music object = 0 (unindexed). Maximal number of index terms per object = 3. Database size = 10,000 music objects. Access rate follows a Poisson distribution with parameter λ=10 accesses per hour (Ghahramani, 2005). Each access has a probability of 0.05 of incrementing the index set by one index term. Figure 9 shows the time for the database to achieve 80% maximal indexing capability (i.e. 8,000 music objects in the database will have reached 3 index terms). Here, the mean time to achieve 80% maximal indexing capability is 2897.75 hours which is about 17 weeks. The standard deviation is 209.31 hours or about 8.7 days.

Figure 8. Test with initial S_t following the uniform distribution U(0.5,1)

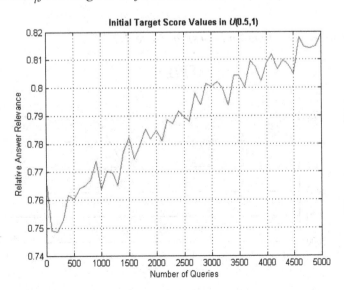

Figure 9. Indexing convergence time (in hours) for Case 1

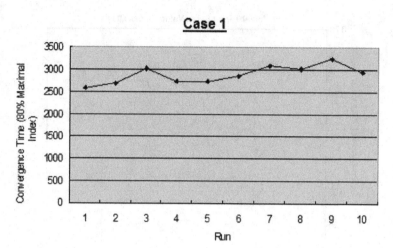

Case 2

Initial number of index terms per object = 3. Maximal number of index terms per object = 8. Database size = 10,000 music objects. Access rate follows a Poisson distribution with parameter λ=10 accesses per hour. Each access has a probability of 0.05 incrementing the index set by one index term. Figure 10 shows the time for the database to achieve 80% maximal indexing capability (i.e. 8,000 objects in the database will have reached 8 index terms). Here, the mean time to achieve 80% maximal indexing capability is 3830.86 hours which is about 23 weeks. The standard deviation is 221.45 hours or about 9.2 days. Thus, even allowing two standard deviations from the mean value (23 weeks + 18.4 days), there is a high probability - over 95% using the Central Limit Theorem approximation to a normal distribution (Ghahramani, 2005) - that 80% maximal indexing capability can be achieved within six months.

Figure 10. Indexing convergence time (in hours) for Case 2

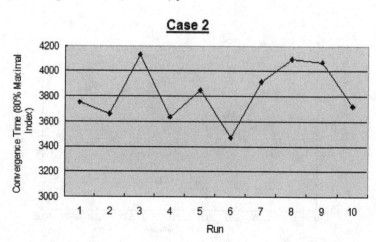

CONCLUSION

We have provided an evaluation of the common Music Information Retrieval (MIR) approaches and have proposed an innovative adaptive approach for music information discovery that overcomes the current limitations. Our indexing approach helps to discover music resources systematically by keeping track of the user query behaviour. By analyzing the search information, the user relevance feedback helps the index hierarchy to evolve towards users' desired preferences. Thus, user satisfaction would be maximized. Our experimental result shows that the index could be fully built after successive use. The present approach, through systematically exploiting collective usage and intelligence, allows the accumulation of expert judgement automatically which substantially enhances the performance of queries involving deep musical semantics.

REFERENCES

Boll, S. (2007). Multitube - where web 2.0 and multimedia could meet. *IEEE MultiMedia, 14*(1), 9–13. doi:10.1109/MMUL.2007.17

Crawford, T. (2005). *Music Information Retrieval and the Future of Musicology*. Technical Report for the Online Chopin variorum Edition project. Bischoff, K., Firan, C. S., Nejdl, W., & Paiu, R. (2008). Can All Tags be Used for Search? In *CIKM '08: Proceedings of the 17th ACM Conference on Information and Knowledge Management*, (pp. 193-202). New York: ACM.

Dannenberg, R. B., Birmingham, W. P., Pardo, B., Hu, N., Meek, C., & Tzanetakis, G. (2007). A Comparative Evaluation of Search Techniques for Query-By-Humming using the Musart Testbed. *Journal of the American Society for Information Science and Technology, 58*(5), 687–701. doi:10.1002/asi.20532

Downie, J. S. (2003). Muisc Information Retrieval. *Annual Review of Information Science & Technology, 37*, 295–340. doi:10.1002/aris.1440370108

Fingerhut, M. (2004). Music Information Retrieval, or How to Search for (and maybe find) Music and Do Away with Incipits. In *Proceedings of the IAML-IASA Congress*.

Futrelle, J., & Downie, S. (2002). Interdisciplinary Communities and Research Issues in Music Information Retrieval. In *Proceedings of ISMIR 2002*, Paris.

Ghahramani, S. (2005). *Fundamentals of Probability with Stochastic Processes* (3rd ed.). New York: Prentice Hall.

Giannakidou, E., Kompatsiaris, I., & Vakali, A. (2008). Semsoc: Semantic, social and content-based clustering in multimedia collaborative tagging systems. In: *ICSC 2008: Proceedings of the 2008 IEEE International Conference on Semantic Computing*, (pp. 128–135). Washington, DC: IEEE Computer Society.

Go'mez, J., & Vicedo, J. L. (2007). Next-generation Multimedia Database Retrieval. *IEEE MultiMedia, 14*(3), 106–107. doi:10.1109/MMUL.2007.56

Goth, G. (2004). Multimedia Search: Ready or Not? *Distributed Systems Online, IEEE, 5*(7). Retrieved from http://ieeexplore.ieee.org/stamp/stamp.jsp?arnumber=1323037&isnumber=29290

Knees, P., et al. (2007). A Music Search Engine Built Upon Audio-based and Web-based Similarity Measures. In *Proceedings of the ACM SIGIR 2007*, Amsterdam.

Lesaffre, M. (2005-2006). *Music Information Retrieval: Conceptual Framework, Annotation and User Behaviour.* PhD thesis, Faculty of Arts and Philosophy, Department of Art, Music and Theatre Sciences, Ghent University, The Netherlands.

Leung, C., & Liu, J. (2007). Multimedia Data Mining and Searching Through Dynamic Index Evolution. In *VISUAL 2007: Proceedings of the 9th International Conference on Visual Information Systems*, Shanghai, China, (pp.298-309).

Musicpedia. (n.d.). *The Open Music Encyclopedia.* Retrieved from http://www.musicpedia.org

Orio, N. (2006). Music Retrieval: A Tutorial and Review. *Foundations and Trends in Information Retrieval, 1*(1), 1–90. doi:10.1561/1500000002

Sebe, N., & Tian, Q. (2007). Personalized multimedia retrieval: the new trend? In *Proceedings of the international Workshop on Workshop on Multimedia information Retrieval*, Augsburg, Germany, September 24 - 29, 2007, (pp. 299-306). New York: ACM.

Snoek, C. G. M., Worring, M., van Gemert, J. C., Beusebroek, J. M., & Smeulders, A. W. M. (2006). The Challenge Problem for Automated Detection of 101 Semantic Concepts in Multimedia. In *Multimedia '06: Proceedings of the 14th annual ACM international conference on Multimedia*, (pp. 421-430). New York: ACM.

Vaughan, T. (2006). *What is Multimedia? Multimedia: Making It Work* (7th ed., pp. 1–17). New York: McGraw-Hill Professional.

Vinay, V., Wood, K., Milic-Frayling, N., & Cox, I. J. (2005). Comparing relevance feedback algorithms for web search. In *WWW 2005: Special interest tracks and posters of the 14th International Conference on World Wide Web*, (pp. 1052–1053). New York: ACM.

Yang, B., & Hurson, A. R. (2005). Ad Hoc Image Retrieval using Hierarchical Semantic-based Index. In *AINA '05: Proceedings of the 19th international conference on advanced information networking and applications*, (pp. 629-634). Washington, DC: IEEE Computer Society.

Yang, Y. H., et al. (2009). Personalized Music Emotion Recognition. In *Proceedings of the SIGIR 2009*, Boston.

Yesilada, Y., & Harper, S. (2008). Web 2.0 and the semantic web: hindrance or opportunity? In *Proceedings of W4a - International Cross-disciplinary Conference on Web Accessibility 2007. SIGACCESS Access. Comput.* (90), 19–31.

Chapter 14
Music Content Analysis in MP3 Compressed Domain

Antonello D'Aguanno
Università degli Studi di Milano, Italy

ABSTRACT

Nowadays more and more audio contents are stored in compressed formats. Especially MP3 music has become very popular with the availability of powerful computation and wide bandwidth connectivity. So that, this chapter will be devoted to present techniques and algorithms, dealing with compressed audio, aimed at content analysis. Since content analysis in compressed domain is an innovative field of applications, the literature review will be extended to methods that extract music content from MP3, even if the algorithms are not focused on music information retrieval. In this chapter, the authors focus on a number of different algorithms dealing with common tasks of the MIR field such as tempo induction, tempo tracking, and automatic music synchronization. They will present an overview of the MusicXML, and IEEE1599 language to represent score and synchronization results, because they have decided to use those formats to represent the score in their synchronization algorithm. The chapter will end showing applications, conclusions, and future works in the field of direct content analysis in compressed domain.

INTRODUCTION

Nowadays more and more audio contents are stored in compressed formats. Especially MP3 music has become very popular with the availability of powerful computation and wide bandwidth connectivity. Consequently, there is a clear advantage in developing analysis systems, which can work directly in compressed formats. The time signature extraction tasks, the BPM (Beat per Minute) detection and tracking or the automatic music synchronization are important parts in the Music Information Retrieval

DOI: 10.4018/978-1-61692-859-9.ch014

(MIR) context. Furthermore, it is very common to find users having music personal collection of more than thousands of songs, for that reason direct analysis will be a key point of audio content analysis both for personal collection than for public database.

This chapter will be devoted to present techniques and algorithms, dealing with compressed audio, aimed at content analysis. Since content analysis in compressed domain is an innovative field of applications, the literature review will be extended to methods that extract music content from MP3, even if the algorithms are not focused on music information retrieval. For example the error concealment in music transmission over noisy channels may found some benefits from beat recognition and tracking.

In the real world algorithms dealing with tempo induction and tracking find application in many software that manage users playlist, E.G. iTunes. In iTunes for example the BPM are used to obtain new listing methods. It should be noted that BPM are key feature for many music professions like disc-jockey. For that profession having a knowledge about the BPM of their music collection would be a key point. Having automatic software that can derive automatically the BPM will be a killer application to speed up their works.

The literature review will also include the state of the art algorithms working on PCM and MIDI domain in order to point out how the PCM-methods have been adapted for the MP3 domain.

The chapter will contain a review of the MP3 standard focused on the WSP feature (Window-Switching Pattern) and MDCT (modified discrete cosine transform).

The WSP is useful information to achieve tempo tracking and time signature on MP3 files, and MDCT coefficients are the key representation of the spectrum in MP3.

In this chapter we will focus on a number of different algorithms dealing with common tasks of the MIR field such as tempo induction, tempo tracking, and automatic music synchronization. We will analyze their implementation and their relation with their counterparts in state of the art of PCM and MIDI domains. We will also compare the results of each algorithm with respect to the results of the related algorithms in PCM and MIDI domain in order to demonstrate limits and advantage of direct analysis.

We will present an overview of the MusicXML, and IEEE1599 language to represent score and synchronization results, because we have decided to use those formats to represent the score in our synchronization algorithm.

The chapter will end showing applications, conclusions, and future works in the field of direct content analysis in compressed domain.

BACKGROUND

MP3

MPEG audio gives a set of standards to lossy audio compression. Algorithms are classified in three layers sorted by complexity and efficiency. They are contained both in MPEG-1 (MPEG1) and MPEG-2 (MPEG2). These standards allow to work on high (32, 44.1, 48 kHz) and low sampling frequencies (16, 22.05, 24 kHz) respectively.

Usually MP3 codecs use a non-uniform quantization on frequency domain driven by perceptual model to compress PCM audio signal into a standard bit stream at various bit rate values.

The time to frequency transform is built by means of a polyphase filter bank and by cascading it with MDCT (hybrid filter bank). Polyphase filter bank gets samples from PCM streaming and represents them, for long window, in 32 frequency sub-bands, further subdivided into 18 finer sub-bands by MDCT.

Psychoacoustic model generates the SMR (Signal to Mask Ratio), this index tells to the quantization block about the bits number that should be allocated for each frequency sub-band in order to get an inaudible quantization noise (Zwicker,2001).

The output of filter banks and perceptual model are the input of non-uniform quantization process. This process decides how to quantize every frequency sub band to respect the SMR value. Huffman lossless compression is performed before bit stream packing. Although MPEG-2 layer 3 frame contains only one granule per frame, MPEG-1 Layer 3 frame is made by two granules.

Further information about MPEG standards can be found in (MPEG1; MPEG2; Noll,1997; Pan,1995).

Window Type Based Detection

MP3 provides 4 different MDCT window types. They are: long, long-to-short, short, short-to-long indexed with 0,1,2,3 respectively.

The short window provides better time resolution for transients (Pan,1995). In a short block there are 3 different windows. Each window has 32 frequency sub-bands, further subdivided into 6 finer sub-bands by MDCT. 3 short windows are then grouped in one granule. The values are ordered by frequency and then by window.

The switch between long and short blocks is not instantaneous. The 2 window types long-to-short and short-to-long, serve as transition between long and short window types. Because MDCT processing of a sub-band signal provides better frequency resolution, it consequently has poorer time resolution.

The quantization of MDCT values will cause errors that are spread over the long time window, so it is more likely that this quantization will produce audible distortions. Such distortions usually manifest themselves as pre-echo because the temporal masking of noise that occurs before a given signal is weaker than the masking of noise after (Pan,1995). This situation appears frequently in music, with strong drums line, when the drummer plays snare or bass drum.

To avoid pre-echo distortions the encoder MP3 will change the window length of MDCT into short window in order to increase the time resolution and decrease the pre-echo effect. The switch between long and short window is leaded by the Perceptual Entropy criterion: if the value of PE (Perceptual Entropy) in one granule is higher than the predefined threshold (*PE_SWITCH* in (MPEG1)) the encoder will change the window length to short. The PE criterion can be used to represent the occurrence of burst signal. But the sudden increase of signal energy is not the only factor to influence the PE. The distribution of the signal energy and the tonality characteristics of the signal are also important factors that influence the PE (Zhaorong,2001).

It should be noted the switching criterion is not a part of the standard MPEG. In (MPEG1) the window dimension is standardized for any kind of window, but the choice of the correct window type is delegated to codec implementation. Many algorithms have been proposed to solve this problem (Zhaorong,2001).

The short block utilization is not required to meet the MPEG standard, because this information is optional. Actually professional codecs implement this information, because it permits a better sound quality reducing the artifacts generated by MP3 compression in faster transients.

IEEE 1599

The development of IEEE 1599 followed the guidelines of IEEE PAR1599, *Recommended Practice Dealing With Applications and Representations of Symbolic Music Information Using the XML Language*. Its ultimate goal is to provide a highly integrated representation of music, where score, audio, video, and graphical contents can be appreciated together.

The following discussion will introduce its key features, which are different from other music-oriented XML-based languages such as MusicXML (Good,2001).

Multi-Layer Structure

As stated before, a comprehensive description of music must support heterogeneous materials. Thanks to the intrinsic capability of XML to provide strongly structures for information, such representations can be organized in an effective and efficient way.

IEEE 1599 employs six different layers to represent information:

- *General* - music-related meta data, i.e. catalogue information about the piece
- *Logic* - the logical description of score symbols
- *Structural* - identification of music objects and their mutual relationships
- *Notational* - graphical representations of the score
- *Performance* - computer-based descriptions and executions of music according to performance languages
- *Audio* - digital or digitized recordings of the piece.

Needless to say, not all layers must, or can, be present for a given music piece.

Richness has been mentioned in regard to the number of heterogeneous types of media description, namely symbolic, logic, audio, graphic, etc. But the philosophy of IEEE 1599 allows one extra step, as each layer can contain many digital instances. For example, the *Audio* layer could link to several audio tracks and even videos for the same piece. The concept of *multi-layered description* - as many different types of descriptions as possible, all correlated and synchronized - together with the concept of *multi-instance support* - as many different media objects as possible for each layer - provide rich and flexible means for encoding music in all its aspects.

Moreover, it is possible to adopt some *ad hoc* encoding in addition to already existing formats to represent information. In fact, while a comprehensive format to represent music is not available, popular existing standards must be taken into account. This is a not a contradiction because of the two-sided approach of IEEE 1599 to music representation, which is: keep intrinsic music descriptions inside of the IEEE 1599 file - in XML format - and media objects outside of the IEEE 1599 file - in their original format.

The Spine

The spine is a sort of glue needed in a multi-layer framework. In this approach, heterogeneous descriptions of the same music piece are not simply linked together, but a further level of detail is provided: whenever possible, media information is related to single music events. The concept of music event is left intentionally vague, since the format is flexible and suited to many purposes. A music event can be defined as the occurrence within the score, or its abstraction, of something that is considered important by the author of the encoding.

The spine consists of a sorted list of events, where the author of the encoding can choose the definition and granularity of events.

The spine has a fundamental theoretical importance within the format. It provides both an abstraction level and the glue among layers; in a certain sense, it represents an abstraction level, as the events identified in it do not have to correspond to score symbols, or audio samples, or anything else. It is the author who can decide, from time to time, what goes under the definition of music event, according to the needs. Since the spine simply lists events to provide a unique label for them, the mere presence of an event in the spine has no semantic meaning. As a consequence, what is listed in the spine structure must have a counterpart in some layer, otherwise the event would not be defined and its presence in the list (and in the MX file) would be absolutely useless.

For example, in a piece made of *n* music events, the spine would list *n* entries without defining them from any point of view. If each event has a logic definition - namely, it is a note or a rest - it is graphically represented in many scores and it is present in a number of audio tracks. These aspects are treated in the *Logic*, *Notational*, and *Audio* layers respectively.

Music events are not only listed in the spine, but also marked by a unique identifier. These are referred to by all instances of the corresponding event representations in other layers. Thus, each spine event can be described:

- In 1 to *n* layers; e.g., in the *Logic*, *Notational*, and *Audio* layers;
- In 1 to *n* instances within the same layer; e.g., in three different audio clips mapped in the *Audio* layer;
- In 1 to *n* occurrences within the same instance; e.g., the notes in a song refrain that is performed 4 times (thus the same spine events are mapped 4 times in the *Audio* layer, at different timings).

The events listed in the spine structure can correspond to one or to many instances in other layers. Thanks to the spine, IEEE 1599 is not a simple container for heterogeneous media descriptions related to a unique music piece. It shows instead that those descriptions can also present a number of references to a common structure. This aspect creates synchronization among instances within a layer (*intra-layer synchronization*), and - when applied to a complex file - also synchronization among contents disposed in many layers (*inter-layer synchronization*).

Synchronization Mechanisms

In order to get synchronization among IEEE 1599 layers, a mechanism based on spine concept has been introduced. Spine allows the interconnection of these layers on space and time domain through a relative measure in spine and an absolute measure in the other layers.

Inside spine, each music event is univocally defined by an identifier (the *id* attribute) and carries information about timing and position. Timing (the *timing* attribute) is expressed in a relative way: the measurement unit is user-defined in function of time domain and its value is the timing distance from the preceding event. For instance, a quarter note may correspond to 1024 timing units, no matter which absolute timing it has. Please note that the absolute timing of a music event depends on the performance, so it is described in the *Audio* layer. The *hpos* attribute, standing for horizontal position, has a similar meaning referred to space domain. A simplified example of spine could be the following one:

```
<spine>
   <event id="e1" timing="0" hpos="0"/>
   <event id="e2" timing="1024" hpos="5"/>
   <event id="e3" timing="512" hpos="10"/>
...
</spine>
```

In the previous example, three music events are listed within the spine structure. The second event occurs 1024 time units after the first one, whereas the third occurs 512 time units after the second one. We have to remark two key points: i) such values are theoretical, i.e. the first score event should last half the second one, but different audio performances could ignore this indication, and ii) those values have no absolute meaning, as neither physical time units nor rhythmical music values are directly involved in their spine definition.

The approach is completely different in the *Audio* layer, where every media linked to IEEE 1599 is mapped to spine events through the *track* tag. This element is a container for a number of *track_event* elements, which contains the spine identifier (the *event_ref* attribute) and absolute references (the *start_time* and *end_time* attributes) that specify the absolute occurrence of the event in the media file. Through this mechanism, each single music event in spine can be physically indexed and recognized within one or many digital objects.

Unlike spine timing, the *Audio* layer contains absolute time references, allowing the use of different measurement units in function of the various kinds of media. As regards the *timing_type* attribute, the default unit is the second, but it is possible to use bytes, samples, or frames as well. This solution provides a more sophisticated time granularity according to the different media structures (PCM, MP3, AAC, etc.) supported by IEEE 1599.

A simplified example of *Audio* layer contents could be the following one:

```
<audio>
  <track file_name="audio/example.mp3"
         encoding_format="audio_mpeg"
          file_format="audio_mpeg">
    <track_indexing timing_type="seconds">
      <track_event event_ref="e1" start_time="0.00" />
      <track_event event_ref="e2" start_time="1.15" />
      <track_event event_ref="e3" start_time="1.67" />
    ...
    </track_indexing>
  </track>
</audio>
```

Thanks to IEEE 1599 it is possible to represent the synchronization data and we shown its capability to act as a specialized container for such information. Timing information can be easily and automatically extracted, converted in any suitable format, and finally used to produce segmentation in a media object.

MusicXML

MusicXML is an XML-based format aimed at representation of common Western musical notation from the 17th century onwards (Good,2001a). MusicXML is designed to meet the interchange needs for all these types of applications: sequencing, musical database, and music notation. At MusicXML website http://www.recordare.com/xml.html it is possible to find many example related to this format.

We decide to use this format to represent score because it offers a better representation of music than MIDI, for example it has explicit time and key signature. Other reasons for choosing to use MusicXML, to represent score, can be summarized as follows:

- A huge number of scores is available in MusicXML format;
- It is supported by the most important notation editor softwares;
- It is aimed at meeting interchange needs;
- It is XML-based, which means easy to understand;

In the future our goal will be the implementation of an MX-based synchronization algorithm. In fact, this format is aimed to represent music symbolically in a comprehensive way, opening up new ways to make both music and music-related information available to musicologists and performers on one hand, and to non-practitioners on the other. Its ultimate goal is to provide a highly integrated representation of music, where score, audio, video, and graphical contents can be appreciated together (Baraté,2005).

In MusicXML, time is represented using three different values *beats*, *beat-type* and *divisions*; *beats* and beat-type are the numerator and the denominator of the fraction representing time in common western notation, respectively. The *divisions* value is the number of beat subdivisions. In the following example A note in the fourth octave is presented. The note duration is provided by the *duration* element and it is expressed in division amount. The *step* element represents the pitch name of the notes.

```
<note>
   <pitch>
      <step>A</step>
      <octave>4</octave>
   </pitch>
   <duration>2</duration>
   <voice>1</voice>
   <type>quarter</type>
   <stem>up</stem>
</note>
```

To lead the frequencies analysis - which will be presented in section "Frequency Analysis For Music Synchronization In MP3" - we have to perform two different operations about the MusicXML score i) verticalization ii) global note duration. The verticalization operator is used to identify the contemporaneous occurrence of notes inside different parts. It is essentially a "selective" function, with a domain defined by all the notes in the score. This function groups notes in chords. Verticalization operator is able to distinguish and manage redundant notes, those frequencies analysis should not consider (Haus,2004). After verticalization the *global note duration* is computed summing the whole duration of the notes having the same name (E.G. Ab, A, A#, B, C and so on) selected after the verticalization. It should be noted that notes having different name but equal fundamental frequency are grouped, for example A# and Bb will be considered as the same note. In subsection MP3 and MusicXML we will present how *global note duration* will be used.

Tempo Induction and Beat Tracking Algorithms in PCM and MIDI Domain

In literature there are various beat/tempo trackers dealing with MIDI signals (Allen,1990; Dixon, 2001; Uhle,2003) or PCM samples (Matthew,2005; Scaringella,2005; Alonso,2004; Dixon,2003; Scheirer,1998; Tzanetakis,2002; Uhle,2004), but only few articles which solve the tempo tracking task on compressed formats have been presented (Wang,2001; (Kurniawati,2004).

These programs find application in tasks like beat-driven real-time computer graphics, computer accompaniment of a human performer, lighting control and many others (Goto,2001). Tempo and beats tracking are directly applicated in MIR systems, for example in the query by tapping systems as proposed in (Eisenberg,2004).

It should be noted that these tasks are not restricted to music with drums; in fact the human ear can identify beats and tempo even if the song has not a strong rhythmical accentuation. Obviously these tasks are more difficult in music without drums. The algorithms that implement tempo and beat tracking actually have less accuracy in music without drums (Goto,2001).

In this contest it is difficult to point out the accuracy rate of the various algorithms because some widespread data set and common methodological evaluation routine are not yet accepted. This situation is partly due to the choice of data set, which often depends on the goals of the system (Dixon,2001a). We choice to follow the guidelines proposed in (Gouyon,2006) using the same data sets.

Various models have been proposed in order to extract the beat from performance data. The primary distinction we want to point out is between real-time and batch algorithms. For example automatic accompaniment systems have to use real-time algorithms. Transcription and analysis software tends to process data off-line, because rhythmically ambiguous sections can be frequently determined analyzing all the beat information found in the song. Thus the choice between real-time and off-line system is directly related to algorithm aim.

Actually the beat tracking system works on a two stage models. The first stage is an onset detector, the second one is an interpretative system, which gets the onset detector output and tries to understand the tempo of the song and the correct beat position.

About the interpretative system is possible to find many different solutions like agents model (Goto,2001; Dixon,2001), or probabilistic systems (Sethares,2005) and so on.

Wang (Wang,2001) proposes the WSP as information to refine the output of an MDCT (Modified Discrete Cosine Transform) coefficient analysis to solve a beat tracking problem. It should be noted that in (Wang, 2001) the beat recognition is not performed to obtain music symbolic information, but to get better error concealment for music transmission in noisy channels. In this work the whole tempo tracking computations are performed by decoder, so it works on every MP3 files.

Later, Wang (Wang,2002) proposed a new error concealment method, based on MPEG-AAC that improved the beat detector in (Wang,2001). Only the SDFT (Shifted Discrete Fourier Transform) coefficients are employed in (Wang,2002), instead of both window types and the MDCT coefficients. The sub-band energy slope (derivative) as FV (Feature Vector) is also used in (Wang,2002). The method proposed in (Wang,2002) works both on codec and encoder so it is necessary to compress the music files with the modified encoder to use this algorithm.

The WSP is used in error concealment contest even in (Kurniawati,2004). (Kurniawati,2004) is based on MPEG-AAC format and uses the WSP to perform better error concealment in non-stationary signals. In this work when the packet lost is a short window granule, the previous short window received replaces it. If a long window granule is lost, to recover the error a frame repetition technique is used.

The state of the art provides several scientific works that propose solutions to solve beat/tempo tracking problem in compressed domain, but the whole studies are related to error concealment and not directly to M.I.R.

Synchronization Algorithms in PCM Domain

Many algorithms that deal with synchronization have been proposed in literature. The majority of them can be subdivided into two steps: in the first one, audio and score are analysed to extract the low level features (Haus, 2004; Goto,2001; Sethares,2005; delacuadra,2001; tzanetakis,2000), the second one links the low level features extracted from audio and the related score.

The typical score analysis phase is performed using a verticalization algorithm. This algorithm groups the notes in the score system that is played at the same time.

The second step can be done implementing a DTW algorithm (Dannenberg,2003; Muller,2004; Arifi2003; Arifi,2004; Dixon,2005; Turetsky,2003), hidden Markov models (Soulez,2003), discriminative learning algorithms (Keshet,2007) or heuristic models (D'Aguanno,2007).

The algorithms proposed in literature use several different systems to implement audio analysis, with well-known tools from audio signal processing. (Arifi,2003) proposes an onset detection followed by pitch detection. In (Muller,2004) the feature extraction procedure performs the following operations: decomposition of the audio signal into spectral bands corresponding to the fundamental pitches and harmonics, followed by the computation of the positions of significant energy increases for each band - such positions are candidates for note onsets.

To select the correct links between audio and score a *template matching technique* (Soulez,2003; Dannenberg,2003; Turetsky,2003) can be used. Such algorithms render a MIDI score to obtain a template of the real execution that is compared to the real audio using a DTW. The correct synchronisation is then obtained from the difference between the agogics of the real execution and that of MIDI. Turetsky (Turetsky,2003a) first convert the score data (given in MIDI format) into an audio data stream using a synthesizer. Then, the two audio data streams are analyzed by means of a short-time Fourier transform (STFT) which in turn yields a sequence of suitable feature vectors. Based on an adequate local distance measure permitting pairwise comparison of these feature vectors, the best alignment is derived using DTW.

TEMPO INDUCTION AND BEAT TRACKING ALGORITHMS IN MP3

Beat Tracking in MP3

Wang (2001) proposes the Window-Switching Pattern (WSP) as information to refine the output of an MDCT coefficients analysis in a beat tracking task in order to perform better error concealment for music transmission in noisy channel.

The algorithm extracts the sub-band MDCT coefficients and then it calculates any sub-band energy. The basic principle of onset selection is setting a proper threshold for the extracted sub band energy values.

A search window is defined then beat candidates are selected in individual bands based on a threshold method in the given search window. Within each search window the number of candidates in each band is either one or zero. If there are one or more valid candidates selected from individual bands, they are then clustered and converged to a single candidate.

A confidence score is calculated for each beat candidate. Based on them, a final confidence score is calculated, which is used to determine whether a converged candidate is a beat.

A Statistical model selects the correct beat from the beat candidate set.

Before a beat candidate is finally marked and stored as a beat, it has to pass a confidence test. Only a candidate with sufficient confidence is selected as a beat. Its position, IBI, and confidence score are stored. The confidence score is also used as a feedback to calculate the confidence score of future beat candidates.

In the last step, the WSP identified by the encoder is used to refine the position, IBI and confidence obtained from the previous analysis.

Because of its aim (error concealment) this algorithm has to work in real-time and it has to calculate the position of the next beat (to select the correct frame which will substitute the corrupted one). It is a matter of fact that WSP does not tackle correctly all the beats in a piece than in this case a frequency analysis it is needed. In tempo induction the aim of the algorithm is totally different (music-BPM content analysis) in fact the algorithm addressing tempo induction do not take into account the correct position of the single beat, so the WSP can be used alone to address that problem.

Tempo Induction in MP3

In (D'Aguanno,2006) it is proposed a template matching technique, based on WSP solely, to reach a general purposes tempo extractor on music with drums. Because the WSP is structured coherently with the drums line it is possible to compare this pattern with a simple template made up by a vector filled with 0 and with a 1 value where is a metronome beat. Any elements of this array represent an MP3 granule. This array has to be matched with the WSP found by the MP3 encoder. An estimation function is required. This function has to yield the distance between the metronome template examined and the real MP3 window-switching pattern. The general schema of that algorithm can be found in Figure 1.

The Metronome Templates

The first step of the algorithm is dedicated to metronome template creation. The algorithm takes into account metronomes that range from 40 to 600 BPM. This assumption is related to the algorithm implementation. The results over 240 BPM are discarded as a consequence of the common metronome range.

Figure 1. Block diagram of tempo induction algorithm using WSP

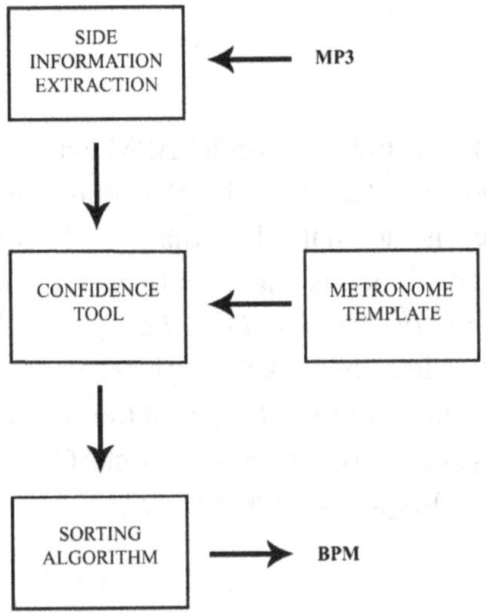

Metronome templates over 240 BPM are used because the algorithm finds the metronome template having the maximum positive distance from its BPM number. A vector filled with 0 and 1 represents each metronome. The number of vector elements is equal to the number of frames.

Confidence Tool

The WSP and the Metronome template selected are multiplied element-by-element. The algorithm takes into account only positive matches because the number of positive matches is about 1/10 of the negative matches. Thus negative matches will always prevail over the positive ones. The result of this operation is stored in a vector which has the same length of the two vectors considered (WSP, Metronome template).

For each vector calculated, one for each metronome considered, the algorithms sums the vector's values and then stores this result into a vector where the index represents the BPM value and the value in the cell represents the number of beats that match. This vector is called *conf*. The Confidence Tool block will end sorting the *conf* vector and saving in *DC* the original indexes; which means that: let *OrdConf* be the result of the sorting operation then *OrdConf(i)=conf(DC(i))*.

Sorting Algorithm

In this section we describe the last step of that algorithm. The first operation performed is:

For each *i*, *BPM (i) = i - DC (i)*, where *i* is the index of the BPM, in other words the BPM name and *BPM* will represent the confidence obtained by the selected BPM.

In this way the algorithm calculates the offset between the metronome starting position (1th for metronome 40, 2nd for metronome 41 and so on until metronome 600 having position 560th) and the vector *DC* resulting from the previous subsection.

The algorithm selects the *max(BPM)* that is lower than 240. This is the algorithm result.

Tempo Induction in MP3 Using Frequency Analysis

The Proposed Algorithm

The aim of the proposed algorithm is trying to solve the BPM extraction problem analysing each MP3 frame, not considering the information from the WSP. This algorithm gets the necessary information directly from the compressed file. In Figure 2 is shown its block diagram. In comparison to (D'Aguanno,2007a), it is possible to note that only the first block is changed. Instead of the first one, three new blocks are used: *Frequency Extraction*, *Spectral Analysis* and *Beat Recognition*. The first extracts the frequencies from the file, the second arranges the data and looks over the spectral part we are interested in, the third contains the rules to detect one beat in a group of frames. After this analysis, the algorithm produces a vector, so that it is possible to use, without any change, the blocks *Confidence Tool*, *Metronome Template* and *Sorting Algorithm* proposed in (D'Aguanno,2007a).

Frequency Extraction

In this section, the algorithm processes the audio file in order to obtain a text file that contains 576 frequency values for each frame normalized from -1 to 1. In this file for every 576 value a sequence of "*" is printed out, which shows the end of one granule and the beginning of the next. This text file is not easy to handle due to its dimension: for a~3 minutes audio file we will have more than 200 MB of space occupied.

In case of mono signal, we will have 576 values every 0.013 s. In a stereo signal instead, the Time-granule remains the same, but the Hybrid will have double values: channels left and right are rotated and appear like two consecutive granules.

Figure 2. Block diagram of tempo induction algorithm using frequency analysis

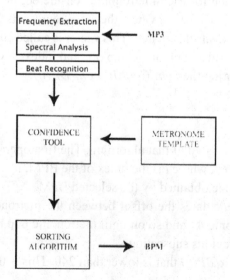

Spectral Analysis

The chosen strategy is quite simple: in the audio file the software tries to identify the drum kick hits. Obviously this kind of approach has a limit: the drum, or a strong percussion source is necessary in order that the algorithm can succeed. The drum kick is chosen because of its:

- Low frequency range
- High energy onset

This frequency range is usually the less crowded in a musical mix and presumably the most regular so even a little variation of intensity is easily detectable. What the algorithm will try to detect is to find out the energy difference at the low frequencies, between two consecutive time instants, for which it can be possible to assume the presence of the beat.

First, the algorithm reads the text file and imports only the first 9 frequency lines for each granule. Now the algorithm counts the modulus of the whole array to remove the minus symbol caused by the phase. At this time the algorithm has a 'time--frequency' system, at this point to be able to value the energy factor for each instant, the algorithm moves on a 'time--energy' system. In order to do that, it calculates a frequency mean first, followed by a temporal mean. One single granule lasts 13 ms, but the analysis on the single granule would not be realistic because no drum kick hit lasts just 13 ms. Therefore the algorithm calculates the mean on a 10 granules block.

Beat Recognition

First of all, the first 999 frames are discarded to avoid silences or instrumental intro without drum. That is an arbitrary condition, which in several cases improves the algorithm precision, because its analysis is not altered from energetic values without rhythmic pattern. The algorithm scrolls the music piece analyzing each line starting from the 100th. At the same time an *analyzing window,* equal to 11 values, is created, and it will always keep the considered line in the centre position. The software reads each line one by one, also moving the analyzing window at the same time. In this way each line is not considered alone, but in the context in which it is. So the algorithm counts the *standard deviation* of the values in the window instant by instant.

Intuitively, the first condition needed in order to consider a line as a beat, is having an energy component above the average of the surrounding values. The algorithm subtracts the standard deviation value to the arithmetic mean of the window.

The next part of the algorithm is composed by 3 rules. When they are all verified at the same time, instant by instant, they return a beat.

The value we are considering must be:

- Greater than the mean value minus the standard deviation of the considered window
- Greater than the previous value
- Greater than the 2 next values

So the algorithm multiplies the cell number inserting the original value repeated 10 times.
After that the algorithms will use the same block proposed in (D'Aguanno,2006)

Tempo Tracking in MP3

At a high level of abstraction our algorithm can be described as an operator that, after having segmented the musical piece into many little blocks, estimates the BPM value for each of them. At this point it finds out how many times specific values appear in contiguous positions and decides which to consider and which to discard. Subsequently the algorithm detects the tempo shiftings and after how many seconds from the beginning of the piece these appear. As said above no frequency analysis is employed.

In Figure 3 it should be noted that the algorithm could be divided into 6 main sections or blocks: first of all the WSP of the considered file is divided into 4 parts and the BPM of each of them are calculated.

In the second block the WSP, following the results of the previous section, is subdivided into many smaller parts and for each of them the BPM value is detected. After that all the values obtained from the previous block are analyzed and the counting of how many times very similar values appear in contiguous positions is performed. The following step, taking into account the previous results, has the task to choose which value is correct and which one it is not. The BPM and the timing of tempo shiftings (if present) are calculated.

BPM Adaptive Detection

The algorithm checks out if the values contained in the four blocks are greater than 130 BPM (empirically chosen value), the algorithm splits the array containig the whole WSP in many blocks, each of which equals to 32 quarter notes at 240 BPM. If the previous condition is not satisfied, the array containing the whole WSP is subdivided into blocks that equal to 32-quarter notes at the higher BPM value found. These conditions have been set after having made many tests in order to observe the algorithm's behaviour in

Figure 3. Block diagram of tempo tracking algorithm

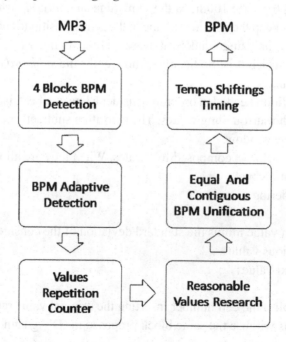

different situations. In fact, if a section of a musical piece has a slow rhytmic pattern, dividing this section using the first method would generate a high number of wrong values and this could compromise the functionality of the algorithm. Once the WSP is divided, the algorithm detects the BPM value for each block using the method described in (D'Aguanno,2007a).

FREQUENCY ANALYSIS FOR MUSIC SYNCHRONIZATION IN MP3

The algorithms in PCM domain cannot be applied directly to compressed domain because they are based on tools from audio signal processing as Short Time Fourier Transform (STFT), or decomposition into spectral bands related to fundamental and harmonic pitches or template matching technique etc.

In MP3 we cannot perform a STFT or similar transformations because this format stores MDCT coefficients of the signal, so a transformation has just been performed. A template matching technique cannot be applied directly to MP3, because at least we should compress the MIDI template into MP3 before the template matching. It should be noted that the compression stage is more cost expensive than decompression, this means more overhead than decompress MP3 into PCM and perform synchronization using one of the algorithms in PCM domain. Thus the MDCT coefficients have to be our starting point for frequency analysis.

The first problem - related to MP3 musical analysis - is the limited frequency resolution in MDCT. For example an MP3 with sample frequency at 44100 Hz has a frequency resolution of 40 Hz. This frequency resolution does not allow differentiating adjacent notes. For example the *A4* has a frequency of 440 Hz, the *A#4* has 466 Hz and *Ab4* has 415 Hz, thus a frequency resolution of 40 Hz cannot discriminate among that notes. We do not try to analyze the short block because in this blocks there are 192 frequency lines, thus the frequency resolution is about 115 Hz that is useless to identify notes.

To address this problem our analysis takes into account first, second and third harmonic of the notes, in this way we can discriminate also the notes in fourth octave. The problem remains for the lower octaves.

We calculate the relative energy of a particular note in one granule:

$$\text{Erel}(n,j) = \sum_{h=1}^{3} (E(n,h,j)) / \sum_{n=1}^{576} E(i,j) \tag{1}$$

Where *n* is the note name selected (see section "MusicXML"), *E(i,j)* is the energy of the *i-th* frequency line in the *j-th* granule and *h* is the harmonic. *E(n,h,j)* is the energy of the frequency line closest to the frequency of the *h* harmonic of note *n* in the *j-th* granule. When this formula is applied to low energy signal it oscillate generating a series of ripple. This behavior is due to the low energy value, which is the denominator of Formula 1. It should be noted that this function has a behavior not stable so the score is needed to identify correctly the notes inside the MP3. In subsection "MP3 and MusicXML" we will show how the MusicXML score can lead the MP3 analysis.

MP3 and MusicXML

Taking into account the high oscillations generated by formula number 1 we have to pay attention to the threshold selection. This threshold is used to discriminate the presence of a note inside an MP3 granule.

Let us introduce the following Formula 2, which tries to identify the number of granules (*x*) where a note (*n*) has to be identified.

$$x(n) = F * gnd(n) / D \qquad (2)$$

Where F is the number of granules composing the MP3, *gnd(n)* is the *global note dration* and D is the number of *divisions* composing the MusicXML score. Formula number 2 can be derived from this observation: the note durations are not absolute values they are relative values. This means that for example for each BPM velocity a quarter note will be double than an eight note. Thus if a note is present (e.g.) in the 30% of the score that note could be present in the 30% of the audio file, without respect to song velocity. In formula:

$$x(n)/F = gnd(n)/D \qquad (3)$$

This assumption may fail when the song has an higher level of variations due to interpretation choices. For example a musician may decide to play a score doubling the duration of the first chord and play the others halving theirs duration. In this case Equation number 3 is violated. In other cases Equation 3 may be still valid even if the musician varies chords duration. For example, he/she can double durations of chord number 1 and 2 and halve the duration of chord number 3 and 4. In this case Equation number 3 is still valid even if the player changes the agogics.

The Formula number 2 is used to calculate a reliable threshold value about *Erel(n,j)* to identify the presence or not of the note n inside the frame j. We set this threshold to a value near to 0 and then we increase this value until the whole granule number containing the note n is equal to *x(n)*. In this way we calculate twelve different thresholds, one for each note name. After this operation we perform a median filter over the result in order to eliminate the false positive identifications due to high variations of Formula number 1 result.

RESULTS OF THE ALGORITHMS

All the algorithms presented in that chapter dealing with tempo and beat induction/tracking obtains results similar to their counterparts acting in PCM domain. For example the algorithm presented in (D'Aguanno,2007a) scored between the second and the eleventh place when it is applied to the same dataset of the MIREX contest 2004, see (D'Aguanno,2007a; Gouyon,2006) for further information.

In general the tempo induction algorithm are evaluated following two metrics:

- Strong Accuracy: the percentage of tempo estimates within 4% (the precision window) of the ground-truth tempo.

Table 1. The results of the algorithms presented

Algorithm	Number of Songs	Accuracy 1	Accuracy 2	Wrong
D'Aguanno 2007	463	55.29%	77.53%	22.46%
Freq Analisys	463	60.77%	81.17%	18.83%
Tempo Tracking	463	62.37%	84.31%	15.69%

- Weak Accuracy: Weak Accuracy: the percentage of tempo estimates within 4% of either the ground-truth tempo, or half, double, three times, or one third of the ground-truth tempo.

In Table 1 are presented the results obtained by the BPM detection algorithm working on MP3:

From Table 1 it should be noted the frequency analysis module, presented in that chapter, leads to an improvement about the 10% of the performances of the algorithm proposed in (D'Aguanno,2007a).

In order to evaluate the tempo-tracking algorithm presented, we use the following criterion: The tempo, shown from that algorithm, having the large number of concurrencies, has been selected.

The above mentioned conditions are suitable for checking the rightness of the BPM values but not for verifying if the number of tempos detected by the tempo tracking algorithm is correct. For these reasons we have to use additional evaluation metrics:

- Perfect Matching: the number of tempos detected by the algorithm agrees with the real number of tempos present in the musical piece.
- Minor Partial Matching: the number of tempos detected by the algorithm is less than the real number of tempos present in the musical piece.
- Major Partial Matching: the number of tempos detected by the algorithm is greater than the real number of tempos present in the musical piece.

Table 2 shows the algorithm is able to find the correct number of tempo shiftings in 75% of analyzed cases. Nevertheless, considering the cases presenting a major partial matching (10%), is possible to find out that the algorithm is not getting all wrong. In fact some of the examined musical pieces have a part in which one of the tempos is not constant but increases (like an accelerando). In this particular situation the algorithm could be able to detect some intermediate values, and that's exactly what happens in our case. Let's now consider the cases where a minor partial matching is found (15%). In these cases some of the tempos of the examined musical pieces have a very short duration ad the algorithm isn't able to track them down. In fact a tempo must last at least 15 seconds otherwise it won't be detected.

Unfortunately the tempo tracking algorithms shows some limits related to time changes detection due to the limited time resolution of the MP3, in fact the timing has to be related to frame timing and than some retards are introduced.

A simple synchronization system to test the synchronization algorithm, about its ability to search notes in MP3 audio, has been developed. The testing system can be summarized has follows:

1. Score verticalization and calculus of formula number 1 for each note name in the MusicXML score;
2. Calculus of formula number 2 for each note name in the score;
3. Threshold level selection;
4. Median filter;

Table 2.

Number of Songs	Perfect matching	Minor partial matching	Major partial matching
102	75%	15%	10%

5. Each verticalized chord in the score is linked with the first frame which contains the notes in the chord.

It should be noted that a frame containing the same notes of the previous one is discarded.

The approach proposed is purely sequential, then if an error occurs it spreads over the whole note sequence. In fact, the algorithm has been tested on short MP3 audio files, about 15s long. Over that duration the algorithm loose synchronization because errors about previous notes cannot be recovered.

Testing this software on 20 excerpts of various music pieces, we obtained a positive degree about 60% of the whole notes in the excerpts. It should be noted that this percentage lowers for real music excerpts to 40% and raises high to 75% for MIDI ones. Its maximum (about 80%) is obtained for MIDI monodic pieces.

In a future will be necessary to develop a real decisional part to link the notes in the score and the notes in the MP3. To do that the same approach used in PCM domain can be used.

CONCLUSION

In this chapter we have presented many algorithms devoted to music content analysis working directly in compressed domain.

The algorithms presented obtain results similar to their counterparts working in PCM, thus the application of that algorithms may lead to music information systems that can produce in a faster way because nowadays the large part of music database stores data in compressed formats, like MP3.

The focus of the algorithms presented in this chapter is not only dedicated to large database, but also to single users because, thanks to MP3 revolution, now it is usual to find users having thousands of song in their private collections. Needless to say, algorithms that can lead to direct content analysis without performing decoding appears very useful for that users.

In the future it would be very interesting to expand the number of algorithm acting in compressed domain with respect to the performed tasks – nowadays only tempo and beat tracking, and music synchronization have been addressed in directly compressed domain.

Another interesting point would be the application of the direct algorithms of content audio analysis even in other formats like AAC or WMA or OGG/Vorbis.

REFERENCES

Allen, P., & Dannenberg, R. (1990). Tracking Musical Beats in Real Time. In *ICMC, Glasgow 1990 Proceedings, International Computer Music Association*, (pp. 140-143).

Alonso, M., David, B., & Richard, G. (2004). Tempo and beat estimation of musical signals. In *Proc. Int. Conf. Music Information Retrieval*, (pp. 158-163).

Arifi, V., Clausen, M., Kurth, F., & Muller, M. (2003). Automatic Synchronization of Music Data in Score-, MIDI-and PCM-Format. In *4th International Conference on Music Information Retrieval, ISMIR 2003*.

Arifi, V., Clausen, M., Kurth, F., & Muller, M. (2004). Automatic Synchronization of Musical Data: A Mathematical Approach. In Hewlett, W., & Selfridge-Fields, E. (Eds.), *Computing in Musicology*. Cambridge, MA: MIT Press.

Baraté, A., Haus, G., Ludovico, L. A., & Vercellesi, G. (2005). MXDemo: a Case Study about Audio, Video, and Score Synchronization. In *Proceedings of IEEE Conference on Automatic Production of Cross Media Content for Multi-channel Distribution (AXMEDIS)*, (pp. 45-52).

D'Aguanno, A., Haus, G., & Vercellesi, G. (2006). MP3 window-switching pattern preliminary analysis for general purposes Beat Tracking. In *Proceedings of the 120th AES Convention*.

D'Aguanno, A., & Vercellesi, G. (2007). Automatic synchronisation between audio and score musical description layers. In *Semantic Multimedia* (*Vol. 4816*, pp. 200–210). Berlin: Springer-Verlag. doi:10.1007/978-3-540-77051-0_22

D'Aguanno, A., & Vercellesi, G. (2007a). Tempo induction algorithm in MP3 compressed domain. In *Proceedings of the international workshop on multimedia information retrieval*, (pp. 153-158).

Dannenberg, R. B., & Hu, N. (2003). Polyphonic Audio Matching for Score Following and Intelligent Audio. In *Proceedings of the 2003 International Computer Music Conference*.

Davies, M. E. P., & Plumbley, M. D. (2005). Beat tracking with a two state model. In *Proceedings of IEEE Int. Acoustics, Speech, and Signal Processing, (ICASSP '05)*, (pp. 241 – 244).

de la Cuadra, P., Master, A., & Sapp, C. (2001). Efficient pitch detection techniques for interactive music. In *Proceedings of the 2001 International Computer Music Conference*.

Dixon, S. (2001). Automatic extraction of tempo and beat from expressive performances. *Journal of New Music Research, 31*(1), 39–58. doi:10.1076/jnmr.30.1.39.7119

Dixon, S. (2001a). An Empirical Comparison of Tempo Trackers. In *Proceedings of the 8th Brazilian Symposium on Computer Music*.

Dixon, S., Pampalk, E., & Widmer, G. (2003). Classification of dance music by periodicity patterns. In *Proc. Int. Conf. Music Information Retrieval*, (pp. 159-165).

Dixon, S., & Widmer, G. (2005). MATCH: A Music Alignement Tool Chest. In *6th International Conference on Music Information Retrieval, ISMIR 2005*.

Eisenberg, G., Batke, J. M., & Sikora, T. (2004). Efficiently Computable Similarity Measures For Query By Tapping Systems. In *Proc. of the 7th Int. Conference on Digital Audio Effects*, (pp. 189-193). Naples, Italy: DAFx.

Good, M. (2001a). *MusicXML for Notation and Analysis. The VirtualScore: Representation, Retrieval, Restoration*. Cambridge, MA: MIT Press.

Good, M., et al. (2001). *MusicXML: An Internet-Friendly Format for Sheet Music*. XML Conference and Expo.

Goto, M. (2001). An Audio-based Real-time Beat Tracking System for Music With or WithoutDrumsounds. *Journal of New Music Research, 30*(2), 159–171. doi:10.1076/jnmr.30.2.159.7114

Gouyon, F., & Dixon, S. (2005). A Review of Automatic Rhythm Description Systems. *Computer Music Journal, 29*(1), 34–54. doi:10.1162/comj.2005.29.1.34

Gouyon, F., Klapuri, A., Dixon, S., Alonso, M., Tzanetakis, G., Uhle, C. & Cano, P. (2006). An experimental comparison of audio tempo induction algorithms. *IEEE Trans. on Speech and Audio Proc, 14*(5).

Haus, G., Longari, M., & Pollastri, E. (2004). A score-driven approach to music information retrieval. *Journal of the American Society for Information Science and Technology, 55*(12), 1045–1052. doi:10.1002/asi.20056

Keshet, J., Shalev-Shwartz, S., Singer, Y. & Chazan, D. (2007). A Large Margin Algorithm for Speech-to-Phoneme and Music-to-Score Alignment. *Audio, Speech and Language Processing, IEEE Transactions on [see also Speech and Audio Processing, IEEE Transactions on], 15*(8), 2373-2382.

Kurniawati, E., & Kurniawan, E. Lau, C.T., Premkumar, B., Absar, J., & George, S. (2004). Error concealment scheme for MPEG-AAC. In *Communications Systems. ICCS 2004. The Ninth International Conference on,* (pp. 240-246).

MPEG1 - Information Technology - Coding of Moving Pictures and Associated Audio for Digital Storage Media at up to about 1.5 Mbits/s - Part 3: Audio I. I. S. I. 11172-3. *(n.d.).*

MPEG2 - Information Technology - Generic Coding of Moving Pictures and Associated Audio, Part 3: Audio I. I. S. I. 13818-3. *(n.d.).*

Muller, M., Kurth, F., & Roder, T. (2004). Towards an Efficient Algorithm for Automatic Score-to-Audio Synchronization. In *5th International Conference on Music Information Retrieval, ISMIR 2004.*

Noll, D. (1997). MPEG Digital Audio Coding. *IEEE Signal Processing Magazine, 14*, 59–81. doi:10.1109/79.618009

Pan, D. (1995). A tutorial on MPEG/audio compression. *IEEE MultiMedia, 2*, 60–74. doi:10.1109/93.388209

Scaringella, N., & Zoia, G. (2004). A Real-Time Beat Tracker For Unrestricted Audio Signals. In *SMC '04 Conference Proceedings.*

Scheirer, E. (1998). Tempo and beat analysis of acoustic musical signals. *The Journal of the Acoustical Society of America, 103*(1), 588–601. doi:10.1121/1.421129

Sethares, W. A., Morris, R. D., & Sethares, J. C. (2005). Beat tracking of musical performances using low-level audio features. *IEEE Transactions on Speech and Audio Processing, 13*(2), 275–285. doi:10.1109/TSA.2004.841053

Soulez, F., Rodet, X., & Schwarz, D. (2003). Improving Polyphonic and Poly-Instrumental Music to Score Alignment. In *4th International Conference on Music Information Retrieval, ISMIR 2003,* (pp. 143-148).

Turetsky, R. J., & Ellis, D. (2003). Ground-truth transcriptions of real music from force-aligned midi syntheses. In *4th International Conference on Music Information Retrieval, ISMIR 2003.*

Turetsky, R. J., & Ellis, D. P. (2003a). Force-Aligning MIDI Syntheses for Polyphonic Music Transcription Generation. In *Proceedings of International Conference on Music Information Retrieval (ISMIR).*

Tzanetakis, G., & Cook, F. (2000). Sound analysis using MPEG compressed audio. In *Proceedings of the IEEE International Conference on Acoustics, Speech, and Signal Processing ICASSP '00*.

Tzanetakis, G., & Cook, P. (2002). Musical Genre Classification of Audio Signals. *IEEE Transactions on Speech and Audio Processing*, *10*(5), 293–302. doi:10.1109/TSA.2002.800560

Uhle, C., & Herre, J. (2003). Estimation Of Tempo, Micro Time And Time Signature From Percussive. In *Proc. of the 6th Int. Conference on Digital Audio Effects (DAFX-03)*.

Uhle, C., Rohden, J., Cremer, M., & Herre, J. (2004). Low complexity musical meter estimation from polyphonic music. In *Proc. AES 25th International Conference*, (pp. 63-68).

Wang, Y., & Streich, S. (2002). A drumbeat-pattern based error concealment method for music streaming applications. In *IEEE International Conference on Acoustics, Speech, and Signal Processing, 2002, (ICASSP '02)*, (Vol. 3, pp. 2817-2820).

Wang, Y., & Vilermo, M. (2001). A compressed domain beat detector using MP3 audio bitstreams. In *MULTIMEDIA '01: Proceedings of the ninth ACM international conference on Multimedia*, (pp. 194-202).

Zhaorong, H., Weibei, D., & Zaiwang, D. (2001). New window-switching criterion of audio compression. *Multimedia Signal Processing, 2001 IEEE Fourth Workshop on*, (pp. 319-323).

Zwicker, E., & Fastl, H. (1990). *Psychoacoustics: Facts and Models*. Berlin: Heidelberg.

Chapter 15
Acoustic Analysis of Music Albums

Kristoffer Jensen
Aalborg University Esbjerg, Denmark

ABSTRACT

Most music is generally published in a cluster of songs, called an album, although many, if not most people enjoy individual songs, commonly called singles. This study proposes to investigate whether or not there is a reason for assembling and enjoying full albums. Two different approaches are undertaken in order to investigate this, both based on audio features, calculated from the music, and related to the common music dimensions rhythm, timbre and chroma. In the first experiment, automatic segmentation is done on full music albums. If the segmentation is done on song boundaries, which is to be expected, as different fade-ins and –outs are employed, then songs are seen as the homogenous units, while if the boundaries are found within songs, then other homogenous units also exist. A second experiment on music sorting by similarity reveals findings on the sorting complexity of music albums. If the sorting complexity is high, then the albums are unordered; otherwise the album is ordered with regards to the features. A discussion of the results of the evaluation of the segment boundaries and sorting complexity reveals interesting findings.

INTRODUCTION

Music can be enjoyed on different time scales, going from the individual notes, to the riffs, as popularized in for instance ring tones, through choruses and full songs, which are popularized through the single format, and to albums, that many consider cannot be listened to other than at full length. This applies in particular to the concept albums. The investigations of albums will lead to the analysis of segmentation of music, to the analysis of sorting of music, and to the analysis of the theories of music perceptions.

DOI: 10.4018/978-1-61692-859-9.ch015

Theories of what homogenous units are to be found in music can be found in the music theory, for instance by the grouping theory of Lerdahl & Jackendoff (1983). Results from memory research (Snyder 2000) can also be used as the ground reference. Snyder refers to echoic memory (early processes) for event fusion, where fundamental units are formed by comparison with 0.25 seconds, the short-term memory for melodic and rhythmic grouping (by comparison up to 8 seconds), and long-term memory for formal sectioning by comparison up to one hour. Snyder (2000) relates this to the Gestalt theory grouping mechanisms of proximity (events close in time or pitch will be grouped together. Proximity is the primary grouping force at the melodic and rhythmic level (Snyder 2000, p 40). The second factor in grouping is similarity (events judged as similar, mainly with respect to timbre, will be grouped together). A third factor is continuity (events change in the same direction, for instance pitch). These grouping mechanisms give rise to closure, that can operate at the grouping level, or the phrase level, which is the largest group the short-term memory can handle. When several grouping mechanisms occur at the same time, intensification occurs, which gives rise to higher-level grouping. Other higher-level grouping mechanisms are parallelism (repeated smaller groups), or recurrence of pitch. The higher-level grouping demands long-term memory and they operate at a higher level in the brain, as compared to the smaller time-scale grouping. The higher-level grouping is learned while the shorter grouping is not. Snyder (2000) further divides the higher level grouping into the objective set, which is related to a particular music, and the subjective set, which is related to a style of music. Both sets are learned by listening to the music repeatedly. Snyder (2000) also related the shorter grouping to the 7±2 theory (Miller 1956), that states that the short-term memory can remember between five to nine elements.

Recently, the chunk has been appointed as an important element of music (Kühl 2007, Godøy 2008). A chunk is a short segment of a limited number of sound elements, corresponding to the working memory of approximately 3 seconds. A chunk consists of a beginning, a focal point (peak) and an ending. Both Kühl and Godøy seems to believe that the chunk is fundamental in music, but while Kühl mainly relates the chunking to the cognition, in particular the memory, Godøy also relates chunking to the action, i.e. physical gestures. Kühl (2007) extends the chunks to include microstructure (below 1/2 second), mesostructure (the present, approximately 3 seconds) and macrostructure (approximately. 30-40 seconds).

Automatic segmentation using dynamic programming has been proposed previously (Jensen et al 2005, Jehan 2005). In Jensen (2007), the dynamic programming is done of self-similarity matrices, created from the original features (rhythm, chroma or timbre) by comparing each time vector to all other time vectors. The dynamic programming will cluster the time vectors into segments, as long as the vectors are similar. By varying the insertion cost of new segments, segment boundaries can be found at different time scales. A low insertion cost will create boundaries corresponding to micro-level chunks, while a high insertion cost will only create few meso-level chunks. Thus, the same segmentation method can create segments of varying size, from short to long.

With the advent of downloaded music on personal computers, the necessity of assisting users choosing music among thousands of songs has arisen. Such a choice can be random (Shuffle play), by automatic playlist generation, or relate to a degree of similarity between songs. Playlist generation can be done on audio features (Foote 1997), for instance based on one song, or audio input, as in the query-by-humming systems (McNab 1996, Rolland et al 1999, Ghias *et al* 2001). Playlist generation can also be based on meta-data (Pauws & Eggen 2002), and collaborative filtering.

Album vs. Single

What is an album? It is a collection of music tracks, that most often has some unifying content, by the composer, musicians, or otherwise. An album has a total duration above half an hour, and generally contains more than 10 tracks. Originally, the album term was designating a bound container of several 78-RPM discs, which individually could contain up to 10 minutes of music.

Assumably, before the start of technology for storing and distributing music, all genres would be performed in a length corresponding to an album or longer, i.e. in excess of half an hour. The technology up to around 1950 (cylinders and discs; acoustic devices from 1877 (the invention of recordings by Edison) to 1925, and electric devices thereafter) did not allow storing more than a couple of minutes on each support (Schoenherr 2005). Only with the advent of the 33-RPM vinyl record was it possible to store a full album on one support. As the cost of producing the 45-RPM single was lower than producing the larger 33-RPM, it retained popularity among the younger and dance-oriented record buyers. But the CD in the 1980ies supplanted the vinyl, and it does not contain the same production cost advantages for the single format, and thus single sales declined (The Sydney Morning Herald 2004). Lately, singles have regained popularity in the internet-based music sales, represented by the iPod/iTunes combination. In addition, different internet download opportunities currently put thousand of songs on many user music players. It seems clear that technology plays a role in the relative popularity of the album as compared to the single. It is only natural that technology also plays a role in helping users choose music in large databases, through the development of automatic playlist generators. These systems generally work by identifying the similarity between songs. The question remains, however, whether similarity is a good measure for grouping songs. Furthermore, are songs in an album homogenous individually, or do album tracks structure differently, either as one more homogenous group, or as smaller sections that are more homogenous that full songs.

It appears that one of the reasons for listening to music is mood regulation. This applies in particular for the adolescent music listeners (Behne 1997, Saarikallio & Erkkilä 2007). Behne (1997) studied changes in adolescent's development of Musikerleben (basically the sum of psychic processes that accompany active music listening). By asking children questions using different questionnaires, the mood managing (compensating) was the main listening mode found. Children with more problems have higher vegetative or sentimental listening style. Different mood management approaches was also found, i.e. coping with anger either by listening to aggressive music; "living out all feelings of anger", or by listening to slow music; "seek consolation in the music". Gender differences were also found; stimulative listening is more pronounced for boys, while sentimental listening is more pronounced for girls. Saarikallio & Erkkilä (2007) develops a theoretical model through group interviews and forms, which describes music mood regulation as a process of satisfying personal mood-related goals. Both Behne (1997) and Saarikallio & Erkkilä (2007) found a number of listening styles/regulatory strategies that are actively used by listeners to compensate for a problem or satisfy mood regulatory goals. It is not clear from these experiments, however, whether shorter or longer music excerpts are necessary or used in mood regulations. Other issues that may determine the choice of single versus album are the lyrics, and the issues of music and identity (Gerstin 1998).

While other studies are necessary in order to understand the full implications of singles vs. albums in mood regulations and identity creation, the work presented here attempts to draw some initial conclusions and replies to these questions through the analysis of the acoustic content of selected albums. First, features related to the common musical dimensions rhythm, timbre and chroma are calculated. Secondly, two experiments are performed on the selected album, using these features. The first experiment involves determining the homogeneity of songs in an album by merging the features of full albums, and then analyzing whether segment boundaries obtained by automatic segmentation fall within or between songs. The second experiment involves determining whether acoustic similarity is related to song position in an album. To determine this, songs in the selected albums are sorted, and the distance to the original order (the sorting complexity) is analyzed, to find if and how each album is ordered.

The work is organized as follows; first, the feature calculations are presented, and then the dynamic programming are presented along with analysis of the result of segmentation experiments. A second experiment regarding the sorting of songs is presented thereafter, along with a discussion of the significance of the results.

FEATURE ESTIMATION

In this work, features corresponding to music perception have been used in order to perform a good segmentation or sorting of the songs, and also to be able to assess the results to some aspects of human listening. Three different features are investigated here; the rhythmic feature (the *rhythmogram*, Jensen 2005) is based on the autocorrelation of the perceptual spectral flux (PSF, Jensen 2005). The PSF has high energy in the time position where perceptually important sound components, such as notes, have been introduced. The timbre feature (the *timbregram*) is based on the perceptual linear prediction (PLP), a speech front-end (Hermansky 1990), and the harmony feature (the *chromagram*) is based on the chroma (Bartsch & Wakefield 2001), calculated on the short-time Fourier transform (STFT). The Gaussian Weighted Spectrogram (GWS) is performed in order to improve resilience to noise and independence on block size for the *timbregram* and *chromagram*. More information of the feature estimation used here can be found in (Jensen 2007). A speech front-end, such as the PLP alters the STFT data by scaling the intensity and frequency so that it corresponds to the way the human auditory system perceives sounds. The chroma maps the energy of the FFT into twelve bands, corresponding to the twelve notes of one octave. Using the rhythmic, timbre, and harmonic features to identify the structure of the music, thus some of the different aspects of music perception are taken into account.

Rhythmogram

Any model of rhythm should have as basis some kind of feature that reacts to the note onsets. The note onsets mark the main characteristics of the rhythm. In a previous work (Jensen 2005), a large number of features were compared to an annotated database of twelve songs, and the perceptual spectral flux (PSF) was found to perform best. The PSF is calculated with a step size is 10 milliseconds, and the block size is 46 milliseconds. As the spectral flux in the PSF is weighted so as to correspond roughly to the equal loudness contour, both low frequency sounds, such as bass drum, and high frequency sounds, such a hi-hat are equally well taken into account.

This frequency weighting is obtained in this work by a simple equal loudness contour model. The power function is introduced in order to simulate the intensity-loudness power law and reduce the random amplitude variations. These two steps are inspired from the PLP front-end (Hermansky 1990) used in speech recognition. The PSF was compared to other note onset detection features with good results on the percussive case in a recent study (Collins 2005). In order to obtain a more robust rhythm feature, the autocorrelation of the feature is now calculated on overlapping blocks of 8 seconds, with half a second step size (2 Hz feature sample rate), Only the information between zero and two seconds is retained. The autocorrelation is normalized so that the autocorrelation at zero-lag equals one. If visualized with lag time on the y -axis, time position on the x-axis, and the autocorrelation values visualized as intensities, it gives a fast overview of the rhythmic evolution of a song. This representation, called *rhythmogram* (Jensen 2005), provides information about the rhythm and the evolution of the rhythm in time. The autocorrelation has been chosen instead of the fast Fourier transform FFT, for two reasons. First, it is believed to be more in accordance with the human perception of rhythm (Desain 1992), and second, it is believed to be more easily understood visually. The *rhythmogram* gives information about the tempo of the song, along with the strength of the tempo, and also to a slighter degree it gives information about the time signature. In a task where different songs are compared for segmentation or for sorting, the tempo difference will probably dominate the calculations.

Timbregram

The timbre is understood here as the spectral estimate and done here using the perceptual linear Prediction, PLP (Hermansky 1990). This involves using the bark (Sekey & Hanson 1984) scale, together with an amplitude scaling that gives an approximation of the human auditory system. The PLP is calculated with a block size of approximately 46 milliseconds and with a step size of 10 milliseconds. The *timbregram* is a feature that is believed to capture orchestration of the music mainly. In the *timbregram*, information about which instruments are participating in the music at the current time step is given, along with indications of what dynamic level the instruments are played. As the *timbregram* gives information on a very small time scale, it is rather noisy. In order to eliminate some of the noise, and improve the use of the *timbregram* data, smoothing is performed, by summing each bin across the full time-scale using a Gaussian that is localized in time. This is called the Gaussian Weighted Spectrogram, GWS (Jensen 2007). Using the GWS, all segments are used at all time steps, but the current block values are weighted higher than the more distant blocks. By averaging, using the Gaussian average, no specific time localization information is obtained of the individual notes or chords, but instead a general value of the time area is given. In this work, the averaging is done corresponding to a −3 dB window of approximately 1 second. After the GWS, the *timbregram* has a stepsize of ½ second.

Chromagram

Note estimation is notoriously error-prone even if a lot of progress is made in the domain currently. There exists one estimate that is robust and related to the note values, the chroma, which is used here. In the chroma, only the relative content of energy in the twelve notes of the octave is found. No information of the octave of the notes is included. The chroma is calculated from the STFT, using a blocksize of 46 milliseconds and a stepsize of 10 milliseconds. The chroma is obtained by summing the energy of all peaks of 12 $\log_2$ of the frequencies having multiples of 12. The *chromagram* gives information about the note value, without information about the octave. This is a rather good measure of which chords are played, and also of the musical scale and tonality. The *chromagram* gives information of each note played, along with information of unvoiced signals that add some noise to the *chromagram*. As with the *timbregram*, the *chromagram* is smoothed in time by the Gaussian Weighted Spectrogram. This removed information about the individual note values, and it retains better information about the tonality and the long-term presence of note values. The averaging using the GWS is done corresponding to a −3 dB window of approximately 1 seconds. After the GWS, the *chromagram* has a stepsize of ½ second.

As an example of the features, the *rhythmogram*, *timbregram* and *chromagram* of Alicia Keys – Songs in A Minor (J Records, 2001) is shown in Figure 1.

In the *rhythmogram*, it is clear from the visual analysis that each song has a different tempo. Of course, whether a tempo is a certain value or the double or half is difficult to ascertain, but the *rhythmogram* certainly gives information about the tempo, along with some information about the rhythm employed in each song. As for the *timbregram*, all songs have energy high up in the trebles, except one or two in the second part of the album. Most songs have a fade-in and fade-out in the beginning and the end of each song. It also seems many songs end up with some sort of crescendo.

AUTOMATIC MUSIC SEGMENTATION

With the features available for full albums, it is now possible to investigate whether automatic segmentation will find segmentation boundaries in between songs, or inside songs.

Automatic segmentation using dynamic programming or other methods has been proposed previously (Foote 2000, Bartsch & Wakefield 2001, Goto 2003, Chai & Vercoe (2003), Jensen 2005, Jensen *et al* 2005, Jensen 2007). These studies have shown that the acoustics of music permit to segment the songs into smaller segment, corresponding to the chorus/verse, or other structures. In an automatic segmentation task, adjacent blocks are grouped together, forming segments. This can for instance correspond to

Figure 1. Rhythmogram (top), timbregram, and chromagram (bottom) of the album 'Song in A Minor' by Alicia Keys

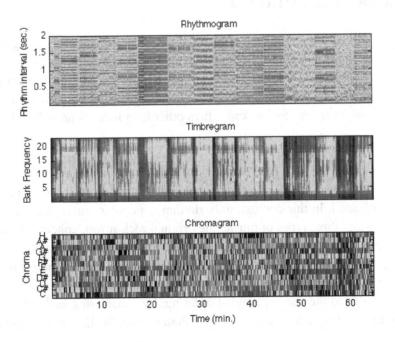

the chorus/verse structure found in most rhythmic music, or to changes in the rhythmic pattern, in the orchestration or in the notes played.

The dynamic programming used here based on the shortest-path algorithm (Cormen *et al* 2001) and done on self-similarity matrices, created from the original features (rhythm, chroma or timbre, Jensen 2007) by calculating the L2 norm of each time vector compared to all other time vectors, using a sequence of N vectors of each song that should be divided into a number of segments. In order to do this, let the *cost c(i,j)* of a segment from block i to j be the weighted sum of the self-similarity and the cost of a new segment be a fixed cost α. In order to compute a best possible segmentation, an edge-weighted directed graph G is constructed with the set of nodes is all the block of the song. For each possible segment an edge exists. The weight of the edge is $\alpha + c(i, j)$. A path in G from node 1 to node $N + 1$ corresponds to a complete segmentation, where each edge identify the individual segments. The weight of the path is equal to the total cost of the corresponding segmentation. Therefore, a shortest path (or path with minimum total weight) from node 1 to node $N + 1$ gives a segmentation with minimum total cost. Such a shortest path can be computed in time $O(N^2)$.

The dynamic programming will cluster the time vectors into segments, as long as the vectors are similar. By varying the insertion cost α of new segments, segment boundaries can be found at different time scales. The same segmentation method can create segments of varying size, from short to long, from the grouping to the form of the music. Kühl (2007) related the different segment sizes in music to the notion of chunks. According to him, the chunk is an important element of music. A chunk is a short segment of a limited number of sound elements; a chunk consists of a beginning, a focal point (peak) and an ending. Kühl (2007) extends the chunks to include microstructure (below 1/2 sec), mesostructure (the present, appr. 3-5 secs) and macrostructure (Superchunks, Kühl and Jensen 2008) (at 30-40 secs). Using the shortest-path segmentation method a low insertion cost will create boundaries corresponding to micro-level chunks, while a high insertion cost will only create few meso-level chunks.

SONG OR CHUNK SEGMENTATION

In this section, a number of full albums are segmented into the same number of segments as there are songs in the album, using the automatic segmentation method based on the shortest path dynamic programming algorithm (Jensen *et al.* 2005). The idea is that if all or most of the segmentation boundaries fall in between songs in the album, then the songs are homogenous between them, while if many automatic segmentation boundaries fall inside songs, then other homogenous areas besides the songs exist.

Database

In order to investigate the issues of album, song or chunk preference, a small collection of representative albums have been collected. In this context, only rhythmic, popular music has been considered. The general idea is to consider three types of music, the original rock-n-roll, concept album and R&B/pop genres. The hypothesis is that there would be a difference in where the segment boundaries are found, dependent on the genre. It is expected that the concept album genre has less boundaries found at song boundaries, and the pop/dance genre has most. The same albums are also used for the experiment on whether similarity is a good measure of playlist ordering, by considering each album a playlist of its own. The original rock-n-roll genre consists of two albums, The Beatles, Sgt Peppers Lonely Hearts

(Parlophone/Capitol, 1967) and Rolling Stones, Exile On Main Street (Atlantic 1972). The concept albums also consist of two albums, Magma - Mekanik Destruktiw Kommandoh (A&M 1973) and Alice Cooper - The Last Temptation (Epic 1994). Finally the pop/R&B genre also consists of two albums, Shakira - Laundry Service (Epic 2001) and Alicia Keys - Songs In A Minor (J Records, 2001). These albums can also be divided into early rhythmic music, from 1967, 1971 and 1972, and recent rhythmic music, from 1994, 2001 and 2001. A second experiment is done using the full Beatles discography.

Segmentation

In order to sort the music, the *rhythmogram*, *timbregram* and *chromagram* features are calculated for each song individually, and then merged together into full album features. The self-similarity matrix is then calculated for each feature, and the shortest-path algorithm is employed using a Newton optimization method to iteratively find the same number of clusters, as there are songs. In this approach, first a low alpha value corresponding to a low cost of inserting new segment and a high alpha value corresponding to a high new segment insertion cost are used to calculate the extreme segmentation boundaries. Then, the average of the two alpha values are used to calculate the segmentation boundaries in between. Now, if the mean segment length is higher than the researched length, the low alpha is set to the mean value, otherwise the high alpha limit is set to the mean value. This is repeated until the alpha limits difference is below a threshold. As the number of segments is decreasing continually with alpha value (Jensen *et al* 2005), this method is guaranteed to converge. Unfortunately, the number of segments often changes in jumps of more than one, which sometimes makes it impossible to find the correct number of segments.

Tempo Normalization

As it is visible that tempo is one of the most changing features between songs, the tempo of the *rhythmogram* is normalized in order to ignore this effect in the segmentation task. Indeed, tempo changes only occur between songs generally, and it would have been dominant in the task of determining the automatic segmentation boundaries for the *rhythmogram*.

The tempo normalization is done as follows. First, the mean *rhythmogram* is calculated for each song of an album. Then the tempo difference of the first and the second song is determined. This tempo difference is estimated by calculating the minimal L2 difference between the mean *rhythmogram* of the two songs, where the second *rhythmogram* is interpolated until it corresponds best with the first song. This is done between a positive and negative tempo difference limit, at 43% of two seconds. The maximum of the L2 difference for all interpolations between the limits is found, and this is the tempo difference between the two songs. For all remaining songs, this same method is used, with the difference that the L2 norm is calculated between the new song and the mean of all songs up to the previous song. As an example of this tempo normalization, the *rhythmogram* of Alicia Keys – Song in A Minor is shown in Figure 2.

In many cases, it is not clear whether a tempo octave error has occurred, and for two songs at the end, there is not much rhythmic presence at all. However, this method of tempo normalization will certainly remove most of the tempo effect on the segmentation.

Figure 2. Original (top) and tempo normalized (bottom) rhythmogram of Alicia Keys – 'Songs in A Minor'

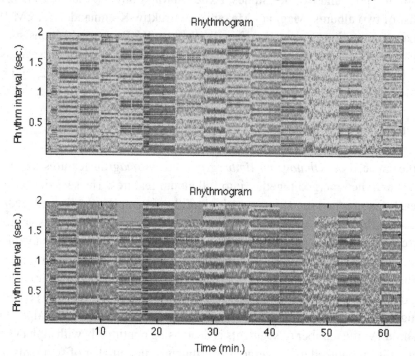

Segmentation Analysis

It is not necessarily an easy task to assess whether the music is homogenous in an album or in each song, or in shortest segments within songs. As a first approach, standard information retrieval performance measures are used in the comparison between the automatic segmentation boundaries and the song boundaries. This will give a first approach to whether the automatic segmentation renders boundaries corresponding to the song boundaries or not. Unfortunately, the automatic segmentation boundaries do not match the song boundaries. For a reasonable distance threshold of 4 seconds, and the mean of the six albums, 3.50 matches were found, of 13.83 song boundaries (Recall=25.30%) & 16.33 *rhythmogram* segments (Precision=15.91%), F_1=0.24, and (for the *timbregram*-based segmentation) 2.17 matched, of 13.83 song boundaries (Recall=15.66%) & 17.83 automatic segments (Precision=9.85%), F_1=0.14. Finally, the information retrieval measures are 2.00 matched, of 13.83 song boundaries (Recall=14.46%) & 17.50 *chromagram* segments (Precision=9.09%), F_1=0.13. As an initial conclusion, the *rhythmogram* boundaries match the song boundaries significantly better than the other features. This, notwithstanding that the *rhythmogram* has been normalized for each song, so as to have the same tempo throughout an album. The six albums have an F_1 value of 0.22, 0.13, 0.16, 0.16, 0.18 and 0.16, respectively. The original rock albums thus have both the best and the worse matches than the concept and pop/R&B albums. These scores are not impressive, though.

All the automatic segmentation boundaries are shown for the six albums together with the song boundaries in Figure 3. The *rhythmogram* boundaries are denoted'+', the *timbregram* 'o', the *chromagram* 'x'. The song boundaries are denoted with vertical lines. If the '+', the 'o', or the 'x' fall on the vertical

Figure 3. Segmentation boundaries for six albums. Rhythmogram boundaries are denoted '+', timbregram 'o', chromagram 'x', and the song boundaries are shown as vertical lines. Time is on the x-axis in minutes, corresponding to the length of each album

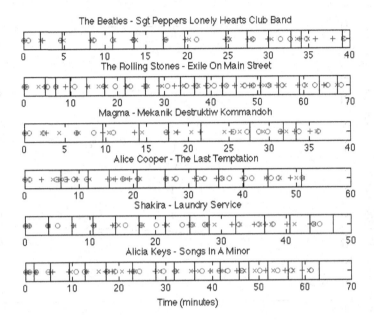

lines, then the corresponding automatic segmentation boundary is a match. The Beatles and Shakira albums seemingly have better matches, which are also reflected in the F_1 values.

While the recall and precision, and the associated F_1 measure give an estimate of the accuracy of the matching between the automatic segmentation boundaries, and the song boundaries, it is believed that these measures are not necessarily giving a full answer to the problem presented here. Instead, the distance of each automatic segmentation boundary to the nearest song boundary is calculated for each automatic segmentation boundary for all features and songs. This measure is presented in a histogram in Figure 4 (top).

If the absolute values of the histogram of distances between the automatic and song boundaries are cumulative summed and divided with the absolute sum, then a measure of the percentages of the automatic segmentation boundaries that are matched to a song boundary within each distance is obtained. This is presented in Figure 4 (bottom) for all six albums and all features. A 95% matching rate is obtained for distances up to 138 seconds. As the mean length of the songs on the six albums is 234 seconds, it would be expected that the automatic boundaries should be matched within half of this. As this is not the case, it can be said that song boundaries is not the main acoustic discriminatory place in music albums. Additionally, the bad recall, precision and F_1 scores also give the same indications. However, giving the intro and outros of the music under test, it may be the case that most automatic segmentations fall within these limits, in which case these boundaries still can be said to belong to the song boundaries. The intro and outro time has been estimated to have an average length of 10 seconds. This includes mainly fade-ins and outs, but also instrumental additions/removals, rhythm changes and occasionally chroma changes. If the matching measures are done on 10 sec thresholds, a better result is obtained, of course. The features match 6.5, 3.5, and 2.5 respectively for the *rhythmogram*, *timbregram* and *chro-*

Figure 4. Histogram of distances to nearest song boundary for all albums and features (top) and cumulative relative number of occurrences (bottom). The 10 seconds mark and 95% matched mark has been indicated in the lower subplot

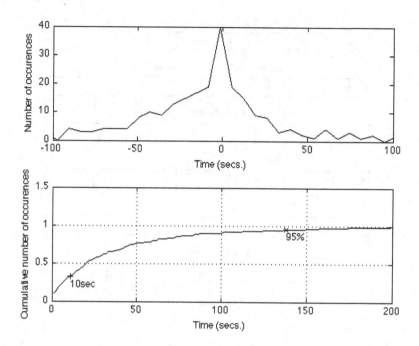

magram. The corresponding F_1 values are 0.43, 0.22, and 0.16. The F_1 values for the six albums are 0.41, 0.27, 0.16, 0.21, 0.29 and 0.26. Significantly better results, but still not so impressive. With the 10 second matching threshold limit, the concept albums have the highest matching scores, which was also the expected result.

Finally, by calculating all distances for all features and songs, 32.13% of the matches are fond within 10 seconds. Thus, approximately one third of the boundaries found from automatic segmentation are matched to the song boundaries.

MUSIC SORTING

Playlist generation is a common topic in music information retrieval today, as it gives technological-based applications to the problem of identifying songs to play in large music databases. Indeed, thousands of songs can exist on music players, with little meta-data (artist, song, genre, etc) to support the retrieval of songs. Playlist generation can be based on either the acoustics of the sound, or some measure of collaborative behavior, or on the metadata belonging to the music. Foote (1997) used the Mel Frequency Cepstral Coefficients (MFCC) and a supervised greedy decision tree growing method and a correlation distance measure on the histogram of the leaf probabilities to sort male and female speech, percussive sounds and music. Other uses of audio features are for instance genre matching (Tzanetakis & Cook 2002). A particular application of music retrieval using acoustics is the so-called query-by-humming systems, in which the singing input is transcribed and pattern matched (McNab 1996, Rolland et al 1999, Ghias *et al 2001)* to the best match in a transcribed music database. Feng *et al* (2003) uses mood as a qualifier for music retrieval. Pauws (2002) uses meta-data of music in an interactive playlist generation process that creates a playlist of similar songs, based on one selected song. In an experiment, Pauws (2002) found indications that this playlist generation created playlist with high rated music than random playlist.

Other uses of meta-data is in the Pandora.com music genome project, in which music experts hand-label the music for better retrieving results. Collaborative music recommendation systems exist in many variants. One example is the iTunes Genius recommendation system.

The approach used here for the experiment on whether album order follows audio similarity or not is based on the Travelling Salesman Problem, which is also used in (Pohle *et al* 2005) for playlist generation. Audio features, the *rhythmogram, timbregram* and *chromagram* are calculated, but only the mean value and the standard deviation of each song are retained. Afterwards, the self-similarity matrix is calculated using the L2 norm. Finally, the travelling salesman problem (TSP) solution is calculated using the concorde software (Concorde 2009). As the optimal solution is NP-hard, and solutions so far are limited to a relatively low number of cities, the Lin-Kernighan (1973) heuristics is used to find a good solution. A travelling salesman problem is related to finding the minimum length that visits each 'city' exactly once. In our case, the cities are songs, and the distances are the L2 norm distance between each song and all other songs. The songs are ordered by the TSP solution in a manner, so as to minimize the total cost from the first song to the last song.

Sorting Complexity

If the songs in an album are sorted in a manner so as to minimize the difference between each adjacent song according to some feature, then the album is considered ordered. If not, then it is considered unordered. In order to verify this, a simple exchange-sorting algorithm is used. This sorting is done in $O(n^2)$. The maximum number of sorting steps is determined to be $0.5n(n-1)$. As the TSP solution may be inversed, this is tested to see if the sorting by the inverse list is done faster.

The TSP algorithm is now used to sorts each album, and the results are compared to the album sequence $(1...n)$, the inverse sequence and all possible circular shifted sequences, i.e. $(2...n, 1; 3...n, 1, 2$, etc). The number of steps necessary to sort the result is divided by the maximum number of sorting steps for randomly ordered sequences, and the square root is taken,

$$C = \sqrt{\frac{Ns}{0.5 \cdot n(n-1)}}, \tag{1}$$

where Ns is the number of sorting steps, n is the number of songs in the album, and C is the sorting complexity of the album. The sorting complexity is equal to one for the inverse order, which is therefore considered ordered. For any random permutation, it does not typically exceed *0.7*. The TSP-based sorting and the estimation of the sorting complexity are done for each feature (*rhythmogram, timbregram* and *chromagram*) individually. If the sorting complexity (C) is above *0.7* then the complexity is maximal, while if it close to zero, the sorting complexity is minimal. The sorting complexity C can be approximately said to be linear with respect to the randomness of the order of the result of the TSP solution. The sorting complexity corresponds to the percentage of an ordered sequence that is scrambled. I.e., if the sequence has N elements, and the first $N/2$ elements a permuted randomly, then $C \approx 0.35$. The alternating sequence, i.e. first odd, then even elements, or on a general level, first multiples of *n*, then the other elements has sorting complexity $C<=0.5$, with the $C=0.5$ for $n=2$. The total sorting complexity for all six test albums are shown in Table 1.

As a first conclusion, all albums have rather high sorting complexity. However, if the sorting complexity is significantly above *0.7* then it has some order different from a random permutation. This is not the case for the ordering found here. Indeed, the mean sorting complexity for all six albums and three features is $C=0.53$, which corresponds for instance to the case where approximately 76% of the songs are in random order. The Rolling Stones album has relatively higher sorting complexity for all three features, while the concept albums have the lowest sorting complexity. In particular, the concept albums have low sorting complexity for the *chromagram*- and *timbregram*-based TSP sorting result. Overall, the *chromagram* has the lowest sorting complexity, with the *timbregram* having the second-lowest sorting complexity.

Finally, if the songs of all six albums are merged together, then the sorting complexity is *0.63*, *0.52*, and *0.63* for the *rhythmogram*-, *timbregram*-, and *chromagram*-based TSP sorting results. If the circular shift sorting complexity maximum is found instead, then the full six albums have a complexity of *0.78*, *0.85*, and *0.78*. This is above the sorting complexity for completely random order, and there must therefore be some hint of a sorting system in the albums. This can be an alternating, an up-down sequence, or a something else, which renders sorting complexity above *0.7*. It is also interesting to observe that the same feature, which renders the lowest sorting complexity for the merged six albums, i.e. the *timbregram*, also renders the highest. This is also an indication that there is some system in the sorted order, in particular perhaps using the *timbregram*.

While it is difficult from the current study to say exactly how the order of the album songs is chosen, it is clear that it is not a random order sequence.

A second experiment using the same method has been performed on the complete Beatles discography. The sorting complexity result of this is shown in Table 2.

In the case of the Beatles discography, the sorting complexity is approximately the same as the six albums of varying genres. The mean sorting complexity is *0.55*, *0.56*, and *0.55* for the *rhythmogram*, *timbregram* and *chromagram*, respectively. While the *timbregram* renders the lowest sorting complexity for 10 out of 13 albums, it does not have lower overall mean sorting complexity. No distinctive difference among the albums or features is otherwise immediately discernible. The merged 13 albums have a sorting complexity of *0.64*, *0.54*, and *0.63*. The maximum sorting complexity within the reversed

Table 1. Sorting complexity values for the TSP sorting results for six albums and three features

Album/Feature	No songs	Rhythmogram	Timbregram	Chromagram	Mean
Beatles	13	0.58	**0.45**	0.59	0.54
Rolling Stones	18	**0.58**	0.62	0.60	0.60
Magma	7	0.53	**0.38**	0.44	0.43
Alice Cooper	10	0.56	0.49	**0.42**	0.49
Shakira	13	0.57	0.52	**0.51**	0.53
Alicia Keys	16	0.54	0.53	**0.52**	0.53
Mean	12.83	0.56	0.51	**0.50**	0.53

Table 2. Sorting complexity for the Beatles full discography

Album/Feature	No	Rhythmogram	Timbregram	Chromagram	Mean
Please Please Me	14	0.57	**0.50**	0.58	0.55
With The Beatles	14	0.58	0.56	**0.44**	0.53
A Hard Days Night	13	**0.47**	0.59	0.62	0.56
Beatles for Sale	14	0.57	**0.56**	0.58	0.57
Help!	14	0.57	**0.52**	0.55	0.55
Rubber Soul	14	**0.52**	0.55	0.56	0.55
Revolver	14	0.58	**0.50**	0.60	0.56
Sgt Peppers	13	0.58	**0.45**	0.59	0.54
The White Album 1	17	**0.51**	**0.51**	0.55	0.52
The White Album 2	13	0.57	**0.48**	0.53	0.53
Yellow Submarine	13	0.60	**0.44**	0.45	0.50
Abbey Road	17	0.55	**0.49**	0.61	0.55
Let It Be	12	**0.55**	0.59	0.63	0.59
Mean	14	0.55	0.56	0.55	0.55

and circular shifted TSP order is *0.77*, *0.84*, and *0.77*. As with the six albums previously, the *timbregram* has both the lowest and the highest possible sorting complexity.

The Actual Order of Albums

While it is clear now, that the albums under test are not in an order that can be recreated with the TSP sorting using the features, the actual order has not been determined. Apparently, according to the sorting complexity, the earlier albums are sorted more on the timbre, mainly, and the rhythm feature, while the later albums are sorted more in accordance with the chroma feature, although the differences between the sorting complexity for the different features are not that big.

While the order is probably not inherently random, it is difficult with the methods presented here, to identify whether there is system in the original order. The resulting TSP order for the six albums of varying genres is shown in Figure 5.

An immediate analysis of the TSP sorting order reveals that most often, the order is shifting up and down with a frequency of 2-6, i.e. 1 to 3 up and 1 to 3 down alternately. The Rolling Stones albums has most up-down order, while the Alice Cooper album has four up, one down, and then six up, with only two inversions for the rhythmogram, and some very similar for the *timbregram*, while the *chromagram* reveals four down and then six up in perfect order. Magma also have more order, this confirming the hypothesis that the concept albums are more homogeneous that the other albums. Overall, however, most albums have alternating up and down order.

The full Beatles discography album TSP order is shown in Figure 6.

The Beatles albums possibly also show a more systematic order in the *timbregram*-based TSP order, in particular for the later albums, which the sorting complexity values also showed previously. For instance, Yellow Submarine (Album 11) has an almost original order, with only few inversions.

Figure 5. Resulting TSP order for six albums, using the rhythmogram (top), the timbregram, and the chromagram (bottom). The x-axis is the original order, and the y-axis is the TSP order. Plus signs at the x-axis denote the album shifts

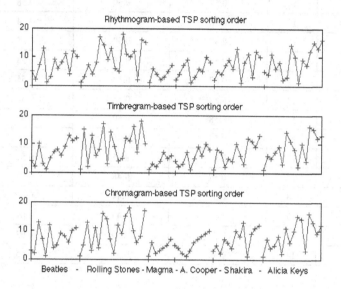

Figure 6. Resulting TSP order for full Beatles discography albums, using the rhythmogram (top), the timbregram, and the chromagram (bottom). The x-axis is the original order, and the y-axis is the TSP order. Plus signs at the x-axis denote the album shifts. Please refer to Table 2 for the album names

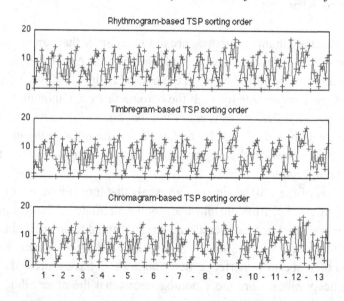

An initial investigation reveals preponderance for a periodicity of four in the TSP result order for the *rhythmogram-* and *chromagram*-based sorting, while the *timbregram*-based sorting reveals a periodicity of three. While this periodicity is not very strong in the autocorrelation, it is nonetheless repeated for both datasets used here. The sample size is too limited, however, to ascertain a truth in this matter with certitude. The order of the albums is neither random, nor ordered, with the exception of the concept albums. The hypothesis of alternating up/down order is plausible given the observations made here.

CONCLUSION

Whether music is sold in individual songs (singles) or through collections of songs (albums) has been more a matter of technology and commercial issues than a matter of user preferences due to the acoustic content of albums according to the literature. Singles were preponderant before approximately 1950 because of technological limitations in the support, and also afterwards, because of the 45 RPM single was cheaper than the 33-RPM album. Only with the CD pressing technology did single lose its price-advantage, which also decreased the relative sale of singles. With the internet-based sales, the price-advantage of singles was restored, and single sales increased again. As music listening is often related to mood regulation or identity building, the actual order of the songs in albums is potentially very important.

This study has investigated whether the acoustic content of music has an influence in the structure of albums. On the question of where the homogeneity is in albums, an experiment has been performed that reveals that approximately half of the segments found by automatic segmentation belong to song boundaries, while the other half is found inside songs. The experiment was based on three features related to music dimensions; the *rhythmogram*, *timbregram* and *chromagram*, that were merged for full albums. Six albums belonging to three genres, rock, concept albums and pop/R&B were used. For each album and feature, the self-similarity was calculated and the shortest-path through the self-similarity distances was calculated using dynamic programming. The intro and outro average duration was determined to be approximately 10 seconds, and the automatic segmentation boundaries was matched to the song boundaries using standard information retrieval measures. The resulting F_1 values below 0.5 are certainly not impressive, and they reveal that a lot of changes inside songs are more important than the changes between songs. Therefore, the conclusion must be that approximately half the homogeneity ruptures in music occurs within the songs, and the other half in between songs. However, this is very dependent on the music genre. The pop music in this study has more distinct songs than e.g. rock and concept albums.

In order to determine the segmentation boundaries for the rhythm, novel tempo normalization has been presented. This allows the comparison of the rhythm between songs, without taking into account the tempo, which would otherwise be to dominant.

A second experiment has investigated the order of the albums. By calculating the mean and the standard deviation of the three features, and calculating the difference between each song, a travelling-salesman problem solution has been employed to sort the songs so as to minimize the total distance between them. In order to compare the novel order with the original order, a sorting complexity measure has been used to investigate whether an album song order is totally random, or if it contains some order. While the *rhythmogram* performs best in the segmentation task, the *timbregram* and *chromagram* performs best in the sorting task. For most more recent songs, the *chromagram* has the lowest sorting complexity, and for the older songs, the *timbregram*-based segmentation renders the order closest to the original order. Further analysis reveals that the concept albums have almost linear order with respect to most features. For most other albums, the order varies up/down with a frequency of two or three.

The preliminary conclusions that can be drawn from this work are the following; Music in commercial albums is not necessarily divided into individual homogenous songs. A lot of the changes happen within songs. Up to two-thirds of segment boundaries has been found inside songs. As for the order of musical albums, it has been found to generally be varied in a way so the rhythm and timbre content variation direction is changed every four songs on average, while the tonal content variation direction is changed every three songs. For the concept albums, a more linear order was found, however.

REFERENCES

Bartsch, M. A., & Wakefield, G. H. (2001). To Catch a Chorus: Using Chroma-Based Representations For Audio Thumbnailing. In *Proceedings of the Workshop on Applications of Signal Processing to Audio and Acoustics (CD)*. Washington, DC: IEEE.

Behne, K. (1997) The Development of "Musikerleben" in Adolescence: How and Why Young People Listen to Music. In I. Deliége & J.A. Sloboda, (Eds.), *Perception and Cognition of Music,* (pp. 143–159). Hove, UK: Psychology Press.

Chai, W., & Vercoe, B. (2003). Music thumbnailing via structural analysis. In *Proceedings of ACM Multimedia Conference*, November.

Collins, N. (2005). A comparison of sound onset detection algorithms with emphasis on psychoacoustically motivated detection functions. In *Proceedings of AES 118th Convention*, Barcelona, Spain, May.

Concorde. (2009). Concorde TSP solver. Retrieved July 1, 2009, from http://www.tsp.gatech.edu/concorde.html

Cormen, T. H., Stein, C., Rivest, R. L., & Leiserson, C. E. (2001). *Introduction to Algorithms* (2nd ed.). New York: The MIT Press and McGraw-Hill Book Company.

Desain, P. (1992). A (de)composable theory of rhythm. *Music Perception, 9*(4), 439–454.

Feng, Y., Zhuang, Y., & Pan, Y. (2003). Music information retrieval by detecting mood via computational media aesthetics. In *Proceedings of the 2003 IEEE/WIC International Conference on Web Intelligence*, Washington, DC.

Foote, J. (1997). A similarity measure for automatic audio classification. In *Proc. AAAI 1997 Spring Symposium on Intelligent Integration and Use of Text, Image, Video, and Audio Corpora*, Stanford, Palo Alto, California, USA.

Foote, J. (2000). Automatic Audio Segmentation using a Measure of Audio Novelty. *Proceedings of IEEE International Conference on Multimedia and Expo, I*, 452–455.

Gerstin, J. (1998). Reputation in a Musical Scene: The Everyday Context of Connections between Music, Identity and Politics. *Ethnomusicology, 42*(3), 385–414. doi:10.2307/852848

Ghias, A., Logan, J., Chamberlin, D., & Smith, B. C. (2001). Query by humming - musical information retrieval in an audio database. In *Proceedings Multimedia,* (pp. 231-236).

Godøy, R. I. (2010). Chunking Sound for Musical Analysis. [). Berlin: Springer.]. *Lecture Notes in Computer Science, 5493*, 67–80. doi:10.1007/978-3-642-02518-1_4

Goto, M. (2003). A chorus-section detecting method for musical audio signals. In *Proceedings of the IEEE International Conference on Acoustics, Speech, and Signal Processing*, (pp. 437-440), April.

Hermansky, H. (1990). Perceptual linear predictive (PLP) analysis of speech. *The Journal of the Acoustical Society of America, 87*(4), 1738–1752. doi:10.1121/1.399423

Jehan, T. (2005). Hierarchical Multi-Class Self Similarities. In *Proceedings of the WASPAA (CD), USA.*

Jensen, K. (2007). Multiple scale music segmentation using rhythm, timbre and harmony. *EURASIP Journal on Applied Signal Processing*, (Special issue on Music Information Retrieval Based on Signal Processing), 68–74.

Jensen, K., Xu, J., & Zachariasen, M. (2005). Rhythm-based segmentation of Popular Chinese Music. In *Proceeding of the ISMIR*, (pp. 374-380), London.

Kühl, O. (2007). *Musical Semantics*. Bern, Switzerland: Peter Lang.

Kühl, O., & Jensen, K. (2008). Retrieving and recreating Musical Form. []. Berlin: Springer-Verlag.]. *Lecture Notes in Computer Science, 4969*, 263–275. doi:10.1007/978-3-540-85035-9_18

Lerdahl, E., & Jackendoff, R. (1983). *A generative theory of tonal music*. Cambridge, MA: M.I.T. Press.

Lin, S., & Kernighan, B. W. (1973). An Effective Heuristic Algorithm for the Traveling-Salesman Problem. *Operations Research, 21*(2), 498–516. doi:10.1287/opre.21.2.498

McNab, R. J., Smith, L. A., Witten, I. H., Henderson, C. L., & Cunningham, S. J. (1996). Towards the digital music library: Tune retrieval from acoustic input. In *Proceeding DL'96*, (pp. 11-18).

Miller, G. A. (1956). The magical number seven, plus or minus two: some limits on our capacity for processing information. *Psychological Review, 63*, 81–97. doi:10.1037/h0043158

Pauws, S., & Eggen, B. (2002). PATS: Realization and user evaluation of an automatic playlist generator. In *Proceedings of the 3rd International Conference on Music Information Retrieval*, Ircam, France, (pp. 222-230).

Pohle, T., Pampalk, E., & Widmer, G. (2005). Generating similarity-based playlists using traveling salesman algorithms. In *Proceedings of Digital Audio Effects*, Madrid, Spain, (pp. 220-225).

Rolland, P. Y., Raskinis, G., & Ganascia, J. G. (1999). Musical content-based retrieval: an overview of the Melodiscov approach and system. *ACM Multimedia*, (1), 81-84.

Saarikallio, S., & Erkkilä, J. (2007). The roles of music in adolescents' mood regulation. *Psychology of Music, 35*, 88–109. doi:10.1177/0305735607068889

Schoenherr, S. (2005). *Recording Technology History*. Retrieved July 1st, 2009, from http://history.sandiego.edu/gen/recording/notes.html

Sekey, A., & Hanson, B. A. (1984). Improved 1-bark bandwidth auditory filter. *The Journal of the Acoustical Society of America, 75*(6), 1902–1904. doi:10.1121/1.390954

Snyder, B. (2000). *Music and Memory. An Introduction*. Cambridge, MA: The MIT Press.

The Sydney Morning Herald. (2004). Pop single still hits right note. Retrieved from http://www.smh.com.au/articles/2004/08/25/1093246622880.html, accessed July 1st 2009.

Tzanetakis, G., & Cook, P. (2002). Musical Genre Classification of Audio Signals. *IEEE Transactions on Speech and Audio Processing, 10*(5), 293–302. doi:10.1109/TSA.2002.800560

Compilation of References

Adjeroh, D. A., & Lee, M. C. (2001). On ratio-based color indexing. *IEEE Transactions on Image Processing, 10*(1), 36–48. doi:10.1109/83.892441

Agrawal, R., Faloutsos, C., & Swami, A. (1993). Efficient similarity search in sequence databases. In *Proc. of the 4th Conference on Foundations of Data Organization and Algorithms*, (pp. 69-84).

Ah-Pine, J., Bressan, M., Clinchant, S., Csurka, G., Hoppenot, Y., & Renders, J.-M. (2009). Crossing textual and visual content in different application scenarios. *Multimedia Tools and Applications, 42*, 31–56. doi:10.1007/s11042-008-0246-8

Allen, P., & Dannenberg, R. (1990). Tracking Musical Beats in Real Time. In *ICMC, Glasgow 1990 Proceedings, International Computer Music Association*, (pp. 140-143).

Alonso, M., David, B., & Richard, G. (2004). Tempo and beat estimation of musical signals. In *Proc. Int. Conf. Music Information Retrieval*, (pp. 158-163).

Alwis, S., & Austin, J. (1998). A novel architecture for trademark image retrieval systems. In *Challenge of Image Retrieval*. Retrieved from http://citeseerx.ist.psu.edu/viewdoc/download?doi=10.1.1.100.1494&rep=rep1&type=pdf doi: 10.1.1.100.1494

Andrews, S., & Hofmann, T. (2004). *Multiple-instance learning via disjunctive programming boosting*. NIPS.

Andrews, S., Tsochantaridis, I., & Hofmann, T. (2003). *Support vector machines for multiple-instance learning*. NIPS.

Antani, S., Kasturi, R., & Jain, R. (2002). A survey on the use of pattern recognition methods for abstraction, indexing and retrieval of images and video. *Pattern Recognition, 35*, 945–965. doi:10.1016/S0031-3203(01)00086-3

Antoniou, G., & van Harmelen, F. (2008). *A semantic web primer* (2nd ed.). Cambridge, MA: MIT Press.

Arifi, V., Clausen, M., Kurth, F., & Muller, M. (2004). Automatic Synchronization of Musical Data: A Mathematical Approach. In Hewlett, W., & Selfridge-Fields, E. (Eds.), *Computing in Musicology*. Cambridge, MA: MIT Press.

Aronov, B., Bronnimann, H., Chang, A. Y., & Chiang, Y.-J. (2003). Cost-driven octree construction schemes: an experimental study. In *Proceedings of the nineteenth annual symposium on Computational geometry*, (pp. 227 – 236).

Assfalg, J., Bertini, M., Colombo, C., Bimbo, A. D., & Nunziati, W. (2003). Semantic annotation of soccer videos: automatic highlights identification. *Computer Vision and Image Understanding, 92*(2-3), 285–305. doi:10.1016/j.cviu.2003.06.004

Auer, P. (1997). On learning from multi-instance examples: empirical evaluation of a theoretical approach. In *Proc. ICML*.

Bailloeul, T., Zhu, C., & Xu, Y. (2008, October). Automatic image tagging as a random walk with priors on the canonical correlation subspace. In *ACM International Conference on Multimedia Information Retrieval* (p. 75-82), Vancouver, British Columbia, Canada.

Banerjee, S. (2008). Improving text classification accuracy using topic modeling over an additional corpus. *Proceedings of the 31st International ACM SIGIR conference on research and development in information retrieval*, 867-868.

Baraté, A., Haus, G., Ludovico, L. A., & Vercellesi, G. (2005). MXDemo: a Case Study about Audio, Video, and Score Synchronization. In *Proceedings of IEEE Conference on Automatic Production of Cross Media Content for Multi-channel Distribution (AXMEDIS)*, (pp. 45-52).

Barnard, K., Duygulu, P., de Freitas, N., Forsyth, D., Blei, D., & Jordan, M. (2003, March). Matching words and pictures. *Journal of Machine Learning Research, 3*, 1107–1135. doi:10.1162/153244303322533214

Barnard, K., Fan, Q., Swaminathan, R., Hoogs, A., Collins, R., & Rondot, P. (2008, May). Evaluation of localized semantics: Data, methodology, and experiments. *International Journal of Computer Vision, 77*(1-3), 199–217. doi:10.1007/s11263-007-0068-6

Barnard, K., Duygulu, P., Guru, R., Gabbur, P., & Forsyth, D. (2003, June). The effects of segmentation and feature choice in a translation model of object recognition. In *The IEEE International Conference on Computer Vision and Pattern Recognition*, (Vol. 2, p. 675-682).

Bartsch, M. A., & Wakefield, G. H. (2001). To Catch a Chorus: Using Chroma-Based Representations For Audio Thumbnailing. In *Proceedings of the Workshop on Applications of Signal Processing to Audio and Acoustics (CD)*. Washington, DC: IEEE.

Basharat, A., Zhai, Y., & Shah, M. (2008, June). Content based video matching using spatiotemporal volumes. *Computer Vision and Image Understanding, 110*(3), 360–377. doi:10.1016/j.cviu.2007.09.016

Beckmann, N., Kriegel, H. P., Schneider, R., & Seeger, B. (1990). The R*-Tree: An Efficient and Robust Access Method for Points and Rectangles. In *Proc. SIGMOD Conference*, (pp. 322-331).

Behne, K. (1997) The Development of "Musikerleben" in Adolescence: How and Why Young People Listen to Music. In I. Deliége & J.A. Sloboda, (Eds.), *Perception and Cognition of Music*, (pp. 143–159). Hove, UK: Psychology Press.

Beitzel, S., Jensen, E., Chowdhury, A., & Frieder, O. (2008). Analysis of varying approaches to topical web query classification. *Proceedings of the 3rd international Conference on Scalable information Systems*, 1-5.

Belkin, M., & Niyogi, P. (2002). Laplacian Eigenmaps and spectral techniques for embedding and clustering. *Advances in Neural Information Processing Systems, 14*, 585–591.

Benitez, A. B., & Chang, S.-F. (2002a, August). Perceptual knowledge construction from annotated image collections. In *IEEE International Conference on Multimedia & Expo (ICME)*. Lausanne, Switzerland.

Benitez, A. B., & Chang, S.-F. (2002b, August). Semantic knowledge construction from annotated image collections. In *IEEE International Conference on Multimedia & Expo (ICME)*. Lausanne, Switzerland.

Benitez, A. B., & Chang, S.-F. (2003, September). Image classification using multimedia knowledge networks. In *IEEE International Conference on Image Processing (ICIP)*. Barcelona, Spain.

Bentley, J. L. (1975). Multidimensional binary search trees used for associative searching. *Communications of the ACM, 18*(9), 509–517. doi:10.1145/361002.361007

Berchtold, S., Keim, D. A., & Kriegel, H.-P. (1996). The X-tree: An index structure for high-dimensional data. In *Proc. 22nd VLDM Conf.*, (pp. 28-39).

Berkley Segmentation Dataset. (n.d.). Retrieved from http://www.eecs.berkeley.edu/Research/Projects/CS/vision/bsds

Berretti, S., Del Bimbo, A., & Pala, P. (2009). 3D Mesh Decomposition using Reeb Graphs. *Image and Vision Computing, 27*(10), 1540–1554. doi:10.1016/j.imavis.2009.02.004

Berretti, S., Del Bimbo, A., & Pala, P. (2010). 3D Face Recognition using Isogeodesic Stripes. *IEEE Transactions on Pattern Analysis and Machine Intelligence, 32*(12).

Berry, M. J. A., & Linoff, G. (2004). *Data Mining Techniques for Marketing, Sales, and Customer Relationship Management*. Indianapolis, USA: Wiley Publishing.

Bertini, M., Cucchiara, R., Bimbo, A., & Prati, A. (2006). Semantic adaptation of sport videos with user-centred performance analysis. *IEEE Transactions on Multimedia, 8*(3), 433–443. doi:10.1109/TMM.2006.870762

Bertini, M., Bimbo, A. D., & Torniai, C. (2006). Automatic annotation and semantic retrieval of video sequences using multimedia ontologies. In *ACM International Conference on Multimedia* (p. 679-682), Santa Barbara, CA.

Bertoline, G. (1998). Visual science: An emerging discipline. *Journal for Geometry and Graphics, 2*(2), 181–187.

Besl, P., & Mc Kay, N. (1992). A method for registration of 3-d shapes. *IEEE Transactions on Pattern Analysis and Machine Intelligence, 14*(2), 239–256. doi:10.1109/34.121791

Birren, F. (1969). *Principles of color - a review of past traditions and modern theories of color harmony*. New York: Reinhold.

Bishop, C. M. (2006). *Pattern Recognition and Machine Learning*. New York: Springer.

Blanz, V., & Vetter, T. (2003). Face recognition based on fitting a 3D morphable model. *IEEE Transactions on Pattern Analysis and Machine Intelligence, 25*(9), 1063–1074. doi:10.1109/TPAMI.2003.1227983

Blei, D. M., & Jordan, M. I. (2003, August). Modeling annotated data. In *The 26th annual International ACM SIGIR Conference*.

Bober, M., Preteux, F., & Kim, W.-Y. Y. (2002). Shape descriptors. In B. S. Manjunath, P. Salembier & T. Sikora (Ed.), *Introduction to MPEG-7*, (pp. 231-260). Chichester, UK: Wiley.

Bobicev, V., & Sokolova, M. (2008). An effective and Robust Method for Short Text Classification. *Proceedings of the 21st Conference of the Association of the Advancement of Artificial Intelligence*, 1444-1445.

Boccignone, G., De Santo, M., & Percannella, G. (2000). Automated threshold selection for the detection of dissolves in MPEG video. *IEEE International Conference on Multimedia and Expo, 3*, 1535–1538.

Boll, S. (2007). Multitube - where web 2.0 and multimedia could meet. *IEEE MultiMedia, 14*(1), 9–13. doi:10.1109/MMUL.2007.17

Bollegala, D., Matsuo, Y., & Ishizuka, M. (2007). Measuring semantic similarity between words using web search engines. In *International Conference on World Wide Web (WWW)*.

Boutell, M. R., Luo, J., Shen, X., & Brown, C. M. (2004). Learning multi-label scene classification. *Pattern Recognition, 37*, 1757–1771. doi:10.1016/j.patcog.2004.03.009

Bowyer, K., Chang, K., & Flynn, P. (2006). A survey of approaches and challenges in 3D and multi-modal 3D+2D face recognition. *Computer Vision and Image Understanding, 101*(1), 1–15. doi:10.1016/j.cviu.2005.05.005

Bradley, P. S., & Fayyad, U. M. (1998). Refining initial points for K-Means clustering. In *Proceedings of the Fifteenth International Conference on Machine Learning*. San Francisco, CA: Morgan Kaufmann.

Bronstein, A. M., Bronstein, M. M., & Kimmel, R. (2005). Three dimensional face recognition. *International Journal of Computer Vision, 64*(1), 5–30. doi:10.1007/s11263-005-1085-y

Bronstein, A., Bronstein, M., & Kimmel, R. (2006). Robust expression-invariant face recognition from partially missing data. In *European Conference on Computer Vision*, (pp. 396–408), Gratz, Austria.

Brostow, G. J., Fauqueura, J., & Cipolla, R. (2009, January). Semantic object classes in video: A high definition ground truth database. *Pattern Recognition Letters, 30*(2), 88–97. doi:10.1016/j.patrec.2008.04.005

Brunelli, R., Mich, O., & Modena, C. M. (1999). A survey on the automatic indexing of video data. *Journal of Visual Communication and Image Representation, 10*, 78–112. doi:10.1006/jvci.1997.0404

Burak Ozer, I., & Wolf, W. H. (2002). A hierarchical human detection system in uncompressed domains. *IEEE Transactions on Multimedia, 4*(2), 283–300. doi:10.1109/TMM.2002.1017740

Cai, D., He, X., Wen, J.-R., & Ma, W.-Y. (2004). Block-level link analysis. In *the 27th annual International ACM SIGIR Conference on Research and Development in Information Retrieval (SIGIR'04)*, (pp. 440–447).

Calic, J., & Izquierdo, E. (2002). A multiresolution technique for video indexing and retrieval. *IEEE International Conference on Image Processing, 1*, 952–955.

Caltech Archive. (n.d.). Retrieved from http://www.vision.caltech.edu/html-files/archive.html

Campbell, N. W., Mackeown, W. P. J., Thomas, B. T., & Troscianko, T. (1997). Interpreting image databases by region classification. *Pattern Recognition, 30*(4), 555–563. doi:10.1016/S0031-3203(96)00112-4

Carbonetto, P., de Freitas, N., & Barnard, K. (2004, May). A statistical models for general contextual object recognition. In *The Eighth European Conference on Computer Vision (ECCV2004)*.

Carneiro, G., Chan, A. B., Moreno, P. J., & Vasconcelos, N. (2007, March). Supervised learning of semantic classes for image annotation and retrieval. *IEEE Transactions on Pattern Analysis and Machine Intelligence, 29*(3), 394–410. doi:10.1109/TPAMI.2007.61

Castelàn, M., & Hancock, E. R. (2005). Improved face shape recovery and re-illumination using convexity constraints. In *International Conference on Image Analysis and Processing* (pp. 487–494). Cagliari, Italy.

Cesa-Bianchi, N., Gentile, C., & Zaniboni, L. (2006). Hierarchical Classification: Combining Bayes with SVM. P*roceedings of the 23ʳᵈ International Conference on Machine Learning*, 177–184, Pittsburgh, PA.

Chai, W., & Vercoe, B. (2003). Music thumbnailing via structural analysis. In *Proceedings of ACM Multimedia Conference*, November.

Chan, J., Koprinska, I., & Poon, J. (2008). Semi-Supervised Classification using Bridging. *International Journal of Artificial Intelligence Tools, 17*(3), 415–431. doi:10.1142/S0218213008003972

Chan, K. L., Xiong, X., Liu, F., & Purnomo, R. (2001). Content-Based Image Retrieval Using Region Representation. In Klette, (Eds.), *Multi-Image Analysis, Lecture Notes in Computer Science* (*Vol. 2032*, pp. 238–250). Berlin: Springer-Verlag.

Chan, S. S. M., Qing, L., Yi, W., & Yueting, Z. (2001). A hybrid approach to video retrieval in a generic video management and application processing framework. *IEEE International Conference on Multimedia and Expo*, (pp. 389 - 392).

Chang, K. I., Bowyer, K. W., & Flynn, P. J. (2006). Multiple nose region matching for 3D face recognition under varying facial expression. *IEEE Transactions on Pattern Analysis and Machine Intelligence, 28*(6), 1695–1700. doi:10.1109/TPAMI.2006.210

Chang, S. K., Shi, Q. Y., & Yan, C. W. (1987, May). Iconic indexing by 2-d strings. *IEEE Transactions on Pattern Analysis and Machine Intelligence, 9*(3), 413–428. doi:10.1109/TPAMI.1987.4767923

Chang, S. K., Yan, C. W., Dimitroff, D. C., & Arndt, T. (1988, May). An intelligent image database system. *IEEE Transactions on Software Engineering, 14*(5), 681–688. doi:10.1109/32.6147

Chang, P., Han, M., & Gong, Y. (2002). Extract highlights from baseball game video with hidden Markov models. In. *Proceedings of IEEE International Conference on Image Processing, 1*, 609–612. doi:10.1109/ICIP.2002.1038097

Chang, C.-C., & Lin, C.-J. (2001). *LIBSVM: a library for support vector machines*. Software available at: http://www.csie.ntu.edu.tw/~cjlin/libsvm.

Chang, E., Goh, K., Sychay, G., & Wu, G. (2003). Cbsa: Content-based soft annotation for multimodal image retrieval using bayes point machines. *IEEE Trans. On Circuits and Systems for Video Technology, 13*(1).

Chau, M., Fang, X., & Sheng, O. R. L. (2005). Analysis of the Query Logs of a Web Site Search Engine. *Journal of the American Society for Information Science and Technology, 56*(13), 1363–1376. doi:10.1002/asi.20210

Chavez, E., Navarro, G., Baeza-Yates, R., & Marroquin, J. L. (2001). Searching in metric spaces. [CSUR]. *ACM Computing Surveys, 33*(3), 273–321. doi:10.1145/502807.502808

Chen, M., Chen, S.-C., Shyu, M.-L., & Wickramaratna, K. (2006). Semantic event detection via temporal analysis and multimodal data mining. *IEEE Signal Processing Magazine. Special Issue on Semantic Retrieval of Multimedia, 23*(2), 38–46.

Chen, S.-C., Shyu, M.-L., Zhang, C., & Chen, M. (2006). A multimodal data mining framework for soccer goal detection based on decision tree logic. *International Journal of Computer Applications in Technology, 27*(4), 312–323. doi:10.1504/IJCAT.2006.012001

Chen, D. Y., Hsiao, M. H., & Lee, S. Y. (2006a). Automatic closed caption detection and filtering in MPEG videos for video structuring. *Journal of Information Science and Engineering, 22*(5), 1145–1162.

Chen, H. T., Chen, H. S., Hsiao, M. H., Chen, Y. W., & Lee, S. Y. (2006b). A trajectory-based ball tracking framework with enrichment for broadcast baseball videos. In. *Proceedings of the International Computer Symposium, 2006*, 1145–1150.

Chen, H. T., Chen, H. S., Hsiao, M. H., Tsai, W. J., & Lee, S. Y. (2007a). A trajectory-based ball tracking framework with visual enrichment for broadcast baseball videos. *Journal of Information Science and Engineering, 24*(1), 143–157.

Chen, H. T., Tien, M. C., Chen, Y. W., Tsai, W. J., & Lee, S. Y. (2009a). Physics-based ball tracking and 3D trajectory reconstruction with applications to shooting location Estimation in Basketball Video. *Journal of Visual Communication and Image Representation, 20*(3), 204–216. doi:10.1016/j.jvcir.2008.11.008

Chen, H. T., Tsai, W. J., & Lee, S. Y. (2009c). Contour-based strike zone shaping and visualization in broadcast baseball video: providing reference for pitch location positioning and strike/ball judgment. *Multimedia Tools and Applications, 47*(2), 239–255. doi:10.1007/s11042-009-0321-9

Chen, S.-C., Shyu, M.-L., & Zhang, C. (2005). Innovative shot boundary detection for video indexing. In Deb, S. (Ed.), *Video data management and information retrieval* (pp. 217–236). Hershey, PA: Idea Group Publishing.

Chen, H. S., Chen, H. T., Tsai, W. J., Lee, S. Y., & Yu, J. Y. (2007c). Pitch-By-Pitch Extraction from Single View Baseball Video Sequences. In *Proceeding of IEEE International Conference on Multimedia and Expo*, (pp. 1423-1426).

Chen, H. T., Chen, H. S., & Lee, S. Y. (2007b). Physics-based ball tracking in volleyball videos with its applications to set type recognition and action detection. In *Proceedings of IEEE Int. Conference on Acoustic Speech Signal Processing*, (Vol. 1, pp. 1097-1100).

Chen, H. T., Hsiao, M. H., Chen, H. S., Tsai, W. J., & Lee, S. Y. (2008). A baseball exploration system using spatial pattern recognition. In *Proceedings of IEEE International Symposium on Circuits and Systems*, (pp. 3522-3525).

Chen, H. T., Tsai, W. J., & Lee, S. Y. (2009b). Stance-based strike zone shaping and visualization in broadcast baseball video: providing reference for pitch location positioning. In *Proceedings of International Conference on Multimedia and Expo*, (pp. 302-305).

Chen, H. W., Kuo, J.-H., Chu, W.-T., & Wu, J.-L. (2004). Action movies segmentation and summarization based on tempo analysis. *ACM International Workshop on Multimedia Information Retrieval*, (pp. 251-258). New York: ACM.

Chen, M., Chen, S.-C., & Shyu, M.-L. (2007) Hierarchical temporal association mining for video event detection in video databases. In *Proceedings of the Second IEEE International Workshop on Multimedia Databases and Data Management, in conjunction with IEEE International Conference on Data Engineering,* (pp. 137-145).

Chen, S.-C., Shyu, M.-L., & Zhao, N. (2005) An enhanced query model for soccer video retrieval using temporal relationships. In *Proceedings of the 21st International Conference on Data Engineering (ICDE 2005),* (pp. 1133-1134).

Chen, X., & Zhang, C. (2007) Interactive mining and semantic retrieval of videos. In *Proceedings of the 2007 International Workshop on Multimedia Data Mining, in conjunction with the ACM SIGKDD International Conference on Knowledge Discovery & Data Mining.*

Chen, Y., Bi, J., & Wang, J. (2006). MILES: multiple-instance learning via embedded instance selection. *IEEE Trans. PAMI, 28*(12).

Cheng, H., & Sun, Y. (2000). A hierarchical approach to color image segmentation using homogeneity. *IEEE Transactions on Image Processing, 9*(12), 2071–2082. doi:10.1109/83.887975

Cheng, C. C., & Hsu, C. T. (2006). Fusion of audio and motion information on HMM-based highlight extraction for baseball games. *IEEE Transactions on Multimedia, 8*(3), 585–599. doi:10.1109/TMM.2006.870726

Cheng, W., Xu, D., Jiang, Y., & Lang, C. (2005). Information Theoretic Metrics in Shot Boundary Detection. In R. Khosla, et al. (eds.), *Knowledge-Based Intelligent Information and Engineering Systems,* (LNCS Vol. 3683, pp. 388-394). Berlin: Springer-Verlag.

Choi, Y., Kim, Y., & Myaeng, S. (2009). Domain-specific sentiment analysis using contextual feature generation. *Proceeding of the 1st international CIKM Workshop on Topic-Sentiment Analysis for Mass Opinion,* 37-44.

Chong, C.-W., Raveendran, P., & Mukundan, R. (2003). Translation invariants of Zernike moments. *Pattern Recognition, 36*(8), 1765–1773. doi:10.1016/S0031-3203(02)00353-9

Ciaccia, P., Patella, M., & Zezula, P. (1997). M-tree: An Efficient Access Method for Similarity Search in Metric Spaces. *The VLDB Journal,* 426–435.

CITIA. (2009). *City of Moving Images - The International Animated Film Festival,* http://www.citia.info/, & *Animaquid Indexing System,* http://www/toondra.com/, Annecy-France.

Coldefy, F., & Bouthemy, P. (2004). Unsupervised soccer video abstraction based on pitch, dominant color and camera motion analysis. In *ACM Multimedia* (pp. 268–271). New York: ACM.

Collins, N. (2005). A comparison of sound onset detection algorithms with emphasis on psychoacoustically motivated detection functions. In *Proceedings of AES 118th Convention,* Barcelona, Spain, May.

Colombo, A., Cusano, C., & Schettini, R. (2006). 3d face detection using curvature analysis. *Pattern Recognition, 39*(3), 444–455. doi:10.1016/j.patcog.2005.09.009

Colombo, C., Del Bimbo, A., & Pala, P. (1999). Semantics in visual information retrieval. *IEEE MultiMedia, 6*(3), 38–53. doi:10.1109/93.790610

Concorde. (2009). Concorde TSP solver. Retrieved July 1, 2009, from http://www.tsp.gatech.edu/concorde.html

Cormen, T. H., Stein, C., Rivest, R. L., & Leiserson, C. E. (2001). *Introduction to Algorithms* (2nd ed.). New York: The MIT Press and McGraw-Hill Book Company.

Cormode, G., & Krishnamurthy, B. (2008). Key differences between Web1.0 and Web2.0. *First Monday, 13*(6).

Cox, T., & Cox, M. (1994). *Multidimensional scaling.* London: Chapman & Hall.

Crawford, T. (2005). *Music Information Retrieval and the Future of Musicology.* Technical Report for the Online Chopin variorum Edition project. Bischoff, K., Firan, C. S., Nejdl, W., & Paiu, R. (2008). Can All Tags be Used for Search? In *CIKM '08: Proceedings of the 17th ACM Conference on Information and Knowledge Management,* (pp. 193-202). New York: ACM.

Csurka, G., Dance, C. R., Fan, L., Willamowski, J., & Bray, C. (2004). Visual categorization with bags of keypoints. In *International Workshop on Statistical Learning in Computer Vision*, (p. 1-22).

Curvature. (n.d.). In *Wikipedia*. Retrieved April 13, 2007, from http://en.wikipedia.org/wiki/Curvature

D'Aguanno, A., & Vercellesi, G. (2007). Automatic synchronisation between audio and score musical description layers. In *Semantic Multimedia* (*Vol. 4816*, pp. 200–210). Berlin: Springer-Verlag. doi:10.1007/978-3-540-77051-0_22

D'Aguanno, A., & Vercellesi, G. (2007a). Tempo induction algorithm in MP3 compressed domain. In *Proceedings of the international workshop on multimedia information retrieval*, (pp. 153-158).

D'Aguanno, A., Haus, G., & Vercellesi, G. (2006). MP3 window-switching pattern preliminary analysis for general purposes Beat Tracking. In *Proceedings of the 120th AES Convention*.

Dannenberg, R. B., Birmingham, W. P., Pardo, B., Hu, N., Meek, C., & Tzanetakis, G. (2007). A Comparative Evaluation of Search Techniques for Query-By-Humming using the Musart Testbed. *Journal of the American Society for Information Science and Technology*, *58*(5), 687–701. doi:10.1002/asi.20532

Dannenberg, R. B., & Hu, N. (2003). Polyphonic Audio Matching for Score Following and Intelligent Audio. In *Proceedings of the 2003 International Computer Music Conference*.

Datta, R., Joshi, D., Li, J., & Wang, J. Z. (2008). Image Retrieval: Ideas, Influences, and Trends of the New Age. *ACM Computing Surveys*, *40*(2), 1–60. doi:10.1145/1348246.1348248

Datta, R., Ge, W., Li, J., & Wang, J. (2006). Toward bridging the annotation-retrieval gap in image search by a generative modeling approach. *Proc. ACM Multimedia*.

Datta, R., Li, J., & Wang, J. Z. (2005, November). Content-based image retrieval - approaches and trends of the new age. In *ACM SIGMM International Workshop on Multimedia Information Retrieval*, (pp. 253-262).

Davies, M. E. P., & Plumbley, M. D. (2005). Beat tracking with a two state model. In *Proceedings of IEEE Int. Acoustics, Speech, and Signal Processing, (ICASSP '05)*, (pp. 241 – 244).

Dayanik, A., Lewis, D. D., Madigan, D., Menkov, V., & Genkin, A. (2006). Constructing informative prior distributions from domain knowledge in text classification. *Proceedings of the 29th Annual international ACM SIGIR Conference on Research and Development in Information Retrieval*, 493–500. New York: ACM Press.

de la Cuadra, P., Master, A., & Sapp, C. (2001). Efficient pitch detection techniques for interactive music. In *Proceedings of the 2001 International Computer Music Conference*.

de Ves, E., Domingo, J., Ayala, G., & Zuccarello, P. (2007). A novel Bayesian framework for relevance feedback in image content-based retrieval systems. *Pattern Recognition*, *39*, 1622–1632. doi:10.1016/j.patcog.2006.01.006

Deng, J., Dong, W., Socher, R., Li, L.-J., Li, K., & Fei-Fei, L. (2009, June). Imagenet: A large-scale hierarchical image database. In *IEEE International Conference on Computer Vision and Pattern Recognition (CVPR)*, Miami Beach, FL, USA.

Desain, P. (1992). A (de)composable theory of rhythm. *Music Perception*, *9*(4), 439–454.

Deschacht, K., & Moens, M.-F. (2007, June). Text analysis for automatic image annotation. In *the 45th annual meeting of the Association of Computational Linguistics*, (pp. 1000-1007), Prague, Czech Republic.

Deselaers, T., & Deserno, T. M. (2008). Medical image annotation in imageclef 2008. In *CLEF Workshop 2008*.

Detyniecki, M., & Marsala, C. (2003). Discovering knowledge for better video indexing based on colors. *IEEE International Conference on Fuzzy Systems*, (Vol. 2, pp. 1177–1181), St. Louis, USA.

Dietterich, T., Lathrop, R., & Lozano-Perez, T. (1997). Solving the multiple instance problem with axis-parallel rectangles. *Artificial Intelligence, 89*, 3171. doi:10.1016/S0004-3702(96)00034-3

Dillon, W. R., & Goldstein, M. (1984). *Multivariate Analysis, Methods and Applications*. New York: John Wiley and Sons.

Dix, A. (2007). Designing for appropriation. *BCS-HCI '07: Proceedings of the 21st British HCI Group Annual Conference on HCI*, 27-30.

Dixon, S. (2001). Automatic extraction of tempo and beat from expressive performances. *Journal of New Music Research, 31*(1), 39–58. doi:10.1076/jnmr.30.1.39.7119

Dixon, S. (2001a). An Empirical Comparison of Tempo Trackers. In *Proceedings of the 8th Brazilian Symposium on Computer Music*.

Dixon, S., & Widmer, G. (2005). MATCH: A Music Alignement Tool Chest. In *6th International Conference on Music Information Retrieval, ISMIR 2005*.

Dixon, S., Pampalk, E., & Widmer, G. (2003). Classification of dance music by periodicity patterns. In *Proc. Int. Conf. Music Information Retrieval*, (pp. 159-165).

Djeraba, C. (2002). Content-based multimedia indexing and retrieval. *IEEE MultiMedia, 9*(2), 18–22. doi:10.1109/MMUL.2002.998047

Dorai, C., & Venkatesh, S. (2001, October - December). Computational media aesthetics: Finding meaning beautiful. *IEEE MultiMedia, 8*(4), 10–12. doi:10.1109/93.959093

Doulamis, A. D., Doulamis, N., & Kollias, S. (2000). Non-sequential video content representation using temporal variation of feature vectors. *IEEE Transactions on Consumer Electronics, 46*(3). doi:10.1109/30.883444

Downie, J. S. (2003). Muisc Information Retrieval. *Annual Review of Information Science & Technology, 37*, 295–340. doi:10.1002/aris.1440370108

Duan, L. Y., Xu, M., & Tian, Q. (2005). A unified framework for semantic shot classification in sports video. *IEEE Transactions on Multimedia, 7*(6), 1066–1083. doi:10.1109/TMM.2005.858395

Duan, L. Y., Xu, M., Chua, T. S., Tian, Q., & Xu, C.-S. (2003). A mid-level representation framework for semantic sports video analysis. In *Proceedings of 11th ACM International Conference on Multimedia*, (pp. 33- 44).

Dubey, P., Chen, Z., & Shi, Y. (2004) Using Branch-Grafted R-trees for Spatial Data Mining. In *Proc. ICCS 2004* (LNCS, pp. 657-660).

Dudani, S. A., Breeding, K. J., & McGhee, R. B. (1977, January). Aircraft identification by moment invariants. *IEEE Transactions on Computers, 26*(1), 39–45. doi:10.1109/TC.1977.5009272

Duygulu, P., Barnard, K., Freitas, J. F. G. D., & Forsyth, D. A. (2002). Object recognition as machine translation: Learning a lexicon for a fixed image vocabulary. In *Proc. The 7th European Conference on Computer Vision*, (Vol. IV, pp. 97–112), Copenhagen, Denmark.

Eakins, J. P. (2001). Trademark image retrieval. In Lew, M. S. (Ed.), *Principles of visual information retrieval* (pp. 319–354). Berlin: Springer-Verlag.

Eakins, J. P., Graham, M. E., & Boardman, J. M. (1997). Evaluation of a trademark image retrieval system. In *Proceedings of the information retrieval research, the 19th annual BCS-IRSG colloquium on IR research*, Aberdeen, UK: BCS Information Retrieval Specialist Group.

Eisenberg, G., Batke, J. M., & Sikora, T. (2004). Efficiently Computable Similarity Measures For Query By Tapping Systems. In *Proc. of the 7th Int. Conference on Digital Audio Effects*, (pp. 189-193). Naples, Italy: DAFx.

Ekin, A., Tekalp, A. M., & Mehrotra, R. (2003). Automatic soccer video analysis and summarization. *IEEE Transactions on Image Processing, 12*, 796–807. doi:10.1109/TIP.2003.812758

Elad, A., & Kimmel, R. (2003). On bending invariant signatures for surfaces. *IEEE Transactions on Pattern Analysis and Machine Intelligence, 25*(10), 1285–1295. doi:10.1109/TPAMI.2003.1233902

Ester, M., Kriegel, H. P., & Xu, X. (1995). Knowledge discovery in large spatial databases: Focusing techniques for efficient class identification. In *Proceedings of 4th International Symposium on Large Spatial Databases (SSD'95)*, Portland, ME, (LNCS, pp. 67-82). Berlin: Springer.

Esuli, A., Fagni, T., & Sebastiani, F. (2008). Boosting multi-label hierarchical text categorization. *Information Retrieval, 11*, 287–313. doi:10.1007/s10791-008-9047-y

Excite. (1999). Excite and other more recent data sets can be downloaded from http://ist.psu.edu/faculty_pages/jjansen/academic/transaction_logs.html

Fan, J., Luo, H., Gao, Y., & Jain, R. (2007, August). Incorporating concept ontology for hierarchical video classification, annotation, and visualization. *IEEE Transactions on Multimedia, 9*(5), 939–957. doi:10.1109/TMM.2007.900143

Fan, J., Luo, H., & Elmagarmid, A. K. (2004). Concept-oriented indexing of video databases: toward semantic sensitive retrieval and browsing. *IEEE Transactions on Image Processing, 13*(7), 974–991. doi:10.1109/TIP.2004.827232

Farkas, L. (1994). *Anthropometry of the Head and Face.* New York: Raven Press.

Fei-Fei, L., & Perona, P. (2005). A bayesian hierarchical model for learning natural scene categories. In *IEEE International Conference on Computer Vision and Pattern Recognition (CVPR)* (p. 524-531). Washington, DC: IEEE.

Fei-Fei, L., Fergus, R., & Perona, P. (2004). Learning generative visual models from few training examples: An incremental bayesian approach tested on 101 object categories. In *International Workshop on Generative Model based Vision.*

Fellbaum, C. (Ed.). (1998). *WordNet: an electronic lexical database.* Cambridge, MA: MIT Press.

Feng, D., Siu, W. C., & Zhang, H. J. (2003). *Multimedia Information Retrieval and Management: Technological Fundamentals and Applications.* Berlin: Springer.

Feng, X., & Huang, H. (2005). A fuzzy-set-based reconstructed phase space method for identification of temporal patterns in complex time series. *IEEE Transactions on Knowledge and Data Engineering, 17*(5), 601–613. doi:10.1109/TKDE.2005.68

Feng, D., Long, F., & Zhang, H. (2002). Fundamentals of content-based image retrieval. In Feng, D., Siu, W. C., & Zhang, H. (Eds.), *Multimedia information retrieval and management: Technological fundamentals and applications* (pp. 7–13). Berlin: Springer-Verlag.

Feng, S. L., Manmatha, R., & Lavrenko, V. (2004). Multiple Bernoulli relevance models for image and video annotation. In *Proc. The International Conference on Computer Vision and Pattern Recognition*, Washington, DC.

Feng, Y., Zhuang, Y., & Pan, Y. (2003). Music information retrieval by detecting mood via computational media aesthetics. In *Proceedings of the 2003 IEEE/WIC International Conference on Web Intelligence*, Washington, DC.

Fergus, R. Li, F.-F., Perona, P., & Zisserman, A. (2005). Learning object categories from Google's image search. In *Proc. ICCV.*

Fernando, W. A. C., Canagarajah, C. N., & Bull, D. R. (1999). Fade and dissolve detection in uncompressed and compressed video sequence. *IEEE International Conference on Image Processing*, (pp. 299-303), Kobe, Japan.

Fingerhut, M. (2004). Music Information Retrieval, or How to Search for (and maybe find) Music and Do Away with Incipits. In *Proceedings of the IAML-IASA Congress.*

Finlayson, G. D., Funt, B. V., & Barnard, K. (1995, June). Color constancy under varying illumination. In *IEEE International Conference on Computer Vision (ICCV)* (pp. 720-725). Cambridge, MA, USA.

Fischer, S., Lienhart, R., & Effelsberg, W. (1995). Automatic recognition of film genres. In *ACM International Conference on Multimedia* (pp. 295-304).

Fisher, R. B. (2004, January 16). *Moment invariants*. Retrieved from http://homepages.inf.ed.ac.uk/rbf/CVonline/LOCAL_COPIES/FISHER/mominv.htm

Foote, J. (2000). Automatic Audio Segmentation using a Measure of Audio Novelty. *Proceedings of IEEE International Conference on Multimedia and Expo, I*, 452–455.

Foote, J. (1997). A similarity measure for automatic audio classification. In *Proc. AAAI 1997 Spring Symposium on Intelligent Integration and Use of Text, Image, Video, and Audio Corpora*, Stanford, Palo Alto, California, USA.

Frasconi, P., Gori, M., & Sperduti, A. (1998). A general framework for adaptive processing of data structures. *IEEE Transactions on Neural Networks, 9*, 768–785. doi:10.1109/72.712151

Friedman, J. H., Bentley, J. L., & Finkel, R. A. (1977). An algorithm for finding best matches in logarithmic expected time. *ACM Transactions on Mathematical Software, 3*(3), 209–226. doi:10.1145/355744.355745

Frisch, A. M., & Allen, J. F. (1982). Knowledge retrieval as limited inference. In Loveland, D. (ed.), *Proceedings of the 6th Conference on Automated Deduction*, (pp. 274-291).

Fu, H., Chi, Z., & Feng, D. (2009, January). An efficient algorithm for attention-driven image interpretation from segments. *Pattern Recognition, 42*(1), 126–140. doi:10.1016/j.patcog.2008.06.021

Fu, H., Chi, Z., Feng, D., & Song, J. (2004, December). Machine learning techniques for ontology-based leaf classification. In *International Conference on Control, Automation, Robotics and Vision* (p. 681-686), Kunming, China.

Furht, B., & Marques, O. (2002). *Content-based image and video retrieval*. New York: Kluwer Academic.

Futrelle, J., & Downie, S. (2002). Interdisciplinary Communities and Research Issues in Music Information Retrieval. In *Proceedings of ISMIR 2002*, Paris.

Gabrilovich, E., Broder, A., Fontoura, M., Joshi, A., Josifovski, V., Riedel, L., & Zhang, T. (2009). Classifying search queries using the Web as a source of knowledge. *ACM Transactions on the Web, 3*(2), 1–28. doi:10.1145/1513876.1513877

Gabrilovich, E., & Markovitch, S. (2005). Feature generation for text categorization using world knowledge. *Proceedings of the Nineteenth International Joint Conference of Artificial Intelligence*, 1048–1053.

Gabrilovich, E., & Markovitch, S. (2007). Harnessing the Expertise of 70,000 Human Editors: Knowledge-Based Feature Generation for Text Categorization. *The Journal of Machine Learning Research, 8*, 2297 – 2345.

Gaede, V., & Günther, O. (1998). Multidimensional Access Methods. *ACM Computing Surveys, 30*(2), 170–231. doi:10.1145/280277.280279

Gao, X., Wang, T., & Li, J. (2005). A Content-based Image Quality Metric. In D. Slezak et al. (eds.), *Rough Sets, Fuzzy Sets, Data Mining, and Granular Computing*, (LNCS Vol. 3642, pp. 231-240). Berlin: Springer-Verlag.

Gao, Y., Fan, J., Xue, X., & Jain, R. (2006). Automatic image annotation by incorporating feature hierarchy and boosting to scale up svm classifiers. In *ACM International Conference on Multimedia* (p. 901-910).

Geetha, M. K., & Palanivel, S. (2007). HMM based automatic video classification using static and dynamic features. *International Conference on Computational Intelligence and Multimedia Applications*, (Vol. 3, pp. 277 – 281).

Genkin, A., Lewis, D., & Madigan, D. (2007). Large Scale Bayesian Logistic Regression for Text Categorization. *Technometrics, 49*(3), 291–304. doi:10.1198/004017007000000245

Gerstin, J. (1998). Reputation in a Musical Scene: The Everyday Context of Connections between Music, Identity and Politics. *Ethnomusicology, 42*(3), 385–414. doi:10.2307/852848

Gevers, T., & Stokman, H. (2003). Classifying color edges in video into shadow-geometry, highlight, or material transitions. *IEEE Transactions on Multimedia, 5*(2), 237–243. doi:10.1109/TMM.2003.811620

Ghahramani, S. (2005). *Fundamentals of Probability with Stochastic Processes* (3rd ed.). New York: Prentice Hall.

Ghamrawi, N., & McCallum, A. (2005). Collective multi-label classification. In *ACM International Conference on Information and Knowledge Management* (p. 195-200). New York: ACM.

Ghani, R. (2002). Combining Labeled and Unlabeled Data for MultiClass Text Categorization. *Proceedings of the Nineteenth International Conference on Machine Learning*, 187–194. San Francisco: Morgan Kaufmann.

Ghias, A., Logan, J., Chamberlin, D., & Smith, B. C. (2001). Query by humming - musical information retrieval in an audio database. In *Proceedings Multimedia*, (pp. 231-236).

Giannakidou, E., Kompatsiaris, I., & Vakali, A. (2008). Semsoc: Semantic, social and content-based clustering in multimedia collaborative tagging systems. In: *ICSC 2008: Proceedings of the 2008 IEEE International Conference on Semantic Computing*, (pp. 128–135). Washington, DC: IEEE Computer Society.

Gliozzo, A., Strapparava, C., & Dagan, I. (2009). Improving Text Categorization Bootstrapping via Unsupervised Learning. [TSLP]. *ACM Transactions on Speech and Language Processing, 6*(1), 1–24. doi:10.1145/1596515.1596516

Go'mez, J., & Vicedo, J. L. (2007). Next-generation Multimedia Database Retrieval. *IEEE MultiMedia, 14*(3), 106–107. doi:10.1109/MMUL.2007.56

Godøy, R. I. (2010). Chunking Sound for Musical Analysis. []. Berlin: Springer.]. *Lecture Notes in Computer Science, 5493*, 67–80. doi:10.1007/978-3-642-02518-1_4

Goh, K.-S., Li, B., & Chang, E. Y. (2005, October). Using one-class and two-class svms for multiclass image annotation. *IEEE Transactions on Knowledge and Data Engineering, 17*(10), 1333–1346. doi:10.1109/TKDE.2005.170

Goldman, S., & Zhou, Y. (2000). Enhancing Supervised Learning with Unlabeled Data. *Proceedings of the Seventeenth International Conference on Machine Learning*, (pp. 327–334). San Francisco: Morgan Kaufmann.

Gong, Y., Han, M., Hua, W., & Xu, W. (2004). Maximum entropy model-based baseball highlight detection and classification. *Computer Vision and Image Understanding, 96*(2), 181–199. doi:10.1016/j.cviu.2004.02.002

Gonzalez, R. C., & Woods, R. E. (2002). *Digital image processing*. Upper Saddle River, NJ: Prentice Hall.

Gonzalez, R. C., Woods, R. E., & Eddins, S. L. (2004). *Digital image processing using MATLAB*. Upper Saddle River, NJ: Prentice Hall.

Good, M. (2001a). *MusicXML for Notation and Analysis. The VirtualScore: Representation, Retrieval, Restoration*. Cambridge, MA: MIT Press.

Good, M., et al. (2001). *MusicXML: An Internet-Friendly Format for Sheet Music*. XML Conference and Expo.

Goth, G. (2004). Multimedia Search: Ready or Not? *Distributed Systems Online, IEEE, 5*(7). Retrieved from http://ieeexplore.ieee.org/stamp/stamp.jsp?arnumber=1323037&isnumber=29290

Goto, M. (2001). An Audio-based Real-time Beat Tracking System for Music With or Without Drum-sounds. *Journal of New Music Research, 30*(2), 159–171. doi:10.1076/jnmr.30.2.159.7114

Goto, M. (2003). A chorus-section detecting method for musical audio signals. In *Proceedings of the IEEE International Conference on Acoustics, Speech, and Signal Processing*, (pp. 437-440), April.

Gouyon, F., & Dixon, S. (2005). A Review of Automatic Rhythm Description Systems. *Computer Music Journal, 29*(1), 34–54. doi:10.1162/comj.2005.29.1.34

Gouyon, F., Klapuri, A., Dixon, S., Alonso, M., Tzanetakis, G., Uhle, C. & Cano, P. (2006). An experimental comparison of audio tempo induction algorithms. *IEEE Trans. on Speech and Audio Proc, 14*(5).

Griffin, G., Holub, A., & Perona, P. (2007). *Caltech-256 object category dataset.* Technical Report No. 7694, California Institute of Technology.

Guan, G., Wang, Z., Tian, Q., & Feng, D. (2009, October). Improved concept similarity measuring in visual domain. In *IEEE International Workshop on Multimedia Signal Processing.* Rio de Janeiro, Brazil.

Guan, H., & Wada, S. (2002). Flexible color texture retrieval method using multi- resolution mosaic for image classification. In *Proceedings of the 6th International Conference on Signal Processing: Vol. 1* (pp. 612-615).

Gueziec, A. (2002). Tracking pitches for broadcast television. *Computer, 35,* 38–43. doi:10.1109/2.989928

Guimaraes, S. J. F., Couprie, M., Araujo, A. A., & Leite, N. J. (2003). Video segmentation based on 2D image analysis. *Pattern Recognition Letters, 24,* 947–957. doi:10.1016/S0167-8655(02)00218-0

Gupta, A., & Jain, R. (1997, May). Visual information retrieval. *Communications of the ACM, 40*(5), 70–79. doi:10.1145/253769.253798

Guttman, A. (1984). R-trees: A Dynamic Index Structure for Spatial Searching. In *Proc. ACM SIGMOD Int. Conf. on Management of Data,* (pp. 47-54).

Haeghen, Y. V., Naeyaert, J. M. A. D., Lemahieu, I., & Philips, W. (2000). An imaging system with calibrated color image acquisition for use in dermatology. *IEEE Transactions on Medical Imaging, 19*(7), 722–730. doi:10.1109/42.875195

Haering, N., Qian, R., & Sezan, I. (2000). A semantic event-detection approach and its application to detecting hunts in wildlife video. *IEEE Transactions on Circuits and Systems for Video Technology, 10*(6), 857–868. doi:10.1109/76.867923

Hagenbuchner, M., Sperduti, A., & Tsoi, A. C. (2003, May). A self-organizing map for adaptive processing of structured data. *IEEE Transactions on Neural Networks, 14*(3), 491505. doi:10.1109/TNN.2003.810735

Haker, S., Angenent, S., Tannenbaum, A., Kikinis, R., Sapiro, G., & Halle, M. (2000). Conformal surface parameterization for texture mapping. *IEEE Transactions on Visualization and Computer Graphics, 6*(2), 181–189. doi:10.1109/2945.856998

Han, B., Gao, X., & Ji, H. (2005). A unified framework for shot boundary detection. In *Pattern Recognition,* (LNCS 3801, pp. 997-1002). Berlin: Springer.

Han, E. H., Karypis, G., & Kumar, V. (2001). Text categorization using weight-adjusted k-nearest neighbor classification. In D. Cheung, Q. Li and G. Williams (eds.), *Proceedings PAKDD-01, 5th Pacific–Asia Conference on Knowledge Discovery and Data Mining,* (LNCS 2035, 53–65. Berlin: Springer.

Han, M., Hua, W., Xu, W., & Gong, Y. (2003). An integrated baseball digest system using maximum entropy method. In *Proceedings of 10th International Conference on Multimedia,* (pp. 347-350).

Hanjalic, A., & Xu, L. Q. (2005). Affective video content representation and modeling. *IEEE Transactions on Multimedia, 7,* 143–154. doi:10.1109/TMM.2004.840618

Haralick, R. M., Shanmugam, K., & Dinstein, I. (1973). Textural features for image classification. *IEEE Transactions on Systems, Man, and Cybernetics, SMC-3*(6), 610–621. doi:10.1109/TSMC.1973.4309314

Hauptmann, A. G. (2005, July). Lessons for the future from a decade of informedia video analysis research. In *ACM International Conference on Image and Video Retrieval* (p. 1-10). Singapore.

Haus, G., Longari, M., & Pollastri, E. (2004). A score-driven approach to music information retrieval. *Journal of the American Society for Information Science and Technology, 55*(12), 1045–1052. doi:10.1002/asi.20056

Heisele, B., Ho, P., & Poggio, T. (2001). Face recognition with support vector machines: Global versus component-based approach. In *International Conference on Computer Vision* (pp. 688–694), Vancouver, Canada.

Hermansky, H. (1990). Perceptual linear predictive (PLP) analysis of speech. *The Journal of the Acoustical Society of America, 87*(4), 1738–1752. doi:10.1121/1.399423

Hernandez, B., Jiménez, J., & Martín, M. J. (2009). Key website factors in e-business strategy. *International Journal of Information Management, 29*(5), 362–371. doi:10.1016/j.ijinfomgt.2008.12.006

Heseltine, T., Pears, N., & Austin, J. (2004). Three dimensional face recognition: an eigensurface approach. In *International Conference on Image Processing* (pp. 1421–1424), Singapore.

Hettich, S., & Bay, S. D. (1999). *The UCI KDD Archive* [http://kdd.ics.uci.edu]. Irvine, CA: University of California, Department of Information and Computer Science.

Hilaga, M., Shinagawa, Y., Kohmura, T., & Kunii, T. L. (2001). 3D Shapes. In *ACM SIGGRAPH* (pp. 203–212). Los Angeles, CA: Topology Matching for Fully Automatic Similarity Estimation of.

Hjaltason, G., & Samet, H. (2003). Index-driven similarity search in metric spaces. [TODS]. *ACM Transactions on Database Systems, 28*(4), 517–580. doi:10.1145/958942.958948

Hollink, L., & Worring, M. (2005). Building a visual ontology for video retrieval. In *ACM International Conference on Multimedia* (pp. 479 - 482), Hilton, Singapore.

Hollink, L., Little, S., & Hunter, J. (2005, October). Evaluating the application of semantic inferencing rules to image annotation. In *International Conference on Knowledge Capture*, Banff, Alberta, Canada.

Hoogs, A., Rittscher, J., Stein, G., & Schmiederer, J. (2003, June). Video content annotation using visual analysis and a large semantic knowledgebase. In *IEEE International Conference on Computer Vision and Pattern Recognition (CVPR)* (pp. 327-334).

Horn, B. (1977). Understanding image intensities. *Artificial Intelligence, 8*(2), 1250–1267. doi:10.1016/0004-3702(77)90020-0

Hotelling, H. (1933). Analysis of a complex of statistical variables into principal components. *Journal of Educational Psychology, 24*, 417–441. doi:10.1037/h0071325

Hu, M. K. (1962). Visual pattern recognition by moment invariants. *I.R.E. Transactions on Information Theory, 8*(2), 179–187. doi:10.1109/TIT.1962.1057692

Hua, W., Han, M., & Gong, Y. (2002). Baseball scene classification using multimedia features. In *Proceeding of IEEE International Conference on Multimedia and Expo*, (Vol. 1, pp. 821-824).

Huan, Z., Xiuhuan, L., & Lilei, Y. (2008). Shot boundary detection based on mutual information and canny edge detector. *IEEE International Conference on Computer Science and Software Engineering*, (pp. 1124-1128).

Huang, J., Kumar, S. R., Mitra, M., Zhu, W.-J., & Zabih, R. (1999, December). Spatial color indexing and applications. *International Journal of Computer Vision, 35*(3), 245–268. doi:10.1023/A:1008108327226

Huang, J., Liu, Z., Wang, Y., Chen, Y., & Wong, E. K. (1999). Integration of multimodal features for video classification based on hmm. In *IEEE International Workshop on Multimedia Signal Processing* (pp. 53-58), Copenhagen, Denmark.

Huang, T. S., & Zhou, X. S. (2001). Image retrieval with relevance feedback: From heuristic weight adjustment to optimal learning methods. In *Proceedings of the IEEE International Conference on Image Processing* (pp. 2-5).

Hubert, L. & Arabie, P. (1985). Comparing partitions. *Journal of Classification*, 193-218.

Hughes, A., Wilkens, T., Wildemuth, B. M., & Marchionini, G. (2003). Text or pictures? an eyetracking study of how people view digital video surrogates. In *ACM International Conference on Image and Video Retrieval*.

Ianeva, T. I., Vries, A. P., & Rohrig, H. (2003). Detecting cartoons: a case study in automatic video-genre classification. *IEEE International Conference on Multimedia and Expo, 1*, 449-452.

IBM QBIC. (2006). *Hermitage Museum*. Retrieved from http://www.hermitagemuseum.org.

Idris, F., & Panchanathan, S. (1997, June). Review of image and video indexing techniques. *Journal of Visual Communication and Image Representation, 8*(2), 146–166. doi:10.1006/jvci.1997.0355

Inkpen, D., & Desilets, A. (2005). Semantic similarity for detecting recognition errors in automatic speech transcripts. In *International Conference on Human Language Technology and Empirical Methods in Natural Language Processing* (pp. 4956), Morristown, NJ.

Ionescu, B., Lambert, P., Coquin, D., & Buzuloiu, V. (2007). The cut detection issue in the animation movie domain. *Academy Publisher Journal of Multimedia, 2*(4), 10–19.

Ionescu, B., Lambert, P., Coquin, D., Ott, L., & Buzuloiu, V. (2006). Animation movies trailer computation. In *ACM Multimedia*. Santa Barbara.

Ionescu, B., Coquin, D., Lambert, P., & Buzuloiu, V. (2007). Fuzzy semantic action and color characterization of animation movies in the video indexing task context. In Marchand-Maillet, S. (Eds.), *LNCS 4398* (pp. 119–135). Berlin: Springer.

Ionescu, B., Buzuloiu, V., Lambert, P., & Coquin, D. (2006). Improved cut detection for the segmentation of animation movies. *IEEE International Conference on Acoustic, Speech and Signal Processing*, (Vol. 2, pp. 14-19), Toulouse, France.

Ionescu, B., Coquin, D., Lambert, P., & Buzuloiu, V. (2008). A fuzzy color-based approach for understanding animated movies content in the indexing task. *Eurasip Journal on Image and Video Processing, special issue on Color in Image and Video Processing, 1*, 20-36.

Ionescu, B., Lambert, P., Coquin, D., & Buzuloiu, V. (2006). Fuzzy color-based semantic characterization of animation movies. In *IS&T CGIV - 3th European Conference on Colour in Graphics, Imaging, and Vision*, University of Leeds, United Kingdom.

Ionescu, B., Lambert, P., Coquin, D., & Dârlea, L. (2005). Color-based semantic characterization of cartoons. *IEEE ISSCS - International Symposium on Signals, Circuits and Systems, 1*, (pp. 223-226), Iaşi, Romania.

Itten, J. (1961). *The art of color: The subjective experience and objective rational of color*. New York: Reinhold.

Iyengar, G., Duygulu, P., Feng, S., Ircing, P., Khudanpur, S. P., Klakow, D., et al. (2005, November). Joint visual-text modeling for automatic retrieval of multimedia documents. In *ACM International Conference on Multimedia*, (pp. 21-30), Singapore.

Jansen, B. J., Zhang, M., Booth, B., Park, D., Zhang, Y., Kathuria, A., & Bonner, P. (2009). To What Degree Can Log Data Profile a Web Searcher? *Proceedings of the American Society for Information Science and Technology*, Vancouver, British Columbia.

Jeannin, S., & Divakaran, A. (2001). MPEG-7 visual motion descriptors. *IEEE Transactions on Circuits and Systems for Video Technology, 11*(6), 720–724. doi:10.1109/76.927428

Jehan, T. (2005). Hierarchical Multi-Class Self Similarities. In *Proceedings of the WASPAA (CD), USA*.

Jensen, K. (2007). Multiple scale music segmentation using rhythm, timbre and harmony. *EURASIP Journal on Applied Signal Processing*, (Special issue on Music Information Retrieval Based on Signal Processing), 68–74.

Jensen, K., Xu, J., & Zachariasen, M. (2005). Rhythm-based segmentation of Popular Chinese Music. In *Proceeding of the ISMIR*, (pp. 374-380), London.

Jeon, J., & Manmatha, R. (2004). Using maximum entropy for automatic image annotation. In *Proc. International Conf. Image and Video Retrieval*.

Jeon, J., Lavrenko, V., & Manmatha, R. (2003). Automatic image annotation and retrieval using crossmedia relevance models. *Proceedings of the 26th Annual International ACM SIGIR Conference on Research and Development in Information Retrieval*, Toronto, Canada.

Jiang, H., Ngoa, C.-W., & Tana, H. K. (2006). Gestalt-based feature similarity measure in trademark database. *Pattern Recognition*, *39*(5), 988–1001. doi:10.1016/j.patcog.2005.08.012

Jiang, X., Marti, C., Irniger, C., & Bunke, H. (2005). Image segmentation evaluation by techniques of comparing clusterings. In Fabio, R., & Sergio, V. (Eds.), *Image Analysis and Processing (ICIAP)* (*Vol. 3617*, pp. 344–351). LNCS. doi:10.1007/11553595_42

Jiang, J., Li, Z., Xiao, G., & Chen, J. (2007). Real-time shot-cut detection in a compressed domain. *SPIE Journal of Electronic Imagining, 16*(4).

Jin, R., Chai, J. Y., & Si, L. (2004). Effective automatic image annotation via a coherent language model and active learning. In *ACM International Conference on Multimedia*.

Jin, Y., Khan, L., Wang, L., & Awad, M. (2005). Image annotations by combining multiple evidence & wordnet. In *ACM International Conference on Multimedia*.

Joachims, T. (2002). The Maximum-Margin Approach to Learning Text Classifiers, *Ausgezeichnete Informatikdissertationen*. In Wagner, D. (Eds.), *GI-Edition - Lecture Notes in Informatics (LNI)*. Bonn, Germany: Köllen Verlag.

Jurie, F., & Triggs, B. (2005). Creating efficient codebooks for visual recognition. In *Proc. ICCV*.

Kaban, A. (2008). A Probabilistic Neighborhood Translation Approach for Non-standard Text Classification. In *Proceedings Discovery Science (DS08)*, (LNAI 5255, 332-343).

Kakadiaris, I. A., Passalis, G., Toderici, G., Murtuza, N., Lu, Y., Karampatziakis, N., & Theoharis, T. (2007). Three-dimensional face recognition in the presence of facial expressions: An annotated deformable approach. *IEEE Transactions on Pattern Analysis and Machine Intelligence, 29*(4), 640–649. doi:10.1109/TPAMI.2007.1017

Kang, F., Jin, R., & Sukthankar, R. (2006). Correlated label propagation with application to multi-label learning. In *IEEE International Conference on Computer Vision and Pattern Recognition*, (pp. 1719 - 1726).

Katayama, N., & Satoh, S. (1997). The SR-tree: an index structure for high-dimensional nearest neighbor queries. In *Proc. 1997 ACM SIGMOD*, (pp. 369 – 380).

Kato, T. (1992). Database architecture for content-based image retrieval. In Jamberdino, A. A., & Niblack, W. (Eds.), *Image storage and retrieval systems* (pp. 112–113). Berlin: Springer-Verlag.

Kaufmann, L., & Rousseeuw, P. (1989). *Finding Groups in Data*. New York: John Wiley and Sons.

Kauppinen, H., Seppänen, T., & Pietikäinen, M. (1995). An experimental comparison of autoregressive and Fourier-based descriptors. *IEEE Transactions on Pattern Analysis and Machine Intelligence, 17*(2), 201–207. doi:10.1109/34.368168

Kawai, Y., Sumiyoshi, H., & Yagi, N. (2007). Automated production of TV program trailer using electronic program guide. *ACM International Conference on Image and Video Retrieval*, (pp. 49-56), Amsterdam.

Ke, Y., & Sukthankar, R. (2004, June). PCA-SIFT: A more distinctive representation for local image descriptors. In *IEEE International Conference on Computer Vision and Pattern Recognition*. Washington, DC: IEEE.

Ke, Y., Sukthankar, R., & Hebert, M. (2007, October). Event detection in crowded videos. In *IEEE International Conference on Computer Vision* (p. 1-8), Rio de Janeiro, Brazil.

Keogh, E., Chakrabarti, K., Pazzani, M., & Mehrotra, S. (2000). Dimensionality reduction for fast similarity search in large time series databases. *Knowledge and Information Systems, 3*(3), 263–286. doi:10.1007/PL00011669

Keshet, J., Shalev-Shwartz, S., Singer, Y. & Chazan, D. (2007). A Large Margin Algorithm for Speech-to-Phoneme and Music-to-Score Alignment. *Audio, Speech and Language Processing, IEEE Transactions on [see also Speech and Audio Processing, IEEE Transactions on], 15*(8), 2373-2382.

Khan, L. (2007). Standards for image annotation using semantic Web. *Computer Standards & Interfaces, 29*(2), 196–204. doi:10.1016/j.csi.2006.03.006

Khan, A., Aylward, E., Barta, P., Miller, M. I., & Beg, M. F. (2005). Semi-automated Basal Ganglia Segmentation Using Large Deformation Diffeomorphic Metric Mapping. In J.S. Duncan, G. Gerig (eds.), *Medical Image Computing and Computer-Assisted Intervention,* (LNCS Vol. 3749, pp. 238-245). Berlin: Springer-Verlag.

Khan, L. & Wang, L. (2002) Automatic Ontology Derivation Using Clustering for Image Classification. *Multimedia Information Systems,* (2002), 56-65.

Kim, W.-Y., & Kim, Y.-S. (2000). A region-based shape descriptor using Zernike moments. *Signal Processing Image Communication, 16*(1-2), 95–102. doi:10.1016/S0923-5965(00)00019-9

Kim, D.-J., Frigui, H., & Fadeev, A. (2008). A generic approach to semantic video indexing using adaptive fusion of multimodal classifiers. *International Journal of Imaging Systems and Technology, 18*(2-3), 124–136. doi:10.1002/ima.20147

Kim, K. I., Jung, K., Park, S. H., & Kim, H. J. (2000). Support vector machine-based text detection in digital video. *Pattern Recognition, 34*(2), 527–529. doi:10.1016/S0031-3203(00)00095-9

Kinoshenko, D., Mashtalir, V. & Shlyakhov, V. (2007). A partition metric for clustering features analysis. *International Journal 'Information theories and applications', 14,* 230-236.

Kinoshenko, D., Mashtalir, V., Vinarsky, V., & Yegorova, E. (2005). Hierarchical partitions for content image retrieval from Large-scale database. In *Machine Learning and Data Mining in Pattern Recognition,* (LNCS Vol. 3587, pp. 445-455). Berlin: Springer-Verlag.

Knees, P., et al. (2007). A Music Search Engine Built Upon Audio-based and Web-based Similarity Measures. In *Proceedings of the ACM SIGIR 2007,* Amsterdam.

Koskela, M., Smeaton, A. F., & Laaksonen, J. (2007, August). Measuring concept similarities in multimedia ontologies: Analysis and evaluations. *IEEE Transactions on Multimedia, 9*(5), 912–922. doi:10.1109/TMM.2007.900137

Krafft, J. (2009). Profiting in the info-coms industry in the age of broadband: Lessons and new considerations. *Technological Forecasting and Social Change, 77*(2), 265–278. doi:10.1016/j.techfore.2009.07.002

Kühl, O. (2007). *Musical Semantics.* Bern, Switzerland: Peter Lang.

Kühl, O., & Jensen, K. (2008). Retrieving and recreating Musical Form. []. Berlin: Springer-Verlag.]. *Lecture Notes in Computer Science, 4969,* 263–275. doi:10.1007/978-3-540-85035-9_18

Kumano, M., Ariki, Y., Tsukada, K., Hamaguchi, S., & Kiyose, H. (2005). Automatic extraction of PC scenes based on feature mining for a real time delivery system of baseball highlight scenes. In *Proceeding of IEEE International Conference on Multimedia and Expo,* (Vol. 1, pp. 277-280).

Kurniawati, E., & Kurniawan, E. Lau, C.T., Premkumar, B., Absar, J., & George, S. (2004). Error concealment scheme for MPEG-AAC. In *Communications Systems. ICCS 2004. The Ninth International Conference on,* (pp. 240-246).

Kushki, A., Androutsos, P., Plataniotis, K. N., & Venetsanopoulos, A. N. (2004). Query feedback for interactive image retrieval. *IEEE Transactions on Circuits and Systems for Video Technology, 14,* 644–655. doi:10.1109/TCSVT.2004.826759

La Cascia, M., Sethi, S., & Sclaroff, S. (1998). Combining textural and visual cues for content- based image retrieval on the World Wide Web. In *Proceedings of the IEEE Workshop on Content-Based Access of Image and Video Libraries,* Santa BarBara, CA, USA.

Laptev, I., Marszalek, M., Schmid, C., & Rozenfeld, B. (2008, June). Learning realistic human actions from movies. In *IEEE International Conference on Computer Vision and Pattern Recognition* (p. 1-8), Anchorage, AK.

Lavrenko, V., Manmatha, R., & Jeon, J. (2003). A model for learning the semantics of pictures. In *The 16th annual Conference on Neural Information Processing Systems.*

Lay, J. A., & Guan, L. (2004). Retrieval for color artistry concepts. *IEEE Transactions on Image Processing, 13*(3), 125–129. doi:10.1109/TIP.2003.822971

Lazebnik, S., Schmid, C., & Ponce, J. (2006). Beyond bags of features: Spatial pyramid matching for recognizing natural scene categories. In *IEEE International Conference on Computer Vision and Pattern Recognition.*

Lecce, V. D., & Guerriero, A. (1999, December). An evaluation of the effectiveness of image features for image retrieval. *Journal of Visual Communication and Image Representation, 10*(4), 351–362. doi:10.1006/jvci.1999.0423

Lee, K. (2005). *Semantic feature extraction based on video abstraction and temporal modeling. Pattern Recognition and Image Analysis* (Vol. 3522, pp. 392–400). Berlin: Springer.

Lee, M.-S., Yang, Y.-M., & Lee, S.-W. (2001). Automatic video parsing using shot boundary detection and camera operation analysis. *Pattern Recognition, 34,* 711–719. doi:10.1016/S0031-3203(00)00007-8

Leonardi, R., Migliorati, P., & Prandini, M. (2004). Semantic indexing of soccer audio-visual sequences: a multimodal approach based on controlled Markov chains. *IEEE Transactions on Circuits and Systems for Video Technology, 14*(5), 634–643. doi:10.1109/TC-SVT.2004.826751

Leonardi, R., Migliorati, P., & Prandini, M. (2004). Semantic indexing of soccer audio-visual sequences: a multimodal approach based on controlled Markov chains. *IEEE Transactions on Circuits and Systems for Video Technology, 14*(5), 634–643. doi:10.1109/TC-SVT.2004.826751

Lerdahl, E., & Jackendoff, R. (1983). *A generative theory of tonal music.* Cambridge, MA: M.I.T. Press.

Lesaffre, M. (2005-2006). *Music Information Retrieval: Conceptual Framework, Annotation and User Behaviour.* PhD thesis, Faculty of Arts and Philosophy, Department of Art, Music and Theatre Sciences, Ghent University, The Netherlands.

Leslie, L., Chua, T.-S., & Ramesh, J. (2007). Annotation of paintings with high-level semantic concepts using transductive inference and ontology based concept disambiguation. In *ACM International Conference on Multimedia,* (pp. 443-452). New York: ACM.

Leung, C., & Liu, J. (2007). Multimedia Data Mining and Searching Through Dynamic Index Evolution. In *VISUAL 2007: Proceedings of the 9th International Conference on Visual Information Systems,* Shanghai, China, (pp.298-309).

Levinson, D. J. (1986). *The Seasons of a Man's Life.* New York: Ballantine Books.

Lew, M., Sebe, N., Djeraba, Ch., & Jain, R. (2006). Content-based multimedia information retrieval: state of art and challenges. *ACM Transactions of Multimedia Computing, Communications, and Applications, 2*(1), 1–19. doi:10.1145/1126004.1126005

Lew, M. S., Sebe, N., & Eakins, J. P. (2002). Challenges of image and video retrieval. *Proceedings of the International Conference on Image and Video Retrieval, Lecture Notes in Computer Science,* London, UK.

Lewis, D. D., & Catlett, J. (1994). Heterogeneous Uncertainty Sampling for Supervised Learning. *Proceedings of the Eleventh International Conference on Machine Learning,* 148–156. San Francisco: Morgan Kaufmann.

Li, C. H., & Yuen, P. C. (2000). Regularized color clustering in medical image database. *IEEE Transactions on Medical Imaging, 19*(11), 1150–1155. doi:10.1109/42.896791

Li, B., Chang, E., & Wu, Y. (2003). Discovery of a perceptual distance function for measuring image similarity. *Multimedia Systems, 8*(6), 512–522. doi:10.1007/s00530-002-0069-9

Li, J., & Wang, J. Z. (2003). Automatic linguistic indexing of pictures by a statistical modeling approach. *IEEE Transactions on Pattern Analysis and Machine Intelligence, 25*(9), 1075–1088. doi:10.1109/TPAMI.2003.1227984

Li, Y., Bandar, Z. A., & McLean, D. (2003, August). An approach for measuring semantic similarity between words using multiple information sources. *IEEE Transactions on Knowledge and Data Engineering, 15*(4), 871882.

Li, J., & Wang, J. Z. (2006). Real-time computerized annotation of pictures. In *the ACM International Conference on Multimedia*.

Li, J., Wang, J. Z., & Wiederhold, G. (2000). IRM integrated region matching for image retrieval. In *proc. ACM Multimedia'2000*, (pp. 147-156).

Li, S., & Chen, Z. (2005) Enhanced Image Management Using an Image Algebra. In *Proc. ISIE 2005*.

Li, X., & Liu, B. (2003). Learning to Classify Text Using Positive and Unlabeled Data. *Proceedings of the Eighteenth International Joint Conference on Artificial Intelligence, 587–594*. San Francisco: Morgan Kaufmann.

Li, X., Chen, L., Zhang, L., Lin, F., & Ma, W.-Y. (2006). Image annotation by large-scale content based image retrieval. In *Proc. ACM Multimedia*.

Li, Z., Qu, H., & Zhang, J. (2008). Real-time fade detection in compressed domain. *IEEE International Conference on Image and Signal Processing, 2*(2), 535-539.

Li, Z., Schuster, G., Katsaggelos, A. K., & Gandhi, B. (2004). Optimal video summarization with a bit budget constraint. *IEEE International Conference on Image Processing*, (Vol. 1, pp. 617-620), Singapore.

Lienhart, R. (1999). Comparison of automatic shot boundary detection algorithms. *SPIE Storage and Retrieval for Still Image and Video Databases VII, 3656*, 290–301.

Lienhart, R. (2001). Reliable transition detection in videos: A survey and practitioner's guide. *International Journal of Image and Graphics, 1*(3), 469–486. doi:10.1142/S021946780100027X

Lin, K.-I., Jagadish, H. V., & Faloutsos, C. (1994). The TV-tree: An index structure for high-dimensional data. *The VLDB Journal, 3*(4), 517–542. doi:10.1007/BF01231606

Lin, S., & Kernighan, B. W. (1973). An Effective Heuristic Algorithm for the Traveling-Salesman Problem. *Operations Research, 21*(2), 498–516. doi:10.1287/opre.21.2.498

Ling, H., & Jacobs, D. (2005). Deformation invariant image matching. In *International Conference on Computer Vision*, (pp. 1466–1473), Beijing, China.

Lippincott, T., & Passonneau, R. (2009). Semantic Clustering for a Functional Text Classification Task. In *Proceedings of the 10th international Conference on Computational Linguistics and Intelligent Text Processing*, (LNCS 5449, 509-522.

Liu, Y., Zhang, D., Lu, G., & Ma, W.-Y. (2007). A survey of content-based image retrieval with high-level semantics. *Pattern Recognition, 40*(1), 262–282. doi:10.1016/j.patcog.2006.04.045

Liu, Y., Zhanga, D., Lua, G., & Ma, W.-Y. (2007). A survey of content-based image retrieval with high-level semantics. *Pattern Recognition, 40*(1), 262–282. doi:10.1016/j.patcog.2006.04.045

Liu, Y., Zhang, D., Lu, G., & Ma, W.-Y. (2007). A survey of content-based image retrieval with high-level semantics. *Pattern Recognition, 40*, 262–282. doi:10.1016/j.patcog.2006.04.045

Liu, J., Li, M., Ma, W.-Y., Liu, Q., & Lu, H. (2006, October). An adaptive graph model for automatic image annotation. In *ACM International Workshop on Multimedia Information Retrieval* (pp. 61-70), Santa Barbara, CA.

Liu, J., Wang, B., Li, M., Li, Z., Ma, W., Lu, H., et al. (2007, September). Dual cross-media relevance model for image annotation. In *the ACM International Conference on Multimedia* (pp. 605 - 614), Augsburg, Germany.

Liu, W., & Tang, X. (2005). Learning an image-word embedding for image auto-annotation on the nonlinear latent space. In *Proc. ACM Multimedia*.

Liu, X., Croft, W. B., Oh, P., & Hart, D. (2004). Automatic recognition of reading levels from user queries. *Proceedings of the 27th ACM International Conference on Research and Development in Information Retrieval*, 548–549, Sheffield, UK.

Lo, Y.-L., & Chen, S.-J. (2002). The numeric indexing for music data. *Proceedings of the 22nd International Conference on Distributed Computing Systems Workshops.* Vienna, Austria.

Loncaric, S. (1998). A survey of shape analysis techniques. *Pattern Recognition, 31*(8), 983–1001. doi:10.1016/S0031-2023(97)00122-2

Lopez, C., & Chen, Y.-P. P. (2006). Using object and trajectory analysis to facilitate indexing and retrieval of video. *Knowledge-Based Systems, 19*(8), 639–646. doi:10.1016/j.knosys.2006.05.006

Lowe, D. G. (2004). Distinctive image features from scale-invariant keypoints. *International Journal of Computer Vision, 60*(2), 91–110. doi:10.1023/B:VISI.0000029664.99615.94

Lu, H., & Tan, Y. P. (2003). Unsupervised clustering of dominant scenes in sports video. *Pattern Recognition Letters, 24*(15), 2651–2662. doi:10.1016/S0167-8655(03)00108-9

Lu, S., King, I., & Lyu, M. (2003). Video summarization using greedy method in a constraint satisfaction framework. In *International Conference on Distributed Multimedia Systems,* (pp. 456–461), Miami, Florida, USA.

Luo, Y., Wu, T. D., & Hwang, J. N. (2003). Object-based analysis and interpretation of human motion in sports video sequences by dynamic Bayesian networks. *Computer Vision and Image Understanding, 92*(2-3), 196–216. doi:10.1016/j.cviu.2003.08.001

Luo, H., Fan, J., Gao, Y., & Xu, G. (2004). Multimodal salient objects: General building blocks of semantic video concepts. In *ACM International Conference on Image and Video Retrieval,* (pp. 374-383).

Lupatini, G., Saraceno, C., & Leonardi, R. (1998). Scene break detection: A comparison. In *Research Issues in Data Engineering, Workshop on Continuous Media Databases and Applications,* (pp. 34–41), Orlando, FL, USA.

Ma, Z. (Ed.). (2009). *Artificial Intelligence for Maximizing Content-Based Image Retrieval.* Hershey, PA: Information Science Reference.

Ma, W.-Y., & Manjunath, B. S. (2000). EdgeFlow: a technique for boundary detection and image segmentation. *IEEE Transactions on Image Processing, 9*(8), 1375–1388. doi:10.1109/83.855433

Manjunath, B., Salembier, P., & Sikora, T. (Eds.). (2002). *Introduction to MPEG-7: multimedia content description interface.* Chichester, UK: Wiley.

Manjunath, B. S., & Ma, W. Y. (1996). Texture features for browsing and retrieval of image data. *IEEE Transactions on Pattern Analysis and Machine Intelligence, 18*(8), 837–842. doi:10.1109/34.531803

Manjunath, B. S., & Sikora, T. (2002). Overview of visual descriptors. In Manjunath, B. S., Salembier, P., & Sikora, T. (Eds.), *Introduction to MPEG-7* (pp. 180–185). Chichester, UK: Wiley.

Manning, C. D., Raghavan, P., & Schtze, H. (2008). *Introduction to information retrieval.* Cambridge, UK: Cambridge University Press.

Markkula, M., & Sormunen, E. (2000, January). End-user searching challenges indexing practices in the digital newspaper photo archive. *Information Retrieval, 1*(4), 259–295. doi:10.1023/A:1009995816485

Maron, O., & Lozano-Perez, T. (1998). *A framework for multiple instance learning.* NIPS.

Marques, O., & Furht, B. (2002). *Content-based image and video retrieval.* London: Kluwer.

Mashtalir, V., Mikhnova, E., Shlyakhov, V., & Yegorova, E. (2006). A Novel Metric on Partitions for Image Segmentation. In *Proceedings of IEEE International Conference on Video and Signal Based Surveillance,* (pp. 18).

McCallum, A., & Nigam, K. (1998). A comparison of event models for naïve Bayes text classification. In *AAAI-98 Workshop on Learning for Text Categorization.*

McNab, R. J., Smith, L. A., Witten, I. H., Henderson, C. L., & Cunningham, S. J. (1996). Towards the digital music library: Tune retrieval from acoustic input. In *Proceeding DL'96,* (pp. 11-18).

Meila, M. (2003). Comparing clustering by the Variation of Information. In B. Scheolkopf, M.K. Warmuth (eds.), *COLT/Kernel 2003,* (LNAI Vol. 2777, pp. 173–187). Berlin: Springer-Verlag.

Meilhac, C., & Nastar, C. (1999). Relevance feedback and category search in image databases. *Proceedings of IEEE International Conference on Multimedia Computing and Systems,* 512-517.

Metaxas, P., Ivanova, L., & Mustafaraj, E. (2009). New Quality Metrics for Web Search Results. *Web Information Systems and Technologies LNBIP, 18*(3), 278–292. doi:10.1007/978-3-642-01344-7_21

Mian, A. S., Bennamoun, M., & Owens, R. (2007). An efficient multimodal 2D-3D hybrid approach to automatic face recognition. *IEEE Transactions on Pattern Analysis and Machine Intelligence, 29*(11), 1927–1943. doi:10.1109/TPAMI.2007.1105

Mikolajczyk, K., & Schmid, C. (2002). An afine invariant interest point detector. In *European Conference on Computer Vision* (pp. 128-142), Copenhagen, Denmark.

Mikolajczyk, K., & Schmid, C. (2003). A performance evaluation of local descriptors. In *IEEE International Conference on Computer Vision and Pattern Recognition.*

Miller, G. A. (1956). The magical number seven, plus or minus two: some limits on our capacity for processing information. *Psychological Review, 63,* 81–97. doi:10.1037/h0043158

Milnor, J. (1963). *Morse Theory.* Princeton, NJ: Princeton University Press.

Mitra, M., Singhal, A., & Buckley, C. (1998). Improving automatic query expansion. In *International ACM SIGIR Conference on Research and Development in Information Retrieval.*

Mochizuki, T., Tadenuma, M., & Yagi, N. (2005). Baseball video indexing using patternization of scenes and hidden Markov model. In. *Proceedings of IEEE International Conference on Image Processing, 3,* 12–15.

Moghaddam, H. A., Khajoie, T. T., & Rouhi, A. H. (2003). A new algorithm for image indexing and retrieval using wavelet correlogram. In. *Proceedings of the International Conference on Image Processing, 3,* 497–500.

Mokhtarian, F., & Mackworth, A. (1986). Scale-based description and recognition of planar curves and two-dimensional shapes. *IEEE Transactions on Pattern Analysis and Machine Intelligence, 8*(1), 34–43. doi:10.1109/TPAMI.1986.4767750

Monay, F., & Gatica-Perez, D. (2003, November). On image auto-annotation with latent space models. In *ACM International Conference on Multimedia,* (pp. 275-278), Berkeley, CA.

Monay, F., & Gatica-Perez, D. (2004, November). PLSA-based image auto-annotation: constraining the latent space. In *ACM International Conference on Multimedia,* (pp. 348-351). New York: ACM.

Monay, F., & Gatica-Perez, D. (2004). PLSA-based image auto-annotation: constraining the latent space. In *Proc. ACM Multimedia.*

Money, A. G., & Agius, H. (2008). Video summarization: A conceptual framework and survey of the state of the art. *International Journal of Visual Communication and Image Representation, 19,* 121–143. doi:10.1016/j.jvcir.2007.04.002

Moreno, A. B., & Sànchez, A. (2004). GavabDB: A 3D Face Database. In *Workshop on Biometrics on the Internet,* (pp. 75-80), Vigo, Spain.

Mori, Y., Takahashi, H., & Oka, R. (1999). Image-to-word transformation based on dividing and vector quantizing images with words. In *The first International Workshop on Multimedia Intelligent Storage and Retrieval Management (MISRM99).*

Moxley, E., Mei, T., Hua, X.-S., Ma, W.-Y., & Manjunath, B. S. (2008, June). Automatic video annotation through search and mining. In *IEEE International Conference on Multimedia and Expo,* (pp. 685-688), Hannover, Germany.

MPEG1 - Information Technology - Coding of Moving Pictures and Associated Audiofor Digital Storage Media at up to about 1.5 Mbits/s - Part 3: Audio I. I. S. I. 11172-3. *(n.d.).*

MPEG2 - Information Technology - Generic Coding of Moving Pictures and AssociatedAudio, Part 3: Audio I. I. S. I. 13818-3. *(n.d.).*

Mu, X. (2006) Supporting semantic visual feature browsing in content-based video retrieval. In *Proceedings of the 29th International ACM SIGIR Conference on Research and Development in Information Retrieval*, (pp. 734-734).

Muller, H., Michoux, N., Bandon, D., & Geissbuhler, A. (2004). A review of content-based image retrieval systems in medical applications-clinical benefits and future directions. *International Journal of Medical Informatics, 73*(1), 1–23. doi:10.1016/j.ijmedinf.2003.11.024

Müller, H., Müller, W., Squire, D. McG., Marchand-Millet, S., & Pun, T. (2001). Performance evaluation in content-based image retrieval: Overview and proposals. *Pattern Recognition Letters, 22*(5), 593–601. doi:10.1016/S0167-8655(00)00118-5

Muller, H., Marchand-Maillet, S., & Pun, T. (2002). The truth about corel-evaluation in image retrieval. In *ACM International Conference on Image and Video Retrieval*, (pp. 38-49).

Muller, M., Kurth, F., & Roder, T. (2004). Towards an Efficient Algorithm for Automatic Score-to-Audio Synchronization. In *5th International Conference on Music Information Retrieval, ISMIR 2004.*

Müller, S., & Rigoll, G. (1999). Improved stochastic modelling of shapes for content-based image retrieval. *IEEE Workshop on Content-based Access of Image and Video Libraries, CBAIVL'99*, (pp. 23-27).

Musicpedia. (n.d.). *The Open Music Encyclopedia.* Retrieved from http://www.musicpedia.org

Naphade, M., Smith, J. R., Tesic, J., Chang, S.-F., Hsu, W., & Kennedy, L. (2006, July-September). Large-scale concept ontology for multimedia. *IEEE MultiMedia, 13*(3), 86–91. doi:10.1109/MMUL.2006.63

Naphade, M. R., & Huang, T. S. (2002). Extracting semantics from audiovisual content: The final frontier in multimedia retrieval. *IEEE Transactions on Neural Networks, 13*(2), 793–810. doi:10.1109/TNN.2002.1021881

Ngo, C., Zhang, H., Chin, R. T., & Pong, T. (2000, June). Motion characterization by temporal slice analysis. In *IEEE International Conference on Computer Vision and Pattern Recognition* (pp. 768-773), Hilton Head Island, SC.

Niebles, J. C., & Fei-Fei, L. (2007). A hierarchical model of shape and appearance for human action classification. In *IEEE International Conference on Computer Vision and Pattern Recognition.*

Nigam, K., McCallum, A., & Mitchell, T. (2006) Semi-Supervised Text Classification Using EM. In O. Chapelle, B. Sch"olkopf, & A. Zien (Eds.), *Semi-Supervised Learning*, 31-51. Cambridge, MA: MIT Press.

Nister, D., & Stewenius, H. (2006). Scalable recognition with a vocabulary tree. In *IEEE International Conference on Computer Vision and Pattern Recognition.*

Noll, D. (1997). MPEG Digital Audio Coding. *IEEE Signal Processing Magazine, 14*, 59–81. doi:10.1109/79.618009

Ojala, T., Pietikainen, M., & Maenpaa, T. (2002, July). Multiresolution gray-scale and rotation invariant texture classification with local binary patterns. *IEEE Transactions on Pattern Analysis and Machine Intelligence, 24*(7), 971–987. doi:10.1109/TPAMI.2002.1017623

Ojala, T., Pietikinen, M., & Harwood, D. (1996). A comparative study of texture measures with classification based on featured distribution. *Pattern Recognition, 29*(1), 51–59. doi:10.1016/0031-3203(95)00067-4

Oliva, A., & Torralba, A. (2001). Modeling the shape of the scene: a holistic representation of the spatial envelope. *International Journal of Computer Vision, 42*, 145–175. doi:10.1023/A:1011139631724

Orio, N. (2006). Music Retrieval: A Tutorial and Review. *Foundations and Trends in Information Retrieval, 1*(1), 1–90. doi:10.1561/1500000002

Ott, L., Lambert, P., Ionescu, B., & Coquin, D. (2007). Animation movie abstraction: Key frame adaptive selection based on color histogram filtering. In *Computational Color Imaging Workshop at the International Conference on Image Analysis and Processing*, Modena.

Ouyang, A., & Tan, Y. P. (2002). A novel multi-scale spatial-color descriptor for content-based image retrieval. In *Proceedings of the 7th International Conference on Control, Automation, Robotics and Vision: Vol.3* (pp. 1204-1209).

Owens, N., Harris, C., & Stennett, C. (2004). Hawk-eye tennis system. *International Conference on Visual Information Engineering,* (pp. 182- 185).

Ozmutlu, S., Ozmutlu, H. C., & Spink, A. (2008). Analytical approaches for topic analysis and identification of Web search engine transaction logs. In Jansen, B. J., Spink, A., & Taksa, I. (Eds.), *Handbook of Web Log Analysis.* Hershey, PA: Idea Group Publishing.

Pan, D. (1995). A tutorial on MPEG/audio compression. *IEEE MultiMedia, 2,* 60–74. doi:10.1109/93.388209

Pan, G., Han, S., Wu, Z., & Wang, Y. (2005). 3D face recognition using mapped depth images. In *Conference on Computer Vision and Pattern Recognition,* (pp. 175–181), San Diego, CA.

Pan, J.-Y., Balan, Y., Xing, E., Traina, A., & Faloutsos, C. (2006). Automatic mining of fruit fly embryo images, *Proc. ACM KDD.*

Pan, J.-Y., Yang, H.-J., Duygulu, P., & Faloutsost, C. (2004, June). Automatic image captioning. In *IEEE International Conference on Multimedia and Expo (ICME)* (Vol. 3, pp. 1987-1990). Taipei, Taiwan.

Pan, J.-Y., Yang, H.-J., Faloutsos, C., & Duygulu, P. (2004, July). Gcap: Graph-based automatic image captioning. In *International Workshop on Multimedia Data and Document Engineering*, Washington, DC.

Pan, J.-Y., Yang, H.-J., Faloutsos, C., & Duygulu, P. (2004). Automatic multimedia cross-modal correlation discovery. In *Proc. ACM KDD.*

Pardo, B. (2006). Music information retrieval. *Communications of the ACM, 49*(8), 29–31.

Park, U., Chen, H., & Jain, A. K. (2005). 3D model assisted face recognition in video. In *Canadian Conference on Computer and Robot Vision,* (pp. 322–329), Victoria, Canada.

Partridge, M., & Jabri, M. (2002). Hierarchical Feature Extraction for Image Recognition. *The Journal of VLSI Signal Processing, 32*(1-2), 157–167. doi:10.1023/A:1016379721504

Pass, G., & Zabih, R. (1999). Comparing images using joint histograms. *Multimedia Systems, 7*(3), 234–240. doi:10.1007/s005300050125

Pauws, S., & Eggen, B. (2002). PATS: Realization and user evaluation of an automatic playlist generator. In *Proceedings of the 3rd International Conference on Music Information Retrieval*, Ircam, France, (pp. 222-230).

Pavel, F. A., Wang, Z., & Feng, D. D. (2009, October). Reliable object recognition using sift features. In *IEEE International Workshop on Multimedia Signal Processing.* Rio de Janeiro, Brazil.

Payne, A., & Singh, S. (2005, October). Indoor vs. outdoor scene classification in digital photographs. *Pattern Recognition, 38*(10), 1533–1545. doi:10.1016/j.patcog.2004.12.014

Perlich, C., Provost, F., & Simonoff, J. S. (2003). Tree induction vs. logistic regression: a learning-curve analysis. *Journal of Machine Learning Research, 4,* 211–255. doi:10.1162/153244304322972694

Persoon, E., & Fu, K. sun. (1997). Shape discrimination using fourier descriptors. *IEEE Transactions on Systems, Man, and Cybernetics, SMC-7*(3), 170–179.

Petra, K., Jenny, B.-P., & Jean-Philippe, D. (2006). Scene similarity measure for video content segmentation in the framework of a rough indexing paradigm. *International Journal of Intelligent Systems, 21*(7), 765–783. doi:10.1002/int.20159

Petridis, K., Precioso, F., Athanasiadis, T., Avrithis, Y., & Kompatsiaris, Y. (2005) Combined Domain Specific and Multimedia Ontologies for Image Understanding. In *Proc. 28th German Conference on Artificial Intelligence*, Koblenz, Germany.

Phillips, P. J., Flynn, P. J., Scruggs, T., Bowyer, K. W., Chang, J., Hoffman, K., et al. (2005). Overview of the Face Recognition Grand Challenge. In *IEEE Workshop on Face Recognition Grand Challenge Experiments*, (pp. 947-954), San Diego, CA.

Platt, J. (1998). Fast training of support vector machines using sequential minimal optimization. In Schoelkopf, B., Burges, C., & Smola, A. (Eds.), *Advances in kernel methods - support vector learning* (pp. 185–208). Cambridge, MA: MIT Press.

Pohle, T., Pampalk, E., & Widmer, G. (2005). Generating similarity-based playlists using traveling salesman algorithms. In *Proceedings of Digital Audio Effects*, Madrid, Spain, (pp. 220-225).

Porter, S. V., Mirmehdi, M., & Thomas, B. T. (2000). Video cut detection using frequency domain correlation. *International Conference on Pattern Recognition*, (pp. 413–416), Barcelona, Spain.

Povinelli, R. J., & Feng, X. (2003). A new temporal pattern identification method for characterization and prediction of complex time series events. *IEEE Transactions on Knowledge and Data Engineering*, 15(2), 339–352. doi:10.1109/TKDE.2003.1185838

Prieto, M. S., & Allen, A. R. (2003). A similarity metric for edge images. *IEEE Transactions on Pattern Analysis and Machine Intelligence*, 25(10), 1265–1277. doi:10.1109/TPAMI.2003.1233900

Qi, G.-J., Hua, X.-S., Rui, Y., Tang, J., Mei, T., & Zhang, H.-J. (2007, September). Correlative multi-label video annotation. In *The ACM International Conference on Multimedia*, Augsburg, Germany.

Qian, G., Sural, S., Gu, Y., & Pramanik, S. (2004). Similarity between Euclidean and cosine angle distance for nearest neighbor queries. In *Proceedings of ACM Symposium on Applied Computing* (pp. 1232-1237).

Queirolo, C. C., Silva, L., Bellon, O. R. P., & Pamplona Segundo, M. (2010). 3D Face Recognition Using Simulated Annealing and the Surface Interpenetration Measure. *IEEE Transactions on Pattern Analysis and Machine Intelligence*, 32(2), 206–219. doi:10.1109/TPAMI.2009.14

QuesTec. (2007). *Umpire Information System*. Retrieved from http://www.questec.com/q2001/prod_uis.htm

Quinlan, J. R. (1986). Induction of Decision Trees. *Machine Learning*, 1, 81–106. doi:10.1007/BF00116251

Raghavan, H., Madani, O., & Jones, R. (2006). Active Learning with Feedback on Both Features and Instances. *Journal of Machine Learning Research*, 7, 1655–1686.

Rahman, A., & Murshed, M. (2008). Temporal texture characterization: A review. *Studies in Computational Intelligence*, 96, 291–316. doi:10.1007/978-3-540-76827-2_12

Rahmani, R., & Goldman, S. (2006). MISSL: multiple-instance semi-supervised learning. In *Proc. ICML*.

Rand, W. M. (1971). Objective criteria for the evaluation of clustering methods. *Journal of the American Statistical Association*, 66, 846–850. doi:10.2307/2284239

Ren, W., Singh, S., Singh, M., & Zhu, Y. S. (2009). State-of-the-art on spatio-temporal information based video retrieval. *Pattern Recognition*, 42, 267–282. doi:10.1016/j.patcog.2008.08.033

Roach, M., Mason, J. S., & Pawlewski, M. (2001). Motion-based classification of cartoons. *International Symposium on Intelligent Multimedia, Video and Speech Processing*, (pp. 146-149), Hong-Kong, China.

Rocchio, J. J. (1971). Relevance feedback in information retrieval. In Salton, G. (Ed.), *The SMART Retrieval System-Experiments in Automatic Document Processing* (pp. 313–323). Englewood Cliffs, NJ: Prentice Hall.

Rodden, K., Basalaj, W., Sinclair, D., & Wood, K. (2001, March). Does organisation by similarity assist image browsing? In *ACM SIGCHI Conference on Human Factors in Computing Systems*, (pp. 190-197), Seattle, WA.

Rojas, R. (1996). *Neural Networks - A Systematic Introduction*. Berlin: Springer-Verlag.

Rolland, P. Y., Raskinis, G., & Ganascia, J. G. (1999). Musical content-based retrieval: an overview of the Melo-discov approach and system. *ACM Multimedia, (1)*, 81-84.

Ronh, J., Jin, W., & Wu, L. (2004). Key frame extraction using inter-shot information. *IEEE International Conference on Multimedia and Expo, 1*, Taiwan. Qian, R., Haering, N., & Sezan, I. (1999). A computational approach to semantic event detection. *Computer Vision and Pattern Recognition, 1*, 206.

Roweis, S. T., & Saul, L. K. (2000). Nonlinear dimensionality reduction by Locally Linear Embedding. *Science, 290*(5500), 2323–2326. doi:10.1126/science.290.5500.2323

Rubner, Y., Tomasi, C., & Guibas, L. J. (2000). The Earth Mover's Distance as a Metric for Image Retrieval. *International Journal of Computer Vision, 40*(2), 99–121. doi:10.1023/A:1026543900054

Rui, Y., & Huang, T. (1999). *A novel relevance feedback technique in image retrieval* (pp. 67–70). New York: ACM Press.

Rui, Y., Huang, T. S., & Chang, S.-F. (1999, March). Image retrieval: Current techniques, promising directions, and open issues. *Journal of Visual Communication and Image Representation, 10*(1), 39–62. doi:10.1006/jvci.1999.0413

Rui, X., Yu, N., Wang, T., & Li, M. (2007). A search-based web image annotation method. In *IEEE International Conference on Multimedia and Expo*, Beijing, China.

Rui, Y., Gupta, A., & Acero, A. (2000). Automatically extracting highlights for TV baseball programs. In *Proceedings of the 8th ACM international conference on Multimedia*, (pp. 105-115).

Rui, Y., Huang, T. S., & Mehrotra, S. (1998). Human perception subjectivity and relevance feedback in multimedia information retrieval. In *Proceedings of IS&T / SPIE Storage and Retrieval of Image and Video Database* (pp. 25-36).

Russ, J. C. (2006). *The Image Processing Handbook*. New York: CRC Press. doi:10.1201/9780203881095

Russell, B., Torralba, A., Murphy, K., & Freeman, W. T. (2008, May). Labelme: a database and web-based tool for image annotation. *International Journal of Computer Vision, 77*(1-3), 151–173. doi:10.1007/s11263-007-0090-8

Saarikallio, S., & Erkkilä, J. (2007). The roles of music in adolescents' mood regulation. *Psychology of Music, 35*, 88–109. doi:10.1177/0305735607068889

Sahami, M., & Heilman, T. D. (2006). A Web-based Kernel Function for Measuring the Similarity of Short-text Snippets. *Proceedings of the Fifteenth International World Wide Web Conference*, 377–386. New York: ACM.

Salembier, P., & Garrido, L. (2000, April). Binary partition tree as an efficient representation for image processing, segmentation, and information retrieval. *IEEE Transactions on Image Processing, 9*, 561–576. doi:10.1109/83.841934

Samir, C., Srivastava, A., Daoudi, M., & Klassen, E. (2009). An Intrinsic Framework for Analysis of Facial Surfaces. *International Journal of Computer Vision, 82*(1), 80–95. doi:10.1007/s11263-008-0187-8

Santini, S., & Jain, R. (1999). Similarity measures. *IEEE Transactions on Pattern Analysis and Machine Intelligence, 21*(9), 871–883. doi:10.1109/34.790428

Santos, S. M., Borges, D. L., & Gomes, H. M. (2008). An evaluation of video cut detection techniques. In *Progress in Pattern Recognition, Image Analysis and Applications*, (LNCS 4756, pp. 311-320). Berlin: Springer.

Sarawagi, S. (Ed.). (2005). *SIGKDD Explorations, Newsletter of the ACM Special Interest Group on Knowledge Discovery and Data Mining*. Reading, MA: AddisonWelsley.

Saur, D. D., Tan, Y. P., Kulkarni, S. R., & Ramadge, P. J. (1997). Automated analysis and annotation of basketball video. In *SPIE Symposium on Storage and Retrieval for Image and Video Databases V*, (Vol. 3022, pp. 176–187).

Savarese, S., Winn, J., & Criminisi, A. (2006). Discriminative object class models of appearance and shape by correlations. In *IEEE Conference on Computer Vision and Pattern Recognition*.

Scaringella, N., & Zoia, G. (2004). A Real-Time Beat Tracker For Unrestricted Audio Signals. In *SMC'04 Conference Proceedings*.

Schapire, R. E., Rochery, M., Rahim, M., & Gupta, N. (2002) Incorporating Prior Knowledge into Boosting. *Proceedings of the International Conference on Machine Learning*, 538–545. San Francisco: Morgan Kaufmann.

Scheirer, E. (1998). Tempo and beat analysis of acoustic musical signals. *The Journal of the Acoustical Society of America*, *103*(1), 588–601. doi:10.1121/1.421129

Schneider, K.-M. (2005). Techniques for Improving the Performance of Naïve Bayes for Text Classification. In *Sixth International Conference on Intelligent Text Processing and Computational Linguistics*, (LNCS 3406, 682–693.

Schoenherr, S. (2005). *Recording Technology History*. Retrieved July 1st, 2009, from http://history.sandiego.edu/gen/recording/notes.html

Schreck, T., & Chen, Z. (2000). Branch grafting method for R-tree implementation. *Journal of Systems and Software*, *53*(1), 83–93. doi:10.1016/S0164-1212(00)00057-1

Schreiber, A. T., Dubbeldam, B., Wielemaker, J., & Wielinga, B. (2001, May-June). Ontology-based photo annotation. *IEEE Intelligent Systems*, *16*(3), 66–74. doi:10.1109/5254.940028

Sebastiani, F. (2002). Machine learning in automated text categorization. *ACM Computing Surveys*, *34*(1), 1–47. doi:10.1145/505282.505283

Sebe, N., & Lew, M. S. (2002). Texture features for content-based retrieval. In Lew, M. S. (Ed.), *Principles of Visual Information Retrieval* (pp. 51–85). London: Springer.

Sebe, N., & Tian, Q. (2007). Personalized multimedia retrieval: the new trend? In *Proceedings of the international Workshop on Workshop on Multimedia information Retrieval*, Augsburg, Germany, September 24 - 29, 2007, (pp. 299-306). New York: ACM.

Sekey, A., & Hanson, B. A. (1984). Improved 1-bark bandwidth auditory filter. *The Journal of the Acoustical Society of America*, *75*(6), 1902–1904. doi:10.1121/1.390954

Sethares, W. A., Morris, R. D., & Sethares, J. C. (2005). Beat tracking of musical performances using low-level audio features. *IEEE Transactions on Speech and Audio Processing*, *13*(2), 275–285. doi:10.1109/TSA.2004.841053

Sfikas, G., Constantinopoulos, C., Likas, A., & Galatsanos, N. P. (2005). An Analytic Distance Metric for Gaussian Mixture Models with Application in Image Retrieval. In W. Duch, et al. (eds.), *Artificial Neural Networks: Formal Models and Their Applications*, (LNCS Vol. 3697, pp. 835-840). Berlin: Springer-Verlag.

Shah, B., Raghavan, V., & Dhatric, P. (2004). Efficient and effective content-based image retrieval using space transformation. *Proceedings of the 10th International Multimedia Modelling Conference*, Brisbane, Australia.

Shi, R., Chua, T.-S., Lee, C.-H., & Gao, S. (2006). Bayesian learning of hierarchical multinomial mixture models of concepts for automatic image annotation. In *ACM International Conference on Image and Video Retrieval*.

Shum, H., & Komura, T. (2004). A spatiotemporal approach to extract the 3D trajectory of the baseball from a single view video sequence. In *Proceedings of IEEE International Conference on Multimedia and Expo*, *3*, 1583–1586.

Shyu, M.-L., Xie, Z., Chen, M., & Chen, S.-C. (2008). Video semantic event/concept detection using a subspace-based multimedia data mining framework. *IEEE Transactions on Multimedia. Special Issue on Multimedia Data Mining*, *10*(2), 252–259.

Sindhwani, S., & Keerthi, S. (2006) Large scale semi-supervised linear SVMs. *Proceedings of the 29th annual international ACM SIGIR conference on Research and Development in Information Retrieval*, 477–484. New York: ACM Press.

Sivic, J., & Zisserman, A. (2004). Video data mining using configurations of viewpoint invariant regions. *Proceedings of the IEEE Conference on Computer Vision and Pattern Recognition,* Washington, DC, USA.

Sivic, J., Russell, B. C., Efros, A. A., Zisserman, A., & Freeman, W. T. (2005). Discovering object categories in image collections. In *IEEE International Conference on Computer Vision.* Washington, DC: IEEE.

Sjoberg, M., Laaksonen, J., Honkela, T., & Polla, M. (2008, August). Inferring semantics from textual information in multimedia retrieval. *Neurocomputing, 71*(13-15), 2576–2586. doi:10.1016/j.neucom.2008.01.029

Smeaton, A. F., Lehane, B., O'Connor, N. E., Brady, C., & Craig, G. (2006). Automatically selecting shots for action movie trailers. In *ACM International Workshop on Multimedia Information Retrieval,* (pp. 231-238), Santa Barbara.

Smeaton, A. F., Over, P., & Kraaij, W. (2006). Evaluation campaigns and TRECVid. *Proceedings of the 8th ACM International Workshop on Multimedia Information Retrieval,* Santa Barbara, CA, USA.

Smeulders, A. W. M., Worring, M., Santini, S., Gupta, A., & Jain, R. (2000). Content-based image retrieval at the end of the early years. *IEEE Transactions on Pattern Analysis and Machine Intelligence, 22,* 1349–1380. doi:10.1109/34.895972

Smith, P., Drummond, T., & Cipolla, R. (2004). Layered motion segmentation and depth ordering by tracking edges. *IEEE Transactions on Pattern Analysis and Machine Intelligence, 26*(4), 479–492. doi:10.1109/TPAMI.2004.1265863

Snoek, C. G. M., Huurnink, B., Hollink, L., de Rijke, M., & Schreiber, G. (2007, August). Adding semantics to detectors for video retrieval. *IEEE Transactions on Multimedia, 9*(5), 975–986. doi:10.1109/TMM.2007.900156

Snoek, C. G. M., & Worring, M. (2005). Multimodal video indexing: A review of the state-of-the-art. *Multimedia Tools and Applications, 25,* 5–35. doi:10.1023/B:MTAP.0000046380.27575.a5

Snoek, C. G. M., & Worring, M. (2005). Multimodal video indexing: A review of the state-of-the-art. *Multimedia Tools and Applications, 25*(1), 5–35. doi:10.1023/B:MTAP.0000046380.27575.a5

Snoek, C. G. M., Worring, M., van Gemert, J. C., Beusebroek, J. M., & Smeulders, A. W. M. (2006). The Challenge Problem for Automated Detection of 101 Semantic Concepts in Multimedia. In *Multimedia '06: Proceedings of the 14th annual ACM international conference on Multimedia,* (pp. 421-430). New York: ACM.

Snyder, B. (2000). *Music and Memory. An Introduction.* Cambridge, MA: The MIT Press.

Soulez, F., Rodet, X., & Schwarz, D. (2003). Improving Polyphonic and Poly-Instrumental Music to Score Alignment. In *4th International Conference on Music Information Retrieval, ISMIR 2003,* (pp. 143-148).

Spink, A., & Jansen, B. J. (2004). *Web search, public searching of the web.* New York: Kluwer.

Spink, A., Jansen, B. J., Wolfram, D., & Saracevic, T. (2002). From E-Sex to E-Commerce: Web Search Changes. *IEEE Computer, 35*(3), 107–109.

Su, Z., Zhang, H., Li, S., & Ma, S. (2003). Relevance feedback in content-based image retrieval: Bayesian framework, feature subspaces, and progressive learning. *IEEE Transactions on Image Processing, 12,* 924–937. doi:10.1109/TIP.2003.815254

Su, C. W., Liao, H.-Y. M., Tyan, H. R., Fan, K. C., & Chen, L. H. (2005). A motion-tolerant dissolve detection algorithm. *IEEE Transactions on Multimedia, 7*(6), 1106–1113. doi:10.1109/TMM.2005.858394

Swain, M. J., & Ballard, D. H. (1991, November). Color indexing. *International Journal of Computer Vision, 7*(1), 11–32. doi:10.1007/BF00130487

Szummer, M., & Jaakkola, T. (2000). Kernel expansions With Unlabeled Examples. [Cambridge, MA: MIT Press.]. *Advances in Neural Information Processing Systems, 13,* 626–632.

Taksa, I. (2005). Predicting the Cumulative Effect of Multiple Query Formulations. *Proceedings of the IEEE International Conference on Information Technology: Coding and Computing,* (Volume II, April 2005, 491–496.

Tamura, H., Mori, S., & Yamawaki, T. (1978). Textural features corresponding to visual perception. *IEEE Transactions on Systems, Man, and Cybernetics, SMC-8*(6), 460–473. doi:10.1109/TSMC.1978.4309999

Tamura, H., & Yokoya, N. (1984). Image database systems: A survey. *Pattern Recognition, 17*(1), 29–43. doi:10.1016/0031-3203(84)90033-5

Tan, S., Cheng, X., Wang, Y., & Xu, H. (2009). Adapting Naïve Bayes to Domain Adaptation for Sentiment Analysis. *Proceedings of the European Conference on Information Retrieval,* (LNCS 5478, 337-349.

Tang, J., Hare, J., & Lewis, P. (2006). Image auto-annotation using a statistical model with salient regions. In *IEEE International Conference on Multimedia and Expo,* (pp. 525-528).

Tao, Y., & Grosky, W. I. (2001, December). Spatial color indexing using rotation, translation, and scale invariant angle. *Multimedia Tools and Applications, 15*(3), 247–268. doi:10.1023/A:1012486900033

Teague, M. R. (1980). Image analysis via the general theory of moments. *Journal of the Optical Society of America, 70*(8), 920–930. doi:10.1364/JOSA.70.000920

Tenenbaum, J. B. (1998). Mapping a manifold of perceptual observations. *Advances in Neural Information Processing Systems, 10,* 682–688.

Ter Haar, F. B., & Veltkamp, R. C. (2009). A 3D face matching framework for facial curves. *Graphical Models, 71*(2), 77–91. doi:10.1016/j.gmod.2008.12.003

The Sydney Morning Herald. (2004). Pop single still hits right note. Retrieved from http://www.smh.com.au/articles/2004/08/25/1093246622880.html, accessed July 1st 2009.

Tien, M. C., Chen, H. T., Chen, Y. W., Hsiao, M. H., & Lee, S. Y. (2007). Shot classification of basketball videos and its applications in shooting position extraction. In. *Proceedings of IEEE International Conference on Acoustics, Speech, and Signal Processing, 1,* 1085–1088.

Tirilly, P., Claveau, V., & Gros, P. (2008). Language modeling for bag-of-visual words image categorization. In *ACM International Conference on Image and Video Retrieval.*

Torralba, A., Fergus, R., & Freeman, W. T. (2008, November). 80 million tiny images: A large data set for nonparametric object and scene recognition. *IEEE Transactions on Pattern Analysis and Machine Intelligence, 30*(11), 1958–1970. doi:10.1109/TPAMI.2008.128

Traina, A. J. M., Traina, C. Jr, Bueno, J. M., Chino, F. J. T., & Azevedo-Marques, P. (2003). Efficient Content-Based Image Retrieval through Metric Histograms. *World Wide Web (Bussum), 6*(2), 157–185. doi:10.1023/A:1023670521530

TRECVID. (2009). *Video retrieval evaluation campaing.* Retrieved from http://www-nlpir.nist.gov/projects/trecvid/

Truong, B. T., & Venkatesh, S. (2007). Video abstraction: A systematic review and classification. *ACM Transactions on Multimedia Computing Communications and Applications, 3*(1), 3. doi:10.1145/1198302.1198305

Truong, B. T., & Dorai, C. (2000). Automatic genre identification for content-based video categorization. *IEEE International Conference on Pattern Recognition, 4,* 230–233, Barcelona, Spain.

Truong, B. T., Dorai, C., & Venkatesh, S. (2000). New enhancements to cut, fade, and dissolve detection processes in video segmentation. In *ACM Multimedia,* (pp. 219–227).

Tsoumakas, G., & Katakis, I. (2007). Multi-label classification: An overview. *International Journal of Data Warehousing and Mining, 3*(3), 1–13.

Turetsky, R. J., & Ellis, D. (2003). Ground-truth transcriptions of real music from force-aligned midi syntheses. In *4th International Conference on Music Information Retrieval, ISMIR 2003.*

Turetsky, R. J., & Ellis, D. P. (2003a). Force-Aligning MIDI Syntheses for Polyphonic Music Transcription Generation. In *Proceedings of International Conference on Music Information Retrieval (ISMIR)*.

Turk, M., & Pentland, A. (1991). Eigenfaces for recognition. *Journal of Cognitive Neuroscience*, *3*(1), 71–86. doi:10.1162/jocn.1991.3.1.71

Tzanetakis, G., & Cook, P. (2002). Musical Genre Classification of Audio Signals. *IEEE Transactions on Speech and Audio Processing*, *10*(5), 293–302. doi:10.1109/TSA.2002.800560

Tzanetakis, G., & Cook, F. (2000). Sound analysis using MPEG compressed audio. In *Proceedings of the IEEE International Conference on Acoustics, Speech, and Signal Processing ICASSP '00*.

Ueda, N., & Saito, K. (2003). Parametric mixture models for multi-labeled text. In *Advances in neural information processing systems* (p. 15). Cambridge, MA: MIT Press.

Uhle, C., & Herre, J. (2003). Estimation Of Tempo, Micro Time And Time Signature From Percussive. In *Proc. of the 6th Int. Conference on Digital Audio Effects (DAFX-03)*.

Uhle, C., Rohden, J., Cremer, M., & Herre, J. (2004). Low complexity musical meter estimation from polyphonic music. In *Proc. AES 25th International Conference*, (pp. 63-68).

Vailaya, A., Figueiredo, M. A. T., Jain, A. K., & Zhang, H. J. (2001). Image classification for contentbased indexing. *IEEE Transactions on Image Processing*, *10*(1), 117–130. doi:10.1109/83.892448

Valle, E., Cord, M., & Philipp-Foliguet, S. (2008). High-dimensional descriptor indexing for large multimedia databases. In *ACM Conference on Information and Knowledge Management* (pp. 739-748), Napa Valley, California, USA.

Van der Maaten, L., Postma, E., & Van Den Herik, H. (2007). *Dimensionality reduction: A comparative review*. Technical Report, Maastricht University.

Vapnik, V. (1998). *Statistical Learning Theory*. New York: John Wiley and Sons.

Varelas, G., Voutsakis, E., Raftopoulou, P., Petrakis, E. G., & Milios, E. E. (2005). Semantic similarity methods in wordnet and their application to information retrieval on the web. In *ACM International Workshop on Web Information and Data Management* (pp. 10-16). New York: ACM.

Vaughan, T. (2006). *What is Multimedia? Multimedia: Making It Work* (7th ed., pp. 1–17). New York: McGraw-Hill Professional.

Velivelli, A., & Huang, T. S. (2006, June). Automatic video annotation by mining speech transcripts. In *IEEE International Conference on Computer Vision and Pattern Recognition Workshop* (pp. 115-122), New York.

Veltkamp, R. C., & Tanase, M. (2000). *Content-based image retrieval systems: A survey* (Technical Report UU-CS-2000-34), Department of Information and Computing Sciences, Universiteit Utrecht.

Vilalta, R., & Ma, S. (2002) Predicting rare events in temporal domains. In *Proceedings of IEEE International Conference on Data Mining*, (pp. 474-481).

Vinay, V., Wood, K., Milic-Frayling, N., & Cox, I. J. (2005). Comparing relevance feedback algorithms for web search. In *WWW 2005: Special interest tracks and posters of the 14th International Conference on World Wide Web*, (pp. 1052–1053). New York: ACM.

Viola, P., & Jones, M. J. (2004). Robust real-time face detection. *International Journal of Computer Vision*, *57*(2), 137–154. doi:10.1023/B:VISI.0000013087.49260.fb

Vogel, J., & Schiele, B. (2004). Natural scene retrieval based on a semantic modeling step. In *ACM International Conference on Image and Video Retrieval*, Dublin, Ireland.

von Ahn, L., & Dabbish, L. (2004, April). Labeling images with a computer game. In *ACM SIGCHI Conference on Human Factors in Computing Systems* (p. 319 - 326). Vienna, Austria.

von Ahn, L., Liu, R., & Blum, M. (2006, April). Peeka-boom: A game for locating objects in images. In *ACM SIGCHI Conference on Human Factors in Computing Systems* (p. 55 - 64). Montreal, Quebec, Canada.

Wang, Y., Ding, M., Zhou, C., & Hu, Y. (2006). Interactive relevance feedback mechanism for image retrieval using rough set. *Knowledge-Based Systems*, *19*, 696–703. doi:10.1016/j.knosys.2006.05.005

Wang, D., Ma, X., & Kim, Y. (2005). Learning Pseudo Metric for Intelligent Multimedia Data Classification and Retrieval. *Journal of Intelligent Manufacturing*, *16*(6), 575–586. doi:10.1007/s10845-005-4363-1

Wang, M., Hua, X.-S., Hong, R., Tang, J., Qi, G.-J., & Song, Y. (2009, May). Unified video annotation via multigraph learning. *IEEE Trans. on Circuits and Systems for Video Technology*, *19*(5), 733–746. doi:10.1109/TCSVT.2009.2017400

Wang, M., Hua, X.-S., Mei, T., Hong, R., Qi, G., & Song, Y. (2009, March). Semi-supervised kernel density estimation for video annotation. *Computer Vision and Image Understanding*, *113*(3), 384–396. doi:10.1016/j.cviu.2008.08.003

Wang, X.-J., Zhang, L., Li, X., & Ma, W.-Y. (2008, November). Annotating images by mining image search results. *IEEE Transactions on Pattern Analysis and Machine Intelligence*, *30*(11), 1919–1932. doi:10.1109/TPAMI.2008.127

Wang, Y., Liu, Z., & Huang, J.-C. (2000). Multimedia content analysis using both audio and visual clues. *IEEE Signal Processing Magazine*, *17*(6), 12–36. doi:10.1109/79.888862

Wang, C., Zhang, L., & Zhang, H.-J. (2008). Scalable markov model-based image annotation. In *ACM International Conference on Content-based Image and Video Retrieval*, (pp. 113-118), Niagara Falls, Canada.

Wang, J. R., & Parameswaran, N. (2005). Analyzing tennis tactics from broadcasting tennis video clips. In *Proceedings of 11th IEEE International Multimedia Modelling Conference*, (pp. 102-106).

Wang, M., Hua, X.-S., Song, Y., Yuan, X., Li, S., & Zhang, H.-J. (2006, October). Automatic video annotation by semi-supervised learning with kernel density estimation. In *ACM International Conference on Multimedia* (pp. 967-976), Santa Barbara, CA.

Wang, M., Hua, X.-S., Yuan, X., & Rong Dai, Y. S. andLi. (2007, September). Optimizing multi-graph learning: Towards a unified video annotation scheme. In *ACM International Conference on Multimedia*, (pp. 862-871), Ausburg, Bavaria, Germany.

Wang, M., Yang, L., & Hua, X.-S. (2009). *MSRA-MM: Bridging research and industrial societies for multimedia information retrieval*, (Technical Report MSR-TR-2009-30). Microsoft Research Asia.

Wang, M., Zhou, X., & Chua, T.-S. (2008, July). Automatic image annotation via local multi-label classification. In *ACM International Conference on Image and Video Retrieval* (pp. 17-26). Niagara Falls, Ontario, Canada.

Wang, S., Wang, Y., Jin, M., Gu, X., & Samaras, D. (2006). 3D surface matching and recognition using conformal geometry. In *Conference on Computer Vision and Pattern Recognition* (pp. 2453–2460), New York.

Wang, X.-J., Ma, W.-Y., Xue, G.-R., & Li, X. (2004). Multi-model similarity propagation and its application for web image retrieval. In *Proc. the 12th annual ACM international conference on Multimedia*, (pp. 944–951), New York City.

Wang, X.-J., Zhang, L., Jing, F., & Ma, W.-Y. (2006). AnnoSearch: Image auto-annotation by search. In *Proc. CVPR*.

Wang, Y., & Streich, S. (2002). A drumbeat-pattern based error concealment method for music streaming applications. In *IEEE International Conference on Acoustics, Speech, and Signal Processing, 2002*, (ICASSP '02), (Vol. 3, pp. 2817-2820).

Wang, Y., & Vilermo, M. (2001). A compressed domain beat detector using MP3 audio bitstreams. In *MULTIMEDIA '01: Proceedings of the ninth ACM international conference on Multimedia*, (pp. 194-202).

Wang, Y., Chiang, M.-C., & Thompson, P. M. (2005). Mutual information-based 3D surface matching with applications to face recognition and brain mapping. In *International Conference on Computer Vision* (pp. 527–534), Beijing, China.

Wang, Z., Chi, Z., & Feng, D. (2002, November). Structural representation and bpts learning for shape classification. In *International Conference on Neural Information Processing,* (pp. 134-138).

Wang, Z., Feng, D., & Chi, Z. (2004). Comparison of image partition methods for adaptive image categorization based on structural image representation. In *The 8th International Conference on Control, Automation, Robotics, and Vision (ICARCV04)* (pp. 676-680).

Wang, Z., Guan, G., Wang, J., & Feng, D. (2008, October). Measuring semantic similarity between concepts in visual domain. In *IEEE International Workshop on Multimedia Signal Processing,* (pp. 628-633), Carins, Australia.

Wang, Z., Hargenbuchner, M., Tsoi, A. C., Cho, S. Y., & Chi, Z. (2002). Image classification with structured self-organizing map. In *IEEE International Joint Conference on Neural Networks (IJCNN2002).*

Weber, R., Schek, H.-J., & Blott, S. (1998). A quantitative analysis and performance study for similarity-search methods in high-dimensional spaces. In *International Conference on Very Large Data Bases,* (pp. 194-205).

Wei, C.-H., Li, C.-T., & Wilson, R. (2006). A content-based approach to medical image database retrieval. In Ma, Z. M. (Ed.), *Database Modeling for Industrial Data Management: Emerging Technologies and Applications* (pp. 258–291). Hershey, PA: Idea Group Publishing.

WEKA. (Version 3.6) [Software], (n.d.). Available from http://www.cs.waikato.ac.nz/ml/weka/

Wen, J.-R., Nie, J.-Y., & Zhang, H.-J. (2002). Query clustering using user logs. *ACM Transactions on Information Systems, 20*(1), 59–81. doi:10.1145/503104.503108

Westermann, U., & Jain, R. (2007). Toward a common event model for multimedia applications. *IEEE MultiMedia Magazine, 14*(1), 19–29. doi:10.1109/MMUL.2007.23

Winn, J., Criminisi, A., & Minka, T. (2005, October). Object categorization by learned universal visual dictionary. In *The IEEE International Conference on Computer Vision* (p. 1800-1807).

Wu, J. K., Lam, C. P., Mehtre, B. M., Gao, Y. J., & Narasimhalu, A. D. (1996). Content-based retrieval for trademark registration. *Multimedia Tools and Applications, 3*(3), 245–267. doi:10.1007/BF00393940

Wu, L., Hu, Y., Li, M., Yu, N., & Hua, X.-S. (2009). Febuary). Scale-invariant visual language modeling for object categorization. *IEEE Transactions on Multimedia, 11*(2), 286–294. doi:10.1109/TMM.2008.2009692

Wu, X., Kumar, V., Ross Quinlan, J., Ghosh, J., Yang, Q., & Motoda, H. (2008). Top 10 algorithms in data mining. *Knowledge and Information Systems, 14*(1), 1–37. doi:10.1007/s10115-007-0114-2

Wu, L., Hua, X.-S., Yu, N., Ma, W.-Y., & Li, S. (2008, October). Flickr distance. In *ACM International Conference on Multimedia* (pp. 31 40). New York: ACM.

Wu, L., Li, M., Li, Z., Ma, W.-Y., & Yu, N. (2007, September). Visual language modeling for image classification. In *ACM International Workshop on Multimedia Information Retrieval*, Augsburg, Bavaria, Germany.

Wu, Y., Chang, E., & Tseng, B. (2005). Multimodal metadata fusion using casual strength. In *Proc. ACM Multimedia.*

Xie, L., Sundaram, H., & Campbell, M. (2008). Event mining in multimedia streams. *Proceedings of the IEEE, 96*(4), 623–647. doi:10.1109/JPROC.2008.916362

Xie, L., Chang, S.-F., Divakaran, A., & Sun, H. (2003). Unsupervised mining of statistical temporal structures in video. In *Video Mining.* Amsterdam: Kluwer Academic Publishers.

Xie, L., Xu, P., Chang, S. F., Divakaran, A., & Sun, H. (2004). Structure analysis of soccer video with domain knowledge and hidden Markov models. *Pattern Recognition Letters, 25*(7), 767–775. doi:10.1016/j.patrec.2004.01.005

Xie, L., Chang, S.-F., Divakaran, A., & Sun, H. (2003, July). Unsupervised discovery of multilevel statistical video structures using hierarchical hidden markov models. In *IEEE International Conference on Multimedia and Expo (ICME)*, Baltimore, MD.

Xiong, Z., Radhakrishnan, R., Divakaran, A., & Huang, T. S. (2005, September). Audiovisual sports highlights extraction using Coupled Hidden Markov Models. *Pattern Analysis & Applications*, 8(1-2), 62–71. doi:10.1007/s10044-005-0244-7

Xiong, Z., Radhakrishnan, R., & Divakaran, A. (2003). Generation of sports highlights using motion activity in combination with a common audio feature extraction framework. *IEEE International Conference on Image Processing, 1*, 5-8, Barcelona, Spain.

Xu, C., Wang, J., Lu, H., & Zhang, Y. (2008). A novel framework for semantic annotation and personalized retrieval of sports video. *IEEE Transactions on Multimedia*, 10(3), 421–436. doi:10.1109/TMM.2008.917346

Yang, B., & Hurson, A. R. (2005). Ad Hoc Image Retrieval using Hierarchical Semantic-based Index. In *AINA '05: Proceedings of the 19th international conference on advanced information networking and applications*, (pp. 629-634). Washington, DC: IEEE Computer Society.

Yang, C., & Dong, M. (2006). Region based image annotation using asymmetrical support vector machine based multiple-instance learning. In *IEEE International Conference on Computer Vision and Pattern Recognition*, (pp. 2057-2063).

Yang, C., & Lozano-Perez, T. (2000). Image database retrieval with multiple-instance learning techniques. In *Proc. ICDE*.

Yang, C., Dong, M., & Fotouhi, F. (2005, November). Region based image annotation through multiple instance learning. In *The ACM International Conference on Multimedia*, (pp. 435438).

Yang, Y. H., et al. (2009). Personalized Music Emotion Recognition. In *Proceedings of the SIGIR 2009*, Boston.

Yao, B., Yang, X., & Zhu, S.-C. (2007, August). Introduction to a large scale general purpose ground truth dataset: methodology, annotation tool, and benchmarks. In *IEEE International Conference on Computer Vision and Pattern Recognition*, (pp. 169-183), Ezhou, China.

Yao, J., Antani, S., Long, R., Thoma, G., & Zhang, Z. (2006). Automatic medical image annotation and retrieval using secc. In *IEEE Symposium on Computer-based Medical Systems*.

Yeo, C., Ahammad, P., Ramchandran, K., & Sastry, S. S. (2008, August). High-speed action recognition and localization in compressed domain videos. *IEEE Transactions on Circuits and Systems for Video Technology*, 18(8), 1006–1015. doi:10.1109/TCSVT.2008.927112

Yesilada, Y., & Harper, S. (2008). Web 2.0 and the semantic web: hindrance or opportunity? In *Proceedings of W4a - International Cross-disciplinary Conference on Web Accessibility 2007. SIGACCESS Access. Comput.* (90), 19–31.

Yilmaz, A., Javed, O., & Shah, M. (2006). Object tracking: A survey. *ACM Computing Surveys*, 38(4). doi:10.1145/1177352.1177355

Yong, W., & Bhandarkar, S. M. Kang Li, (2007). Semantics-based video indexing using a stochastic modeling approach. *IEEE International Conference on Image Processing, 4*, 313-316.

Yu, X., Leong, H. W., Xu, C., & Tian, Q. (2006). Trajectory-based ball detection and tracking in broadcast soccer video. *IEEE Transactions on Multimedia*, 8(6), 1164–1178. doi:10.1109/TMM.2006.884621

Yu, H., Li, M., Zhang, H.-J., & Feng, J. (2002). Color texture moments for content-based image retrieval. In *Proceedings of the International Conference on Image Processing 2002*, (Vol. 3, pp. 929-932).

Yu, X., Xu, C., Leong, H. W., Tian, Q., Tang, Q., & Wan, K. W. (2003). Trajectory-based ball detection and tracking with applications to semantic analysis of broadcast soccer video. In *Proceedings of 11th ACM International Conference on Multimedia*, (pp. 11-20).

Zelikovitz, S., Cohen, W. W., & Hirsh, H. (2007). Extending WHIRL with Background Knowledge for Improved Text Classification. *Information Retrieval, 10*(1), 35–67. doi:10.1007/s10791-006-9004-6

Zezula, P., Amato, G., Dohnal, V., & Batko, M. (2006). Similarity Search. In *The Metric Space Approach, Advances in Database Systems*, (220 p). New York: Springer Science+Business Media, Inc.

Zha, Z.-J., Mei, T., Wang, Z., & Hua, X.-S. (2007). Building a comprehensive ontology to refine video concept detection. In *International Workshop on Multimedia Information Retrieval* (pp. 227-236), Augsburg, Bavaria, Germany.

Zhang, R., & Zhang, Z. (2006). BALAS: Empirical Bayesian learning in the relevance feedback for image retrieval. *Image and Vision Computing, 24*, 211–233. doi:10.1016/j.imavis.2005.11.004

Zhang, R., Tsai, P.-S., Cryer, J., & Sham, M. (1999). Shape from shading: A survey. *IEEE Transactions on Pattern Analysis and Machine Intelligence, 21*(8), 690–706. doi:10.1109/34.784284

Zhang, D., & Lu, G. (2002). A comparative study on shape retrieval using Fourier descriptors with different shape signatures. *Signal Processing Image Communication, 17*(10), 825–848. doi:10.1016/S0923-5965(02)00084-X

Zhang, D., & Lu, G. (2003). A comparative study of curvature scale space and Fourier descriptors for shape-based image retrieval. *Journal of Visual Communication and Image Representation, 14*(1), 41–60. doi:10.1016/S1047-3203(03)00003-8

Zhang, D., & Lu, G. (2003). Evaluation of MPEG-7 shape descriptors against other shape descriptors. *Multimedia Systems, 9*(1), 15–30. doi:10.1007/s00530-002-0075-y

Zhang, M.-L., & Zhou, Z.-H. (2007, July). ML-KNN: A lazy learning approach to multi-label learning. *Pattern Recognition, 40*(7), 2038–2048. doi:10.1016/j.patcog.2006.12.019

Zhang, R., & Zhang, Z. (2007). Effective image retrieval based on hidden concept discovery in image database. *IEEE Transactions on Image Processing, 16*(2). doi:10.1109/TIP.2006.888350

Zhang, Z., Masseglia, F., Jain, R., & Del Bimbo, A. (2006). KDD/MDM 2006: The 7th KDD multimedia data mining workshop report. *ACM KDD Explorations, 8*(2), 92–95. doi:10.1145/1233321.1233336

Zhang, H., Rahmani, R., Cholleti, S., & Goldman, S. (2006). Local image representations using pruned salient points with applications to CBIR. In *Proc. ACM Multimedia*.

Zhang, L., Qian, F., Li, M., & Zhang, H. (2003). An efficient memorization scheme for relevance feedback in image retrieval. In *Proceedings of the IEEE International Conference on Multimedia & Expo*.

Zhang, Q., Goldman, S., Yu, W., & Fritts, J. (2002). Content-based image retrieval using multiple instance learning. In *Proc. ICML*.

Zhang, R., Zhang, Z., Li, M., Ma, W.-Y., & Zhang, H.-J. (2005, October). A probabilistic semantic model for image annotation and multi-modal image retrieval. In *The IEEE International Conference on Computer Vision*, (pp. 846-851).

Zhao, W., Chellappa, R., Phillips, P. J., & Rosenfeld, A. (2003). Face recognition: A literature survey. *ACM Computing Surveys, 35*(4), 399–458. doi:10.1145/954339.954342

Zhaorong, H., Weibei, D., & Zaiwang, D. (2001). New window-switching criterion of audio compression. *Multimedia Signal Processing, 2001 IEEE Fourth Workshop on*, (pp. 319-323).

Zhong, D., & Defee, I. (2007). Perfomance of similarity measures based on histograms of local image feature vector. *Pattern Recognition Letters, 28*(15), 2003–2010. doi:10.1016/j.patrec.2007.05.019

Zhou, X. S., & Huang, T. S. (2003). Relevance feedback in image retrieval: A comprehensive review. *ACM Multimedia System Journal, 8*, 536–544. doi:10.1007/s00530-002-0070-3

Zhou, X., Wang, M., Zhang, Q., Zhang, J., & Shi, B. (2007). Automatic image annotation by an iterative approach: incorporating keyword correlations and region matching. In *ACM International Conference on Image and Video Retrieval*, (pp. 25-32), Amsterdam, The Netherlands.

Zhu, X. (2007). *Semi-Supervied Learning Literature Survey*. Madison, WI: Computer Sciences Technical Report, University of Wisconsin-Madison.

Zhu, X., Wu, X., Elmagarmid, A. K., Feng, Z., & Wu, L. (2005). Video data mining: semantic indexing and event detection from the association perspective. *IEEE Transactions on Knowledge and Data Engineering, 17*(5), 665–677. doi:10.1109/TKDE.2005.83

Zhu, G., Huang, Q., Xu, C., Xing, L., Gao, W., & Yao, H. (2007a). Human behavior analysis for highlight ranking in broadcast racket sports video. *IEEE Transactions on Multimedia, 9*(6), 1167–1182. doi:10.1109/TMM.2007.902847

Zhu, C.-Z., Mei, T., & Hua, X.-S. (2005). Video booklet - natural video browsing. In *ACM Multimedia*, (pp. 265-266), Singapore.

Zhu, G., Huang, Q., Xu, C., Rui, Y., Jiang, S., Gao, W., & Yao, H. (2007b). Trajectory based event tactics analysis in broadcast sports video. In *Proceedings of 15th ACM International Conference on Multimedia*, (pp. 58-67).

Zhu, G., Xu, C., Huang, Q., Gao, W., & Xing, L. (2007c). Player action recognition in broadcast tennis video with application to semantic analysis of sports game. In *Proceedings of 14th ACM International Conference on Multimedia*, (pp. 431- 440).

Zhu, Q., Yeh, M.-C., & Cheng, K.-T. (2006). Multimodal fusion using learned text concepts for image categorization. In *Proc. ACM Multimedia*.

Zhu, T., Greiner, R., & Haeubl, G. (2003). Learning a model of a web user's interests. *Proceedings of the 9th International Conference on User Modeling*, (LNCS 2702, 65–75. Berlin: Springer.

Zhu, X. (2008, July). *Semi-supervised learning literature survey*. Technical Report TR-1530, University of Wisconsin Madison, Madison, WI.

Zimmer, M., & Spink, A. (2008). *Web Searching: Interdisciplinary Perspectives*. Dordrecht, The Netherlands: Springer.

Zuo, W., Zhang, D., & Wang, K. (2006). Bidirectional PCA with assembled matrix distance metric for image recognition. *IEEE Transactions on Systems, Man, and Cybernetics, 36*, 863–872. doi:10.1109/TSMCB.2006.872274

Zwicker, E., & Fastl, H. (1990). *Psychoacoustics: Facts and Models*. Berlin: Heidelberg.

About the Contributors

Chia-Hung Wei is currently an assistant professor of the Department of Information Management at Ching Yun University, Taiwan. He obtained his Ph.D. degree in Computer Science from the University of Warwick, UK, and Master's degree from the University of Sheffield, UK, and Bachelor degree from the Tunghai University, Taiwan. His research interests include content-based image retrieval, digital image processing, medical image processing and analysis, machine learning for multimedia applications and information retrieval. He has published over 10 research papers in those research areas.

Yue Li received his Ph.D. degree in computer science from University of Warwick, UK, in 2009, M.S. in Information Technology from Department of Computer Science, University of Nottingham, UK, in 2005, and B.Sc. in Mathematics from Nankai University, China, in 2003. He is currently an assistant professor of Collage of Software, University of Nankai, China. He serves as a member of editorial review board of International Journal of Digital Crime and Forensics. His research interests include digital forensics, multimedia security, digital watermarking, pattern recognition, machine learning and content-based image retrieval.

* * *

Antonello D'Aguanno receives his M.S. degree in Computer Science (2005) from the Università degli Studi di Milano. In 2009 he receives his Ph.D. degree in Computer Science at the Università degli Studi di Milano. Now he is a research associate in the same university. His current research activity focuses on both the theoretical aspects and the applications of digital signal processing applied on content analysis of music signal. His other research interests include database models for music, audio and video driven by contents.

Stefano Berretti received the Lurea degree in Electronics Engineering and the Ph.D. in Information and Telecommunications Engineering from the University of Florence, Italy, in 1997 and 2001, respectively. In 2000, he received the post-Laurea degree in "Multimedia Content Design," from the University of Florence. Since 2002 he is an Assistant Professor at the University of Florence, where he teaches "Operating Systems" and "Fundamentals of Computer Programming" at the School of Computer Engineering. Since 2001 he also teaches "Database Systems" at the post-Doctoral school in "Multimedia Content Design" of the University of Florence. His scientific interests are pattern recognition, content based image retrieval, 3D object partitioning and retrieval, 3D face recognition.

Alberto Del Bimbo is Full Professor of Computer Engineering, President of the Foundation for Research and Innovation, Director of the Master in Multimedia, and Director of the Media Integration and Communication Center at the University of Florence. He was the Deputy Rector for Research and Innovation Transfer of the University of Florence from 2000 to 2006. His scientific interests are Multimedia Information Retrieval, Pattern Recognition, Image and Video Analysis and Natural Human Computer Interaction. He has published over 250 publications in some of the most distinguished scientific journals and international conferences, and is the author of the monography "Visual Information Retrieval". From 1996 to 2000, he was the President of the IAPR Italian Chapter, and, from 1998 to 2000, Member at Large of the IEEE Publication Board. He was the general Chair of IAPR ICIAP'97, the International Conference on Image Analysis and Processing, IEEE ICMCS'99, the International Conference on Multimedia Computing and Systems and Program Co-Chair of ACM Multimedia 2008. He is the General Co-Chair of ACM Multimedia 2010 and of ECCV 2012, the European Conference on Computer Vision. He is IAPR Fellow and Associate Editor of Multimedia Tools and Applications, Pattern Analysis and Applications, Journal of Visual Languages and Computing and International Journal of Image and Video Processing, and was Associate Editor of Pattern Recognition, IEEE Transactions on Multimedia and IEEE Transactions on Pattern Analysis and Machine Intelligence.

Alice W.S. Chan received the BS Honours degree in computer studies (information systems) from Hong Kong Baptist University, Hong Kong, in 2007. She is currently an MPhil candidate in the Department of Computer Science, Hong Kong Baptist University, supervised by C.H.C. Leung. She has held technical positions in industry before, and she takes part in music education in her spare time. Her research interests include semantic multimedia retrieval, internet search and music technology.

Min Chen is an Assistant Professor at the Department of Computer Science, University of Montana, Missoula, MT, USA, since August 2007. She received her Master's and Ph.D. degrees from the School of Computing and Information Sciences at Florida International University, Miami, FL, USA in 2004 and 2007, respectively. Her research interests include multimedia database systems, image and video database retrieval, and multimedia data mining. She has authored and co-authored more than 30 technical papers published in various prestigious journals, referred conference/workshop proceedings and book chapters. She was the program co-chair of the 2009 IEEE International Workshop on Semantic Computing and Multimedia Systems and publicity co-chair of the 2009 IEEE International Symposium on Multimedia.

Sherry Y. Chen is a Reader in the School of Information Systems, Computing and Mathematics at Brunel University. She obtained her PhD from the Department of Information Studies, University of Sheffield, UK. Her current research interests include human-computer interaction, data mining and e-business.

Hua-Tsung Chen received his B.S. and M.S. degree in Computer Science and Information Engineering from National Chiao Tung University, Hsinchu, Taiwan in 2001 and 2003, respectively, and the Ph.D. degree in Computer Science from National Chiao Tung University in 2009. He is currently a Postdoctoral Research Fellow with National Chiao Tung University, Hsinchu, Taiwan. His research interests include computer vision, video signal processing, content-based video indexing and retrieval, multimedia information system and music signal processing.

Zhengxin Chen is a professor of Computer Science at College of Information Science and Technology, University of Nebraska at Omaha. He received his PhD degree in Computer Science from Louisiana State University in 1988.

Wing-yin Chau graduated with a first class degree from the Department of Computer Science at the University of Warwick, UK in 2007. During the final year of her study, her research project is one of a few best project of the year. Her research interests include content-based image retrieval, digital image processing and information retrieval.

Didier Coquin received the Ph.D. degree in signal processing and telecommunication from University of Rennes I, France, in 1991. He is currently an Assistant Professor of telecommunication and network engineering at the Savoie University (Technological Academic Institute) and works in the Informatics, Systems, Information and Knowledge Processing Laboratory (LISTIC), Annecy, France. His research interests include image processing, pattern recognition, image and video indexing, data fusion, and fuzzy logic.

Antonello D'Aguanno receives his M.S. degree in Computer Science (2005) from the Università degli Studi di Milano. In 2009 he receives his Ph.D. degree in Computer Science at the Università degli Studi di Milano. Now he is a research associate in the same university. His current research activity focuses on both the theoretical aspects and the applications of digital signal processing applied on content analysis of music signal. His other research interests include database models for music, audio and video driven by contents.

(David) Dagan Feng received his ME in EECS from Shanghai JiaoTong University in 1982, MSc in Biocybernetics and Ph.D in CS from UCLA in 1985 and 1988 respectively. He has served as Head of Department of Computer Science and Head of School of Information Technologies, University of Sydney. He is the Founder and Director of the Biomedical & Multimedia Information Technology (BMIT) Research Group, Professor of School of Information Technologies, Associate Dean of Faculty of Science, University of Sydney; Chair-Professor of Information Technology, Hong Kong Polytechnic University; Advisory Professor and Chief Scientist of the Med-X Research Institute, Shanghai JiaoTong University. He has published over 500 scholarly research papers, pioneered several new research directions, and made a number of landmark contributions in his field. He is Fellow of Australian Academy of Technological Sciences and Engineering, ACS, HKIE, IET and IEEE.

Christos Faloutsos is a Professor at Carnegie Mellon University. He has received the Presidential Young Investigator Award by the National Science Foundation (1989), the Research Contributions Award in ICDM 2006, thirteen ``best paper'' awards, and several teaching awards. He has served as a member of the executive committee of SIGKDD; he has published over 200 refereed articles, 11 book chapters and one monograph. He holds five patents and he has given over 30 tutorials and over 10 invited distinguished lectures. His research interests include data mining for graphs and streams, fractals, database performance, and indexing for multimedia and bio-informatics data.

Zhen Guo is a Ph.D student in Computer Science department at State University of New York at Binghamton. He has the B.Sc and M.Sc degrees both in Electrical Engineer from Xi'an Jiaotong University,

China. He was a senior software engineer at UTStarcom Inc. at Shenzhen, China. He also worked as an Intern student at NEC Laboratories American at Cupertino, CA and Yahoo Labs at Santa Clara, CA. His research interests are machine learning and the applications to data mining, information retrieval, and computer vision. He has published several peer-reviewed academic papers in the premier data mining conferences and book chapters, and has served as reviewers or program committee members for many international journals and conferences.

Ling Guan is a Tier I Canada Research Chair in Multimedia and a Professor of Electrical and Computer Engineering at Ryerson University, Toronto, Canada. He received his Bachelor's Degree from Tianjin University, China, Master's Degree from University of Waterloo, Canada and Ph.D. Degree from University of British Columbia, Canada. Hs research interests are in image, video and multimedia signal processing and have published extensively in the field. Dr. Guan currently serves on the editorial boards of IEEE Transactions on Multimedia and IEEE Transactions on Circuits and Systems for Video Technology. He chaired the 2006 IEEE International Conference on Multimedia and Expo in Toronto, and co-chaired the 2008 ACM International Conference on Image and Video Retrieval in Niagara Falls. Dr. Guan is a Fellow of the IEEE, a Fellow of Engineering Institute of Canada and a recipient of the 2005 IEEE Transactions on Circuits and Systems for Video Technology Best Paper Award.

Bogdan Ionescu is currently a Lecturer with University "POLITEHNICA" of Bucharest-Romania. He holds a B.S. degree in applied electronics (2002) and an M.S. degree in computing systems (2003), both from University Politehnica of Bucharest. He also holds a Ph.D. degree in image processing and informatics (2007) from, both, the University of Savoie and University "Politehnica" of Bucharest. Between 2006 and 2007, he held a temporary Assistant Professor position with Polytech'Savoie, University of Savoie. Between 2003 and 2007, he has attended the International Animated Film Market, Annecy, France, presenting solutions for the symbolic/semantic analysis of the animated movies. At the present time, he is in-charge with the Romanian CNCSIS Video Indexing RP2 project. His scientific interests cover electronics engineering, artificial intelligence, image processing, computer vision, software engineering, and computer science. He is a Member of IEEE, SPIE, ACM, and GDR-ISIS.

Kristoffer Jensen obtained his Masters degree in 1988 in Computer Science at the Technical University of Lund, Sweden, and a D.E.A in Signal Processing in 1989 at the ENSEEIHT, Toulouse, France. His Ph.D. was delivered and defended in 1999 at the Department of Computer Science, University of Copenhagen, Denmark, treating signal processing applied to music with a physical and perceptual point-of-view. This mainly involved classification, and modeling of musical sounds. Kristoffer Jensen has been involved in synthesizers for children, state of the art next generation effect processors, and signal processing in music informatics. His current research topic is signal processing with musical applications, and related fields, including perception, psychoacoustics, physical models and expression of music. Kristoffer Jensen has chaired 3 major conferences, been the editor of 6 books and conference proceedings, and he currently holds a position at the Software and Media Technology Department, Aalborg University Esbjerg as Associate Professor.

Dmitry Kinoshenko, completed MD in 'Applied mathematics' in 2004 and PhD in 'Systems and Means of Artificial Intelligence' in 2008 in Kharkov National University of Radio Electronics, Ukraine, where currently obtains position of Senior Researcher. Has over 40 publications including ones published in Springer and IEEE. In 2008 got the first place in 'The best young scientist of the region' competitions in 'mathematics and informatics' field. Science interests include image retrieval, database indexing, image and video processing.

Patrick Lambert received the engineer degree in electrical engineering in 1978 and the PhD degree in signal processing in 1983, both from the National Polytechnic Institute of Grenoble, France. He is currently Professor at the School of Engineering of University of Savoie, Annecy, France. His research interests include color image processing and video analysis.

Clement Leung received the BSc degree (with first class honours) in mathematics from McGill University, the MSc degree in mathematics from the University of Oxford, and the PhD degree in computer science from the University of London. Before joining the university sector, he has held various technical positions in industry in the United Kingdom. Before joining Hong Kong Baptist University as a professor, he held the foundation chair in computer science at Victoria University, Melbourne, and prior to that, held an established chair in computer science at the University of London. His services to the research community include serving as a program chair, program co-chair, keynote speaker, and panel expert of major international conferences. In addition to contributing to the editorship of six international journals, he has served as the chairman of the International Association for Pattern Recognition Technical Committee on Multimedia and Visual Information Systems, as well as on the International Standards (ISO) MPEG-7 Committee, which was responsible for generating standards for digital multimedia.

Suh-Yin Lee received the B.S. degree in electrical engineering from National Chiao Tung University, Taiwan, in 1972, and the M.S. degree in computer science from University of Washington, Seattle, U.S.A., in 1975, and the Ph.D. degree in computer science form Institute of Electronics, National Chiao Tung University. Her research interests include content-based indexing and retrieval, distributed multimedia information system, mobile computing, and data mining.

Jiming Liu is a Professor and the Head of Computer Science Department at Hong Kong Baptist University. He was a Professor and the Director of School of Computer Science at University of Windsor, Canada. His current research interests include: Autonomy-Oriented Computing (AOC), Web Intelligence (WI), and self-organizing systems and complex networks, with applications to: (i) characterizing working mechanisms that lead to emergent behavior in natural and artificial complex systems (e.g., phenomena in Web Science, and the dynamics of social networks and neural systems), and (ii) developing solutions to large-scale, distributed computational problems (e.g., distributed scalable scientific or social computing, and collective intelligence). Prof. Liu has contributed to the scientific literature in those areas, including over 250 journal and conference papers, and 5 authored research monographs, e.g., Autonomy Oriented Computing: From Problem Solving to Complex Systems Modeling (Kluwer Academic/Springer) and Spatial Reasoning and Planning: Geometry, Mechanism, and Motion (Springer). Prof. Liu serves as the Editor-in-Chief of Web Intelligence and Agent Systems, an Associate Editor of IEEE Transactions on Knowledge and Data Engineering, IEEE Transactions on Systems, Man, and Cybernetics – Part B, and Computational Intelligence, and a member of the Editorial Board of several other international journals.

Alexandru Marin received an MSc degree in applied electronics from University "Politehnica" of Bucharest (2009). The graduation project entitled "Applying Stein's principle in SENSE pMRI reconstruction", was developed jointly with the Informatics Laboratory of the Institut Gaspard Monge, Paris-Est University. Between 2006 and 2009 he held several position as software consultant, software engineer, Java software developer with several international companies in the field. His main scientific interests cover image processing and analysis, data mining and computer science.

Francisco Josè Silva Mata graduated in Electronic Engineering in the Higher Polytechnic Institute José A. Echeverría (ISPJAE), Havana Cuba, in 1982, and received the certificate of Associated investigator in 2002. He is at the moment an expert in Image Processing of the Department of Pattern Recognition of CENATAV. Engineer Silva has focused his main investigations in the Representation and Analysis of shapes. He has acquired a great experience in the representation area and analysis of shapes in connection with the problems of capturing, processing, storing and interpreting digital images.

Vladimir Mashtalir, completed MD in 1979 in 'Applied mathematics', completed PhD in 'Cybernetics and Information Theory' in 1984 and Habilitatus in 'Systems and Means of Artificial Intelligence' in 2002. All in Kharkov National University of Radio Electronics, Ukraine. Since 2003 is Professor and Dean of Computer Science Faculty ibid. Has over 100 publications including monographies, papers and conference proceedings published all over the world. Research interests include image and video processing, pattern recognition.

Alfredo Milani is an Associate Professor of Computer Science at University of Perugia. His research interests include automated planning, evolutionary algorithms, web based adaptive systems and knowledge based multimedia retrieval. He has been researcher at the Institute for Computational Linguistic of the Italian National Research Council at Pisa, and visiting scientist in major universities and research centers including Jet Propulsion Laboratory and Hong Kong Baptist University. He has served as chair and program committee member of several international conferences and workshops, editorial board member of international journals and Executive Committee member of the European Network of Excellence in Planning.

Pietro Pala received the Laurea degree in 1994 from the University of Firenze. From the same University, he received the Ph.D. in Information and Telecommunications Engineering in 1997. Presently, he is Associate Professor at the University of Firenze where he teaches "Image and Video Analysis" and "Database Management Systems'" at the school of Information Engineering and "Fundamentals of Multimedia and Programming Languages" at the Master in Multimedia Content Design. Pietro Pala is a member of the Board of the PhD in Informatics, Multimedia and Telecommunications, a member of the Board of the Master in Multimedia Content Design and a member of the MIUR Center of Excellence Media Integration and Communication Center of the University of Firenze. Pietro Pala is also President of the Board for Quality Assessment (CRUI Model of Quality) for both the Master in Multimedia Content Design and the school of Information Engineering. Pietro Pala carries out scientific research and technological experimentation in the area of Multimedia Information Processing and Analysis. In particular, recent research activities have focused on the analysis and definitions of models to support image based object recognition, content based retrieval of images and 3D models, segmentation of 3D models, 3D face recognition.

Jiaxiong Pi received his Master degree in Computer Science from University of Nebraska at Omaha in 2005. Since then, he has been working as a programmer in Valmont Industries, Inc.

Yong Shi is Charles & Margret Durham Distinguished Professor of Information Technology at College of Information Science and Technology, University of Nebraska at Omaha. He received his PhD degree in Management Science from University of Kansas in 1991.

Vladislav Shlyakhov, completed MD in 1979 in 'Applied mathematics' in Moscow State University, completed PhD in 'Cybernetics and Information Theory' in 1984 in Kharkov National University of Radio Electronics where currently obtains position of Lead Researcher. Has over 80 publications including monographies, papers and conference proceedings published all over the world. Science interests include multialgebraic systems, granular computing, metrical properties of n-arity relations.

Amanda Spink, Professor of Information Science, Queensland University of Technology has a BA (ANU), DipLib (UNSW), an M.B.A. in IT Management (Fordham) and a Ph.D. Information Science (Rutgers). Her research focuses on studies in information science, including theories, models and empirical studies related to information behavior. Professor Spink's research has been supported by the National Science Foundation, Australian Research Council, NEC, IBM, Lockheed Martin, Alta Vista, Infospace, Vivisimo, Excite and the Andrew R. Mellon Foundation. She has over 330 publications and her recent books include Information Behavior: An Evolutionary Instinct (Springer), Web Search: Multidisciplinary Perspectives (Springer) and Handbook of Research on Web Log Analysis (Idea Group). Professor Spink was ranked the second most highly cited scholar in the field of Library and Information Science for 2001-2004, and was recently noted as having the second highest citation h-index in the field of Library and Information Science.

Isak Taksa, Associate Professor in the Department of Computer Information Systems at Baruch College of the City University of New York (CUNY). His primary research interests include information retrieval, knowledge discovery and text and data mining. He has published extensively on theoretical and applied aspects of information retrieval and search engine technology. His publications include a Handbook of Research on Web Log Analysis (Idea Group) and papers in journals including Information Retrieval, Journal of the American Society for Information Science. He teaches both undergraduate and graduate courses, as well as mentoring Ph.D. students in various research and educational efforts.

Constantin Vertan holds an image processing and analysis tenure at the Image Processing and Analysis Laboratory from the Faculty of Electronics, Telecommunications and Information Technology at the „Politehnica" University of Bucharest (UPB). He was an invited professor at INSA de Rouen and University of Poitiers (France). For his contributions in image processing he was awarded with UPB's „In tempore opportuno" award (2002) and with the Romanian National Research Council „In hoc signo vinces" award (2004). His research interests are general image processing and analysis, CBIR, fuzzy and medical image processing applications. He is a member of SPIE, senior member of IEEE and secretary of the Romanian IEEE Signal Processing Chapter.

Sarah Zelikovitz, Associate Professor of Computer Science at the College of Staten Island of the City University of New York. She received her B.S. with honors and M.A. from Brooklyn college of

CUNY. She graduated with a PhD from Rutgers University in 2002 for work in text classification. Since that time, she has spent much time researching the effect of background knowledge in text categorization. Over the last decade she has published in machine learning, artificial intelligence, and information retrieval journals and conferences on this topic.

Zhiyong Wang received his B.E. and M.E degrees from South China University of Technology, Guangzhou, China, in 1996 and 1999, respectively. He earned a Ph.D. degree from Hong Kong Polytechnic University, Hong Kong, in 2003. In 2003, he joined the School of Information Technologies, University of Sydney as a Postdoctoral Research Fellow and is currently a Lecturer in the school. His research interests include multimedia information processing, retrieval and management, Internet-based multimedia data mining; human centered multimedia computing; pattern recognition and machine learning.

Elena Yegorova, completed her MPhil in 'Information Technologies, Data Mining and Knowledge Discovering' in 2006 in Wessex Institute of Technology, UK and PhD in 'Systems and Means of Artificial Intelligence' in 2007 in Kharkov National University of Radio Electronics, Ukraine where currently obtains position of Senior Researcher. In 2008 was a guest editor of Graphic Vision and Image Processing, Cairo, Egypt. Has over 20 publications. In 2007 got the first place in 'The best young scientist of the region' competitions in 'mathematics and informatics' field. Science interests include image processing and pattern recognition.

Rui Zhang is affiliated with the Ryerson Multimedia Research Laboratory, Ryerson University, where is currently pursuing a Ph.D. degree. He received his Bachelor's and Master's Degrees from Tianjin University, China, in 2002 and 2004. His research interests include statistical machine learning, pattern recognition, image retrieval and annotation. He has been with Microsoft Research Asia as a research intern in the summer of 2009.

Zhongfei Zhang is an associate professor at the Computer Science Department at State University of New York (SUNY) at Binghamton, and the director of the Multimedia Research Laboratory. He received a B.S. in Electronics Engineering (with Honors), an M.S. in Information Sciences, both from Zhejiang University, China, and a PhD in Computer Science from the University of Massachusetts at Amherst, USA. He was on the faculty of Computer Science and Engineering Department, and a research scientist at the Center of Excellence for Document Analysis and Recognition, both at SUNY Buffalo, before he joined the faculty of computer science at SUNY Binghamton. His research has been funded by a number of US federal government agencies, industry research labs, as well as a number of private foundations and foreign funding agencies. He holds more than ten inventions, is an author of two monographs and over 100 peer reviewed papers, and is currently in the editorial boards for several journals.

Index